Alex Hiam and Charles Schewe have developed both an objective and tactical approach that makes global marketing sense: Focus on the customer worldwide; simplify and change strategic planning; drive marketing knowledge and skills to all levels of an organization. I highly recommend this book.

Scott H. Creelman
Vice President-International
Spalding Sports Worldwide

THE PORTABLE MBA IN MARKETING breathes life into the conceptual frameworks of marketing with a generous dose of exciting real-world case histories. It's a great introduction to the foundations of marketing and engaging refresher for marketing managers.

David G. Fubini
Managing Director
McKinsey & Company, Inc., Boston

Few books connect a sound vision of the marketing concept with useful how-to guidance. Hiam and Schewe have forged a seamless continuum between the marketing imagination and the real world by including not only descriptions of actual experience but also useful prescriptions. Their ingenuity gives *THE PORTABLE MBA IN MARKETING* hands-on value for marketing professionals and strategic executives alike.

Dirk Coburn
Product Marketing Manager
Pilot Executive Software

This book not only provides the reader with the basic foundation of marketing but adds to the structure using contemporary issues such as globalization, innovation, quality management, and customer service.

Gordon W. Paul
Professor of Marketing
University of Central Florida

THE PORTABLE MBA IN MARKETING has clarity and style . . . it is full of real-world examples that make the conceptual material jump out of the pages. This book will sharpen and hone your marketing skills. I guarantee it.

Stephen H. Winchell
President
Stephen Winchell & Associates
A Direct Response Agency

Engaging, easily digestible concepts built on a sea of real-world examples. . . . Finally, I've received my MBA in Marketing . . .

Bruce R. McBrearty
Transamerica Marketing Services, Inc.

THE
PORTABLE MBA
IN MARKETING

The Portable MBA Series

The Portable MBA, Eliza G.C. Collins and Mary Anne Devanna
The Portable MBA in Marketing, Alexander Hiam and Charles D. Schewe
The Portable MBA in Finance and Accounting, John Leslie Livingstone

Forthcoming Titles

The Portable MBA Desk Reference, Donna Carpenter
The Portable MBA in Management, Allan R. Cohen

THE PORTABLE MBA IN MARKETING

Alexander Hiam
Charles D. Schewe

John Wiley & Sons, Inc.

New York • Chichester • Brisbane • Toronto • Singapore

Library of Congress Cataloging-in-Publication Data
Hiam, Alexander.
     The portable MBA in marketing / by Alexander Hiam, Charles D.
  Schewe.
         p.   cm.
     Includes index.
     ISBN 0-471-54728-X (cloth) 0-471-11984-9 (paper)
     1. Marketing—Management.   I. Schewe, Charles D., 1942–
  II. Title.
  HF5415.13.H47   1992
  658.8—dc20   91-37515

Printed in the United States of America.

10 9 8

DEDICATION

This book not only is about marketing, but is also very much about a revolution in management thought and practice—a revolution that is reshaping the corporation to better meet and anticipate customer needs and competitive challenges. We dedicate our book to the courageous managers whose efforts to recreate their organizations are setting a new standard of excellence in management. Their work holds great promise for recapturing the preeminent position of U.S. business, both in its home markets and throughout the world.

We also wish to acknowledge the support of our families, assistants, and publisher—special thanks are due to Happi Cramer of Word for Word—and Hiam wishes to acknowledge the influence of Schewe's *Marketing: Principles and Strategies,* the book that provided the cornerstone on which the current volume was erected.

ALEXANDER HIAM
CHARLES D. SCHEWE

Amherst, Massachusetts, 1992

TRADEMARKS

Acustar is a registered trademark of Tymeshare.

Agree is a registered trademark of S.C. Johnson.

Ajax is a registered trademark of Colgate-Palmolive Company.

Armor All is a registered trademark of McKesson Corporation.

Baby Ninja is a registered trademark of Kawasaki Motor.

Band-Aid is a registered trademark of Johnson & Johnson.

BehaviorScan is a registered trademark of Information Resources.

Big Mac is a registered trademark of McDonald's.

Blistex is a registered trademark of Blistex, Corp.

Borden is a registered trademark of Borden.

Brawny is a registered trademark of James River Corporation.

Budweiser is a registered trademark of Anheuser-Busch.

Caress is a registered trademark of Lever Brothers.

Chaps is a registered trademark of Ralph Lauren.

Charmin is a registered trademark of Procter & Gamble.

Cherry Coke is a registered trademark of Coca-Cola.

Chewy Granola Bars is a registered trademark of Quaker Oats.

Chloraseptic is a registered trademark of Procter & Gamble.

Citrus Hill is a registered trademark of Procter & Gamble.

Clearasil Adult Care is a registered trademark of Richardson-Vicks.

Clearasil is a registered trademark of Richardson-Vicks.

CoAdvil is a registered trademark of American Home Products.

Coke Classic is a registered trademark of Coca-Cola.

Coors Light is a registered trademark of Coors.

Crest is a registered trademark of Procter & Gamble.

Cricket Lighter is a registered trademark of Gillette.

Cuisinart is a registered trademark of Conair Corporation.

Cup-a-Soup is a registered trademark of Thomas J. Lipton.

Cycle is a registered trademark of Gaines Food.

DBase is a registered trademark of Ashton-Tate.

Dewey Stevens is a registered trademark of Anheuser-Busch.

Dipps is a registered trademark of Quaker Oats.

Dockers is a registered trademark of Levi Strauss.

Dorito is a registered trademark of Frito Lay/Pepisco.

Dove is a registered trademark of Lever Brothers.

Dristan Sinus is a registered trademark of American Home Products.

Dustbuster is a registered trademark of Black & Decker.

Eagle is a registered trademark of Anheuser-Busch.

English Leather is a registered trademark of Yardley.

Eraser Mate is a registered trademark of Gillette.

Escort Wagon is a registered trademark of Ford Motor Company.

EXPRESS is a registered trademark of Information Resources.

Fab 1-Shot is a registered trademark of Colgate-Palmolive Company.

Finesse is a registered trademark of Helene Curtis.

Fresh Chef is a registered trademark of Campbell Soup Company.

Friskies is a registered trademark of Nestlé.

Gatorade is a registered trademark of The Gatorade Company.

Great Starts is a registered trademark of Campbell Soup Company.

Green Giant is a registered trademark of Pillsbury Company.

Guess is a registered trademark of Guess, Inc.

Head and Shoulders is a registered trademark of Procter & Gamble.

Healthy Choice is a registered trademark of Campbell Soup Company.

INF°ACT is a registered trademark of A.C. Nielsen.

Intuit is a registered trademark of Noumenon Corporation.

Jell-O is a registered trademark of General Foods.

L'eggs is a registered trademark of Hanes.

Lean Cuisine is a registered trademark of Stouffer.

LeMenu is a registered trademark of Campbell Soup Company.

Levis is a registered trademark of Levi Strauss.

Lotus 1-2-3 is a registered trademark of Lotus Corporation.

Macintosh is a registered trademark of Apple Computer.

Marlboro is a registered trademark of Philip Morris, Inc.

McLean Deluxe is a registered trademark of McDonald's.

Miller Genuine Draft is a registered trademark of Miller.

Minute Maid is a registered trademark of Coca-Cola.

Mr. Clean is a registered trademark of Procter & Gamble.

Mr. Pibb is a registered trademark of Coca-Cola.

Neutrogena is a registered trademark of Neutrogena, Inc.

Nova is a registered trademark of Chevrolet.

Nuk is a registered trademark of Gerber Products Company.

NutraSweet is a registered trademark of G.D. Searle.

Obsession is a registered trademark of Calvin Klein.

Old Milwaukee Light is a registered trademark of Stroh.

Onestep is a registered trademark of Poloroid Corporation.

Ortho is a registered trademark of Johnson & Johnson.

Oskar is a registered trademark of Sunbeam.

PC_{jr} is a registered trademark of IBM.

Pepsi Light is a registered trademark of Pepsico.

Philadelphia Cream Cheese is a registered trademark of Kraft.

Pinto is a registered trademark of Ford Motor Company.

Polishing Pen is a registered trademark of Chesebrough-Ponds.

Prego is a registered trademark of Campbell Soup Company.

Primaxin is a registered trademark of Merck.

PS/1 is a registered trademark of IBM.

Quarter Pounder is a registered trademark of McDonald's.

Quatro Pro is a registered trademark of Borland International.

Raid is a registered trademark of S.C. Johnson.

Rally is a registered trademark of Wilson Sporting Goods Company.

Ritz is a registered trademark of RJR–Nabisco.

Ruffles is a registered trademark of Frito Lay/Pepsico.

Salon Selectives is a registered trademark of Helene Curtis.

Savage is a registered trademark of Suzuki.

Scope is a registered trademark of Procter & Gamble.

Scrabble is a registered trademark of Selchow and Richter.

Sensor is a registered trademark of Gillette.

Sheer Indulgence is a registered trademark of Kayser-Roth.

Slice is a registered trademark of Pepsico.

Snickers is a registered trademark of Mars, Inc.

Souper Combos is a registered trademark of Campbell Soup Company.

Souptime is a registered trademark of Nestlé.

Spiffits is a registered trademark of DowBrands.

Steri-Strip is a registered trademark of 3M.

Street Rocker is a registered trademark of Huffy.

Suave is a registered trademark of Helene Curtis.

Sudafed 12-Hour Capsules is a registered trademark of Burrough Wellcome, Inc.

Sun Camera is a registered trademark of Poloroid Corporation.

Sun Light is a registered trademark of Lever Brothers.

Surf is a registered trademark of Lever Brothers.

Swanson's Homestyle Recipe Entrees is a registered trademark of Campbell Soup Company.

Switchit is a registered trademark of Innovative Sport Systems.

Tempo is a registered trademark of Ford Motor Company.

Tercell is a registered trademark of Toyota Motor Corporation.

Tide is a registered trademark of Procter & Gamble.

Timex is a registered trademark of U.S. Time.

Touch 'n Curl is a registered trademark of General Electric.

Trac II is a registered trademark of Gillette.

Tropicana is a registered trademark of Seagrams.

Tylenol is a registered trademark of Johnson & Johnson.

Ultra-Wheels is a registered trademark of First Team Sports, Inc.

Viva is a registered trademark of Scot Paper Company.

Whirlpool is a registered trademark of Whirlpool Corporation.

Whopper is a registered trademark of Burger King.

Xerox is a registered trademark of Xerox Corporation.

FOREWORD

I have been thinking and writing a lot lately about the importance of customer service—and I have come to believe that the secret to competitive success is to give customers service so far above their expectations it becomes legendary. Many managers are rediscovering the power of positive word-of-mouth and realizing that to generate it you have to deliver *more* than customers expect. Your attention to customer needs and problems can differentiate what would otherwise be a commodity product and lead to larger market share and profits. It's that simple—and that difficult. It's difficult because many companies are not used to a 100 percent focus on adding value for their customers. They are not used to listening well, trusting their employees, and making continuous improvements, yet these are the keys to competitive success today.

Here is a book that may become a legend in its own right because it shows how managers can achieve competitive success by building on the core concepts of marketing. The authors argue that the marketing concept is at the root of all the exciting new directions in management, and they show readers how to nurture their service and quality efforts and many other programs with the concepts and tools of marketing.

One of the most basic principles I teach in my service workshops is that today, if you're not getting better, you're getting worse. Continuous improvement simply means that you have to continually find ways to do things better, faster, different to be a leader in your industry. Where do new ideas for continuous improvement come from? This book shows how ideas can be stimulated by looking at the entire corporation (not just the marketing department!) from the customer's perspective. Schewe and Hiam use the term "marketing imagination" to describe the powerful force this perspective creates, and the unexpected benefits it produces for customers.

One way to look at this is to draw a box representing the product. Around this box is a second, larger box. It represents everything the customers expect to be bundled with that product—local distribution, timely repairs, and a warranty, for example. This second box is what's expected, so it is the price of admission. But you don't win the game just by getting onto the playing field. So now you have to draw a third, even larger box, this one representing what is *possible*. Many things are possible that the customer may not expect, may not even have imagined. But your task as a manager is to figure out how to deliver these extras. It is in the third box that markets are won and lost, that the battle for U.S. companies to regain leadership of industries like consumer electronics, textiles and automobiles is fought. This book maps the terrain and defines the strategies and tactics for competing in the third box.

In fact, *The Portable MBA in Marketing* is a fine illustration of the strategy of giving what's possible, rather than just what customers expect. As readers, we expect this book to present the MBA marketing curriculum and make it relevant to managers. It does this, more than adequately, but it goes far beyond the expected by showing how any manager, in any department, can create positive change and achieve competitive advantage by applying the marketing concept. In the effort to give more than readers expect, the authors may have rewritten the marketing curriculum forever. This is not just marketing at the MBA level, this is the *new* marketing, and I think it will serve as a user's manual for the quiet revolution that is now percolating in U.S. businesses.

I want to end this foreword with another observation from my work on customer service with all sorts of organizations: I believe that listening is one of the most underutilized skills in business today. Your best resources for information about your business are your customers, your suppliers, and your employees. You need to track costs and read the accounting reports, sure, but you won't ever find a source of competitive advantage in them. And how do you listen better? In part, this means gathering more and better information, and again I recommend this book for both the basic principles and for new ideas and insights on the whole subject of marketing information. And in part, it means listening with commitment.

There is a big difference between commitment and interest. Most managers are interested in what their customers, suppliers and employees think and feel. But I'm not sure how many managers are *fully committed* to hearing what they have to say and acting on it. So ultimately better listening comes down to commitment, and that's an eight inch job; it's all in your head. When managers start working on that job, all sorts of incredible achievements are possible. You've already taken the first step; that's why you are reading this book. I recommend making the study of marketing—and rethinking what the marketing concept means in your work—a top priority when you do your One Minute Goal Setting.

Years ago in *The One Minute Manager* I wrote that 80% of your really important results will come from 20% of your goals, which means you shouldn't waste time on any but the three to six most important goals. But these goals deserve full attention, and you should track your performance on them carefully. Well, I don't know what every reader's top few goals are right now, but I can guess they generally have to do with improving business performance, rising to competitive challenges, and striving for excellence in management. What I *do* know is that developing and applying your marketing imagination ought to be among those goals because it is very likely to help you achieve them.

KEN BLANCHARD
Co-author of
The One Minute Manager

CONTENTS

INTRODUCTION

The man who will use his skill and constructive imagination to see how much he can give for a dollar, instead of how little he can give for a dollar, is bound to succeed.

—*Henry Ford*

Why marketing? Simply put, all the important new directions in management thought and practice are marketing oriented.

Quality marketing programs align manufacturing and service standards with customer preferences and competitor capabilities. The new emphasis on service excellence is defined by customer perception and driven by customer needs. The shift toward flexible production systems is designed to make manufacturing more responsive to the marketplace. So, too, is the drive toward faster product development cycles. Organizations are trading in their bureaucratic layers for a new, "flat" structure so as to be closer to their customers. It is no wonder that financial and strategic plans are now based on market-oriented planning at most U.S. companies.

Within the typical company, growing interest in work and family issues and the management of diverse workforces presents a host of internal marketing challenges. Beyond the company's doors, the pursuit of specialized markets—whether women, the elderly, Hispanics, blacks, overseas buyers, or baby boomers—leans heavily on the principles and techniques of marketing. Also, due to the growing need for appropriate responses to environmental issues, the corporation seeks direction from the customer, via the marketing information that reveals the customer's viewpoint.

Even the shift from regional or national to global arenas of competition is contributing to the marketing movement by forcing international marketing into

1

the forefront of management issues. As Laszlo Papay, IBM's director of quality, observed, "Competitiveness is decided neither by the industry nor by the companies; it is created by the final arbiter—the customer. This notion is often forgotten by U.S. companies."[1] How U.S. companies will respond to the current challenges and threats of international competition is in large part a marketing issue. The importance of marketing to the modern U.S. corporation cannot be underestimated. To demonstrate this, we provide a tour of Omni Consumer Electronics in the introduction to Part One.

Yet marketing as a corporate function has not kept pace with the emergence of marketing as a critical success factor. Marketing departments have not always grown in size or power, despite the greater importance placed on marketing. Perhaps this is as it should be, for what is happening instead is that managers and staff throughout the organization are learning to *think* like marketers. They are using marketing concepts and marketing information to bring the customer's perspective to life as a basis for better decisions in manufacturing, service, finance, product development, billing, and many other nonmarketing functions, as well as in advertising, sales, and all the traditional marketing tasks.

Managers are finding that their newly found marketing intelligence offers a potent source of competitive advantage—after all, the ultimate bottom line is the customer, and anything that can be done to give customers more for their money will translate into a stronger competitive position upon which to build revenue and profit growth. Managers are learning the wisdom of Peter Drucker's advice that "Marketing is so basic it cannot be considered a separate function. . . . It is the whole business seen from the point of view of its final result, that is, from the customer's point of view."[2]

Thus, every manager and would-be manager needs to know marketing cold. The chief executive officers (CEOs) and senior vice presidents (VPs) whose schooling predated modern marketing are now going in search of updated information and instruction; the junior managers and new recruits who had the good fortune to study marketing as students in master's of business administration (MBA) programs now recognize a need to refresh and expand their knowledge; and those who have not had the time or the need to attend business school, or who did not study marketing while in school, find it increasingly important to be fully up to speed in this critical area. Finally, with the growing importance of marketing strategy and the customers that drive it, the many marketing experts—specialists in everything from conducting focus groups to developing direct mail programs—are increasingly called upon to bring a broader view of their field and its principles to their companies or clients. This change requires a "back-to-basics" effort on the part of these experts to broaden their knowledge base and reacquaint themselves with the many other marketing specialties. In short, almost everyone in the modern corporation needs to know more about marketing.

Of course, all these managers could go back to school—and some of them do, through either evening MBA programs or specialized seminars and workshops. But there ought to be an easier way. Unfortunately, the only other option to date has been to sit down with a pile of textbooks from MBA courses and a heap of trade magazines and marketing journals—an option that appeals only to insomniacs (and, incidentally, is an excellent cure for their affliction). In recognition of this lack of options, we have designed this book to capture the spirit and practice of marketing for a management audience.

Our key criteria during the writing were readability and relevance, and our editors have held us to these twin standards quite heartlessly. Whenever something could be explained more simply, they have pushed us to do so. Whenever material could be made more interesting and relevant by illustrating it with real-life examples or anticipating future trends, they have encouraged us to do so. The result is, we believe, a first: a book that answers the manager's need for marketing expertise by presenting the facts of an MBA program and the wisdom of practitioners in a series of easily digested chapters that are amply illustrated with current case histories and examples.

As you read and use this book, remember that its purpose is to help you manage better by being more customer oriented and by outperforming your competitors. These are the benefits marketing brings to a company. The tools and ideas of marketing allow you to maximize sales in the short term, and to position all aspects of the organization most advantageously for the long term. As such, marketing touches on the work of everyone within the modern corporation—or ought to. Whether you are pursuing a career within the boundaries of a marketing department, or are focusing on another functional area, you will benefit from a deeper understanding of marketing and a stronger emphasis on serving your customers.

A PERSONAL NOTE

The writing of this book has had a strange and rewarding effect upon its authors. Both of us have many years of experience, as consultants and managers, in the practical side of marketing. Between us, we have taught marketing courses and workshops to MBAs, undergraduates, and managers for hundreds, perhaps thousands, of hours. We expected this project to require a fairly routine presentation of the marketing curriculum for those unfamiliar with it. Instead it has been an inspiring journey, leading us to reassess our vision of management. It is almost as if we were seeing this material for the first time, for it certainly shone in a new light as we examined it in view of the many dramatic changes in management thought and practice that are now gathering momentum in this country.

Marketers have spoken for years about the coming marketing revolution. Every marketing major leaves school with the (optimistic) impression that marketing departments will soon be the largest and best funded areas in the corporation. But it turns out that this view of the marketing revolution is far too parochial. The revolution is under way all right, but in many companies it started in manufacturing, or quality control, or the CEO's office, and not in the marketing department. Although this revolution is based upon the field of marketing, it is transforming every function, even marketing itself. The transformation of marketing reflects the reality that managers facing the need to achieve global competitiveness must take no prisoners. Much of the doctrine of management thought is within their sights, even in the field of marketing.

What seems to be happening is that marketing is recreating the U.S. corporation, and the U.S. corporation is recreating marketing. Management will never be the same, but neither will marketing. What amazed us as we wrote this book was the extent to which both management and marketing are changing in tandem. The material seemed new in large part because it is being transformed, either directly, through the development of new practices, or indirectly, because it is now being used in a different and broader context and thus must be understood from a fresh vantage point. The average MBA curriculum has not yet caught up with these revolutionary changes in management thought and practice.

As a result, we must recommend this book not only for those who have not studied marketing, but (and perhaps especially) for those who think they know marketing already. We believe that all managers need to refresh and renew their understanding of marketing and, through the lenses of this important discipline, their understanding of their company and its customers as well.

PART ONE

THE MARKETING CONCEPT

A VISIT TO OMNI:
MARKETING AND THE
MANAGEMENT REVOLUTION

"Good morning, Ms. Jones. I understand you want to learn about marketing here at Omni Consumer Electronics. Would you like a tour of our operations?"

Ann Jones was standing in a long corridor of Omni's headquarters building, talking with Jim Berman, president and CEO. Berman began the tour by explaining that the marketing department was on the other side of the building. Jones indicated that she did not mind the walk.

First he led Jones past a heavy set of double doors marked "Factory Personnel Only." Opening them, he waved toward rows of large equipment and conveyor belts, the production lines. The nearest one had stopped, and five workers were huddled over a piece of equipment.

"What's the matter?" Jones asked.

"Let's see," said Berman, as he approached the group. A brief conversation revealed that the workers had stopped the line to adjust a machine because one worker noticed it had moved out of adjustment.

"You see," explained the worker, "I plot this machine's performance on a chart, and whenever I see it drifting away from our standard, I stop the line. If I didn't, the products would probably be sent back by our customers later, so it's better to get it right the first time."

This did not sound like Jones's idea of a manufacturing operation. Where were the supervisors, the engineers, the quality control specialists? Why were line workers permitted to decide when to stop the line and what standard of quality to build to? Noting Jones's puzzled look, Berman explained that a new quality program had set performance standards for products based on customer requirements, and then given the workers responsibility for meeting those customer requirements. "We are even experimenting with having factory workers respond to customer complaints," he added.

Customer complaints? Customer quality requirements? It sounded like marketing, not manufacturing, to Jones. But Berman was already leading her off the floor and back down that long corridor. "Here," he said, gesturing through a large glass window, "is where all our invoices are processed. Would you like to see?" Not waiting for a response, he pushed open another door and led Jones into rows of desks, each with a computer terminal and piles of correspondence and forms. Dozens of clerical workers were busily entering data into computers, but several were talking and laughing into telephones. Berman strode up behind one, a young woman who was too preoccupied with her conversation to notice his approach. Jones hovered in the background, wondering how tough the president of Omni was on his employees. As Berman approached, the woman was just finishing her conversation, and you could hear her wishing someone a good day.

Seeing Berman, she spun in her chair and said, "Hi, Mr. Berman!" He introduced Jones to the woman, who explained that she had been on the phone to a customer: "Sam's Electronics is a small chain, and one of their stores held up payment on an invoice because the goods were delivered late. When I saw the note the store manager sent in with his bill, I called our shipping department to find out what happened. They looked up the shipment and discovered that it had arrived at Sam's central warehouse on time—the delay must have been on their end. So I called the store manager and explained what happened. He was very nice on the phone, and promised to pay the bill right away."

Berman interrupted to ask how the problem could be prevented in the future. "Well," explained the young woman, "I told him about our new direct shipment program, and suggested that he bypass his central warehouse when delivery time is especially important. I am also going to send a note to our sales department. I think they have a team that could go into Sam's central warehouse and help them solve whatever problems they are having. But that probably has to be arranged with Sam's headquarters, not through an individual store."

"Good idea," said Berman. "Keep up the good work!" Jones breathed a sigh of relief, glad to know that her visit wouldn't result in anyone getting fired. As Berman led Jones back into the corridor, he explained, "That's another part of our new quality program. Everyone who has direct customer contact is being trained to solve customer problems. The people in that department used to be evaluated based on how many bills they processed an hour, and as a result they were very efficient. But our surveys showed us that our wholesale customers were unhappy with these employees' performance, so we changed the entire system."

Noticing that Berman again mentioned customers in relation to a nonmarketing function, Jones commented, "I thought that type of thing was what the marketing department did."

Berman laughed and continued, "The customer service center is another example. We staff a phone bank to handle end users' complaints and problems, and recently we gave these operators the freedom to offer replacements, to cross-sell repair plans, even to consult with our engineers or factory workers when they see a problem we could . . . oops!"

Rounding a corner, Berman almost ran into three middle-aged men in suits, walking slowly the other way and apparently deep in conversation. "Oh, what good luck!" said Berman, "Ms. Jones, I'd like you to meet our director of sales and two of our senior engineers. Gentlemen, Ms. Jones is studying marketing."

"What a coincidence," said one of the engineers, "We were just talking about a marketing problem. We are trying to work out some of the final details on a new product." Berman joined the conversation, and Jones gathered that the issue concerned how to reduce the cost of certain components so that the new product could be introduced at a price the sales force preferred.

After the conversation was over, Jones commented that it sounded more like a technical problem than a marketing problem. "I guess you're right," said Berman, "But you see, we use product development teams here, and they include marketing, sales, and manufacturing people as well as our product development engineers. That way we get products that the market really needs, and it takes less time to bring them to market because everyone gets in their two cents worth at the beginning. We used to send new products from engineering to manufacturing for review, and they would often have to go back to engineering for redesign. Then we'd send them to sales and marketing for review—and more redesign. Now everyone cooperates. Sometimes we even have customers on our product development teams."

As Jones followed Berman down the hall, she tried to make sense of what she had seen so far. Customers designing products? Engineers talking with salespeople about prices? Clerks solving distribution problems for customers? Factory line workers determining product quality? Jones wondered whether anything would be left for the marketing department to do by the time she made it to the other side of the building.

"Here we are," said Berman, as he and Jones entered a side corridor with an open room off it. "Our product managers work here," he added, gesturing toward the cubbyholes spreading across the open area.

"Do they manage Omni's marketing department?" Jones asked hopefully.

"Not really," explained Berman with another laugh. "Actually, they manage Omni's products, rather than any of its employees. Each one is in charge of seeing that a specific product is designed, packaged, produced, sold, shipped, and advertised as well as possible. Of course, since they are not formally in charge of the design, packaging, sales, distribution, or advertising functions, they have to collaborate with people in each of these areas. A product manager is like the hub of a wheel, and all the necessary functions form the spokes."

A middle-aged woman, sitting nearby, cut into the conversation. "More like a dentist, trying to pull teeth!" she quipped.

Berman smiled and introduced Joan Miller, "You see," he explained, "sometimes product managers have to fight for the support they think their product deserves. Joan is in charge of our line of electric toaster ovens. She is working on the promotion plans for two new products."

"You mean some product managers handle more than one product?" Jones asked, suspecting that the marketing department might be as confusing as the rest of Omni.

"I am actually called a line manager," explained Miller. "In some cases, we find it works best to coordinate the marketing of closely related products. I handle all the toaster ovens so that the marketing is consistent and appropriate across the whole product line. Except, of course, for the new models," she added with a reproachful look at Berman.

Berman laughed and explained that Miller was currently lobbying for an advertising campaign on prime-time television for two new toaster ovens. "You see, the advertising manager thinks that their budgets should be in proportion with their sales, which are pretty low so far. But Joan says they need a big up-front investment in advertising to tell consumers about their special features."

"What are you going to decide?" Jones asked Berman, hoping the question was not out of line.

"Nothing," he explained. "It's not my decision. But I expect that Joan will manage to talk the advertising manager into it. Dentists usually get their teeth," he added, with a smile at Miller, then he asked, "What does the consumer research show?"

Miller pulled a sheaf of computer paper out from under a pile and thumbed to a table in the middle of it. "This is from a telephone survey of 300 consumers done just last month. Here it shows that 87 percent of households know that Omni makes toaster ovens, and that 58 percent say they would like the very features we offer in the two new models. But, on the next page, you can see that only 4 percent of them have heard of our new models. No wonder they aren't buying—they don't know about the new models yet. We obviously need to spread the word."

"I think you're right," said Berman. "But how do you know prime-time television is the best way to build awareness?"

"The advertising agency actually came up with that idea," answered Miller. "They looked at the cost of reaching our target customers in various ways—everything from cable TV to home magazines—and their media buyers are convinced that prime time is most efficient in this case. For one thing, it reaches consumers when they have food—and ovens—on their minds."

"Well, good luck with the new products, Joan," said Berman. "Let me know what happens, will you?" With that, he knocked on an open door and led Jones into a large, comfortable office. "I thought you would like to see where those survey numbers come from," he remarked as he introduced Jones to Roger Freeman, the director of marketing research.

Jones looked around the office suspiciously. "Do you do surveys?" she asked, wondering how Freeman could have talked to 300 consumers regarding toaster ovens last month.

"No, not really," he laughed. "Actually, most of our marketing research is done by specialized subcontractors. We use several research firms that have large staffs of interviewers. I work with people at Omni to decide what answers we need, and then I hire a research firm to do a study that will give us those answers."

"What are you working on today?" Berman asked.

"Earlier," said Freeman, "I met with the research firm that does our European surveys. With 40 percent of our sales coming from exports now, we have to track customer opinion in many countries. And I was just talking with Mary Flushing—she's our chief financial officer," he explained, turning to Jones. "She wants to do a study of her customers, and she asked us here in marketing research to help out."

"I didn't know finance had anything to do with Omni's customers," Jones said, puzzled.

"True," explained Freeman, "but the finance department's customers are the people who use the reports and services it provides—mostly Omni's employees and stockholders. Mary feels that many managers are not getting the kind of information they need from finance, and she wants to find out what they think. Also, she suspects that a lot of accounting reports are not read, and would like to save the time and paper for something more useful."

"Who are the marketing department's customers?" Jones asked Freeman, wondering how far the idea of a "customer" could be taken.

"Well, at Omni, the marketing department is a staff function, and its role is to support sales, manufacturing, and any other department that needs information about customers or competitors. Also, marketing is responsible for all the advertising and sales promotion Omni does, which makes Omni's customers ours too. And, last but not least, senior management at Omni is a marketing department customer. For example, when Omni does its annual strategic plan, the marketing department gives management a detailed analysis by product and market segment and a proposed strategy and budget for each product."

"Does every department at Omni have its own customers?" Jones asked Berman.

"We like to look at it that way," he answered. "Why should we distinguish between external and internal customers? Anyone who consumes the products or services deserves to be treated like a customer, and the best way to improve the work the company does is to concentrate on serving customers better."

"It's too bad John and Betty aren't here," interrupted Freeman. "They are Omni's director of marketing and advertising manager. They went over to the agency this morning to review the new corporate campaign. You see," he added for Jones's benefit, "we don't develop most of Omni's advertisements and promotions here, either. We work with an advertising agency that translates our strategies into specific advertisements. They have dozens of artists and writers who specialize in that kind of work."

"What is a corporate campaign?" Jones asked.

Berman fielded that one: "Oh, that's a new direction for Omni. The idea is to do some advertising and public relations—newspaper articles and the like—to tell the public about Omni as a company. We think that a stronger image for the company will help us sell individual products, and will also boost Omni's stock price."

"I'm sorry I can't introduce you to the head of the marketing department," he added. "I hope you are not disappointed. I'm afraid I have not been able to show you very much of our marketing department today."

"That's OK, Mr. Berman," Jones responded. "I think I have learned a great deal about what marketing means at Omni—even without the full tour of the marketing department."

"Yes, I guess that's right," responded Berman. "Marketing isn't confined to a single department any more, is it?" Jones nodded in agreement.

1 THE ESSENCE OF MARKETING

The Customer First, Last, and Always

Nothing is worthwhile unless it touches the customer.

—*Edgar Woolard, CEO, DuPont*[1]

There was a time when companies had never heard of marketing. Either they sold products or they didn't sell them, depending upon the success of the salespeople or retailers who were charged with making the sale. The idea of marketing—focusing on how to satisfy consumers—has been with us in a formal way only since the 1950s. Many businesses today still do not go in for formal marketing. The roadside vegetable stand has no marketing department, and does not need one. But, marketing department or no, however, every organization in this day and age must do marketing to survive.

L.L. Bean had no marketing department in 1912 when it first began mailing catalogs (they were called circulars back then). Nonetheless, unlike many catalog retailers that have failed in the interim, L.L. Bean had a clear vision of the marketing concept. The 1912 catalog contained the following message from founder Leon Leonwood Bean:

I do not consider a sale complete until goods are worn out and customer still satisfied.

We will thank anyone to return goods that are not perfectly satisfactory.

Should the person reading this notice know of anyone who is not satisfied with our goods, I will consider it a favor to be notified.

Above all things we wish to avoid having a dissatisfied customer.[2]

11

Was this guy nuts? Some people thought so, and many managers would still hesitate to apply L.L. Bean's guarantee to their businesses. How many businesses advertise, as L.L. Bean does today, that "We'll accept returns at any time for any reason. Your purchase will be replaced, or we will refund your money or credit your credit card." The very thought strikes fear into many managers' hearts because it requires that they *trust* their customers. But trusting the customer is certainly part of the ephemeral essence of marketing: If you can't trust them, why should they trust *you?*

Marketing is the sum total of activities that keep a company focused on its customers and, with good management and a little luck, ensure that the company's offerings are valued by its customers. At the roadside vegetable stand, marketing includes a host of decisions concerning location, pricing, the choice of vegetables to grow, and the quantities to offer. It might also include issues such as whether to switch to organic produce, whether and where to post signs or run ads to attract customers, and how to handle complaints and returns. No marketing department exists in this type of business because the principals are best suited to handling marketing decisions and activities themselves, and, mercifully, because the business is simply not large enough to justify specialization and division of labor and the bureaucracy it often brings. However, the management of a roadside stand is of necessity at least partially marketing oriented, as is any other business, whether for-profit or not-for-profit, unless it is so protected by regulation or economic monopoly that it can afford to ignore its customers. It is difficult to find examples of such protected organizations, especially over the long run, because they simply do not prosper.

The U.S. Postal Service may be an exception. It has, after all, a protected partial monopoly. Nevertheless, it seems to do a decent job of moving millions of pieces of mail to their intended destinations. Before firms such as Federal Express and United Parcel Service began competing with it, most people would have given the Postal Service high marks.

However, the fact that private companies now carry mail faster and more reliably illustrates an important essence of marketing-oriented management that is missing at the Postal Service: the drive to find new ways to satisfy customers, *even* if customers have not already envisioned and demanded them. Fred Smith knew mail could be delivered overnight, even though the Postal Service and its customers did not. Although Smith's company, Federal Express, cannot by law deliver mail to mailboxes, it can and does hand deliver mail overnight at a lower cost and more reliably than the Postal Service.

This drive to innovate and improve upon current service standards is a natural outgrowth of the sincere conviction that "a customer is the most important person in this office," as Leon Bean warned his employees in 1912. None of his employees would have written as self-important a letter as the following one, sent by a U.S. Postal Service manager to a customer, Mr. Hiam, who had filed a customer complaint card after waiting 25 minutes in line at a post office:

Dear Mr. Heam:

This letter is to acknowledge receipt of your consumer service card. I wish to apologize for any inconvenience you experienced due to the line at the University Drive Post Office. As in any business, we experience peak times of the day, early morning, late afternoon, which requires some amount of delay time to our customers. I'd like to assure you that this is not a situation we wish to put our customers through. Every effort is made to anticipate such times and schedule employees accordingly.

In an effort to save you time in the future, I am enclosing a stamps by mail envelope. This service will provide stamps through mail delivery for you and will make it unnecessary to come to the Post Office. Our vending machines in the lobby area are also available from 5:30 a.m. to 5:30 p.m. A new scale device in our lobby area can provide you with information as to costs and available services.

Thank you for taking the time to express your concerns to us. Your business is important to the Postal Service and every effort will be made to improve delays in the future.

Sincerely,

xxx xxxxxx
Acting Window Supervisor
Amherst Post Office
Amherst, MA 01002-9998

At first, this looks like a good marketing effort: A personal letter, signed by a manager, is sent to a customer after the customer complains. No doubt this letter is the outgrowth of one of the many customer service programs that have taken seed across the nation. Actually, however, the letter is an example of how *not* to do marketing.

The letter opens with a misspelling of the customer's name, clearly starting off on the wrong foot. The writer then explains that it is difficult to staff the post office properly. But customers do not care *why* service is bad—this is not the customer's problem. Most significantly, the second paragraph, despite its polite tone, implies that the Postal Service does not want the customer to come to the post office in the future. "Ah, wouldn't it be peaceful around here if it weren't for those irritating customers," one imagines the managers grumbling.

The acid test of a marketing-oriented organization is whether the managers look to change *their* behavior or that of their customers when something goes wrong. The Postal Service employee who responded to the complaint flunks this test. Meanwhile Federal Express gains a greater share from the U.S. Postal Service yearly by passing the test. John West, Federal Express' manager of quality improvement, explains their philosophy: "We won't be happy until we have 100% customer satisfaction and on-time delivery."[3]

The difference between good and bad marketing can be subtle. Although West's statement does not seem very different from the Postal Service's response—"I'd like to assure you that this is not a situation we wish to put our customers through?"—the structure of these two statements is worlds apart. West's quote uses "won't," short for the definitive "*will* not," whereas the Postal Service employee used "I'd," short for the conditional "I *would*." This latter choice of words unintentionally betrays a lack of conviction.

Why split hairs? Because many people and many managers think U.S. organizations have already adopted the marketing concept, whereas in fact *its essence is still missing at most companies.*

The view that the consumer is the focal point of the firm is the fundamental principle of the marketing concept—captured in the slogan, "The Consumer is King." Here are some other slogans that express this point of view:

"We Do It All for You"—McDonald's

"You're the Boss"—United Airlines

"Nobody Else Like You Service"—Equitable Life Insurance

"Chosen #1 in People Pleasin"—Holiday Inn

Of course, it is easier to put the marketing concept into a slogan than into practice. In fact, often consumers feel more like serfs than kings. Poor service, low product quality, inconvenient locations, rude salespeople, excessively high prices, and other frustrations suffered by consumers attest to the fact that companies are still struggling to apply the marketing concept in full, and that most firms are not yet truly customer oriented.

Even in the 1990s, the marketing concept represents a major challenge for managers. Yet, when we showed the first draft of this book to an expert editor, he responded to the preceding paragraph with the comment, "Is this still true? Haven't a lot of businesses made strong efforts to implement the marketing concept?" We think it is still true, more true than ever, *even though* many organizations (including the U.S. Postal Service) have made strong efforts to implement the marketing concept. This is why it is important to split hairs.

Perhaps the distinction between good and poor marketing is hard to make because real customer-driven management and its results—excellent products and service—are so rare we hardly know them. Professor Peter Senge of the Massachusetts Institute of Technology's (MIT's) Sloan School of Management argues that "Most Americans don't know good service. They haven't had it."[4]

In a large part, U.S. companies are learning what the marketing concept truly means by watching their Japanese rivals. The Japanese companies' passionate pursuit of customer-defined product and service quality has given them an edge over domestic competitors in the U.S. markets. Japan's enthusiastic pursuit of its country's Deming Award for quality spawned the Baldridge Award in the United States, inspiring companies such as recent winner American Express. But the Japanese concept of quality has not remained static, as Senge explains:

Japanese firms' view of serving the customer has evolved. In the early years of total quality, the focus was on "fitness to standard," making a product reliably so that it would do what its designers intended it to do and what the firm told its customer it would do. Then came a focus on "fitness to need," understanding better what the customer wanted and then providing products that reliably met those needs. Today, leading edge firms seek to understand and meet the "latent need" of the customer—what customers might truly value but have never experienced or would never think to ask for.[5]

From fitness to standard, to fitness to need, and now to fitness to latent need, the Japanese version of the marketing concept has proved a moving target for U.S. businesses. The irony is that it all started in the United States. W. Edwards Deming, of Japan's Deming Prize, is American, but at first U.S. companies would not listen to him. Of course, early pioneers such as Leon Bean also knew about fitness to latent need. He didn't invent the special Bean boot, with leather upper and rubber lower parts, because *customers* asked for it, but because *he* knew they needed a new kind of boot that gave both the comfort of leather and the waterproof quality of rubber. L.L. Bean listens well to its customers—this is what fitness to standard demands—but it goes beyond this to address customer needs in a creative manner.

We might call this the *marketing imagination,* and it is as essential to the marketing concept as are good products and service and a willingness to listen and respond to customers. Fred Smith's marketing imagination created overnight parcel service. Mazda's marketing imagination inspired the successful Miata. As a Detroit executive explained to Peter Senge, "You could never produce the Mazda Miata solely from market research. It required a leap of imagination to see what the customer *might* want."[6] This is why Senge believes that "Most changes don't come from listening to the customer. Most major innovations come from some 'crazy people' in the organization who have an idea for something that will work and add value."[7] Thus, how a company manages innovation and how it manages all its employees becomes a part of the essence of marketing. Good marketing is not as easy as simply listening to the customer. But it may be the best way for U.S. companies to regain their leadership in marketing and management. U.S. companies are the original innovators in this area. As Paul Allaire, CEO of Xerox, explains, "We're never going to outdiscipline the Japanese on quality. To win, we need to find ways to capture the creative and innovative spirit of the American worker. That's the real organizational challenge."[8]

Also essential is the basic strategic vision a company sets for itself—its self-image, if you will. The U.S. Postal Service sees its task as moving mail around, and this it does with great gusto. But Federal Express sees its task as satisfying each and every customer, so it is far more able to take a customer complaint or problem seriously than is the Postal Service. While the U.S. Postal Service collects, but does not learn from, customer complaints through the relatively passive medium of complaint forms, Federal Express actively seeks information about problems through 2,100 customer interviews every quarter of the year. What Federal Express has learned from its customer interviews since beginning the process in 1985 is regularly incorporated into its Service Quality Indicator, the measure by which every employee's performance is evaluated daily.[9] Because of its customer-oriented vision of itself, Federal Express is able to *learn* from what it hears customers say, whereas the U.S. Postal Service does not. To truly adopt the marketing concept, an organization must *go beyond listening to its customers*. It must apply its own imagination to what it hears the customer say. This is what successful Japanese companies are learning to do, and what U.S. companies are rediscovering. But the process is slow and difficult, and it is by no means over. The process requires dramatic changes, even for companies that already stand out as leaders. Which explains why Allaire of Xerox says, "I have to change the company substantially to be more market driven."[10]

We stated that a company's basic strategic vision is relevant to its marketing concept. The reverse is true as well. This thought was presented most forcefully by Theodore Levitt in a 1960 article called "Marketing Myopia."[11] He observed that, because the railroads saw themselves as in the business of laying track instead of transporting goods and people, they passed over opportunities to profit from new technologies such as autos and trucks, airplanes, and even telephones. Thus, the railroads declined even though the demand for passenger and freight transportation grew. Similarly, because the oil companies refused to pursue natural gas, renegade executives left to start competing gas companies. Companies often miss growth opportunities by failing to define themselves in terms of the benefit they provide to customers.

As long as companies view their business creatively and from the customer's perspective, they will find opportunities to grow and prosper. According to Levitt "Every major industry was once a growth industry . . . . In every case the reason growth is threatened, slowed, or stopped is *not* because the market is saturated. It is because there has been a failure of management." He continues, "In truth, *there is no such thing* as a growth industry, I believe. There are only companies organized and operated to create and capitalize on growth opportunities."[12]

In his 1975 retrospective commentary, Levitt observes that his famous 1960 article had done both good and bad. Although many companies broadened their vision most profitably—from oil company to energy company, for example—others developed what he calls "marketing mania," becoming "obsessively responsive to every fleeting whim of the customer."[13] Uncontrolled brand and line extensions, compulsive redrawing of organization charts, and riotous growth of sales and marketing departments are not the answer. The marketing concept does not call for more marketing; what it demands is better management. But some companies fail to grasp this essential point.

This dichotomy of views leads to two interpretations of the chapter's opening quote from DuPont's CEO—"Nothing is worthwhile unless it touches the customer"—because a touch can be welcome or unwelcome. The fact that the number of telemarketers has risen fourfold since 1984 to 300,000[14] is evidence that many managers believe more touch is what the marketing concept requires. The corresponding fact that "the Direct Marketing Association has counted roughly 1,000 new state bills on telemarketing this year, about one-third of which would curb unsolicited sales calls,"[15] is strong evidence that customers will not tolerate unwanted touches for long. Companies need to touch, and be touched by, their customers, but the *quality* of this contact is (or ought to be) the key concern of marketing.

Steven Star, director of the Marketing Center at MIT's Sloan School, argues that this may be the central challenge of marketing. He writes, "If you think for a moment about the process of trying to practice the marketing concept carefully, you quickly see how things will necessarily go wrong."[16] The following, according to Star, summarizes how they go wrong: "No matter how specialized our media, how carefully computerized our audience data, how sophisticated our protocols of market analysis, there remain, as always, major misfits among products, audiences, messages, and media." The result is usually that for every targeted customer who welcomes the touch of a marketing program, many more "frustrated, distracted, or irritated customers" are touched more or less accidentally as an artifact of the program's implementation. (Star's article is illustrated by a cartoon of a bald-headed man on the street, surrounded by billboards and taxi and bus posters, all advertising hair sprays.)

From the company's perspective, this misfit between message and audience is a costly waste and, quite possibly, a source of consumer ill will. From the customer's perspective, it is also costly, but more because of the increasing din of misdirected marketing messages it creates than because of any tangible impact. Still, if you believe, as Leon Bean did, that "the customer is the most important person" in your company, the last thing you want to do is shout something at customers that they don't want or need to hear!

When looked at from these multiple perspectives, marketing seems at once more challenging and more essential than it is usually thought to be. The essence of the marketing concept is difficult to grasp, and even more difficult to implement. But implementing it is a practical necessity, both broadly, in how the organization defines and organizes itself, and more narrowly, in how the managers conceive of and implement specific marketing programs.

Program design and implementation are constrained by the tools available to management. These tools are conventionally thought of as including the "four Ps"—product, price, place, and promotion—although, as we discuss below, the implementation of the marketing concept may require additional elements in this mix. How these elements of the marketing mix are utilized is the general issue in development of a marketing program.

Product

The focal point of the marketing mix is the product. A product includes more than a good or service that is designed, produced, and offered for sale. It includes all the planning that precedes actual production; it includes research and development; and it includes all the services that accompany the product, such as installation and maintenance. Consider videocassette recorders (VCRs). Buyers found that several steps were involved in installing and programming a VCR, and that the instruction booklets often were not much help. When Sony became aware of this problem, it began making a VCR with a set of synthesized vocal instructions that guided the user through the installation and operation procedures. This instructional mode was as much a part of the product as was the actual machine.

Price

Price is the cost, or what the buyer must give up, to receive the product. Although price usually means an amount of money, some exchanges involve the giving of goods and services by both parties. Price is not static. For example, the price of a VCR was high upon introduction, but fell as competition intensified and manufacturers learned to produce machines at lower cost.

Place

Place, or distribution, involves making sure that the product is available where and when it is wanted. Marketers can choose among many ways of moving products to consumers. For example, they may choose among different types of outlets and store locations. Distribution also involves such decisions as how much inventory to hold, how to transport goods, and where to locate warehouses. Manufacturers initially placed VCRs in retail stores that sold TVs, but now catalogs and discounters also carry VCRs.

Promotion

Promotion, the final P, is perhaps the most visible to consumers. Promotion is the broad term used to describe the entire field of sales communication—advertising, personal selling, sales promotion, and public relations. These activities result in consumer awareness of a product's existence, as well as knowledge about its unique and desirable features. In short, promotion informs and persuades, and sometimes irritates, as Steven Star observed. When VCRs were first introduced, press coverage was very important in educating consumers. Now competing manufacturers advertise to build brand image and trumpet new features, while retailers use sales promotions and in-store selling to encourage purchase.

A MARKETING MIX FOR THE 1990s

Dick Berry, a professor from the University of Wisconsin—Madison, recently surveyed a sample of marketing managers, customer service managers, product managers, and senior executives to find out which marketing variables they consider to be most important. He started with the four Ps, breaking each into subcategories, and added an S to represent customer service elements of the marketing mix and two Cs to represent customer sensitivity and convenience. Some marketers argue that customer service deserves as much attention in planning as do product, price, place, or promotion decisions. In fact, *Fortune's* 1991 special issue on the hottest ideas for the 1990s features the idea that managers should market every product as though it is a service. According to this concept, there are no products, only services! This means, for example, that Xerox should focus on the quality of the service performed by and with its photocopiers, rather than on the machine itself. But let's get back to Berry's study.

He analyzed his results to identify the elements of the marketing mix that managers currently consider most important, and ranked them by importance. The three new items on this list—the S and two Cs—as well as the traditional four Ps all have to do with how the company responds to and serves its customers. Below are the seven elements of the marketing mix, as ranked in Berry's study from most to least important.[17]

1. *Customer sensitivity*—Employee attitude, customer treatment, and response to customers.
2. *Product*—Product quality, reliability, and features.
3. *Customer convenience*—Availability to the customer, customer convenience, and selling.
4. *Service*—Postsale service, presale service, and customer convenience.
5. *Price*—Price charged, pricing terms, and pricing offers.
6. *Place*—Provider accessibility, provider facilities, pricing terms, and availability to customer.
7. *Promotion*—Advertising, publicity, selling, presale services, and pricing offers.

Note that Berry's respondents ranked customer sensitivity—a variable that was not even considered in the traditional four Ps structure—as the most important variable in the marketing mix. To manage sensitivity to customers, the marketer needs to manage the attitudes of all employees whose work affects the customers. Berry's survey results expand our vision of what a marketing program consists of: It must now involve almost everyone in the business. The more recent items—the two Cs and the S—need to pervade a company's use of the traditional four Ps in a way that is not traditional in U.S. business.

THE MARKETING EQUATION

The decisions that make up the marketing mix, when implemented, are the basis for providing satisfaction to consumers in a particular market segment. Satisfaction comes from an exchange. But an exchange takes place only when each party will receive greater satisfaction from what is received than from what is given up. In other words, the price paid by the buyer must be equal to or less than the total satisfaction obtainable from the bundle of benefits received. This can be expressed in equation form as follows:

$$\text{Price} \leq \begin{cases} \text{Product} \\ \text{Place} \\ \text{Promotion} \end{cases}$$

If the buyer perceives the price to be greater than the benefits received, the value of those benefits is not "worth" the cost and the exchange will not happen.

Marketers can manipulate either or both sides of this equation. They can lower the price (or make it appear lower; we will discuss psychological pricing later) and/or increase the degree of satisfaction offered (through better goods and services, more convenient distribution, and/or more effective promotion). They can also stimulate exchanges.

There are two ways to look at the marketing equation and the exchange it implies, but again the distinction requires us to split hairs. The most obvious and common view is distributive: The buyer and seller cut up a pie, and each tries to get a bigger piece. In this approach, the company worries about recovering its costs plus a decent margin, while the customer tries to get the best price possible. The other view of the marketing equation tries to give both parties more by making the pie bigger. According to this view, marketing imagination and constant advancement on the part of the seller engender more commitment and trust in the buyer by adding value beyond what was expected. If any single perspective can be said to capture the essence of marketing, this is it.

Paul Allaire of Xerox has said, "If we do what's right for the customer, our market share and return on assets will take care of themselves."[18] This is an unusual statement in that it reflects a remarkable faith in the marketing concept. Many CEOs assume that the marketing department will take care of customers, and that their own job is to take care of the bottom line— forgetting that the bottom line is nothing more than the end result of the exchange equation. But managers with Allarie's insight see everything differently. For example, Henry Ford, speaking long before the fall of Detroit (the Japanese appear to have listened to him, although his U.S. successors did not), said, "We have never considered any costs as fixed. Therefore, we first reduce the price to the point where we believe more sales will result. Then we go ahead and try to make the prices. We do not bother about costs. The new price forces the costs down."[19] This view attacks the marketing equation backward, from the customer's end, starting with a desirable price and believing (it has to be a matter of faith) that the company can learn to make the desired product for that price. Perhaps the essence of marketing is that *simple*—attack everything backward, from the customer's perspective instead of the company's. Although Ford Motors rose to greatness on the strength of this perspective, the vision was eventually lost, allowing foreign automakers to champion the consumer's cause. Now Ford is struggling to regain the vision—and its status—through a grueling total quality program. Perhaps the essence of marketing is also that *difficult,* for it is easy to lose this vision, to come down with marketing myopia, and to spend all one's time squinting at accounting reports instead of listening and imagining on behalf of the customer.

2 PLANNING

Using Tested Concepts and New Ideas for Marketing Strategy

If the purpose of strategy is to gain competitive advantage, then by implication theories of strategy should be continually in flux. Any new insight that obtains wide currency . . . loses value in providing additional competitive advantage . . . This self-destructive aspect of strategic insight . . . has received limited attention, as has the attendant need to be continually innovative and creative.

—Paul Schoemaker,
Graduate School of Business,
University of Chicago[1]

If there's a hell for planners, over the portal will be carved the term "cash cow."

—Stephen Hardis,
vice president of planning,
Eaton Corporation.[2]

"Strategic planning is dead; long live strategic planning!" seems like an appropriate way to begin this chapter, for it is necessary both to mark the passing of the old strategic planning and to note the exciting emergence of entirely new approaches, much as the succession of kings was once heralded. Since its birth in the 1950s and 1960s, strategic planning has reigned, giving managers a new and exciting set of more marketing-oriented tools for analysis, planning, and control. Innovators such as the Boston Consulting Group and General Electric discovered the wisdom of identifying opportunities based on market analysis rather than solely on financial analysis, and their philosophy and techniques spread rapidly throughout the 1970s and into the 1980s. But strategic planning's growth stalled in the 1980s, with many companies abandoning their large planning staffs and forsaking more complex analytical methods and planning processes, and by the beginning of the 1990s it was moribund. When Gary Reiner of the Boston Consulting Group wrote in 1989 that "planning is passé," it was clear that a succession was imminent.[3] The problem was that the old king had left no offspring, so managers must find their own. They face the daunting task of planning in the face of great uncertainty and rapid change. As Michael Porter of the Harvard Business School sees it, "The state of practice in this area is very primitive."[4]

If any single factor can be blamed for the death of strategic planning, it must be the failure of the U.S. economy to compete globally. This failure became painfully obvious in the 1980s as the trade imbalance in categories such as autos, machine tools, consumer electronics, semiconductors, and textiles took a nasty turn for the worse on the economist's charts. A report from MIT's Commission on Industrial Productivity summed up management's initial response to the problem:

> The decline of the U.S. economy puzzles most Americans. The qualities and talents that gave rise to the dynamism of the postwar years must surely be present still in the national character, and yet American industry seems to have lost much of its vigor. In looking for ways to reverse the decline, it is only natural to turn to the methods that succeeded in the golden years of growth and innovation. Many business managers have adopted just this strategy. The results, unfortunately, are rather like those of a man who keeps striking the same match because it worked fine the first time.[5]

This failure to measure up to global competition left the people at Xerox looking through their pockets for another book of matches. Xerox's story is an excellent illustration of what is happening to planning in U.S. businesses.

In 1974, Xerox had a stunning 86 percent world market share for photocopiers. What could possibly go wrong? As discussed shortly, conventional planning models assume that strength and profits flow from strong market shares. But as new competitors, such as Ricoh and Canon, entered the market, Xerox fell back, all the way to a 17 percent market share in 1984.[6] If strategic planning really was king, Xerox's managers would have been beheaded! The company began to climb back out of its hole in the latter half of the 1980s, regaining lost share and improving quality. Along the way, Xerox invented new ways of planning and implementing strategy, and adopted many of the best techniques from its Japanese competitors. But, rather than skip that entire decade, we start with a quick review of the planning models that led companies such as Xerox into so much trouble.

It is easy to dismiss the old approach to planning as worthless, but this is not fair. Managers today cannot ignore the old wisdom, but they also cannot rely on it to provide competitive advantage. One must know yesterday's techniques to play the game, and must pioneer tomorrow's to win it. One must realize that the changing environment requires new tools, and the old tools by nature lose their edge when everyone learns to use them. As this chapter's opening quote suggests, there is a sort of arms race in strategy, with the advantage going to the innovators. But, although "smart missiles" may now carry the day, it would still be folly to enter the battlefield without a rifle. Business strategy is similar: Today's planners must master both the old and the new.

THE OLD STRATEGIC PLANNING

Strategy is conventionally thought of as the overall "game plan" or blueprint that guides the organization toward achieving its objectives. *Tactics* are the detailed, individual activities that the organization undertakes to carry out the strategy. They specify how the elements of the marketing mix—the four Ps discussed in Chapter 2—will be allocated, and they allocate manufacturing, capital, people, and other resources as needed. With the help of a strategic plan, members of the organization can develop tactical plans that are much more detailed than the strategic plan. A written plan permits others to evaluate the reasoning and assumptions that underlie the firm's objectives. The plan helps to coordinate the activities that must be implemented to carry out the plan. It also serves as a control device: Actual results can be compared with the intended results outlined in the plan, and adjustments can be made if necessary. This formal view of the plan has not been entirely abandoned, but managers today are more likely to see vision or mission as driving the company, above strategy in the strategy–tactics hierarchy. They also may allow more leeway for employees than formal tactics and controls once did.

Marketing plays an important role in the firm's strategic plan by providing specific information about the firm's current market position and its opportunities for future market positions. Marketing also participates in the organization's planning process by developing specific strategies and tactics for products, customers, distribution channels, and the like. These will be incorporated in varying degrees into the organization's formal strategic plan, and will also generally form a stand-alone marketing plan to be followed by people in sales, product development, and other functions.

The process of strategic planning rests upon assumptions held by the planner. Assumptions concerning expected responses to marketing actions will shape the marketing strategy and tactics. Assessment of the outcomes allows the planner to validate those assumptions or create new ones. The importance of sound assumptions cannot be overemphasized. Feedback provides the basis for evaluating and revising assumptions. Learning by feedback comes through experiencing the plan–execution–feedback process illustrated in Exhibit 2.1.

EXHIBIT 2.1. Learning through feedback at American Express.

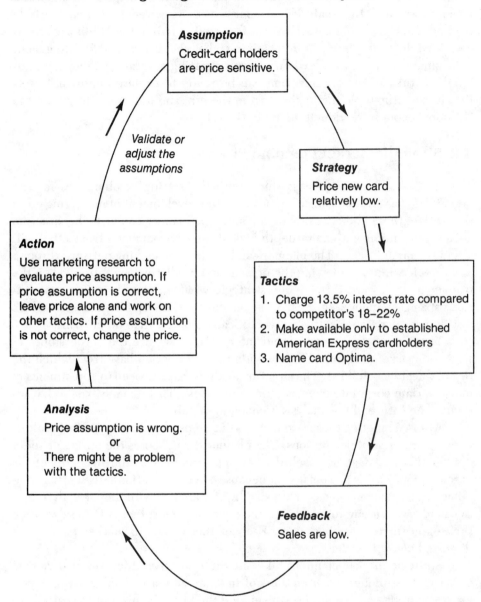

In the "top–down" approach, which was once the norm for most compa-nies, the task of charting an overall strategy for an organization rests mainly with top management. That strategy then guides the decision making of man-agers at each organizational level. More firms now employ "bottom–up" plan-ning, in which plans developed at the lower levels of the organization are blended together into a master strategic plan. Such a plan may turn out to be more marketing oriented than a plan formulated by the top–down method, mostly because it is created by those in daily touch with the customers, the competitors, and the realities of operations. As a recent *Fortune* article pointed out, the strategic watchwords for the first half of the 1990s are "focus and flexibility." *Focus* means determining what you do best and building on it. It originates at the top. *Flexibility* means drafting several possible scenarios for the future so the organization can be ready to explore opportunities as they arise without having to shoot from the hip, and it also means giving the "bottom" enough freedom to be truly flexible.[7]

The Strategic Market Planning Process

The strategic planning process starts with the setting of objectives for the organization as a whole and continues with the development of marketing goals that reflect those objectives. Next the strategic planner conducts the situation analysis, beginning with an in-depth look at the environmental trends that will affect the organization. The planner can be said to be looking outward through a "strategic window," viewing the present and predicting the future. Then the planner looks inward through the strategic window to analyze the organization's strengths and weaknesses. A key purpose of this step is to assess the firm's distinctive competencies, that is, what it can do better than other firms.

These two steps, external and internal analysis, are the cornerstones of strategic market planning. They provide the information base from which the rest of the process follows. The situation analysis may also lead to adjustments to inappropriate corporate or marketing objectives. (This remains true today, although the nature of the analysis is changing rapidly.)

After completing these two fact-finding steps, the planner generates alternative plans or strategic options. The planner then chooses the option or set of options that best matches each market opportunity with the strengths of the organization. This is a crucial step because the organization's distinctive competencies may be only occasionally and briefly aligned with those required by a dynamic external environment. Strategic planners must be ready to seize upon such opportunities as they arise. Each of these steps in market planning is discussed below in order.

Strategic market planning takes its direction from the overall organizational goals. Although we often think of an organization as simply setting targets for sales, profits, return on investment, and the like, organizations usually have broader, less measurable objectives. An organization is, or ought to be, guided by the invisible hand of its purpose or mission. In this sense, the mission of computer companies is to provide information, and that of telephone companies is to facilitate communication. Rather than considering itself a copier company, Xerox sees itself as an "office of the future" company. Some organizations have even more abstract missions: Consulting firms can be seen as providing education, museums as preserving a cultural heritage, and so on. These missions guide the organization's marketing efforts.

The corporate mission depends on how the organization defines its business. That definition is based on the answers to two questions: "What business are we in?" and "What business *should* we be in?"

Sometimes too broad a business definition can create problems for an organization. For example, Levi Strauss, a leader in the apparel industry, added many new lines throughout the 1970s, including sportswear, youth wear, and ski clothes. In a 1979 talk to securities analysts, the company's president stated that Levi Strauss should be looked upon "as a consumer-products company that just happens to be in the garment business." As one worried analyst told *Fortune*, "If they ever really start to believe that, it's trouble." Such a broad business definition would allow the company to add a whole range of products with which it has no marketing experience—cereals, automobiles, detergents, watches, and so on.[8]

Although it did not take such a wildly divergent approach, Levi Strauss did move into higher priced, more fashion-oriented lines. And the skeptical analyst apparently was correct. The period from 1980 to 1982 produced a 10-percent drop in sales for Levi Strauss and a 76-percent plunge in net income. In 1982, the company eliminated many of its upscale product lines and returned to its emphasis on mid-priced, middle-class–oriented apparel, especially its well-known jeans. Its president then told *BusinessWeek* that "we've realized that just putting Levi's name on something isn't enough to gain instant marketing acceptance."[9] Now it sees itself as an "adaptable" company, able to take advantage of opportunities to which its distinctive competencies are applicable. For example, with the apparent emergence of a global generation of teens with similar tastes and values, Levi Strauss has been quick to try its hand at global marketing. It sells a 1960s style across the planet, and it is even gaining popularity back in the United States.[10]

The company's product mix is now somewhere between the narrow jeans-only strategy of its early years and the unfocused consumer-products focus of the early 1980s. New products generally have some tie-in with the jeans identity and market, meaning that it makes sense to consumers for Levi Strauss to sell them. The current star of its product line illustrates this point. Dockers is a line of casual slacks for men, made from a cotton twill that is softer and more comfortable than denim. It is targeted at aging baby boomers, the same customers who made jeans a runaway success in the 1960s and 1970s. According to Alan Millstein, editor of *Fashion Network Report*, "Levi Strauss really understood the forty-something generation," who "have been living off beer, pretzels, and microwave popcorn. Their waistlines have expanded . . . and they can't fit into their jeans."[11] But they can fit into Dockers, and the success of this product has fueled a surge in Levi Strauss' income in 1991. The line is now expanding to include men's shirts and clothing for women and children.

Despite the wisdom of customer-oriented market definitions, it can be very dangerous to move into unfamiliar territory, as Anheuser-Busch discovered along with Levi Strauss in the 1980s. Anheuser-Busch's management felt that its single-minded emphasis on the domestic beer business did not give it any way to use the excess cash it generated. As a result, the company redefined itself as a global food and beverage business and introduced the premium-priced Eagle brand of pretzels, corn curls, tortilla chips, and nuts. It also increased emphasis on its Dewey Stevens, a diet wine cooler; low-alcohol LA; and soda and bottled waters. The company's focus was on making better use of the firm's distinctive competency in beer distribution and developing new products for its existing markets.

By 1988, the company was retrenching heavily, having put up for sale its three bottled water products and its California winery. "The beer guys weren't wine or water guys," said a former company executive. The company "didn't know how to sell the stuff properly."[12] And in the wine cooler market, where all products are already perceived as "light," Anheuser-Busch could not establish a foothold. Perhaps the greatest trouble spot, however, rested with the company's Eagle brand of snacks. On top of tremendous capital expense for the start-up product, Eagle managed to lose several million dollars each year following its inception. There is no question that Anheuser-Busch's distribution network is an awe-inspiring distinctive competency, but it is not as muscular in the supermarkets as it is in the package stores and bars. The company's expensive misfirings in nonbeer businesses have refocused its attention back to the business it knows and conducts best—beer—and successfully too. By 1990, Anheuser-Busch held a 43.4 percent share of the market, up from 28.2 percent in 1980.

These cases lead us to sound a cautionary note—it can be hubris to pursue unfamiliar products and markets, even if the customer demand is clearly there. There appear to be practical constraints on how far afield a company should go in pursuit of the marketing concept. However, to be fair, a single-minded focus on a firm's familiar products and technology also can land it in big trouble. Remember Levitt's "marketing myopia" described in Chapter 1: When cars and trucks came along, railroad companies ignored them—and entered a long, slow decline. Why? Because they saw themselves as specializing in laying track rather than in transporting people and freight. There is often a fine line between this sort of marketing myopia and the overconfidence of Anheuser-Busch. The success of Levi's Dockers illustrates the importance of expansion that makes sense to the customers: Another product line for established customers is a safer bet than something totally new to the company.

From the corporate mission, the organization is supposed to develop a set of objectives that will direct it over a 3- to 5-year period. These objectives are generally stated in terms of sales growth, market share improvement, profits, innovation, acquisitions, and risk reduction. (In the new strategic planning, however, the validity of long-term forecasts and plans is no longer taken for granted; the environment changes too rapidly.)

From general corporate objectives flow more specific marketing goals. These goals may focus on overall sales increases, but usually they are somewhat more detailed, calling for sales increases by product class, geographic region, or type of customer. It is generally assumed that market share improvement translates into higher sales volume, and higher volume means lower production costs and higher profits. Thus, marketing goals are often expressed in terms of improvement in market share, or the percentage of the total market served by the company. Market share is the chief measure of how well an organization is doing relative to its competitors.

Because of the importance of assumptions about market share, a group of professors with The Strategic Planning Institute (SPI) has assembled a highly detailed database of information on the performance of thousands of individual businesses and business units over four years or more. It tracks the standard financial measures, plus many of the marketing and strategy variables thought to drive financial performance. In this Profit Impact of Marketing Strategy (PIMS) database, two striking trends can be documented. First, on average, market share and return on investment (ROI) vary together. A smaller share is typically associated with lower ROI, and vice versa. In fact, the relationship is virtually a straight line, varying from an average ROI of 11 percent for businesses with market shares of 10 percent or less, up to an ROI of 40 percent for businesses with shares of 50 percent or more. Professors Buzzell and Gale of SPI write that:

> The primary reason for the market share–profitability linkage, apart from the connection with relative quality, is that larger share businesses benefit from scale economies. They simply have lower per-unit costs than their smaller competitors. These cost advantages are typically much smaller than those once claimed by overenthusiastic proponents of "experience curve pricing strategies," but they are nevertheless substantial and are directly reflected in higher profit margins.[13]

Second, as their brief aside about quality hinted, the data also show a clear relationship between quality relative to competitors, as perceived by customers, and both market share and ROI. The data support the arguments of quality advocates that there does *not* need to be a trade-off between quality and cost. Higher quality seems to be associated with higher share and lower costs (thus higher margins and ROI) in actual operating data from thousands of companies.

So what happened to Xerox? If firms gain 3.5 points of ROI for every 10 points of market share on average, as the PIMS database indicates, Xerox's 86-percent share in 1974 should have given it a greater than 25 percent lead in ROI over its closest competitors. How could anyone possibly afford to challenge Xerox? This is exactly what its management assumed, and what many leaders in other industries assumed as well. (The U.S. auto industry is the classic example.) But this assumption ignores the impact of quality. Higher profits do not *guarantee* dominance—it depends on how you spend them! Xerox did not use its cost advantage to maintain its leadership in quality and product superiority, and customers do not share planners' regard for market position. Market share represents customers' *past* purchases, not their future purchases—something planners tend to overlook—and if a better product comes along, future purchases will not remain consistent with past purchases. Market share is a good objective for management, but it is not an impenetrable shield against competitors, as Xerox learned.

The Situation Analysis

In the next step of strategic planning—the situation analysis—planners analyze information about the firm's environment, especially its customers and competitors. This environmental scanning involves looking at the present state of the environment and forecasting trends in its various aspects. Planners also look inward and analyze their organization's strengths and weaknesses. They assess not only tangible, observable resources, but also intangible resources, such as the skills of personnel and the company's image. The focus then shifts to matching the opportunities that exist in the environment with the firm's particular strengths. The outcome of this analysis is an understanding of how to take advantage of the opportunities by using the distinctive competencies of the organization. It may also require some revision of previously set goals. This crucial step in the strategic market planning process may utilize analytical tools such as the Boston Consulting Group's growth–share matrix, which will be discussed shortly. It also draws on an organization's ongoing efforts to scan and monitor its business environment—the topic of the next chapter.

The Organization—Looking Inside the Strategic Window

Once the external environment has been analyzed, planners examine of firm's resources, both tangible and, often more important, intangible. Planners should thoroughly review the tangibles—the firm's financial resources, production and distribution systems, and the like. They also should analyze intangible resources, such as the company's image and culture, the creative and administrative talent of its personnel, employee attitudes toward the company, and the company's vulnerability to competition. These intangibles, though difficult to assess, can make the difference between success and failure.

Strategic Business Units and Portfolio Analysis

Perhaps no company has contributed more to the "old" strategic market planning than General Electric (GE). In the 1970s, GE reorganized its 48 divisions and nine product lines into strategic business units (SBUs). Each SBU consists of one or more products, brands, company divisions, or market segments that have something in common, such as the same distribution system, similar customers, or the same basic technology. At the same time, each SBU has its own mission, its own distinct set of competitors, and its own strategic plan. About 20 percent of the largest manufacturing firms in the United States have adopted the SBU system. Recently, for example, Campbell Soup Company established eight SBUs: soups, beverages, pet foods, frozen foods, fresh produce, main meals, grocery, and food service. The SBU structure's great merit is that it defines the company according to the markets it serves—one SBU per market. Smaller companies are often focused on a single market, but larger ones easily lose their marketing orientation without the SBU structure to force it.

The Boston Consulting Group (BCG) suggested in the 1970s that SBUs should be managed as a portfolio the way financial investments are managed (see Exhibit 2.2a). Different SBUs may have different missions, but all work together to achieve the organization's overall objectives. Top management decides which business units to build up, maintain, phase down, or eliminate. In short, the organization is continually attempting to improve its portfolio of SBUs by divesting itself of units that do not perform well and, at the same time, acquiring promising new ones (see Exhibit 2.2b).

EXHIBIT 2.2a.   The BCG portfolio matrix.

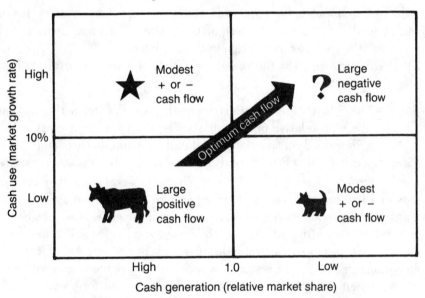

EXHIBIT 2.2b.   Possible changes in the portfolio over time.

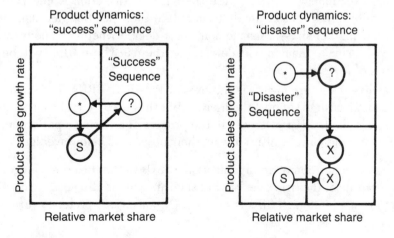

The BCG approach focuses on three factors: market growth, the SBU's relative market share, and cash flow. An SBU's relative market share is determined by dividing its market share by that of its largest competitor. Thus, if Gillette's razors-and-blades SBU has a 65-percent share of that market while Schick, its largest competitor, has 16 percent and BIC has 11 percent,[14] their relative market shares are:

Gillette	4.1	(65%/16%)
Schick	0.3	(16%/65%)
BIC	0.2	(11%/65%)

The dividing line between high and low relative market share is set by 1. Only the market leader can lie to the left of this point. The more dominant the leader's share, the stronger its position in the marketplace.

SBUs are categorized by the amount of cash they generate, resulting in the following four categories:

1. *Stars*—These SBUs are in industries with high sales growth rates, and they have a high relative market share. The stars are the leaders in their markets. They need continual inputs of cash to maintain their high growth rates. Eventually that growth will slow and they will become cash cows.

2. *Cash cows*—Cash cows are SBUs with a higher market share than competitors in a low-growth market. They have high sales volume and low costs. Thus, they generate more cash than they need; the excess cash can be used to support other SBUs. At Gillette, the razors-and-blades SBU generated 32 percent of the company's 1989 sales revenues, but 64 percent of its profits. Profit margins on this SBU were a whopping 34.7 percent, compared with 15.2 percent for stationary products and 6.9 percent for toiletries.[15] Domestic beer is a cash cow for Anheuser-Busch, supporting the new product lines discussed earlier.

3. *Question marks*—These high-growth, low-market-share SBUs are problems for management because their future direction is uncertain. They require a lot of cash simply to maintain their position, let alone increase their market share. Management must decide whether to pour in enough cash to make them into leaders; if not, these SBUs probably will be phased out of the portfolio.

4. *Dogs*—Dogs are low-growth, low-market-share SBUs. They may provide enough cash to support themselves, but they are not a substantial source of funds. Such SBUs often are in the process of entering a particular market or phasing out of it. Either way, their position is below average.

The distribution of an organization's SBUs in the different categories provides a profile of the firm's health. But such an analysis also needs to consider the direction in which each SBU is moving. Organizations prefer to turn question marks into stars and, as growth slows, into cash cows that can be used to fund other question marks. This is precisely the sequence that occurred at Gillette, where the excess cash from the razor blade business was funneled into disposable lighters. Eventually Gillette's Cricket lighter became a star.

The portfolio approach aids in the setting of marketing strategies. The following basic strategies are closely related to this approach:

- *Build*—This strategy is appropriate for question marks if they are to grow into stars. The firm invests heavily to improve product quality, develop promotional campaigns, or subsidize price reductions—all in an effort to beat the competition.
- *Hold*—This strategy is used to protect cash cows and stars that are strongly entrenched. The market leader simply defends its market share and maintains customer loyalty.
- *Harvest*—When the future looks dim for a weak cash cow, a dog, or even a question mark, the best strategy may be to harvest as much profit from it as possible before letting it go. Marketing (especially promotion) and research and development expenditures are curtailed; economies of production are emphasized; and customer services are reduced. In short, all costs are lowered as the SBU is "milked" of its cash-generating potential.
- *Divest*—When a dog or question mark has no future, it is sold off or dropped from the portfolio because the cash needed to fund it can be used better elsewhere.

Competitive Position Matrix

The matrix can be modified to analyze the position of products relative to their competitors (see Exhibit 2.3). In the example illustrated, the top ten beer brands are plotted using 1990 data. The market growth rate is not used, because it is the same for every brand in this market (total 1990 U.S. beer sales grew 3.1 percent over 1989, but were flat for the three previous years). Instead, the growth in each brand's sales is used to show which grew faster. Sometimes, as in this illustration, each brand's growth is made relative to the growth of the market to show whether its share is growing or shrinking. (To do this, divide a brand's annual revenue growth or unit growth by the market's annual growth, or by dividing current market share by last year's market share to find the percentage of change in market share, as in Exhibit 2.3.)

Exhibit 2.4 shows the data we used to create a competitive position matrix for the U.S. beer market. As the exhibit illustrates, this kind of analysis can show the market in a new light. The leader in sales, Budweiser, had a strong relative market share, but was weak on the growth dimension of the matrix—its share was slipping. The hot brands were Coors Light and Miller Genuine Draft, which gained a significant share in 1990. The cash flow implications of the BCG matrix do not necessarily apply, however, because competing brands may be owned by

EXHIBIT 2.3. Competitive position matrix for leading beer brands, 1990.

```
                  ┌─────────────────────┬─────────────────────────┐
                  │ Why is no brand     │                 MILLER  │
                  │ in this quadrant?   │                 G.D.    │
             20   │                     │                         │
                  │                     │                         │
             15   │                     │                         │
                  │                     │     COORS               │
             10   │                     │     LIGHT               │
                  │                     │        BUD              │
              5   │                     │     LIGHT               │
  Growth          │                     │                         │
    in    0       │                     │  MILLER     MILW'S      │
  Market          ├─────────────────────┤   LITE        BEST      │
  Share   -5      │ BUD                 │         BUSCH           │
   (%)            │                     │                         │
            -10   │                     │       OLD MILW.         │
                  │                     │                         │
            -15   │                     │     MILLER H.L.         │
                  │                     │                         │
                  │                     │          COORS          │
                  └─────────────────────┴─────────────────────────┘
                  3             1            .5              .1
```

◀── Relative Share of Market (Log Scale)

different companies. This analysis can be taken a step farther by identifying each brand's brewer and comparing the company portfolios, or by plotting companies instead of brands. One could learn, for example, that Anheuser-Busch had the largest share, 43.4 percent, and that its sales grew 7 percent, more than twice as fast as the total market. Also, one would find that brewer's share is closely related to performance. The top three, Anheuser-Busch, Miller and Coors, were responsible for all the market growth in 1990.

EXHIBIT 2.4. Competitive position analysis.

Brand	1990 Share of Shipments	1989 Share of Shipments	% Change in Share	Relative Market Share, 1990
Budweiser[a]	25.2%	25.9%	−2.7%	2.40
Miller Lite	10.5	10.5	0	.42
Coors Light	6.2	5.6	10.7	.25
Bud Light	6.1	5.7	7.2	.24
Busch	4.6	4.8	−4.2	.18
Milwaukee's Best	3.6	3.6	0	.14
Old Milwaukee	3.3	3.6	−8.3	.13
Miller High Life	3.2	3.8	−15.8	.13
Miller Genuine Draft	3.0	2.4	25.0	.12
Coors	2.2	2.7	−18.5	.09

[a] Calculations:
  $25.2/25.9 = 0.97; 0.97 - .1 = 0.027 \times 100 = -2.7\%$
  $25.2/10.5 = 2.4$

One might also plot a matrix that compares light and regular beers, which would indicate that, of the top 25 brands, the only light beer to lose share was Old Milwaukee Light. Altogether, light beers in 1990 had about a 30-percent market share and annual growth of 12.5 percent. And some background reading on the beer industry would reveal that Old Milwaukee Light's sliding share reflected the financial problems of its parent brewer, Stroh, which cut Old Milwaukee's advertising and other marketing expenses in 1989 in an effort to harvest profits from its brands and thus lost 12 percent of its volume. This analysis would indicate that light beers are currently the high performers of the beer market.

This example illustrates a fundamental principle of the new strategic planning: The firm must use available techniques and information creatively to gain new insights into its position and opportunities. It is not enough to crank out the same old matrices that were used last year, even if they are as venerable as the BCG matrix. It is important to ask intelligent questions ("Are light beers fueling the growth in the beer industry?" "Is the leading brand losing share?"), and to take a creative approach to analysis to answer such questions clearly. The firm that asks an intelligent question before its competitors do may be able to seize an opportunity first.[16]

The GE Business Screen

Some critics of the BCG portfolio approach believe that an analysis of the organization's resources should not be reduced to relative market share and market growth. They feel that too great an emphasis on this factor masks many other factors that make a business attractive and indicate its strengths. Also, relative share is of greatest importance where economies of scale and "experience curve" effects give the largest producer a significant cost advantage. (An experience curve reflects a decline in unit costs as more units are produced; it is the result of learning or "experience" in contrast to straight economies of scale.) This is not always the case. As a result, many strategic planners have gone beyond the BCG approach to other approaches that rely on multiple measures of a firm's ability to compete successfully. One of the first and best known of these alternative approaches is the investment opportunity chart or business screen developed by GE.[17]

In the business screen approach, a strategic business unit is classified according to how well it rates on certain success measures, referred to as its business strength. The industries in which SBUs operate are classified on the basis of measures of opportunity, referred to as industry attractiveness. Among the measures of business strength are the SBU's product quality, price sensitivity, knowledge of the market, technological capability, image, and so on, whereas industry attractiveness is measured by such factors as intensity of competition, seasonality of sales, legal constraints, importance of technological change, and the like (see Exhibit 2.5). Clearly, not all these factors can be measured as objectively and precisely as market growth, relative market share,

EXHIBIT 2.5.   The GE business screen.

Business strength
—Domestic market share
—World share
—Share growth
—Share relative to leading competitor
—Product quality
—Technology skills
—Cost efficiency
—Marketing skills
—Relative profitability

Industry attractiveness
—Market size
—Growth
—Profitability
—Cyclicality
—Government regulation
—World scope
—Technology requirements

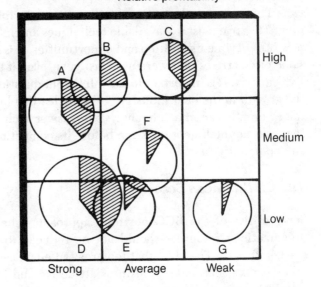

and cash flow. On the other hand, the GE method offers much greater flexibility and comprehensiveness than the BCG approach.

The business screen is used in the following way: The nine cells shown in the illustration are placed in three zones. GE colored these zones green, yellow, and red; hence, this is often called the stoplight approach. The three zones at the upper left indicate industries that are attractive and match the SBUs' strengths. They have a "green light" for investment. The three cells along the diagonal indicate industries of medium interest. They have a "yellow light" to denote caution; usually these SBUs warrant a strategy geared toward maintaining their present market share. The three cells at the lower right show weak SBUs for which a harvesting or divesting strategy may be the best option. The circles A through G represent the SBUs; their size is in proportion to the size of the industries in which they compete. The pie slices represent each SBU's market share within its industry.

The GE business screen's history is representative of the history of strategic planning. Developed in the 1970s by William Rothschild at GE with Mike

Allen of the consulting firm McKinsey & Company, the tool was carefully—and laboriously—applied in annual planning and forecasting by GE's large central planning staff. Now, however, according to GE spokesman Bruce Bunch, the business screen "takes too much time" and is not used at GE any more.[18] In fact, neither GE nor McKinsey will claim ownership of it today (in response to inquiries concerning permission to reproduce it for publication). Once the heir apparent of the strategy throne, this method is a homeless orphan! (It remains a standard in the business school curriculum and important for the concepts it represents, even though it is no longer in widespread use.)

What happened? The SBUs of GE and many other firms that were identified as winners according to the business screen were not necessarily better than other SBUs. They *ought* to have been—nobody could dispute that these represented great business opportunities. However, GE line managers did not necessarily know how to pursue the opportunities, and someone else—perhaps someone from Europe or Japan—might have pursued an opportunity more effectively. As a result, bigger companies, GE included, pushed planning back to the line managers and cut central staff. For example, in 1984, Michael Naylor, General Motor's director of strategic planning, declared that "planning is the responsibility of every line manager," and added that "the role of the planner is to be a catalyst for change—not to do the planning for each business unit."[19]

The case of GE's Major Appliance Business Group is instructive. The group's central planning staff numbered in the 50s at the beginning of the 1950s. Although some of the planners' calls were right—for example, they identified the Japanese threat back in the 1970s—operating managers resisted the growing authority of planning staff and tended to ignore them. They insisted on ignoring Japan and treating Sears as their major competitor, for example. In other cases, planners were dead wrong—their focus on numbers blinded them to realities of implementation. As GE's Roger Schipke concluded when he took over the major appliance group (and booted out planners) in 1982, "An awful lot of conclusions were drawn by that group somewhat in isolation. We had a lot of bad assumptions leading to some bad strategies."[20]

BusinessWeek performed an interesting study in 1984, tracking a random sample of 33 planning strategies described in the magazine in 1979 and 1980. The tally: 19 clear failures and only 14 clear successes.[21] A lot of planners lost their jobs that year!

THE NEW STRATEGIC PLANNING

So what does GE do now? Its circuit breaker business provides a good example. This stagnant SBU in a mature industry would have flunked all the screening tests, but with a billion in yearly revenues, it hardly seemed appropriate to divest it and leave the market to competitors Seimens and Westinghouse. Besides, if any lesson had come out of the old planning models, it was that profits did not necessarily come from high-share, high-growth SBUs. (As Stephen Hardis, Eaton Corporation's vice president of planning, put it, "It's great to say, 'Why don't we all go into growth businesses?' But those are not all highly profitable. If there's a hell for planners, over the portal will be carved the term 'cash cow.'")[22] Instead of divesting, GE consolidated operations—from six circuit breaker plants to only one (in Salisbury, North Carolina).[23] Solving this problem in just one location seemed like enough of a challenge.

Then management assessed the problem, but not in the conventional way, by asking planning staff and consultants for a report. Instead they formed an interdisciplinary team with specialists from manufacturing, marketing, and design, and asked them to figure out how to make the manufacturing process profitable. The group decided to compete on the basis of speed, and adopted the goal of reducing manufacturing time from three weeks to three days.

This radical change could not be accomplished given the existing process, in which GE engineers designed a unique box for each customer using a selection from GE's 28,000 parts, then factory workers assembled the boxes by hand. So the team redesigned the product line, paring parts to 1,275 while still allowing customers the ability to customize their boxes. Next the team developed an expert computer system that could automatically convert customer requirements into instructions for the factory machines. This eliminated the engineers and the delay needed for custom designing. The team also added more machines, increasing the automation of the production process.

Finally, the team tackled personnel problems on the factory floor. The key issue was delays associated with decision making. According to a *Fortune* reporter:

> the solution was to get rid of all line supervisors and quality inspectors, reducing the organizational layers between worker and plant manager from three to one. Everything those middle managers used to handle—vacation scheduling, quality, work rules—became the responsibility of the 129 workers on the floor, who are divided into teams of 15 to 20. And what do you know: the more responsibility GE gave its workers, the faster problems got solved and decisions made.[24]

Because of these changes made at GE, costs have dropped, quality has improved, and customers believe they have more features from which to choose. Delivery is made in three days, as hoped; the backlog has shrunk from two months to two days; employee morale is up; and market share is growing now despite the flat market. The 1989 statistics, for example, are quite amazing: Productivity is up 20 percent, and ROI is above 20 percent. But it was not easy to turn this dog into a star; the project began in 1985, four eventful years before the stunning results we report. *Everything* had to change, from product line through production process to corporate structure and culture. Not every line manager is capable of leading such a transformation, but it definitely takes a line manager to do it. No central planning staff would undertake such goals, or succeed if it did. Still, the new planning approaches are tougher on management. Managers must champion change; they must be willing to push authority down into the organization; and they must learn to use, and work in, teams. As GE's Roger Schipke puts it, "Now it's a question of 'Can they develop a strategy for their business?' Some will make that cut, some won't." When he took over the major appliance group, only one of the four top managers reporting to him made that cut. The others were fired.[25]

Success with the new planning approach also requires reducing the barriers between company and customer—touching customers and listening in the proactive sense described in Chapter 1. For example, GE now promotes an answer center in TV ads and on product packaging. Staffed 24 hours a day, the center may be reached via a toll-free call. Several million calls are logged annually. Frank Sonenberg of Ernst & Young's Consulting Group says that, "by making information easily available to consumers [General Electric] builds brand loyalty in a tough competitive field."[26]

Planning to Be the Best

In the old strategic planning, goals often reflected desired financial returns or conventional wisdom about what was reasonable in the circumstances. But the Japanese competitors did not play by the same rules. They saw nothing wrong with tilting at entrenched leaders in photocopiers or autos, for example, even though entering the U.S. markets for these products meant violating the prescriptions of the BCG and GE portfolio models. And GE's circuit breaker business went way beyond conventional expectations, making such radical improvements that it was able to grow profits, quality, and share despite a no-growth market. Where do goals such as these come from, and how can they be implemented when the more modest goals of the old strategic planning were so often missed? The case of Xerox will help answer these critical questions.

In 1983, when Xerox CEO David Kearns decided to stem the flood of competition, he announced the beginning of a total quality campaign. To the uninitiated, total quality sounds like tougher quality control, more inspections. It is not. Inspired by the Japanese (who in turn were inspired by U.S. statistician W. Edward Demming in the 1950s), total quality programs *eliminate* quality inspection and focus on doing it right the first time. ("It" may be fitness to standard, fitness to need, or fitness to latent need, as discussed in Chapter 1.) This means every person must do his or her job right, or stop the process if he or she does something wrong. Total quality involves suppliers and distributors as well. (McAlpin Industries, a Xerox supplier, now sends its managers to a Xerox quality course, designs its parts with a Xerox team, and endures Xerox auditors on its factory floor.[27] Total quality touches every process in the company, from manufacturing processes to sales and customer service processes. To accomplish total quality, Xerox puts in charge those people who know each process best: the front-line workers.

This type of program involves a big change for most companies—a change in corporate culture. Employee initiative must be encouraged, and employees can no longer be punished for mistakes. They will not report them otherwise.

Employees must be trained in the statistical methods needed to monitor and improve the quality of their own work. And they must learn to work together in teams to solve problems or think of ways to work better.

The first move Kearns made to kick off Xerox's quality program was an appeal to the company's 100,000 workers—the task of championing customer needs would fall to them.[28] And they have proven more than able to meet such challenges. For example, in 1990, a team of people from sales, distribution, and accounting determined how to save Xerox $200 million in inventory costs.[29]

Perhaps the hardest part of changing the corporate culture is admitting openly what is wrong with the old one. Whatever is wrong, however, is at the root of any problems and must be grubbed out. The old culture becomes a conservative force, preventing employees and managers from focusing on customer needs and limiting the rate of organizational learning and change. At Fuji Xerox, the company's total quality program began by admitting that there were some rather serious problems, and that they were systemic rather than the fault of any one manager or group. Hideki Kaihatsu, one of Fuji Xerox's directors, explains:

> The first step was to understand the problems facing the company and why these problems occurred. This soul-searching analysis revealed many surprising facts:
>
> - Our leadership had become fragmented and inconsistent;
> - Our managers had become complacent, arrogant, and had lost their sense of urgency;
> - We did not pay close enough attention to customer requirements;
> - We found our product development process particularly sloppy and not acceptable;
> - We depended too much upon U.S. design capability;
> - The product development process was slow and there was little cross-functional cooperation; and
> - We did not recognize the value of maintaining strong bonds with our suppliers.[30]

In the days of the old strategic planning, a manager's career could have been ruined for coming forward with even one of these criticisms. In fact, that's one reason consulting firms flourished: When one knew the messenger would be killed, one was eager to hire someone else to deliver the message, regardless of price! But Xerox's disastrous performance forced its managers to put these games behind them and take an honest look at their company. The result was an almost incredible list of major problems.

Solving them was not as simple, however, as setting the solutions as strategic goals. How could change be accomplished, and how much change was a reasonable goal? How could the goals be broken down into smaller, more attainable tasks? The answers could not be found within Xerox; the needed changes were too radical. But surely they could be found *somewhere*; there were undoubtedly companies that could provide role models, companies that were the best at each of the individual processes Xerox had to rebuild. With this realization in mind, Xerox created one of the most important of the new planning techniques: *benchmarking*.

Benchmarking at Xerox

Benchmarking began at Xerox in 1979 as a way to analyze competing products. According to Robert Camp of U.S. Marketing for Xerox's Business Services, "Selected product comparisons were made; operating capabilities and features of competing copying machines were compared; mechanical components were taken apart and scrutinized."[31] This reverse engineering of competing products was a natural response to the inroads made by Japanese competitors. But with Xerox's quality program, benchmarking was extended beyond product comparisons, to include process comparisons and companies from other industries.

For example, Xerox used L.L. Bean for benchmarking. Camp tells the story:

> When [we] first informed our management that we were going to assess ourselves against L.L. Bean . . . there was disbelief. But we had much to learn from them. The L.L. Bean statistics that dealt with their warehouse order picking . . . showed that they were able to do it almost three times faster than Xerox.[32]

This meant that L.L. Bean could fill customer orders faster than Xerox. When Xerox adopted a computerized system like L.L. Bean used, one that "made a conscious effort to sort the orders and minimize the picker's travel distance" according to Camp, Xerox also was able to fill orders faster. This is an example of what Xerox now calls "functional benchmarking." The following are the definitions of the four benchmarking methods Xerox uses:

1. *Internal benchmarking* compares a company's operations with an internal exemplar, for example, a plant that has innovated successfully in certain areas.

2. *Competitive benchmarking* makes comparisons with individual competitors; reverse engineering of a competing product is one example.

3. *Functional benchmarking,* according to Camp, is when "we compare function against function across wide sections of different industry types," as in the L.L. Bean comparison.

4. *Generic benchmarking* looks at fundamental business processes that tend to be the same in every industry, such as taking orders, servicing customers, and developing strategies. For these generic practices, Xerox "looks at a wide cross-section" from different industries "to make sure that we have in fact identified those industry best practices," again according to Camp.

The benchmarking process in its various forms gives Xerox a practical way to set radical goals—the company simply finds some other company that is the best in a certain (often narrow) area, and studies how the company became best. CEO Kearns of Xerox defines it succinctly as "the continuous process of measuring products, services and practices against the toughest competitors or those companies recognized as industry leaders."[33] It must be a continuous process, according to Kearns, because "we realize we are in a race without a finish line. As we improve, so does our competition."[34] Xerox cannot afford to become complacent, and the new planning tools give the company the ability to compete effectively in the current environment. Kearns adds that "Five years ago, we would have found this disheartening. Today we find it invigorating."[35]

The Learning Organization

In the days when strategic planning mean plotting a bunch of growth–share matrices, it was widely assumed that organizational learning occurred in lockstep with the number of units produced. As more units were produced by a firm, it became more proficient at producing them and costs dropped correspondingly. This was one reason why BCG plotted relative market share on its matrix. The firm that held the largest share had presumably produced more units, and therefore had learned how to lower costs the farthest. Now that the Japanese have demonstrated both that a low-share competitor can learn faster and that learning can improve quality as well as reduce cost, U.S. managers are forced to rethink their whole notion of learning. In the emerging view, the kind of changes made by both GE and Xerox are successful because they greatly increase the rate of organizational learning.

Ray Stata of Analog Devises has argued that an organization's rate of learning is the key to its competitiveness. Specifically, he argues that "at Analog Devises, and many other U.S. companies, product and process innovation are not the primary bottleneck to progress. The bottleneck is management innovation."[36] After deciding to tackle the issue of management innovation at Analog Devises, Stata discovered that organizational learning drove management innovation: "I see organizational learning as the principal process by which management innovation occurs. *In fact, I would argue that the rate at which individuals and organizations learn may become the only sustainable competitive advantage.*"[37] This conclusion focused his attention on how to use the strategic planning process and a total quality program to increase the rate of learning in his company. Incidentally, *how* he arrived at his conclusions is an example of the new approaches managers are beginning to take in their quest for organizational learning. Stata joined a group of managers working with two MIT professors to develop and exchange ideas in this field.[38] For example, Stata's recognition of the key role played by organizational learning can be traced to the influence of fellow group member Arie deGeus, director of group planning at Shell International.

A learning organization is an adaptive organization. It is able to rethink its structure and function and redefine itself in response to market challenges and customer needs. The need for faster and smarter change is obvious: Many managers believe adaptability is the key to success, and are making it the cornerstone of their strategy. This requires pushing both authority and initiative down into the organization, encouraging people to think and learn harder—and giving them the freedom to do so. But as Stata also observes, "Organizations can learn only as fast as the slowest link learns,"[39] and, in many cases, the slowest link is management.

The Learning Manager

In 1983, around the time Xerox began its total quality drive, Professor Elliot Carlisle of University of Massachusetts at Amhurst wrote a story—a parable actually—about a harried manager who bumps into a successful mentor-like manager on an airplane and learns from him a new way of thinking about management. Here is what the mentor had to say about thinking:

> "You know," he mused, "when you get right down to it, it's almost impossible to get any real thinking done at work. Not just because of interruptions, but almost more importantly, the whole psychological and physical environment in which managers work tends to discourage contemplation and encourage activity. The higher the level in an organization, the more critical is the role of reflection and the less important that of activity, but so often we've become conditioned on the way up through the ranks. How many bosses would give a word of encouragement to a subordinate if they were to come upon him sitting at his desk, chair tipped back, foot resting on an open drawer, and staring into space with an abstract expression on his face? They'd be far more likely to ask him what the hell he's doing, and if the unfortunate replied, 'Thinking,' he'd probably be advised to stop thinking and get back to work."[40]

Although there is now widespread recognition of the need to think harder— and, on the other side of the coin, to learn and adapt more quickly—managers still suffer from that conditioning referred to in the quote. In fact, this conditioning is stronger the higher up you go in the organization. According to Harvard Business School professor Chris Argyris:

> Any company that aspires to succeed in the tougher business environment of the 1990s must first resolve a basic dilemma: success in the marketplace increasingly depends on learning, yet most people don't know how to learn. What's more, those members of the organization that many assume to be the best at learning are, in fact, not very good at it. I am talking about the well-educated, high-powered, high-commitment professionals who occupy key leadership positions in the modern corporation.[41]

In this view, it is senior management that stands in the way of organizational learning and adaptability, and thus in the way of success in the marketplace. The problem, according to Argyris, is that people habitually reason defensively, unconsciously protecting themselves, maintaining their control, and suppressing conflict and negative views. Their behavior blinds them and their organizations to challenges and opportunities that truly open-minded, productive reasoning and learning would reveal. Thus effective, lasting change in any organization must start at the top with self-examination and behavioral change by the leaders.

The effects of the new strategic planning and the market challenges that drive it put this issue front and center. As Rosabeth Moss Kanter, another Harvard Business School professor, sees it, "competitive pressures are forcing corporations to adopt new flexible strategies and structures." And this is forcing changes in the nature of management's work:

> The old bases of managerial authority are eroding, and new tools of leadership are taking their place. Managers whose power derived from hierarchy and who were accustomed to a limited area of personal control are learning to shift their perspectives and widen their horizons. The new managerial work consists of looking outside a defined area of responsibility to sense opportunities and of forming project teams drawn from any relevant sphere to address them. It involves communication and collaboration across functions, across divisions, and across companies. . . . Thus rank, title, or official charter will be less important factors in success at the managerial work than having the knowledge, skills, and sensitivity to mobilize people and motivate them to do their best.[42]

An example of this concept in action is provided by Raymond Gilmartin, CEO of medical equipment maker Becton-Dickinson: "We're creating a hierarchy of ideas. You say, 'This is the right thing to do here,' not 'We're going to do this because I'm boss.'" This means the vision still comes from the top, but strategies well up from Becton-Dickinson's 15 divisions, and Gilmartin must be content to sit back and let this more informal approach to strategy work.[43]

When GE pushed down planning to the line managers, this was not simply the outcome of a struggle for authority between corporate staff and operating divisions (as many saw it at the time). It was the beginning of this transformation of managerial work that Kanter speaks of. And when, in words that proved prophetic, Michael Naylor of GE declared in 1984 that line managers had to be catalysts of change through their planning, he was anticipating the new strategic role of the manager. This role requires flexibility and rapid learning, and it requires that managers teach these traits to others, for these are the traits that a company needs today to identify and implement successful strategies.

Xerox's benchmarking is an example of adaptable, accelerated learning, in that it casts a broad net in the effort to learn how to do something better. The fact is that Xerox *can* learn from L.L. Bean, and vice versa—insight can and must come from all available sources. The truly interesting thing about the new strategies is the way they are pushing (in some cases, dragging) management along this path. As the new strategic planning unfolds in the 1990s, two things are bound to become clear. First, it is management (starting at the top) that is the greatest obstacle to change, and that can become the greatest catalyst. (Stata's quest led Analog Devises to superior performance, logging an incredible 50-percent improvement in product failure rates every three to six months, for example.) Second, the entire thrust of the many new strategic directions and organizational changes is toward the marketing concept. Managerial companies are struggling to learn and adapt in order to serve customers better—better than they did before, better than their customers expect, and better than their competitors do.

This implies a never-ending process, and never-ending change. It is a frightening thought—this notion of chasing a moving finish line—and it takes strategy well beyond the bounds of yesterday's comfortable matrices. Yesterday's solutions become today's problems. Take Xerox's benchmarking against L.L. Bean to speed up delivery of products. It was an exciting innovation in the copier business last year, but this year Xerox is already looking beyond it. Although Xerox learned to deliver products faster than its competitors, studies showed that customer satisfaction was still suboptimal—only 70 percent. The problem was that customers wanted to know exactly *when* their copiers would arrive. Speed was fine, but uncertainty remained a problem. So a new team was convened, with people from distribution, accounting, sales, and so forth, and a new solution developed. Xerox now tracks the progress of every copier through the distribution process so that salespeople can tell customers exactly when they will receive their products, thus providing speed *and* predictability. Now customer satisfaction with product delivery measures at 90 percent instead of 70 percent.

But satisfaction still is short of 100 percent, and if it ever reaches 100 percent, competitors may innovate and push it down—satisfaction is, after all, a relative concept. So Xerox cannot stop now—it must search for and explore the next frontier. This is the nature of the new strategic planning. As PepsiCo's CEO, Wayne Calloway, explains, "The worst rule of management is 'If it ain't broke, don't fix it.' In today's economy, if it ain't broke, you might as well break it yourself, because it soon will be."[44]

3 THE MARKETING ENVIRONMENT

Understanding Forces You Can't Always Control

The things that are hurting John Reed (CEO and President, CitiCorp, America's largest bank) now are not of his own making; they're external events.

—Thomas Hanley, Saloman Brothers

In Chapter 2, we recounted many strategic responses to recent changes in the business environment. The very nature of management is changing to meet the growing challenges of international competition and to take advantage of opportunities presented by this and other changes in the environment. But in one sense, talking strategy puts the cart before the horse. A navigator would not plot a course without first establishing his ship's position and examining the chart with care. Nor should a manager develop strategy without examining the environment. As a practical matter, it is essential to simultaneously monitor the business environment and develop and refine strategy on an ongoing basis.

In this chapter, we explore the various components of an environmental monitoring effort, looking at many of the factors that companies need to monitor routinely. In the next chapter, we focus closely on one of the critical trends that pops out of this analysis: the globalization of markets. We look both at the changes in this area and at their implications for management and strategy.

Many of the forces that shape and direct a company's marketing operations cannot be controlled. Managers must adapt to these external forces as they plan and carry out their strategies and activities, because the manager's success or failure is determined largely by how well he or she recognizes and adjusts to these forces. For this reason, planning must be combined with continuous monitoring of the environment.

To add to the manager's woes, environmental forces often are totally unpredictable. Remember the first Tylenol poisoning incident, which resulted in the deaths of seven people in the Chicago area in September 1982? Some still unknown person placed cyanide in Tylenol capsules. This clearly was not the fault of Johnson & Johnson (J&J), the marketer of Tylenol. Even though the Federal Drug Administration (FDA) cleared J&J of any wrongdoing, the impact on J&J of this totally uncontrollable and unforeseeable disaster was devastating. Tylenol was immediately recalled from the market, and it was not until the following January that a triple-sealed tamper-resistant package allowed Tylenol to return to store shelves. The cost to J&J in lost profits was estimated at $50 million. Moreover, the company had to develop an entirely new marketing campaign to reestablish trust in the Tylenol brand. Unfortunately, that was not the only incident. In 1991, two deaths from cyanide-laced Sudafed 12-Hour Capsules resulted in another massive nationwide recall. John Lister, a consumer products consultant, says of the Sudafed case, "This proves once more that no consumer product is tamper-resistant. The over-the-counter health products makers have done more than any other consumer category to make tamper-resistant packages, and yet it is their products that people bent on poisoning take on as a challenge."[1]

Product tampering has not been limited to over-the-counter drugs. It also has affected some of the country's largest packaged goods companies. Some of the other products hit by "product terrorism" include General Foods's Jell-O, Seagram's Tropicana orange juice, Procter & Gamble's Chloraseptic mouth spray, and Borden skim milk. Pepsi-Cola incurred a $500,000 expense to take its Slice drink temporarily off the shelves after a false threat.

Consider these highly unpredictable events and their implications for marketing strategy and tactics:

- When press coverage of financial problems at Mutual Benefit Life Insurance spooked its customers, they withdrew $500 million from the company over three months, forcing a takeover by regulators. Although Mutual Benefit suffered from excessive investments in real estate, the general wisdom was that it would have been able to pull through. According to consultant Louise Firth of Arthur D. Little, "Mutual Benefit could have worked out the problems. The run did them in."[2]

- The National Institutes of Health report that aspirin taken once a day may lower the incidence of heart attacks in healthy men created an unexpected opportunity for makers of the product. Sterling Drug, the producer of Bayer aspirin, developed a consumer education advertising campaign around the heart attack theme. It also introduced a four-week pack, or "calendar pack," to help high-risk heart patients remember to take the drug each day.

- The war in the Persian Gulf raised concerns about terrorism and scared many would-be travelers. Travel agency bookings fell as much as 50 percent in the early spring of 1991 as a result of recession and the war, and U.S. airlines lost about $2 billion in the first quarter of 1991.[3]

- The Gulf War also affected other markets. Flag sales were way up in 1991. Hallmark rushed out patriotic cards for consumers to send to soldiers in the Persian Gulf, based on those it used to produce during World Wars I and II. But sales of large appliances, such as washing machines and refrigerators, went down—Whirlpool forecast a 5-percent drop as a result of the war.[4]

These positive and negative events are difficult to anticipate, but their implications for marketing are readily apparent. The firm that monitors its environment best is most likely to be prepared for such events. Since the Tylenol tampering case, firms are also attempting to prepare for unpredictable disasters, not by forecasting them, but by learning how to handle disasters in general. Capsugel, the company that made the capsules containing Tylenol, suffered more than J&J during the tampering crises, and its management developed a formal crisis planning process afterward. The cornerstone of their method is simply to sit around a table and think about all the horrible things that could possibly happen, such as "What if the janitor builds pipe bombs in the basement and one goes off by accident during a board meeting?" After making as long a list as possible, the managers rank them in order of likelihood. The janitor is unlikely to be a terrorist in his spare time, but the chance of an underground gasoline tank leaking is relatively high, for example. With this list in hand, senior management develops likely responses, and also considers ways of reducing the probability of the crises.

Capsugel also developed a number of guidelines to help during the actual management of a crisis. Their advice, as related by Charles Hoover of Capsugel at a Conference Board conference, includes the following[5]:

- Have an alternative product or technology standing by.
- Act quickly—the first few days are the most important.
- Make sure the company's side of the story is included in news coverage of the crisis.
- Stay close to your market through surveys and conversations with customers.
- Look for opportunities for you or your competitors as a result of the crisis.
- Don't assume a hostile environment, open, clear information sharing with customers and the press is usually the best policy.

Opportunities and Threats

The environment comprises all the forces external to the organization that influence the marketer's ability to plan and implement. The same external forces can affect different marketers in different ways. Each is confronted with a unique set of opportunities and threats. Often there is only a limited period of time during which the organization's distinctive competencies match the opportunities provided by the environment. Marketers must be able to set and execute an appropriate strategy on short notice so that opportunities are not missed and the impact of threats is minimized or averted.

The forces in the environment have been referred to as "uncontrollable." By this we mean that marketers and planners cannot manipulate the forces to their own advantage. Exxon and General Motors could not stop the energy crisis of 1973. Changes in birthrates affect companies such as Procter & Gamble, with its disposable diapers, and Gerber Products Company, with its baby foods. Of course, Gerber cannot force people to have more children. The decline in birthrates, however, forced the company to diversify from baby products and into insurance, printing, and meals for single diners. Its familiar motto "Babies are our business—our only business" was changed to "Babies are our business—and have been for over 50 years." Then in 1988, Gerber redefined itself as a "family foods company" and began introducing foods for older children and adults. Although Gerber cannot *control* changes in environmental forces, it can *adjust* its strategy in response to them. But strategies built on false assumptions about the environment are doomed; because there is lag between conception and execution of strategy, uncontrolled environmental change often muddies the waters. Exhibit 3.1 lists a number of strategies that bit the dust in the 1980s because their underlying assumptions about the environment proved false.

Firms influence their environment. Many companies have representatives such as trade associations that make their wishes known to public officials and political leaders. For instance, the National Association of Broadcasters lobbied for the defeat of proposals to eliminate beer and wine advertising on radio and television, whereas the National Coal Association urged protection against unreasonable rate hikes by railroads. And certainly the trade agreement between the United States and Japan's Ministry of International Trade and Industry would not have come about had the U.S. semiconductor makers not been so vocal. Technological advances made by some companies influence the technologies available to others. The products and advertising of all companies influence the values we hold as a society. Although managers cannot control these external forces, they can and do influence them in many ways.

Environmental Scanning

Many companies have set up procedures for collecting information about such external areas as resource availability, recent and pending legislation, patents applied for, competitors' actions, and other issues that might affect their future. For example, Levi Strauss conducts environmental scanning at the international, domestic, and industry levels. It regularly gathers data on topics such as fashion trends in European markets, foreign countries' import policies, world gross national product, and world inflation. Domestic economic forces monitored by Levi Strauss include the state of the U.S. economy, inflation, taxes, wages, expenditures on clothing, and growth of apparel and department stores.

EXHIBIT 3.1   Strategies that failed.

Company Strategy	Unanticipated Environmental Problems
Lone Star Industries Focused on cement-related businesses and sold off other operations	Anticipated cement shortages and higher prices did not materialize
Oak Industries Diversified into TV and cable TV equipment	Cable TV competition was greater than expected, and TV equipment technology changed rapidly
Shaklee Streamlined product lines to become the leading nutritional products company	Recession, high sales force turnover
Toro Capitalized on reputation for quality mowers and snowblowers by expanding into other home products	Snowless winters
General Motors Tried to gain market share by out-spending U.S. competitors in the race to offer small fuel-efficient cars	Popularity of competing imports grew
U.S. Home Planned to use economies of scale in land development and its financial clout to become a dominant player in homebuilding	Interest rates rose and home sales fell
Wang Laboratories Planned to become the leader in office computer systems by introducing new products that combined data and word processing	Rise of personal computers

Based on "The New Breed of Strategic Planners," *Business Week*, Sept. 17, 1984, pp. 64–65.

It is equally important to forecast changes in environmental conditions. Correctly anticipating the future can make the difference between disaster and appropriate, sometimes astoundingly profitable, action. Years ago, Sears, Roebuck and Company hit paydirt when it anticipated the passage of legislation requiring that all sleepwear be flameproof. The firm recognized this need early and stocked its stores with nonflammable merchandise, thereby keeping the cost of reacting to the legislation to a minimum. S.C. Johnson, a maker of floor waxes and other chemicals, eliminated fluorocarbons from its aerosol sprays three years before the government required this action.

In sum, environmental changes have vast implications for strategic planning, marketing, and management. All firms must anticipate change, plan appropriately, and carry out the correct responses. In the remainder of this chapter, we examine some of the key forces in the organization's environment, much as a company ought to as part of its routine environmental scanning effort. In Chapter 4, we focus on one important trend—internationalization of markets—and look at how this affects companies and how they should respond.

THE SOCIAL/CULTURAL ENVIRONMENT

From the beginning of this book, we have stressed the need for marketing to focus on the market to be served. Without a firm grasp of the market's wants and needs, an organization has little reason for existence. It is fitting, then, that we begin our environmental analysis by looking at the market, that is, at the firm's social and cultural environment.

Environmental scanning must focus on the beliefs, values, and norms of behavior that are learned and shared by the people in the firm's environment. Values are a person's likes and dislikes, the positive and negative feelings that color his or her view of the world and influence his or her behavior. Less obviously, they are the source of the wants and needs that marketers must satisfy. It is therefore essential to follow shifts in customer values.

Values can shift quickly and dramatically. In Japan, for instance, husbands customarily hand over their paychecks to their wives. Hence, women control 80 percent of household budgets, which are increasingly being spent on Western-style products. A survey has shown that Japanese women are showing dissatisfaction with their traditional home-based role and are seeking careers. They are becoming more selective about product quality and are seeking sports equipment, home computers, and electronic devices, such as microwave ovens, that will allow them more time outside the home. A Japanese social writer has analyzed the change: "We're in a historic transition period. This is a society with a strong sense of roles, and the roles are changing."[6] The Japanese, particularly the young, are exhibiting less commitment to work, more interest in individual expression, and a greater quest for possessions than in generations past.

The United States also has seen changes—some so dramatic that they have left marketers bewildered and dazzled. In virtually no aspect of life does the United States of the 1990s resemble that of the 1950s, and the pace of change is likely to quicken in the decades to come. Already, family life has been vastly changed by the rush of women into the workforce. The youth movement of the 1960s has given way to a more settled lifestyle. Minority groups are playing a bigger role in business, politics, and community life. Americans of all ages and races are being challenged by rapid technological advances, notably the extremely widespread use of computers. The postwar baby-boom generation has left the schools and moved into the prime buying years. This has had a tremendous impact on homebuilders, furniture manufacturers, and auto companies. The company that anticipates such changes can develop strategies to take advantage of them, whereas the company that does not may be surprised by what it later sees as uncontrolled environmental shifts. Control can be as simple as anticipating that something will happen and being prepared for it.

We do not mean to imply that tracking changing values is simple. It requires both formal research—such as the Japanese survey described above—and an ear to social discourse. For example, managers ought to take note when a book about values stays on the best seller lists as long as has Robert Bly's *Iron John: A Book about Men*. In it, he defines a new image of the American male, more assertive, whole, and at peace with his father and his masculinity. He argues that the American male has changed dramatically in recent years:

> The fifties males . . . got to work early, labored responsibly, supported his wife and children, and admired discipline. . . . Many of his qualities were strong and positive, but underneath the charm and bluff there was, and there remains, much isolation, deprivation, and passivity. Unless he has an enemy, he isn't sure he's alive. . . . During the sixties, another sort of man appeared . . . some men began to notice what was called their *feminine* side and pay attention to it. . . . In the seventies I began to see all over the country a phenomenon that we might call the "soft male." . . . They're lovely, valuable people. . . . I like them—they're not interested in harming the earth or starting wars. . . . But many of these men are not happy. You quickly notice the lack of energy in them.[7]

In Bly's workshops for men, given across the country, he finds that "blue-collar workers and woodsmen . . . are just as thoughtful and sensitive as any professors, CEOs or therapists,"[8] so this is not a simple class or profession issue. In his view, changing patterns of parenting now fail to give boys the proper role models and rites of passage, leaving them weakened and ashamed of the maleness of the "wild man" in them. The popularity of his workshops and book suggest that this diagnosis strikes a common chord in our society. This apparent value shift—anticipated by a writer long before researchers' statistics will reflect it—represents an opportunity for the bold and creative among managers to figure out how to profit by the change. (We revisit the subject of values and the broader issue of anticipating changes in customer behavior in Chapter 5.)

THE COMPETITIVE ENVIRONMENT

In the last decade, growth has abated in many markets; hence, growth by individual firms must come at the expense of their competitors. This situation has been characterized as marketing warfare, in which markets are the battlefields.[9] These battles are becoming more and more a "world war."

John Reed, Citicorp chairman and CEO, said in a recent interview, "I approach competition a little like the Chinese board came GO. You see where the other players have put their chips, figure out why, and decide where to put your chips."[10] In GO, however, your competitors have a known number of chips—in management, competitors sometimes surprise you by acquiring new chips.

Reed may have been surprised by the July 1991 merger announcement from Chemical Banking Corporation and Manufacturers Hanover Corporation. The merged entity will displace BankAmerica as the second largest American bank (Citicorp is first), with $135 billion in assets versus Citicorp's $217 billion.[11]

Worse yet, the merged Chemical–Hanover will take the lead in deposits in the tough, and vitally important, New York market. The problem actually began before the merger. Citicorp's consumer deposits grew by only 1.3 percent between March 1989 and March 1990. Chase, the number two New York bank before the merger, experienced deposit growth of 20.2 percent. Chemical and Hanover's deposits grew at 12.7 percent and 11.6 percent, respectively.[12] Now Citicorp must both turn this trend around and cope with a new and larger U.S. competitor. It is CEO Reed's turn to play, but the board doesn't look like he expected it to.

Even as we write, however, rival BankAmerica has announced its plans to acquire Security Pacific for $4.47 billion, and rumors are that Shawmut National Corporation and several other banks may be acquired by BankAmerica.[13] According to *The Wall Street Journal* reporter Fred Bleakley, "When John S. Reed was named chairman seven years ago, Citicorp was, by almost every measure, America's leading bank, first in assets, earnings, equity capital and branch offices. With the pending merger of BankAmerica and Security Pacific, it will have forfeited all these titles but one."[14] Citicorp will still hold the top position as measured by total assets—but tenuously.

In banking, unlike GO, competitors can always buy more chips—if they have the money. Access to money is another of Citicorp's problems. The company went heavily into real estate before the bust, and it has a generous serving of nonperforming Third World debt. The prospect of losses on these loans has forced the bank to set aside $4 billion in reserves, and it has been strapped for capital as a result. Even with a recent stock sale (for half of Citicorp's AMBAC insurance subsidiary), the bank is less able to compete through acquisitions than some of its competitors.[15]

One more thing. GO is not an American game, nor is banking. In fact, the largest bank in the world is Japanese. And so is the second largest. And the third largest. And the fourth largest. And the fifth largest. In fact, Citicorp ranks a sorry eighteenth globally as measured by total assets.[16]

This example is intended to illustrate the impact of competition on a company's environment. But it is also interesting to consider the strategic implications. Reed's strategy will have to begin with the consumer banking operation and will have to focus on its home turf. Consultant Donald McNess (of Cresap/Towers Perin) argues that "The consumer bank is the one cylinder of the [Citicorp] engine that has been firing consistently over the past three to five years, but it is showing signs of getting tired."[17] The following are Citicorp's plans for reviving it:

- Acquire about 200,000 new customers in 1991 by emphasizing convenience, for example, by joining the large Cirrus ATM (automatic teller

machine) network and by increasing the capabilities of its 24-hour telephone banking service.

- Improve branches by extending hours, adding ATMs, adding a retail brokerage service for investors, and increasing staff expertise.

- Convert credit card holders to banking customers. Of Citicorp's 1.5 million New York area card holders, 900,000 do not bank at Citibank, and
about 225,000 of these live within five miles of a branch: These people are
sitting ducks for a marketing program, according to Citibank's New York
area marketing director, Loren Smith. She points out that 80,000 of them
already visit Citibank branches regularly to pay their bills.[18]

- Emphasize global growth. Reed argues (despite Citicorp's ranking) that
"We are the only global bank." Citicorp's far-flung operations and international focus give it, he believes, a unique advantage in consumer banking
worldwide. Most of Citicorp's senior managers speak at least one foreign
language, for example. Reed believes "Our global human capital may be as
important a resource, if not more important, than our financial capital." In
contrast, he argues, the Japanese banks "are not global in the financial
services business. Almost all of their earnings are domestic."[19]

- Cut costs throughout the corporation by trimming middle and upper management, but not the customer contact positions Reed feels are vital to
Citicorp's growth. Cuts to date number 5,000 from an initial staff of
95,000, and 10,000 more cuts are targeted by 1993. These cuts accompany a shift to thinner management, less bureaucracy, and more emphasis
on management judgment versus formal, long-term plans.[20]

Now that Citicorp has played, who has the next move?

Citicorp's case illustrates the most common vision of what competition
means with close rivals elbowing for leadership. But Harvard professor Michael
Porter, from whom we will hear more in Chapter 4, popularized a new vision of
competition in the 1980s. He observed that competition can come from any
direction, not only from the company's direct "competitors." Suppliers, distributors, and many others can compete for resources. The environmental scanning
effort must be broad.

Levitt's concept of "marketing myopia" (see Chapter 1) also is relevant. If
Citicorp's credit card division thinks of itself myopically as in the credit card
business, it will fail to note that other financial services provide competition as
well. According to Reed, "We don't say, 'Consumers need credit cards.' We say,
'Consumers need ways to buy things easily.' That may mean credit cards,
checks, or easy access to lots of cash. In Chile, for example, merchants accept
checks because if you bounce a check, you go to jail."[21]

The need for breadth of vision in assessing competition was brought home to
a very distant competitor of Citicorp—Sealy Posturepedic, the mattress manufacturer. The challenge came not from its conventional competitors, and not even
from banks convincing consumers to keep less cash under their mattresses, but
from within its ranks of licensees. Sealy was loosely structured as a federation of

EXHIBIT 3.2   Characteristics of the four types of competition.

	Pure Competition	Monopolistic Competition	Oligopoly	Monopoly
Number of competitors	Unlimited	Many	Few	One
Product	Homogeneous, undifferentiated	Differentiated, many close substitutes	Either differentiated or undifferentiated	Few if any substitutes
Barriers to entry	Few	Some	Many	Restricted
Knowledge of the market	Perfect	Imperfect, but better than in oligopoly	Imperfect	Perfect
Importance of price competition	Not important	Very important	Price competition is avoided	Not important
Importance of promotion	Not important	Somewhat important	Very important	Not very important
Examples	Some agricultural products	Watches, toothpaste, coffee	Autos, airlines, car rentals	Public utilities

smaller manufacturers, operating under license agreements, until a 1989 leveraged buyout (LBO) reorganized it as a centrally managed national manufacturer. The LBO was the end result of Sealy's struggle with its chief licensee, Ernest Wuliger. His firm acquired other licensees and built its own mattress empire. Eventually, it grew so large that Sealy management could no longer get a good night's sleep. Endless court battles later, Wuliger emerged with a victory, and Sealy was slapped with $77 million in antitrust charges. Wuliger took control over additional licensees in lieu of the cash, and emerged with control over the Sealy empire. It was his firm, not the original licensees or management, that was purchased in the 1989 LBO for $980 million.

The intensity and nature of competition is strongly influenced by the number of competitors. In some cases, the concentration of market share can have a similar influence on competition. Exhibit 3.2 shows the economist's classification scheme for market structure and its implications for management. This exercise is often useful to classify a firm's industry as part of the environmental scanning effort.

THE TECHNOLOGICAL ENVIRONMENT

Technology fosters opportunities to increase consumer satisfaction and thereby gain a competitive edge over other marketers. Today many products exist that were not available a few years ago—compact discs, computers, communication satellites, fiber optics, antilock braking systems, and birth control pills, to name only a few. In the near future, we have been promised household robots, cancer cures, artificial intelligence, videodiscs, debit cards, and practical solar energy.

Often a technological improvement can dramatically change the way we live. The cellular phone boom is one example. Being able to phone while driving means less wasted time, increased productivity, quicker arrival of ambulances, and more effective police forces. More than a million Americans have mobile phones. While now *de rigueur* for salespeople, senior managers, and construction executives, mobile phones have been attached to wheelchairs and tractors as well. One corn farmer was able to let his 20 distributors place orders direct to the field, boosting revenues by 15 percent. Americans are not the only users. Cellular phones abound in Scandinavia and Britain. Over 1,000 of London's distinctive black cabs have mobile phones from which customers can make credit card calls.

The United States has long been the world leader in innovative technology. The transistor, the laser, the semiconductor, xerography, and instant photography were all invented in the United States. But the country's command of technological innovation is weakening. In the 1950s, 82 percent of major inventions brought to the market were American. That share had dropped to 55 percent by the late 1960s, and it continues to fall. Throughout most of the 1970s, the United States devoted a reduced share of its gross national product to research and development (R&D). Spending on R&D more than doubled during the 1980s, but is again falling. This spending grew 5.5 percent in 1990 and is expected to grow at only 2.4 percent in 1991.[22]

Technology has been called the process of "creative destruction" in that new developments create new markets, but destroy many existing ones. The popularity of compact discs and cassette tapes has all but driven vinyl phonograph records from the marketplace, for example. And digital technology is waiting in the wings. The process of creative destruction often catches companies flat-footed. Consultant and historian Alan Kantrow describes the typical pattern:

> When a superior technology appears, corporate management is faced with a difficult and risky challenge: When do we switch? Timing is critical. . . . In practice, studies have shown that most companies tend to switch *too late* from obsolescent to more promising technologies. A striking example is illustrated by the fate of two major producers of mechanical cash registers: Burroughs (now Unisys Corporation) and NCR Corporation. Both companies recognized early the importance of an emerging technology, electronic computers, and, in fact, both tried for a while to compete with IBM in the electronic data processing business. Burroughs switched early (1971) from electromechanical to electronic cash registers. In the same year, NCR decided to stick to electromechanical technology and invest heavily in improving its existing plants. The results of this decision were traumatic for NCR. The market share of electromechanical cash registers declined from 90 percent in 1972 to 10 percent in 1976. NCR was forced to write off $140 million of new, but technologically obsolete, equipment. The CEO was fired, 80 percent

of the top executives lost or changed their jobs, 20,000 workers were let go, and the stock price fell from $45 to $14 per share.[23]

Environmental monitoring plays an important role in the firm's technology strategy by identifying and tracking the development of new technologies. If firms know that their technology is about to become obsolete, they can switch in time. But they often do not. The routine monitoring of the existing technology by the company's technical staff and management is not enough, because new technologies may arise from outside sources. A remarkable inquisitiveness is required to stay on the cutting edge as new technologies displace old ones.

Although we tend to think of technology as the hard-core R&D done by engineers, programmers, and chemists, in fact innovation and new technology occur in every field. Factories must be kept productive through adoption of new production technologies, both tangible and intangible. A fancy new piece of equipment is a tangible innovation. The new total quality programs are based on intangible innovations, such as quality circles. Intangible innovations are the most important innovations in manufacturing at the present time.

New technologies also affect the field of marketing and management in general. For example, the first competitors in an industry to adopt a new distribution channel can be thought of as taking advantage of a new technology. The development of supermarkets is the classic example. This distribution innovation was made possible by developments in both the transportation industry and the nation's roads. Producers and customers could travel longer distances to do business with grocers than before. In general, however, it was not the corner grocery stores that saw the opportunity to innovate; new entrants displaced them. Now that supermarket food has been modified for lengthy transportation and storage, the renegade independents, not the dominant chains, are pursuing the new opportunity to provide ripe and fresh foods again in lieu of five-mile-per-hour tomatoes[24] and "fresh-frozen" fish.

Sometimes shifts in the environment necessitate technological change as a way to cope with new challenges. This shift currently is happening in the accounting business, as the results of a recent survey show: At 50 accounting firms surveyed, "the incidence of coronaries, ulcers and back problems among partners has risen 30% over the past three years."[25] Why are partners having heart attacks? Because several factors have combined to shrink the audit business and make accounting much more competitive and cutthroat. Mergers have reduced the number of clients dramatically, litigation and public outcries over accountants' roles in the failure of Savings and loans and LBO disasters have dampened enthusiasm for accounting, and the recession has forced many clients to cut back on accounting services. According to Steven Oppenheim, a partner at the New York firm of Grant Thornton, "many of us are in a panic, wondering whether the profession will survive."[26]

The profession will survive, but not the firms that fail to innovate. Firms are leaping into marketing now; deregulation made this possible years ago, but it took environmental challenges to force change. Even the structure of accounting firms may be replaced in time—a number of the traditional partnership arrangements have fallen apart in litigation as firms ran into problems, and there are frequent defections, generally producing litigation, these days. The accounting industry is under incredible environmental pressure to innovate, and the first companies to develop and adopt new technologies will likely be the winners.

THE ECONOMIC ENVIRONMENT

Vagaries in the national economy have a dramatic impact on the marketing environment, as we have already seen. Companies have a strong incentive to anticipate major changes, yet they don't seem to be very successful at such predictions. The current recession (with luck, the "last" recession by the time you read this) is a good case in point. It took most of the nation by surprise.

A recession is officially declared when the gross national product (GNP) drops for two quarters in a row. In 1990, the GNP did *not* drop for two consecutive quarterly periods. Instead, it alternated between almost zero- and about $1^{1}/_{2}$-percent growth, actually ending the year on a slight upswing. But compared with the several-percent annual rates that characterized the GNP in 1989, the 1990 figures were miserable. With job opportunities, housing, inventories, and many other indicators heading south in early 1991, the recession proclaimers of the National Bureau of Economic Research gave up on the traditional definition and proclaimed the country in a recession anyway.

If the nation was caught unawares by the beginning of the recession, it certainly seemed prepared for its end. The ink was still wet on the recession proclamation when the first predictions of recovery hit the streets. What is troubling about these forecasts, even the really expert ones, is that they do not even *begin* to agree.

For example, in January 1991, *The New York Times* published three forecasts by leading economists:

- Michael Levy, chief economist of CRT Government Securities, forecast a bad first quarter, but recovery and growth starting in the second quarter of 1991.
- Donald Ratajczak, director of the Economic Forecasting Center at Georgia State University, predicted negative GNP growth until the third quarter of 1991, with a gradual recovery afterward.
- A. Gary Schilling, an economic consultant, forecast GNP shrinkage through the end of 1991, with recovery in 1992.[27]

Whom should people believe? No one, most likely. Any strategy that bets on one of these forecasts is likely to fail. For all we know, the recession could last for years instead of quarters! The GNP (or at least the initial estimates of it)

EXHIBIT 3.3. Annual growth (%) of GNP by quarter.

Year	1991				1992			
Quarter	I	II	III	IV	I	II	III	IV
Actual	−2.8	0.4	?	?	?	?	?	?
Forecasts:								
Levy	0.5	1.1	1.6	1.8	2.1	2.3	2.3	2.3
Ratajczak	−2.3	−0.5	1.4	2.1	1.7	2.0	2.3	2.5
Schilling	−4.5	−4.5	−3.5	−1.5	1.0	2.0	2.0	2.5

continues to be weak as we write, with a 0.4-percent annual growth rate in the second quarter of 1991, following the 2.8-percent drop of the first quarter.[28] The actuality falls somewhere among the three forecasts, but not quite like any. Exhibit 3.3 compares the forecasts with reality—a somewhat sobering experience. Is Jean Dixon available for economic consultation? (Readers may enjoy filling in the "actual" line in this table as new data is released by the Department of Commerce. It will be interesting to find out which forecast was best— and how inaccurate it was. Call the Department of Commerce at (800) 833-8723 for the latest figures.)

Even if one of these economists' forecasts were to be accurate, it now appears that GNP recovery is *not* the critical issue. According to economist James Smith of the Rand Corporation, "The real question is whether our incomes are going to grow at a faster rate than inflation. If not, or if the gain is only 1 percent a year, who wants to wait 20 years to feel better?"[29] Thus, the general concern of forecasters with GNP recovery overlooks a critical issue driving consumer, and thus management, behavior.

Even assuming managers could forecast the economy accurately, it is rarely clear what impact the economy will have on a single industry. Halfway through 1991, some industries seem to be in the grips of a deep recession, whereas others are quite spry. Weekly production figures for steel are down 11.9 percent versus the same period last year, and crude oil refining is down 5.4 percent. But lumber is up 17.8 percent, auto production is up 10.3 percent, and paper is stagnant at 0.7 percent.[30] Are these managers setting strategies in the same economy? Their environments must differ dramatically for their production figures to be so disparate.

One would expect that good times might help all businesses, but this is not true either. The following are examples of how some industries fared after a previous recession. In these examples, business deteriorated. Although firms in these industries are now doing well, they can expect trouble again when this recession ends.

- *Shoe repairers*—"People are repairing shoes less today," complained the owner of Fantastic Shoe Service in Los Angeles. "My business is down from what it was two years ago." Apparently when people have more money they would rather buy new shoes than have old ones repaired.

- *Pawnshops*—Pawnshops prosper during recessions. When times are good, "people still come in but over 70 percent return to claim their pawned items," says Sid Rainey, president of Sandy Springs Pawn Shop in Atlanta. The previous year's figure was 60 percent.
- *Garden supply stores*—When consumers have more money in their pockets, they are more likely to buy their food than to grow it themselves. Gardens for All, the gardening trade association, says that the number of homes with gardens declined from 38 million in 1982 to 35 million as the recession ended in 1983.
- *Security firms*—Although there is plenty of business for security firms, it is hard for them to get good help. "As the economy gets better, a lot of the good people we hire as security guards get called back to their regular jobs," says James Dunbar, president of Loughlin Security Agency in Baltimore.
- *Direct sales*—Many direct-sales companies, such as Dart & Kraft's Tupperware International and Avon, have sales staffs composed largely of women who are unable to find full-time work. But now many of Tupperware's best salespeople switch to nine-to-five jobs, after a recession or, as their husbands go back to work, simply quit. Tupperware's profits fell by 15 percent between 1982 and 1984.[31]

THE POLITICAL/LEGAL ENVIRONMENT

Closely intertwined with economic conditions are the political climate and laws that regulate business activities. Society recognizes that inequities develop when the economic and social systems are left to their own devices. Therefore, at least in theory, government represents the wants and needs of citizens and makes laws in their behalf. Just as citizens are responsible for knowing and obeying traffic laws, managers must be aware of the laws and regulations affecting their activities. Violations not only subject management to prosecution, but are costly in terms of the adverse publicity received by the firm.

The political and legal environment includes both international and domestic boundaries. International political situations, trade agreements, and laws affect marketing activities. The break-up of the Soviet Union, as this book goes to press, will have dramatic effects on businesses around the world. Although the fallout from this distant event may have settled (and hopefully will not be radioactive) by the time this book reaches its readers, there will inevitably be new events and crises on the political landscape.

The international environment can present both opportunities and barriers to exchange. For example, the seizure of U.S. hostages in Iran and the Soviet invasion of Afghanistan created a mood of patriotism among many Americans that translated into problems for companies engaged in trade with those countries. During a single year, 1980, Russian tanks rolled into Afghanistan, the

United States boycotted the Moscow Olympics, and a grain embargo was imposed on Russia. U.S. sales of the popular Russian vodka Stolichnaya suffered dramatically. Between 1979 and 1980, "Stollie" sales dropped from 380,000 cases to 265,000. The brand did recover—in fact, sales rose to 530,000 cases in 1982—but not until the marketing mix was adjusted. To minimize the vodka's association with Russia, Monsieur Henri Wines, the company that imports Stolichnaya, switched the slogan from "The Russian Vodka" to "*The* Vodka." Clearly the political climate can affect marketing decisions.

In contrast, the situation post-1988 is very different. Gorbachev, wanting to revitalize his nation's economy under *perestroika*, attracted U.S. know-how by improving business relations between the two countries. Joint ventures with U.S. companies were solicited to help improve agricultural production, renew Soviet factories, and market consumer products from toothpaste to tires. Two Pizza Huts shops in Moscow, a Soviet partner for RJR–Nabisco to make cookies and snacks, and a Russian version of *PC World* are all part of the plan. The Soviets allowed Western companies to own up to 49 percent of Soviet enterprises for the first time in 50 years. Clearly, the attitudes of both the United States and the Soviet Union (now The Commonwealth of Independent States) have changed dramatically, affecting many marketing decisions as a result. Now the pendulum may be swinging the other way again. For Stolichnaya's slogan to keep up with the political environment, it would have had to change from "The Russian Vodka" to "The Vodka," back to "The Russian Vodka" as Gorbachev ascended, and now back to "The Vodka" again.

Government regulation generally has two purposes: to protect companies from one another and to protect individuals and society at large from unethical business practices. Until the mid-1900s, most such laws focused on maintaining a proper level of competitive activity. The second purpose of regulation is social and consumer protection. As long ago as the mid-1800s, companies were prohibited by law from adulterating food and drugs. In 1906, the Meat Inspection Act focused on sanitary conditions in meat-packing plants. However, in recent years consumer protection legislation has mushroomed, particularly at the federal level. Inequities are noted by lawmakers, and consumer advocates such as Ralph Nader have focused on improving products and helping buyers become better informed.

As the consumer movement gained momentum in the mid-1960s, a rash of consumer protection laws came into being. These laws focused on reducing injustices to consumers and improving product safety, labeling and packaging, warranties, and protection of the natural environment. The magnitude of this surge of consumer-related regulation is apparent when we look at 1976, for instance. That year, the federal government took action in the following areas: food labels, nursing homes, real estate, color additives, prescription drugs, automobile odometers, housing, consumer information, energy, credit leasing, product safety, medical devices, warranties, airline overbooking, and product recalls.[32] Although regulation slowed down during the Reagan era, it seems to be picking up steam again, fueled by increasing concerns over social and environmental impacts of business and by strong lobbying efforts. For example, the powerful American Academy of Pediatrics is currently lobbying for a ban on advertising of all food products that target children. Although this concept will appeal to parents, it probably won't fly in Congress—but it will influence marketers by forcing them to "self-regulate" sufficiently as to avoid such a ban in the future.[33] Clearly, then, the regulations set up by the government, and even proposed regulations, have a substantial influence on the activities undertaken by marketers. No dimension of the marketing mix is untouched by legislation.

The impact of regulation depends largely on how managers and the courts interpret the laws and how they are enforced.[34] Federal, state, and local governments all have agencies to enforce regulations and set guidelines that influence the decisions of marketers. Notable among these are the Federal Trade Commission, the Food and Drug Administration, and the Consumer Product Safety Commission.

The Federal Trade Commission (FTC) has broad powers to influence marketing decisions. When it sees a violation, the FTC can issue a complaint. If the activity is not halted, the FTC can issue a cease-and-desist order. Although it does not have direct authority to imprison or fine, the agency can seek civil penalties of up to $10,000 per day for each violation of a cease-and-desist order. The FTC can also obtain preliminary injunctions or temporary restraining orders to stop firms from undertaking unfair and deceptive practices. In regulating a variety of business practices, the FTC allocates a large amount of its resources to combating false advertising, deceptive packaging and labeling, and misleading pricing practices. In the last few years, state attorney generals have also begun to pursue false advertising claims, and a great many legal actions have arisen in this area. Deceptive claims, ranging from misleading labels to "faked" demonstrations in commercials, are likely to be policed more aggressively in the coming years.

THE NATURAL ENVIRONMENT

Marketers must also contend with natural resources—or the lack of them. They must be aware of the challenges and opportunities that the natural environment provides. Changes in the environment can have positive effects on some marketers and, simultaneously, negative effects on others.

Natural resources vary in the nature of supply. Some, such as water and air, seem to be in infinite supply—yet even these can be serious limitations. For example, in 1988, the worst drought in the United States since 1934 withered crops from Montana to Georgia. Record heat combined with a rainless summer to reduce grain production by 31 percent and corn output by 37 percent. But the severe crop loss was good news for farmers in such countries as Brazil, Argentina, and Australia, who were able to snare larger shares of international markets.

Even the air can cause problems for managers. Researchers said that the fluorocarbon gases used in aerosol sprays could impair the atmosphere's ability to screen out excess ultraviolet radiation. Accordingly, consumers turned away from aerosol cans. As a result, roll-on deodorants increased their market share from 10 percent to about 34 percent, and aerosols lost proportionately.

Although the many finite, renewable resources, such as forests and food, are not likely to disappear, they are subject to drastic change. For example, the 1980 eruption of Mount St. Helens devastated nearly 70,000 acres of Weyerhaeuser's timberland. In 1985, the worst drought of the century wiped out half of Brazil's coffee bean crop, which normally accounts for one-third of the world's supply of coffee. Thus, while some resources can be renewed, their supply is subject to fluctuations.

Clearly, the most critical resources are those that are finite and nonrenewable. The most important of these has been energy. The economic and political environment is strongly affected by the problems of the oil cartel, the Organization of Petroleum Exporting Countries (OPEC), and most recently the 1990–91 Persian Gulf War. High gasoline and fuel oil prices create new opportunities. Coal—which is plentiful in the United States—becomes a popular substitute, for example.

In addition to dealing with the problem of resources, marketers must reckon with natural phenomena that affect their markets. Earthquakes, hurricanes, rain, snow (or lack thereof), tornadoes, extreme heat, and severe cold all have consequences for marketers. Minneapolis's Toro Company, for example, is locked in a seesaw battle against Mother Nature. In the winter of 1978–79, record snowfalls left Toro's snowblower inventory depleted. After the company boosted production by 100 percent for the next year, the virtually snowless 1979–80 winter in the Northeast and Midwest forced the company to offer $30 rebates to lure buyers. In the 1983–84 winter, Toro came up with a new promotional gimmick. Beginning in the fall of 1983, its dealers advertised a "S'no risk" program, promising rebates geared to the amount of snowfall between July 1, 1983, and May 31, 1984. If a given area experienced less than 20 percent of its average snowfall, Toro promised a 100-percent refund. If 30 percent of the average fell, a 70-percent refund was made; 40 percent led to a 60-percent rebate; and 50 percent led to a 50-percent refund. Mother Nature appeared to take Toro's side at last: Sales were higher than the company's projections and snowfall was normal. But low snowfalls in 1989–90 caught Toro and similar companies by surprise again. Sales of snowblowers, shovels, and de-icing pellets were down. According to Tom Hall of Ace Hardware, "Last year we just plain missed our primary season." No amount of clever marketing can completely insulate Toro and its competitors from the weather's influence.[35]

Other companies are learning to put variations in the weather to good advantage. For example, some advertisers schedule advertising based on the weather. This can be as simple as advertising suntan lotion in the summer, or as complicated as the systems Connecticut Radio Network has developed. It measures temperature, humidity, and wind to produce a daily chapped-lips index for scheduling Blistex ads, for example. It also tracks storm forecasts in 30 cities so that Campbell Soup Company can advise consumers to "stock up before the storm." Weather can have strong and unexpected effects on consumption patterns. For instance, a recent heat wave in the eastern United States stimulated the market for art museums, libraries, and bars. At the Detroit Institute of Art, attendance was up 28 percent and Atlanta's High Museum of Art attracted more than double the normal crowd for its annual summer party. After visiting the nearest climate-controlled museum, consumers apparently made tracks to the closest air-conditioned bar. For example, the Grand Slam U.S.A. sports bar in Pittsburgh reported a 50-percent increase in business during the heat wave.[36] It's nice to know that someone will be happy about global warming! Actually, jokes about global warming are considered to be in poor taste these days. The phenomenon illustrates the power of the natural environment to align the long-term interests of companies and consumers because increasingly environmental issues seem to come down to survival issues.

Scientists are concerned that a man-made greenhouse effect will seriously affect our way of life throughout the world. The decade of the 1980s produced the six hottest years in the weather records.[37] Carbon dioxide released into the atmosphere by the burning of fossil fuels such as coal, oil, and gasoline is rapidly accumulating in the atmosphere. The gases act like the glass in a greenhouse, letting in sunlight but trapping the heat. The result is a relentless warming of the planet. Scientists forecast that the busiest waterways in the world, the Great Lakes, will become ice-free 11 months of the year; more icebergs will endanger shipping in Newfoundland and Nova Scotia; India and Bangladesh will be belted by more typhoons and flooding; the tropical rain belt in equatorial Africa will shift northward, wetting parched Chad, Sudan, and Ethiopia; and skin cancer will proliferate globally. All these changes will have profound effects on agriculture, transportation, consumer demand, and government regulation. Although the effects are not yet completely clear, they are likely to cause many related problems. One expert sees it this way: "The winners from global warming are going to be those who think ahead of time and plan. The losers are going to be those who respond only when the crisis arrives, on the spur of the moment."[38] But an increasing number of managers see that everyone is more likely to win if the crisis is averted in the first place.

The solid waste problem clearly illustrates this changing focus. Where companies and conservationists once automatically took conflicting views, collaboration is beginning to emerge. It is not always an easy collaboration, but it is no doubt the first step along a path that more and more managers will have to take, because many companies now have a determining effect on the problem. McDonald's, for example, is the world's largest consumer of polystyrene for disposable packaging. Lately its customers have expressed concern over

McDonald's impact on the natural environment. New Jersey high school student Kurtiz Schneid has made numerous appearances dressed as the clown Ronald McToxic, spreading his "The planet deserves a break today" parody of the Ronald McDonald message.[39] The efforts of McDonald's and the Environmental Defense Fund to cooperate in the analysis of McDonald's solid waste policies is instructive, and are depicted in the following scenes.[40]

Scene 1. August 1990. As the curtain rises, McDonald's announces a taboo-blasting six-month collaborative study with the Environmental Defense Fund (EDF). (Cast includes Frederic Krupp, EDF's executive director; Terri Capatosto, a McDonald's flack-catcher; and Edward Rensi, president of McDonald's U.S.A.)

Krupp: As far as we are concerned, it [the Big Mac box] is under discussion and on the table. We are looking at alternative forms of packaging including reusable plates. The use of polystyrene is not a foregone conclusion.

Capatosto: There is no point in doing this if we are not willing to look at options. But we still have to meet customer expectations. (Winks to polystyrene suppliers in wings.)

Capatosto and Krupp exit stage right while Ronald McToxic makes a cameo appearance to juggle polystyrene burger boxes.

Scene 2. November 1990. McDonald's announces it will ignore EDF recommendations, stick with polystyrene packaging, and institute a plastic recycling program instead.

Krupp: When we learned they were planning to go to comprehensive recycling, we reacted strongly. We had access due to the program [the McDonald's study].

Rensi: Fred [Krupp of EDF] called me on Thursday while I was in New York. When I got back to the office on Friday, I called Shelby Yastrow, who heads our environmental work, and told him to get some people together and study whether we should get rid of foam and switch to paper.

Krupp (purportedly): _____. [Expletive deleted.]

Rensi: This is an indication of how business, consumers, and environmentalists can meet, discuss issues, and create a partnership without a fight. We recognize that not all our decisions are right.

Scene 3. A few days later, Krupp and Rensi are joined by John Giroux, president of McDonald's supplier Amoco Foam Products Company, and by Joseph Bow, president of the Foodservice and Packaging Institute, for a noisy grand finale. McDonald's has just retracted its previous statement and announced it *will* replace polystyrene packaging with paper to reduce the environmental impact.

Giroux (looking disgruntled): This is an environmental attack on the throwaway, fast-food life style and the company with the highest profile. This is not about polystyrene. (Giroux doesn't notice that Ronald McToxic has snuck up behind him and is making bunny ears over his head.)

Rensi: Our customers just don't feel good about it, so we're changing.

Krupp: The hierarchy is: reduce, reuse and recycle. The new packaging has 90-percent less bulk than the foam.

Bow (puts arms around polystyrene makers): This is a big deal to us because of the fact McDonald's bowed to public pressure. We want to see a free economy where materials are used on the basis of their advantages not on the wishes of powerful groups.

Rensi: We're dealing with the consumer and how best to satisfy the consumer. We want to do what we can to encourage the customer to use our product. We want our guests at our restaurants to feel comfortable.

The fact is that consumers *are* increasingly uncomfortable about environmental problems. If the town landfill is full and trash removal costs its citizens more as a result, the people start thinking about issues such as whether Big Macs really have to be packaged in plastic, and whether recycling plastic might not use up more energy than the product is worth. Anyway, Rensi certainly felt his consumers were ready for a "greener" package, even if his suppliers didn't like it. But it was a new twist to have a McDonald's president taking calls from environmentalists—and taking them seriously enough to change the company's policy. A new paradigm seems to be emerging in which managers play a more activist environmental role—but it is not emerging smoothly. The quotes used in the short "play" above are taken directly from news conferences. Although the players did not perform this farce on stage, the press provided a theater with a far larger audience than Broadway could have.

Environmental changes have vast implications for management decision making. It is imperative, therefore, that environmental scanning become an integral part of the strategic planning process. This becomes even more important as key environments change increasingly rapidly. One of the greatest sources of change is the globalization of markets. Firms that once worried about the weather in Chicago now must worry about the weather in Europe, the stability of the Commonwealth of Independent States, and the latest R&D in Japan. In the next chapter, we examine the international arena and its impact on marketing and management.

4 THE INTERNATIONAL CHALLENGE

Going Global with the Flying Pigeon Bicycle Group

> While it is true that a good product knows no national boundaries, there are subtle differences, from country to country and from region to region, in the ways a product is used and what customers expect of it.
>
> —*Hideo Sugiura, Honda Motor Company*[1]

> If U.S. and European companies continue business as usual, they will either fail outright or become, in effect, local design and marketing subsidiaries of Japanese companies.
>
> —*Charles Ferguson, Center for Technology and Policy Development, MIT*[2]

The United States is a global nation when you look at the population statistics, but remarkably insular when you talk to company managers. Most managers have little experience in or knowledge of other nations and cultures. Perhaps this lack of first-hand knowledge explains their tendency to leap onto each new bandwagon—and to fall off quickly if the journey proves difficult for whatever reason. International marketing is fad prone. Managers flock excitedly around the globe, trying out the latest ideas and visiting the latest hot spots, yet only a minority of U.S. businesses have been able to operate on a truly global scale.

The latest hot spots are the many communist countries now opening up their economies to free-market forces—and often to U.S. businesses. But the transition to a free-market system is not as easy as it might seem, either for the domestic companies or for eager U.S. interlopers. The Flying Pigeon Bicycle Group is one example.

Flying Pigeon Bicycles

The Flying Pigeon Bicycle Company is one of China's largest bicycle manufacturers—and one of the first state-controlled manufacturers in that country to attempt the transition to a marketing orientation. Its flight away from a strict production orientation and toward its customers' desires is a migration that will have to be made by hundreds of state-run manufacturers in China, the Russian republics, what was East Germany, Poland, Hungary, Czechoslovakia, Bulgaria, and Yugoslavia. (Little in the way of reform is expected, however, in Romania or Albania.) The barriers these businesses face are similar in many respects to those faced by Western businesses operating in these countries.

Henry Ford's dictum that "they can have cars any color they like as long as it's black" didn't last long in the face of competition from other automakers. Today, we take for granted the diversity of colors and styles available to consumers. But Flying Pigeon bicycles have always been black—until September 1990, that is, when an unsold inventory of two million black bicycles convinced managers that making more of the same was not a good idea. Nobody wanted to buy black bikes anymore. Thus, Flying Pigeon introduced yellow and red bicycles and entered, albeit in low gear, the modern age of marketing. According to *U.S. News and World Report,* "This simple innovation helped Flying Pigeon's sales take off."[3]

Modifying the product—the first of marketing's "four Ps" discussed in Chapter 1—is a big step for any business accustomed to producing according to a central economic plan and selling into a market characterized by chronic shortages. As *U.S. News and World Report* explains, "China's political leaders are encouraging cash-starved inventory-burdened factory managers to flirt with a novel idea: producing goods customers actually want to buy—refrigerators that keep food cool, shoes that don't fall apart in five days and bicycles in a choice of colors and styles." In some cases, making a product more customer oriented is as simple as making it legal. For example, *Newsweek* reports from Russia that "Moscow's new found tolerance for Soviet rock and roll has enticed big American record companies."[4] CBS/Sony Records recently signed up Boris Grebenshikov, lead singer for the Leningrad-based group Aquarium. Just three years ago, the KGB was breaking up Grebenshikov's concerts.

However, the transition to marketing-oriented management is not as simple as it might seem. Even control over the product—what and how much to produce—is still at issue in countries such as China and the Russian republics. According to *Time,* "Gorbachev's determination to force industry to become "self-financing"—to fund current production from the proceeds of past sales—has run into bureaucratic snags, with central planners continuing to exert control over factory operations by placing 'state orders' that effectively determine how much factories produce."[5] Even with the breakup and the price decontrols in the republics, vestiges of the old Soviet planning bureaucracy still remain. In China, "Flying Pigeon has restructured; but despite a 20-month-old economic slump and a nationwide inventory overhang of more than $24.2 billion worth of unsold merchandise, few other state-run enterprises are following suit."[6] Perhaps this explains how a full third of China's state-controlled enterprises are operating at a financial loss, requiring $8.5 billion in direct bailout subsidies and another $4.25 billion in price subsidies by the central government in 1990. It not only pays to be marketing oriented; it costs not to be.

There are often problems with marketing's other three Ps as well. Price controls have maintained prices that are decades out of date in many centralized economies, and loosening the controls can inadvertently permit inflation rates to become airborne. In China, buyers of Flying Pigeon bicycles and other essentials (bikes are for transportation in China, not fun) must now contend with annual inflation rates of 20 to 30 percent. Poland and the Russian republics are currently wrestling with similarly high inflation rates. In Russia, a parliamentary deputy explains that "Prices are not so much an economic category as political," and politics make it difficult to eliminate state-subsidized prices.[7] Now that prices have been freed in Russia, inflation has become the most important political issue in the republic. Pricing is further complicated in many Eastern European countries by the fact that their currencies are "funny money," and, as the economies open up to outsiders, it is becoming harder to maintain their currencies at what *Business Week* refers to as "ridiculously overvalued rates."[8] A black market for these currencies with prices often an order of magnitude different makes it less than clear what a product's actual price is and what the product is truly worth. The elimination of the East German ostmark was considered an essential first step toward revamping East Germany's economy when the two Germanys merged.

Even when prices are deregulated aggressively, problems are plentiful. Ask Chinese farmers next time you find yourself bicycling next to a privately owned rice paddy, and you will probably hear them complain about China's partial decontrol of prices that forced them to buy fertilizer and other supplies at market rates but sell their crops at state-controlled, and unprofitably low, fixed prices.

The complexities and politics of price decontrol make centralized pricing one of the most durable barriers to a free-market economy in Eastern Europe and China. The status of Hungary's economic reforms is a case in point:

> for all its progress creating new institutions for a market economy, such as fledgling stock and bond markets, loans for private entrepreneurs, and privatization laws, problems persist. The country passed a bankruptcy law in 1986, but it still controls prices, taxes heavily, and continues to throw up bureaucratic roadblocks that discourage entrepreneurs.[9]

Distribution ("place" in the four Ps) is also an obstacle to marketing in centralized economies. East Germany's "state-controlled distribution system is hobbled by bureaucracy,"[10] the former Soviet Union's 1990–91 winter food shortage was greatly exacerbated by its inability to distribute available food efficiently, and China restricts the number and location of retail outlets for many products. For example, the Chinese Academy of Sciences reports that only two stores are licensed to sell color TVs in all of China.

U.S. and Western European companies see great opportunities in the opening of socialist and communist economies worldwide. They present massive, growth-stage consumer markets. There are 38 million people in Poland, for example, and only 3.5 million autos. In East Germany, 16.8 million people own only 6,182 autos.[11] But limited retail outlets, inefficient and overburdened distribution channels, and unreliable transportation make such newly opening consumer markets hard to reach, both for domestic producers such as Flying Pigeon and for foreign companies coming into these markets from the United States, Western Europe, and Japan. As Samik Sherif, a vice president of Procter & Gamble, puts it, "Making sure our product is available on a constant basis to the housewife is the key." This project is daunting—Sherif is referring to Procter & Gamble's joint venture that makes and markets laundry and personal care products in China. Sherif is responsible for the company's 1988 investment of $10 million in a Cantonese joint venture and for the company's pursuit of the one billion consumers living in China.[12]

The practice of marketing in these centrally managed economies is also limited by the fourth P, promotion. A marketer of consumer nondurables, such as Procter & Gamble, employs aggressive TV advertising for many products. But in these countries, few consumers have TVs. Only one-tenth of Poland's population does, and roughly one-fifth of East Germans do. Even in the Russian republics, 90 million TVs cannot provide full access to the 284 million residents. In addition, advertisers must cope with regulated, often state-run, media and strict legal limits on advertising. When advertising is not *legally* restricted, it can still be restricted by a lack of advertising space and less media interest in advertisers than Western marketers are accustomed to. J. R. Cerny, vice president of advertising for the two Czech TV channels, explains that, "The media don't depend on advertising yet. They're sponsored by the state. But the situation is changing." Most advertising in Czechoslovakia is in magazines, but publishers are plagued by paper shortages, and most magazines carry only a "handful" of ads.[13]

Despite the many obstacles, marketing is coming to communist and once-communist countries. Flying Pigeon bikes, in their multicolored splendor, are now advertised on Chinese billboards and in magazines. The first Eastern European chapter of the International Advertising Association was established in Hungary in 1989. Procter & Gamble, RJR–Nabisco, and other Western companies are marketing products such as Ritz crackers, Tylenol, Head and Shoulders shampoo, and Band-Aids in China. A.C. Nielsen Company is researching the buying patterns of East Germans. Meanwhile, entrepreneurs have found U.S. and European markets for consumer and industrial goods produced in Eastern

Europe, China, and Russia. In the United States, we can now purchase sweat-shirts from Russia that say "Siberia—Land of Opportunity," and *Radio Silence*, Grebenshikov's first album for CBS/Sony, is now available. Keep your eyes open for Flying Pigeons!

International Marketing and the Firm

If a U.S. company decided to start selling bicycles in China, how should it proceed? There are a variety of ways in which a firm can become involved in international marketing (see Exhibit 4.1). As the exhibit indicates, the degree of a firm's involvement in foreign markets can range from casual to total. Per-haps the most common form of involvement, at least for U.S. firms, is casual. The firm does not actively seek international trade, and is not particularly sensitive to the needs of international markets. A small German toy manufac-turer that sells its products at the 400-year-old Nuremberg Christmas market is a casual international marketer. If a French buyer contacts the manufacturer, the toymaker may be willing to fill a one-time order, but it is unlikely to systematically examine international market opportunities as part of a long-term strategy. Our hypothetical U.S. bicycle maker might fill a one-time order to China's Olympic bicycle racing team; this also would be a casual approach.

Somewhat less casual is the involvement of the indirect exporter, which sells mainly to domestic customers, some of which might be in the export busi-ness. Some organizations in effect serve as the export department for other, less involved firms. Such organizations are known as export merchants or export brokers. These firms may be used on a one-time or a continuing basis, depending on the preferences of the manufacturing company.

The various forms of direct export represent a greater degree of a com-pany's involvement in international marketing. A firm may have an export

EXHIBIT 4.1. Degrees of involvement in international marketing.

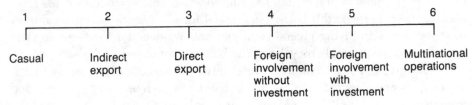

1	2	3	4	5	6
Casual	Indirect export	Direct export	Foreign involvement without investment	Foreign involvement with investment	Multinational operations

1. Not actively seeking international trade.
2. Sells to domestic customers, some of which sell internationally.
3. The firm itself sells to international customers.
4. Uses funds of partners in host countries to establish production facilities there.
5. Uses own funds to establish production facilities in host countries.
6. Views the world as a set of markets and sources of supply.

department or may sell to an import house in another country; in either case, the company views international markets as a long-term opportunity for sales and profits. Many organizations do not advance past the direct export level of commitment. Indeed, for small and medium-sized organizations, this may be the best strategy. But it probably would not work for our U.S. bike manufacturer—production and shipping costs would be prohibitive, even assuming its product is better made than a Flying Pigeon model. It would have to manufacture overseas, perhaps in China, to compete in the Chinese market.

Next on the continuum between casual and total involvement is foreign involvement without investment. A company might license the sale of a product, set up a franchise organization, or enter into a contract with foreign nationals to produce the product abroad or manage the marketing of it. AT&T, for example, recently entered into a reciprocal agreement with Compagnie Génerale d'Electricité (CGE) in which AT&T would help the French firm sell its digital telephone switches in the United States. AT&T also agreed to purchase $200 million worth of CGE equipment over a four-year period. In return, AT&T gained 16 percent of the French telephone switch market, about $150 million in annual sales, by having the French company market its product in France. Our bicycle company might well find this model appropriate. A license agreement with Flying Pigeon might allow the U.S. company to offer its models on the Chinese market without having to invest in local production facilities.

Foreign investment represents an even greater degree of commitment to international marketing. Once a market becomes important enough or a company is offered sufficient incentive by a host country, the firm may decide to invest its own capital in physical facilities abroad. There are many forms of foreign investment, ranging from joint ventures to complete ownership. Joint ventures are strategically beneficial in helping companies penetrate distribution networks in new countries and in helping defray the cost of massive development and production projects. In South America, Ford and West Germany's Volkswagen have formed Autolatina; this organization will produce both VWs and Fords on the same assembly line in a factory previously owned by Ford. To be successful, joint ventures should bring together complementary skills from each partner. Perhaps this is the best model for our bicycle manufacturer: A joint venture with Flying Pigeon could not only produce for the Chinese market, but also could supply bicycles to the U.S. market at reduced cost.

The greatest involvement in international marketing is that of multinational corporations (MNCs), which do not distinguish between domestic and foreign markets. A multinational corporation is based in one country, called the parent country, and produces goods and/or services in one or more countries, called host countries. MNCs make all decisions within a global framework, viewing the world as a set of alternative markets, sources of supply, and locations for productive and distributive facilities. Such companies work toward developing standardized products that can be altered to meet the unique demands of different countries. IBM follows this strategy. Said an IBM executive,

"Our overall concept is to develop a worldwide product line. Each development lab has responsibility for a product from cradle to grave. It is also responsible for identifying customer requirements all around the world, irrespective of the lab location. What is important is that the concept of adaptability is built into the product."[14] Hence, IBM can adjust products to match local markets. Its keyboards, for instance, are all modifiable to meet different language needs. Europe alone needs 20 such keyboards.

Should our hypothetical U.S. bicycle maker follow this model? It might mean building plants and local expertise in Europe, Asia, Africa, and Latin America, for example, and it might mean having a worldwide product line that is customized for local markets. It might mean acquiring or forming a joint venture with Flying Pigeon in China, then building its capacity and updating its designs to supply all of Asia from this location. This would be a dramatic step—probably best not taken all at once. But, for the right company, it might lead to global dominance of the bicycle industry.

The remainder of this chapter focuses disproportionately on the practical and strategic issues faced by exporters and MNCs. The casual international company, although common enough, cannot truly compete globally. It cannot meet the challenge of international markets. To get serious, it needs to think and act like a multinational. But how exactly should the MNC think and act? A simple answer is impossible. The international environment is challenging and strategy must be responsive to it. Furthermore, the optimal global strategy is currently a matter of fierce debate. We must examine both the environment and strategy to answer the question. And because governments play a major role in the environment, we will start with their role.

THE GLOBAL ENVIRONMENT

Basically, governments control the rules of international trade, making them a bigger part of the global business environment than most managers expect. Government policies determine not only what procedures must be followed in importing and exporting foods and services, but also what goods may be traded and even who will be allowed to engage in international trade.

As multinational corporations grow in both size and power, there is some concern that they may be beyond the control of any government. Although no single agency has power over international trade, certain roles that governments can and do play have a major influence on how trade is carried out. Among these are the role of buyer in international markets and that of supporter and regulator of international trade.

Governments themselves buy products. They purchase industrial products such as airplanes, tanks, oil refineries, and typewriters. Many governments have some form of "buy national" policy, requiring their agencies to purchase goods and services in domestic markets whenever possible. However, for products that are not manufactured domestically, the government market represents a large opportunity for foreign firms.

Governments as Regulators and Supporters

Governments also formulate policies that regulate the international marketing efforts of both domestic and foreign firms. Such policies can have far-reaching effects. For example, businesses may request that the government set tariffs (i.e., taxes) on certain imported goods, which raises the prices paid for those goods by the ultimate consumer. Governments also regulate trade, either explicitly or implicitly. In the United States, the government is often said to have no policy toward trade, whereas in fact it does. However, U.S. policy does not often directly support the international marketing activities of a U.S. company. Rather, it attempts to establish "rules of the game" that will allow companies based in the United States to compete fairly in international markets. Other governments, such as that of Japan and Korea, have an explicit policy of aggressively supporting exports.

The Impact of Government Policies

The most visible and controversial international trade policy today is protectionism, or the erection of trade barriers in an attempt to protect domestic industries from foreign competition. Such barriers can take a variety of forms, of which the most common are tariffs and quotas. There are three types of tariffs: specific, ad valorem, and mixed. A *specific tariff* is based on the number of items exported or imported. An *ad valorem tariff* is based on the value of the product; a 20-percent ad valorem tax on a $3,000 motorcycle would result in a tax of $600. *Mixed tariffs* combine the other two types, as in a $50 tax on each item plus 20 percent of its value. Tariffs have generally lost their bite as a protection measure. Among the world's trading countries, the monetary value of tariffs now amounts to only about 5 percent of the value of the goods that carry tariffs, compared to about 50 percent in 1933.

A *quota* is a specific limit on the number of items of a particular kind that may be imported. A more extreme form of quota is an *embargo*, which totally bans imports in designated categories. Other barriers to trade are administrative in nature, such as requiring emission controls on all imported cars.

As a result of the dramatic climb of the U.S. trade deficit in the mid-1980s, the call for measures to protect domestic industries has gained widespread support. Although the deficit is greatly reduced now, concerns over long-term competitiveness of U.S. industries continue to fuel the protectionist movement. Proposed protectionist measures range from broad trade barriers (e.g., import quotas on shoes), to a tougher stance against foreign trade practices that U.S. companies consider unfair (e.g., South Korea's ban on foreign sales of life and fire insurance), to appointing a coordinator to help formulate a comprehensive U.S. trade policy. By the beginning of the 1990s, about 22 percent of goods imported to the United States were under some kind of special protection—up from 12 percent in 1980.

The pursuit of trade protection is a consuming passion for some companies and their executives. For example, Lee Iacocca, chairman and CEO of Chrysler Corporation, says,

> For years, I've been telling anyone who would listen that we're heading for economic disaster with a U.S. market that is wide open to the Japanese market while the Japanese market remains effectively closed to us. That's only possible because the U.S. government is wide open to the Japanese while their government is closed to us. . . . Americans have always been able to make themselves heard in Washington. But now they are being drowned out by more powerful voices from Japan."[15]

Clearly, rhetoric is at least as important as fact when companies lobby for protection.

Bolstering the manufacturing base (with its positive effect on the trade deficit) is only one reason behind the pressure for protectionism. It is estimated that over two million U.S. jobs are lost each year as a result of foreign competition. However, enacting protectionist measures is not all positive; once legislated, they are difficult to retract. The U.S. glassware industry, for example, has been protected since 1922, the dairy industry since 1953, and textiles since 1957. Prices to consumers for protected goods can rise as supply is limited. When the Japanese had an import quota imposed on automobile imports to the United States in the early 1980s, they chose to export more expensive models. In fact, the quota probably forced them to do so, as the only way to increase revenues when volume is restricted is to increase price, which means learning to make better cars.[16]

Trade barriers may limit consumer choice as well as elevate consumer prices. Most damaging, however, barriers can provide artificial isolation from world markets and world competitors; protected firms tend to learn and change more slowly, becoming less competitive over time. This slow change is more likely in a larger country than a smaller one, because the firms in a smaller one tend to look outward for growth and to engage in global competition out of necessity. Thus, Japanese manufacturing is currently leading the world in manufacturing process innovations, even though their home markets are protected. In contrast, U.S. firms have in many cases retreated to their protected domestic markets and failed to pursue global markets with the same aggressiveness.

The United States is not alone in building trade barriers. Italy has defined its import laws so restrictively that only a few thousand Japanese automobiles have been sold there since 1957. France makes all Japanese videotape recorders come into the country through an out-of-the-way customs office in Poitiers. Brazil disallows import licenses for all products produced domestically. This hits 90 percent of imports and bars U.S. exports of textiles, steel, and aircraft, among others.

In 1978, China initiated an "open-door" policy as part of its economic reform program. Until recently, U.S. companies have tried unsuccessfully to grab a share of the Chinese consumer market of one billion people. Chinese trade officials sought foreigners to invest in export industries or high-technology projects. Consumer companies such as Coca-Cola Company and Kentucky Fried Chicken Corporation were limited to licensing and low profits. But gradually China's attitude changed and political logjams for foreign trade were lifted. For example, the Chinese no longer demand majority or at least 50–50 ownership. China also sees more value in low-technology imports. As a result, U.S. companies rushed to the Chinese mainland. Procter & Gamble began a $10 million project to produce laundry and personal-care products in Canton. RJR–Nabisco began to sell its Ritz crackers in China. Chinese consumers are beginning to buy Agree shampoo, Raid insect killer, Band-Aids, and Bausch & Lomb contact lenses.

The activities of foreign firms in China came to a precipitous halt after the massacre of Chinese student protesters in Tiananmen Square on June 4, 1989. Non-Chinese staff was withdrawn and business activity ceased temporarily. Foreign firms put growth plans on hold while waiting to see the full extent of the government clampdown. By now, however, most Japanese and U.S. firms that do business in China have resumed their operations in full. Interestingly, Hong Kong firms have taken a more cautious approach since the massacre and crackdown on political liberties in China—events convinced many of their owners that they needed to move their operations to other countries before Hong Kong reverts to Chinese rule in 1997.

Governments also affect international trade through the agreements they reach with one another. Perhaps the most important international trade pact is the General Agreement on Tariffs and Trade (GATT). Established in 1948 under United Nations auspices, GATT binds 90 of the world's trading nations (and about 95 percent of world trade) to mutual agreements that set limits on both tariff and nontariff barriers. Each decade since GATT was created, special sessions (called "rounds") have been convened to discuss current problems in international trade.

The so-called Uruguay Round of trade talks began in 1987 and will continue until 1992. On its agenda are the issues of consumer price increases due to agricultural subsidies, restrictions on internationally traded services, and the erection of nontariff barriers. The delegates hope to reduce all these protectionist barriers to free trade. Such talks, although long and complicated, offer one of the few realistic hopes for the lowering of barriers to trade among nations.

Billed as the most important U.S. trade agreement in the past two decades, the U.S.–Canada Free Trade Agreement phases out all tariffs and quotas between the two countries by 1999. This pact is intended to improve each country's GNP, employment, and consumer spending. In addition to ending tariffs, the agreement will halt future restrictions on cross-border trade in services; guarantee U.S. access to Canadian oil, gas, and uranium; and set new procedures for resolving trade disputes between the countries.

Other multinational trading agreements exist. At one extreme is what is called "most favored nation" status, in which special treatment is given to a specific trading partner, or set of trading partners, in connection with specific products. The United States, for example, gives developing nations limited duty-free (i.e., tariff-free) access to certain markets. Under a trade program for developing economies called the Generalized System of Preferences (GSP), 140 countries are given GSP status, resulting in exemption for $15 billion of their exports. In 1988, Asia's "Four Tigers"—South Korea, Taiwan, Hong Kong, and Singapore—were removed from GSP status; their exports to the United States resulted in $37 billion of the 1987 U.S. trade deficit, up from $6.1 billion in 1981. Meanwhile, these countries have been resisting opening their markets to U.S. products.

At the other extreme from most favored nation status is the economic cooperation among several nations, such as is found in the European Economic Community (EEC), which was formed in 1957 by six countries and has since expanded to embrace most of Western Europe. In a sweeping program, the EEC is wiping away a sea of red tape, regulation, and fiscal restriction that has grown over the decades to protect member nations. By the end of 1992, the 320 million consumers of the 12 countries will be unified into one market regulated by a common set of trade laws. In effect, people, products, and services will be able to move across country borders with the same ease that they move among the state borders in the United States. It is expected that protectionist regulations will be raised to favor member nations and insulate the EEC from outsiders, especially Japan and the United States. However, foreign companies already firmly entrenched in the EEC nations will fare well. Furthermore, a recent surge in foreign investments, joint ventures, and even mergers within EEC nations is a strategic move by foreign companies to establish themselves in the EEC before 1992. With Europe becoming one, vast economies will come to marketers. Transportation will be quicker and less expensive without the border stops, fewer product alterations will be needed as product requirements are leveled, and much advertising will become standardized across nations.

On a broader scale, the ability to engage in international marketing at all is contingent upon the permission of the governments involved. In the early 1980s, for example, Caterpillar had a major contract to work on a gas pipeline in the former Soviet Union. The Reagan administration demanded the cancellation of that contract, primarily in response to the Soviet invasion of Afghanistan. Large portions of the contract were reassigned to Japanese competitors. Coca-Cola Company left India when the government demanded that the company turn over its secret formula to an Indian company. However, because India has a population of 800 million and annual sales of 2.4 billion bottles of name-brand soft drinks, PepsiCo agreed in 1988 to tough conditions imposed by the Indian government to gain entry to India. PepsiCo agreed to export five times the value of components imported to India. Failure to comply will result in none of its profits being allowed out of the country. In defense of the company's decision to enter India, the president of PepsiCo International indicated, "We're willing to go so far with India because we wanted to make sure we get an early entry while the market is developing. The Indian middle class is beginning to emerge, and we see that as a big growth market."[17] Such examples point up the importance of uncontrollable environmental forces in international marketing, a subject that is discussed in detail in the next section.

THE LOCAL ENVIRONMENT

The most obvious problems in global marketing result from language, laws and restrictions, time zones, customs inspections, transportation, and customary business practices. For instance, haggling is never done by the Dutch, often by Brazilians, and always by the Chinese. Financing and currency swings can also cause trouble. Because exporting entails abnormally high overhead, many private banks are not willing to bankroll beginning exporters. And the volatility of currencies can deeply affect profitability. When the dollar soared in the early 1980s, many companies became financially traumatized; in the later 1980s, many companies recouped their losses as the dollar's strength changed.

To develop an international marketing strategy, a company needs to assess five major areas: economic, cultural, technological, political/legal, and geographic environments.

The Economic Environment

In Manila, Marlboro cigarettes are sold singly, not by the pack or carton. "It's too expensive to buy the whole pack, so I get a few at a time," explained a Filipino taxi driver.[18] The point of this example is that if consumers cannot afford a company's products, the company does not necessarily have to ignore that market. Instead, it can reorganize its marketing mix to take limited economic resources into account. Product and price adjustments may be useful in marketing to consumers in affluent nations as well. For example, Mercedes-Benz cars are priced higher in the United States than in Germany, where they are made. The cars carry a premium image in the United States and are given a premium price to match.

These examples emphasize the importance of a country's level of economic development. Countries are frequently classified based on gross domestic product per capita into three economic categories: less developed, developing, and highly developed. The differences among these categories are considerable. For example, the least developed countries have per capita GNPs of less than $400, whereas the most highly developed ones may have per capita GNPs of over $110,000.

The economic gap between the poorest and richest nations is widening as economic growth is offset by rapid population growth. Except for Asia, with its newly industrialized countries, less developed countries have made much less progress than the industrialized nations.

Nations that have achieved a long-term record of economic growth are classified as "developing." Examples include Brazil, India, and Taiwan. India, where food once accounted for 25 percent of total imports, now produces its own and even exports grain to Russia.

Still other countries are classified as highly developed. Many of these are members of the Organization for Economic Co-operation and Development (OECD), which was formed after World War II to provide a forum for discussion of the economic relationships among member nations. Together, the 24 OECD nations (which include most of Western Europe, New Zealand, Australia, Canada, the United Kingdom, Turkey, and the United States) account for well over 70 percent of world trade and have shown the most consistent growth patterns over the years. Their export growth has been higher than the world average, in contrast to that of less developed countries, whose export growth is only about 10 percent of the world average.[19]

What does all this imply for marketing? The fact is that more than two-thirds of the world's population lives in the developing nations—an enormous market. Perhaps the greatest challenge facing marketers is the low level of disposable income in those countries. The per capita income in many developing countries is less than $200 per year. Low or negative economic growth rates, coupled with high birthrates, result in a situation in which fewer economic resources must be allocated among more people. This leaves very little to be spent on imported goods on a per capita basis. However, many companies see developing countries as a major source of growth markets in the future.

The Cultural Environment[20]

Culture may be thought of as a set of shared learned behaviors based on group values. Among the elements of culture are language, religion, values and attitudes, ethics, education, and social organization.[21]

The importance of cultural factors to a firm that engages in international marketing can be seen in the following example. A company marketing baby food in Sweden, which has a 99-percent literacy rate, could advertise the product in various magazines and newspapers, perhaps including information about the product's nutritional content. In Yemen, however, where the literacy rate is about 30 percent, an approach based on the use of visual media, such as posters, would be more appropriate. Even then, the company might run into problems. One company that hoped to market baby food in central Africa put a picture of a cute baby from a local tribe on the jar. Consumers responded all right, but not in the way the company expected. The literacy rate in the area was practically zero, and consumers had come to expect that the picture on the package represented its contents. They concluded that the baby food jars contained processed baby!

The baby food didn't sell, of course. But behind that failure is more than bad luck—there is a lack of interest in the critical social factors. To avoid stupid mistakes, and to find opportunity in the unique culture of each country and market, managers need to acquire deep, personal knowledge of a culture. If they can't do this personally, they need to hire people from the culture and rely on their expertise.

Language

Language is perhaps the most important element of culture from the standpoint of international marketers. Chevrolet once attempted to introduce its Nova into Spanish-speaking countries. In Spanish, however, the word *nova* means "It doesn't go." Needless to say, Chevrolet's venture was not a success. A similar problem arose for a German exporter of chocolates, which introduced its product to the U.S. market under the brand name Zit. Such stories are amusing, but it is important to realize that both companies incurred substantial losses as a result of these mistakes. They could, of course, modify their brands, but such changes take time and money while leaving the market open to competitors.

Edward T. Hall's concept of the "silent language" of time and space is indicative of another source of problems for unwary international marketers.[22] In India "time is a river," whereas in the United States "time is money." The notions of deadlines and delivery dates are very different in the two cultures. Space also is viewed differently in different cultures. U.S. marketers sometimes feel uncomfortable when negotiating with Jordanian counterparts because Jordanians tend to stand closer to others than is generally considered acceptable in the United States.

Religion

Religion and ethics play key roles in people's responses to marketing activities. An example is the reaction of consumers in Saudi Arabia to an airline ad showing a female flight attendant serving champagne to smiling business people. This ad violated at least two norms related to the Moslem religion: the appropriate roles for women and the prohibition of alcoholic beverages. It was seen by Saudis as an attempt to change their religious values and eventually had to be canceled.

Values and Attitudes

Cultures differ in their values and attitudes toward work, success, clothing, food, music, sex, social status, honesty, the rights of others, and much else. For example, attitudes toward personal care—and hence personal-care products—vary considerably. Pepsodent's claim that its toothpaste helps create white teeth did not go over well in parts of Southeast Asia where people chew betel nuts to stain their teeth.

Values and attitudes are frequently translated into rules of conduct and sometimes into laws that can directly affect international marketing. The ban on comparative advertising in Germany, for example, causes problems for U.S. advertisers that are used to claiming their products are stronger, faster, or cheaper than those of competitors. Unwritten rules of conduct are almost as important as formal laws. A gesture such as putting one's feet on one's desk can be interpreted quite differently in different cultures. In the United States, this action is taken as a sign of relaxation or contemplation. In most Middle Eastern countries, by contrast, it is considered in very poor taste. There, the sole of the foot or shoe is considered offensive because it comes into contact with the ground.

Ethics

When in Rome, do—or don't do—as the Romans do? Determining what constitutes ethical practices when conducting business at home is not always easy. When doing business on foreign turf, the question becomes even more difficult to resolve. A barrage of global actions by U.S. marketers have come under question. Multinational companies have striven to change deep-seated cultural values. For example, U.S. consumer products such as deodorants, toothpaste, fast foods, and breakfast cereals have been introduced and pushed in Third World countries where they were previously unknown. Birth control devices and infant formula to replace breast feeding have been marketed in many illiterate countries. Is it ethical to attempt to change cultural values to obtain greater sales for U.S. companies? In most Third World countries, the per capita consumption of cigarettes is zooming. In such countries, advertising is not regulated; packaging is not mandated to include health warnings. U.S. tobacco companies have aggressively targeted these countries to offset the lack of growth in markets at home. Is this ethical marketing?

In the United States, bribery is considered a sin. But in parts of Asia, Africa, and the Middle East, certain forms of bribery are considered another cost of doing business. Gifts in the form of outright money, products, even services can be demanded of U.S. companies without a blush. For instance, executives wanting to operate in Qatar were requested to make a staggering $1.5 million "gift" to the country's minister of oil. An official of Indonesia's government-owned oil company asked U.S. suppliers for contributions to an Indonesian restaurant in New York City to "enhance" the Indonesian image in the United States. Ethical? Extortion? Or simply normal business practice?

America's aversion to bribery is mirrored in the law. In 1977, Congress enacted the Foreign Corrupt Practices Act which prohibits U.S. companies from "providing or even offering payments to foreign political parties, candidates, or officials with discretionary authority under circumstances that might induce recipients to misuse their positions to assist the company to obtain, maintain, or retain business." Corporations can be fined up to $1 million. Some foreign countries also have legislated against bribery. In Malaysia, long imprisonment can result from bribery. In the old Soviet Union, officials found guilty of accepting bribes could be executed. Yet in most countries where antibribery laws are on the books, deep-rooted traditions replace the law. Foreign companies have the option of treating the request as illegal or as local custom. In fact, in some cultures, what outwardly appears to be a bribe is truly local custom. The act may be a signal of intent to do business, or it may symbolize gratitude, friendship, or even a release of some obligation. In East Africa, for instance, a monetary gift called *Zawadi* is generally requested and, as dictated by tradition, is used to provide a feast in the honor of the donor.

The ethical boundaries of non-Western practices are defined by laws, traditional commercial practices, and social norms. Violation may well rest with interpretation and with general business attitudes tempered by understanding of the local tradition. What may be viewed by Americans as bribery, begging, or blackmail may simply reflect local custom and be nothing more than cross-cultural courtesy or friendship building.[23]

Education

As shown in the baby food example, education and the resultant increase in literacy rates have an enormous impact on the options open to international marketers. Of the elements in the marketing mix, promotion is most affected by this aspect of culture. In India, for example, where the literacy rate is about 33 percent and television and other means of modern mass communication are not widespread, advertising objectives are often met through pictorial outdoor advertising (e.g., transit posters and billboards) and filmed commercials aired in movie theaters. In contrast, newspaper advertising is the largest sector of the advertising industry in the United States.

Social Organization

All societies have some kind of social-class structure. Members of a given class tend to behave in similar ways, especially when compared with members of other social classes. Comparing social classes across societies is difficult. A middle class Frenchman and a middle class German do not share the same values and preferences. However, people in the upper classes in most societies seem to be more similar to each other than to members of other classes within their own societies.[24] Interestingly, there may be a shift in this pattern with the emergence of a global generation of youth with many shared values and tastes; we discussed Levi Strauss' effort to court this new market in Chapter 2 on strategy.

Social mobility, or movement from one social class to another, also varies considerably from one culture to another. In India, traditional Hindu religious values dictate that people accept their social status, at least for this lifetime. In the United States, by contrast, Judeo-Christian religious values encourage people to strive for higher social status in this lifetime. But people are seldom completely honest about social class and/or cannot always take such conventional wisdom for granted. Class mobility in the United States may be more limited than generally assumed, a point to which we'll return in Chapter 7 on consumer behavior. Meanwhile, mobility in India is increasing.

Members of the middle and upper classes are more likely than members of the lower classes to use imported products. This makes countries with large lower class populations, such as Chile, less attractive to international marketers than countries with larger middle and upper classes, such as Sweden.

The Technological Environment

A nation's level of technology directly affects the assortment of goods and services that a marketer is able to sell there. For example, sales of mainframe computers in China are limited because buildings there are not cooled to the correct temperature range. Meanwhile, in India, water buffalo remain the dominant source of energy for farming. Obviously, the level of technology that prevails in some societies is lacking in others, and in still others, technological advances occur in fits and starts. Even the meaning of *technology* varies from one nation to another. The U.S. Agency for International Development (AID), which assists nations in their efforts to develop economically, once donated small tractors to farmers in a Latin American nation. When AID representatives returned a year later, they discovered that the tractors had not been maintained—the oil had not been changed, tune-ups had not been performed, and so on. The farmers had never heard of "preventive maintenance" and were quite surprised when the tractors stopped working. (This anecdote says as much about the assumptions of AID workers as it does about Latin American farmers.)

The Political and Legal Environments

Throughout this chapter, we have discussed instances of differences in the political and legal environments of various countries. Exhibit 4.2 illustrates the differences among various Western European countries in the regulation of advertising. Imagine the problems involved in developing an advertising campaign that would meet all these requirements and still deliver the desired message to the consumer! However, many of these regulations will undoubtedly change as the EEC unifies the European market in 1992.

Governments frequently block investment by foreign firms. Many less developed nations view such investment as exploitive, because the return on the investment does not remain in the host country. But several countries with high levels of foreign debt have changed their policies and are aggressively seeking foreign investment.

Repatriation (i.e., transfer back) of profits from foreign countries is also restricted in some countries. To circumvent such restrictions, a strategy known as transfer pricing is sometimes used. This might occur, for example, when a firm in Switzerland has an affiliate in Argentina that is permitted to transfer only a certain amount of profit to the parent firm each year. The Swiss firm may therefore

EXHIBIT 4.2. International regulations on advertising.

Country	General Regulations		Limitations of Specific Products		
	Comparative Advertising	Advertising to Children	Alcoholic Beverages	Tobacco	Drugs and Medicine
Germany	Banned	Voluntary for TV and radio	Voluntary limits by industry	Banned on TV and radio	Banned in all media
Italy	Direct comparisons banned; indirect OK if substantiated	Cannot show children eating	Some restrictions on TV ads	Banned in all media	Copy clearance needed
Netherlands	OK if comparison is fair and detailed	Voluntary restraints	Voluntary restraints on TV and radio	Voluntary restraints on TV and radio	None
Sweden	Banned if denigrating	Ban on showing children in danger	Voluntary control on ads for wine and hard liquor	Banned in all media	Prescription drug ads banned
Switzerland	None	None	Banned in all media	Banned in all media	Banned in all media
United Kingdom	Banned if denigrating	Voluntary rules designed to protect children	No commercials before 9 P.M.	Cigarette ads banned on TV and radio	Voluntary control

Source: Adapted from Courtland L. Bovee and William F. Arens, *Contemporary Advertising*, 3rd ed., Richard D. Irwin, 1988.

charge the affiliate $125 for a product that is normally priced at $100. The effect is to transfer an extra $25 of profit from the affiliate to the parent firm.

It is sometimes difficult to determine which country's laws govern an international contract; there is no international code or law in this area. Thus, most international contracts include a jurisdiction clause that specifies which set of laws will apply if a dispute arises. An often-quoted piece of advice for resolving such disputes is "negotiate, arbitrate, litigate"; that is, try to settle disputes out of court if at all possible, because court cases are even more lengthy and costly in an international dispute than in a domestic one.

Political issues are another major concern of international marketers. For example, Hong Kong's political status will change entirely in 1997, when it is transferred from British to Chinese control. Although some large firms seem to view this political shift as an opportunity to penetrate Chinese markets more deeply, they are nervous about the possibilities of nationalization or expropriation. Nationalization occurs when a government takes over the ownership or management of a business organization. Expropriation is a more radical action in which the host country denies a foreign corporation the right to engage in business there and seizes its assets. When copper mines and plants in Latin America were expropriated in the 1970s, foreign-owned corporations lost millions of dollars worth of their assets. Confiscation is expropriation without compensation.

Geographic Environments

Products must sometimes be modified to accommodate differences in topography and climate. In Lesotho, a small, mountainous nation in southern Africa, breakfast cereals are sold in bags rather than boxes. Because products are delivered to Lesotho over very rough, unpaved roads, boxes tend to be damaged during shipment. Cereals packed in bags survive the trip without damage. Similarly, Quaker Oats uses special vacuum-sealed tins to protect its cereal products in hot, humid countries. Desert driving conditions in the Middle East require that cars be equipped with supplementary air filters and special clutches.

Natural resources are a major determinant of a nation's production potential. The United States has a variety of minerals, many navigable rivers, and a diverse climate. Thus, it can produce a wide assortment of goods and distribute them efficiently. This has allowed Americans to achieve a high standard of living without relying on imports and exports. Japan, on the other hand, faces a shortage of resources and has been forced to rely on imports and exports to survive economically.

STRATEGIC ALTERNATIVES

We have just described some of the external forces that shape success or failure when doing business in the global arena. Knowledge of these environments directly affects the determination of an appropriate global strategy. International marketing begins with the choice of an entry strategy. Once a company is established in a foreign market, other strategies can be employed to seek competitive success.

Global Entry Strategies

The easiest way to enter international markets is through exporting. Most commonly companies beginning exporting use indirect export. Little investment is needed. The company simply employs salespeople outside the company who provide various services plus international selling expertise. Most indirect exporting is done through domestic-based export merchants who buy domestic products and sell them abroad, and through domestic-based export agents who never own the goods but merely seek out foreign buyers for a commission. Some indirect exporting is done through cooperative organizations where many producers band together and collectively administer the exporting activities.

When the marketer's foreign business has grown sufficiently, the company will likely shift to direct export by setting up of an export department or division. The exporter contacts foreign buyers and conducts the marketing activities. Such greater involvement may include the hiring of international manufacturers' representatives, overseas agents who sell related noncompetitive products for a small number of exporters. Alternatively, the exporting company could use import houses, merchants located abroad who buy directly from the exporter and resell to wholesalers, retailers, and industrial users in their countries. Because these import houses do not have exclusive territorial rights, an exporter might use a number of such import houses within a country. This, however, dilutes their loyalty to the exporter. Another alternative is to set up a sales office in the foreign country, staffed with salespeople from the home or foreign country. Because it entails actual presence on foreign soil, this alternative should be considered a form of investment.

Mead Corporation's coated board division has been a successful direct exporter. The company recently began building a new $500 million plant in Alabama to double its capacity to produce coated paperboard used in packaging. Most of the additional capacity is earmarked for Pacific Rim countries. To ensure meeting the local needs of Japanese customers, Mead signed an agreement with Seibu Saison Group, a $20 billion retailer, which will function as the sales representative. The deal will ensure that Mead knows the ultimate customer's wants and will be able to tailor boxes to specific products.

Investment without capital investment means joining with a foreign partner in some sort of arrangement that leads to some production abroad but without bearing the cost of that production. Licensing is an easy way to conduct global marketing. The licensor agrees with a licensee in the foreign country to allow the use of the licensor's production processes, trademark or brand name, patent, marketing know-how, or some other valued asset. In return, the licensee pays the licensor a fee or royalty. A.G. Spalding, the marketer of athletic goods, now has more sales revenue from licensing than from direct production of products. Gerber Company grabbed entry to Japan through licensing. However, because the licensor has less control over the licensee than with its own manufacturing, this strategy is rather risky. Sometimes the licensor finds that at the end of the contract, a direct competitor has been created. Constant innovation by the licensor is the best way to avoid this.

Popular with consumer goods, franchising has become a frequently used entry strategy. In a franchise, the franchisor contracts with a franchisee, as in licensing. The franchise agreement spells out the specific rights and responsibilities of each party. Generally much more is involved than with licensing. Capital requirements, location restrictions, and merchandising programs are often set for the franchisee to ensure needed control. The franchisor in turn receives financial remuneration. Holiday Inn, McDonald's, and Kentucky Fried Chicken have expanded to foreign markets via franchising.

Production contracting involves agreeing with a local producer in the foreign country to make a product. Generally, the company retains the marketing activities, often through its foreign sales branches. Although a company cannot maintain good control over production, contracting provides quicker access to foreign markets than setting up one's own manufacturing facilities. Many Japanese companies have used this strategy to enter U.S. markets. Sapporo Breweries contracted with Southern California's Hansen Foods to bottle soft drinks for sale in the United States, and Kirwin Brewery Company has an agreement with Molson Breweries of Canada to bottle Japanese beer for sale in the United States.

With management contracting, the domestic firm provides management skills and knowledge to the exporting firm in return for capital for the operation. Hilton and Marriott both operate many hotels in foreign countries using this strategy.

Joint venturing exists where foreign companies join together in a partnership in which they share ownership and control—and risk. Three options exist: The domestic company may buy a share in the existing operation of the foreign company, the foreign investor may buy an interest in the local company, or the two partners may form a completely new company. The joint venture is particularly effective when one party needs the financial, production, labor, or marketing expertise of the other partner. Some foreign governments demand joint venture, often offering less than 50-percent ownership to the foreigner, as a condition of entry.

In the quest for greater worldwide market share, joint venturing has become an increasingly popular strategy.[25] India's leather processing subsidiary of Tata has joined with France's TFR to challenge the Italians' dominance in upscale leather goods. America's Caterpillar is teaming with Japan's Mitsubishi to manufacture enormous earthmoving equipment. Some joint ventures seek world dominance. Philips, the Dutch electronics conglomerate, has joint ventures with many partners to grab the lion's share of the optical disc market. The major alliance is with U.S. DuPont to develop, produce, and market optical storage media. Sometimes these joint ventures produce industries not feasible otherwise. South Korea's Jindo Corporation's joint venture with Siberian sable ranches received the blessing of the Soviet government (but may now have to be renegotiated with Siberian authorities, illustrating the impact political events can have on globel strategy). Bringing Jindo's designers and stitchers together with the pelt producers created a $265 million annual fur business.

The greatest involvement comes with the direct investment in manufacturing abroad. When sufficient expertise in the foreign country exists and/or when the market appears large enough, the company may decide to build its own production plants. This strategy maintains control; creates jobs in the foreign country, which enhances the company's image politically and culturally; and builds relationships with the government, people, suppliers, and local distributors. However, this strategy exposes the company to greater risk from unstable governments, changing markets, and even possible expropriation.

Investment on foreign soil has been a recent trend to gain stronger foreign footholds, increase global market share, and maintain stronger competitive position. Many mergers, particularly in Europe, are taking place to help companies compete against the United States and Japan. Others are coming together to be holding a stronger position when the EEC countries become one marketplace in 1992. The fall of the U.S. dollar has made U.S. companies attractive to foreigners. Firestone Tire & Rubber Company sold to Japan's Bridgestone Corporation to gain a Japanese source for tires for the Japanese automobiles produced in the United States. General Mills sold its Pioneer Products subsidiary, which makes Betty Crocker cake decorations, to a West German corporation, Schwartauer Werke. At the same time, a rash of foreign production, especially by Japanese and other Asian countries, has been transplanted to the United States. About 250,000 American workers work for Japanese companies located in the United States, for example.

Exhibit 4.3 summarizes the risks associated with each method of market entry, rating each from very low to high. The table also rates three areas of market concern associated with each method. Under Risk Factors, the heading Necessary Capital refers to the risk a firm encounters when it invests its own capital to support the strategy. Political/Economic Risk refers to the degree to which the strategy is vulnerable to political or economic pressures within the host country. Adaptability to Trade Barriers refers to the strategy's ability to respond to newly imposed trade barriers. Under Market Concerns, the heading Stability of Relationships examines the nature of the interaction between organizations in the host and home countries. For example, indirect exporting occurs on an ad hoc basis, with no thought to the long-term potential of that relationship, whereas joint ventures require partners that maintain a mutually rewarding relationship over the long run. Availability of Information refers to the

EXHIBIT 4.3. Risk factors and market concerns in international market entry strategies.

Alternative	Risk Factors			Market Concerns		
	Necessary Capital	Political/ Economic Risk	Adaptability to Trade Barriers	Stability of Relationships	Availability of Information	Control
Indirect export	VL	VL	L	VL	VL	VL
Direct export, export department	M	M	L	M	M	L
Sales representatives	L	L	L	L	M	M
Import house	VL	VL	L	L	L	VL
Sales office	M	M	M	M	H	M
Involvement without capital investment						
Licensing	L	M	H	L	L	VL
Franchising	M	L	M	M	H	M
Product contract	VL	H	M	M	M	L
Management contract	L	M	M	M	H	M
Involvement with capital investment						
Joint venture	M	M	H	M	H	H
Manufacturing abroad	H	H	H	H	H	H

VL = Very low; L = Low; M = Medium; H = High.

marketing information required for the strategy to be successful. Finally, Control refers to the amount of influence the firm will have over marketing activities in the host country.

A brief look at the table shows that each method of market entry involves trade-offs between risk and market concerns. Indirect exports, for example, rate very low on all risk factors but also rate low in terms of the firm's ability to influence the market. In other words, if a firm sells its products to an export broker, the broker assumes the risks of international marketing, but the seller gives up control over how its product is marketed. On the other hand, the risks of establishing a manufacturing plant abroad are very high, but this method of market entry gives the marketer the greatest potential influence on the market.

Global Marketing Strategy

The degree of adaptation to local cultural and business conditions is one consideration in deciding on a strategy. One popular, though controversial, strategy is referred to as the global marketing strategy (GMS).[26] This approach has been defined as "selling the same product, the same way, everywhere."[27] GMS is based on the notion that consumers around the world are growing more and more similar and that a standardized product and marketing mix can achieve enormous economies, especially in advertising, packaging, and distribution because they would not be changed. The strategy is controversial because it seems to flaunt the many factors that make it difficult to move into a new national market, factors much of this chapter is dedicated to analyzing.

Proponents of this strategy believe that modern technology has created a commonalty among people around the world. Global travel and communication have exposed more and more people to products and services that they have heard about, actually seen, or even experienced—and now want. Although differences exist in consumer preferences, shopping behavior, cultural institutions, and promotional media, those who support GMS believe that these preferences and practices can and will change to be more similar. The general strategy of offering high-quality, lower priced products will prevail in any global market.

A few companies, such as Coca-Cola, McDonald's, Exxon, and recently Levi Strauss, have achieved great success through strategies that allow them to operate in a standardized fashion in diverse markets. The "Marlboro Man" advertising campaign has worked well around the world. Coca-Cola is the most recognized soft drink brand on this globe. Yet many companies have been unsuccessful in using this approach. These companies have found it necessary to adapt their strategies to different markets. Exhibit 4.4 lists some factors that appear to affect the success of a global marketing strategy.

The 1992 EEC elimination of barriers to trade in Europe could present greater opportunity for successful use of a global marketing strategy—at least on a pan-European basis. Already companies are treating Europe as one market. Johnson & Johnson, traditionally a country-by-country marketer, has

EXHIBIT 4.4. Factors influencing the success of a global marketing strategy.

	Favoring Global Strategy	Favoring Individualized Strategy
Environment		
Unique cultural factors affecting consumption	Not present	Present
Legal environment	Similar	Different
Geographic factors	Similar	Different
Government involvement in business	Laissez faire	Controlled
Attitude toward change	Flexible	Inflexible
Market characteristics		
Character of resident population		
Degree of urbanization	Largely urban	Largely rural
Size of total population	Very large	Small
Sophistication of marketing institutions	Sophisticated	Primitive
Product		
Breadth of market appeal	Narrow	Broad
Technical complexity of product	Simple	Technical
Cost of financial factors		
Level of R&D cost	High	Low
Importance of price	Important	Unimportant
Availability of investment capital	High	Low

launched a sanitary product throughout Europe and backed it with a multimillion-dollar advertising campaign. Satellite television transmissions to all of Europe provide a medium for sending the standardized campaign. Some companies are producing new products for the mass European market, whereas others are redesigning existing products for a more unified look. With increased travel among European countries, marketers strive to offer standardized brands, retail locations, and even shelf space. But this task is not easy. As a London-based consultant said, "Brands that grew up in different countries are often perceived as different characters. Making them into an international brand is a real job."[28]

What is the answer, then—go international with a single global strategy, or focus locally with individualized strategies and offerings? The answer is not yet clear—there are successes and failures in both cases—but it is beginning to appear that both strategies need to be implemented at once. This is the "think globally, act locally" strategy.

Honda is the third largest manufacturer of automobiles, *in the United States*. Although it is a Japanese company, it has made such a large investment in U.S. operations that it is also a major U.S. manufacturer. It might be considered an extreme examplar of the localization strategy. Hidea Sugiura, Honda's previous chairman (still an active adviser to the company) explains that, "More than 60 percent of our total sales take place outside of Japan; our products are marketed in well over one hundred countries. Moreover, we manufacture products at seventy-seven plants in forty countries outside Japan."[29] Sugiura goes on to explain that "we place the utmost importance on localization—adapting our activities to those practiced in the countries where we operate. This overseas strategy consists of four concepts: localization of products, profit, production, and management."[30] This means that products are tailored to the needs of local markets, profits from local markets are reinvested (which often makes the difference between being a welcome or unwelcome guest in a foreign country), production occurs in major local markets, and authority and control are decentralized to the local management.

This strategy would be a recipe for disaster without a strong centralizing force to tie together every local market and keep the Honda mission and identity at the fore. At Honda, this comes from a transfer of corporate culture to the local enterprise. According to Sugiura, "It involves the transfer of a philosophy, that is, the corporate culture that constitutes the basis of technology and management, developed within a corporation since its founding."[31]

U.S. auto companies take the opposite approach, traditionally building most of their cars in the United States for export to foreign markets and not customizing the product or even the marketing message for the local market. U.S. cars with the steering wheel on the left are still offered in many foreign countries where traffic laws require one to drive on the left even though most cars have the wheel on the right. To these U.S. auto companies, Honda's incredibly localized strategy seems very appealing, but difficult to implement. From Honda's perspective, the centralized control over marketing and product development that Ford or Chrysler maintains no doubt seems efficient and simpler to manage.

This contrast appears in a study of many multinational corporations by professors Cristopher Bartlett and Sumantra Ghoshal, published in the University of California–Berkeley's *California Management Review*. They reported that,

> In the course of a study of some of the world's leading Japanese, European, and American multinationals, we found that these globalizing and localizing forces are working simultaneously to transform many industries. But for historical reasons, few companies have built the organizational capabilities to respond equally to both of these forces.[32]

In other words, although both centralized and localized models have appealing features, it is difficult for managers to transform either model into the other. What the authors recommend instead is a linkage of central and local structures that combines strengths of each, allowing the company "to do what it must to survive in today's international environment—think globally and act locally."[33] To be effective, this hybrid approach needs to be characterized by:

- Interdependence between local operations through shared resources and responsibilities

- Devices to force integration of operations among local units, for example, through communications and cooperation by managers
- Strong, shared corporate identity and philosophy, such as Honda uses to keep its local operations focused on the central goals and mission

Of these characteristics, the operational interdependence of local units is most important. According to Bartlett and Ghoshal,

> Perhaps the most important requirement of the transnational organization is a need for the organizational configuration to be based on a principle of reciprocal dependence among units. Such an interdependence of resources and responsibilities breaks down the hierarchy between local and global interests by making the sharing of resources, ideas and opportunities a self-enforcing norm.[34]

Perhaps the simplest way to state this principle is to say that the organization needs to be designed so that local managers work with local managers from other countries, not merely their own. This is the essence of thinking globally but acting locally.

Other Strategic Options

In addition to a GMS or an individualized approach, other strategies are open to international marketers. One of these is called modular marketing, a centrally coordinated strategy that is carried out in local units or modules. The modules may be either demographic or geographic. They may even cross national boundaries. This approach is used by Procter & Gamble in selling soap. A soap with the same chemical properties may be marketed in the Western European module and the Asian module using the same basic advertising theme (cleanliness), but the soap may be positioned differently according to the cultural meaning and importance of cleanliness in each module. The packaging may also appeal to different cultural traits through the colors and artwork used.

Another strategic option for international marketers is the use/need approach.[35] In this strategy, the product mix and the promotional mix are either extended (used in the same manner) or adapted (modified) according to an evaluation of whether the product use and the need being served are the same or different in various markets. Thus, bicycles sold in China or Holland might be physically similar to bicycles sold in the United States, but the manner in which they are promoted would be quite different because the needs they satisfy are different. In China and Holland, a bike is needed for transportation; in the United States, the chief need satisfied is recreation. In this situation, a single, global strategy is unrealistic. Flying Pigeon is no more prepared to sell bikes for recreation than Schwinn is for transportation. A more localized approach that takes into account local use and need would therefore be appropriate. Products would have to differ dramatically between transportation- and recreation-oriented bicycle markets.

U.S. INDUSTRIAL COMPETITIVENESS

Thus far, we have focused on the individual firm's strategic choices, looking at the environmental and strategic considerations that would help management decide, for example, whether and how to enter the Chinese bicycle market. These decisions are of practical short-term importance to managers, who see many opportunities and threats abroad. If a U.S. manufacturer could sell bicycles in China, it could participate in a far larger market (on a unit basis) than any other in the world. If the manufacturer could produce bicycles in China for U.S. or European markets, say through a joint venture with Flying Pigeon, it could probably lower its costs dramatically. If, however, it did nothing about China, and Chinese firms such as Flying Pigeon began exporting bicycles to the U.S. market, the U.S. company might find itself challenged by a new low-cost competitor. Thus, the focus on short-term issues and strategies is important.

But when we add up all the specific cases, discussed in this chapter, and notice the number of affected industries, another, perhaps more pressing question becomes apparent. What if U.S. businesses fail to respond effectively to the challenges and opportunities presented by the new global markets? What if they do not manage to penetrate the Chinese market for bicycles, but Flying Pigeon does penetrate the U.S. market? And what if this happens time and again, in business after business and industry after industry? Pretty soon the U.S. economy's strength will be eroded and its industries pushed from their leadership positions. The individual companies within them will not only have to deal with domestic competitors, but will have to face far larger and more successful foreign competitors. The fate of the U.S. economy therefore seems tied to the success of individual managers and their companies in the global competitive arena. Many observers think the first battles have already been lost.

The statistics alone tell much of this story. Where U.S. businesses once dominated the global business scene, they now share the stage with a crowd of

EXHIBIT 4.5.   Ten largest public companies.

Rank	Company	Country
1	NTT	Japan
2	IBM	U.S.
3	Royal Dutch/Shell	Netherlands, U.K.
4	General Electric	U.S.
5	Industrial Bank of Japan	Japan
6	Exxon	U.S.
7	Toyota Motor	Japan
8	Fuji Bank	Japan
9	Sumitomo Bank	Japan
10	Dai-Ichi Kangyo Bank	Japan

Source: Morgan Stanley, "The World's 100 Largest Public Companies," *The Wall Street Journal,* September 21, 1990, p. R28.

Japanese companies, and the momentum favors the Japanese firms, not the U.S. firms. Exhibit 4.5 shows the ten largest public companies, ranked by their market value, according to investment bankers Morgan Stanley.

When critical industries are examined, the track record is grim. A recent study by MIT's Commission on Industrial Productivity reports, "Much of the evidence we have gathered points to the manufacturing sector as the area where the American advantage in cost and quality has been most severely eroded. The problem is particularly evident because many U.S. manufacturers now compete directly with foreign rivals in both domestic and overseas markets."[36] Any number of U.S. industries can be used to illustrate this erosion and the impact it has on the businesses within the industry. The computer industry is an especially good example because it is one in which the United States is generally assumed to excel in contrast to many of the old-line industries where production has already fled overseas. Charles Ferguson, previously with IBM and now at MIT's Center for Technology, describes the current status of the computer industry:

> On the surface, no crisis is visible. The world market share of the U.S. computer systems industry has declined only modestly—from 70% in 1980 to approximately 60% today. Japan holds only 20% of this market. But market share is measured in gross revenues; and U.S. and European computer companies have been paying an increasing fraction of those revenues to vertically integrated Japanese components and hardware suppliers, who are also their primary future competitors. Japanese industry may well control more than 50% of the hardware content of world-wide personal systems markets within five years.[37]

The Japanese companies are becoming the dominant mass producers of a wide variety of computer components, just as they already have become with semiconductors—four of the six largest semiconductor manufacturers are Japanese companies. The trend, taken to its extreme, might turn the United States into what entrepreneur Roy Manns of Polyfiltronics describes as "a nation of shopkeepers and shoppers."[38] Ferguson does his own prognosticating, as provided in one of this chapter's opening quotes, and concludes that Japanese companies "will dominate a $1 trillion world hardware industry." He goes on to describe an endangered list that includes "most of the U.S. computer, office equipment, and imaging industries."[39] The prospect of these high-tech industries following the same disastrous path that steel, textiles, machine tools, and other industries already have is alarming to say the least.

Ferguson's analysis of computers leads him to focus on the Keiretsu system in Japan, by which some of the larger Japanese companies form loose federations with supplier companies, banks, and so forth, to achieve greater scale and focus than their U.S. competitors. This explanation is only one of many that have been advanced—the higher relative quality of Japanese products being one of them—but Ferguson argues that a similar effort to combine forces is necessary in the U.S. computer industry. He calls for the formation of a U.S. computer keiretsu (which raises the issue of how to avoid violating U.S. antitrust laws while still achieving coordinated effort).

The findings of Michael Porter of Harvard Business School are perhaps especially relevant, as they share a philosophical perspective with Ferguson and also with the "think globally, act locally" strategy discussed previously. Porter spent four years studying the market share trends of ten countries in hundreds of separate industries. He found, for example, that between 1978 and 1985, the United States increased its share by 15 percent or more in 82 industries, but lost 15 percent or more of its share in 97 others, producing a net loss. What is particularly interesting about his findings is his explanation of why these trends occurred. Competitive advantage occurs, according to Porter, when an industry has four conditions that are favorable to successful business development in that industry:[40]

1. *Factor conditions* — The natural resources needed in the industry and the ability to turn them into a specialized advantage (the resources do not help competitiveness if many other countries also have them).

2. *Demand conditions* — A large, sophisticated domestic market to spur innovation and development in the industry.

3. *Related and supporting industries* — According to Porter, "An industry striding toward the top needs worldclass suppliers" and strong indirect competitors that, together, can form what he calls an industrial cluster in which accelerated innovation occurs. (Silicon Valley is an obvious example.)

4. *Company strategy, structure and rivalry* — The factors that determine how a company is "created, organized, and managed." For example, a highly competitive domestic industry will tend to produce companies that are more competitive on the global level.

Porter's findings are relevant to government policymakers, but we are especially interested in their implications for managers. For example, what do they say about the U.S. computer industry? It has favorable factor conditions, such as a highly educated workforce (although national policy has not focused on maintaining this advantage). It has favorable demand conditions, with a large, sophisticated, and demanding U.S. consumer base. It also has fierce, sophisticated rivals to provide domestic competition.

So what could be wrong? Does it have the critical mass of related and supporting industries that Porter talks of? Do the industrial clusters of Silicon Valley and Boston's Route 128 fill this role adequately? Perhaps not. Ferguson's findings seem to point to a weakness in this area, one that is not immediately obvious because it is happening under the surface. More and more Silicon Valley companies are sourcing critical components overseas, and doing the bare minimum of assembly here. This means that the power of this industrial cluster is fading, and it no longer contains a critical mass of related companies, all innovating and competing together to advance the computer industry.

What should U.S. companies do to remain competitive worldwide? Some of the success factors Porter identifies are difficult for individual companies to control—how do you single-handedly create an industrial cluster, or keep one from losing its vitality? But perhaps even a problem of this magnitude can be addressed. As we discussed in Chapter 3 on the marketing environment, firms often make some headway on such issues through trade groups and lobbying efforts, providing they agree that the issue deserves their attention.

At the level of the individual firm, Porter interprets the results as indicating a need to build global strategy on a firm "home-base" strategy. By this, he means that "A company has only one home base for each particular business, and its health is essential to the company's capacity to prosper in the long run."[41] The home base should be the country and location that provides the four critical success factors an industry needs, as defined above, and the company's strategy should be designed to be closely tied to this home base.

Porter explains that "Today's competitive advantage is a matter of knowledge and skill. These are shaped by local institutions, local values, local suppliers, local customers. . . . The capacity to compete globally arises from the advantages created at home."[42] This means, for example, that although in the short run a company might achieve cost advantages by buying products from abroad, in the long run it will become less competitive because it will no longer have the advantage of capable home-base suppliers. The company's management must both select a good home base and nurture that home base so that it will in turn nurture the company for global competition.

Porter's arguments could be taken as a conservative call for fully centralized management of multinationals. They are not. On the marketing side, to be successful, companies need to maintain a local presence, and to know thoroughly a country's culture, values, and needs. This means acting locally, through vertical integration into the foreign country for distribution, even for production in many cases. But this must be balanced by a dynamic home base, one that ensures a long-term supply of leading-edge innovations and that allows the company to lead the market in the effort to give customers more for their dollar—or yen. Honda's successful local strategy is based on a strong Japanese home industry, and much of Honda's know-how, ideas, and components comes from Japan, even though many of its cars and motorcycles are built overseas.

When Porter's arguments concerning the need for a strong home base are considered, we can conclude that three strategic components seem essential to a company's global competitiveness. First, as discussed earlier, the firm must have a global vision. It must think globally and have sufficient mechanisms to ensure that local managers rub shoulders—and share ideas—with other managers on a global as well as a local level. Second, also as discussed earlier, a strong local presence in each foreign market is essential. This is the "act locally" component of the multinational's strategy. Third, the company must pick a domestic home base for each of its industries that can give the company home-base advantages in each industry. This strategy is not simple to follow—it is much more complex than the strategies required to succeed in a domestic market. But, then again, the problem of how to achieve global leadership is not a simple one!

PART TWO

MARKETING KNOWLEDGE

OMNI'S NEW RECRUIT

"If you are going to work here, there is one thing you have to get straight," said June Smith.

"What's that?" asked Ann Jones, regarding her new boss with what she hoped would appear to be her full attention. (In fact, now that the excitement of her first day on the job was wearing off and the reality sinking in, she couldn't help thinking about the unknowns of a career in marketing compared with the pleasant routine of her old job in cost accounting.)

"Are you listening, Ann?" Smith's voice brought the new employee to attention. "What you need to understand is that this department is in the knowledge business. We supply knowledge—to Omni's management, to our sales force, to distributors and retailers, even to our own staff of product managers. We do a lot of other things, of course, but I think that is our most important task."

"I understand the importance of information to the firm," answered Jones. "After all, I've been in accounting for six years and that's how we saw our business, too. For instance, the purpose of the cost accounting system my firm developed for Omni was to provide better cost and profitability information on each of your products."

The director of marketing stared at Jones for a minute, as if (it seemed to Jones) she couldn't believe Omni had hired her. "I said *knowledge*, not information," corrected Smith crisply. "The distinction is important. We gather lots of data, both from formal sources such as surveys and informal sources such as conversations with customers. We convert this data to information by analyzing it and organizing it. And we help the users of this information convert it to knowledge by thinking about what the information *means*."

Smith paused for a moment to tip her chair back and peer at Jones, perhaps still suspicious that the recruit was not paying full attention. "For example," she continued, "we sometimes find competitors or firms in other industries that seem to perform a function better than Omni does, and with our research capabilities, it makes sense for us to initiate a benchmarking effort to find out how they do it better. But the effort has to involve a team from whatever function is in question—they need to share in the research process so that they learn from it." Jones thought about the cost accounting system she had helped develop for Omni a few years ago, wondering if all the trouble users had with it could have been avoided if a team approach had been used. Smith continued, "I view this department as responsible for stimulating organizational learning. Management insight needs to flow from information about the market, and the market is our department. We have to play a proactive role in the company, not be passive report writers."

"Like accountants?" thought Jones, wondering if her new boss did not care for the accounting profession. "I see your point," she added aloud. "Is that why you said earlier that in a way everyone at Omni works in the marketing department?"

"Yes," laughed Smith, "I meant that the entire company is our project. I'm not empire building. I merely agree with Peter Drucker's observation that marketing is the whole firm, viewed from the customer's perspective. This means we have to help Omni see itself as its customers do. As a product manager, you are going to be narrowly focused on the two new ovens you are in charge of. But you also have to keep this broader perspective in mind. Information that helps you design a better marketing campaign can also help others at Omni better understand the market and the customer's behavior. Remember you don't have any direct authority as a product manager, so you can only get things done if other managers see the wisdom of your requests. You can think of this as an education task. But I don't mean to give a speech—do you have any questions?"

Jones thought about her initial conversation with Miller, the toaster oven category manager, back when Jones first visited Omni's marketing department. "Will I have trouble getting support for my products?" she asked. "I remember Joan was concerned they wouldn't get the advertising they needed."

"Yes, I remember that debate. We eventually agreed to try a prime-time campaign. In fact, that's why you are here. The response was so strong that it was obvious the new models were a hit, and Joan asked us to bring someone on board to help her handle them. They are your products now, but it is still her category, and you will find her very helpful if you need to do a little arm-twisting." Smith laughed again, giving Jones the impression that Miller must be a good arm-twister. "In fact, I'm going to turn you over to Joan for the rest of the morning. You'll find her at her desk. She'll bring you up to date on the ovens, and I'm sure she can answer most of your other questions too. But please step in if you have more questions for me. Oh, and I have arranged for us all to go to lunch with Jim Berman at 1:00. Will that work out for you?"

"That's great, June. Thanks. I'll see you later." Jones headed out of the marketing director's office, turned left, stopped, turned around, and headed right, hoping Smith wouldn't see her pass by the office door again. She was too distracted to keep her directions straight—most of her attention was focused on an internal debate over what exactly Smith had meant about marketing knowledge, and how this differed from the information she was accustomed to providing as an accountant. One thought struck her as she found her way to Miller's desk: Accounting information after all was focused on what happened in the *past,* whereas marketing knowledge obviously was more concerned with how customers and competitors would behave in the *future.*

5 MARKETING RESEARCH AND INFORMATION

Figuring Out What the Customer Wants

We spend hundreds of millions of dollars trying to figure out what the customer wants.

—*Maryanne E. Rasmussen, Senior VP of Quality,
American Express Travel Related Services Company*

Do you remember *Fatal Attraction,* the popular movie in which Michael Douglas has a brief extramarital fling with Glenn Close, who pursues him psychotically for the rest of the film, then commits suicide in the ending scene?

What? That doesn't sound quite right? Well, actually, it isn't. The Close character commits suicide in the *original* version of the movie. However, after a prerelease test screening received low marks from the viewers, the ending was remade, with Close going on a murderous rampage in Douglas's house, and almost doing in both Douglas and his wife before they do her in. The remake was a success, and the movie became a blockbuster hit. But if management had not obtained detailed test results, the movie might have flopped.

Perhaps you also remember the American Express TV commercial in which a successful young businesswoman breaks in her new credit card by taking her (also successful) husband to dinner. It aired nationally for a short time, but was pulled after tests suggested that some people found the ad intimidating. In an interesting study, Ogilvy & Mather, the ad agency handling this campaign, asked consumers to imagine that they were *talking* with American Express cards. One subject imagined the card saying, "You're not really my type—you can't keep up."[1] Ogilvy shifted to "a more laid-back crew of cardholders. Still handsome, still elegant, but in more relaxed settings—two people off on a spontaneous vacation, for instance," as *Forbes* described it. Decisions like this, based on detailed consumer information, are not uncommon at American Express. The company takes advantage of its regular contacts with cardholders to amass a great deal of information about them. For example, their computers are reported to maintain, with weekly updates, 450 pieces of information about each cardholder.[2] This information is used to target specific groups of customers for ancillary sales of everything from magazine subscriptions and stereo equipment to the exercise video *Buns of Steel*, which American Express chairman James Robinson reportedly uses for his workouts—but which presumably is not sent to cardholders identified by the database as being overweight, conservative, and averse to exercise.

Many success stories in marketing are based on successful acquisition and interpretation of marketing information. But useful information can be hard to come by. Managers often complain about the marketing information available to them. There is generally too much information of the wrong kind, but not enough of the information they need. Does American Express truly need all 450 pieces of information it collects about each cardholder? And why, with all this information, did the company not know its advertisement was a flop until Ogilvy & Mather asked viewers to talk to their cards?

Managers frequently complain that information is scattered throughout the company and hard to find, or that it arrives too late to be useful. They also worry about the accuracy of their marketing information. These complaints reflect the essential role of marketing information, and the frustration managers experience when they must make decisions based on imperfect information.

To overcome many of these problems and to increase the value and quantity of information, managers can pursue the following strategies:

- Increase the sources of information
- Reduce error
- Design studies better
- Report information more clearly
- Manage the company's marketing information system more aggressively

In this chapter, we discuss how each of these strategies is implemented to improve the quantity and quality of marketing information. We do this in considerable detail, as it is increasingly important for all managers to understand and use marketing information.

SOURCES OF INFORMATION

Numerous sources of information exist—many more than most marketers use. Some sources provide formal information, such as a carefully written report describing survey results, whereas others present information informally. But all are valuable. The following are some categories of marketing information:

Books and periodicals

Consultants and research firms

Customers

Friends inside your company

Friends outside your company

Grapevine

Marketing information system (company's internal records)

Marketing research

Other managers

Public documents from competitors

Staff

Subordinates

Superiors

Suppliers

Customers are often the most valuable source, and most marketing research focuses on them. But other sources, from employees to competitors, can also be useful.

Informal Sources

American Express, Sony, Whirlpool, Procter & Gamble, and other companies have begun to solicit complaints from customers as a supplement to the formal customer surveys they conduct. GE's Answer Center in Louisville, Kentucky, handles three million calls via the company's toll-free number each year, and about 10 percent of them are complaints. The complaints are used by marketing to identify problems and improve products and service. Twenty-five percent of the callers ask for help with prepurchase decisions, giving GE a chance to influence 500,000 purchases. American Express spends $150 million annually to help customers with problems. The communication lines, data banks, computers, personnel, and specialized training that go into this operation produce a tremendous amount of marketing information for use in decision making. Coca-Cola's (800) GET-COKE number logged more than 12,000 calls a day when New Coke replaced the old formula in 1985. Ninety percent were complaints, and Coke Classic was introduced soon after.

Informal information from customer complaint lines and centers is sometimes supplemented by information from other sources. United Airlines decided to provide better flight information because a company executive overheard passengers discussing their difficulties. Montgomery Ward lowered its prices when its chairman discovered many employees shopping at Kmart. At Minnesota Mining & Manufacturing (3M), the sales force is the main source of new product ideas. When its salespeople saw workers in automobile factories choking on the dust produced by dry sandpaper, 3M developed a sandpaper that could be used wet. The firm also came up with disposable surgical staplers and Steri-Strip, a tape for closing incisions, as a result of its salespeople's observations of problems that occurred in operating rooms.

Formal Sources

Formal sources are those that follow specified procedures, which increases their accuracy in some cases, and makes it much easier to assess their reliability in all cases. Formal systems usually start with a manager's information request, then collect and analyze raw data to answer the manager's question. Formal sources include *primary sources* (or original sources), such as customers, and *secondary sources*, which report on information already gathered from primary sources. Most of this chapter focuses on formal sources.

Often-Missed Sources

Are you overlooking good sources of information? The following is a list of sources most commonly overlooked by managers:

- *Government patent fillings*—Watching such data discloses potential technological advancement within a firm's industry.
- *Competitors' annual reports*—In an attempt to enhance stockholders' image of the firm, the annual report may disclose new technology in research and development or other useful information.
- *Competitors' employment ads*—Such ads may suggest a competitor's technical and marketing directions.
- *Professional associations and meetings*—The competitors' products, research and development, and management philosophy are often disclosed in displays, brochures, scientific papers, and speeches.
- *Various governmental agencies*—Under the 1966 Freedom of Information Act, many federal agencies must provide requested documents, files, or other records of a federal agency, such as the Federal Drug Administration's inspection reports of competitors' plants, competitors' cost data in a competitive bid, and reports filed with the Federal Trade Commission to support advertising claims.

- *Newspaper and magazine reports*—Tracking events at competitors' sites and in the industry and environment as a whole. It is often worthwhile to assign someone the task of clipping articles and compiling a weekly circular of the important ones.

THE ROLE OF RESEARCH

According to a recent report, American Express uses its customer research to "divine the preferences of its card members and potential card members, primarily by surveying them relentlessly and extensively refining and test marketing new ideas. Amexco knows, for example, just which card 'enhancements'—automatic car-rental insurance, 24-hour phone lines for service—really make a difference to customers but don't break the bank to provide."[3] Furthermore, American Express uses its marketing information to segment customers into groups based on lifestyle and income. They pitch different products and services to each group. Customer research also provides the foundation for American Express' quality program, which aims to improve customer service through efforts such as the employee training performed at its Quality University in Phoenix. In fact, research plays many roles at American Express, as it does at most companies. It is important to understand thoroughly the role of research in marketing. Too many people are confused about research, and too few take full advantage of the marketing information it can provide. In the following sections, we answer basic questions in an effort to pin down the role of research in modern business.

What?

Marketing research focuses on understanding customers. This usually involves asking them questions and interpreting their answers. Questions are asked, and answers found, through systematic, objective research that focuses on gathering information relevant to a specific marketing problem.

It is essential that marketing research be:

- *Systematic*—The research needs to be a planned, well-organized process.
- *Objective*—The information must not be biased by the researcher or the research process.
- *Useful*—The process needs to produce information that helps managers make decisions.
- *Specific*—The information should focus on a specific problem.
- *Decision oriented*—When gathered, the information should result in a decision. Otherwise it was a waste of time and money.

Why?

Most companies perform research to identify the characteristics of the market and to measure market potential. Research is also commonly used to support short-range and long-range forecasts, and to study competitive products and develop or evaluate new products.

Who?

Marketing research as a field dates back only to the 1920s. It is now used in a large majority of medium and large companies. Use of marketing research has grown substantially in recent years, and is spreading to many not-for-profit and service organizations. For example, since 1970, the number of financial service companies conducting research has grown from negligible to over 70 percent. Research is performed by marketing departments, and also with increasing frequency by product development, customer service, quality management, and other customer-oriented functions.

How Much?

On average, businesses spend from 25 to 50 percent of their marketing research budgets on the services of specialized research firms. A single customer survey may cost as little as $10,000, but many cost a great deal more. In-house information gathering can also be expensive: GE's telephone answer center, for instance, costs $8 million per year.

The Role of Specialists

Most research is performed by specialist research firms and purchased by marketing departments, on either an as-is or a customized basis. There are three types of research firms. *Syndicated services* compile specific types of data for sale to marketers. For example, A.C. Nielsen Company, the world's largest marketing research firm, provides demographic profiles of television audiences. The American Research Bureau provides both television and radio audience data, whereas Simmons Market Research Bureau and Target Group Index do the same for magazine readership. These and other syndicated firms provide significant amounts of useful information.

The *custom research firm* designs a customized study in collaboration with the client, collects the information, and provides a report (and presentation if desired) for the client firm. Although the research staffs of these companies include statisticians, psychologists, and experts in survey design, one cannot expect direct access to the most expert staff without a specific request.

The final category of commercial research suppliers is the *specialty line supplier.* Such firms specialize in one aspect of the research process. Perhaps the most common firm of this type is the field interview firm, which specializes in personal interviewing. If a company has considerable in-house expertise in research, it may subcontract portions of a study to specialty research firms and do the rest in-house. Some full-service custom research firms use these specialty line suppliers as subcontractors as well.

A company usually selects a research firm by identifying a handful of firms in the region that have some experience in similar studies and markets, describing the project to each in detail, and asking each to present a proposal and bid. The choice should be based not only on cost, but also on the competence and interest of the firm's personnel, their prior experience, and the quality of their study design and proposal. Small differences in key assumptions (e.g., response rate) can lead to very different price quotes, so compare assumptions and ask for explanations if the quotes differ dramatically.

Syndicated Marketing Research Services

It is always less expensive to purchase available information than to hire a firm for a custom study. The trade-off is that the available information may not be as relevant. However, a great deal of information is available from syndicated research firms, and it is essential to check with them before doing original research. The following is a list of the major syndicated research services and their products:

- *A.C. Nielsen Company, Northbrook, Illinois*—The specialty of Nielsen, the world's largest marketing/advertising research company, is monitoring TV program viewing. Its "audimeter" device is attached to 1,700 household TV sets throughout the nation. The company also provides syndicated and custom audits of retail product sales.
- *Arbitron Ratings Company, New York*—The focus of this company is measurement of radio and TV audiences in local markets. The company also offers a computerized program that provides audience data merged with information on viewer lifestyle.
- *Burke Marketing Services, Cincinnati*—Burke provides both syndicated research services and various customized services through its multiple divisions. It offers pre-and post-TV advertising copy testing and custom survey research, educational seminars, special market modeling, television campaign testing in controlled laboratory settings, and psychological measurement of reactions to advertising.
- *The Gallup Organization, Princeton*—Gallup specializes in quantitative attitude and public-opinion research and provides syndicated surveys in the areas of packaged goods, video, and financial services.
- *IMS International, New York*—IMS's research activities consist mainly of syndicated audits in the pharmaceutical, medical, and health care industries throughout the world. The company tracks the movement of products through panels of doctors, drugstores, hospitals, medical laboratories, nursing homes, and the like.

- *Information Resources, Chicago*—This company's main business is its BehaviorScan system, which collects product sales data via in-store scanner equipment; monitors buying behavior through a panel of households that use an identification card tied to the optical scanner; controls TV advertising to selected homes via cable to test the relationship of advertising to purchase behavior; and measures in-store promotions.
- *NFO Research, Toledo*—The main business of NFO is to track purchases of beverages, home furnishings, women's tailored apparel, and home computers and video games, using a fixed panel of 240,000 households.
- *Simmons Market Research Bureau, New York*—Simmons conducts an annual survey of 19,000 adults regarding their media usage, purchase behavior, and demographic characteristics. These data are combined with the Dun & Bradstreet databank to produce measures of advertising effectiveness by geographic area.
- *Yankelovich, Skelly & White, New York*—This marketing and social research company offers two widely used services: Monitor, a survey of opinions and trends in special segments of society, and *Laboratory Test Market*, a market simulation that evaluates new products in the planning stage.

A number of consulting and research firms produce occasional special reports on specific markets, either presold to a group of clients or sold as high-priced publications to an industry after publication (e.g., The Yankee Group of Boston produces detailed studies of the telecommunications and computer industries). Check with a research librarian and the research staff of relevant trade associations to find out what is available from these sources.

STAGES IN A MARKET RESEARCH PROJECT

If the information a company requires is unavailable from syndicated research firms, and no existing source of information provides an adequate substitute, then a customized research project is the only alternative. Research projects have a number of standard stages, and it is helpful to review them before planning a project. Analyzing a project stage by stage is also necessary when trying to estimate the cost of research, as is often done when deciding whether to spend the money on research or to simply "wing it" on the basis of whatever information is already available.

Research projects are usually managed by the marketing manager or research manager, but sometimes by a president, division manager, or other manager. This person should guide the project through the following stages:

1. Formulate the problem.
2. Determine information needs and sources.
3. Select the research technique.

4. Design the sample.

5. Process and analyze the data.

Skipping a stage is an easy way to run into trouble or produce information that is not helpful to management.

The first and last steps of the research process are the most critical. The last, reporting and using the information, is critical because it focuses on the action needed to make the decision and solve the problem. However, the first stage, formulating the problem, is often the most difficult task in the process. Marketers often have only a vague notion of what their problems are, but researchers need a concrete definition of the problem. The definition will guide the entire research process. An inaccurate definition of the problem will inhibit or even preclude proper use of the results.

Stage 1: Formulate the Problem

Define the problem. A problem is identified when something other than the usual happens. For instance, the New England Aquarium in Boston, one of the region's most frequently visited attractions, recently found attendance down after a period of rapid growth. This was not the problem, however; it was a symptom. It was a sign to management that something was wrong and needed attention. The problem was eventually diagnosed as the museum's inability to attract visitors from the local community.

The researcher and manager need to work together to define the problem correctly. The decision maker should describe the action that will be taken on the basis of the research results. This forces him or her to focus on information that will be useful rather than simply nice to have. The researcher needs to understand the events that brought the problem to management's attention—this helps the researcher get a better understanding of the problem.

When the New England Aquarium's managers realized they needed to focus on local visitors, for example, they were able to give researchers a clear definition of the problem and the decisions that research should support. Research was used to find out how local visitors differed from other visitors and to support the scheduling and marketing of special events, programs, and exhibit openings to match visitor preferences.

Set specific objectives. Once the problem has been defined, the actual goals of the research project can be set. Those goals should be stated in very precise terms, because they will guide the rest of the research process. Moreover, they must be stated in such a way that specific action can be taken on the basis of research findings. In the aquarium study, for example, the following objectives were stated:

1. To know whether different types of people attend on weekends versus weekdays.

2. To determine what affects their decision to visit the aquarium.
3. To find out whether visitors differ from season to season.
4. To learn what percentage of visitors come from the Boston area versus out-of-town.

The analysis of objectives can be taken even further. For example, it is often helpful to add to the list of objectives a short description of the decisions affected by each objective, and possibly to outline likely actions for several different research outcomes. The more thought given to the decisions that management might make, the more action oriented the research can be. It is at this first stage, formulating the problem, that the usefulness of the study is usually determined. A problem formulation that is not very action oriented will probably yield marketing information that management will later complain was "nice to know," rather than necessary to know. "*Need* to know" information should be the ultimate goal of every research project.

Stage 2: Determine Information Needs and Sources

In the aquarium study, the marketing manager might hypothesize that more families visit the museum on weekends than during the week. This hypothesis flows from a discussion of Objective 1. It seems reasonable, but to act on it, the hypothesis must be proved or disproved. The aquarium would commission the researcher to collect data on whether visitors are attending alone or with other people and, in the latter case, whether those people are members of the visitor's family. The marketing manager might also ask the following questions:

- Are more children coming on weekdays than on weekends?
- What are the educational levels of visitors who come at different times of the week?
- What percentage of weekday visitors are from Boston-area colleges?

At this point, the researcher should conduct an informal investigation to answer these questions. Likely sources of information include people both inside and outside the organization, including various managers, salespeople, and customers. Hanging around the aquarium and talking to visitors could provide some answers and could help in deciding what additional information should be sought. For example, tourists who travel more than 500 miles might be looking for a glimpse of a live whale. Without such information, the researcher might not become aware of the need to focus on this particular attraction.

Caution! Check secondary sources. It is tempting at this stage to begin primary research. But the project manager should check secondary sources first. Company sales records and other internal sources may be helpful. Some useful reports can be easily obtained from industrial trade associations and the government. For the aquarium project, for example, the National Association of

Museums provided demographic data on visitors to museums throughout the United States. This secondary source indicated the kinds of visitor characteristics the aquarium should focus on in its research.

Stage 3: Select the Research Technique

If the researcher and manager decide that there is not enough information available to solve the problem, and that the research problem is important enough to justify spending additional money and time, they may choose to collect primary data. The first step along this path is taken by the researcher, who must develop a research design that specifies the kind of research and how it will be conducted. The key decision at this point is the research method to employ. A good place to start is to decide whether the research is primarily descriptive or causal in its focus (simpler observational methods are more likely to work with descriptive studies than with causal studies).

Descriptive studies focus on demographic information about markets and their composition. The aquarium study provides a good example. In that case, the manager wanted to find out where visitors came from, and compare that data to day of the week and season of the year.

Causal studies are required when the problem demands exploration of the cause-and-effect relationships between various phenomena. For example, what is the effect on attendance when the aquarium increases its advertising? Will weekend visitors come during the week if the weekend admission fee is raised? In addition to deciding whether the study should be descriptive or causal, the manager and researcher need to select one of the following three methods: observation, experiment, or survey.

Observation

In observational studies, the researchers do not actually interact with the subjects. Toy companies often use the observational method when deciding whether to market certain products. Fisher-Price, for example, runs an on-site nursery school where designers observe children through one-way mirrors. They watch for such things as general interest, safety features, and ease of play. The true test of a toy is its "play value," that is, whether the child plays with a new toy for a few minutes and then goes back to an old favorite or whether the new toy is interesting enough to be used repeatedly.

There are many observational techniques. Two Detroit companies, Urban Science Applications and R.L. Polk, collect license plate numbers at shopping center parking lots. These are fed into a computer and compared with auto registration data to show where the shopping center's customers live. Such a study showed Taubman Company, a shopping center developer, which customer groups were not coming to its centers. A direct-mail campaign aimed at those groups increased sales by 40 percent at one San Francisco area center.

Other observational techniques involve the use of mechanical devices, such as counting machines, cameras, and recorders. As mentioned earlier, A.C. Nielsen plants an audimeter in selected homes to record when the TV set is in use and which programs are being watched. This is the source of the widely used Nielsen popularity ratings. AGB Television Research has a similar product. Marketers usually refer to these types of studies as "people meters." Along similar lines, Chicago-based Information Resources has developed BehaviorScan, which monitors store purchases by people who agree to carry special shopper identification cards. As purchases are made, the point-of-sale equipment records the information and assigns it to a specific household.

Sherlock Holmes learned much about his subjects without using any of the modern research techniques. Some market researchers employ very simple but often ignored observational techniques. For instance, an attraction such as the New England Aquarium might like to know which exhibits people visit first. They could find out by surveying customers or, more simply, by observing the dirt patterns on the floors on a snowy day. During the summer months, scuff marks on a polished floor might provide the same information. Libraries can use circulation figures to decide what kinds of books to add to their collections.

If observational techniques will help achieve research objectives, they definitely should be used. It is almost always less expensive to observe than to run an experiment or to question people.

Experiment

In a controlled experiment, the effect of a particular variable is measured. The researcher makes changes in the conditions experienced by a test group (usually customers) with respect to a variable (e.g., the amount or type of advertising). The results are compared with those of a control group that did not experience the change; in this way, the effect of the change can be measured.

In a laboratory experiment, people are brought to a specific location and given the experimental treatment. In such settings, it is easier to eliminate outside influences that might cause invalid conclusions. The laboratory can be equipped with one-way mirrors, recorders, videotapes, and the like. For example, one group of consumers watches a series of commercials in a movie theater. A second group then watches the same series, except that one commercial is different. Both groups are asked to rate the commercials. Differences between the two sets of ratings can be ascribed to the effects of the different commercials.

Field experiments are much harder to conduct than laboratory experiments because it is more difficult to hold extraneous factors constant. For instance, how can a researcher testing the effect of a price reduction regulate competitors' advertising? Moreover, it is often hard to gain the attention, interest, or cooperation of respondents. Also, it may be difficult to measure the relevant variable, such as how many sales of the product actually resulted from the price reduction rather than from friends' suggestions, advertising, or plain luck. Despite these drawbacks, field experiments are used more often than laboratory experiments.

Information Resources' BehaviorScan provides a good example of field experimentation. This system has been set up in several small cities. In each city, purchase data are collected from 12,000 households that have cable television service. On the basis of their purchase behavior, certain households receive specific commercials whereas others do not. Each household's subsequent buying behavior is monitored and related to the commercials seen.

Survey

Questionnaires and surveys are used when personal information is needed. Observing people under natural or experimental conditions reveals only what they do. Surveys are required to learn what they *think*. However, people do not always tell the researcher what they are thinking—they do not necessarily even know what they think—so survey technique must wrestle with the issue of how accurately subjects can report their thoughts and feelings. There are three major survey techniques: the personal interview, the telephone interview, and the mail interview.

The personal interview is a perennial favorite of interviewers because it allows face-to-face interaction with respondents. The interviewer can explain complex questions; use audiovisual aids, such as records, pictures, diagrams, and actual products; and can spend more time with the respondent. Face-to-face contact builds confidence and usually permits in-depth probing by the researcher.

On the negative side, personal interviews (especially in-home interviews) can be expensive. Moreover, the presence of the interviewer can introduce two kinds of bias. On the one hand, some respondents may alter their responses so as to appear in a positive light. On the other hand, the way in which the question is presented, the tone of voice, or even the body language of the interviewer can influence the answers given. Extensive training of interviewers is the best antidote to the latter problem.

Today the shopping mall intercept has largely supplanted the in-home interview. In this technique, interviewers approach or "intercept" people as they pass a particular spot in a shopping mall. This technique is very popular: A survey of major consumer goods and service companies by Market Facts found that 90 percent of them use this technique—it was surpassed only by telephone interviewing.

Another popular technique is the focus group, also used by 90 percent of consumer goods and service companies. Groups of eight to ten people are brought together to offer their views on an issue, idea, or product. These informal sessions are conducted by a moderator, who structures the discussion by asking specific questions. One major use of focus groups has been in the early stage of research, when the researcher wants to gain greater insight into the problem. For example, a computer company might want to know whether users of personal computers (PCs) are concerned about the amount of random access memory (RAM) available to them. Through a focus group session, the company might learn that people tend to think in terms of the number of pages of text a machine can hold. The company could then develop a survey that asks a larger sample of PC users questions about the number of pages their computer could hold, rather than the number of bytes of RAM—and the researchers would be more likely to obtain meaningful responses as a result. This technique can be very helpful in refining a problem definition, learning what further questions to ask, determining how they should be phrased, and even learning what answers to expect. Focus group sessions often are held in front of a one-way mirror and recorded on camera or tape. Managers can sit behind the mirror to observe the session or review the tape later.

Much can be learned from conducting three focus groups on the same topic. The small group sizes tend to produce significant variation among groups. If findings from the second group differ from the first, the third group can act as a tiebreaker. One should not expect quantitative results from a focus group, or believe them if they are offered.

The telephone interview is the most frequently used method of marketing research. It is the fastest and has a relatively high response rate—mostly because it involves little effort by the respondent. Although people are more likely to hang up than to close the door on an interviewer, the response rate is significantly higher for telephone interviews than for mail surveys. Telephone interviewing eliminates the high cost of travel, and is often the least expensive survey method. With the use of WATS, even national surveys can be cost-effective. An advantage of telephone interviewing is that it allows the interviewer to probe. Respondents generally are willing to participate for a period of 10 to 20 minutes, particularly when the caller indicates the length of time the interview will take when the call begins.

On the other hand, telephone interviews do not allow for observation or audiovisual aids. Moreover, when there is no face-to-face contact, the respondent feels anonymous. This promotes less rapport between researcher and respondent, leading to more difficulty in obtaining personal information such as the respondent's age and income. Also, the potential respondents are limited to those with telephone numbers listed in a directory, which excludes a significant percentage of U.S. households. Certain groups of people are more likely than others to have unlisted numbers—notably blacks, people aged 16 to 34, those who live in the West, and residents of metropolitan areas. As a result, responses to telephone surveys are automatically biased against these groups. A number of techniques can be used to avoid this problem. In random-digit dialing, the caller adds four random numbers to a telephone prefix. In plus-one sampling, numbers are taken from a directory, but one digit is changed. These methods allow the researcher to reach any phone number that is operating, regardless of whether it is in the directory.

Telephone interviewers can now use computer-assisted telephone interviewing (CATI). In CATI, answers are entered directly into the computer, eliminating the cost, time, and errors of manually coding data. Computer systems also make it possible to design more elaborate and flexible surveys. It is advisable to use a research firm with this capability.

The mail survey is the least flexible data collection technique. Because the questionnaire must be highly structured and standardized, it provides little room for probing. This drawback can be overcome to some degree by asking open-ended questions. However, questionnaires must be short and easy to complete to keep the amount of effort required of the respondent to a minimum.

Because the mail survey is standardized, interviewer bias is reduced or eliminated. Moreover, questionnaires can be returned anonymously, allowing some respondents to be more frank than they would be in a personal interview. One frequently encountered problem is that the appropriate mailing list can be difficult or impossible to obtain. Perhaps the greatest disadvantage of mail surveys is their low response rates—often less than 25 percent. This creates concern about the answers that would have come from people who did not respond—nonresponse error can be high. However, mail surveys are sometimes less costly than telephone surveys, and are always less costly than personal interviews.

Techniques for increasing mail response rates include notifying people that they will be receiving a questionnaire (via mailgrams, postcards, phone calls, or letters), personalizing the questionnaire package, offering monetary or gift incentives, including a self-addressed return envelope, and sending a follow-up letter or postcard one to three weeks after the questionnaire mailing. For consumer surveys, the follow-up letter and a prepaid monetary incentive have been found most effective. Many marketing research studies now consist of a preliminary phone call, followed by a mailed questionnaire, followed by another phone call.

A variation of the mail survey is the consumer panel, in which people are given some form of remuneration for participating in an ongoing study. These individuals receive a series of questionnaires or keep detailed records of their purchase behavior. This technique allows researchers to track brand loyalty, the effectiveness of advertising campaigns, and rates of consumption of products and brands.

Stage 4: Sample Design

An important part of the research process is selecting the respondents. The choice of respondents will influence the types of questions asked, as well as the methods used to ask them. It usually is unrealistic and unnecessary to include every possible respondent in a survey. Instead, researchers select a sample of respondents who represent the population being surveyed. (A population includes all the individuals who have a particular characteristic about which conclusions will be drawn.) Sampling offers researchers a number of benefits that would not be available if the entire population were surveyed. In conducting personal interviews, for example, researchers can save both time and money through sampling, since fewer respondents are interviewed. Moreover, sampling can actually be more accurate than surveying the whole population. In many cases, it is virtually impossible to interview an entire population—imagine trying to talk to all the tennis players in the United States, for example.

Because respondents' thoughts, impressions, and feelings can change, by the time the last member of the population is interviewed, many of those already spoken to may have changed their minds.

There are two basic kinds of sampling procedures: *probability sampling*, in which all members of the population have a known chance of being included in the sample, and *nonprobability sampling*, in which respondents are selected partly on the basis of researchers' judgment. Probability sampling is done according to statistical rules that leave no room for judgment on the part of the researcher or interviewer. (Note that we said each member of the population has a *known* chance of being selected for the sample; this is not the same as having an *equal* chance. With a known chance, the researcher can calculate the probability of a certain person's being selected.) We discuss three probability sampling techniques: simple random sampling, stratified random sampling, and area (cluster) sampling.

In simple random sampling, researchers obtain a complete list of the members of the population and choose the sample in a random fashion. For example, the names of all the individuals in the population might be written on cards and mixed thoroughly in a barrel. The researchers then choose the sample by pulling out cards without looking or otherwise influencing the choice. This gives every member of the population not only a known, but also an equal, chance of being included in the sample.

In the stratified random sampling technique, the total population is divided into subgroups, or strata, each of which is treated like a simple random sample. This approach is often followed when certain subgroups of the population might have an unusual impact on the results. For instance, suppose the research objective is to determine the average amount of time people spend playing tennis. Those who have higher incomes than the general tennis-playing population are more likely to play year-round and to do so indoors. Thus, to ensure that the sample does not reflect too many year-round players, the researchers might divide all tennis players into groups based on income or indoor-club membership. They could then use simple random sampling to select individuals from each of the strata.

In many cases, it is difficult to obtain a list of the total population, but data about specific geographic areas, such as city blocks, can easily be obtained from the U.S. Census Bureau. An area (cluster) sample is chosen by simply taking a random sample of the geographic areas on the list. Then each household in the geographic unit is interviewed, or a second random sample is taken from each of the geographic units and those households are interviewed.

In nonprobability sampling, the selection of the sample is based to some extent on the researchers' judgment. There is no known chance of any particular person's being selected. Nonprobability sampling is used when probability sampling is not possible—when no list of the population exists, when the population is not stable over time, and so on. We examine three nonprobability sampling techniques: convenience sampling, judgment sampling, and quota sampling.

As the name implies, convenience samples are selected to suit the convenience of the researchers. Examples include asking people to volunteer to test products, using the mall intercept method discussed earlier, using students as subjects in an experiment, and conducting "on the street" interviews on television. In all these cases, either the sample members volunteer out of interest in the project, or researchers select them because they are available. However, with such samples, it is unclear exactly what population is represented; the members of the desired population do not all have an equal or known chance of participating.

In the judgment sampling technique, samples are selected on the basis of criteria that the researchers believe will result in a group that is representative of the population being surveyed. In test marketing a new product, for example, researchers may turn to the U.S. Census Bureau to make a judgment about which cities are similar to national markets.

Quota sampling is a special form of judgment sampling. In this case, researchers take specific steps to obtain a sample that is like the overall population in terms of some specified characteristic or set of characteristics. For example, an interviewer may be instructed to select half the sample from people over 30 and half from people under 30 because the researcher knows that the population is divided in half at the 30-year mark. Moreover, this simple example uses only one characteristic. To get a truly representative sample of a population, researchers must use a number of characteristics, making effective quota sampling very difficult.

Stage 5: Process and Analyze the Data

Once the researchers have developed the questionnaire and selected a sample, data can be collected using the methods described earlier. When the data have been collected, they can be analyzed. First, however, the questionnaires must be scanned for obvious errors or incomplete responses. Faulty questionnaires are ignored.

Marketing researchers use a variety of statistical techniques to turn raw data into useful information. First, they tabulate the data, or count the frequency of each type of response. In doing so, they produce three different kinds of numbers: the mode, the median, and the mean. These simple statistics provide the foundation of more advanced statistical analysis. The *mode* is the number that occurs most frequently. The *median* is the middle number; it divides a list in half so that 50 percent are above the median and 50 percent are below it. The *mean*, or average, is the sum of all the numbers divided by the number of scores. These calculations are illustrated in Exhibit 5.1, using data from research on family size in a suburban neighborhood.

The next step is to cross-classify the data, that is, to look for frequencies of responses by different categories of respondents. Finally, more sophisticated analytical techniques can be used to extract further information from the data. These techniques can be complex, and special training in data analysis is needed

EXHIBIT 5.1. Mode, Median, and Mean Calculations

Question:	How many children do you have?

1	2	3	4	5	6 or more

Results: (Population of 200 families)

1	2	3	4	5	6 or more
55	45	50	35	10	5

Mode: 1 child

Median: Between 2 and 3—50 percent have 2 or fewer and 50 percent have 3 or more

Mean:
$55 \times 1 = 55$
$45 \times 2 = 90$
$50 \times 3 = 150$
$35 \times 4 = 140$
$10 \times 5 = 50$
$5 \times 6 = 30$

$515/200 = 2.575$ children per family

---

to use them properly. For example, statistical tests may be performed to determine whether a result is explainable simply due to the error that is likely to occur by chance, or whether the result is attributable to some determining cause. Generous use of graphs and tables is helpful in conveying this information. Recommendations for action should be included.

Exhibit 5.2, taken from an actual marketing report, shows concise, easy-to-read recommendations that were presented to the Kalamazoo Metro Transit system by a marketing research team. This example features four recommendations, each backed up by research findings. The recommendations are referenced to the numbers of the questions asked in the survey and to the page numbers of the report that provide further details. This is a good example of effective interpretation and presentation of marketing information.

Procter & Gamble's Citrus Hill introduction demonstrates the importance of data interpretation. A recent case study in *Marketing Week* concluded that "from its birth as a result of misread market research, the story of Citrus Hill is a series of large and small disasters." (However, P&G's version of this story was not included in the article.)

P&G decided to enter the orange juice market with a product innovation that would give them a quality advantage. But an ex-P&G marketing executive now says, "If you look at consumer acceptance of orange juice, the perceived difference between the best and the worst product in the category is narrower than in any other category. P&G needs to compete in categories where they can create a discernable difference and market the heck out of it. Orange juice had less room for improvement than anything."[4] That was mistake number one.

While P&G engineers labored to produce a better orange juice concentrate, P&G marketers introduced Citrus Hill in a few local markets to gain valuable marketing experience against the dominant brands, Minute Maid and

EXHIBIT 5.2. Actual marketing report.

Recommendations (Based upon results of an initial (1980) and follow-up (1981) telephone survey of public transit attitudes and awareness in Kalamazoo, Michigan)

Target Advertising Featuring the Benefits of Riding the Bus to:	Target Advertising to *Nonriders* Outlining the Fare Structure for Riding the Bus	Target Advertising to *Nonriders* Emphasizing How Close Bus Stops Are to Certain Kalamazoo Area Residents	Target Advertising to *Nonriders* Emphasizing Frequency of Bus Service, *i.e.,* How Often the Bus Comes by
• *Males* for "work," "personal business," "school," and "when I don't have a car/when car is in garage" purposes . . . • *Females* for "personal business," "shopping," and "visits or recreation" uses. Radio spots could feature male and female announcers.	*Reason:* a 12% increase among *nonriders* who did not know the cost for a ride on the bus.	*Reason:* 48% of *nonriders* in both surveys, who live 1 to 2 blocks from the nearest bus route, chose not to use the bus during the last year.	*Reason:* Approximately seven out of 10 *nonriders* were initially unaware of the frequency of bus service, and remained so during follow-up interviewing.
Reason: There was an increase in the number of *males* and *females* who used the bus for the purposes mentioned above.	Question 10 (p. 16 of report)	Question 12 (p. 24 of report)	Question 14 (p. 17 of report)
Question 6 (p. 36 of report)	• *Change negative attitudes that bus riding is inconvenient (via news stories for particularly good or unusual service).* • *Point out comparative costs of auto use versus public transit.*	*Target advertising to nonriders who own only one car.* *The message: "take the bus and save the family car for use by other members of the household."*	*Continue using "other" media and "radio" advertising in addition to newspaper and television advertising.*
Service improvements (where feasible) in the areas of more convenient routes and more courteous drivers.	*Reason:* More than nine out of 10 *nonriders* in both surveys reported "car" as their usual means of transportation.	*Reason:* Approximately one-third of *nonriders* in both surveys reported having only one automobile in their household.	*Reason:* Follow-up results for "other" media show a higher percentage of recall over initial survey results for *heavy* and *other* users, and for *nonriders*. Similar results were found for *moderate* users regarding recall of "radio" advertising.
Reason: An increase among certain Kalamazoo area *bus riders* and *nonriders* who reported a need for the improvements mentioned above.			
Question 20 (p. 33–35 of report)	Question 34 (p. 25 of report)	Question 35 (p. 26 of report)	Conclusions (p. 51–54 of report)

Nancy L. Frederick's "2-Part Report Format Attracts Attention of Research Users," Marketing News, May 13, 1983, p. 18.

121

Tropicana. Citrus Hill scored a little higher than its competitors in blind taste tests that paired it with one competitor at a time. It was preferred by 60 percent vs. 40 percent for a competing brand. According to the P&G executive, "All that means is that 10 people out of 100 can tell the difference, but everyone was running around like that was a big deal." Misinterpreting the statistics was mistake number two. On the strength of these results, combined with discouraging reports from the product development engineers, P&G took its Citrus Hill brand through test markets and eventually went national. The brand's share peaked at 17.5 percent with high introductory promotion, but stabilized at 8.5 percent by the end—too low a percentage to be profitable. P&G was forced to relaunch with an improved Citrus Hill Select.

CONCLUSIONS

Congratulations! You have just made it through a much more rigorous tour of the marketing research function than Ms. Jones experienced in her brief visit to Omni's research department in the beginning of this book. The many options for gathering market research and the complex, five-stage process for conducting original (or primary) research make this a difficult topic to understand. Add a little math anxiety, and most managers find it positively repellent. Perhaps this is why research is left to specialists at most companies. Firms usually delegate research to a research manager, who in turn subcontracts all major studies to specialized research firms. In other cases, firms rely on their advertising agency's research department to design studies and hire the appropriate researchers. In either case, the arms-length relationship between research and general business management is potentially unhealthy. The more closely involved the entire marketing department and the entire management team are in the generation and interpretation of marketing information, the closer to the customer the company can be. This point is illustrated by American Express' efforts to improve the quality of its services.

Jim Robinson, CEO of American Express, is fond of saying that "quality is the only patent protection we've got."[5] Years ago, as head of the company's Travel Related Services division, he introduced the methodology used to measure the quality of customer service. Today, his company uses dozens of unusual research techniques to further refine its understanding of customer desires and its measurement of service quality. According to Maryanne Rasmussen, senior VP of quality at Travel Related Services:

> We spend hundreds of millions of dollars trying to find out what the customer wants. One sophisticated external customer satisfaction market research program is our transaction-based surveys. We consider a transaction every contact a customer has with us—telephone calls, billing inquiries, a charge authorization question, etc. This is the most difficult element to measure. Companies can determine customer expectations, measure transaction time, and analyze error rates. But we

go beyond that: through unique transaction-based surveys we focus on how customers perceive a particular single contact with us.[6]

When American Express learns that customers are frustrated with a specific kind of contact, the company uses developed mechanisms to translate this finding into specific goals and actions aimed at improving that contact. For example, each general manager is expected to set annual goals for improving customer service. The transaction-oriented customer surveys are used to maintain a "worldwide service tracking index" for each market in which the company competes, and general managers set their goals according to this index. This means *customers* write the managers' report cards.

American Express also brings marketing information into the management process through the use of regular "on-site business reviews" by Rasmussen's group of quality specialists. The several-week audits look at strategy and marketing plans and, most importantly, focus on the quality of customer service. For example, the auditors read customer correspondence and "ask employees from all levels of the organization what they believe affects internal and external customer quality."[7]

Efforts such as these are beginning to break down the traditional boundaries between research and other marketing functions, and to move marketing information into a more central position in the management of a business. This is an appropriate trend from the customer's perspective, as the marketing information generally represents customer needs. But it requires managers to work with, and understand, marketing information—and, we hope, makes the effort you have put into digesting this chapter all the more worthwhile. A word of caution is also in order, however: The innovative efforts of companies such as American Express are producing new practices in the field of market research that do not always fit the standard categories and descriptors. Rasmussen's transaction-based surveys and service tracking index are both innovations, and neither has been clearly described in the marketing literature to date. A hands-on knowledge of marketing research techniques helps managers at companies such as American Express improve products and services and outcompete rivals. For this reason, a detailed understanding of marketing research is increasingly useful to managers, even if they do not have direct responsibility for this function. With this is mind, we have added several special topics as an appendix to this chapter. You may wish to read them now, or you may prefer to proceed on to the next chapter and come back to these topics later.

It seems fitting to end this chapter on research with an unanswered question—perhaps you will figure out how to answer it using your newfound knowledge of marketing research. Even as companies such as American Express embrace marketing information and build their in-house databases of customers and prospects, the $2.5 billion market research industry is experiencing a decline. Inflation-adjusted revenues dropped slightly in 1990 and are dropping again in 1991 after growing at an annual average of 8 percent in the 1980s.[8] Some managers argue that "Market research just hasn't delivered," as Jim Figura, research VP at Colgate-Palmolive Company puts it.[9] And there certainly are cases in which extensively researched new products have failed dramatically. Perhaps his firm's disastrous launch of Fab 1-Shot laundry detergent and fabric softener explains his attitude. It did well in simulated test markets, but the tests used family shoppers, while its market (since it comes in individual packages) is individuals, not families. The product didn't prove popular with families once it was introduced, and its market share now stands at a miserable tenth of one percent. After reading this chapter, you were no doubt quick to notice that the Fab 1-Shot story includes a methodological error from Stage 4, sample design, and thus cannot truly be considered as evidence against well-designed research projects. Perhaps it is more accurate to say that *bad* research doesn't deliver. The fact is, however, that managers generally have a love–hate relationship with research, and right now there seems to be a swing toward the negative end of the spectrum.

Another way to view the decline in industry sales is to see it as evidence that companies are following American Express' lead and bringing more of their marketing research in-house. Although American Express reports that it spends "hundreds of millions of dollars trying to find out what the customer wants," you can be certain that all of it does not trickle down to market research firms. The company performs a great many surveys, but, on the other hand, it also does extensive in-house number crunching and database analysis to develop its 450-item profile of customers. This is a new vision of customer research, in which someone's response, say to a bill-stuffer selling stereos, adds to the company's understanding of that person and his or her consumer behavior—without the aid of the market research industry. In any event, we are left with an interesting paradox: If marketing research is growing in importance, as it certainly seems to be, why is the industry experiencing declining sales?

APPENDIX: SPECIAL TOPICS IN MARKETING RESEARCH[10]

International Marketing Research

Undertaking marketing research in the burgeoning international arena adds a layer of complexity to the process. Three particularly annoying problems exist: studying many markets, locating secondary data, and collecting primary data.[11] A study replicated in many countries increases the costs and problems. Although some economies are conducive to multiple uses of the research design, these are offset by increased implementation costs—for example, multiple-interviewer recruitment and training, questionnaire translation, and acquisition of population lists. Each country's differences must be factored into the study. For example, a study in one country resulted in the respondents being 64 percent women, whereas in another they were 80 percent men.[12] This sampling problem creates havoc with cross-cultural comparisons. In Lesotho, respondents holding up their thumb and first finger in response to a question about household size would be counted as two by an American interviewer. However, in Lesotho, people start counting on the little finger and continue over the thumb to represent six. Thus the actual answer would be seven. Such peculiarities multiply the problems of international marketing research.

Secondary data sources are much less available in many foreign nations, and statistical data are often unreliable. Most governments conduct censuses, but the quality varies. Laos and Oman never have, however, and Zaire took its last census in the 1950s. Because probability sampling is severely limited, most international studies employ convenience samples. Furthermore, cross-cultural comparisons are limited because secondary sources offer different measures. Classifications are different, and base years are seldom the same. Such terms as *wholesaler* or *commercial vehicle* can also vary in meaning by country.

A company trying to collect its own data meets with "people problems." Language is an obvious difficulty. Not all English words exist in other languages. The different dialects within a country can further complicate translation. In Zaire, for example, the official language is French; however, most Zairians speak one of four *lingua francas* of the country, and they use their tribal language when speaking of emotional issues. Translation of questionnaires for international use is not a simple operation. One technique that is used is *backtranslation*, in which a questionnaire is translated into a second language and then translated back into the original language. The two versions are compared and any inconsistencies resolved in drafting the final version. Coupled with the use of local researchers, this technique can be very effective.

Primary data collection is also confounded by social differences between countries. In many nations, the household includes grandparents and aunts and uncles. This complicates isolating decision makers and key influencers. The role of women around the globe also is not uniform. In Muslim countries, a woman may not be allowed to talk to a male interviewer if her husband is not present, and in many countries, women cannot work as interviewers. Obtaining responses is still another problem. Literacy, reluctance to talk about personal concerns, and even differences in thought patterns all add to the challenge of conducting global marketing research.

It is easy to see international marketing research as a problem. Although it presents many challenges, it also can provide interesting cultural insights and can be a source of ideas and opportunities for marketers. Sometimes it puts researchers in touch with interesting research techniques from other countries. For example, the "antenna shops" used for new-product research in Japan may soon be imported into the United States. Major Japanese manufacturers, from Sony to Nissan, have opened their own stores to have direct access to shoppers and their opinions. Matsushita Electric Industrial Company's antenna shop, Works, does not even sell products. Instead, customers come in to talk about the novel product ideas that the store displays. This antenna store played a central role in the development of the new Musica from Panasonic, a telephone/answering machine/alarm clock combination. The idea of antenna stores is gaining momentum in Japan, and there is even an antenna restaurant, run by Japan's largest fish-processing company, Nissui.[13] Perhaps U.S. companies will add this technique to their marketing research portfolio.

Marketing Information Systems

The recognition that successful marketing requires useful information has given rise to widespread use of what is called a *marketing information system* (MIS): "A set of procedures and methods for regular, planned collection, analysis, and presentation of information for use in making marketing decisions."[14] Although MIS often uses a computer, one is not always necessary. What is necessary is the planned, orderly, and continuous collection, analysis, and presentation of the correct information for marketing decisions. Thus, a library with its reference sources or an employee armed with a file cabinet can be considered a marketing information system.

The concept of an MIS can be used by all marketers—not merely by large firms such as Procter & Gamble or American Airlines, but also by a local grocery store or a small restaurant. The purpose of an MIS is to provide the information needed for decision making so that the use of guesswork can be reduced. These may sound like the same comments that could be made about marketing research, but the two are not synonymous. In fact, MIS and marketing research differ in a number of ways. First, marketing research generally focuses on one problem at a time, and information is collected for the sole purpose of solving that problem. In contrast, an MIS continuously collects and stores data that may be relevant to a variety of problems. Perhaps more important, the MIS provides information that can alert marketers to possible future problems. In this sense, the MIS functions as both a crisis preventer and a problem solver. (American Express' routinely updated record of 450 facts per cardmember is an MIS. The company's one-time study of what consumers imagined American Express cards would say to them was marketing research.)

Another difference between marketing research and MIS arises from how data are collected. In most cases, data for marketing research come from external sources, such as consumers, competitors, and the government. The MIS, by contrast, relies more heavily on data generated within the firm (e.g., sales and accounting data). Much of the original data in the MIS remain "raw" until they are combined or analyzed in some meaningful manner. Then the information is presented to decision makers in the form of reports. Often information obtained through marketing research is stored in the MIS as well.

The following are components of the computerized MIS:

- *Data bank*—Stores raw data that come in from both the external environment and internal records.
- *Statistical bank*—Offers statistical techniques to be used in analyzing data.
- *Model bank*—Contains mathematical marketing models that show relationships among various marketing activities, environmental forces, and desired outcomes.
- *Display unit*—Permits the user to communicate with the system.

IMS International provides a good example of a global MIS. The company developed sales management systems (SMSs) to provide pharmaceutical companies with access via telephone lines to data such as prescriptions filled in drugstores, number of sales presentations made to physicians, medical journal circulation figures, monthly sales volumes of major pharmaceutical products by brand, and number of product samples sent. Data are collected from a worldwide panel of 100,000 physicians, drug wholesalers, and drugstore chains. All data are maintained for each physician market segment and identified by medical specialty, age, and region where doctors' practices are located. In addition to retrieving data, the SMS user can run statistical programs or use a complex model to identify sales increases due to changes in promotional methods. Various marketing programs can be tested and the anticipated volume of new prescriptions determined. Thus, the usefulness of the system depends on the interaction among its various components.

Marketing Intelligence Systems

The marketing intelligence system is the set of activities whose purpose is to monitor the external environment for emerging trends or events. In practice, it often focuses on what competitors are doing. Marketing intelligence is gathered in many ways. Salespeople can be trained to notice, track, and report relevant changes. Wholesalers, retailers, and sales representatives are prime sources of intelligence, as are suppliers. Some companies even have specialists devoted to gathering intelligence. In addition, outside data agencies collect and sell valuable information. Market Research Corporation of America, for example, maintains a panel of 7,500 households and can supply weekly information on competitors' market shares, product package sizes, prices, and promotional deals. The Chicago Hospital Association provides the occupancy rates of all its member hospitals. Companies can also obtain information from government agencies by requesting it under the Freedom of Information Act. For instance, by scanning competitors' bids on government contracts, one can learn their bidding strategies and costs. However, it should be noted that the requests themselves are public documents, so competitors can monitor attempts to obtain information about their bids!

The growth in global marketing strategies has been accompanied by a growth in the need for international marketing intelligence systems. A coherent global strategy rests on a foundation of solid business information. Many sources for foreign intelligence are readily available right here in the United States. Special foreign newspaper subscription services exist. Overseas Courier ships Japanese periodicals worldwide; German News Company is a similar source for European print media. Foreign trade organizations and international chambers of commerce are also excellent resources. Foreign brokerage houses, many of which are in New York City, provide analytic reports on their country's international environment, and developing global communication networks is becoming a top priority as firms expand their market boundaries.

Strategic Intelligence . . . or Unethical Spying?

Today it is not money that makes the world go around, but information. Successful global and domestic marketing strategies are built on a solid base of business information. Generally, managers from other industrialized nations tend to be better informed than U.S. managers. Before entering a market, the Japanese, for instance, studiously analyze the country to be entered, gathering intelligence about language, key environmental trends, technologies in vogue, and the cultural values. To keep abreast, British executives reportedly read three times as many newspapers as U.S. managers. Strategic intelligence is the backbone of effective global strategies, as it is of domestic marketing strategies.

Ethically borderline methods are sometimes used to capture competitive insights. Public document scanning, bogus job interviews with in-depth grilling of applicants, even piecing together of torn memos from corporate trash are part of the growing game of corporate sleuthing. Consultants are hired or seminars taken to ensure effective snooping. Some detectives act as reporters in quest of corporate stores. Others, using a technique of "benchmarking," literally tear competitor's products apart looking at how they achieve the quality they provide. Even observing noncompetitors helps. Xerox, for example, has dramatically improved its order handling process by studying the mail-order champion, direct mail cataloguer L.L. Bean. Other companies visit Japanese competitors, finding them surprisingly open about their plans. Said one executive after visiting a Japanese competitor, "It was sort of like them telling us, this is how we are going to kill you. Get ready."

Other methods used by corporate sleuths include:

- *Plant tours*—Firms often give tours of their plants to the public or to potential clients. Observation of the plant can be a dead giveaway.
- *Analysis of help wanted ads*—Help wanted ads are, in effect, press releases. The kinds of people a company wants to hire are potent clues as to what it will be up to next.
- *Buying competitors' garbage*—Once trash has left a competitor's premises, it is legally classified as abandoned property. Sometimes valuable information is thrown out in the trash. Smart competitors shred any documents that contain information that could be used by rivals.

Criminal action proceedings can occur when corporate intelligence exceeds legal limits. Procter & Gamble sued Frito-Lay, Keebler, and Nabisco for allegedly stealing its patented recipe for soft-center chewy cookies. In the suit, P&G claimed that Keebler took photographs of its plant from an airplane, that a Frito-Lay intelligence agent posed as a customer to gain entry to a secret sales meeting, and that Nabisco's spy sneaked by a security guard to get into a kitchen where "secret cookie-making technology was being used."

This kind of intelligence gathering rings of "007" tactics. However, improper sleuthing is unnecessary, because other approaches are quite ethical and substitute creativity for ethical transgressions. One consultant was used by the Internal Revenue Service to estimate the revenues of a house of prostitution; he resorted to using the data on restroom paper towel usage obtained from the brothel's supplier, which he was able to correlate with revenues. A Japanese company measured the amount of rust on the train tracks coming out of a competitor's plant—and estimated the factory's production. Also creative are the suggestions offered by intelligence trainers on how not to let out important information. They suggest that businesses flag sensitive information not for public or competitive consumption, and that executives should not work on airplanes where others can uncover secrets by reading over one's shoulder.

Marketing Decision Support Systems

The marketing decision support system (MDSS) is defined as "a coordinated collection of data, models, analytic tools, and computing power by which an organization gathers information from the environment and turns it into a basis for action."[15] This sophisticated system focuses on the marketing decision itself. The manager is viewed as a strategist who must perceive and analyze the environment, consider strategic options, and choose the best one available. The emphasis is on analysis. The MIS answers such questions as "What were sales of Brand X in September?" and "Did we meet our marketing budget?" The MDSS carries the analysis further to include cause and effect: "What changes in our competitor's marketing mix may have caused sales to change?" The MDSS also asks "What would happen if?" questions. In short, the MDSS amplifies the skills of the manager by eliminating certain barriers to problem solving.

To aid managers in coding, analyzing, and reporting data, some generalized commercial programs have been developed. One such program is Acustar, designed and developed by Tymeshare of Stamford, Connecticut. Acustar automatically integrates data from different sources, both external and internal. Adjustments are made to accommodate the fact that different sources collect data for different time periods (e.g., by week vs. by month); then the data are stored in data banks or files. Within the files, information is held mostly by product, geographic area, and brand. Acustar is only one of the available commercial decision support services. A.C. Nielsen has INF°ACT, a time-sharing service that helps clients make use of its database. Information Resources offers EXPRESS, a computer language that allows integration of varied data sources and access to statistical analysis. Many other such services are likely to become available as technological advances continue to make it easier to collect, store, and combine information in highly sophisticated ways.

Guide to Questionnaire Design

Designing a questionnaire is an art; much creativity may be needed. Fortunately, there are some established principles for developing successful questionnaires.

The questions should be directly related to the research objectives. Every questionnaire item must be capable of being translated into a specific decision that will aid in solving the problem. All questions should be as easy to answer as possible. For example, checklists are more convenient to answer than open-ended questions. Personal questions, such as the respondent's age, should be asked only if necessary and put in the form of a range rather than an exact figure. Care should be taken to use simple and unambiguous words and phrases. (How would one interpret the information that most consumers find Pert shampoo "good"?) Finally, the earlier questions should not influence the answers to later questions. (Five questions asking for an evaluation of Saab automobiles might well affect the answer to the later question, "What is your favorite European automobile?").

Before the questionnaire is used, it must be pretested. This involves showing people the draft questionnaire and having them explain to the researcher what each question means to them. Many hidden problems can be uncovered in this way. For instance, a soup company may want to know what kinds of soup its customers prefer. It may design its questionnaire to ask, "What kind of soup do you like?" Through pretesting, it might discover that instead of naming beef barley or chicken noodle, respondents are likely to give such answers as "Mom's," "homemade," "hot," "any kind I don't have to make myself," or "Hector's Diner"!

As part of the questionnaire design process, researchers must decide which questioning technique to use. If they are seeking very simple information—such as whether the respondent is male or female—they can use a simple, direct question. But when they need to learn about respondents' feelings, attitudes, opinions, intentions, or motivations, they may find that simple, direct questions will not obtain the desired information. In that case, the researchers must use an indirect approach.

EXHIBIT 5.3. Structured questioning techniques.

1. *Likert Scale*

Presents respondents with a number of provocative statements and asks them the extent to which they agree or disagree with each statement. Quantitatively measures respondents' attitudes toward different products, brands, and so on.

Example

Following are a series of statements about tennis rackets. Please indicate the extent of your agreement or disagreement with each statement. Be sure to "X" one number for each statement.

Definitely disagree	Generally disagree	Moderately disagree
1	2	3
Moderately agree	Generally agree	Definitely agree
4	5	6

1. I spend a lot of time shopping for price when I buy a tennis racket.   1 2 3 4 5 6

2. I believe gut strings give better control than nylon strings.   1 2 3 4 5 6

3. No racket priced below $69.00 will last long.   1 2 3 4 5 6

2. *Semantic Differential*

Determines the connotative meanings of words and the intensity of those meanings as perceived by respondents. A scale is inscribed between two bipolar words (such as *good/bad* and *hot/cold*); respondents select the point that represents the direction and intensity of their feelings. Identifies words with favorable or unfavorable connotations.

Example

Spalding Tennis Racket

Durable						Nondurable
Bad						Good
Stylish						Nonstylish
Inexpensive						Expensive

EXHIBIT 5.3. *(Continued)*

3. *Word Association*

Respondents are given a list of words and are asked to match each word with one of their own choosing. Answers are usually timed. Provokes quick, unrestrained answers that reveal strongest attitudes. First answer is important.

Example

What is the first word that comes to mind when you hear the following?

Spalding

_____

Pressureless tennis ball

_____

Boris Becker

_____

Ceramic tennis racket

_____

4. *Sentence Completion*

Respondents are shown the first parts of incomplete sentences and are asked to complete them. Requires respondents to take a position or express an attitude. Provides an unrestrained response; first answer is considered most revealing.

Example

1. When I purchase a can of tennis balls, the most important consideration in that decision is

_____

_____

2. If I were given a Spalding tennis racket as a gift, I would feel like

_____

_____

EXHIBIT 5.3. *(Continued)*

5. *Importance Scale*

Rates the importance of some characteristic or set of characteristics from "not at all important" to "extremely important."

Example

How important are each of the following features in determining which tennis racket to purchase?

	Not at All Important 1	Somewhat Unimportant 2	Unimportant 3	Neither Important nor Unimportant 4	Important 5	Somewhat Important 6	Extremely Important 7
Balance	1	2	3	4	5	6	7
Texture of grip	1	2	3	4	5	6	7
Flexibility	1	2	3	4	5	6	7
Weight	1	2	3	4	5	6	7
Appearance	1	2	3	4	5	6	7

6. *Rating Scale*

Rates something on a scale from "Extremely Bad" to "Excellent."

Example

Rate the following types of tennis rackets on the following characteristics:

	Extremely Bad 1	Very Bad 2	Bad 3	Neither Bad nor Good 4	Good 5	Very Good 6	Excellent 7
Graphite							
Flexibility	1	2	3	4	5	6	7
Weight	1	2	3	4	5	6	7
Power	1	2	3	4	5	6	7
Ceramic							
Flexibility	1	2	3	4	5	6	7
Price	1	2	3	4	5	6	7
Weight	1	2	3	4	5	6	7

EXHIBIT 5.4. Unstructured Questioning Techniques

1. Story Completion	Example
An extension of the sentence—completion approach (Exhibit 5.3), but less structured. Repondents are given the beginning of a story and are asked to complete it. Details of the story may be vague to avoid influencing responses. In completing the story, respondents reveal concerns, preferences, attitudes, and other important aspects of purchasing behavior.	Last weekend, Jim and I were trying to decide where to go for an outing. When I suggested the New England Aquarium, Jim remembered his last visit there. Now you complete the story.

2. Picture Frustration	Example
Respondents are asked to identify with cartoon characters by supplying dialog that reflects their feelings about the situation pictured. Gets at deep–seated, subconscious feelings. Analysis requires well–trained, skillful interpreter.	Fill in the empty balloon. 

3. Thematic Apperception Test (TAT)	Example
An extension of the picture–frustration approach. Respondents are shown an even more ambiguous picture or series of pictures and are asked to explain the scene, tell what is happening, and describe the characters. Sometimes respondents are asked to make up a story about what is happening now and what may happen in the future. Reveals hidden feelings and suppressed desires. Requires a skilled technician to give the test, which must be interpreted by a psychologist.	Now make up a story about what these two people are doing. Make up any kind of story you want. 

4. Open–Ended Question	Example
A question that respondents can answer any way they wish.	What is the most important attraction at the New England Aquarium?

The questioning techniques used in marketing research can be divided into two kinds: structured and unstructured. *Structured questions* usually limit respondents to a specific set of replies. Examples include multiple-choice questions and simple checklists with a question such as "Which of the following brands of detergent do you think cleans well?" Structured questions are easier to use than unstructured questions. They require less skill on the part of the interviewer, and the data they yield are more easily analyzed. *Unstructured questions* give respondents more freedom. Often they do not set a limit on the length of responses, and they may not provide specific directions for replies. Some unstructured questions are designed only to get respondents to talk about a given subject. However, such questions require skilled interviewers, and it is difficult to analyze and compare the responses. (See Exhibits 5.3 and 5.4.)

6 PROFILING MARKETS AND FORECASTING SALES

The Art and Science Behind the Numbers

The belief that populations changed slowly in times past is pure myth. Or rather, static populations staying in one place for long periods of time have been the exception historically rather than the rule. In the twentieth century it is sheer folly to disregard demographics. The basic assumption must be that populations are inherently unstable and subject to sudden sharp changes—and that they are the first environmental factor that a decision maker, whether businessman or politician, analyzes and thinks through.

—*Peter F. Drucker*[1]

Companies are digging deeper and deeper into the data to fine-tune their products. And they are integrating a more sophisticated awareness of demographics into their strategic planning.

—*The New York Times*[2]

If someone had told me 20 years ago that I was going to produce a whole week on divorce, I never would have believed them.

—*Mister Rogers*[3]

How would you forecast sales of Clearasil? You might look at the number of teenagers, and discover that the number dropped in the 1980s as the baby boomers were displaced by a smaller number of young "baby busters." Another

135

possibility is to look at the trends in pimples—young people have fewer today, it turns out. Based on these data, the sales of Clearasil should be way down, right? This scenario illustrates why forecasting is such a hazardous activity.

Surprise! Baby busters buy more acne medicines even though they have fewer pimples. Surprise, surprise! Older consumers are buying more acne medicines, helping make up for the drop in teenagers. If this marketer had been in charge of forecasting in the 1980s for Richardson-Vicks, the makers of Clearasil, he or she probably would have been dead wrong. The company was. Jody Phelps, the marketing manager handling Clearasil, explains, "The problem we expected never materialized."[4] The company waited nervously for a drop in Clearasil sales throughout the 1980s. Now the company is looking for sales growth as the number of teens grows again in the 1990s. But will they be right this time around?

To develop sound strategies to satisfy consumers' wants and needs, marketers must learn as much as possible about consumers. This learning process has three stages: description, understanding, and prediction. Before marketers can do anything about understanding and predicting consumer behavior, they need to be able to *describe* the market they plan to serve by answering such questions as, Who will buy? When will they buy? How will they buy? Where will they make their purchase? How often will they buy? But this step results in only a two-dimensional sketch of the consumer. By seeking to *understand* consumers' exchange behavior, marketers get a much more complete picture of the people whose needs they must satisfy. With this more accurate, multidimensional portrait of the consumers in their chosen market, marketers can better *predict* consumers' reactions to their strategies and marketing programs.

The term *demographics* is used to refer to statistics about a population: its size, location, and other characteristics. For example, a journal called *American Demographics* reports on trends in populations and markets in this country (and, incidentally, is wonderful reading for anyone in management). Managers frequently analyze demographic trends to identify important changes in the markets they serve. In this chapter, we examine some demographic variables that help marketers describe consumers in general as well as particular markets. In the process, we discuss (in addition to acne medicines) why the baby boom is like a pig swallowed by a python, what makes Gerber think it is a good time to refocus on baby products, why many marketers forget to look at demographics, and what we can learn about the United States today by reading an 1890 census form. But we also must do a little math, review many statistics, and look at a variety of forecasting techniques to emerge with a leading-edge understanding of this important field. Stay tuned!

We have used the term *market* frequently in the early chapters of this book. We loosely defined it as including both actual and potential buyers of a given product. Before we go on, it is necessary to define it more precisely. A market consists of a group of people with unsatisfied wants and needs who are willing to exchange and have the ability to buy. The members of this group must be interested in buying and must possess the resources—money, goods, services—that might be given in an exchange. The combination of desire to buy and ability to buy is referred to as *effective demand.*

One other factor is needed to explain a market fully. In some cases, people meet the three criteria just given, yet do not have the authority to make a purchase. Children with large trust funds but small allowances may want things, but be unable to buy them. It would be a mistake to market sports cars to them on the assumption that they were rich and therefore big spenders. Convicts in a penitentiary may have the desire and even the money to purchase certain items, yet they are prevented from doing so. It would also be a mistake to market hacksaw blades to convicts. Neither category of people ought to be included in the definition of a market. Thus, we must qualify our definition of a market by noting that the potential for exchange must be present for a market to exist.

In this chapter, we focus on the first two components of a market—people and purchasing power. The third component, willingness to exchange, is a matter of understanding that most slippery of all marketing topics—human behavior—and is the subject of the next chapter. We start by looking at demographics, the mass of statistics that helps marketers describe what is going on right now in their markets. We then examine forecasting, the various techniques whereby marketers try to anticipate what will happen in their markets tomorrow based on what happened yesterday. Forecasting is best viewed as a necessary evil—necessary because every business must plan for the future, and evil because no forecaster can predict the future with certainty (as the marketers of Clearasil learned). Therefore, before we proceed to the meat of this chapter, it seems appropriate to offer some words of advice from C. Northcote Parkinson, the originator of Parkinson's law: "Heaven forbid that students should cease to read books on the science of public or business administration—provided only that these works are classified as fiction."[5] Our book should, of course, be considered an exception to that rule. But when it comes to forecasting, the reader will do well to remember that the field is as closely tied to fiction as to statistics. There are no sure forecasts—in fact, the only certainty is that the forecast will be wrong, and the key question is by how much it will be wrong.

DEMOGRAPHIC FACTORS

Demographics, the analysis of population statistics, seems pretty dry to most marketers. Few if any specialize in it. But demographics underlies almost every marketing program, and is often a source of potent insights and opportunities for marketers. Peter Drucker, the famed management "guru," argues that demographic statistics are the single best source of business opportunity because they are often overlooked, and because they can be forecast reliably. If you know how many one-year-olds there are today, for example, you can make a darn good guess how many 21-year-olds there will be in 20 years. (But you cannot be as certain about what they will do. For example, will they have large families and create another baby boom? Or will they marry late and have few children? Surveying them about their intentions would not be particularly useful at this date!)

As a simple example, one must follow the shifts in the numbers of Americans of different ages to understand why Gerber, the baby food producer, recently diversified into baby bottles, strollers, and humidifiers after scrambling for many years to find ways of diversifying *out* of baby products. (It went as far as packaging food for adults in larger versions of its baby food bottles, but they did not sell.) Its demographic analysis revealed that the number of potential buyers of such products is increasing, contrary to the general perception that, post–baby boom, the demand for baby products must be going down. These statistics are presented in a few pages, but first we will look briefly at the global picture.

Global and Domestic Populations

It took all of human history until the early 1800s for the world population to accumulate to 1 billion persons. In 1974, that number hit 4 billion; in 1987, it reached 5 billion; and in 1999, it will be 6 billion! By then, cities will hold half the world's population. The world's population growth is slowing, however, having peaked at just over 2 percent a year in the late 1960s. The present growth rate of 1.7 percent will result in the global population growth stopping, but not until the beginning of the twenty-second century. By then, the world's population is projected to total 10.2 billion. (This forecast rests on assumptions concerning future mortality and fertility rates—assumptions that may prove wrong.)

The vast majority of this growth will occur in developing countries. For every child born in a developed country, ten will be born in a developing country. The lion's share of the population (76 percent) now live in Africa, Asia (excluding Japan), and Latin America. In the year 2095, 8.8 billion of the world's 10.2 billion people will inhabit these areas. With a 3-percent growth rate, sub-Saharan Africa's growth is double that of the rest of the world, making it the fastest growing region in the world.

Asia accounts for 55 percent of the world's population and 69 percent of the population of the developing world. Latin America has slowed its growth rate, but faces large population booms as its large number of youths come into their family formation years.

Reflecting a definite shift in values away from family and to individual rights, birthrates in Western Europe have been falling. By the late 1980s, Austria, Denmark, Hungary, and West Germany slipped into natural population decline with birthrates below the replacement fertility level of 2.1 children per woman. With a fertility rate of 2.3, Communist bloc countries will be growing at a moderate rate.

These facts point to a number of marketing-related concerns. Third World consumers with lower per capita incomes will be less able to purchase Westerners' more sophisticated and expensive goods, such as automobiles and electronic products. Overcrowding in certain regions will focus demand on food products and other survival goods. As the free, modern world—which now comprises 15 percent of the world—shrinks, Western values that are reflected in the marketplace will likely be overridden, or at least rewritten, by those of less developed nations.

U.S. Demographics

In 1990, the population of the United States stood at just over 250 million. The total population is expected to be 268 million in 2000 and 309 million in 2050. Since the turn of the century, two distinct changes in the birthrate have had a substantial impact on the composition of the U.S. population, both present and future. From 1930 to 1945, because of the Depression and World War II, the birthrate was unusually low; then, from 1946 to 1964, it increased by an extremely high rate that has been described as the baby boom. After that, it dropped again. In 1988, American women bore an average of only 1.8 children, compared with an average of 3.8 in 1957. For three decades in a row, the rate of growth of the U.S. population has been slowing. In the 1970s, the population grew at its second-lowest rate in history.

While the birthrate in the United States remains low, births to women over 30 have been rising steadily for a decade, whereas births to women under 25 have been declining. One child in four now is born to a woman over 30, compared with one in six in 1976. Two separate but related trends account for this. The over-30 age group is larger because the baby boom is getting older; hence, this "baby boomlet" is referred to as the "echo effect." In 1988, there were 26.3 million women between the ages of 30 and 44, compared with 17.7 million in 1970. Additionally, women are waiting until a later age before having their first child. The percentage of women aged 25 to 29 who are childless has risen from 31 percent in 1976 to 41 percent in 1988. Throughout the 1980s, first-time births accounted for over 40 percent of all births. This was the highest percentage of first-time births since the last golden age of child-bearing—the baby boom.

The increase in first-time births is welcome to marketers, because research has shown that parents and grandparents spend ten times more on firstborn infants than on subsequent children. Parents spend some 25 percent of their income on firstborns. Such statistics are extremely helpful to some firms in their strategic planning. Gerber Products Company, for example, although it is best known for its food products for babies, has recently acquired the following companies: Reliance Products, marketers of Nuk brand orthodontic bottle nipples and pacifiers; Century Products—car seats, walkers, and high chairs; Bilt-Rite Juvenile Products—playpens, carriages, and furniture; Walter Moyer—baby wear; Palo Alto Educational System—day-care centers; Hankscraft—vaporizers and humidifiers; and Nursery Originals—lamps, mobiles, and toys. Gerber expects first-time parents to purchase many of these items in the coming years. First-time parents often need other products and services, as well. They are likely to change their car-buying preferences, to remodel or purchase homes, to purchase insurance and medical services, to buy maternity wear, and to buy specialized books and magazines. It is interesting to think of the many ways marketers might take advantage of this opportunity.

These first-time births are to a different type of parent than in prior boom periods. Today's first-time parents are older, better educated, more affluent ($35,000 + annual household income), more socially aware, and less concerned with being like their own parents. Statistics show that two-thirds of mothers return to work within the first three months after giving birth. This affects baby food marketers in that parents are more likely to use prepared formulas and baby foods. Meanwhile, day-care centers have expanded to meet the needs of dual-career couples.

America's Changing Age Structure

Exhibit 6.1 shows how the age structure of the U.S. population changed between 1986 and 1990, and how it is expected to change between 1990 and 2000. This

EXHIBIT 6.1.   Age structure of the U.S. population.

Age Range	Year	Number (in millions)	Percentage of Total
under 5	1986	18.1	7.5
	1990	18.4	7.4
	2000	16.9	6.3
5–17	1986	45.1	18.7
	1990	45.6	18.2
	2000	48.8	18.2
18–24	1986	27.7	11.5
	1990	26.1	10.4
	2000	25.2	9.4
25–44	1986	75.9	31.5
	1990	81.8	32.6
	2000	81.1	30.2
45–64	1986	45.1	18.6
	1990	46.9	18.7
	2000	61.4	22.9
65 and over	1986	29.2	12.1
	1990	31.6	12.6
	2000	34.9	13.0
Total	1986	241.1	100
	1990	250.4	100
	2000	268.3	100

information comes from the Bureau of the Census, a part of the U.S. Department of Commerce, and was extracted from a useful publication called the *Statistical Abstract of the United States* (which, like many demographic reports, can be ordered from the Government Printing Office in Washington, D.C.).

Clearly, the largest group is the 25- to 44-year olds. But can we tell from the table which are the fastest growing groups, and how fast they are growing? Probably not without a pocket calculator—which is exactly what should be used for examining demographics. It is often helpful to rework statistics to answer a specific question or test a hypothesis. For example, if all we want to know is whether there is more growth in the numbers of young people, middle-aged people, or older people, we might want to combine the six age groups in this table into only three. To simplify the data even more, we could calculate the percentage of change in the numbers of each group from 1986 to 2000. (To do that, we divide the difference between starting and ending numbers by the ending number and multiply by 100 to find the percentage of change.) This reduces the information to only three numbers, which makes the table easier to read, but of course also sacrifices some of the detail (see Exhibit 6.2). (For example, the rapid growth in the 45-and-over category might warrant closer attention, leading us to want to break it down further.)

From Exhibit 6.2, the most important trend pops right out of the page. Our population is experiencing a rapid increase of older people, in contrast to minimal growth in the younger groups. If we break down the 45-and-over category further, we find growth of a whopping 36.3 percent in the 45- to 64-year-old group, and less rapid, but still striking, growth of 19.6 percent in the 65-and-over group. We might also think to ask where all these older people are coming from. Most Americans—and the majority of marketers—find these statistics a surprise. But you can be confident that Americans are not having older babies. The movement of the baby boomers into middle age is driving these statistics, and the trend has been predictable, if not widely anticipated, for decades.

Many companies are beginning to feel the effects of these trends, and the companies that follow demographic trends are already planning how to cope with the changes. For example, Levi Strauss introduced a line of roomier pants for the men who have stopped playing football but are now watching it. And Johnson & Johnson is working both sides of the street: While it advertises its shampoo as appropriate for older people as well as babies, it also owns Ortho

**EXHIBIT 6.2.   Growth of U.S. population,
condensed into three groups.**

Age Range	Percent Change, 1986–2000
Under 18	+3.9
18–44	+2.6
45 and over	+29.7

Pharmaceutical Corporation, one of the largest producers of contraceptives for people who want to avoid buying baby products.

In the following sections, we take a closer look at each of these age groups.

The Youth Market

Teenagers have long been a profitable market segment for producers of records, cosmetics, movies, clothing, and soft drinks. However, this market is dwindling: The Census Bureau estimated in 1990 that the number of teenagers in the United States was slightly over 10 percent of the population, down from 14 percent in 1975. Even so, teenagers numbered 23 million in 1990. And three out of five teenagers hold either a part- or full-time job. Adding teenagers' weekly earnings of about $600 million to about $80 million in allowances, marketers find the clout of the teen market at the cash register to be about $35 billion annually—nearly all of it spendable. An even larger sum—$40 billion in family funds—is being spent by teenagers, mostly for groceries and household items. In response to statistics such as these, Bausch and Lomb's Soflens division has featured teens in its television commercials and placed ads in magazines such as *Co-ed* and *Tiger Beat*. Because 63 percent of teenage girls and 39 percent of teenage boys do some family grocery shopping, Nabisco and Nestle's advertise their food products on AVC-TV's American Bandstand. Campbell's Chunky Soups produced a special MTV ad that shows a teenager lip-synching a popular song as he warms soup in his family kitchen. Sara Lee cakes, the National Dairy Association, and Ralston Purina cat foods also advertise on the cable music video channel. Said a marketing researcher, "Typically, they'll [the parents] leave money and a note, 'Get two pounds of hamburger, a loaf of bread, soda, soup and a box of Tide.' That leaves an awful lot of decision-making power in the hands of one teen."[6]

Marketers serving youth markets can look outside the United States for sizable numbers of youths in other countries. Kenya, for example, has a median age of only 14. In Europe, Portugal and Ireland are important youth markets, as are Singapore, Hong Kong, South Korea, Sri Lanka, Turkey, the Philippines, and China in Asia, and Reunion, Mauritius, Cape Verde, and trendsetter Egypt in Africa. The opportunities to serve the sometimes unique needs of these pockets of teenagers are fashioned by when they start to work, the trade climate for an infusion of U.S. goods, and the median income of youths, to name just a few determinants of success. In Costa Rica, for example, 20 percent of its 2.6 million inhabitants are between the ages of 15 and 24. Although the economy is rather stable, the GNP per capita is only $1,070 per year.

The Baby Boomers

As noted earlier, the Depression and World War II combined to keep the U.S. birthrate very low during the 1930s and early 1940s. In 1990, as a result, a relatively small number of Americans are in the 45-to-60 age category. But the birthrate exploded in the years immediately after World War II, hit a peak in 1958, and stayed at that level until 1962. As a result, in 1990, there were 55 percent more people aged 30 to 44 in the United States than people aged 45 to 60. The baby boom thus created a demographic bulge—often likened to a pig swallowed by a python—that affects everything from the housing market to job opportunities.

The baby boomers have spawned a number of trends that have revolutionized the way marketers satisfy needs and especially wants. The buying behavior of this key demographic segment has some important ramifications for marketers. Sometimes referred to as the "boutique generation," many two-income families use their affluence to indulge their taste for upscale products. They are at the age when most people buy their first house and begin raising a family— and discover the vast needs that accompany these two major life changes. Thus, they are an ideal target market. Additionally, the baby boom generation has a preference for premium goods and services, which has resulted in a dramatic increase in the number of small businesses catering to these tastes: upscale ice cream parlors, running shops, fresh pasta and cheese stores, cafes. The baby boomers are also the largest users of discount stockbrokers and automated teller machines in banks.

A number of marketers are turning their attention to this segment. Soft drink companies are introducing older faces into their ads, as well as introducing new products. Pepsi Light, a diet soda with a slightly drier taste, is aimed at adults aged 18 to 49.

A recent "Real Life, Real Answers" advertising campaign for John Hancock Mutual Life Insurance perfectly communicated with today's baby boomers. Showing everyday scenes such as a fortieth birthday party or a young parent telling his daughter about a recent raise, the ads created a brief financial profile of the person featured in the ad: "Age: 40, Salary (dual): $67,000, Home equity: $98,000." The theme of the campaign was that John Hancock understands your financial future.

The Middle-Aged Segment

Changes in the age structure of the population are like glaciers—they change the market landscape, often at such a slow pace that people fail to notice the movement. One such change is the increasing age of the baby boomers. These consumers will be in their prime spending years by the year 2000, yet marketers are only now beginning to learn how to meet the wants and needs of a less youthful population segment. Cosmetics advertising, for instance, has always stressed the value of youth as a sign of beauty. But because the number of women between 35 and 44 will grow by 56 percent by the year 2000, cosmetics firms are changing their tune. Cosmetics companies are introducing "anti-aging" skin care products that claim to hold back the ravages of time. Mid-40ish Linda Evans floats down a staircase in a Clairol ad to announce

"Forty isn't fatal." And Joan Collins (mid-50s) has her own line of perfume. There are similar products to help men grow older—and to help them avoid the realization that they are growing older. Hair dyes, hairpieces, skin care products, and health clubs are in great demand. John Forsythe (over 70) promotes his man's fragrance called Carrington. Marketers are recognizing that people over 49 spend more than others on travel, restaurant meals, and recreational vehicles. In fact, Coachmen Industries has taken away part of its recreational vehicle advertising budget from *Trailer Life* and allocated it to *Good Housekeeping*, *Popular Mechanics*, and other magazines that are popular among older subscribers.

The Elderly Market

The elderly age segment presents many opportunities for marketers. Today 12 percent of the U.S. population is over 65—more than 29 million people, or about one in every nine Americans. That proportion is expected to grow to 13 percent by the year 1999, and, with further improvements in medical knowledge, it can be expected to increase still further in the twenty-first century. Among the elderly, the fastest growing segment is the over-85 population.

Today's elderly do not conform to the common stereotype of them as a relatively disadvantaged group. Most elderly people live in paid-for homes and have enough income to enjoy their leisure years. They are not physically infirm—only 5 percent live in nursing homes. And they are independent. Only 9 percent live with their children, compared with 31 percent in 1950. Financially, they are quite well off. The poverty rate of the elderly is 14.1 percent, compared with 15.4 percent for the population as a whole. Members of this segment prefer to spend their money rather than pass it on to their children. With an annual purchasing power estimated at $60–200 billion, senior citizens offer a market opportunity of sizable proportions.[7]

This mature segment has a thirst for services, particularly those focusing on the home—lawn care, home security, home maintenance, and the like. They have high levels of demand for travel, leisure activities, and health care services. The elderly have also been found to be among the most frequent buyers of stocks, bonds, furs, jewelry, and expensive clothing.[8] They tend to prefer department stores over discount stores, and they like to be singled out and given special attention by store personnel. They do not seem to be price conscious and generally do not favor the use of food stamps, coupons, generic products, and unit pricing. The elderly are the prime users of mass media, especially television. They are the heaviest subscribers of newspapers and use them as guides to help them in their shopping.

Although these facts are well known, marketers have been reluctant to target this neglected market. Some of this reluctance is diminishing as marketers are becoming more aware of the tremendous opportunities open to them in this segment. For example, Price Chopper Discount Foods, a 53-store

New York–based chain, runs free buses that provide round-trip transportation for elderly shoppers. Whirlpool Corporation has developed a line of washers and dryers with large-print instructions and dials to accommodate for diminished eyesight that accompanies aging. Time Fitness Centers, a Sunbelt chain, offers aerobic classes for the silver generation; its exercise program is conducted to the tranquil strains of Guy Lombardo and Glenn Miller rather than a driving disco beat. In sum, like other age groups, the elderly have unique needs that marketers must try to satisfy.

The explosion of elderly is not unique to the United States; all developed countries will be home to increasingly older populations. The world's oldest populations include Sweden (with 17 percent of its population aged 65 and older), West Germany (15 percent), and Denmark (15 percent). By the year 2025, every Western European country will have 18 percent or more of its population aged 65. Although this older segment does not constitute a significant share of developing countries' populations, it is important to note that in Brazil, Mexico, India, Indonesia, and the Philippines, the proportion of the population over age 65 will double between 1985 and 2025.

In Japan, the realization that those over 65 will grow from 10 percent presently to over 20 percent by 2025, as well as comprise a $1 trillion market, has perked up the interest of commercial endeavors. Many small service businesses have emerged to tend to housekeeping, bathing, and the equivalent of the U.S. Meals on Wheels. With average savings of $93,000, compared with $54,000 as a national average, Japanese oldsters are flocking to brokerage houses to improve their savings growth over the 1-percent passbook savings rate. Many U.S. companies are joint venturing to gain entrance to this burgeoning opportunity. Beverly Enterprises, a California retirement home developer, has joined with Japanese construction giant Shimuza Corporation to erect senior living communities.

Some Contemporary Trends

Clearly, populations are changing and will continue to change. Some of the trends accompanying these changes have already drastically altered the fabric of U.S. society—and, hence, the nature of the marketplace. An analysis of these trends can yield fascinating insights into where society is today and where it may be headed. How marketers make use of this knowledge will have a significant effect on how society is served.

To begin with, the family in its traditional form is disappearing from the U.S. scene. In years past, the typical U.S. family consisted of a father who worked outside the home, a mother who took care of the home, and two children. Census data from 1980 show that only 7 percent of the 82 million households in the United States fit that model. Furthermore, the Census Bureau has reported that 73 million single adults lived in the United States in 1989. This is a whopping increase of 35 million in only 20 years. Many sociologists and demographers believe that this constitutes a demographic revolution with far-reaching and un-predictable consequences.

The following sections describe some of the other major trends that are reshaping U.S. society.

Later Marriage

For men, the median age at first marriage is almost 26; for women, it is 23.6. These figures are considerably higher than those of a decade earlier—yet close to the medians that existed in the earlier part of this century. Statistics tell us that 10 percent of young adults will never marry, double the rate that prevailed in the 1970s. In fact, college-educated women still single at age 35 have only a 5-percent chance of ever getting married. This trend has resulted in greater demand for apartments, recreational services, and sporty automobiles.

Fewer Children

We noted earlier in the chapter that the birthrate has been substantially lower in recent decades than it was earlier in the century. The number of families with three or more children under 18 has declined sharply since 1970—from 10.4 to 6.9 million. The average family size is now 3.2 for whites, 3.7 for blacks, and 3.9 for Hispanic Americans. Gerber and Beech-nut (food), Fisher-Price (toys), and Parker Brothers (games) have all felt the pinch of this trend.

More Frequent Divorce

The United States has the highest divorce rate in the world. In the past few years, the divorce rate has leveled off after a dramatic surge in the 1970s. But demographers predict that 50 percent of first marriages and 60 percent of second marriages will end in divorce. As a result, the number of one-parent households has increased by 100 percent since 1970. Nine of ten one-parent families are maintained by the mother, but the proportion of single-parent families maintained by the father has more than doubled and is expected to increase as child custody and divorce laws are modified.

Greater Acceptance of POSSLQs

The 1980s witnessed a trend toward the formation of POSSLQs, or households made up of "persons of the opposite sex sharing living quarters" without being married. In Northern and Western Europe, cohabitation is increasingly accepted as normal, and there are indications that possibly as few as 50 to 60 percent of men and women in future generations will ever marry. In fact, the proportion of out-of-wedlock births has reached 45 to 46 percent in Denmark, Iceland, and Sweden. In those countries, the average age of women at first marriage is now higher than their average age at which they first give birth.

In the United States, almost half of Americans aged 25 to 35 have lived with someone of the opposite sex outside of marriage. This trend has become more acceptable with younger people. Although only 11 percent of Americans marrying between 1965 and 1974 had experienced this kind of living arrangement, 44 percent of those marrying between 1980 and 1984 had. Cohabitation is even more prevalent between marriages; 58 percent of recently remarried people had lived with someone of the opposite sex before remarrying. Sixty percent of those living together end up getting married. This kind of living arrangement is becoming increasingly tolerated in our society. Said a government demographer, "Cohabitation has not simply become increasingly common. If recent trends continue, it will soon be the majority experience."[9] However, the POSSLQ arrangement is transitory; most cohabiting couples marry or separate within a few years. Because the partners in a POSSLQ are less committed to each other than are partners in a marriage, such households are reluctant to purchase durable goods that would be difficult to dispose of if the relationship should end.

More People Living Alone

Since 1960, America's live-alones have tripled to 21.2 million in 1986. They now represent close to one-fourth of households. One in ten adults lives alone, and, by the year 2000, an additional 7.4 million people will be added to these ranks. Later marriages, more frequent divorces, and greater longevity have contributed to this trend. The number of live-alones in the age group 25 to 34 rocketed up 346 percent between 1970 and 1986. Singles aged 35 to 44 rose by 258 percent. The number of single individuals aged 65 and over leaped to 8.8 million in 1987. Eighty percent of these individuals are women, since they tend to outlive men by almost 6 to 1. Hallmark Cards provides unmarrieds with special greeting cards to commiserate by mail about the ebbs and flows of dating. Campbell Soup Company has successfully marketed Le Menu frozen dinners and Swanson's Homestyle Recipe Entrees for singles. Pillsbury offers pint-sized cakes, microwavable in 10 minutes. Singles also can list preferred gifts at Bloomingdale's Self-Registry, a service similar to any bridal registry.

More Women at Work

In 1988, 52 percent of U.S. women 16 years of age and older held jobs outside the home, compared with 32 percent in 1960 and 37 percent in 1970. Fifty-six percent of working women are married, compared with 36 percent in 1940 and only 14 percent in 1890. The female labor participation rate in the United States exceeds that of almost every other industrialized nation. Sweden, with 80 percent of women working, holds the highest ranking. In Japan, Hong Kong, and Taiwan, 55 percent of women aged 15 to 64 now work. Fully three-quarters of Chinese and Thai women in this age category work. Meanwhile, in West Germany, the participation rate has remained constant, at 38 percent, for the past decade. The full-time housewife has dramatically disappeared from the household scene in most developed countries. This forces, for instance, a retargeting for major appliance marketers around the world toward working husbands and wives.

The trend toward greater labor force participation by U.S. women is particularly significant because it affects many families with young children. Fifty-four percent of mothers with children under 17 have full- or part-time work outside of their homes. Besides increasing the demand for child-care services, this trend boosts sales of briefcases, cars, credit cards, insurance, education, air travel, hotel rooms, and clothing. Companies are springing up to provide working parents with services ranging from take-out meals to after-school activities for their children. Reddi Maid in Chicago, for example, provides maids to serve breakfast, make the beds, touch up the bath and kitchen, and even fetch children from school and take them to the doctor. Knowing the importance of customer satisfaction, the maid will even call the day after a doctor's visit to inquire about the child's health! Established businesses also are changing their activities to meet the needs of working women. Hairdressers open earlier and close later. Hotels have increased their security procedures, and headwaiters have learned to ensure that no one bothers solitary female diners.

Growing Ethnic and Racial Subcultures

The United States has been described both as a "melting pot" and as a "salad bowl," reflecting the many ethnic subcultures that coexist and mix within its boundaries. The ties of Americans to their many and varied ancestral backgrounds are strong, and modern life provides more opportunities than ever to learn about other people's cultural origins. A glance at the frozen food section of any supermarket offers proof enough: from blintzes to tacos to pizza, ethnic dishes of every variety compete for our attention.

The 1970s were clearly the "decade of the immigrant"—during the last three years of that decade, the number of immigrants to the United States surpassed the figure for any year since 1924. The greatest number of newcomers came from Asia—refugees from Southeast Asia; families from Korea, Taiwan, and the Fiji Islands; medical students from the Philippines. The total of Asian immigrants increased by 128 percent in the 1970s. Yet in absolute numbers—just over five million people—this segment is small. In this section, therefore, we look at two of the largest subcultural groups in the United States: black Americans and Hispanic Americans.

There are nearly 30 million black Americans, representing $200 billion in buying power. This group constitutes 12 percent of the population and has increased by more than 17 percent since 1970. Some general observations have been made about the buying behavior of this group. They include the following:

- Compared with white Americans, blacks spend proportionately more of their income on clothing, home furnishings, transportation other than

automobiles, and savings; they spend proportionately less on food, housing, medical care, automobile transportation, and insurance.

- Especially at the lowest income levels, black consumers tend to do their
  food shopping close to home.
- At all income levels, black women are at least as fashion conscious as white
  women, and this trait increases with income.
- Advertisements that use integrated models seem to have no adverse effects
  on either blacks or whites.
- In their television viewing, blacks show a greater preference than whites
  for family entertainment and variety shows.[10]

The second largest subcultural group in the United States is the Hispanic
minority. This group, numbering 18.9 million in 1988 (25 million if illegal
aliens and part-time residents are included), is composed mainly of Mexican
Americans, Puerto Ricans, and Cubans, and spends $140 billion annually. Hav-
ing increased by 29.4 percent since 1980, this segment of the population is
growing much faster than the black segment. The states with the largest Hispanic populations are California, Texas, New York, and Florida. On the average,
members of this population are younger, have larger households, and are more
loyal to church and family than the average U.S. citizen. Although they are
poorer and have less schooling than the average American, their income and
educational levels are increasing, as is their purchasing power. Like black
Americans, Hispanic Americans exhibit some distinctive buying patterns:

- Hispanic Americans spend more on food than members of other groups,
  mainly because of larger average family size.
- The Hispanic shopper feels lost in giant supermarkets and inhibited about
  asking questions of store personnel, yet Hispanics still do most of their
  shopping in large stores rather than in small shops.
- Hispanic consumers visit fast-food restaurants more frequently than non-
  Hispanic consumers do.
- Inhibited by difficulties with the English language, many Hispanic Ameri-
  cans are confused by multiple pricing and cents-off labels.
- Hispanics are highly brand loyal.[11]

Generalizations about minority markets can be dangerously simplistic, however. Among Hispanic Americans are many who speak English better than
Spanish, for instance. Among blacks, many do not fit the standard profile referred
to above. The marketer must focus intelligently on a specific target consumer
when marketing to minorities, just as in any marketing effort. In an increasing
number of cases, market segments cross ethnic and racial boundaries. For example, black graduates of Ivy League law schools may have more in common with
their white classmates than with other blacks when it comes to marketing many
consumer durables.

A headlong rush for the Hispanic market has been mounted. Advertising campaigns have appeared featuring Latin athletes touting Miller Lite because it is *mas sabrosa and no llena*. Madge the manicurist pushes Palmolive to her *clientela*. To pitch their *pollo* and *hamburquesas*, Frank Perdue and Ronald McDonald are even speaking Spanish. Aware that the family plays a very important part in the life of Hispanics, Ford Motor Company advertises its family vehicles, such as the four-door Tempo and Escort Wagon with the slogan *"De familia a familia"*—"From family to family." American Telephone and Telegraph Company courts Hispanics by showing them longing for their relatives and picking up the telephone with the slogan "This close—only with AT&T." AT&T's market share among Hispanics is 12 percent higher than for the market as a whole.

Marketers are recognizing that the Hispanic market is far from homogeneous. Anheuser-Busch and Campbell Soup both vary the background music and Spanish voice-overs depending on whether their commercials will be aired in Mexican California, Cuban Florida, or Puerto Rican New York. Just like marketing in international markets, the sometimes subtle cultural differences must be accommodated for. When Pacific Bell pushed its advertising agency to run Spanish ads suggesting that Hispanics make international calls on weekends to save as much as 50 percent, the agency pointed out that Hispanics do not want to feel cheap, particularly when it comes to the family. "If I waited until the rates went down to call home, that would be an insult," said the Hispanic advertising agency director.[12]

A Nation on the Move

Different geographic locations are often associated with different consumer preferences and rates of product usage. As a result, marketers need to be attuned to geographic population shifts. The biggest population increases will occur in the South and West as large numbers of Americans move to the Sunbelt—the warmer states extending from southern California to the Carolinas. This reflects a shift in American values toward increased emphasis on year-round outdoor activities, a more relaxed lifestyle, a lower cost of living, and lower rates of crime, congestion, and pollution. In the 1980s, half of the population growth in the country occurred in only three states: Texas, California, and Florida—all Sunbelt states. Between 1980 and 1989, the population of Texas grew 19.4 percent, the population of California 22.8 percent, and the population of Florida 30.0 percent. Rapid growth also occurred in several states with smaller populations, including Nevada (38.8 percent), Alaska (31.1 percent), and New Hampshire (20.2 percent).[13] Population losses occurred in the Midwest and in some of the older industrial cities that have not recovered from the economic downturns of the last decade. The largest losses were in Iowa (−2.5 percent), Washington, D.C. (−5.3 percent), and West Virginia (−4.8 percent).

The difference between population growth of 20 or 30 percent and static or slipping population amounts to millions of consumers lost in some states and millions gained in others—and a major impact on the businesses in those states! For example, a business operating in Florida could have gained hundreds of thousands of potential customers as the state's population grew by 2.9 million people over the last decade. The following chart shows the shifts by geographic region for the entire country during the 1980s, according to Census Bureau estimates:

Region	Share of U.S. Population, 1989	Percent Change, 1980–89
New England	5.3	5.7
Middle Atlantic	15.2	2.6
Midwest	24.2	11.7
South	34.5	13.5
West	20.9	20.0

The Movement to the Suburbs

Within every region of the nation, there has been a steady movement out of cities and into suburbs. This trend, however, is less pronounced than it was in the two decades following World War II. Growth in the suburbs is expected to be held down by greater congestion; higher energy costs; increased crime, pollution, and racial tension; and housing shortages. Nevertheless, suburbia still dominates the nation's economic and social life. Beautiful shopping malls, sprawling office parks, and high-tech industrial centers have made the suburbs vibrant centers for jobs, shopping, and entertainment.

Income Factors: Ability to Buy

Thus far in this chapter, we have focused on the "people" component of markets through our examination of demographics. However, people without money or some other means of making exchanges are not part of a market. In most situations, ability to buy is based on income. Before we look at this key determinant of buying behavior, however, we first look at two key factors that affect income: education and occupation. In general, the more education one has and the higher the prestige associated with one's occupation, the more income one can expect to receive.

Education, Occupation, and Income

The average education level in the United States has risen dramatically in the twentieth century, and this has major implications for marketers. In 1970, only

52 percent of Americans 25 years of age and over were high school graduates, and only 11 percent had graduated from college. Now more than 75 percent have finished high school, more than 33 percent have attended at least one year of college, and about 20 percent have completed four years of college. Marketers, therefore, not only are called upon to satisfy a more sophisticated, wiser consumer, but also must meet a wider range of wants and needs. Better educated consumers are smarter in their buying behavior, and more likely to be well informed and choosy about the level of quality they receive. Education also affects the lifestyles and interests of consumers—and their income. Today persons under 30 with a college degree will earn four times as much annual income as a high school dropout.[14]

Closely related to education as a determinant of income is occupation. Between 1980 and 1988, the United States produced an astounding 89 percent of all new jobs created in the Western world. European employment expanded only 1.4 percent in those years, while U.S. jobs increased 13.2 percent. Even economically exploding Japan generated new jobs at only half the U.S. rate. Starting late in 1982, the beginning of the U.S. economic recovery, and up to 1988, the latest data available, 16.2 to 17 million new jobs were created. (The rate of job creation has recently begun to fall, however, with the economic downturn of 1990.) Most of those new jobs are ones that require the most training and hence pay the most. The biggest category of U.S. occupations is managerial and professional employment (25 percent of all jobs); this category accounted for 36 percent of jobs added between 1983 and 1987. Over 90 percent of these jobs are full time. The end result has been rising incomes, at least until the beginning of the 1990s.

The rate of unemployment is a significant factor in the amount of income consumers have available to spend. In Chapter 3, we say how troubled the U.S. economy had been into the early 1980s due largely to the 1973 oil crisis, and how the invasion of Iraq created a smaller oil crisis in 1990 and 1991 that also had a negative impact on the U.S. economy. As the economy dips, unemployment rises. During 1981 and 1982, unemployment rates reached levels that had not been seen since the Great Depression of 1932; at the end of 1982, unemployment reached 11 percent, meaning one of every nine Americans looking for a job did not have one. During such depressed periods, purchases of many nonessential goods and services are curtailed. Sales of durable goods and luxury items suffer as people put off such purchases until their financial situation has improved.

Disposable and Discretionary Income

Before 1930, the vast majority of U.S. households had low buying power—just above the subsistence level, in fact. Meanwhile, a small number of households, an elite pocket of the population, held a sizable amount of the total income. By 1960, this pattern had changed, and many people had substantial incomes.

Throughout the 1960s and 1970s, median household income increased. But in the late 1970s, it turned downward, largely because of inflation.

Consumers' incomes take many forms, including wages and salaries, dividends, social security, and interest. Marketers are most concerned with *disposable income*, the amount of income available for spending after taxes have been deducted. To be meaningful, income figures must be stated in terms of *real income*, that is, income that has been adjusted for the effects of inflation. Like median household income, disposable income has been on the decline since 1978. But between 1981 and 1986, the real median incomes of full-time, year-round workers rose 3.8 percent for men and 9.8 percent for women.

Marketers are also interested in *discretionary income*, the amount of disposable income left over after spending on the essentials (i.e., needs), such as food, clothing, transportation, shelter, and utilities. Because discretionary income goes toward satisfying wants rather than needs, it is far more difficult to predict how this income will be spent. Discretionary income is used to purchase luxuries such as boats, second homes, travel, and other top-of-the-line products.

Marketers must pay attention to how income is distributed, as well as to changes in total real income. The distribution of income in the United States is distinctly skewed. The top fifth of the population gets 43.7 percent of all income, while the bottom fifth receives 4.6 percent. Entrance to the top 20 percent requires an income of $53,000. The top 5 percent now get nearly two-thirds of their income from wages and salaries, compared with the dividends, trust funds, and capital gains source of the top 5 percent 25 years ago. Today's richest have earned their wealth by elbowing aside the old money. These new rich are much more ostentatious than the older rich; they are the prime targets for marketers of $60,000 cars, $2,000 watches, and $3 million houses. In the middle is the middle income class that has incomes grouped around the typical U.S. family income of $29,458. This income is a full 50 percent higher than the $19,500 average family income of 1960. At the bottom are the 13.5 percent who live below the official poverty level.

Although many people imagine the top rungs of the income ladder as living in ever-increasing luxury while the bottom falls into deeper financial misery, that picture is not quite true. Statistics show that 44 percent of people in the lowest fifth of incomes in 1971 had moved up and out in seven years—in fact, 6 percent made it to the top fifth. Meanwhile, half of those in the top 20 percent fell out of the top quintile, with 3.5 percent landing in the bottom fifth. The recessionary period the nation entered in the early 1990s has seen unprecedented layoffs of higher income, white-collar workers along with the layoffs of middle income and low income workers. Income mobility is remarkably high in the United States, with the exception that the very poor probably do not move out of poverty at high rates.

The gap between the world's richest and poorest countries is widening. The world's 38 poorest countries, with 54 percent of the world's population, accounted for a mere 5.6 percent of the world's total income in 1982, averaging only $270 per person. The 38 richest countries, on the other hand, had only 18 percent of the global population, but accounted for 77 percent of the world's total income, averaging $11,390 per person. In 1987, gross domestic product per person in the United States was above $18,000, while it was between $10,000 and $15,000 for many European countries and below $2,000 for most Third World countries.[15]

Some Contemporary Trends

No discussion of income in the United States would be complete without some mention of the trends that have helped shape income and spending behavior in the country in recent decades. We have already seen the extent of female participation in the U.S. labor force. Women hold two-thirds of the jobs created in the past decade. Yet until the beginning of the 1980s, women's wages seemed to be stuck at about 60 percent of what men were paid for a comparable job. Some progress has occurred in this area—in 1991, women were earning 72 percent of what men earn. Although this is a far cry from 100 percent, the additional income brought in by women's wages has boosted the discretionary incomes of many households. In 1965, only 13 million families, or about 28 percent, had earnings exceeding $25,000 a year. Now that number is 29 million and represents more than 36 percent of all families.

Another important factor affecting incomes is inflation. As prices move upward, the value of the dollar is reduced. Compared with the dollar of 1900, the dollar of 1982 was worth a mere 8 cents! The double-digit inflation rates of the late 1970s were the main cause of the decline in Americans' real income. The prices of many items soared, and wage rates did not keep up with them. Peaking at 13.5 percent in 1980, the rate of inflation has since fallen significantly. The belief that prices of consumer goods and services will not increase dramatically has created an optimistic outlook for consumer spending.

As the inflation rate fell, however, interest rates became a matter of increased concern. High interest rates inhibit borrowing, and hence spending; especially hard hit are purchases of houses and durable goods. Borrowing at an interest rate of 11 percent instead of 17 percent can make a huge difference. In the spring of 1985, an easing of mortgage rates resulted in a surge of "move-up" buyers, people buying bigger and fancier houses. This was the first time in five years that repeat buyers were a large segment (62 percent) of the housing market. The shift was a direct result of lower interest rates and pent-up demand, and a powerful example of the influence of economic factors on ability to buy.

Also important to spending patterns is saving. Economists like to see high levels of personal saving. A country's savings are the ultimate source of its investment, and investment is the ultimate source of jobs, economic growth, and a rising standard of living. One problem that has plagued the U.S. economy in recent years is a low rate of personal saving, the percentage of after-tax income that individuals have chosen to squirrel away instead of spend. Between 1950 and 1970, that rate averaged about 7 percent, and it was nearly 8 percent from 1970 to 1976. Then it sagged to a low of 3.7 percent in 1987—its lowest level since the 1940s. Americans today display the lowest saving rate in the developed world, compared with 15 percent for the Japanese and 7 to 10 percent for Europeans.

Consumer Spending Patterns

If consumers are not saving, they must be spending. But *how* are they spending? Spending patterns for different product categories have changed over the years. The percentage spent on food, clothing, and personal care has been going down, while that spent on housing, transportation, medical care, and recreational pursuits has been increasing.

It does not take a genius to know that richer households spend greater amounts of money on goods and services than poorer ones. In the nineteenth century, a German statistician, Ernest Engel, explored the expenditure patterns of families as their wealth improved. He found that: as family income increases, the percentage spent on food decreases, the percentage spent on housing and household operations is basically the same, and the percentage spent on all other categories as well as the amount saved increases.

Other studies have corroborated these results, which have since become known as *Engel's Laws*. Note that these laws refer to *proportional* changes in expenditures. As income increases, the absolute amounts spent increase in all categories. Exhibit 6.3 shows recent U.S. patterns of spending on various categories of goods and services by income group. They do not conform exactly to Engel's Laws. For example, the proportion of expenditures going to housing drops significantly from low to high income groups. But in general, they support these theories from the previous century—which may very well make Engel one of the most successful of ecomonic forecasters. Most marketers are

EXHIBIT 6.3.   Buying patterns by income group.

Category	Low Income	Middle Income	High Income
Housing	34%	30%	28%
Transportation	17	22	20
Food	19	16	13
Personal insurance and pensions	4	8	13
Apparel and related services	5	5	6
Entertainment	4	5	6
Health care	7	5	3
Education	2	1	2
Other	8	8	9
Average annual expenditures	$11,006	$19,183	$42,374

Source: Adapted from "Upscale Buying in the Eighties," *Sales & Marketing Management*, Dec. 1987, p. 25 (based on Bureau of Labor Statistics data for 1985).

quite happy if they can forecast successfully even one year in advance, as we discuss in the following section of this chapter.

FORECASTING

At best, demographics provides a quantitative view of the marketplace *as it is today*. Why do we say "at best"? Because of the lag in the publication of demographic data, such data describe the recent past rather than the present. You may have noticed that the data we refer to in this chapter are, at best, current through 1990, and are sometimes several years older, reflecting the availability of information at the time of writing. Yet marketers are making decisions today that will be implemented tomorrow. They want to know the probable size of various market segments in the future, the effects of past demographic trends on the future composition of target markets, and expected sales in various markets. In short, marketers want to look into a crystal ball and forecast the future composition of markets and future sales. Armed with sound forecasts about the future, marketers can make the right decisions today.

Predicting the future is no easy task. The U.S. government, some very sophisticated forecasters, and some of the largest companies use the latest techniques and employ the most highly skilled statisticians—yet forecasting is difficult even for them. Consider the plight of video game makers trying to produce sufficient quantities to meet consumer demand. The "darling" industry of the 1982 Christmas season miscalculated the dropoff in demand and lost more money in 1983 alone than it had ever made in the good years—over $1 billion! Manufacturers reportedly dumped over 30 million video game cartridges on the market at distress prices in 1983. A more recent example of the difficulty of forecasting sales is provided by the auto industry. The recession of 1990 took the automakers by surprise, leaving them with excess inventories of new cars and resulting in a dramatic escalation of rebates and other sales promotions.

Because so much forecasting is directed at predicting sales (in dollars or in units of product), our discussion here focuses on sales forecasts. Although marketers are also interested in forecasting demographic trends, they generally start with government forecasts when looking at these trends. When marketers do try to forecast population shifts, they use the same basic tools as in sales forecasting. Sales forecasting begins with a forecast for the entire industry, because conditions in an industry have such a great impact on the sales of any firm within that industry. Competition, consumer preferences, and other external forces affect the potential sales of any given firm.

From projected industry sales, the forecaster usually develops a *sales potential forecast* for the firm. Potential sales provide an absolute upper limit. Then forecasts are developed for specific products or markets; each product offered or market served is used as a basis for specialized forecasts. Such forecasts are made for the long term (three to five years), the medium term (one to three years), and the short term (usually six months to one year).

Some Commonly Used Forecasting Techniques

Some forecasting methods are qualitative in that the prediction is based more on subjective opinions than on objective facts. (These techniques assume that opinions are based on accumulated experience, which can be viewed as a type of fact.) Other methods are quantitative—they involve mathematical manipulation of objective facts or observations. There are many sources of quantitative data. Government at all levels is a tremendous reservoir of data. There are also many commercial data sources, as discussed in Chapter 5. Industries have trade associations that collect and distribute many kinds of data. Also, companies have internal records from which they may obtain useful data. They can also collect data for forecasting purposes from suppliers, customers, salespeople, executives, and many other sources.

Simple Trend Analysis

In simple trend analysis, managers review historical data and use the rates of change to project future trends. For example, in recent years, the soft drink industry has seen a rather constant pattern of 1-percent growth in sales per year. Because 1988 industry sales were $26 billion, companies such as Coca-Cola and Pepsi might well have projected another 1 percent, or $260 million more in sales, for 1989. The problem with this technique is that it ignores environmental changes. Changes in consumer tastes, economic conditions, competitors' strategies, and a host of other factors may change the simple trend. Thus, although it is easy to use, trend analysis can be misleading in that it assumes that the future will be just like the past. One need only consider the impact on the soft drink industry of the reformulation of Coke, the introduction of NutraSweet, and reduced consumer interest in caffeine-free soft drinks. More complex statistical techniques have been developed to compensate for such environmental changes. Although a marketer may not be expert in statistics, it is essential to be aware of the kinds of issues that ought to be considered in a forecast. By knowing what factors are likely to drive industry sales of soft drinks, one can always find a specialist to model these factors. However, a statistician who understands sophisticated modeling techniques is unlikely to also have a good gut feel for the soft drink market.

Trend analysis of various kinds is often applied to demographic data. For example, if family size has gotten consistently smaller in this country for many generations, it might seem reasonable to assume it would continue to shrink. This is exactly what demographers assumed in 1938. Peter Drucker describes what happened:

> The most prominent population experts called together by Franklin D. Roosevelt predicted unanimously in 1938 that the U.S. population would peak at around 140 million people in 1943 or 1944, and then slowly decline. The American population—with a minimum of immigration—now stands at 240 million. For in 1949, without the slightest advance warning, the United States kicked off a "baby boom"

that for twelve years produced unprecidentedly large families, only to turn just as suddenly in 1960 (actually 1964) into a "baby bust," producing equally unprece-dented small families.[16]

At the beginning of this chapter, we noted that the growth of the U.S. popula-tion has been slowing for three decades, and that the population is therefore expected to be 268 million in 2000 and 309 million in 2050. Will these fore-casts prove accurate? They are basically advanced forms of trend analysis, so they depend on the continuation of trends in an expected direction. But demog-raphers do not truly know what drives family size, for example. Why did family size increase for the dozen years of the baby boom? And why did it drop again? The importance of the baby boom on marketers today has been emphasized throughout this chapter. We also need to emphasize that we do not know how to predict a future baby boom with any accuracy. Knowing what one *doesn't* know is often the best defense when it comes to producing, or using, forecasts. In this example, because we do not really understand why family size varies, we must discount the future population forecasts. It might be more appropriate to use scenario analysis, as described shortly.

Market Share Analysis

Market share analysis starts with the assumption that the firm's market share will remain constant. Then, if the firm expects that total industry sales will grow by, say, 10 percent in the next year, it can expect that its sales will grow by 10 percent in that year.

This technique may be satisfactory in relatively stable industries. For ex-ample, over the past 10 years, Gillette has held 60 percent of the razor blade market. But when an industry is characterized by rapid change or growth, as is true of high-tech industries, the assumption that the firm's market share will remain constant could prove disastrous.

Test Marketing

Sometimes there are no historical data on which to base projections. An obvious example is the case of a new product. In such situations, firms often conduct test-marketing programs in which the product is introduced in a few specific markets. The firm uses the results to estimate total sales for the region in which the product will be introduced. The main problem with this approach is that political, economic, competitive, and other environmental conditions are not necessarily the same from one locality to the next. Furthermore, competitors often employ disruptive tactics, such as increasing their advertising, to distort test-market results. Sometimes competitors even investigate products brought out in test markets and use that information to improve their own products. This happened to Procter & Gamble when it introduced its new Duncan Hines soft-center cookies; by the time the cookies were distributed nationally, Nabisco,

Frito-Lay, and Keebler all had introduced new and improved versions of their own cookies, thereby taking away P&G's taste advantage.

The Market Buildup Technique

The market buildup method is similar to test marketing in that the firm uses one of the other forecasting methods to gather information on a few specific market segments, and then aggregates them to arrive at a total sales forecast. Those segments may be based on geographic areas, age categories, ethnic groups, or even product uses. For instance, a maker of petroleum jelly may know that there are two basic types of users of its product: people who use it as a moisturizer and people who use it to remove makeup. The firm may first estimate sales for each segment and then aggregate them.

The Market Breakdown Approach

The market breakdown technique is the opposite of the buildup approach. In this case, the sales potential for some large unit—an entire industry, for example—is forecast using one or more of the other approaches. This figure is broken down into forecasts for smaller units, such as firms within the industry or individual product lines or market segments.

Consumer Surveys and Panel Discussions

It may be advantageous to contact consumers directly to find out how they would react to a planned change in a product or service. Purchase intentions, rate of consumption, and changes in brand loyalty are only some of the many kinds of information that can be obtained from consumer surveys and panels. (These techniques were discussed in Chapter 5.) On the basis of consumers' responses regarding intention to buy, the forecaster can create a quantitative measure of market potential. As long as proper sampling techniques have been used, the resultant estimate can be quite accurate.

Statistical Techniques

Market analysts can identify a variety of quantifiable factors that may influence the event they are attempting to forecast. Historical data are collected for each variable and fitted into a mathematical model. An example of such a technique is regression analysis. With the help of a computer, an equation is developed that shows how each variable affects the event being forecast. Then the analyst "plugs in" values for each variable to come up with a forecast. For example, a model for sales might be:

Units sold = 10,000 − 10,000 (price) + 0.5 (advertising expenditure).

The marketer plugs in the price of the item and the level of advertising, and the model predicts sales. If the price will be set at $10 and the firm plans to spend $500,000 on advertising, the equation will predict 160,000 units sold [10,000 − 10,000(10) + 0.5(500,000)]. Although this example has only two variables, price and advertising, the models developed by large corporations would likely contain many more variables.

How might one develop such a model? These models usually are driven by a theoretical understanding of what factors drive sales. In our equation, price and advertising are assumed to drive sales. A more sophisticated model might add demographic factors, such as the change in the target market's population size; economic factors, such as interest rates; and competitor actions, such as price increases, advertising levels, and sales promotions. A model might even incorporate survey data on perceived quality of the product. Once data on all these factors have been collected for a number of historical periods, a linear regression or other statistical analysis might be performed on a computer to find shifts in sales levels that correspond to shifts in any of the factors thought to drive sales. The forecaster might start with one or two of the most obvious factors (as in the above formula), then keep adding factors until the computer program produced a formula that explained a large percentage of the historical variation in sales. This formula could then be applied to current data in an effort to forecast the future.

Advanced statistical modeling is now within reach of most marketers. Programs such as Lotus 1-2-3 make it fairly painless to perform the regression analysis needed to try out this method—but not completely painless. The user must review the basic concepts of statistical regression, then read the instructions and examples in the manual for the spreadsheet program. Even after mastering the technique, the forecaster may not be able to forecast sales with high accuracy. One of us spent several weeks some years ago on the formulation of a model to forecast purchase of freight services. When every possible factor had been quantified and added to the analysis, the model still explained only a little more than 50 percent of the variation in purchase of freight transportation services nationwide. This meant, for example, that to determine whether industry sales would go up or down in the next period, one would do just about as well as the model by simply flipping a coin. This was a disheartening realization after two weeks of number crunching!

Scenario Analysis

When using scenario analysis, researchers try to paint a subjective picture of several possible futures. One common approach generates three different pictures of the future: optimistic, pessimistic, and most likely. Each depicts an internally consistent situation in which several events are analyzed in terms of their effect on each other and on the future. Most often scenarios are developed for the purpose of establishing contingency plans for strategic management. Such plans indicate what the reaction should be if a particular event occurs.

Scenario building identifies cause-and-effect relationships and then follows them to their logical conclusions in much the same way that good science fiction writers do. Typically, scenario analysis begins with a question such as, "In the event that solar power is perfected, how will it affect the oil industry?" How far a scenario should look into the future depends on the industry in which the firm operates. A solar energy firm might want to look 20 years or more into the future, whereas a firm that produces fashion clothing may look a year ahead at most. Generally, scenario analysis is confined to forecasting aggregate conditions and is most accurate for long-term forecasts.[17]

The Delphi Technique

In the Delphi technique, a panel of experts is asked to assign rankings and probabilities to various factors that may influence future events. For example, the oil industry knows that hydrogen is potentially a very clean and efficient energy source and that the world's oceans provide a virtually limitless supply. The industry may want to determine the probability that in the next 20 years hydrogen could be extracted from water at a cost competitive with that of extracting oil, and if so, how that would affect the oil industry. It could assemble a panel of experts to answer these questions.

The Delphi technique has several important characteristics. First, panel members remain anonymous and responses are submitted in writing. Second, panel members review each other's responses and give written feedback. Third, the process continues for several rounds until there is consensus or at least close agreement. It is hoped that the anonymity of panel members will increase the reliability and objectivity of the results.

Jury of Executive Opinion

In the jury of executive opinion technique, executives from various departments of a company are asked to estimate market potential and sales for several years into the future. They then try to reach a consensus. This method combines historical data and experienced judgment as bases for decision making. It is one of the oldest and simplest methods of forecasting and has the advantage of being able to be completed quickly.

Like trend analysis, however, this method has drawbacks. Environmental conditions change, and therefore historical data may not be useful in predicting the future. Moreover, some executives may be out of touch with the market and may overlook important factors. Depending on these conditions, this method may produce either very good or very poor results.

Salespeople's Estimates

Another method is similar to the jury of executive opinion, except that it is a "bottom–up" approach in that salespeople, rather than executives, are the source of the forecasts. Salespeople are asked to estimate sales in their own territories. These estimates are then aggregated to produce a total sales forecast. Salespeople are assumed to be more aware of buyers' wants and needs and their likely reactions to changes in the marketing mix. They may also have a feel for how consumers may react to changes in competitors' products. Again, this method has some limitations. Salespeople may be unaware of relevant changes in the nation's economic health or may not be aware of planned changes in their company's marketing mix or in the marketing programs of competitors. This method is very inexpensive to implement, however, and it can provide valuable information. For these reasons, salespeople's input should not be ignored.

Barometric Techniques

Barometric techniques involve the analysis of past trends to predict the future. John Naisbitt employed such a technique to identify the ten "megatrends" in his bestselling book by that name and the newer trends in his book on the future of the U.S. corporation.[18] Naisbitt's firm, the Naisbitt Group, receives 6,000 newspapers a month, from which news stories are clipped and classified by subject. The subject categories are then analyzed in terms of frequency of occurrence, and forecasts of future trends are based on the resulting data. Naisbitt's is one of several organizations that develop indices of trends as a barometer of things to come.

Composite Methods

In general, it is not wise for an organization to rely on only one technique in formulating its sales forecasts. All forecasting techniques have both strengths and weaknesses. Many firms, therefore, use several techniques simultaneously. If they all produce roughly the same results, greater confidence can be placed in the forecast than if only one technique were used. Similarly, if the use of several techniques fails to produce a consistent forecast, the firm should check its assumptions and the accuracy of its data.

READING BETWEEN THE LINES

Some people believe, as the old saying goes, that when all else fails, a person should read the directions. When it comes to understanding the demographic patterns that underlie markets, and when it comes to anticipating shifts in populations, markets, or product sales, working from the numbers is analogous to reading the directions. However, there are some fairly serious limitations to these directions. In fact, the majority of anecdotes in this chapter, from Clearasil's sales forecasts to Roosevelt's population projections, illustrate the dangers of taking the numbers literally. It is not enough to read from the directions.

Forecasting is as much art as science, and therefore it is probably more appropriate to say, "When all else fails, throw out the directions." Before we close this chapter, we want to dwell for a moment on what this means as a practical matter for managers and marketers.

For starters, it is important to look between the lines of population statistics or sales records for insight. Rather than expect a long-standing trend to continue, ask what might reverse it. Rather than market to the groups the data indicate exist, ask whether the survey or census collected data on the right kinds of groups. Look at the questions asked and the methodology used, and see whether they are biased by the values of the designers. Look at society, and make sure something new isn't going on that the demographers haven't gotten around to studying yet. Read between the lines, even if it means entering the world of fiction for awhile. Then go back to the world of hard numbers and test new ideas.

A simple example of the power of this approach is found in the U.S. census forms. Few people read the forms—only the data that they are used to collect. But the forms themselves tell a fascinating story about changed values and demographics, a story that is easily hidden by the mass of statistics. For example, the 1990 census form adds a number of questions and categories designed to collect information that the 1980 census did not:

- Two new categories are added to the relationship list—stepson/stepdaughter and grandchild.
- Space is allotted for Hispanic respondents to identify their background for the first time (i.e., if they are Mexican, Columbian, Dominican).
- The top value category for dwellings has been raised from $200,000 and over to $500,000 and over.
- A question is added to determine if monthly rents include any meals.

There are several explanations for these changes. The dramatic rise in divorce must be leading to a growing number of stepchild relationships, and the combination of a growing number of very poor, an increase in single parents, and growth in the number of surviving elders has thrown child-care duties increasingly to the grandparents. The rapid increase in Hispanic populations from many countries of origin makes it more important to break down the group into subgroups. Also, as a nation, we are probably moving away from seeing Hispanics as a single ethnic group. The price of houses keeps going up, and up, and up (and perhaps the growing gap between rich and poor means that wealthy respondents' houses go way off the old scale). Finally, the increase in elderly has led to a large number of special-care living arrangements in which food and other services are provided. In a way, these four points at which the nation outgrew its old census form, are the most striking and important of the changes that occurred over the decade. However, they are as much a matter of perception and values as they are a matter of statistical fact, an idea that might horrify the statistician, but is the marketer's bread and butter, for in the final analysis, it is the customers' perception of reality that determines what is bought and sold, not the statistician's perception.

To take this idea ten times farther, the 1890 census form differed even more dramatically from the 1990 form. When it asked women if they had children, it added a question to find out how many were still alive; a reflection of the incredibly high infant mortality rates of the time. One question asked whether the respondent was a "prisoner, convict, homeless child or pauper," grouping categories that we would not care to lump together today! The 1890 census takers were given very careful instructions concerning how to categorize blacks: "The word 'black' should be used to describe those persons who have three-fourths or more black blood; 'mulatto,' those persons who have from three-eighths to five-eighths black blood; 'quadroon,' those persons who have one-fourth black blood; and 'octoroon,' those persons who have one-eighth or any trace of black blood." From these instructions, we can easily visualize a society so racist that the government felt it essential to quantify the extent of intermarriage between blacks and whites and to pigeonhole each person by the amount of "black blood" in his or her veins—even the expression is offensive today. The nature of work also has changed so dramatically that instructions concerning jobs such as livery stable keepers and telegraph messenger boys stand in stark contrast to today's preponderance of more modern service professions.[19]

Another way to read between the lines of the forecasts and statistics is to ask customers what *they* think. The data may show that distinct Hispanic groups are emerging, but does this mean that a company should address each group separately in its marketing communications and product offerings? Do *they* see themselves as distinct? If so, do they identify with the group as defined by the census? A company had better make certain, or its marketing is liable to offend a great many potential customers.

Sometimes perceptions differ from the realities the statistics suggest. For example, earlier in the chapter, we reviewed current statistics on expenditures, which showed that Americans spend the largest amount of their money on housing, followed by transportation and then food. We might reasonably conclude that Americans are most concerned about paying for housing, followed by transportation, followed by food. Wrong. A recent Gallup Organization survey of 757 adults found that more people list "finding and paying for good health care" as their top concern over anything else, even though it ranks seventh in the list of expenditures, costing on average about one-sixth of what Americans spend on housing.[20] Exhibit 6.4 contrasts the survey results with the spending statistics from earlier in the chapter.

If you are trying to decide whether to acquire a new product line in health care or in food services, and want to make sure you move into the market that is most important to Americans in the long run, you would have to use the statistics with caution. On the one hand, food accounts for a great deal more of the typical American's spending. On the other hand, Americans are not particularly worried about feeding themselves, but are most worried about finding and

EXHIBIT 6.4. Share of spending vs. share of worry.

Item	Percentage of Total Spending*	Percentage of Respondents Who Worry about It Most
Housing	30%	17%
Transportation	22	NA
Food	16	NA
Personal insurance pensions	8	12
Apparel	5	NA
Entertainment	5	NA
Health care	5	21
Education	1	16
Day care for children	NA	9
Caring for elderly parents	NA	9

* For middle-income Americans.

paying for good health care. Although the health care market is smaller in dollars spent, it is clearly much larger in need and opportunity. You might say that health care has a smaller share of spending but a higher share of worry. However, it takes some creativity and insight to combine different kinds of numbers and ask different questions before you can reach a conclusion such as this one. If you come away from this chapter on profiling the market and forecasting sales with nothing else, be sure you take with you a willingness to read between the lines. This is probably the marketer's most important skill.

It is a lesson Jody Phelps learned the hard way in her disastrous effort to forecast Clearasil sales in the 1980s. The costs of learning this lesson the hard way can be unusually high, but a good forecast can be invaluable, provided that you remember it is pure fiction.

7 UNDERSTANDING BUYER BEHAVIOR
Customers on the Couch

The human being is a wanting animal and rarely reaches a
state of complete satisfaction except for a short time. As
one desire is satisfied, another pops up to take its place.
When this is satisfied, still another comes into the fore-
ground and so on. It is a characteristic of human beings
throughout their whole lives that they are practically always desiring something.

—Abraham H. Maslow[1]

The more you know about the customer the better. You
never know when a small fact might lead to a better
product.

*—R. Stephen Fountaine, vice president
of market research, Kimberly-Clark Corporation*

You're somewhat in the Ruffles camp. You *must* have confidence to dress that way, so flat chips aren't for you. You
aren't taking a trip on the wild side, though; not exciting
enough for jalapeno-flavored. Maybe on a Friday night
you'll try cheddar to really step out. Bean dip too if you
loosen up.

*—Howard Davis, chairman of Frito Lay's
advertising agency, Tracy-Locke[2]*

If demographics and forecasting are all about identifying the customer, consumer behavior is all about understanding that customer. In many ways, understanding is a far more difficult task. As the psychologist Abraham Maslow

observed, people practically always desire something. But it takes a great deal of insight to know *what* they desire.

Howard Davis has a clear understanding of chip desires. It comes from hundreds of hours of thought and research on the topic. In the above quote, he is sizing up a visitor to his office at the ad agency Tracy-Locke based on a quick assessment of the man's clothing and appearance. Clues like boat shoes, khaki pants, red tie, plain blue shirt, navy socks, and a matching plastic pen provide the raw material for his Sherlock Holmes-style deductions. He thinks he can narrow down the visitor's preferences to only a few of Frito Lay's 85 varieties of corn and potato chips. Is he right? Unfortunately, the journalist who reported this conversation did not say.[3]

But the odds of being right are strongly in Davis's favor because Tracy-Locke goes to incredible lengths to understand the personalities of each Frito Lay brand and its users. The agency gets a head start from Frito Lay, which operates an elaborate laboratory near Dallas dubbed the Potato Chip Pentagon. Staffed with close to 500 psychologists, chemists, and engineers, the lab studies everything from chip thickness to flavor patterns. For example, researchers have learned that people prefer their chips to break under approximately four pounds of pressure per square inch, and that they do not like the "Frito Breath" and "Dorito Breath" that people have after eating these chips. (Incidentally, Frito Lay is experimenting with ways to reduce the effect.) The reason Frito Lay invests so much in chip research comes down to a startlingly simple observation of human behavior. As Dennis Heard, senior VP of technology, explains, "We have to be perfect; after all, no one really *needs* a potato chip."

Nonetheless, Howard Davis is determined to find out who *wants* chips, and which chips they want. To start with, the agency does consumer surveys to find out what people say they want (Frito Lay's research queried a total of 500,000 people last year). But for some reason, people rarely tell the truth about their chip passions. Davis explains that "a lot of people who say they feed their families only alfalfa sprouts also eat potato chips." And careful tests have revealed that consumers actually eat about a third more chips at one sitting than they say they do. (How did they find this out? By giving people premeasured large bags of chips at a movie theater, then measuring the leftover chips afterward.) Perhaps people are not entirely honest about their chip behavior because chips are, with all that salt and fat, a somewhat unhealthy indulgence. And chip consumption is essentially a private affair—research shows that 65 percent of all chips are eaten in private.

Thus, Frito Lay's survey research, psychographics, and other standard research must be supplemented with creative insight. The insight starts with projective research designed to learn more about consumers than they know about themselves. Respondents are shown photographs, for example, each depicting different people in different situations. Questions such as "Is this person likely to eat potato chips?" are used to get at underlying attitudes and values. (Some of the results are amusing: someone with an umbrella is not likely to eat chips, whereas someone watching TV is very likely.) Tracy-Locke combines the insights from this qualitative research with the mass of survey research to develop personality profiles, and then prepares videotapes portraying the types of people whom they expect to eat various types of chips. Each of these tapes comprises images collected from modern culture—bits of ads, movies, and TV shows. The videos are then kept strictly under wraps, for use only by the agency's copywriters.

The public will never see these videos, but thanks to the diligence of a *The Wall Street Journal* reporter, we can at least read a quick review of them:

> The videos reflect distinct personality differences among eaters of various snacks. Some examples:
>
> Lay's Potato Chips: Consumers of these flat chips are seen as "affectionate, irresistible, casual and a fun member of the family." Scenes show bubbling streams, puppies, flowers, a couple exchanging wedding vows, a farmer driving mules and a little girl stroking a cat. The music theme is the soft-rock "Little Pink Houses" by John Cougar Mellencamp.
>
> Ruffles Potato Chips: Customers are depicted as "expressive, aware, confident enough to make a personal statement." Scenes show people getting into a BMW and other new cars, a man opening champagne, wind surfers and a woman working out in a fashionable outfit. The music is from the fast-paced soundtrack from "Caddyshack."[4]

These videos are the culmination of an incredible effort to understand the people who eat chips. We don't even want to *think* about how much this effort costs Frito Lay, and Frito Lay does not want to reveal how much it costs either. But the results of the research pay handsomely. Americans will eat more than six pounds of chips each in 1991, spending a total of $4 billion in the process. And Frito Lay's share of the market has grown from 25 percent a decade ago to 33.5 percent at present. With pretax profit close to 20 percent of retail sales, it is difficult to visualize the potential *earnings* from this market! For example, a 1-percent gain in Frito Lay's market share would be worth about $8 million in profits. The value of knowing your consumer's behavior a little better than the competitors do can be incredibly high.

In this chapter, we examine the foundations of consumer behavior upon which programs such as Frito Lay's are built. This requires reviewing a number of important concepts before we can apply them to the management task.

Understanding Exchange Behavior

Earlier in this book we defined the exchange process as involving two parties, each of whom has an unsatisfied want or need and something to exchange. Frequently, however, there are more than two parties involved in an exchange. Instead of only one receiving party, as many as six parties, each with a different role, may be involved:

1. *Initiator*—the person who first recognizes an unsatisfied want or need.
2. *Influencer*—the individual who provides information about how the want or need may be satisfied.
3. *Decider*—the person who finally chooses an alternative that will satisfy the want or need.
4. *Buyer*—the purchaser of the product.
5. *Consumer*—the user of the product.
6. *Evaluator*—the individual who provides feedback on the chosen product's ability to satisfy.

Sometimes all these roles are undertaken by one person ; at other times, different people enter the picture at each stage in the exchange process. Marketers must identify all the important people in any given purchase situation. (By the way, rather than trying to memorize terms such as these, try to *use* them. For example, think of cases in which you play each of these roles as consumers. You will find you have become familiar with the terms and remember them painlessly as a result. Now if you could only figure out how to create this kind of involvement among readers or viewers of your company's advertising!)

Understanding that modern-day mothers increasingly are working outside the home rather than in it, General Foods, a subsidiary of Philip Morris Company, is directing more of its marketing of food products toward children. A marketing manager told *The Wall Street Journal*, because "kids have more and more influence over food purchases, we felt we had to market increasingly toward children."[5] In one year's time, the proportion of Kool-Aid's advertising devoted to children jumped 200 percent. In addition to the time-honored roles of initiating, influencing, and evaluating, children are taking an increasing role in buying. Black & Decker Corporation is looking to the future by putting its brand names on miniature toy replicas of its small appliances. Said a company analyst, "Youngsters don't buy Black & Decker drills. But they might someday, if they start out on toy Dustbusters."[6]

In this chapter, we look at major influences on people's willingness to exchange, including culture, social class, reference groups, and family. Each of these can take one of three roles: It can act as an initiator (i.e., we see products that others have and want them for ourselves), an influencer (i.e., we talk with other people to obtain information that may help us satisfy our wants), or an evaluator (i.e., we look to others for approval of our buying behavior).

Culture

Culture is the most all-encompassing aspect of our social environment. It has been defined as "a complex of values, ideas, attitudes, and other meaningful symbols created by [human beings] to shape human behavior and the artifacts of that behavior as they are transmitted from one generation to the next."[7] As such, culture is the basic determinant of much of our decision-making and buying behavior. It has a lot to do with why some people prefer Lay's Potato Chips and others prefer Ruffles.

Each of us belongs to several cultural groups. The largest of these is the nation of which we are citizens. With the Iraqi war, Americans have exhibited a resurgence of patriotism, a renewed spirit of love of country. This is a sign of devotion to one's national heritage. Many marketers have taken advantage of this trend (see Exhibit 7.1).

Miller beer is "made the American way," and fashion designer Perry Ellis offers "sportswear for all America—looks you'll pledge allegiance to." Searching for a single identity to represent its passenger car and truck lines, General Motors settled on the highly acclaimed "Heartbeat of America" theme to pump life into its sagging market share. The theme has been so successful for GM that it is still in use, four years later. This nationalistic advertising theme is not entirely consistent with the foreign origins of many GM cars, but this has not seemed to limit its appeal. Remember that in marketing one must be concerned

EXHIBIT 7.1. Cultural environment.

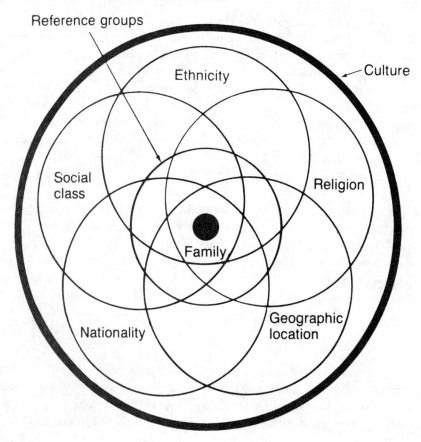

with perceptions as much as reality (although this is no excuse for deceptive advertising, which to some minds is exactly what GM's advertising is).

We are also members of smaller groups, subcultures within the larger society. These often reflect geographic, religious, or ethnic differences. For example, there are regional differences in taste for beer: New Yorkers seem to prefer a somewhat bitter beer, Californians like a lighter beer, and Texans prefer their beer chilled to 32 degrees.

Frito Lay spends a great deal of time tailoring products and their distribution to the preferences of different regional subcultures. Vinegar-flavored chips sell in the Northeast, mesquite-flavored chips sell in the Southwest, and sour cream-flavored chips sell in the Midwest. This marketing approach might be viewed as simple opportunism—if a discrete regional market can be developed through regional product development and marketing, Frito Lay can make more money and protect its market position better. But it also can be put into the context of the movement toward more customer-oriented marketing and management, a move that is beginning to change everything from manufacturing quality to customer service—and is bringing the customer into the loop earlier in the product development and planning process so that more focused offerings are now practical, even for behemoths such as Frito Lay and its parent, PepsiCo.

Taken one step further, marketers can focus on subcultures as small as the neighborhood around a single grocery store. Firms such as Frito Lay are now experimenting with customized product selections and in-store displays and promotions based on careful analysis of a store's neighborhood. The detailed data from scanners at checkout give companies the ability to see whether their experiments work.

For example, Kraft experimented last year with store-by-store variations in their cream cheese offerings, as this report details:

> Shoppers in a big Midwestern city early last year found extra rows of strawberry-flavored cream cheese at one supermarket. Just miles away, another store had almost no strawberry but lots of the diet version. Still another had mostly large, 12-ounce cartons of Philadelphia Cream Cheese.[8]

Although these variations might seem accidental to the consumer, in fact they reflect the careful analysis of store-specific data. The research firm Market Metrics in Lancaster, Pennsylvania, now gathers data that include economic, social, and ethnic profiles; traffic patterns; per capita food expenditures; and information on store sales for each of 3,000 supermarkets.[9] Now marketers can take the kind of personality profiles that Tracy-Locke developed for Frito Lay and match them with individual stores. For example, Coors Light Beer is targeted toward 21- to 34-year-old, male, middle to upper income, suburban or urban heads of households who belong to a health club, buy rock music, travel by plane, give parties and cookouts, rent videos, and are heavy TV sports viewers.[10] This description is so specific that you could probably pick out one of them just by his clothing, as Howard Davis can with his potato chip profiles. The combination of this profile and store-specific information allows Coors to identify, for example, the three top stores for Coors Light: the Food Emporiums at 1498 York Avenue and First & 72nd Street, and the Gristedes Supermarket at 350 East 86th, all in New York City. This is a subculture of importance to Coors, but one that sociologists might find a bit odd because it is identified primarily by its preference for a specific brand of beer. From a marketing perspective, however, it is just as legitimate as any regional or ethnic subculture—and probably much more useful.

The Nature of Culture

Culture develops because we live together with other people in a society. Living with others creates the need to determine what behaviors are acceptable to all members of the group. To meet this need, groups develop rules of conduct, or norms. Norms are situation specific—they inform the members of a particular cultural group what behavior is correct in certain situations. For the Ruffles customer Howard Davis pegged in the chapter's opening quote, for example, wearing boat shoes with blue socks, khaki pants, and a red tie is no doubt accepted within his reference group or subculture, although it might be considered odd by other groups.

Underlying cultural norms are values, the deeply held beliefs and attitudes of the members of a particular society. Values give direction to the development of norms. The process by which an individual learns cultural values and norms is called socialization or enculturation. We absorb cultural values, ideas, and attitudes primarily from our families, but also through the educational process and religious training. In later years, our behavior is refined by the influence of friends, peers, and the culture at large—everything from fine art to television— and even by marketers as they present ideas through their promotional campaigns. The constellation of attitudes and preferences that go into one of Frito Lay's brand-user profiles reflects a common history of family, educational, and social influences. This constellation has a certain stability—they are a real reflection of our culture as experienced by a certain group of people.

Cultural norms are a shifting landscape. Today, the Ruffles consumer may wear blue socks with his boat shoes; tomorrow, boat shoes may be out and loafers in. However, the underlying values are more constant. The Ruffles eater's attitudes toward the importance of work, for example, are unlikely to change dramatically when he changes his shoes.

Although these values are more constant, they are not unchanging. When cultural values do shift, the impact on society, and on businesses in particular, is dramatic. The marketing impact is so central to any major cultural value shift that when *Time* reported in the spring of 1991 that the United States was shifting toward simpler, home and family-oriented values, the magazine found that the easiest way to describe the trend was by listing the products representing it. The following is *Time's* shopping list for the new simple life of the 1990s:

> Macaroni and cheese. Timex watches. Volunteer work. Insulated underwear. Savings accounts. Roseanne. Domestic beer. Local activism. Sleds. Pajamas. Sentimental movies. Primary colors. Mixed-breed dogs. Bicycles. Cloth diapers. Shopping at Wal-Mart. Small-town ways. Iceberg lettuce. Family reunions. Board games. Hang-it-yourself wallpaper. Push-it-yourself lawn mowers. Silly Putty.[11]

Behind these often trivial commercial symbols is a fundamental and significant change in values and lifestyles. Thousands of "dropout" managers such as Peter Lynch, who left his star position at Fidelity for family life, and Barry Blake, who left an executive position in the liquor industry to run an apple winery in Vermont, are literally forsaking the corporate chase of the 1980s for a more meaningful lifestyle, and, one supposes, are starting to push mowers again instead of ride them as part of this transition. What does this value shift mean for marketers? The researchers at ad agency Foote, Cone & Belding do not know, but they are determined to find out. To do so, they have moved undercover investigators into a small town in the Midwest (they won't say which one) to observe the simple life firsthand. According to one report, the researchers "are eavesdropping at school-board meetings, at the local cafe and even at funerals (they say eulogies really sum up the town's values)."[12] According to Dan Fox, the project's director, they are learning that "Everything that is important seems to be tied directly to children. And helping one's neighbors is not just something do-gooders do. It's all-pervasive." Observations such as these may seem corny— or, perhaps, a simple reflection of the culture shock a New Yorker might experience in moving to a small town. But the agency thinks there is more to it, and so do the many businesses that are trying to understand changes in consumer behavior. You might have noticed that *Time's* shopping list, for all its lack of systematic method, touched on dozens of industries. Everything from banking to entertainment to lawn care may be affected by this value shift.

Another, more long-term value shift of importance to U.S. businesses is the change in sexual mores. Society definitely views sex differently today than it did 30 years ago. Whereas in the past, sex was viewed primarily in terms of reproduction, this aspect of sex is given less attention today, and attitudes toward sexuality have become far less strict. Sexual values have changed in part as a result of birth control products, which, incidentally, are an excellent example of how products can and do drive even the most fundamental of cultural values. In the marketplace, these changes are reflected both in the goods and services offered, and in the promotional activities related to them. Few would argue that marketers have not kept pace with these changes in cultural values. Some marketers have used subtle sexual overtones to their advertising, such as the appeal, "All my men wear English Leather—or nothing at all." Other marketers test the outer limits of the

U.S. value system: The highly suggestive and controversial Guess jeans print advertisements and the male nudity in the Obsession perfume commercials are examples. But these ads are probably not popular in Foote, Cone & Belding's secret Midwestern village. It will be interesting to see what impact the emerging constellation of simple-life values will have on the use of sex in advertising during the 1990s.

In some cultures, the use of sex in advertising is more blatant. In Brazil, risqué advertising is the norm: In commercials for Playboy shampoo, a young couple is shown in bed, whereas another TV ad shows two women talking about why people think they are homosexuals. In Japan, sexy ads are commonplace. Only three unwritten taboos exist: no frontal nudity, no depiction of sexual acts, and no advertising using sexual themes during the hours that children watch TV. In Sweden, frontal nudity in ads is not only acceptable, but common. Yet the Swedish government, which distills and sells vodka nationwide, bans any form of advertising of hard liquor. In sharp contrast, in Malaysia, ads cannot show bare shoulders or armpits on female models, or touching, kissing, sexy clothing—or even blue jeans. Although the logic of cultural values sometimes escapes marketers, we must acknowledge the values nonetheless.

Social Class

Social classes are relatively permanent and homogeneous categories of people within a society; the members of a class have similar values, lifestyles, interests, and behavior. In some countries, social class is very detailed and rigid. Over 3,000 subdivisions exist in India, and traditionally social mobility between classes or "castes" is impossible. In the United States, the social class system is appreciably more loose and flexible. An American's social class is determined by many factors. Generally, educational credentials and occupation are the most accurate indicators of social class. But one's social position is also affected by one's interpersonal skills, status aspirations, community involvement, cultural background, family history, recreational habits, and physical appearance.

People tend to look up to those in higher social classes, wanting many of their privileges and advantages. Many people in lower social classes try to emulate those in higher classes by buying similar goods and services, and their consumer behavior is therefore strongly influenced by their perception of social class. Thus, to the extent that a marketer can position a product so as to assist in the consumer's personal goal for upward class mobility, the marketer can add significant value to the product. This makes class an important topic for marketers. But it is also a confusing and potentially troubling subject, for notions of class structure have implications far beyond the world of marketing, and the very notion of a class-based society is controversial in the United States. For these reasons, it is especially interesting to take a look at the current debate over class.

The Class Debate

Benjamin DeMott, an English professor at Amherst College, refers to "the myth of classlessness." He argues that Americans suffer from the illusion that this country does not have a class-based society. In his view, Americans are restricted in their opportunities, especially their employment opportunities, by their class affiliations. In a book subtitled "Why Americans Can't Think Straight about Class," DeMott describes many "rationalizations that help to suppress consciousness of social differences."[13] If DeMott's theory is true—and it does seem to be at least near the bull's eye—it means that managers must be cautious in the use of class-oriented appeals lest they touch on issues that consumers prefer to suppress. A company cannot simply say, "Hey, you're strictly lower middle class, but if you'll start eating potato chips with ridges, we can help you do something about it."

Others take issue with DeMott's thesis that class structure is a well-kept secret in the United States. Andrew Hacker, a professor of political science at Queens College, argues that "American society can be explained by privilege and inequality, even exploitation; but not necessarily by a system of classes. There is too much movement, too many crosscutting factors like race and religion."[14] Hacker reaches back to the vision of the nation's founders, quoting James Madison's prescription that "the society itself will be broken into so many parts, interests, and classes of citizens, that the rights of the minority will be in little danger from interested combinations of the majority."

If the United States does not have a formal class structure, it definitely does have dramatic disparities in income and lifestyle. Internal Revenue Service data from income tax returns show that the number of millionaires has increased dramatically in recent years, from 41 per million tax returns in 1978 to 595 per million in 1988, a 15-fold increase in 10 years (these figures are adjusted for inflation). The rich apparently do keep getting richer.[15] In contrast, author and educator Jonathan Kozol argues that the United States now has 13 million poor children and that we need to recognize a new lower-class group of poor children that he calls "the new untouchables."[16]

Perhaps it is this growing disparity between rich and poor that Americans wish to avoid when they duck the issues of class. (Social class and income level are two separate issues, but sociologists generally view income as a reward of social class.) DeMott's complaint that we avoid the topic has a truthful ring about it, but Hacker is convincing when he argues that individual mobility and the sheer number of social groupings are inconsistent with the notion of a formal class structure. Although U.S. society is deeply divided, and wealth is distributed unevenly, it is also true that class boundaries are porous and ill defined. We are a society divided more by wealth than by class. But our democratic ideals and egalitarian rhetoric leave us uncomfortable with this notion, and unwilling to define ourselves categorically by class or income as a result.

What does this mean for marketers? Most obviously, the ambivalence of attitudes toward class suggests the need for caution when it comes to class-based product pitches. There may be a fine distinction between the appealing and the offensive. Additionally, the potential for mobility is a powerful source of marketing strategies—some might say the most powerful. Many products succeed because they provide consumers the emblems and symbols of a higher social group to which they aspire. What makes a Range Rover worth more than twice the price of a Jeep? The United States may not have social classes, but nonetheless the class aspirations of Americans are reflected strongly in much of consumer marketing. It is evident that social class, or at least income level and associated lifestyle, is an important theme in consumer marketing today. Consumers may not talk about class, but they certainly seem to *think* about it when making purchase decisions. Thus, marketers are well advised to think about it too.

Reference Groups

In addition to culture and social class, both of which are traditionally viewed as large aggregations of people, smaller groups also affect buyer behavior. A reference group is any set of people that influences an individual's attitudes or behavior. The group serves as a reference point in the individual's evaluation of his or her own behavior. There are many types of reference groups. Some, called primary groups, are small enough and intimate enough that all their members can communicate with one another face to face. Examples include the family, a group of close friends, and one's coworkers. Larger, less intimate secondary groups also influence our behavior. Trade unions, religious organizations, and professional associations are examples of such groups.

Some researchers have examined the influence of reference groups on purchases of various product categories, as well as of brands within those categories.[17] The researchers defined *private products* as those that other people are not aware that one has; *public products* are those that others know that one has and uses. Remember the statistic that 65 percent of chips are consumed in private? That makes chips closer to a private product—but not without a public side. Research shows that each category includes a variety of products and a wide range of prices. The nature of the product and its price do not seem to determine whether purchases of a particular product or brand are influenced by reference groups. However, the research indicates that when products or brands are socially visible and conspicuously consumed, our buying habits reflect the influence of our reference groups. No one has to know whether we buy a floor lamp or which brand we buy. But a new car is another matter—people notice.

Opinion Leaders

Because of their special skills, intelligence, appearance, or gregarious personality, certain individuals within a reference group are viewed as experts and their opinions are trusted by other members of the group. These people often have a much greater impact on a company's sales than its advertising does, because they are perceived as more credible than company-sponsored promotion. Some people are looked to for information about personal computers, software, and peripheral equipment, yet they would not be considered an appropriate source of information about fashion clothing or sports equipment. These opinion leaders are exposed more than most people to the influence of the mass media (e.g., advertising), and they, in turn, influence others. (This is known as the two-step flow of communication.)

The Gillette Company's Paper Mate Division mailed 60,000 samples of its new Eraser Mate erasable-ink pens to such opinion leaders as U.S. senators, English teachers, baseball players, bankers, television news personalities, and advertising agency executives. When other consumers were interviewed shortly thereafter, 40 percent had heard of the product and 13 percent knew the brand name—before any advertising was done!

Sometimes companies try to weave the appeal of an opinion leader into their marketing, for example, by using a respected spokesperson. When Frito Lay arranged a cross-promotion with MCA Records, they associated their product with the rock group, the Jets, presumably opinion leaders within some reference group of rock fans, by printing discount coupons for a Jets album on 120 million packages of Doritos.[18]

People belong to many reference groups, and marketers often have difficulty identifying the group that is most influential for a particular type of consumer. When this happens, they may turn to two other aspects of the individual's relationship to groups: role theory and self-image.

Role Theory

When Shakespeare wrote, "All the world's a stage, and all the men and women merely players," he effectively summed up role theory. Role theory recognizes that people conduct their lives by playing many roles. People look to others in their reference groups to learn which roles to play and how to play them. Role theory holds that for every position in society, there is a certain range of acceptable behaviors. An individual is expected to behave in a certain way to carry out the requirements of a given social position.

Behavior that is acceptable in one role may be unacceptable in another. For instance, a woman might occupy such positions as wife, mother, bridge club member, company executive, president of a neighborhood association, and tennis partner. Each position requires different behaviors, different skills, and different talents. Her position as a mediocre bridge player contrasts with her authoritative position as a mother and an executive, and with her prestige as head of the neighborhood association. Her performance in these roles is also affected by the fact that she must constantly change from one role to another during the course of a week or even a single day.

How a person performs in a given role is determined by role expectations; that is, the rights and privileges—and duties and responsibilities—that go with a role. As noted earlier, most people look to their reference groups to learn how they should behave. Thus, role expectations can be viewed as norms. Those who perform a role poorly may meet with the disapproval of other members of their reference group.

In the late 1980s, men's fashion fancy turned to the rugged, outdoor attire of hunters, fly fishermen, and even those going on safari. Magazines were thick with outdoorsy ads as consumers shot their wads on preppy Duck Blind outfits from L.L. Bean, paraffin-coated canvas hunting jackets from British Khaki, and even the rough-and-ready, and extremely pricey, British-made Range Rover "sport-utility vehicle." A harsh black-and-white photograph in a Guess jeans advertisement shows a father and son, looking predatory near a pond. The youngster has a rifle in his hand. The subliminal message is that Guess jeans go with having a masculine experience with one's son. Said a psychologist, "These ads show men in complete control of their environment. Men are buying a role."[19]

Self-Image

Each person has a mental picture of what he or she is like. This view, called real self-image, directs behavior. But it often happens that a person's real self-image is at odds with how others actually see that person. For instance, a business executive whose hair is turning gray may see that as a sign of diminishing youthfulness and vitality, whereas other people are amazed by his energy and competence. As a result of his *real* self-image, he may seek out such products as exercise equipment and hair coloring. Whether or not he actually needs these products, his real self-image influences his buying behavior.

Each person actually has three self-images. In addition to real self-image, people have a view of how they would *like* to be—*ideal* self-image—and a view of how they believe others see them—*other's* self-image. In comparing oneself with others, a person may wish to be better looking, more intelligent, healthier, wealthier, or happier. People also have a sense of the way they appear to others. These self-images also affect buying behavior.

The Role of the Family

Family life is such an everyday, commonplace situation that it may seem unnecessary to discuss it. Yet some features of family living are very important to marketers—and they are not all obvious. One interesting feature of family structure is that most individuals are actually members of *two* families. The family a person is born into is the family of orientation; later, many people also marry and establish a family of procreation. This pattern results in a *nuclear family*, consisting of parents and children living together, and an *extended family*, which includes the nuclear family as well as aunts, uncles, grandparents, and in-laws. All these people influence a person's life and buying behavior.

People's membership in two families has some definite effects on marketing. To begin with, most young couples start from scratch in purchasing housing, furniture, cars, and hundreds of other products. Obviously, this creates a huge market to be served. Also, family life and structure are affected by many of the trends discussed in earlier chapters—fewer children, more women working outside the home, high divorce rates, greater geographic mobility, more single parents, more dual-income households, and increased leisure time.

The behavior of various family members at each stage of the purchase decision is of major importance to marketers. The members of a household are confronted with various decisions that reflect the needs of the family unit: Who will pay the bills? When will the grocery shopping be done? Who will wash the clothes? Three patterns of decision making in these areas have been noted:

1. *Husband dominated*—The husband has the greatest weight in the buying decision.
2. *Wife dominated*—The wife carries the greatest weight.
3. *Joint*—Both partners share about equally in the buying decision.

Who has more say in the purchase decision differs for various products and services. Joint decision making is most prevalent in decisions about vacations and housing. Life insurance tends to be the domain of the husband, whereas grocery purchases are usually the responsibility of the wife.[20] However, the relative influence of family members is changing. Husbands still dominate automobile purchase decisions, but they are influenced by their wives far more than they were a few decades ago. Moreover, women and, to a greater extent, men have been found to be influenced by their parents in deciding what household tasks they will perform.[21]

Knowing the relative influence of husbands and wives is basic to effective marketing; marketers need to target their messages toward the appropriate family member. For many products, such as toys, games, movies, and snacks, children can be a major force. Exhibit 7.2 shows the results of a study of children's influence on cereal purchases. One can see why Quaker Oats and Kellogg's direct much of their advertising toward children. At the same time, many critics argue that such directed advertising creates unnecessary wants in impressionable children, and thereby generates conflict within the family. A number of marketers of children's products have responded by curbing their pitches toward children.

The Family Life Cycle

As one is born into a family, grows older, and establishes one's own family, many changes in one's values and behavior occur. The differences that arise as people journey through the family life cycle are important to marketers. Developmentally, infants are totally dependent upon their parents, and do little beyond the house except, in some cases, attend nursery school. They need a wide variety of

EXHIBIT 7.2.   Influence of children on cereal purchases.

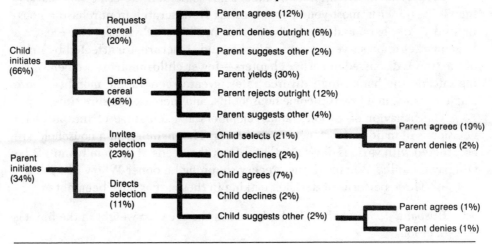

Source: Charles K. Atkin, "Observation of Parent–Child Interaction in Supermarket Decision Making," *Journal of Marketing, 4,* (4), October 1978, pp. 41–45.

products, but play little role in their selection. These characteristics change rapidly and radically with age, however. One schema recognizes 16 discrete stages in the family life cycle, from infancy through young marrieds, young divorced, parents, and so forth, on to various middle-aged categories (married, not married; with or without children) and a variety of stages of later adulthood and retirement (see Exhibit 7.3).

Although this kind of descriptive effort can verge on the obvious, it is often an essential first step toward understanding the needs of a clearly defined target segment and focusing products and marketing messages on that segment. The fact is that people's needs and preferences change in important ways as they move through their own family life cycle. And it is also important to recognize that different people have different life cycles. In general, however, everyone in the same situation or stage will have in common a constellation of behaviors that create common needs and desires.

Situational Influences

Thus far, we have emphasized the influence of other people on individuals' purchase decisions. But other people are not the only outside influence; marketers must also recognize that the selection of a particular product or brand depends on *how, when,* and *why* the consumer is going to use it. These outside factors are called situational variables.

Consumers are influenced by the circumstances surrounding the purchase of a product. When a shopper looking for a favorite brand of potato chips is confronted with a change in price, an out-of-stock condition, or an attractive coupon on another brand, the favorite brand may lose out. Such possibilities have

EXHIBIT 7.3. Family lifestyle cycle stages.

Age Group	Age	Behavioral Characteristics	Products of Interest
Early childhood	Birth–5	Total dependency on parents; development of bones and muscles and use of locomotion; accident- and illness-prone; ego-centered; naps; accompanies guardian shopping; may attend nursery school.	Baby foods; cribs; clothes; toys; pediatric services; room vaporizers; breakfast cereals; candy; books; nursery schools.
Late childhood	6–12	Declining dependency on parents; slower and more uniform growth; vast development of thinking ability; peer competition; conscious of being evaluated by others; attends school.	Food; toys; clothes; lessons; medical and dental care; movies; candy uniforms; comic books.
Early adolescence	13–15	Onset of puberty; shifting of reference group from family to peers; concern with personal appearance; desire lot more independence; and transition to adulthood begin.	Junk food; comic books and magazines; movies; records; clothing; hobbies; grooming aids.
Late adolescence	16–18	Transition to adulthood continues; obtains working papers; obtains driver's license; concern with personal appearance increases; dating; active in organized sports; less reading for fun.	Gasoline; auto parts; typewriters; cameras; jewelry and trinkets; cigarettes; books and magazines; sporting goods.
Young singles	19–24	Entrance into labor market on a fulltime basis; entrance to college; interest in personal appearance remains high; increased dating; varying degrees of independence; activity in organized sports decreases.	Auto; clothing; dances; travel; toiletries; quick and easy-to-prepare foods.
Young marrieds	25–34	First marriage; transition to pair-centered behavior; financially optimistic; interest in personal appearance still high; learning to be homemakers, working wives, and husbands.	Home renting; furniture; major appliances; second auto; food; entertainment; small household items.
Young divorced, without children	28–34	Life style may revert back to young single; both males and females financially worse off than when married; most men and women will remarry.	Discos; therapists; clothing; auto; household goods; apartments.
Young parents	25–34	Transition to family-centered behavior; decline in social activities; companionship with spouse drops; leisure activities centered more at home.	Houses; home repair goods; health and nutrition foods; family games; healthcare services; early childhood products (see above).

181

EXHIBIT 7.3. *(Continued)*

Age Group	Age	Behavioral Characteristics	Products of Interest
Young divorced, with children	28–34	Wife usually retains custody of children; husband provides child support; woman must look for employment; low discretionary income.	Child-care centers; household goods; condominiums.
Middle-aged, married with children	35–44	Family size at its peak; children in school; security-conscious; career advancements; picnics; pleasure drives.	Replacement of durables; insurance; books; sporting equipment; yard furniture; gifts.
Middle-aged, married without children	35–44	Small segment, but increasing in size; life style less hectic than when younger; emphasis on freedom and being "care-free."	Vacations; leisure-time services; athletic products; personal health-care services; party-related products.
Middle-aged, divorced without children	35–44	Small segment; major life style adjustment for both spouses; financial condition dependent on occupation and socioeconomic status; very unlikely ever to have children.	Self-help books; therapy; cruises; vacations; condominiums; household goods.
Middle-aged divorced with children	35–44	Life style changes are significant; some children may have resumed some responsibility for family's livelihood; divorced father has financial constraints; mother seeks employment if not already employed.	Condominiums; sports equipment; financial planning services.
Later adulthood	45–54	Children have left home; physical appearance changes; increased interest in appearance; community service; decline in strenuous activity; pair-centered.	Clothing; vacations; leisure-time services; food; gifts; personal health-care services.
Soon-to-be-retired	55–64	Physical appearance continues to decline; interests and activities generally continue to decline; pair-centered.	Gifts; slenderizing treatments; manicures and massages; luxuries; smaller homes.
Already retired	65 and older	Physical appearance continues its decline; mental abilities and health may decline; home-body and ego-centered behavior.	Drugs; dietetic canned foods; retirement communities; nursing home care; vacations; home care services.

Source: Adapted from Fred D. Reynolds and William D. Wells, *Consumer Behavior* (McGraw-Hill, New York, 1977); Patrick E. Murphy and William A. Staples, "A Modernized Family Life Cycle," *Journal of Consumer Research*, vol. 6 (June 1979). pp. 12–22. Reprinted by permission of the *Journal of Consumer Research*.

direct implications for a marketer's pricing, distribution, and sales promotion strategies.

Consumers are also influenced by the consumption situation. The way the purchase is going to be consumed affects product and brand choices. The greeting card industry understands the importance of the consumption situation. The industry leaders, Hallmark, American Greetings, and Gibson, have designed cards that reflect the growing number of occasions for which greetings are typically offered. Now card givers can congratulate or sympathize with people for getting their driver's license, buying a new car, moving into a new home, obtaining a divorce, getting a job, losing a pet, or successfully completing a diet. The projective research for Frito Lay in which respondents were asked whether people in the photographed situations would be likely to eat chips provided situational information of value in the development of new products and packages, the content and style of advertisements, and the management of product distribution. For example, if it were revealed in the study that people are likely to eat chips while driving home from work, an effort could be made to increase the availability of chips in vending machines at worksites.

Also of interest to the marketer is the communication situation. Where was a newspaper ad read—at home, on the train heading to work, or at the newsstand? (Lately, more people have been reading ads for the first time as they bundle their papers for recycling. What does this suggest for advertisers?) Was a TV commercial viewed alone or with friends? Was the commercial aired during a program that was important to the consumer?

Situational factors such as these have definite implications for marketers. Market segmentation is often influenced by the consumption situation. The paper towel market, for example, can be segmented on the basis of how the towels are used: heavy-duty uses (cleaning windows, washing cars, cleaning ovens) and light-duty uses (napkins, placemats). Market analysis in terms of situational variables can uncover new marketing opportunities, and situational factors help direct promotional activities. In the case of paper towels, advertising to the light-duty segment would stress absorbency, whereas strength would be emphasized for the heavy-duty segment.

The Japanese have coined a term for marketing to situationists—TOP marketing, which stands for *T*ime, *O*ccasion, and *P*lace. Japanese families, for instance, own multiple cameras, each for a different situation. Their sophisticated single-lens reflex 35-mm camera is reserved for weddings and overseas travel; a simple aim-and-shoot camera is for parties; and a weatherproof, underwater version is used for the beach and camping.

INDIVIDUAL INFLUENCES ON PURCHASE BEHAVIOR

We have covered a broad range of behavioral influences, including culture, class, reference group, and family, each of which can be vital to the success of a marketing effort. However, we have left out an important side of the equation, for all these factors are external to the individual. Learning what goes on inside people's heads and bodies is also important in understanding their behavior.

Studying the consumer's psychological side has been compared with looking inside a black box. Marketers can see the stimuli that precede behavior, and they can monitor the responses, but they cannot see what goes on inside the consumer's mind. For example, although Frito Lay's researchers know the optimal thickness, diameter, and breaking point for a potato chip, they do not know *why* people have these preferences.

As consumers, we are bombarded with stimuli that lead to certain responses. In marketing terms, these stimuli include the marketing mix, competitors' marketing mixes, social influences, and the situation that prevails at any given time. On any given day, we are exposed to about 300 ads! After being exposed to certain stimuli, an individual may be motivated to seek more information, to buy, or to do nothing.

Even though they cannot directly observe the inner workings of the consumer's "black box," marketers and behavioral scientists have come far in exploring the inner workings of consumers' minds. In the remainder of this chapter, we examine some research evidence on these phenomena and explore the problem-solving process consumers go through in making their purchase decisions.

Motivation

A motive is a need or want that is activated by a particular stimulus and initiates behavior toward some goal. We are filled with potential needs and wants; only when they are aroused do they lead to actual behavior.

Motives generally are classified into two broad groups. Some motives are *biogenic;* they arise from physiological states of deprivation, such as lack of food, drink, sex, or bodily comfort. Others are *psychogenic;* they are psychological states of tension arising from the need or want for prestige, belonging, pride, recognition, and the like.

Consider Neutrogena skin care soap, the amber-colored, transparent bars that look attractive, smell nice, and do not irritate the face. At over $2 a bar, Neutrogena is billed as a mild soap for people who want healthy skin and are willing to pay a premium for it. This successful company understands both the biogenic and psychogenic motives that activate the consumer. As its president told *Forbes*, "What people think they're getting is what's important. With skin, half the problems are here," he said, touching his wrist, "and the other half are here," he added, pointing to his temple.[22]

Abraham Maslow has proposed a well-known five-level hierarchy of needs as a way of understanding motivation.[23] Basically, his theory states that a person has many kinds of needs with varying degrees of importance. The five levels of needs he has identified are listed below and shown in Exhibit 7.4.

EXHIBIT 7.4. Maslow's hierarchy of needs.

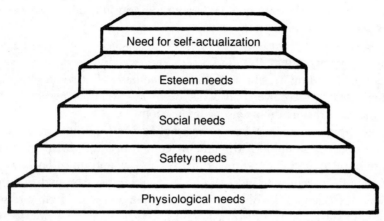

1. *Physiological*—the need for food, sex, drink, and shelter.
2. *Safety*—the need for security, protection, and order.
3. *Social*—the need for affection, belonging to a group, and acceptance.
4. *Esteem*—the need for self-respect, prestige, reputation, and status.
5. *Self-actualization*—the need for self-fulfillment.

A person focuses on satisfying the most important needs first. Those needs, according to Maslow's theory, are at the physiological level. The person then progresses to higher levels of the need hierarchy. Once a need has been satisfied, its motivating power ceases and the person is activated to satisfy the next most important need. For example, people who are very hungry seek only food. However, once they have eaten McDonald's Quarter Pounder with cheese or Burger King's Whopper, their focus turns to the need for safety. Of course, need satisfaction is not as rigid a process as Maslow's model suggests. More than one need can be satisfied by the same action. Eating a five-course dinner (physiological) at the Four Seasons restaurant in Manhattan (esteem) with one's closest friends (social) is a good example.

A motivated person is ready to take action. Arousal has started the process that will result in behavior of some kind. But what shapes and influences that behavior? The answer lies in perception.

Perception

It is not reality that drives our behavior, but rather our perception of reality. Again. It is not reality that drives our behavior, but rather our perception of reality. We know the sentence is repeated, but it is the most commonly overlooked fact in the world of marketing. For example, it is easy to assume that, because your company sells a better product at a cheaper price, customers will go wild over it. But what makes it better? If it is not yet perceived as better by potential customers, then its quality is your perception, not theirs—and the market is your competitors', not yours!

Perception is the process by which a person attaches meaning to the various stimuli he or she encounters. Besides sensory impressions, perception involves an individual's own "filling in" of the picture on the basis of previous experiences. Very often a person perceives only what he or she wants to perceive; that is, people sometimes distort their sensory impressions.

For example, after Lever Brothers launched Sun Light dishwashing liquid by distributing free samples of the lemon-scented product, nearly 1,000 consumers added it to iced tea and mixed drinks and wound up in hospital emergency rooms. Researchers found that the consumers had stopped reading the label when they reached the phrase, "With real lemon juice," failing to see the equally important message, "dishwashing liquid." No one was seriously injured as a result of misperception of Sun Light dishwashing detergent. In fact, Sun Light's sales actually benefited from the publicity generated by the incident (which is not to be construed as an argument in favor of this as a general sales tactic—the company is darned lucky nobody died).

To gain entry into consumers' perceptual arenas, marketers first must get their attention. Think of the last time you watched television. How many commercials can you recall? Probably not many; perhaps none. This is an example of selective perception. From the vast number of stimuli available in our complex world, we choose which ones we pay attention to. This is called *selective exposure*. We sift and funnel stimuli, paying attention to considerably fewer than we are exposed to and understanding even fewer. Finally, we remember only some of the ones we understand. This is called *selective retention*. In short, what we learn about our environment—what we perceive—is the outcome of a very selective process.

If you have raised children, you know that we learn early in life to ignore what our parents say—in fact, children appear to be *selectively deaf*. It is not a great leap for children as they grow up to become selectively deaf and blind to TV commercials, for example, or even to zap them (no doubt many children would love to be able to use the TV remote control to zap their parents as well). Marketers have been working long and hard to create advertisements that gain attention and are captivating enough to penetrate this selective perception. But it is an increasingly difficult task as the number of advertising messages per person increases daily. And now that we can zap TV commercials so easily, it is estimated that exposure to commercials has dropped by 30 percent. (Nevertheless, the price for air time keeps going up!)

To counter this trend, advertisers use all kinds of gimmicks. In magazines, advertisers have used pop-ups, three-dimensional advertisements that stand up as readers turn the page, scent stripes, and even musical microchips to grab maximum impact. During the 1987 Christmas season, for example, Carillon Importers, and Brown-Forman Beverage Company inserted a musical microchip in magazine ads for Absolut vodka and Canadian Mist whiskey that played *Deck the Halls* when the advertisement's page was opened. Because research indicates that "anything that startles—a loud noise, a flash of light—involuntarily triggers the brain to direct attention to the stimulus,"[24] some TV ads have used surprise to grab the viewer's attention. For example, the early Bud Light commercials based on the line, "Don't just ask for a light . . . ," put on startling light shows to grab viewer attention and proved extremely memorable.

Sensory Thresholds

One of the more surprising results to come out of Frito Lay's Potato Chip Pentagon is that consumers can detect, and will complain about, variations in chip thickness as small as .008 of an inch. (The standard for flat chips is .036 of an inch; for Ruffles, .091.) Apparently people like chips at the standard thickness and can tell with a high, and measurable, degree of accuracy when chips deviate from standard. But people do not necessarily detect other changes with as much sensitivity. For example, do you know what you last paid for a bag of potato chips, and do you think you would notice if the next one cost 10 percent more? This threshold is probably fairly high in light of the high profit margins in the chip industry.

Sensory thresholds, or limits, are obviously a key aspect of perception. Every human sensory process has an upper threshold, the point at which further increases in intensity will not be noticed, and a lower threshold, the point at which further decreases in intensity will not be noticed. What is of particular interest to marketers is the so-called difference threshold, that is, the smallest change in the intensity of a stimulus that can be noticed.

There are times when marketers do *not* want to exceed the difference threshold. In fact, the entire practice of downsizing is predicated on the consumer's inability to perceive small changes that do not exceed difference thresholds. Downsizing is one of the marketing terms not taught in MBA programs; in fact, it is almost a dirty word. Perhaps we should call it the "D" word. Anyway, downsizing is the reduction of package size without a corresponding reduction in price, performed in such a way as to minimize the number of customers who notice it. For example, tuna fish cans held 6½ ounces of tuna for 30 years, until StarKist modified its can in 1990. It now holds ⅜ of an ounce less, but the price stayed the same.[25] This repackaging in effect gave StarKist a price increase of 5.8 percent without attracting consumer attention to it. Downsizing is essentially a deceptive practice; a simple price rise of this amount would undoubtedly have crossed the difference threshold of many StarKist buyers.

On the other hand, there are times when companies wish they *had* exceeded the difference threshold. Frito Lay found itself in court over this issue last year when the gravelly voiced singer Tom Waits filed suit with the claim that a Tracy-Locke commercial for a spicy Frito Lay corn chip featured an impersonation of his voice. The jury agreed that the singer in the commercial sounded like

Tom Waits, and awarded Waits about $2.5 million in compensation.[26] That amounts to a lot of chips: 909,000 pounds of them at retail to be exact.

Difference thresholds likely vary depending upon the situation. A recent study of TV advertising found that viewers evaluate dramas on the basis of how true to life they seem, whereas they evaluate argument-oriented ads based more on whether they seem factual and consistent than on whether they are true to life. This implies that viewers apply a different threshold for detecting consistency when viewing argument-oriented ads than when viewing ads that tell a story.[27] And a person's physical condition no doubt affects the difference threshold, which may explain the incredible claims the makers of cold medicines get away with. For example, one ad claims that "Only Dristan Sinus combines the leading decongestant with the modern pain reliever ibuprofen."[28] In fact, American Home Products manufactures both Dristan Sinus and CoAdvil—and they have the same active ingredients in the same doses. As a spokesperson for the company conceded, "In terms of chemicals, they're identical." This might be said for many of the other 85 brands of cold medicines on the U.S. market as well, but the fact is that a consumer with a terrible cold is not likely to worry about such details.

Learning

Closely tied to perception is *learning*, which may be defined as changes in our behavior that result from our experiences. Learning and perception are related because we can experience, and learn from, only what we perceive. Besides changes in physical behavior, learning includes changes in mental behavior, such as feelings, emotions, and personality. Learning in markets is ideally a two-way street, with consumers learning from product use experiences and marketing information, and with companies learning from customer research, the sales performance of their products, and other feedbacks. Furthermore, the company's learning can be beneficial to, and in tandem with, the consumer's learning, as when Hewlett Packard worked with customer groups to find out what people wanted in laser printers, then introduced a better, cheaper printer for owners of PCs. Hopefully this is the direction in which marketing is going. But it can also go the other way, with companies learning to take advantage of consumers, as downsizing takes advantage of difference thresholds. Think about these two options in the context of the quote from Henry Ford that we used to open this book: "The man who will use his skill and constructive imagination to see how much he can give for a dollar, instead of how little he can give for a dollar, is bound to succeed." Not every business uses marketing based on the objectives Ford articulated.

What do we learn, in general as individuals in society, and specifically in response to marketing efforts directed at us? We learn what objects are and what their functions are. We learn tastes—to like certain things such as spinach or Scotch. We also learn what is tasteful in clothes and in social behavior. And we learn wants and needs. We learn to want Ralph Lauren polo players on our

clothes, and that excessive amounts of salt, sugar, and caffeine are not healthful. The list is endless. The point is that marketing plays a role in the learning
process for every individual in a society.

Learning through Association

The process of building mental associations, or connections, is one form of learning. We build associations between two or more stimuli or between a stimulus
and a response. Mental associations are a convenient way of understanding the
information we receive.

Quaker State Oil Refining Corporation, the country's largest refiner and
marketer of motor oil, knows the importance of mental associations. Quaker
State consumers have unusually strong brand loyalty, stemming largely from
their association of Quaker State with the so-called Penn-grade variety of crude
oil, a light greenish crude that was used to refine the first motor oils used in the
United States. The consumer's belief in the high quality of Pennsylvania motor
oil is so widespread that many oil companies add green dye to their Texas or
Middle Eastern crude-based oils.

In their efforts to create mental associations, marketers employ *signs* that
communicate what the buyer can expect. Food marketers use the word "light"
to convey low calories. The scent of lemon is put into cleansers, furniture
polishes, bath oils, and the like to communicate freshness. In the superpremium
ice cream market, U.S. marketers use the Swedish-sounding Häagen-Dazs as a
sign that their ice cream has a Scandinavian "all-natural" quality. In fact, the
brand name Häagen-Dazs is not Swedish and has no meaning in any language.

Global marketers must be careful in choosing the correct signs to avoid
creating a cross-cultural problem. McDonnell Douglas Corporation had to revise its television commercial to be shown in China because the Chinese government objected to footage of a plane flying into a map of China, a national
symbol the Chinese do not want commercialized. Similarly, showing a man
giving flowers to a woman in the United States is a sign of romance; in some
Arab countries, it is a sign of death. The associations we attach to symbols such
as these are often very powerful—but exactly which associations consumers
will make when confronted with a symbol is sometimes a tricky issue. Focus
group research can be informative in these cases.

The Learning Process

It is helpful to review some of the jargon of behaviorists, because these terms
reveal a great deal about how the learning process works:

- A *cue* is an environmental stimulus that is perceived as a signal for action.
- A *drive* is a strong motivating tendency that arouses an organism toward a
  particular type of behavior. Usually it is synonymous with *motive*.

- A *response* is whatever occurs as a reaction to an aroused need.
- *Reinforcement* is the extent to which satisfaction is derived from a response.
- *Retention* is the extent to which one remembers what one has learned.

Although marketers cannot create drives within consumers, they can affect the amount of learning that takes place by the way they handle the cues that stimulate learning. The *frequency* with which cues are presented is one important factor. When consumers are exposed repeatedly to the same cue, they are more likely to remember it than when they are exposed to many cues at once. On the other hand, massive exposure to cues can lead to faster learning. Often marketers who are introducing a new product will expose consumers to frequent cues in large doses. *Getting consumers to participate* also enhances learning. Using the automobile industry tactic of test driving, Apple Computer promoted its Macintosh by encouraging the prospective buyers to take home a computer for a 24-hour trial period. The ads said, "Take home a Macintosh for a test drive" or "Take home a Macintosh. No purchase required."

In general, the greater the reinforcement, the greater the learning. Total reinforcement, in which a reward is given each time a certain behavior occurs, results in faster learning. However, partial reinforcement, in which a reward is received for only some responses, leads to learning that is more difficult to extinguish. This can mean that once a brand has been used satisfactorily for some time, a single negative experience with that brand (partial reinforcement) may not change the opinion of the consumer.

Low-Involvement Learning

Recently marketers have noted that the way consumers learn depends on how much they care about or are interested in a given product. Automobile and home purchases are very important to the consumer, but most purchases are not. Bicycles, facial tissues, toothpaste, potato chips, and many other products show relatively low consumer involvement.[29] In the case of such low-involvement products, learning is done passively. Instead of actively seeking information to evaluate products before buying, consumers pick up pieces of information at random. Reference groups have little influence on product choice, at least for very low-involvement products, which are not likely to be related to the values of groups. Television is a good medium for conveying information to a passive audience, because its animation has attention-getting value and frequent repetition of commercials fosters the acquisition of random information. For example, Frito Lay TV ads for Doritos featured the personality of comedian Jay Leno more than anything specific in the line of product information. The ads are funny and attention getting, and happen to express aspects of the careful user profile developed for this brand. Putting a comedian in front of a passive audience turns out to be a good way to hold attention and slip in a little product awareness in through the back door.[30]

Memory

Information acquired by an individual undergoes a set of mental operations known as *cognitive processes* by the behavioral scientist. Two concepts are useful in this regard: leveling and sharpening. Leveling can be compared with forgetting: The information we retain becomes shorter and more concise. We tend to remember only certain aspects of an experience. For instance, when we think about a particular brand of after-shave lotion, we may recall its sting and not its pleasant scent. Sharpening is the opposite of leveling: Much of what we recall is more vivid and important than the event itself. The sting of the after-shave lotion may have been sharp, but not as intense or painful as we remember it to be, just as the strength of Dorito breath is probably not as strong as some consumers remember it to be.

Evaluative Criteria

Buyers and consumers can be viewed as decision makers. Their cues and drives create a perceived problem—a goal for the consumer. Consumers' goals are reflected in the evaluative criteria they apply when making a purchase decision. Some contemporary U.S. evaluative criteria are convenience, service, healthfulness, and quality.

Evaluative criteria also apply to noncommercial marketing. For instance, people who donate to charitable organizations expect their money to be put to a stated use. The choice of a political candidate depends on what the voter expects that person to do once he or she takes office. To provide satisfaction, marketers must know the consumer's evaluative criteria as thoroughly as possible. They must know how many criteria are involved, the importance of each, and the strength of each.

In some purchase situations, consumers may use only one criterion to make a decision. They may buy a pencil because it is available. In other situations, they may use many criteria. In buying a car, such features as style, safety, price, dependability, service, economy, color, accessories, and status may all be involved. On average, however, only five or six criteria come into play, and some of these may be far more important than others in the evaluation process. In the case of the car purchase, price, style, and economy may rank high on a consumer's list of priorities, whereas color may be less important. Finally, a particular criterion may be stronger in one exchange situation than in another. For instance, style may exert a stronger influence when one is buying a car than when one is buying a kitchen clock. Exhibit 7.5 shows the mental process that may be involved in buying an automobile. A number of strategies can emerge from analyses of evaluative criteria.

If a marketer's brand matches a highly-prized evaluative criterion, this can and should be communicated to the market. For instance, when the healthful effects of lower cholesterol became known to the public, Quaker Oats Company pushed in a print advertisement the cholesterol-lowering properties of its

EXHIBIT 7.5.   Evaluative criteria as applied to automobile purchases.

Criteria	Weight	Rating (poor match . . . good match)					Total
		1	2	3	4	5	
Style	10					X	50
Price	9				X		36
Economy	8				X		32
Dependability	6			X			18
Service	6				X		24
Accessories	4			X			12
Safety	3		X				6
Color	1	X					1
							179

product: "You know by now that lowering your cholesterol level can lower your risk for heart trouble. Studies say that just 2 ounces of Quaker Oats a day, along with a low-fat, low cholesterol diet, can help lower you cholesterol almost 10%. Other studies say that's enough to reduce your risk of heart attack by nearly 20%." By the time this claim was determined to be false, or at least exaggerated, quite a number of consumers had increased their consumption of oatmeal.

If a marketer finds that its product is perceived as being poor on an important criterion, the marketer can attempt to improve the product's performance on that criterion. To combat its image as the purveyor of junk food, McDonald's confronted that negative perception with an advertising campaign stressing the nutritional value of the fast-food giant's menu. In the spring of 1991, McDonald's took a more substantive step toward improving its position on this criterion by introducing an innovative McLean Deluxe burger that is only 9-percent fat but still tastes (or is supposed to taste) like the typical 20-percent fat burger because it uses a carrageenan binder.[31]

Another strategy is to make consumers aware of criteria they have not considered before. Automotive companies have turned to high-tech terminology to sway car buyers in their favor. General Motors focused on the "16-valve, dual-overhead-cam Quad 4 engine" on its 1988 Oldsmobile Calais, whereas Chrysler pushed the "2.5 liter EFI balance-shafted engine and power-assisted rack-and-pinion steering" on its LeBaron coupe. Another strategy is to change the importance placed on a particular criterion. Detergents have long been promoted for making clothes smell fresh and fragrant, but Lever Brothers Company promoted its Surf laundry detergent with a stronger claim of "odor-fighting" and quickly captured an 8-percent market share.

Attitudes

Attitudes are our feelings of liking or disliking objects in our environment. Attitudes have three components: The *cognitive* component reflects one's evaluation of the characteristics of an object; the *affective* component is the emotional feeling of favorableness or unfavorableness that results from the evaluation; and the *conative* component is the resultant intention or tendency to act. In marketing terms, consumers have attitudes about products, brands, retail outlets, salespeople, and advertisements. Marketers obviously are interested in developing specific attitudes among consumers.

An important point for marketers to remember is that attitudes can develop only after consumers learn that an object exists and what its attributes are (the cognitive component). The affective or feeling component of an attitude is formed by perceiving information about an object and evaluating that information. Not before a lot of consumer education had taken place did attitudes form toward such products as wine coolers and Sizzlean (a soybean-based bacon substitute). Consumers' attitudes toward a product come from their assessment of the product's ability to meet their evaluative criteria. When we like a product, we tend to see only its good features; we selectively reject information about its weaker qualities. Thus, although our attitudes influence our behavior, our behavior (purchase and use of products, in this case) also affects our attitudes.

Marketers are concerned about consumers' attitudes because favorable attitudes lead to favorable exchange behavior. But marketers must also be concerned with consumers' intentions (the cognitive component). If favorable attitudes can be developed, consumers will intend to make a purchase, and this intention will lead to an actual purchase. In many cases, however, constraints intervene between attitudes and behavior, and may override the influence of attitudes. For example, a person may have a favorable attitude toward a sports car, yet may not buy one. The reason may be simple: The car is too expensive. Or it may be very complicated: The person may feel that it is a sinful waste to spend so much money on a car.

Much of what marketers do is directed toward the development of favorable attitudes, which depend on the topics we have discussed thus far. Exhibit 7.6 summarizes the steps in the development of attitudes that lead to exchange. Nothing can be bought or sold until the consumer moves through this process, step by step. The ultimate goal of marketing can therefore be seen as ensuring that consumers move through this process. Insight into the black box of human behavior is essential to this effort.

THE CONSUMER DECISION-MAKING PROCESS

In this chapter, we have examined several social, situational, and psychological concepts that add to marketers' understanding of consumers and their purchase behavior. It is wrong to assume that perception alone, or social class alone, or any of these concepts alone is enough to explain exchange behavior. In some cases, one or more of these concepts may dominate the exchange situation. But a more realistic view is that all these elements interact, as they seem to in the complex, multifaceted personality profiles that Howard Davis uses to sell different brands of potato chips for Frito Lay, as discussed in the beginning of this chapter. What may seem to be an instantaneous decision by the buyer is

EXHIBIT 7.6.   Attitude development steps.

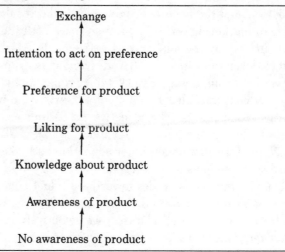

Exchange

↑

Intention to act on preference

↑

Preference for product

↑

Liking for product

↑

Knowledge about product

↑

Awareness of product

↑

No awareness of product

Source: Robert J. Lavidge and Gary Steiner, "A Model for Predictive Measurements of Advertising Effectiveness," *Journal of Marketing, 25* (4), October 1961, p. 61.

actually a result of the interaction of mental and social phenomena. Below, we take a closer look at the process by which consumers make purchase decisions.

Problem Recognition

The first step in the decision-making process is problem recognition. This occurs when the consumer perceives a difference between an actual state and an ideal state. You find that the battery in your wristwatch is not working; stepping on the scale reveals that you have gained two pounds during vacation; a particularly attractive person asks you to dinner on Saturday. All these events create problems that cry out for solutions. They create different levels of anxiety. Timex, Lean Cuisine, and Calvin Klein have all provided ways of solving these kinds of problems.

Some problems are shelved until later, but others are attended to very quickly—especially those that reflect a large discrepancy between a real state and a desired state and those that touch off a key internal drive. When one realizes that one is shaving with the last blade in the pack, a particular behavior is likely to occur quite soon. The complexity of the decision also has an impact on the decision process. Buying another nine-pack of Trac II blades, a brand you have been loyal to for years, is quite a different matter from purchasing a personal computer, which involves considerations of user friendliness, memory capability, software availability, price, appearance, speed of response, peripheral equipment needs, service, and guarantee.

Marketers can uncover consumer problems by conducting marketing research. Problem recognition is at the root of good marketing and, clearly, at the heart of consumer decision making.

The sporting goods industry is seizing on opportunities to solve what it believes is a widespread consumer problem—poor athletic skills that are due to poor equipment or could be enhanced by better equipment. "We've had a lot of people leave these sports [golf and tennis] because it was tougher than they thought," says a Wilson Sporting Goods Company executive. "They get frustrated, embarrassed, self-conscious."[32] In an effort to lure consumers back to golf courses and tennis courts, Wilson is trying to make these sports easier. After using a computer to sort through hundreds of golf ball designs, the firm settled on 432 dimples to provide the greatest possible accuracy and distance. The company has also created Rally, a larger-than-normal tennis ball that is "more forgiving."

Internal Information Search

When faced with a problem, the consumer first tries to recall any information he or she already has about possible solutions. What comes immediately to mind is termed the *evoked set*. Much of the communication engaged in by marketers is aimed at getting us to recall their products and brands when we have a particular problem. When you are hungry—think Snickers! When you have bad breath—think Scope! We search our memory for whatever bits of information about these possible solutions we have stored there. These are summoned and measured against the evaluative criteria we use to judge each possible solution to our problem. Generally, if we find a satisfactory solution among those in the evoked set, we make a decision based on our internal search.

Not all problems have satisfactory solutions in the evoked set. In such cases, we seek more information from sources outside our own memories. Certain circumstances influence the likelihood that we will search for more information. For example, some decisions are seen as riskier than others. The degree of *perceived risk* can dictate the amount of additional search in which we engage. Certain products by their nature are high in perceived risk—complex items (stereo equipment, computers), expensive goods (houses, typewriters), and high-involvement products (cars, clothing) are examples. When the consumer has limited knowledge about existing products and brands—when the consumer knows little about them and the proper evaluative criteria to use—more risk is felt and more information seeking takes place. Also, when the decision is very relevant to the consumer and high involvement exists, the consumer actively seeks further information from external sources.[33]

External Information Search

Sources of additional information can be either personal or nonpersonal. On the personal side, consumers turn to salespeople, friends, relatives, and opinion leaders—even doctors. Food marketers are using physician endorsements to capture sales. Procter & Gamble, for example, sends doctors brochures that outline the nutrition and health benefits of their products and counts on doctors to recommend them to their patients. Kellogg Company has used a physician in print advertisements to endorse its high-fiber cereals. Today's consumers are more attuned to the need for improved nutrition and healthfulness—and are turning to health professionals for advice. Said a medical advertising agency executive, "Companies are recognizing that professionals—dentists, doctors, teachers, and veterinarians—can be used as a medium to endorse products. It's like turning each professional into a little TV set."[34]

Nonpersonal sources are also key influences. Consumers turn to magazines, directories, and advertising to shed light on the alternatives available to them. Consider the choice of a personal computer—we have already noted the complexity of this decision. The software decision isn't any easier. For help in making these decisions, consumers are turning to a variety of nonpersonal sources. Many personal-computer magazines find that their software reviews are among their most popular articles, and a number of companies have issued massive directories that catalog thousands of programs.

The extent of a consumer's search for information depends on the perceived risk and uncertainty that surrounds the decision: The higher the risk and uncertainty, the greater the search. Studies have shown that better educated and higher income consumers conduct more extensive information searches,[35] as do those with lower self-confidence and greater anxiety.[36]

The Decision

Once the consumer has acquired information through internal and external searches, a choice can be made. Basically, one can do nothing, seek more information, or choose one of the known and considered alternatives. The decision not to buy may result when none of the alternatives appears to solve the problem satisfactorily—or, worse yet, when the purchase would create other problems. The desired choice may meet with social disapproval or cause financial strain, for instance. When uncertainty remains and there is no pressure to make a choice, the consumer may decide to seek additional information.

Postdecision Evaluation

Consumers do not stop with the purchase decision itself. They evaluate the amount of satisfaction they have derived from the decision. Such an evaluation cannot happen until the product has been consumed or used. Consumers' experiences are generally the strongest influence on what they believe about the product or brand and its attributes. A positive experience will strengthen positive beliefs, improve attitudes, and thereby increase the likelihood of repeat purchases. Furthermore, a satisfied customer can be a key influence on others.

Although satisfaction or dissatisfaction can come immediately with some products (as in downing a soft drink on a hot day), most purchase decisions are evaluated after a certain period of time. We have a natural tendency to assure ourselves that our decision was the best one. We need this assurance, because by choosing one alternative we have given up all the others. Each alternative had some positive attributes; those attributes have been passed up. This situation creates some degree of anxiety or postpurchase uneasiness, which is called *cognitive dissonance*.

People who have made a purchase decision use a variety of tactics to reduce or minimize cognitive dissonance. One approach is to seek more information that confirms the appropriateness of the decision. We perceive more ads now than we did before the purchase. We look for positive evaluations of our decision from peers. Postpurchase contact with consumers by marketers is particularly effective in reducing dissonance; among the techniques used for this purpose are letters of congratulation, guarantees, and toll-free customer complaint and problem-solving telephone lines. Consumers may also play down the advantages of the unchosen alternatives and emphasize those of the one they chose. In general, cognitive dissonance occurs more often when the purchase is important to the consumer and the alternatives that were not chosen are highly desirable.

The Big Picture

The consumer's decision-making process as we have presented it seems logical, yet some decisions seem not to fit this pattern. Many decisions, such as whether to buy chewing gum or a magazine, involve neither information seeking nor evaluation. Such decisions are habitual and routine, because the consumer has amassed much prior information and is satisfied with his or her past purchases. In other buying situations, the consumer has some knowledge of alternatives and their attributes, but a new brand comes on the market. In such cases, some information may be sought and added to what is already known. The greatest information-seeking effort is needed in cases that involve new problems or highly innovative solutions, such as cellular telephones and facsimile machines. The least effort generally comes with frequently used, low-priced items.

This decision-making process also can be interrupted at any time by external factors, such as the social influences noted earlier in this chapter. For example, the immediate problem of hunger may be squelched by the cultural value of wanting to look fit. Thus, you may forgo a snack as a result of reference group influence—perhaps someone mentioned that you were putting on a bit of weight—or you may skip dessert because of your ideal self-concept—you would like to be a lot thinner than you are. At the same time, other nonsocial situational factors may intervene—you are out of money, no food is available at the moment, and so on. Such interruptions can occur at any time in the decision-making process.

Frito Lay recognizes this possibility and addresses it with a new line of "healthy" chips. Starting with test markets for low-oil Doritos and Ruffles Light in 1988,[37] the company went on to introduce a line of four light chips nationally in 1990. For some chip consumers, the urge to eat chips can be interrupted by thoughts of fat and salt. Through demographic research and the application of concepts of consumer behavior, Frito Lay developed a profile of these people. Their demographics are "white-collar workers, 35 to 54 years old, earning more than $35,000." To target these consumers, Frito Lay used the new store-specific databases to select stores with a high proportion of these customers. "By increasing promotional spending, running in-store taste programs and lobbying retailers to give more space to the pricier chips in the selected stores, Frito Lay got the line off to a running start."[38]

But it is not always this easy. Marketers must remember that consumer behavior is complex and individualized. Although the models suggest logical, predictable behavior, in fact, behavior can be difficult to understand and predict. Understanding consumer behavior is more an art than a science, and it provides marketers with many of their greatest challenges and opportunities. Both the challenges and the opportunities arise from the essential fact that consumer behavior involves consumers, and consumers are people in all their complexity and individuality. Perhaps the only certainty is that people "are practically always desiring something," as stated by Maslow in the chapter's opening quote. The uncertainty arises when marketers need to decide exactly what consumers desire in any specific situation, as we have discussed. As the humorist Josh Billings used to say, "It's better to know nothing than to know what ain't so." Study consumer behavior to form hypotheses, but don't take them too seriously or you are very likely to find you know what ain't so!

PART THREE

THE TOOLS
OF MARKETING

OMNI, THREE MONTHS LATER

"Are you *serious*, Ann?" asked Joan Miller, a puzzled look on her face. "Who in the world would buy an *oven* through the mail?"

"That's not the point, Joan," answered Ann Jones, warming to her topic.[1] "Direct marketing doesn't have to be done by direct mail. The point is that we could target potential customers much more efficiently by building a database of prospects. We know a lot about the target—two-income households, college grads, young kids, people in a hurry but who still value good food—we even have a good idea what kinds of neighborhoods they live in. So why waste our advertising on all the other people who watch TV and read the papers? And why waste their time, for that matter?"

"Well, Ann, when Jim Berman said he was looking for new marketing ideas, I don't think he had anything *that* radical in mind."

"Joan, what's the value of new blood if you don't give their ideas a fair trial? I've only been here a few months, so I don't know what the sacred cows are yet. If he doesn't like the idea, you can blame it on me. Anyway, I think he is trying to be open-minded, don't you?"

"Sure, Ann, I agree. He's been much more receptive to ideas since he got on that quality kick. And we probably ought to work up a direct mail option just to see what it looks like. But I have to admit I hate direct mail. I must throw away tons of that junk every week!"

"Direct marketing, Joan, not direct mail. And it doesn't have to be done as poorly as most of that stuff you throw away. Did you hear about Porsche's new direct marketing campaign? They are writing personalized

---

[1] No pun intended.

letters to the few hundred thousand people out of the millions of car owners who match the profile of a Porsche buyer exactly."

"Funny, I didn't get a letter yet," Miller interjected.

"I've been reading a new book called *MegaMarketing*," Jones continued. "The authors argue that it will soon be possible to target each individual with a personal marketing message. Now that's really getting to know
your customer, don't you agree?"

Miller pushed back her chair, stood up, and began pacing. "I've read
the book too, and others like it. But I just don't think individualized marketing makes sense."

"Why not?"

"Think about the last few times you tried to talk a friend into doing
something. Did you prevail? Probably not in every case. People are relatively resistant to suggestion, even from someone they know well. And
think how much you know about your friends—you know thousands of
intimate details about their lives, habits, values, beliefs, and preferences.
You know from long experience how to talk them into something, and how
not to. After all, we all have our weak spots, and we certainly all have our
hot buttons that raise defenses and virtually guarantee we will not be
swayed."

"Like you and junk mail?"

"Right," laughed Miller. "I just don't think marketers can ever get
close enough to the customer to know what each individual's hot buttons
are. I think direct marketing can be personal*ized,* but it can never be truly
personal."

"You make it sound like a law of nature."

"Maybe it is," responded Miller. "Isn't there some principle of uncertainty in modern physics? We can call this one the 'principle of marketing
uncertainty.' A company doing business with tens of thousands of people
can't ever become best friends with all of them, so it will never be able to
predict their behavior with certainty."

"Yes, and maybe they don't want to be friends with a company, either,"
laughed Jones.

"No, seriously, I think it is an important point," Miller protested. "Maybe
it explains why marketing communications are so complicated compared
to just talking with or writing to a friend. The whole transaction has to be
structured much more formally, and the message has to be simplified and
broadcast more powerfully if anyone is going to hear it. That's why we need
to worry about the four Ps in customer exchanges—it's an artificial kind of
relationship when compared with a truly personal one."

"Well, what about all the advanced techniques we have for segmentation and targeting, Joan?" Jones asked. "Companies can target a narrow
customer profile and position a product specifically for that customer. My
ovens are a good example."

"Yes, that's true, but I'm just saying we can never get to know each individual well enough to do truly personal marketing."

"Perhaps," responded Jones, "but we could certainly know our customers better than we do. What about American Express? They collect 450 facts on each cardholder. All we know about our customers is what comes back on the warranty cards. With even half the information Amex has, we could mount a pretty good direct marketing effort."

"What does happen to those warranty cards?" asked Miller. "Let's check up on that."

"Yeah, maybe that should be the starting point. We could develop a direct program for existing customers. Send them a quarterly newsletter with recipes and cooking tips. Cross-sell our other appliances to them. We could even add a line of cookware that goes with our ovens."

"As long as you're talking about cross-selling, Ann, why not a whole bundle of related products in some sort of special package, with cheaper pricing. We'll have scale economies to justify it. And you could include a single long-term warranty covering everything in the line."

"Sure, Joan, and we could even promote it as a club—call it the Omni-Club or something. I think we should use relationship pricing, you know, a club discount or a 'friends of Omni' discount. People would join the club for the pricing and convenience of direct shopping, and we could fill their orders direct."

"What about the dealers? They'll be steamed if you start marketing a buying club that bypasses them and their markup."

"Hmm. We might have to have designated dealers in each area who receive a pass-through cut on the direct sales in order to keep the existing channel happy while we develop a new one."

"You are full of ideas today, Ann! I hope you're going to write some of them down. By the way, who knows about direct mail—sorry, direct marketing—here at Omni? How would we forecast the response rates and the details of the cost side for an idea like the Omni Club?"

"I have an old friend from when I was at the accounting firm. He's working on American Express' direct marketing program now. Maybe he would be willing to help us."

"Yes, they just won one of those national Baldrige Awards for quality, didn't they? I think that means they are supposed to share information about how they do things."

"About their quality program," Jones corrected. "I don't know how far they'll take that, but my friend should help out anyway. We don't compete, after all."

"Say, Ann, as long as you have an 'in' there, why don't you see if they would like to market some of our appliances? We could even do a line under a different brand name to avoid conflict with the retailers."

"Didn't you just say nobody would buy an oven through the mail?"

"Okay, okay, but I'm sure we could improve our promotion effort by building a customer database, and it might prove useful to product development too. I'm not saying we should start a direct campaign—that's a whole new distribution channel we have never used, after all. But we probably ought to look at it, and if it has any merit we better do it *first*."

Jones nodded in agreement. "Are you thinking about Somitsu? I can't believe they already came out with competitors for our new models. It took them less than six months. I've heard of fast-cycle product development, but that's ridiculous!"

"Which reminds me of another project," added Miller. "We've been asked to help out the benchmarking team that's working on product development. We should try to get some information on Somitsu's methods, don't you think?"

"I guess there's always another project," sighed Jones with a glance at the wall clock over their heads. "What do you think we should do first?"

"Lunch. It's already 12:30. And we can swing by engineering and see if anyone from the benchmarking team can come with us. Two birds with one stone, you know."

"Great idea. Do you like Chinese?" Jones asked.

"Sure. The leftovers warm up so well in the new OmniWave model!"

SEGMENTATION, TARGETING, POSITIONING

8

From Mass Marketing to One-on-One with the Customer

The fifties and sixties were the heyday of mass marketing. There was one kind of Coca-Cola soft drink for the thirsty. One kind of Clairol hair dye for hair coloring. One kind of Holiday Inn motel for the traveler. The seventies became a decade of segmentation and line extension. It was followed in the early eighties by intensified niche marketing that sliced markets into smaller and smaller groups of consumers—each group with particular needs and wants to satisfy. By the mid-eighties, Robitussin was offering four kinds of medicine for four kinds of coughs. . . . From mass marketing to segmented marketing to niche marketing to tomorrow's world of one-to-one marketing—the transformation will be complete by the end of the eighties.

—*Stan Rapp and Tom Collins*[1]

Were the gurus of direct marketing correct in predicting that all marketers would be focusing their products and pitches on individual consumers by the 1990s? Yes and no. As a practical matter, one-to-one selling is not always a cost-effective way to market products and services. On the one hand, companies generally run into problems of scale when they try to break down their markets into ever-smaller groups. On the other hand, many products that were once designed and advertised to the entire country have now splintered into a variety of more specialized products and sales messages. The revolution is not complete—perhaps it never will be—but the increasing power of computerized customer databases continues to drive marketing toward more narrowly focused products and marketing campaigns. At the root of this trend is the simple observation that no two consumers are alike.

This is easy to see in the consumer market. Think about all the material goods that your friends possess. No two individuals have the same set of possessions. Each person wants a unique combination of goods and services. And think about how numerous people are, how spread out over the country and the world they are, and how diverse their buying habits are. Meeting their needs is far from a trivial task. In their efforts to perform this task, marketers divide the market as a whole into smaller segments on the basis of some kind of similarity among consumers, such as age or sex, buying behavior, or psychological traits. Most managers believe that they cannot compete successfully in every market and that it is in their interest to focus on a few segments that seem more attractive than others. This is the basis of target marketing.

Porsche recently sent the following letter to potential customers: "Your preeminent position in society and your success as a doctor demonstrate that you pursue excellence in all things, a quality you share with Dr. Ferry Porsche, the creator of the original Porsche automobile. . . . Since you already own a luxurious European car, I would like to introduce you to another—the Porsche." The recipient may not have taken the bait, but he was bound to be surprised that Porsche knew he was a European-car-driving doctor. Steven Judge of Rapp Collins Marcoa, Porsche's direct-marketing agency, explains, "We've been successful in obtaining a great deal of information about our prospects, such as their profession, their income range, the type of cars they currently drive, where they live, and what type of neighborhood they live in." This research has allowed Porsche to select 300,000 likely prospects from an initial list of 80 million car owners. It cost the company 6 months and $250,000 to generate the list, but the benefits of targeting this segment will far outweigh the costs of development if it turns out, for example, that middle-aged male doctors who drive Mercedes, earn more than $150,000 per year, and live in affluent suburbs are very likely to buy Porsches.[2]

Before discussing market segmentation in detail, however, we need to consider a broader approach that marketers sometimes use. Instead of dividing the total market into smaller, more homogeneous segments, they may treat all consumers as one large group—an aggregate. Thus there are two basic strategies available to marketers: market aggregation and market segmentation. We examine the objectives, methods, costs, and benefits of each strategy.

MARKET AGGREGATION—THE STRATEGY OF MASS MARKETING

When marketers follow the strategy of market aggregation, also called mass marketing or undifferentiated marketing, the total market is not divided into segments. Rather, a single marketing program is used to offer the same product to all consumers. Because of the diversity of the consumers' wants and needs, the market aggregation approach will not completely satisfy every potential buyer. Marketers use this strategy when they believe enough consumers will buy the product as it is. This strategy has been used by marketers of standardized goods, such as sugar, many farm products, gasoline, salt, paint, and liquid bleach, as well as standardized services, such as dry cleaning, appliance repair, lawn maintenance, and house painting. It has also been used for some products that people may not think of as standardized, such as beer, cigarettes, coffee, and household cleansers.

The market aggregation approach is used when consumers perceive little or no difference between the products of different firms, that is, when competing products seem virtually the same physically and chemically. For this approach to be successful, therefore, a large number of people must have the same basic need or want. Also, the marketer must be able to design a single marketing mix that will satisfy various potential customers. If these two conditions are not met, mass marketing is doomed to failure.

Organizations that use the market aggregation approach realize that consumers may have different wants and needs, but they also believe that a sufficient number of consumers are similar enough to be treated as a homogeneous group. In short, consumers are expected to compromise by accepting a product that may not suit their needs perfectly. This approach is exemplified by Henry Ford's famous remark about potential buyers of his Model T. A firm believer in mass marketing, he is reported to have said that the market "can have any color it wants as long as it's black." Contrast this with the way Porsches are sold today.

The major advantage of the market aggregation strategy comes from lower production and marketing costs. Only one product is made and production techniques do not have to be changed for different models, styles, and the like. This is extremely efficient; Ford's Model T offered consumers more value for their money because standardized mass production lowered the cost of production. Advertising costs also may be lower because often only one advertising campaign is used.

Despite the advantages in terms of costs and efficiency, there are built-in dangers in the market aggregation strategy. By using an approach that may leave some consumers' wants unsatisfied, marketers expose themselves to challenges from competitors. This is especially true when the firm serves a large market. In trying to meet the entire market's needs reasonably well, marketers are vulnerable to competitors who satisfy those needs more precisely. Henry Ford was forced to offer a choice of colors when competitors started to.

Marketers that use the market aggregation approach often employ promotion and other marketing activities to get consumers to perceive their product as different from and better than those of competitors. This strategy is known as *product differentiation*.[3] It involves creating a perception of uniqueness and superiority and, thus, a preference for a particular product. The actual product may not be different from competitors' products, but consumers believe it is different. To create that perception in the minds of consumers, marketers rely heavily on creating a positive image for the product or associating it with something that is valued by the consumer.

Consider the bath towel business. Can you honestly tell the difference between two bath towels? In recent years, towel manufacturers have created an industry in which consumers consider most bath towels as the same. Even designer brand sheets and towels have been sold at rock-bottom prices to bargain-seeking customers. In an effort to differentiate its products from those of competitors, Fieldcrest has begun marketing only its most fashionable, high-profit products under its corporate brand name. While most of its competitors sew their corporate names on all their products and sell them through all kinds of outlets—discount stores and mass merchandisers as well as prestigious department stores—Fieldcrest stitches its name only on its finest quality towels and markets them exclusively through department stores.

The chances of success with a differentiation strategy are greater under certain conditions. First, there should be some way for consumers to distinguish between the offerings of two or more competitors. The differences between Fords and Porsches are obvious, but can you tell one brand of sewing needle from another? Second, the differences between competing products should not be so small that they are trivial. Third, the consumer must care about the product; otherwise the differentiation strategy will not have much impact. Furthermore, the product features that are emphasized must be desired by a substantial portion of the population.

Product differentiation can be costly. Creating a difference in consumer perceptions often requires a major investment in promotion, packaging, branding, and the like. The marketer must be able to afford the expense that will be incurred by taking this approach. On the other hand, the rewards of this strategy, if it succeeds, can be substantial. Many consumers purchase the well-known Clorox brand of bleach over lower priced brands even though the products are chemically identical.

Over time, markets seem to move from a mass-marketing approach to increasing product differentiation, and ultimately to splintering into an increasing number of segments. Ford's Model T competed against a great many fewer competitors than Porsche does in today's auto market. Now that the auto market has splintered into dozens of regional, behavioral, and psychographic segments and many hundreds of product offerings, mass marketing is out of the question. The only way to get ahead in the auto market is to focus more narrowly and more accurately than the competitors—as Porsche is doing in its new direct-mail campaign. When this logic is extended to other products, it implies a competitive force pushing companies inexorably toward finer targets and more segments, presumably at ever-higher marketing costs. In fact, this does seem to be the case. There are certainly more products and more segments every year. Differentiated marketing is a difficult game to play, and the final moves are still unclear. Will the game really end in one-on-one marketing? The differences between business and personal relationships make this possibility unlikely, as discussed in the introduction to Part Three. However, there is certainly room to maneuver between current efforts at segmented marketing and this one-to-one ideal. After reviewing the standard concepts and tools of market segmentation, this chapter explores two tools that are on the leading edge of this drive.

MARKET SEGMENTATION—THE STRATEGY OF SUBDIVIDING THE MARKET

When they choose to use a segmentation strategy, marketers view a particular market as consisting of many smaller parts whose members share certain characteristics. Market segmentation thus involves breaking down a large, heterogeneous market into small, more homogeneous segments as Porsche did when it targeted 300,000 of the 80 million U.S. car owners. Separate marketing programs, generally with a different product, are developed to meet each segment's particular needs. In this way, the company is able to provide a product and marketing mix that "fits" a relatively homogeneous part of the total market. As a result, market segmentation results in a better match between what the marketer offers and what the market desires.

This approach has its drawbacks, however. For one thing, research expenditures increase as more market segments are investigated. Production costs rise because production runs are shorter and the efficiency of mass production is lost. Finally, sales in one segment may be sacrificed as another segment is served—for example, Coca-Cola's addition of Cherry Coke cut into its sales of Mr. Pibb. On the whole, then, segmentation provides a better match between the product and the consumer, but not without substantial costs.

Markets can be broken down in many ways, as we discuss shortly. What marketers look for are distinctive groups of consumers within the total market. Sometimes there is no such group—that is, the market is totally homogeneous (see Exhibit 8.1). At one extreme, for example, is the market for rubber bands. Because there are no sets of consumers with different wants in this market, the market aggregation strategy is the proper approach. At the other extreme, carpenters, homebuilders, tailors, and furniture upholsterers face consumer demands that are highly diverse in that each individual has a unique set of requirements. The marketer can try to serve all, many, or some of those markets' diverse desires. As noted earlier, however, the costs are likely to be high; there is little opportunity for mass production standardization, which is one reason why houses and Porsches are so expensive.

For market segmentation to work well, marketers need to find a pattern of similarities in which consumer preferences form distinct clusters. Exhibit 8.1 shows different patterns of consumer needs. Only Market C offers the clusters of distinct groups that lend themselves to segmentation.

EXHIBIT 8.1.   Basic product preference patterns.

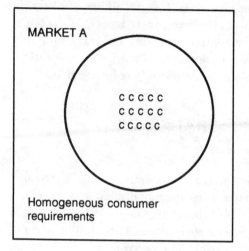

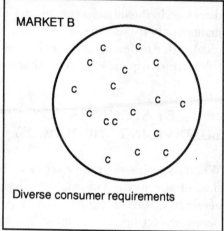

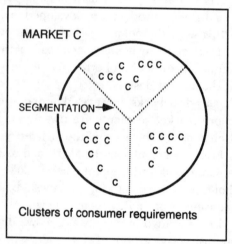

Effective Use of Market Segmentation

Market segmentation is not always the best strategy. For it to be effective, the marketer must answer the following questions:

1. *Can the market be identified and measured?* Marketers must be able to identify which consumers are members of a particular market segment. There must be a shared characteristic that can be used to include or exclude consumers from the group, and that characteristic must be measurable. How can marketers identify and measure consumers whose vision is poor or whose scalps itch? These are difficult, perhaps impossible, traits to measure—yet marketers of contact lenses and shampoos probably wish they could do so.

Gaines Foods markets its Cycle dog food to clearly identified market segments. The company found that many dog owners think of their pets as four-footed humans with special needs. These owners respond favorably to Cycle because it is formulated to match their dog's age and activity pattern. Four products are marketed under the Cycle label, each designed to meet the needs of an identifiable segment: Cycle 1 for puppies, Cycle 2 for young adult dogs, Cycle 3 for overweight dogs, and Cycle 4 for older dogs. You might say Cycle segments both pet owners and pets, targeting dog food buyers on the basis of the age and condition of their dogs.

2. *Is the segment large enough to be profitable?* Because market segmentation can be costly, unless a segment is large enough to generate a sales volume that will ensure a profit, it is not worthwhile to design a unique marketing program for that segment. Some segments are small yet have enough purchasing power to be profitable. For example, only about 10 percent of fur coats are sold to men, but this small segment's profit potential is very high.

3. *Is the market reachable?* For a segmentation strategy to succeed, marketers must be able to communicate effectively and efficiently with each segment chosen for attention. Some segments, even though they may be quite large, cannot be reached effectively. For example, potential buyers of inexpensive watches are not likely to read any one magazine or view any one television program. Thus, much of the promotion cost would be wasted in that it would be directed at people who are not interested in the product. Compare the ability of furniture companies to reach their market through magazines such as *Metropolitan Life* and *Better Homes and Gardens.* Sometimes direct marketing can be used to make a market reachable for the first time. Porsche's investment in list development gives it better access to its market than its competitors have.

4. *Is the segment responsive?* Unless a segment is likely to react to the marketing program, there is little reason to develop a unique program for that segment. Clearly, members of the segment must be willing to purchase the product in response to a particular marketing mix. For example, in a market known for flat sales, Orville Redenbacher found a responsive segment for his "gourmet popcorn," which claims to be lighter, fluffier, more tender, and bigger than ordinary popcorn. He markets to the segment that wants to pay more for better quality. Other popcorns, however, use mass marketing. There is probably *no* responsive segment of people looking for cheap popcorn, for example.

5. *Is the segment expected not to change quickly?* Designing and executing a marketing program aimed at a particular market segment takes time. For it to be profitable, the segment should be stable with respect to the wants and needs of its members over a considerable period of time. If it is not, the strategy chosen by the marketer may turn out to be inappropriate for that segment. Some markets, such as those for clothing and accessories, are known for their fickleness and must be approached with great care.

Potential Bases for Market Segmentation

How do you segment a market? This question is both complex and critical. It is complex because there are many possible ways to market a segment, and it is not always obvious which one to use. It is critical because how you segment the market often determines the success of your marketing strategy. Also, many new products arise from new ways of segmenting the market. Creative approaches to segmentation offer considerable opportunity to the marketer. Exhibit 8.2 lists many of the ways in which markets are segmented.

Descriptive Bases for Market Segmentation

One of the most frequently used methods of subdividing a market is *demographic* or *socioeconomic* segmentation. Demographic variables include age, sex, family size, marital status, race, religion, and place of residence; socioeconomic characteristics include income, occupation, and education. These variables are most helpful in describing market segments because they are easy to measure and often prove to be good indicators of consumer wants, needs, preferences, and product usage. The following are some examples:

- Noting that the number of young adults aged 20 to 24 who have skin problems now exceeded the number of teenagers with blemishes, Richardson-Vicks introduced Clearasil Adult Care. Adults are now an important market segment for acne medicine as we learned in Chapter 7.

- Learning that 15 percent of cookware customers are male, San Francisco–based Williams-Sonoma, a 26-store cookware chain, purchased mailing lists from men's magazines such as *Gentlemen's Quarterly* to boost its catalog sales.

- With the growth of older "silver" segments, Selchow and Richter markets a version of its Scrabble board game with tiles that are 50 percent larger than normal.

Geographic differences are another commonly used basis for market segmentation. In this case, a market is divided according to consumers' locations, which influence many of their needs and wants. Marketers use nations, states, regions, counties, cities, or even neighborhoods as bases for segmentation. For example, New Englanders scoop up an average of 23.1 quarts of ice cream a year, more than consumers in any other region. In the sunny Southeast, the average is only 11.57 quarts. What you drink may also be influenced by where you live. The South, with 32 percent of the population, accounts for 48 percent of tea consumption and only 21 percent of wine drinking. People in the Northeast, with 22 percent of the population, drink 19 percent of the tea and 30 percent of the wine.

Marketers going international are compelled to perform geographic segmentation. The traditional "multinational" segmentation approach has been to

EXHIBIT 8.2. Commonly used bases for market segmentation.

Descriptive Bases

Demographic variables

Age	Under 6, 6–11, 12–19, 20–34, 35–49, 50–64, 65+
Gender	Male; female
Income	Under $5,000; $5,000–10,000; $10,001–20,000; $20,001–30,000; $30,001–50,000; over $50,000
Occupation	Managerial, professional, office worker, skilled trade, technical, homemaker, general laborer, student, sales, farmer, foreman, craftsman, public official
Education	Less than 8 years, 9–11 years, high school graduate, technical/vocational school, 1–2 years college, 3–4 years college, college graduate, graduate or professional degree
Family size	1–2, 3, 4, 5+
Family life cycle	Young single; young married–no children; young married–youngest child under 6; young married–youngest child at least 6; older married with dependent children; older married with no children at home; older couple–retired; widow or widower
Religion	Catholic, Jewish, Protestant
Nationality	American, British, German, Chinese, Japanese, Italian, French, Spanish, Scandinavian, Latin American, Middle Eastern

Geographic variables

Region	Northeast, Midwest, West, Southwest, Southeast, Atlantic, Mountain
Density	Urban, surburban, rural
Climate	Warm, cold
Population	Under 5,000, 5,000–20,000, 20,001–50,000, 50,001–100,000, 100,001–250,000, 250,001–500,000, 500,001–1 million, over 1 million

Behavioral Bases

User status	Nonuser, ex-user, potential user, first-time user, regular user
Brand loyalty	Loyal, switcher
Usage rate	Heavy user, light user, nonuser
Benefits sought (toothpaste market)	Taste, decay prevention, brightness, plaque prevention, low price
Personality	Gregarious, achieving, egotistical, ambitious
Lifestyle (American men)	Quiet family man, traditionalist, discontented, ethical, highbrow, pleasure oriented, achiever, he-man, sophisticated
Social class	Upper, middle, lower
Occasion	Special, usual
Readiness to buy	Unaware, informed, interested, intending to buy

partition the world on political boundaries and to create a separate marketing mix for each country. With at least 125 countries in the world, however, the difficulty of treating each as an individual market can easily be seen. Many companies group nations into segments, but this is not always appropriate. Consider the Middle Eastern countries of Iran, Iraq, Saudi Arabia, Kuwait, the United Arab Emirates, Egypt, Syria, Israel, and Lebanon; they are all quite different. The Emirates, for instance, have no formal business laws, whereas the Egyptian legal system is very old and based on French law. Furthermore, these markets are all highly nationalistic in their cultures, creating even greater heterogeneity. Although they seem culturally similar to outsiders, they may view each other as different, and even as enemies—witness the Iran–Iraq war and Iraq's invasion of Kuwait. Although geographic segmentation based on grouping nations is an often-used method of dividing the world, it is not the best; it overlooks many political and cultural differences among countries.

Behavioral Bases for Segmenting Markets

Descriptive variables can be a useful basis for dividing up markets; however, these variables do not get beneath the surface. Behavioral variables can give the marketer greater insight into the motivations of consumers in a particular market segment. Thus, behavioral variables can be a much more powerful means of segmenting markets than descriptive variables. They can be viewed as determining variables, whereas descriptive variables are qualifying variables, that is, variables that "qualify" a person to be a member of a certain market, but do not determine what he or she will buy.

One behavioral basis for market segmentation is *user status*. Some members of the market have never been users of the marketer's product or brand. These consumers represent a special challenge, because they must be persuaded to change their buying behavior—and they will tend to resist such a change. If the wealthy doctor who received the Porsche letter (described in the beginning of this chapter) has always favored restored MGs, it will be difficult to convince him another sports car is better. Then there are ex-users, those who have switched to another product or brand. This group also needs to have its perceptions changed—again, a difficult task. First-time users are another segment, one that is likely to be more responsive to marketing efforts.

With the percentage of women buyers of motorcycles growing from 7.5 to 10 percent of the market in the last decade, motorcycle marketers have taken steps to convert more of these traditional nonusers. The first step was to raise cycle consciousness through a nearly $1 million promotional campaign cosponsored by the four leading Japanese manufacturers: Honda, Yamaha Motor Corporation, Suzuki, and Kawasaki. The "Discover Today's Motorcycling" campaign's objective was to take the "motorcycle mama" image out of cycling and to show it as a leisure activity in line with the ideals of the women's movement. It seemed to work; in 1987, women purchased 21 percent of Kawasaki Motor's smaller sized 250 "Baby" Ninja model and 16 percent of Suzuki's more powerful 650 Savage bikes. (Yes, these shares of product sales are far higher than the 10 percent market share cited earlier because the Baby Ninja and 650 Savage are targeted at female buyers.)

Segments can also be based on *brand loyalty.* Some consumers are brand loyal. Others are constant switchers; their next purchase is totally unpredictable. Naturally, marketers would like consumers to be loyal to their brands. They entice consumers to try specific products through such strategies as free samples and cents-off deals in the hope that brand loyalty will develop. Such loyalty will happen when the fit between the attributes of the product or brand and the needs of the consumer is strong. Marketers also constantly attempt to maintain the loyalty of consumers who have already developed a preference for their brand. Postpurchase service and attention to product quality are ways of achieving this.

Segmentation by *product usage* involves distinguishing heavy users of a product or brand from light users and nonusers. Marketers who examine product usage rates often find the "80–20 principle" at work—20 percent of the market accounts for 80 percent of the sales. Although this rule of thumb cannot be applied to every product, it indicates the importance of a rather small group of buyers to the well-being of many firms.

Exhibit 8.3 shows the results of two studies, conducted 20 years apart, that examined purchase and consumption behavior for 16 categories of products. Users were assigned to the "light half" or the "heavy half" depending on whether their usage was low or above the median for the category. Certain product categories, such as cola, frozen orange juice, and bourbon, were found to contain segments in which one heavy-half household purchased as much as eight light-half households. This clearly illustrates the value of usage segmentation.

The heavy half is more attractive to many marketers because it is often relatively easy to identify and measure. For example, department stores can analyze the buying behavior of charge account customers, banks can assess how their services are used, and many syndicated services provide information about heavy users of consumer products.

An increasingly popular and extremely powerful approach to market segmentation is *benefit segmentation.* This approach focuses on the primary benefit that the consumer seeks. The marketer analyzes information about consumers' desires and translates that information into marketing programs that will satisfy those desires. This approach assumes that differences in benefits sought are the basic reason for the existence of different market segments. Although consumers seek as many benefits as possible from the products they buy, the value they attach to various benefits can differ significantly. That is, consumers do not often expect a product to provide many benefits all at once; rather, they are looking for one overriding benefit. Buyers of Levi's jeans seek "durability"; buyers of Elmer's Glue-All want "adhesion"; and buyers of Lego Toys' building blocks are looking for "possibilities." As a perceptive marketer

EXHIBIT 8.3. Examples of product usage segmentation.

Product	Light Half		Heavy Half		Nonusers	
	1962[a]	1982[b]	1962[a]	1982[b]	1962[a]	1982[b]
Soaps and detergents	19%	25%	80%	75%	2%	6%
Toilet tissue	26	29	74	71	2	5
Shampoo	19	21	81	79	18	6
Paper towels	17	25	83	75	34	10
Margarine	17	23	83	77	11	12
RTE cereals	13	20	87	80	4	14
Cake mixes	15	17	85	83	27	26
Frozen orange juice	11	16	89	84	28	32
Sausage	16	18	84	82	3	31
Cola	10	17	90	83	22	33
Hair fixative	12	19	88	81	54	47
Beer	12	13	88	87	67	59
Lemon and lime drink	9	13	91	87	42	61
Dog food	13	19	87	81	67	70
Hair tonic	13	25	87	75	52	78
Bourbon	11	5	89	95	59	80

[a] Chicago Tribune Panel Data.
[b] Simmons Study of Media and Markets.
Source: Victor J. Cook, Jr., and William A. Mindak, "A Search for Constants: The 'Heavy User' Revisited!" *Journal of Consumer Marketing, 1,* Spring 1984, p. 80.

once remarked, "Consumers do not buy three-quarter-inch drill bits; they buy three-quarter-inch holes." When using benefit segmentation, the marketer must identify the basic need that consumers seek to satisfy and apply this knowledge in developing the marketing mix. Selling Porsche on the basis of fuel economy would be a waste of time, regardless of how well the marketing program was executed.

A recent study of marketing managers found 65 percent agreeing that consumers' tastes for certain goods and services are becoming increasingly similar worldwide.[4] Consumers in different countries will differ demographically and culturally, but they may seek the same benefits. Nestlé, for instance, found cat owners' concerns for feeding their pet the same throughout Europe. Focusing on the universally recognized independent nature of cats, Nestlé created a pan-European campaign for its Friskies Dry Cat Food that stressed dry cat food as better than wet foods, given cats' indifference to eating (wet cat food dries before they finish it).

Personality segmentation has also been used to divide markets. The underlying concept is that if personality segments can be identified, products and brands can be given "personalities" that are consistent with those of the different personality segments. Marketers therefore have tried to use certain personality traits—dominant/passive, conservative/liberal, impulsive/thoughtful, and the like—to identify market segments. Most efforts along these lines have met with frustration, however; personality traits don't seem to be much help in understanding buying behavior.[5]

Recently marketers have looked at personality from a different angle and found a more promising way of identifying market segments. Called *lifestyle* or *psychographic segmentation*, this method divides the market into segments based on how consumers live, as reflected in their values, attitudes, and interests. Exhibit 8.4 offers some dimensions on which lifestyle is measured.

In researching the lifestyle patterns of consumers, marketers measure three things: activities, interests, and opinions. Opinions include beliefs, attitudes, or values.[6] Stanford Research Institute (SRI) blended demographic and lifestyle variables (called VALS, for Values and Lifestyles) to create psychographic portraits of nine categories of Americans. SRI conducted a mail survey that drew responses from over 1,600 adults. Analysis of the data resulted in four broad categories of Americans—need-driven, outer directed, inner directed, and combined outer and inner—which were subdivided into nine lifestyle segments, each with a distinct set of values, needs, beliefs, drives, dreams, and special perspectives.[7] Recently, SRI updated VALS on the basis of a new survey, VALS2. These two surveys are especially popular with advertisers, although some marketers think they are a waste of time. (See the special discussion of VALS at the end of this chapter.)

Some evidence suggests that the VALS categories have counterparts in other countries.[8] Three cross-cultural psychographic segments have been identified: international sophisticates, semisophisticates, and provincials. The first segment has become increasingly important to global marketers, including the purveyors of such designer goods as Gucci, Louis Vuitton, Burberry, and Hermes. American Coach Leatherware, marketer of fine leather handbags and accessories, has gone international to compete with other well-known leather goods boutiques. In 1988, the company opened its first stores abroad in London and in Japan. "The Japanese have a fairly high awareness of Coach already because of the number of business travelers," said Coach's vice president of marketing.[9] In Japan, stores will be opened in four Mitsukoshi department

EXHIBIT 8.4.   Lifestyle dimensions.

Activities	Interests	Opinions
Work	Family	Themselves
Hobbies	Home	Social issues
Social events	Job	Politics
Vacation	Community	Business
Entertainment	Recreation	Economics
Club membership	Fashion	Education
Community	Food	Products
Shopping	Media	Future
Sports	Achievements	Culture

Source: Joseph T. Plummer, "The Concept and Application of Lifestyle Segmentation," *Journal of Marketing, 38,* Jan. 1974, pp. 33–37.

stores and advertisements placed in Japanese versions of internationally recognized magazines *Yes* and *Elle*.

Other Bases for Segmentation

Marketers sometimes employ *social-class segmentation*. As noted in Chapter 7, sociologists have suggested many ways of dividing the population into social classes; no one system is agreed upon by all. Yet at the basis of any breakdown of the population into classes is evidence of homogeneity in values, ideas, attitudes, lifestyles, and behavior within each class. The 300,000 recipients of the Porsche letter are no doubt similar in many ways. One way to view Porsche's strategy is as a class-based segmentation of the auto market.

West German household appliance manufacturer Braun AG has segmented the U.S. market on social class and targeted young, upscale "nouveau riche" consumers whose conspicuous consumption and deep pockets provide a match with its brand's high-quality performance and stylish European design. Priced 10 to 30 percent higher than U.S. counterparts, the appliances nonetheless sell well.

Occasions can also be used to segment markets. Certain occasions have special meanings. Significant events in our lives, such as graduation, marriage, and retirement, as well as holidays and other special events, often involve the use of special products. Candy, watches, flowers, and greeting cards can be marketed to segments based on special occasions.

Stage of buyer readiness is another helpful basis for segmentation. Sometimes consumers can be classified on the basis of how much they know about a product or brand and how interested they are in buying it. Some people are totally unaware of the product; others are aware of it; and still others are informed about it, interested in it, even intending to purchase it. Each stage requires a marketing program with a slightly different slant. For instance, the marketer needs to catch the attention of the unaware segment and make it aware. For those who intend to buy, the marketing program must emphasize price and other factors that will prompt them to buy the product.

Single- versus Multivariable Segmentation

Segmentation can be based on one or more of the variables just described. Using only one basis for dividing a market is easier than using more than one; however, using one variable clearly is less precise than using more than one, since most markets are complex.

For example, beer drinkers can be broken down by age. Consumption is highest in the 18- to 24-year-old group; 61 percent reported in a survey that they drank beer during the last month. Next highest is the group aged 24 to 34 at 58 percent, then the 35- to 39-year-olds at 44 percent. Only 25 percent of over-40s report drinking beer in the last month. With this data, the marketer could target younger people. But this is still a large, undifferentiated group.

The survey results also indicate that 83 percent of beer drinkers
and only 17 percent are women. By combining this data with the age
marketer could focus on younger men. Although the target is bette
the group is still diverse.

The picture becomes clearer when market research data on the benefits
consumers seek in beer are also included. For example, 76 percent care most
about taste, and 5 percent about calories. Using benefits sought, age, and sex, the
marketer can define much more specific segments. For example, a brand could
be targeted at 18- to 24-year-old men who seek good taste in a beer—a smaller
and more homogeneous segment than any based on only one or two of the variables.[10] A visual representation of this three-variable segment is provided in the
"How Do You Like Your Beer?" diagram. (Exhibit 8.5).

Steps in the Market Segmentation Process

Having explored the concept of market segmentation, we can now look at how
marketers actually carry out this process. The six steps in the market segmentation process are discussed below.

1. *Determine market boundaries.* The first step is to define the market to
be served. The marketing manager must keep in mind the business definition
outlined in the strategic marketing plan. If the company is in the low-cost
modular-housing business, for example, a different definition of the market
should result than if the firm's focus is on luxury condominiums. The marketer
should also consider the types of competition discussed in Chapter 2—
generic, form, and brand. Given the broad definition of the firm's business,
what are its generic competitors? In the low-cost modular-housing business,
generic competition would come from trailer homes, apartments, rental
houses, other low-cost houses, and so on. Thinking about these questions
forces the marketer to consider the basic wants and needs of the market to be
segmented.

2. *Decide which segmentation variables to use.* We have discussed many
variables that can be used to segment a market. An important step in the segmentation process is to sort through these variables and decide which are most
likely to be useful. Sometimes marketers simply collect data on as many potentially useful variables as possible and then use data analysis to cluster people
into segments. This "hunting expedition" approach is useful in some instances,
particularly lifestyle segmentation, but in general it is more effective to select
appropriate bases for segmentation in advance. Marketers have also found that
product-specific variables are more closely tied to marketing decision making.

3. *Collect and analyze segmentation data.* This step is the domain of marketing research. At this point, appropriate questionnaire items are developed
and samples designed. Once the data have been collected, the marketer can use

EXHIBIT 8.5.

a. Percentage of age segments who drank beer in the past month

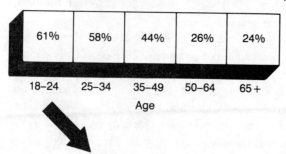

b. Percentage of men and women who drank beer in 1984

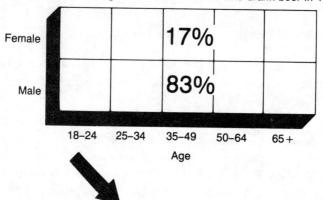

c. Percentage of men and women seeking various benefits

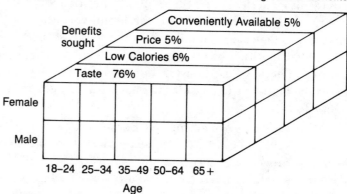

a wide range of analytical techniques to determine which segments of the market have the greatest within-segment homogeneity and between-segment heterogeneity. The entire process of market segmentation is focused on identifying groups whose members have the same unsatisfied wants and needs. Thus, the segments that emerge should be based on behavior-related variables such as benefits or lifestyles.

4. *Develop a profile of each segment.* The next step is to select from the vast array of possible descriptive variables an appropriate set to fill in the portrait of the segment. Demographic and geographic variables create a more complete picture of each segment of the market. These variables should be related in some way to the actual buying behavior exhibited within the segment.

5. *Target the segments to be served.* Now the marketer can look for opportunities. Which segments offer the most attractive opportunities? Where is the best fit between the organization's resources and those opportunities? How many and which segments should be pursued? The competitive situation and the firm's financial resources, special skills, unique technologies, image, objectives, and mission must be taken into consideration. The size of the market segment and its potential profitability must not be ignored.

6. *Design a marketing plan.* Once the segments to be served have been targeted, the marketer must decide how to go about serving them. The attributes of the product that appeal to the members of each segment must be identified. The segments served by competitors must also be identified, and then a strategy for getting the attention of consumers in each segment must be developed. The product's features must be designed or redesigned and the promotional campaign structured to create the image that the marketer intends.

SELECTING TARGET MARKETS

The market segmentation process identifies the segments that the marketer may choose to address. The marketer must evaluate those segments and decide which one or ones to serve. Most marketers would agree that they want to direct their efforts toward the segments that are potentially most profitable. Closely allied to profitability is *response sensitivity,* that is, the likelihood that a given segment will react to a marketing program with the desired buying behavior. However, research has shown that these bases for targeting are rarely used. Marketers often use the number of consumers in a segment as a basis for targeting that segment. A survey of consulting firms that conduct segmentation studies uncovered the following bases for targeting: "'the best target had the heaviest users,' 'these people are looking for product benefits our client's brand can deliver,' and 'more women 18 to 34, the group the client has always gone after, were in this target segment than in any other.'"[11]

Although marketers often target the largest segment of the market, that segment does not always offer the best opportunity. Often the largest segment faces very heavy competition; often, too, consumers in that segment are very satisfied with competitors' products and brands. In many cases, the best choice is a segment that has been neglected by the competition—consumers who are likely to be dissatisfied with existing products and brands. The marketer that focuses on such segments has a better chance of success.

Low income shoppers have not been targeted by most companies, and they might now qualify as an attractive segment simply because they are so commonly overlooked. A quick look at the demographics confirms the hypothesis that low income households represent a marketing opportunity. This is a high-growth segment. The retail consulting firm Management Horizons calculated in late 1990 that low income households make up 36 percent of U.S. households, versus 31 percent in 1970.[12] (The factors driving this growth include declining union influence; rising divorce rates, creating smaller and poorer households; and the shift from manufacturing to low-paying service jobs.)

This means about 40 million families are being overlooked by most marketers. Although their spending power is clearly low, they do spend. For example, if each family spends only $100 a month on clothing, this represents a $48 billion segment of the clothing market! You might say this segment is at the opposite end of the spectrum from Porsche's targeted segment, in that the marketer would need to make many small sales versus the few large ones Porsche makes, but either strategy can work in the right circumstances. And the circumstances are right for The Limited.

This retailer had purchased Lerner's in 1985, a chain characterized by *BusinessWeek* as "a struggling, poorly lit chain of bargain emporiums serving lower-income working women."[13] Lerner's was a downscale store targeted for a downscale market, but that formula wasn't working for Lerner's. Was the opportunity in this segment an illusion? To jump ahead in the chapter for a moment, The Limited rethought Lerner's positioning, starting with the realization that low income clothing buyers were shopping for image as well as warmth and protection. Although less affluent, they were looking for the same benefits from clothing that other shoppers were. So Lerner's was remodeled and repositioned. *BusinessWeek* describes the new positioning: "Lerner's flagship Manhattan store, for example, boasts a peaches-and-cream color scheme, a high rotunda, and a tuxedo-clad piano player. But a rayon dress costs only $60, while a cardigan sweater goes for $25." The strategy has been a success, so far, with sales growing from $675 million to $1 billion (in 800 stores) in four years.

When the marketer has evaluated the potential of each possible market segment, the next task is to decide how many and which segments will become the targets of the organization's marketing programs. The marketer has three target strategies from which to choose: concentration, differentiation, and atomization. (That is to say, there are *currently* three commonly used strategies. However, someone will eventually discover a new approach, and its novelty will provide an advantage. As you learn "truths" such as these, always look for creative ways to extend them.)

When marketers decide to serve a single market segment, they are pursuing a *concentration* strategy. Companies that have taken this approach include Volkswagen, 7-Up, Hallmark, U.S. Time (Timex), and of course Porsche with its narrow focus on upper-class sports car drivers. A concentration strategy allows the marketer to direct all of its efforts toward satisfying a single group's desires.

This targeting strategy is not always best, however. It ties the firm to a single market segment; if that segment declines in size or consumer tastes change, the firm stands to lose. Not only will the company's financial resources be threatened, but the marketer's image may be tarnished as well. Furthermore, when a marketer becomes firmly focused on one segment, it may be unable to move into others. When Porsche introduced its 924S model in 1987 and priced it at $19,999 to appeal to middle-of-the-road buyers, the company's image was seriously hurt. Sales dipped 45 percent. In response, Porsche removed the low-end models and jacked up prices 23 percent to resecure its luxury, high-price image in the United States where it markets half of its annual production.

Most marketers that employ market segmentation find it profitable to direct their efforts toward several market segments. This is known as *differentiated* marketing, or the multisegment strategy. It involves varying the marketing mix through products, prices, promotional efforts, distribution arrangements, or a combination of these elements. Sometimes companies pursue different segments under different brand names, as The Limited does through its Lerner's subsidiary.

In a market *atomization* strategy, each individual consumer is treated as a unique market segment. Although forecasts suggesting that all consumer markets would be atomized by the 1990s proved false, this approach is popular among industrial firms. It is based on the idea that each customer has unique needs and concerns that the marketer must satisfy. This approach is used for certain consumer goods, including custom-built homes, tailor-made suits and shirts, and furniture reupholstering.

Alert readers will recognize the atomization strategy in Rapp and Collins's forecast of a switch to one-to-one marketing as quoted in this chapter's opener. However, their timetable for a complete switch to one-to-one marketing— "the end of the eighties"—was incorrect. In a new book, *The Great Marketing Turnaround*, they predict that "individualized marketing" will predominate by the end of the 1990s.[14] And many other experts are now hailing "micromarketing" with the same enthusiasm. It is important to remember, however, that most of these experts, including Rapp and Collins, have a stake in direct-mail or direct-marketing agencies, and stand to profit from the conversion of managers to their point of view.

Nevertheless, there is a gradual move toward the atomization strategy, whether under this name or under the micromarketing or individualized marketing banners. For example:

> Stash Tea Co. included a tiny ad for its catalog on its tea-bag wrappers. About 150,000 tea drinkers responded . . . many mentioning such personal details as their favorite brew. Stash . . . sent just a catalog to one group of customers. Another group received the catalog and a chatty note that used information that the customers had included in their letters.[15]

The result of this experiment in personalized marketing was three times as many responses from the group receiving both letter and catalog (30 percent versus 10 percent). The Porsche letter quoted in the beginning of the chapter is another example. But not every effort toward atomization is a success. For example, Quaker Oats recently began a series of coupon mailings to 18 million households, intending to track each household's response via a unique identity number on coupon bar codes so that future coupon mailings can be personalized to each household based on prior responses. But the high cost (and, one suspects, an underwhelming result) has put this program on hold.[16] As we observed in the introduction to Part Three of this book, many practical obstacles remain to truly personalized marketing—so many that it is hard to imagine that most companies could ever develop *truly* personalized relationships with customers. It will be interesting to see where this trend leads us over the decade . . . and what the experts will predict in the year 2000!

In selecting a targeting strategy, the marketer must consider a number of factors. For instance, the firm's resources must be substantial if it plans to target several segments. Offering a wider selection of products and marketing programs greatly increases the costs of doing business. If resources are limited, a concentrated strategy may make more sense. A firm with a homogeneous product, perhaps a commodity, would be more likely to succeed using a concentrated strategy. Closely allied to product homogeneity is market homogeneity. If the market has the same basic wants, needs, and preferences, serving multiple segments may be difficult, if not impossible. Competitors' strategies must also be kept in mind. When competitors are employing a multisegment strategy, it may be appropriate to follow suit.

STRATEGIC POSITIONING

In Chapter 2, we saw how competitive activity can be likened to doing battle, complete with aggressors and defenders, attack plans, and actual assaults. The battlefield on which that warfare takes place has been said to be the mind of the consumer.[17] Consumers' behavior is guided by their perceptions of reality. Their interpretation of what they sense shapes their behavior. Marketers compete for consumers' attention by presenting various sensations that will allow them to arrive at a certain conclusion about a product or brand: Charmin is soft, Dove is for dry skin, Crest fights cavities. In this way, marketers' actions establish a distinct place for a product or brand in the minds of consumers. All the ways in which the marketer communicates with the consumer determine the psychological place that will be held by the product. Positioning, then, consists of all the actions taken by marketers to achieve this goal of managing the marketplace's perception.

Positioning Strategies

Strategic positioning is a result of communicated perceptions about a product or brand. It is different from image. Image is a global impression about a product, whereas a position assumes a reference point in the mind of the consumer, a point that is generally set in relation to the competition. The strategy is to find one or more characteristics that can be used to set apart the product or brand from competitors. Thus, in the highly fragmented shampoo market, which is overflowing with brands that promise body or control, renewed life for dull or damaged hair, elimination of split ends, and avoidance of dandruff, S.C. Johnson offered Agree, the shampoo that fights the "greasies." This unique positioning strategy quickly gained Agree a 7-percent share of the shampoo market.

Effective marketers understand the value of establishing a solid position in the minds of consumers. The following sections discuss some alternatives among which marketers can choose in deciding on a positioning strategy.[18]

Product Attributes

The most frequently used approach to positioning attempts to associate a product with a specific feature or characteristic. Beers, for example, have been positioned against one another on the basis of lightness versus heaviness, imported versus domestic, light versus dark color, and the like. A company's own brands also can be positioned on the basis of product features—Miller High Life versus Miller Lite on the calorie dimension, Beck's Light versus Beck's Dark on the color dimension. A new product can be positioned on the basis of a feature that has been ignored by competitors. Other products can be positioned on the basis of existing features. Thus, whereas most paper towels have established positions on the basis of absorbency, Viva was introduced with the advertising slogan "keeps on working," pushing durability, and was followed closely by Brawny with its emphasis on strength.

Sometimes marketers attempt to broaden their market by positioning their brand with respect to two or more product features. Tylenol, for example, was advertised as "more powerful but safer" than aspirin. Although this strategy has been successful for Johnson & Johnson, marketers must not try to be all things to all people. If too many product characteristics are added to the positioning strategy, the market can become confused and the product's position can become cloudy.

In global marketing in which the brand image is standardized over many cultures, the features of "high tech, high touch" (function/emotion) seem to transcend cultural boundaries and provide a mechanism to position products in multicultural markets.[19] BMW is positioned worldwide as "The Ultimate Driving Machine," whereas print advertisements for VISA in Saudi Arabia and other places display the card with a backdrop of high-quality, high-price possessions. These extremes of high tech and high touch hit at universally understood appeals and can result in high involvement on the part of the consumer. The thrill of driving is known the world over, as is the desirability of owning gold and diamond jewelry.

Benefits, Problem Solutions, and Basic Needs

Closely allied to positioning on the basis of product features is positioning on the basis of the consumer's reason for buying the product. Yogurt has been positioned as "healthful," diet soft drinks as "keeping America trim," and light (i.e., low-calorie) beer as "less filling." Brands as well as products have been positioned in this way. Procter & Gamble introduced gender-specific disposable diapers in the United States, Europe, and Japan to solve what consumers indicated were the biggest problems with existing diapers—leakage at the waist for boys and at the legs for girls. The new diapers feature a "leak-guard zone" in the front for boys and in the middle for girls. "Boys and girls won't change, so we did," says a Belgian commercial. "Vive la difference."

Price and Quality

Marketers can gain a competitive advantage by offering products that are perceived as high in quality. A high price sometimes acts as a signal of quality. (Porsche's prices are predicated on this theory.) Often marketers offer more in terms of service, added features, or other advantages to warrant the higher price. Thus New Balance, the Boston-based athletic shoe company, offered the following print ad for its top-of-the-line 1300 running shoe: "Mortgage the house. The New Balance 1300 costs more ($130) than any running shoe you've probably ever owned. But, then, it *offers* more." The ad goes on to explain what the product offers in the way of added comfort and protection, finishing with: "The 1300. Proof that in running, it pays to dig deep."

Specific Use

Products can also be positioned on the basis of a special use. Gatorade has been positioned as a beverage for athletes who need to replace body fluids; AT&T has positioned itself as an emotional link to distant loved ones; and Campbell's has long spelled out for consumers the value of serving soup for lunch. Arm & Hammer has suggested numerous uses for its ubiquitous baking soda—it can be used not only as a baking ingredient, but as a toothpaste, a bath salt, and a deodorant for refrigerators, garbage cans, sink traps, and kitty litter boxes.

Product User

Numerous marketers have established a position for their brand or product by associating it with some well-known personality. Star athlete Bo Jackson ("Bo knows") has sold Nike sneakers; Jim Palmer has advertised Jockey underwear; and Bill Cosby has characteristically and comically touted JELL-O pudding pops. Such positioning is not limited to profit-driven firms. For example, the former president's wife lends her name to the Betty Ford Center in Rancho Mirage, California, a drug rehabilitation center, and publicly promotes its benefits.

Marketers also position products on the basis of user categories. In 1968, Oshkosh B'Gosh was a small Wisconsin clothing manufacturer with children's clothes making up only 15 percent of its sales. When a local mail-order house displayed in a catalog the company's bib overalls for children, 10,000 orders resulted. The next year Bloomingdale's and other children's specialty stores picked up the line. By 1988, the company's sales had increased 2,160 percent, with children's clothes accounting for 90 percent of sales.

Positioning against a Competitor

Another approach to positioning is to take an explicit or implicit stance against a competitor. When a competitor has a well-entrenched position, it can often be exploited by a direct reference to it. One of the best known examples of this approach is Avis's "We're Number Two. We try harder." The implication is that Hertz, the leader, has become "fat and flabby" and that Avis offers better service because it must to survive. Gentlemanly advertising has been the rule for 75 years at discount clothier Jos. A. Bank. But recently it took off the gloves and fired a punch at its higher priced competitors. Ads indicated that Bank tailors literally rip apart the suits of competitors Brooks Brothers, Hart Schaffner & Marx, and Chaps by Ralph Lauren. The message further states that its suits are equal in quality, but 20 to 30 percent lower in price.

Comparative advertising has been used for years in the cola wars. But the approach is not accepted in Japan, where a taboo against competitive advertising is still strong despite an easing of rules on advertising by Japan's Fair Trade Committee four years ago. Pepsi plans to change all that. With only 2 percent of Japan's soft drink market versus Coke's 30 percent, Pepsi needs a radical approach to rise above the 5,500 other soft drinks for sale in Japan. Their solution: to run an ad comparing Coke and Pepsi. The *Wall Street Journal* describes it this way: "The ad features M. C. Hammer, the popular rap artist, drinking Pepsi between energetic gigs on stage. After switching to Coke, the rapper suddenly starts crooning the syrupy "Feelings," shocking his audience. But after he sips a Pepsi handed to him by an eager fan, the singer regains his high-energy rhythm."[20]

Positioning in Relation to Other Kinds of Products

Some products are positioned in relation to particular classes of products. For example, granola bars are positioned in relation to candy bars, other snack foods, and even desserts. Stouffer's Lean Cuisine line of low-calorie dishes is positioned against dinner entrees. Lever Brothers's Caress hand soap, instead of being pitted against other toilet soaps, is positioned as a bath oil product.

DEVELOPING A POSITIONING STRATEGY

The development of a positioning strategy is highly dependent on the techniques of marketing research. The procedure for identifying an appropriate position involves a series of seven steps that have been refined and improved in recent years.

1. *Determine the relevant product/market.* Many products are intended to satisfy more than one want or need. A candy bar, for example, is a source of energy, a snack, a dessert, a reward, and even a substitute for a meal. A product thus can be positioned in many different markets. The first step in positioning, therefore, is to list the possible wants and needs that the product may satisfy (i.e., the product/markets that might be served).

2. *Identify the competitors.* An upscale beverage such as Perrier bottled water has a variety of competitors, including soft drinks, other natural spring waters, alcoholic beverages, beer, even tap water. Generally there are both primary and secondary competitors. *Primary competitors* are those that compete to satisfy the core need—other natural spring waters in Perrier's case. *Secondary competitors* are indirect competitors, those that do not come immediately to mind when one thinks about what the consumer wants or needs. Marketing research can be very valuable here. Consumers can be asked what products they use to meet a particular need: "When you come in hot and thirsty after engaging in some athletic event, what do you usually do to quench your thirst?"

3. *Determine how consumers evaluate options.* When faced with a problem, people generally evaluate the possible solutions to see which one is most likely to satisfy their needs. The standards on which such an evaluation is based are the foundation on which product positions are built. The marketers must understand these standards and the relative importance of each one in the consumer's decision. Again, marketing research is needed.

4. *Learn how competitors are perceived.* The marketer must also identify the positions held by competitors. Those positions could be based on product attributes, usage situations, or user groups. Exhibit 8.6 shows the positioning of various domestic and foreign automobiles along two dimensions: product attributes and user groups.

5. *Identify gaps in positions held.* An analysis of the positions of competing products will often reveal areas in which there are many competitors. In Exhibit 8.6, for example, such a position is held by Lincoln, Cadillac, and Mercedes. A close inspection of the chart indicates, however, a gap in the lower right-hand corner. No one has provided a product that is reasonable in cost yet also has a high-spirited snazzy sports car appeal. This does not necessarily

EXHIBIT 8.6.   Perceptual map of brand images.

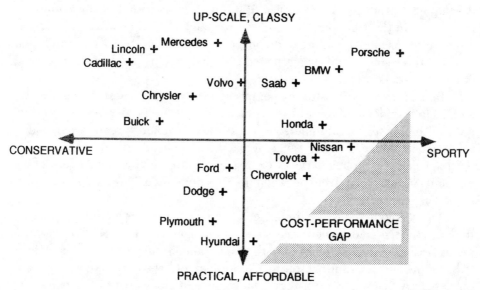

mean that efforts should be directed toward filling that gap; some analysis of the market segment represented by the gap must be made. That segment must meet the segmentation criteria of size, accessibility, identification, responsiveness, and stability.

6. *Plan and carry out the positioning strategy.* Once the target market has been selected and the desired position determined, the marketer must design a program that ensures that every piece of information about the product or brand that is transmitted to the market will create the intended perception in the mind of the consumer. This means that the product's characteristics and price must be consistent with the desired position and that the outlets chosen to distribute the product must also communicate the appropriate message. The promotional campaign is at the center of the positioning strategy—the promotional messages must also convey the appropriate information to the market.

7. *Monitor the position.* We have discussed how the environment in which marketers operate shifts over time. It is extremely important to make sure that the intended position is the one actually achieved by the product or brand. The actual position should be continually monitored and any needed adjustments made through changes in the marketing program.

TARGETING IN PRACTICE

We have focused thus far on the nuts and bolts of segmentation, targeting, and positioning. Taken together, they form three dimensions of the same picture, allowing the company to identify a group, target its marketing message on the group, and achieve a distinct position in that group's perception. Porsche's list development produced a segment of 300,000 car buyers out of the 80 million car owners in the United States. A careful analytical and creative process was required to develop a mailing and companion print advertising campaign that targeted this segment and strengthened Porsche's unique positioning relative to other sports cars.

Behind every successful segmentation, targeting, and positioning effort is an in-depth understanding of the segment. While the mass marketer can get away with only a general understanding of the customer, targeting demands a fuller acquaintance. The full range of analytical tools described in Part Two of this book must be applied in the effort to make a three-dimensional image of the targeted consumer pop from between the two-dimensional lines of the available marketing information.

This struggle to clarify the image of the customer is a recurring theme—both in modern management and within the pages of this book. Therefore, it seems fitting to end this chapter with two detailed examples of current efforts to bring the customer into better focus. Both are efforts of well-known marketing research firms, and both represent important steps toward the fantasy of "one-to-one marketing" described in this chapter's opening quote. In the first, the effort occurs at the neighborhood level, on the assumption that neighborhoods are characterized by common demographic and social attributes. In the second, the marketers focus on the value systems of consumers, trying to find useful patterns and groupings. Are these efforts useful? It depends on the marketer's situation and needs. You be the judge!

Marketing by the Neighborhood

Thomaston, Georgia, is a city where people gobble up the *National Enquirer;* zero in on roller derby; and are prodigious buyers of curling irons, hair-setting lotions, and deviled ham. They worship Hardee's. And they are much like the folks in Tarboro, North Carolina, and those in Childersburg, Alabama. In sharp contrast is Huntington, New York, where new homes, new station wagons, country club membership, and electric toothbrushes and depilatories are the shoppers' rage.

Through its computer system Prizm, Claritas crunches census data on the 240,000 neighborhoods in the United States into 40 different prototypes that often very accurately profile life within them, including the purchase behavior exhibited, from amount of aspirin in the medicine chest to number of above-ground swimming pools. From this mountain of information, Claritas is able to show differences in what would seem to be very similar communities.

Consider the yuppie communities of what Claritas calls Young Suburbia—a subdivision of River Mist, northeast of Atlanta—and Young Influentials— Vinings, Georgia. People in predominately white-collar, baby-boomer communities play a lot of tennis, belong to health clubs, play backgammon, and purchase the same number of umbrellas. Yet many more River Mist yuppies have children than those in Vinings. This explains why people in Vinings buy three times as much Irish whiskey, take twice the number of cruises, and buy pregnancy tests, which are shunned in River Mist.

This kind of information is invaluable to marketers wanting to rifle their marketing campaigns. A marketing manager for Mountain Bell Telephone Company in Denver believed his best prospects for his call-waiting and call-forwarding services were Young Suburbanites and other parents: "Our internal analysis showed that kids were it." Prizm showed that his best potential customers were childless Young Influentials—ambitious, active, and hating to miss that critical phone call!

Not all of Claritas's insights have proven fruitful. Prizm was not helpful in marketing medical encyclopedias, for instance. Buyers tend to be hypochondriacs, and they live in all neighborhoods. When Pillsbury Company used Prizm to locate eaters of its Green Giant frozen corn on the cob, Prizm indicated that they were predominantly black. But with such a huge market, Pillsbury could not put coupons in everyone's mailbox as it hoped it could do. It needed a finer tuned analysis. Also, Prizm's geodemographic analysis offers little in the way of understanding the personal touches needed to meet demand. It merely creates assumptions about the "why" that drives marketplace behavior—assumptions that marketers have to test. Yet Prizm is still hailed as a giant step forward in market segmentation.

General Motors's Buick division, for example, uses Claritas to keep a sharp eye on market goings-on. Its Buick Electra, at one time a status symbol akin to the Cadillac, had dropped its presence in wealthy, upscale neighborhoods and become the prestige car in rural areas. Said a GM marketing researcher, [These rural people] "liked to buy cars for image and like them to be big, prestigious, bulky." So when GM brought out a shorter, sleeker Electra, the company was understandably worried. But Prizm showed Buick to be right on the money: The new model had success, to use Prizm's terms, in the Furs and Station Wagon neighborhoods, in the Young Suburbias, and in the Pools and Patios, but lost ground in the Sharecropper neighborhoods.[21]

VALS and VALS2

Whereas Claritas divides the nation into 40 types of neighborhoods, SRI divides it into eight psychographic groups. This very different way to look at the nation is as powerful as Prizm when it comes to targeting products and services to specific consumer groups.

The original VALS, introduced in 1978, became the first psychographic segmentation system to be widely accepted in business. Many ad agencies use VALS to help them create fuller, more human targets than demographic statistics alone can provide, and a variety of marketers position their products to appeal to specific VALS segments. To create VALS, SRI drew on psychologist

Abraham Maslow's classic hierarchy of needs (see Exhibit 7.4), dividing the U.S. population into nine segments. The bottom segment comprises the Survivors, who are focused on the most basic survival needs. At the top, as in Maslow's hierarchy, are the Integrateds. Two separate paths lead to the top. The outer-directed path moves from Belongers to Emulators and, just below Integrateds, the Achievers. The inner-directed path leads from I Am Me's, to Experientials, to the Societally Conscious.

What do these titles mean? They are defined briefly below. (To make this list more interesting to read, determine which group describes you best.)

Need-Driven Segment

- *Survivors*—Very poor, mostly elderly women. Purchases focus on necessities. Buy used cars, household cleaners, hot cereals. Total 7 million.
- *Sustainers*—Poor, angry, resentful. Majority under 35 and without high school education. Purchase cigarettes, pancake mixes, candy, canned soups at high rates. Total 12 million.

Outer-Directed Segment

- *Belongers*—Aging, traditional, patriotic, content. Purchase American cars. Buy homes, freezers, and recreation equipment at high rates; high-tech stuff at low rates. Half of the Belongers graduated from high school. Total 64 million.
- *Emulators*—Ambitious, competitive, ostentatious. Emulate people they see as richer and more successful than themselves. Purchase more foreign and specialty cars, also home electronics. Consume high rates of beer and vodka. Graduated from high school. Total 17 million.
- *Achievers*—Successful, materialistic, hardworking, middle aged. Include lawyers, doctors, and business managers. A quarter graduated from college. Purchase luxury and mid-sized cars, various home appliances, wines. Total 35 million.

Inner-Directed Segment

- *I-Am-Mes*—Young, impulsive, experimental, very active. A third have college degrees, and many are still students. Income fairly low. Buy used, foreign subcompact cars, bicycles, stereos, jeans, beer. Total 5 million.
- *Experientials*—Youthful, often artistic. Seeking direct experience, action, personal development. Over a third are college graduates. Fairly well off. Purchase new foreign cars, camping and sports equipment, wines, yogurt. Total 8 million.

- *Socially Conscious*—Concerned and mission oriented, often active in social and political issues. Mature and successful. Three-fourths have college degrees. Purchase foreign cars, dishwashers, food processors, exercise/camping equipment. Consume higher than average rates of alcohol and seafood. Total 20 million.
- *Integrateds*—Psychologically mature. Open-minded and understanding. Consumption is quite varied. Total 1 million.

Did you decide which group best describes you? If publishers marketed books using VALS (they don't), this book would probably be targeted at Achievers—the successful professionals looking for additional insight to bring to their work—and at Emulators and Experientials as they begin to advance in their careers. The reason publishers don't use VALS is obvious when you think about how they distribute their products. Bookstores deliver to a broad cross-section of the book-buying public, and do not collect any detailed information about their customers. A highly targeted marketing strategy for a book would run into trouble when it came time to distribute it, because bookstores cannot supply publishers with specific market segments. (The situation is different with professional books, which can be targeted at specific professional groups quite accurately through direct-mail solicitations. If the publisher advertised this book to you through the mail, it was because of your job title or magazine subscriptions, not your VALS classification.)

In fact, many marketers find it difficult to put the VALS typology into practice. Although it may be helpful to visualize the target consumer as fitting the Integrateds profile, it may be impossible, or at least impractical, to focus distribution and advertising efforts on the less than 2 percent of Americans who fit this profile. These people don't hang out at any particular mall or even read any specific magazine. (Newsstands are crowded with titles, but presumably not with *Integrateds Life*.) Easier by far are efforts to target larger VALS segments, such as the 40 percent of Americans who fit the profile of Belongers. But the larger categories also create problems for marketers. As Jane Fitzgibbon, a senior vice president at the ad agency Ogilvy and Mather, explains, marketers would often say, "If 40 percent are Belongers, why should we bother with the rest?" Other users found the variations in segment size a problem. For example, when WISH-TV in Indianapolis used VALS to profile its audience, it found that two-thirds fell into only two segments. This turned out to limit the kinds of advertisers the station could attract. In addition to these practical problems, SRI decided that "the link between values and lifestyles and purchasing choices seems less strong than it had been," as Edward Flesh, the director of SRI's VALS program, puts it. So SRI went back to the public with a survey of 2,500 people in 1988, and gave birth in 1989 to VALS2.

VALS2 uses eight psychographic groups of almost equal size. They are said to be based on "unchanging psychological stances" rather than the more changeable lifestyles and values of the earlier VALS groups. Although some of the names are similar, SRI insists that the new groups are completely different.

At the bottom of the scheme are the Strugglers who, like the Survivors of VALS, tend to be elderly and poor. At the top are the Actualizers, replacing the old Integrateds, and characterized by high self-esteem and high incomes. Between these two extremes are six groups, arrayed in a two-by-three matrix based on whether they have high or low resources (economic, social, and psychological resources), and on whether they are principle-oriented, status-oriented, or action-oriented. These six groups are the core of the consumer market, and they are explained further below. (Again, which of these types best fits you?)

Principle-Oriented Segment

The purchases of these two groups are guided by views of how the world should be.

- *Fulfilleds*—High resources. Mature, responsible professionals. High education levels. High incomes, but value-oriented shoppers. Openminded.
- *Believers*—Low resources. Modest incomes, conservative attitudes. Focused on family and the church. Patriotic.

Status-Oriented Segment

The purchases of these groups are guided by the actions and opinions of others.

- *Achievers*—High resources. Focused on work; successful. Enjoy their jobs and families. Conservative, favor established products. Proud of their success and believe it is important for others to be aware of it.
- *Strivers*—Low resources, but values similar to Achievers. Style is important to them.

Action-Oriented Segment

The purchases of these groups are guided by desire for social or physical activity and risk.

- *Experiencers*—High resources. Young (median age of 25), and full of energy. Avid consumers, favoring new fashions and designs.
- *Makers*—Low resources. Self-sufficient and narrowly focused on their immediate environment of family, work, and recreation. Favor practical, functional purchases.

Is the new VALS2 much ado about nothing? Probably not. WISH-TV is certainly happier now that VALS2 shows the station's audience as falling into three major and four minor segments, rather than only two as in the old VALS.

More important, however, SRI has created a new standard that many advertisers and marketers find helpful in visualizing their target markets. It is based on 1988 survey data, giving it a 10-year advantage over the old VALS, and its categories are proving useful to a variety of consumer-products marketers.

It remains difficult, however, to find VALS segments using conventional marketing. But since the first VALS was introduced, considerable progress has been made in targeting individuals and narrowly defined segments. Four firms now specialize in providing what the trade affectionately calls "geodemographic cluster systems." Claritas was profiled previously. CACI, Donnelley Marketing Information Services, and National Decision Systems also specialize in delivering narrowly defined groups of consumers that share a cluster of common characteristics. Their customers, like SRI's, generally purchase annual subscriptions that give their marketing departments full access to the provider's databases and reports. SRI now collaborates with each of these research firms so that VALS2 profiles of their clusters are available to marketers. This means that a marketer can now use one of these databases to actually identify neighborhoods, mailing lists, or other practical groupings that are rich in a targeted VALS segment. VALS has come of age, and so, too, has targeted marketing.[22]

ADVANTAGE OR ADVERSITY

Regis McKenna recently argued that marketers must operate in a new "age of adversity," and many others seem to agree with his thesis that marketing is increasingly difficult.[23] The proliferation of brands and the growth of targeted marketing make success in most markets more difficult than ever before. A startling possibility is that the very tools that seem to solve our current marketing problems may create worse problems in the future! A continuing drive toward segmentation forces all players to move down this path simply to maintain parity with their competitors. If your competitors adopt segmentation schemes from Claritas and SRI, you may have to as well. And next year you will try to be the one who adopts the new ideas *first*. Aggressive, innovative pursuit of market segmentation, targeting, and positioning is now a major source of competitive advantage. As Rapp & Collins forecast in the chapter's opening quote, marketing does seem to be driving toward smaller and smaller groups, perhaps even to groups of one where market structure permits.

But, aside from the potential adverse effects on marketers' budgets and database systems, there may be some natural checks on this segmentation trend. In most markets, buying patterns eventually defy the logic of this process. There is often some limit beyond which further breakouts do not improve explanatory power. (Quaker Oats's coupon program may have bumped into one of these limits.) The world may simply refuse to divide neatly into ever-smaller boxes. A clue that this may be the case comes from the on-the-job observation of Larry Gibson, a former research director at General Mills, that "You can never find a way of classifying consumers so one group accounts for all the purchasing . . . there are always a distressing number of other people who use your product."[24] While distressing at first blush, this fact sounds an encouraging counterbeat to the truly distressing vision of ever-increasing market diversity and the adversity it creates for marketers. The tools of segmentation are exciting and in any event requisite in today's markets. But it is encouraging to think there may be some optimal level of segmentation in each market, as opposed to the now popular vision of segmentation *ad infinitum*, or at least to the smallest possible unit, the single customer.

Come to think of it, the individual might not be the smallest possible unit. One might imagine a further breakdown—for example, one based on role. A company could conceivably target individuals only in their role as grandparents, for instance, to make a personalized pitch for toys or baby clothes. Another pitch might focus on the same individuals, but with *different* personal information and in a different role. This game might truly go on *ad infinitum!* But we will leave such prognostications for the direct-marketing gurus—after all, they will be looking for a new pitch in a few years anyway.

9 PRODUCT DEVELOPMENT

The Business of Innovation

Good ideas don't begin around the conference table. They begin with the consumer.

—Charles Hooper, executive vice president and chief operating officer, Helene Curtis[1]

What's usually missing is going to the field and asking dumb questions, and smelling and feeling and getting in bed with the problem so that you understand the other side of it.

—Joe McPherson, director of innovation programs, SRI International[2]

What we have neglected is the ability to nurture fragile ideas into sturdy products before someone uneasy with the unfamiliar snips the idea at the stem. The nurturing process is called management, and innovation withers without it.

—BusinessWeek[3]

Proponents of the concept of a product life cycle maintain that every product moves through a series of four life stages, from introduction, to growth, to maturity, and finally to decline and eventual death. In fact, the product life cycle model is one of the most often-cited concepts in marketing. There is a great deal of circumstantial evidence to suggest that the model is valid, but little in the way of hard facts or clear theory to explain why it should be.

As a result, we will examine the model's underlying assumptions with a skeptical eye. But we do that later in the chapter. The model is too useful as a descriptive framework to abandon. In fact, it not only provides a good starting point for developing product strategies, but it also provides a fine scaffolding for our two chapters on product. This chapter takes the product from development (actually earlier, because how companies first devise product ideas is vital) to introduction (and failure, when things do not work out). Chapter 10 follows the product through its initial growth to its maturity and decline—or its revival, if innovations in product management and design can be applied successfully. Sometimes it is possible to foil the product life cycle and renew a product. Unlike people, products may have more than one life. (See Exhibit 9.1.)

We said the product life cycle has four stages, which it does as generally presented. However, the first stage of the life cycle is more accurately the inception and development of the new-product concept, although product inception is usually left out of the model—at least by authors less prurient than we are. Curiously, although in this modern society we now have a clear understanding of where babies come from, we remain a little vague about where new products come from. The creative process that generates new-product ideas is poorly understood and, in most companies, poorly managed. That the product life cycle model conventionally starts with the development stage and overlooks the inception of the idea in the first place is indicative of the lack of focus on product inception, both among academics and managers. Time and money traditionally go into product development and testing, but not into brainstorming, customer focus groups, and other sources of creative new-product ideas. Likewise, until recently, little emphasis has been placed on nurturing and evaluating new ideas within companies.

But before we move onto the exciting topic of inception, we review quickly what is meant by *product*. The product is, most simply, the tangible object a customer buys: a car, a box of paper clips. It can, however, be intangible. In marketing, services such as automobile repair and clerical work also

EXHIBIT 9.1. The product life cycle.

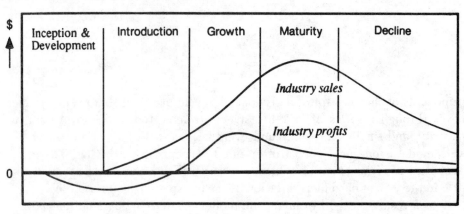

are considered products. It is immensely helpful, however, to broaden this simple view of the product to include a number of abstract concepts.

First, a product can be viewed as containing a certain amount of potential satisfaction; the full amount is not always realized. Perhaps you have heard the joke, "How do you know if a family has any teenagers living at home?" Answer: "The clock on the VCR isn't flashing." A recent survey by ad agency Ogilvy & Mather found that a pitiful 3 percent of VCR owners' total viewing time goes to watching programs they prerecorded—the potential for this and other fancy uses is not realized by most VCR owners even though manufacturers compete to cram more programming and other gimmicks into their products every year.[4]

A second way to look at the product is as a set of benefits sought by consumers. Often there is a core need—some primary, overriding desire for satisfaction. Such primary needs and wants provide individual buyers with their most important criteria for making an exchange decision. For instance, if a tennis racket buyer is seeking power as a core benefit, he or she will emphasize attributes such as high-tension strings, a strong metal frame, and a heavy handle above others, such as attractiveness, size of the sweet spot, or lightness. Closely allied to this concept of core need is the idea that the product presents a solution to a problem. In fact, it is through recognition of problems that many products are first conceived. No one would ever think of a paperweight unless they were working at their desk next to an open window on a windy day; there is no problem when the window is closed, and thus no need to be addressed by a new product. Few marketers have expressed the role of product as solution better than cosmetics maker Charles Revson, who is said to have stated that "in the factory we make chemicals, but in the drugstore we sell hope."

Another perspective portrays the product as a set of tangible and intangible attributes that are assembled into an identifiable form. (You might find it helpful to think of services as being mixes favoring the intangible attributes over the tangible ones.) In this view, each separate product category is defined by a commonly understood descriptive name—pillows, vacuum cleaners, shirts, personal computers. These categories are called generic products. The product life cycle model is most applicable at the level of the generic product. In other words, while individual models of personal computers may be on the market for only a year or two, it is the slower maturation of the category of personal computers in general that fits the descriptive and prescriptive elements of the life cycle model, as we will discuss shortly.

Customers have certain expectations about the products they buy, and it is helpful to recognize what is termed an *expected* product. The *generic* product is the core idea of a product. Yet consumers have expectations for it—what it will do, convey, and so forth. This is the expected product. In many cases, the manufacturer tries to offer a product that exceeds the customer's expectations—this is termed the *augmented* product. Thus, there are three nested definitions of the product, each a little broader and more elaborate than the preceding: generic product, expected product, and augmented product.

There is, however, an additional necessary layer of complexity. The product actually consists of a great deal more than merely the tangible or intangible item purchased. It has a core benefit or service, to be sure—a little bent piece of metal that holds papers together, for example. But in most cases the core benefit is supplemented by a series of additional attributes that, together, combine to make up the tangible product: packaging, styling, quality, brand name, and so on. In addition, these attributes are augmented by services, warranties, postsale service, delivery and installation, and so forth. Although these aspects of the product are trivial for a box of paper clips, they are sometimes of overriding importance for products such as personal computers.

As we think about the conception, development, and introduction of products, we need to think of products in all their complexity. A new product may look and work exactly like an old product, for example, but have a completely different set of associated services and be distributed in a different manner. Or it may simply be a different quantity and packaging of the same core or generic product. These are as much product innovations as the more traditional innovations involving actual modification of the makeup and workings of the core product itself. And all are fair game in the creative stage of the life cycle.

PRODUCT INCEPTION

New-product ideas can come from a recognition of need, as when 3M salespeople noticed that users of their sandpaper were troubled by the dust in their workplaces. From this definition of a problem came the idea for a solution: sandpaper that can be used wet so that no dust is created. Wet sandpaper is now a large category for 3M as a result of the problem solution it offers. Also, and probably more often, new-product ideas can be stimulated by technical developments. The advances in microchip design and the rapid decreases in their cost have stimulated the development of a host of consumer products with complex internal logic. Everything from personal computers to children's games takes advantage of this technology, representing creative ways to apply it to offer new benefits to consumers.

Which way is best? In theory, technology-driven product development is looking in the wrong direction. Simply because something comes out of the lab does not mean it is the most valuable thing for consumers. Better to be customer driven than technology driven in new-product development. But as a practical matter, many companies are strategically dependent on their mastery of certain technologies. The core technologies in which they specialize are what defines them and gives them competitive advantage. If they were to discover customer needs that their technologies did not address, it would probably be a mistake to try to satisfy these needs. The companies would soon find their efforts scattered and without focus, and they would soon lose their competitive strength if they strayed too far from their core technologies. As a practical matter, many companies' new-product ideas must be narrowed and focused by issues such as their areas of technical expertise, their distribution capabilities, and their customers' perceptions of them. Ideas are not easily constrained by such boundaries, so in practice companies evolve dozens of ways—unfortunately many of them unintentional and unmanaged—to discourage the bulk of the clever ideas their people generate. (This is the main obstacle to innovation, both in products and in all the various work processes of the company. But more on this point later.)

Having argued that customer-driven innovation must be tempered by other considerations in technology-based companies, we must now qualify this remark with the observation that in most cases technology-driven companies could go much farther toward balancing technical innovation with customer input. The evolution of the VCR industry provides a fine example.

Early VCRs were notorious for their complexity and incredibly confusing instruction manuals. According to a recent article on the topic, the typical first-generation VCR required the operator to hit the "set" and "select" buttons eight times simply to set the clock. Programming, for that 3 percent of the time when owners dared to try it, required the operator to hit the "on/off," "select," and "set" buttons 14 times![5] Designed by engineers and programmers, these technological nightmares were so unusable that they undoubtedly spread through the U.S. market more slowly than they might have otherwise. (The rate at which a novel product, or idea, diffuses through a market is an important issue in product introductions, and it can be slowed by poor design and marketing.) The cited article about VCRs concludes, in rather grim tones, that:

> The marketing implications of overwhelming consumers with all these complex and rarely used features may be more profound than companies realize. Manufacturers of consumer products are not only losing the interest of their customers but they're also alienating them. People have come to believe that somehow its their fault that they can't master these products. They have been made to feel like technological illiterates. And they don't like it.

Here, here! The failure of VCR manufacturers (and many other consumer-products companies) to design to the customer's requirements in the first place has created an opportunity for a second generation of product innovations—driven by customer needs, not technology. A manager with the Japanese VCR manufacturer, JVC, explains that "We've been getting more and more complaints about the difficulty of using VCRs. All video makers have been working hard to make them simpler."[6] On-screen programming is one innovation that resulted from this effort, and in fact VCR makers have hardly tapped the rich vein created by the initial user hostility of their products. User friendliness is emerging as a major product attribute—it is on its way to being part of the expected product—and the focus of product innovation is shifting at VCR makers as this dimension becomes more important in brand competition. Customers are now brought into the lab so that engineers can observe their machines in use. Customer complaints and opinions are solicited. The VCR industry is, albeit slowly, discovering marketing.

Regis McKenna, the public relations guru of Silicon Valley, has been marketing high-tech companies for decades, and he sees no reason why a technology-based company cannot be marketing oriented. In fact, "marketing oriented" fails to capture the full impact of his vision—the phrase seems to suggest a larger budget for the marketing department, whereas what McKenna envisions is an entire company that thinks marketing, even in the labs and product development facilities:

> Marketing is not a new ad campaign or this month's promotion. Marketing has to be all-pervasive, part of everyone's job description, from the receptionists to the board of directors. Its job is neither to fool the customer nor to falsify the company's image. It is to integrate the customer into the design of the product and to design a systematic process for interaction that will create substance in the relationship.[7]

Several fascinating concepts are presented in this quote. First, it is clear that the kinds of activities that firms such as our fictional Omni Consumer Electronics are undertaking—total quality programs, employee empowerment, and the like—are in keeping with McKenna's view that marketing ought to be part of everyone's job description. We are seeing the beginning of a revolution, but not a complete revolution—merely a 180-degree turn, putting the customers and the people who interact directly with customers at the top of the organization chart instead of the bottom. This means management must now be at the bottom, providing the support and nourishment needed to sustain these all-important customer relationships, much as the roots of a tree support and nourish its foliage. Traditionally the company has existed to serve its managers—a feudal model, if you will. (Don't believe for a minute the old saying that companies serve their shareholders—you don't see shareholders flying around on company planes.) In the traditional model, the company could serve its management either by focusing on customer-defined needs or by focusing on applications of its core technologies. But now the trend is to create firms that exist to serve their *customers*—surely this is what McKenna means when he refers to "substance in the relationship"—and these firms are by nature customer oriented—or for a better term, customer driven—whether or not they have a strong technical base. If this sort of firm's strategy is to nurture a core technology, it is only because this is the best way for customers to obtain improved solutions to a set of problems. The technology is truly secondary from the customer's perspective, and so must be from the company's as well.

Technology-rich DowBrands visualizes the balance of customer and technical considerations in a formula for innovation. According to Rob Grant, the marketing VP for new products, innovation is "the sum of consumer trends, leveraging of technology, and listening." Listening is accomplished through programs such as an Innovator's Club to recognize good new product ideas and the employees who generate them. The judges are typically line employees who use the products at home. Dow also gives awards and recognition to employees for new-product ideas, and has given away $30,000 to date in what Grant calls "an important investment in the intellect of our people."[8]

Raychem Corporation, maker of electronic and fiber-optic products for telecommunications and other industries, is another example of a very technically oriented company that nonetheless seems able to stay focused on customer needs with remarkable clarity. Raychem's founder and CEO, Paul Cook, sees a danger in being focused on the market without a complementary focus on the technology. He explains the company's balancing of technology and customer viewpoints as follows:

> Too many American companies are only immersed in their markets. They bring along whatever technology they think is necessary to satisfy a market need. Then they fall flat on their faces because the technology they deliver isn't sophisticated enough or because they don't know what alternatives the competition can deliver. We think of our business differently. Raychem's mission is to creatively interpret our core technologies to serve the marketplace. That means we don't want to be innovators in all technologies. We restrict our charter . . . to niches that can sponsor huge growth over a long period of time and in which we can be pioneers, the first and best in the world . . . Then we draw on those core technologies to proliferate thousands of products in which we have a powerful competitive advantage and for which our customers are willing to pay us lots of money relative to what it costs us to make them.[9]

However, Raychem's customer will be willing to pay high prices only if it reaps significant benefits from Raychem's mastery of its core technologies. Raychem adds value from the customer's perspective primarily by virtue of its leading knowledge in various technologies.

Also interesting is McKenna's vision of marketing's purpose as being "to integrate the customer into the design of the product and to design a systematic process for interaction that will create substance in the relationship." The upside-down organization designed to serve the customer is no longer focused on making and selling products. It is, or ought to be, focused on *developing* products. This is a subtle but profound insight. From the customer's perspective, everything within the organization's walls is transparent and trivial. Only the delivered product and the transactions needed to deliver it matter. Moreover, the delivered product is never good enough. Life is not yet perfect, so customers are eager for new and better products. They wish to solve problems more easily and at decreasing cost, and they are open to new problem definitions and new products to solve these problems. This puts the product at the very core of the new marketing-driven company. (Perhaps it is fitting that this issue is covered in the center of this book.) It also puts greater weight on new-product development than ever before, necessitating, as McKenna indicates, a "systematic process" for customer-driven innovation. This process, both in its conventional forms and in the newly evolving forms designed for the new customer-driven companies, is the subject of the next section.

DEVELOPMENT

Exactly what is a "new" product? This question can be answered in many ways. From the perspective of management, a new product is anything that an organization believes to be a new product. This approach makes some sense, because in most cases such "newness" results in new research, new organization, new advertising campaigns, and other new ingredients in the marketing mix.

What ultimately matters, however, is whether the customer sees anything new and important in the product's introduction. Many me-too products spark only management's imagination these days! Think for a minute about the new products you noticed on the shelves of your local grocery store last year. A few? Dozens? And how many did you adopt? Whatever the number, it falls incredibly short of the 10,301 new food products and the 2,863 nonfood products introduced to grocery stores during 1990![10] (And the number of new products grows every year—15,401 were introduced to grocery stores in 1991.)[11] One of Campbell's hard-and-fast rules (one it should have established earlier, as we discuss shortly) is that new products must be substantially better than the old ones with which they compete, *from the customer's perspective.* This means they must be given a preference rating in consumer tests of 1.6 or more to 1 when compared with the competition. This is a substantial difference—and a hurdle that most of those 13,164 new grocery-store products from 1990 would have failed to clear. As Gordon McGovern, CEO of Campbell's, puts it, "The consumer is ready for improved quality and service. Delivering it is the true secret of new product success."[12]

New products can be modifications, minor innovations, or major innovations. A major innovation is an item that has never been sold by any other organization, as in Intel's introduction of the semiconductor and Searle's development of NutraSweet. But not all innovations need be so astounding. Inspired by a Magic Marker, Chesebrough-Ponds developed a nail polish in a pen. Called "Polishing Pen," this product brought quick praise from the cosmetics industry. Said an industry expert, "It's the best concept I've seen in cosmetics in 10 years."[13] But it may also have been the simplest. Rather than offer a new kind of nail polish, the developers simply changed its packaging—and changed the ways the product can be used as a result.

A recent study has shown that 70 percent of the new products brought to market by large U.S. firms are modifications, 20 percent are minor innovations, and 10 percent are major innovations.[14] The same study showed that major innovations receive greater support from top management, a key ingredient in the success of new products.

Booz, Allen & Hamilton uses a model that groups new products into six categories:[15]

1. *New-to the-world products*—products such as cellular telephones and robotics, which result in entirely new markets.
2. *New product lines*—new categories of products that allow entry into new markets. R.J. Reynolds, for instance, added a chain of bagel stores to its line of cigarettes.
3. *Additions to existing product lines*—taking an established product line (e.g., Jell-O Pudding Pops) and extending the product or brand (e.g., Jell-O Gelatin Pops).
4. *Improvements in or revisions of existing products*—providing greater perceived value or satisfaction or replacing existing products with better products. Coca-Cola replaced its regular Coke with its slightly sweeter New Coke.
5. *Repositioning*—changing the perception of an existing product, as when Kellogg's advertising linked its all-bran cereals to cancer prevention (until the FDA forced the company to drop the claim).
6. *Cost reductions*—offering similar value at a lower cost. Scott Paper has offered its facial tissues, toilet tissue, and paper towels at prices up to 30 percent lower than competitors' products.

Conventional wisdom has recently shifted toward favoring the bottom half of this list. For example, many managers and expert commentators have been struck by the fact that Japan's competitiveness, and losses by the United States to Japanese manufacturers in many markets, seems to be driven by an emphasis on small, incremental innovations by the Japanese companies. The U.S. companies hit an occasional home run, but the Japanese companies hit single after single and ultimately win the game. As a result, product developers are now urged to add extensions to existing brands or improve their performance rather than to chase fundamental innovations that result in new-to-the-world products. But this is stupid advice, to put it politely.

The Japanese firms may have been weak historically in fundamental R&D, but they compensated for this with better overall product inception and development—better because it is more customer oriented, more efficiently managed, and far more rapid. Now they are beefing up their research as well, and will soon be hitting both home runs and singles. If U.S. firms bench their heavy hitters in the effort to learn how to hit singles, they will lose much more market share. The issue boils down to leadership, leadership of a market in the customer's eyes, which means advancing the customer's cause through product development more often and consistently than competitors. As McKenna says, "in marketing, what you lead, you own. Leadership is ownership."[16] The successful Japanese companies own their markets because they have led them, and if U.S. competitors mistake the issue and focus on small-scale innovation with an eye toward small-scale market share goals rather than market leadership, they will only strengthen the position of the Japanese leaders in the customer's mind. On the other hand, if they can continue to lead in major innovations, and also learn how to hold onto their lead with continuous smaller innovations, market leadership will be a realistic goal.

Competition, both foreign and domestic, is a major force in spurring innovation. But this incentive is countered by social and governmental constraints (e.g., regulations designed to protect the environment and increase consumer safety), the high costs of research (particularly for small companies), the tendency of firms to emphasize short-term return on investment, and the high cost of borrowing funds. Nevertheless, the key to success in world markets is innovation, and frequently the door to marketing superiority is improved technology.[17] As Richard Swingle, Compaq Computer Corporation's director of strategic marketing, says, "50% of our revenues are from products introduced in the last year. We eat our own children. If we don't, someone else will. Last year we introduced 12 new computers."[18]

Older products lose their luster and are withdrawn from the market, creating a need for new products to take their place. New products can renew a faltering image, reduce the firm's overall risk, and open up new markets and distribution channels. It is therefore alarming to see that R&D spending is again shrinking in the United States after a decade of growth.[19]

Organizing for New-Product Development

At most companies, responsibility for new products takes one of four basic forms. Many companies use the product or brand manager approach. Each manager has complete responsibility for one product or brand—determining objectives, developing strategies, setting prices and advertising budgets, and working with the sales force. The manager is also responsible for creating new-product concepts and shepherding them through the development process. Often, however, managing both new and existing products is too extensive a job for one person. Some companies therefore use a system in which each new product is given to another manager after it has been successfully launched. R.J. Reynolds, for instance, has a management group whose sole task is to dream up new cigarette brands. Once a new brand has proved itself in test markets, it is assigned to another group within the company.

Other companies form new-product committees, generally composed of top managers from several departments. These committees meet to develop new ideas; once the task is complete, their members return to their regular positions. Although this approach has the advantage of getting top managers involved in new products right away, it has certain drawbacks: It takes up valuable executive time, and committee members have a tendency to put their own interests above those of other members. Also, new-product committees tend to take a long time to devise recommendations.

Other organizations set up permanent, full-time new-product departments. Such a department usually is high in the corporate structure and has considerable power. Sometimes it works in conjunction with a temporary new-product committee. Generally this department plans and coordinates all the activities involved in new-product development—from generating ideas to supervising the development process.

A newer approach is the venture team. At larger companies such as Dow Chemical, Monsanto, and Westinghouse, groups of managers, each a specialist in a certain area, are given the task of bringing a specific new product to market. The team combines needed resources and expertise, such as product design, engineering, capital management, market analysis, accounting, and marketing. To promote creativity, members in such a group are usually excused from regular duties and report directly to top management.

The key, but unspoken, issue in any of these structures is how they relate to the customer (the traditional emphasis is unfortunately on how the new-product developers relate to the rest of the *firm*, not to the customer). If they have an arms-length relationship with customers—for example, through close-ended surveys conducted by the marketing department's subcontractors—then they are unable to play the catalytic role McKenna sees for product development in the new marketing-driven firm.

We discuss in the following sections the typical stages in the development of new products. These seven stages are generating ideas, screening ideas, developing and testing the concept, conducting a business analysis, product development, test marketing, and commercialization.

Stage 1: Generating Ideas

The sources of new-product ideas are many and varied.[20] Customers sometimes write letters suggesting new products. One study of technological innovation found that in 74 percent of 137 cases studied, the source of the new idea was the customer.[21] Many companies encourage their employees to make suggestions. General Electric gives out $2 million annually in bonuses to employees who contribute successful product ideas, whereas 3M gives trophies and certificates to innovative employees. In addition, a firm's scientists and technicians often make discoveries that lead to new products. There is evidence that innovative companies give their employees a great deal of freedom to tinker with new ideas. At 3M, one story has it that a fired scientist kept sneaking back into the lab to develop an improved asphalt shingle and eventually won a promotion to vice president! Top managers are another source of new-product ideas. There are also consulting firms that specialize in idea generation. These "think tanks" assess the client's resources and objectives and devise concepts.

One widely used method for generating ideas is called brainstorming. This approach is based on the recognition that the really new ideas often mix several previous ideas to produce something that is nonobvious and exciting. (Brainstorming is a widely used *term*, but for some reason the *practice* is rarely used, even though it is simple, easy, and beneficial.) Group discussion sessions are held to generate as many new ideas as possible. The group generally consists of six to ten people. A specific problem or goal is set at the beginning of the meeting, but group members are encouraged to be as wild as they want in suggesting solutions. Practicality is not important in a brainstorming session. No idea is criticized, and hence no ideas are held back. As ideas start to flow, one leads to another. Within a short time, hundreds of ideas can be on the table, so it is important to have someone write down ideas on a chalkboard or pad. Only after ideas are generated freely and noncritically can the group look at them critically and sort out the most promising.[22]

A study of over 700 companies found that firms are increasingly combining the idea-generation step with an analysis of the firm's overall business and new-product strategy.[23] In this way, new-product ideas are more likely to reflect the company's overall goals. This process includes the establishment of strategic roles for new products, as well as formal financial criteria to be used in measuring the performance of new products. This firmer understanding of the purpose of new products has greatly reduced the mortality rate for new-product ideas. In 1968, it took 58 new-product ideas to come up with one successful new product. In 1982, the mortality rate was reduced to an average of seven ideas per successful new product,[24] and the mortality rate is thought to still be declining gradually.

Although no quantitative studies are available yet to prove it, a trend is occurring toward incorporating customer ideas and evaluation into the idea-generation stage. This is done indirectly when companies such as DowBrands, GE, and 3M encourage employees to generate ideas, for this pushes the employees to think like consumers and to make informal observations of consumers in their daily lives. It is also done directly—many more focus groups and new-product testing labs are now used in which customers are directly exposed to new-product concepts and even asked to help develop or refine them. The Japanese antenna shops, in which experimental products are displayed to see how consumers react to them, are one indication of where this trend is going.[25]

Stage 2: Screening Ideas

Once a large pool of ideas has been generated, the next step is to reduce it to a more manageable size. Three general criteria for screening ideas have been suggested.[26] New-product ideas should fit into the organization's overall strategy. They should also build on the company's resources and skills—financial, technological, and managerial. Finally, an idea must have sufficient market potential to justify further consideration. (Again, this is the conventional wisdom, but an explicit evaluation by customers does not come into the equation.)

Marketers often establish a formal method for choosing which ideas they want to examine more closely. For example, The Center for Concept Development uses an elaborate new-product evaluation form.[27] It rates product ideas on dozens of factors, such as effectiveness, reliability, appearance, design, potential volume, entry position, and regulatory environment. (In general, firms will want to develop their own lists rather than use the factors that are important to someone else.) Each factor is then lumped with similar ones into a factor group, which in turn is combined with other groups into what this consulting firm calls "major aspects." There are only four of these: item, company, environment, and venture. To understand what they mean, examine the factor groups of which these aspects are comprised:

- *Item*—performance, salability, defensibility, marketing.
- *Company*—technology, production, market.
- *Environment*—competition, suppliers, government.
- *Venture*—support, investment, strategy.

If you want to use this structure for rating new-product ideas, develop specific criteria for each factor group. For example, list the factors that ought to be related to the performance of the new product. Then rate each idea on each factor using a 1–3 (weak to strong) scale, and sum scores across until you know on which major aspects the idea is weak and strong.

Richard Swingle of Compaq, cited earlier, explains that "We don't worry about how to save face. Some new products get 'critical mass' that is unstoppable at some companies, no matter what. It's going to market, no matter what. Not at Compaq." He is talking about a powerful force that both limits initial acceptance of ideas and, equally dangerous, limits the company's ability to derail a new product when it isn't holding up to expectations. This force is inertia, the tendency for organizations to resist change. It is much easier to keep any company going in the same direction than to make it do an about-face. This is why it is often difficult for companies to become good at recognizing and using novel ideas. Even if they do become innovative in this way, inertia can get them on the backswing by institutionalizing a product development effort. A company must evaluate a new product periodically during development, *as if it were under evaluation for the first time.* Whatever screening and analysis is performed to select ideas in the first place ought to be repeated as they are developed, perhaps at periodic benchmarks, so that losers can be spotted by management rather than by the market.

Stage 3: Developing and Testing the Concept

Throughout the stages of idea generation and screening, product developers work only with the kernel of an idea, a general concept. In this third stage, they try to make that idea more specific. For example, if they have determined that they will produce a new candy bar, the answers to the following questions might help them formulate a more specific concept from the general idea:

1. *Who will buy the new product?* A candy bar can appeal to children, adults, or the elderly—or to all three groups.
2. *What is the primary benefit of the new product?* A candy bar may appeal as a sweet, a high-energy snack, or an emergency food for diabetics.
3. *Under what circumstances will the new product be used?* A candy bar may be offered to children as a reward, or used as a meal substitute, or eaten by diabetics suffering from too much insulin.

After a concept has been developed, the next step is to test it. Consumer reactions are obtained by using a verbal description or a picture of the product and asking for candid opinions. At this point, the developers want to know how they can improve the product idea, and the best way to find out is to ask the consumer. This is commonly accomplished in the toy industry by simply inviting kids to come and play in a new-toy lab—and watching what they do and don't play with. When the company has a winner, this method makes it obvious. For example, when Huffy's new Street Rocker kid's bike with a radio on the handlebars was tested, new-product development manager Wayne Beiser found that the product "was so popular, we eventually had to pull it from the research cells because we couldn't get information on any of the other products we were testing."[28] In the computer industry, the products are brought to business or industrial consumers at designated test sights, and developers work closely with these consumers to spot problems and refine designs. This approach is applicable in any concept-testing effort, and companies increasingly look for ways to use consumers in concept testing.

The scale of new-product development sometimes works against effective new-concept testing, especially at larger companies. When Compaq develops dozens of new computers, or Campbell Soup develops hundreds of new foods, it is difficult to give each product the individual attention it deserves. In fact, this may be why Campbell Soup has a relatively poor success record with new products. Throughout the 1980s, the company pushed hard to expand lines and introduce new products. It introduced over 700 new items from 1980 to 1990. A few of these really took off—Great Starts breakfasts and Le Menu frozen dinners, for example. But most went unnoticed or, like Fresh Chef ready-to-eat soups and salads, died expensive deaths. (This line lost $20 million before Campbell gave up on it.)[29]

Oddly, Campbell seemed to have a surfeit of new-product ideas in the 1980s, but to be inept at distinguishing good ideas from bad. The cost of this failure was high—the company's earning per share grew at 8.8 percent from 1980 through 1989, lower than eight other food companies, and well below the industry average of 12.9 percent.[30] The company underwent a costly restructuring in 1989, cutting 2,800 manufacturing jobs and closing nine factories in one of the most striking recent examples of the impact of product development processes on company performance. According to Anthony J. Adams, Campbell's VP of marketing research, "We're definitely blowing the whistle on mindless line extensions."[31]

Stage 4: Business Analysis

The next step in the new-product development process is to project costs, profits, return on investment (ROI), and cash flow if the product is placed on the market. Business analysis is not a haphazard process; it is a detailed, realistic projection of maximum and minimum sales and their impact on the company's financial health. Projections of potential sales at various prices need to be made, as well as detailed cost projections for different volumes of production. Start-up and continuing costs, fixed and variable costs, and the impact of economies of scale need to be determined. Tentative marketing plans need to be set, along with the costs associated with them. Finally, a set of full-blown budgets is required to estimate the potential return on the product. The outcome of this analysis is key, for it is not enough to produce a new product that consumers like—it must also be profitable for the company to make and sell the product. Every new-product concept must satisfy the parties on both sides of the equation, not only on one side or the other!

The assessment of sales and costs is not an easy task, and sometimes the rules for evaluation can be too stringent. Campbell's Prego spaghetti sauce almost failed in the business analysis stage. Corporate policy required a new product to show a profit in one year, but Prego was not expected to do so for three years. Astute managers, realizing that the one-year policy held back product development, changed the rules—and, luckily for Campbell, Prego went national.

The business analysis must also include an assessment of the amount of risk the company will face if the new product is introduced. In general, the greater the degree of newness, the greater the risk. Production facilities, because of the huge investment they require, and marketing activities, because of their importance to consumer satisfaction, are two key areas to analyze in terms of risk. If the new product can be produced using existing production and marketing capabilities, the risk is lower. Less investment in new plant and equipment will be needed, and the marketer can benefit from already acquired knowledge of the market. On the other hand, greater tolerance of risk can lead to greater rewards. The study mentioned earlier found that the highest risk ideas (accounting for 30 percent of all new-product introductions) provided 60 percent of the "most successful" new products.[32]

Stage 5: Product Development

In the next stage, the new-product concept is given a tangible, concrete form: A prototype is made. The prototype can be seen and held, and its benefits and attributes can be demonstrated. Production engineers and R&D specialists construct a model; the marketer develops a brand name to match the idea or concept; packaging is designed; and the major elements of the marketing mix are put together. The positioning strategy is also examined.

Gillette Company uses a unique method to test its shaving products during this stage. Each day about 1,000 men and women in a dozen countries use Gillette prototype products either at home or at the company's facilities. They rate the products in terms of the closeness and comfort of the shave. In addition, numerous testing devices are employed: High-speed cameras and electronic gadgets measure whisker length to within millionths of an inch. Plastic casts of shaved faces are used to compare the closeness of shaves, and technicians measure and weigh the amount of stubble removed. These data—along with reports from physicists, statisticians, and metallurgists—are fed into computers that store knowledge about every aspect of shaving accumulated over some five years.

At the product development stage, many new ideas bog down for months or years, or wander off track completely. At this stage, many different functional areas of the firm are called upon to cooperate in the creation of prototypes and the development of production or delivery processes, marketing plans, and the other elements required to make the idea a reality. The traditional, and most logical, approach is to move the product from functional area to area sequentially, so that each element of product development is handled in turn. But this approach is no longer viable, as *Business Week* recently reported:

> Many laggards have clung to a product development process derisively dubbed the "bucket brigade." Someone in a research lab comes up with an idea. Then it is passed on to the engineering department, which converts it into a design. Next, manufacturing gets specifications from engineering and figures out how to make the thing. At last, responsibility for the finished product is dumped on marketing. . . . Plans are constantly pushed back down the chain to fix problems that could have been avoided. . . . The outcome: slow response times, high costs, and shoddy quality. Compare that system to the system most Japanese companies use. They take what's called a "fast cycle" approach to development—whipping out new product and reacting in a flash to shifts in consumer preference. To accomplish that, managers make communication a top priority at the earliest stages of a project. They pull together a team of experts from each business function to anticipate glitches and to guide the project through the organization from start to finish.[33]

Our separation of the product development discussion into stages should not be misinterpreted as indicating that the product should be developed in a series of separate stages. These various tasks must be accomplished, but they need to be integrated into a whole, to be pursued simultaneously via constant, detailed communication among all parties involved. This is the fast-cycle approach the Japanese have perfected, and one good way to make it happen is to form multidisciplinary product development teams. But how do you create and manage teams so as to achieve a fast product development cycle? According to

Derwyn F. Phillips, vice chairman of Gillette, one of the secrets is to avoid heavy top–down management of the process:

> The tendency for walls to exist between functional groups is common. For example, people in the product development cycle may throw an idea over the wall and hope the other functional group will run with it. However, I think that U.S. companies are recognizing this and trying to build more team approaches to new product development. There is a focus on putting individuals together in teams, agreeing to a set of objectives, and letting them get on with it without all of the hierarchical intervention that has gone on in some of the historic structures.[34]

Tom Peters, an advocate of the team-based approach, has proposed a variety of factors that ought to help teams succeed:

- *Multifunctional involvement*—The team needs to include everyone with an interest in the new product, including customers.
- *Simultaneous full-time involvement*—The key team members need to be fully committed to the project, not torn between the new product and their regular tasks.
- *Colocation*—The entire team should work in the same physical location.
- *Constant communication*—Ongoing communication must cross all the functional boundaries, and all team members need to be involved in routine decision making.
- *Fully committed resources*—The team should not have to share resources between the new-product development and any ongoing activities of the firm.
- *Outside involvement*—Customers, suppliers, and other external groups with an interest in the product need to be participants in the entire development process.[35]

Note that these rules are likely to strain the average company's organization and culture, which helps explain why product development efforts are commonly fraught with difficulty!

Stage 6: Test Marketing

During test marketing, marketers attempt to measure the reactions of potential consumers of an actual product in a real-world setting. They observe the performance of the product in selected markets and evaluate its probability of success in larger markets. The company can learn about distributors' attitudes toward the product, as well as gauge the reactions of competitors. A test market often provides information that can be used to improve the marketing strategy, such as what type of advertising to use or how to devise point-of-purchase displays.

In a test market, the firm advertises, prices, and distributes the product, just as it will when it goes national. If it finds, for example, that retailers will not give the product the necessary point-of-purchase space, the firm can correct the problem at small expense before encountering it on a national scale. Most companies realize that it is preferable to spend $1 million in a test market than to spend $20 million on a product failure in a national market.

Many marketers have become less enthusiastic about test marketing in recent years. Test marketing is slow, expensive, and open to competitive spying and sabotage. For example, when General Foods tried to test-market frozen baby food, Gerber, Libby, and Heinz bought up all the product in the test markets. Thus, many marketers today are avoiding test markets. Quaker Oats grabbed 40 percent of the granola snack market with its Chewy Granola Bars and chocolate-covered Dipps without test marketing these products, and P&G successfully launched its Folgers instant decaffeinated coffee without test marketing. But not all firms are successful in taking this approach. For example, Campbell's Pepperidge Farm Star Wars cookies took a beating when the Star Wars craze faded soon after the product was rushed onto the market without a test.

Stage 7: Commercialization

Once a new product has been tested successfully, it is ready for commercialization, or full-scale production and distribution to the target market. Although the previous steps are expensive, the major investment in terms of both production and marketing is made at this stage. Miller Brewing Company, for instance, invested $247 million to build a highly automated plant in Albany, Georgia, to brew its Lite beer. Fortunately, the company bet on a winner; the light beer market grew rapidly and is still in the growth stage of its life cycle, while regular beer is in a no-growth maturity.

Innovation is inherently risky, and any strategies that help innovators minimize their exposure to investment risk during the early stage of the product life cycle are especially valuable. Merck, the New Jersey–based pharmaceuticals company, often invests large sums in manufacturing facilities for a new drug well before the FDA has given it permission to market the product. However, the firm tries to minimize its risk by postponing this kind of gamble as long as possible, even if it means living with difficult and expensive makeshift production at first. For example, rather than erecting a $200 million plant to make Primaxin, a new antibiotic that wipes out most bacteria known to science, Merck produced it in ten complex steps at several of its existing plants.

Companies rarely enter national distribution all at once. Rather, they roll out the new product, going from one geographic area to another. (This can be seen as another way to reduce risk during product introduction.) For example, U.S. Pioneer Electronics Corporation brought its videodisc to market in 1980. It began by test marketing the disc in four cities: Syracuse, Dallas–Fort Worth, Minneapolis–St.Paul, and Madison. Every 60 to 90 days thereafter, Pioneer added four additional cities. The rollout was not completed until 1981. Rolling out makes it possible to spread the substantial costs of a new-product launch over a longer period and provides an opportunity to fine-tune the marketing program as the rollout progresses.

FROM INCEPTION TO BIRTH

When the product is first introduced to the market, it enters the second stage of its life cycle. This move from inception to introduction is a critical transition because the product is now put before customers for the first time, at least outside of the artificial environment of concept evaluation and product testing. To keep with the life cycle analogy, the product is born into its market. The challenges facing the company are many and varied as the focus of innovation expands from the internal product development effort to the challenges of bringing the innovation to life in the market. As Paul Cook of Raychem Corporation sees it:

> Innovation is as much about sales or service or information systems as it is about products. We spend twice as much on selling as we do on research and development, so creativity from our sales force is just as important as creativity from the labs. How do you sell a product no one has seen before? How do you persuade a customer to accept you as a sole source for an important component?[36]

According to the product life cycle model, sales at introduction are expected to start slowly, then grow at an accelerating rate as early adopters—the innovators in the market—try the product, and others then hear about it and give it a try. If the product has no competitors, as is often the case with a truly novel and original product, it owns the entire market at this stage. But the market is small; that is, the served market is small, as the new product has not yet penetrated most of its potential market. How long the first entry has before competitors join it will determine to some extent how much of an advantage the first entrant will have in later competition.

The life cycle model elaborates even further on the basic situation at introduction. The typical introductory stage is generally characterized by low and gradually growing sales, with high costs and low margins for the producers. The producers are not very experienced at making the product yet, and are not doing it at high enough volume to achieve any potential economies of scale. Fortunately, little competition exists at this stage, although the company usually spends a lot of time worrying about how and when new competition will enter. A protectable product (through patents, trade secrets, or other high barriers to entry) is an obvious advantage in this game.

Because the product is new, the major marketing task is to educate potential consumers. Awareness and knowledge of the new product must be built from scratch in many cases. (You may be accustomed to grabbing a vacuum cleaner when you want to clean the rug, but think for a minute how you might talk people into buying one if they have never used anything but a broom.

Would it be difficult to convince them to give you 20 or 30 times the cost of a broom for this unfamiliar contraption?)

Although segmentation and targeted marketing may be all the rage in mature consumer products right now, you are unlikely to see them in introductory-stage products. A generalized approach to the marketing task, with a mass-market positioning, is common in the introductory stage. (As the product and its market matures, an increasing number of competitors will begin to carve niches out of the mass market that is created in the introductory and growth stages of the life cycle.)

Much of the most visible marketing in our society is generated in the growth or maturity stages of the life cycle, not in the introductory stage. Marketing budgets are usually low in introduction, and in fact the markets themselves may seem quite small. Who would have guessed the size of the personal computer market back in Apple's early days? And who would have imagined Apple might be buying ad time during the Super Bowl within a decade! Because big U.S. companies seem to have trouble innovating, many of the producers of novel introductory-stage products are entrepreneurial and not accustomed to, or financed for, high-profile marketing. As a result, managers rely heavily on word-of-mouth, public relations (for generating news coverage), and, in many markets, direct sales.

The producer of an introductory-stage product is generally very close to its customers, at least the few who have discovered it and are willing to take a risk on the new product. This is especially true in business-to-business products and services, but is also true in consumer products. The marketer of an introductory-stage product simply cannot afford to be anything but customer focused. Customers must be found and convinced that the new product is worth a try, which means marketers must really understand what the new product does for a customer, what the switching costs are, and how their product generally fits into the customer's world. These issues are considered vital at this stage, and all of management's attention is focused on how the initial customers react. The product may be modified constantly and extensively, and the sales and marketing strategy may evolve rapidly, in response to this early customer feedback. (Often management is directly involved in customer support and in sales.)

The customer orientation that characterizes most introductory-stage products and their managers is of special interest given the current effort in companies to capture this kind of customer orientation in later stages of the product life cycle. The new vision of the corporation, with strong customer ties, little hierarchy, and rapid learning based on market experience, is in many ways a description of the entrepreneurial marketer of growth-stage products. This vision can be seen as an effort to return to childhood for many companies and products.

Oddly, this customer orientation that characterizes the introductory stage is not even mentioned in standard write-ups of the product life cycle model. Yet it is clearly an important and natural element of product introduction—and apparently one that companies lose as their products mature and they begin to jockey for position in a growing field of competitors. At least if a product idea has sprung from recognition of a customer need, management enters the product life cycle with a pure customer orientation. As the concept moves from inception to development and is then introduced to the market, this purely customer-oriented concept is shaped by a variety of practical concerns, many of them adding technical and operational orientations to the concept. But if the core customer benefit has been preserved through this process, it is still there upon introduction, and the task of management is to communicate the benefit and refine the product's ability to deliver this benefit. If the concept has been displaced by internal concerns, or was simply misconceived to begin with, introduction will reveal this fatal flaw rapidly: Customers won't buy the product.

One way to look at the introductory stage of the product life cycle is as the beginning of a fall from grace. Even if customers buy the concept and new-product sales start to grow, the practicalities of manufacturing, selling, delivering, and supporting the new product generally take their toll on that initially pure customer orientation. The management begins to worry about cutting costs, building volume, negotiating lower commissions for the sales reps, and so forth, and spends less time thinking and worrying about the customers' needs. The production facilities, product–management hierarchy, and other internal structures that initially were designed to meet customer needs begin to take on a life of their own. In the typical introductory stage, management begins a long, slow, almost imperceptible shift in orientation, from its initial focus on customer needs, to the strong focus on company needs that characterizes the end of the product's life cycle. In fact, we suspect that this gradual shift in focus is what makes products mortal. It is something inherent in the way companies manage products, not in the products themselves. But this discussion is jumping way ahead of the chapter and, incidentally, ahead of the existing literature on this model, so it is better left to the end of the next chapter and our critical evaluation of the model.

With introduction comes the threat of failure, which means there are suddenly two paths the product can take. Sales can go up, or they can go down. Results can satisfy management, or they can fall far short of expectations. As in the life cycles of living creatures, product mortality rates are often highest at and shortly after birth. The product life cycle is characterized by high infant mortality.

PRODUCT FAILURES

The reasons for failure are many. Some new products do not match a company's unique skills and competencies. Other times, the firm overestimates the size of a market segment. RCA had forecast annual sales of 600,000 videodiscs by 1984, yet actual sales totaled only 500,000 by the time it scrapped its videodisc player system. RCA's loss can be attributed mainly to competition from VCRs.

As a Japanese competitor told *Business Week,* "RCA's problem was they tried to compete with the VCR and focused only on one function—playback."[37] Most frequently new products fail because there is no need or want for them; they don't solve a real consumer problem. (What makes a customer problem real? Not whether management or the company's scientists see a problem they want to solve, but whether the customers agree that they have a problem and perceive the company's new product to be a fine solution to it. The only way to verify this is to introduce the product.)

Various studies have shown that the failure rate for new consumer products ranges from a low of 20 percent to a high of 90 percent; new industrial products fare somewhat better.[38] The most recent study we have seen, in which The Conference Board surveyed 148 mid-sized and large U.S. manufacturers, reported a failure rate of one in three for major products launched in the last five years. (Respondents faulted their marketing research, along with technical problems and poor timing of introductions, for these failures.)[39] The 33-percent failure rate in this study conforms with another major study, which found that 30 to 35 percent of all consumer goods and 25 percent of all industrial products do not meet the expectations of the firms that develop them.[40] This failure is most likely because the products did not live up to *customer* expectations—a misunderstanding of customer expectations and needs is probably what lies behind The Conference Board's finding that marketing research was most often at fault in product failures. The chairman of the American Marketing Association (AMA), Calvin L. Hodock, argues that the failure to keep customers in focus while pursuing technology is at the root of many product failures:

> RCA poured millions into the videodisc; Sony chased the Beta format, but VHS won the war. Consumers did not lay down their bag of potato chips for Pringles, because the taste was not as innovative as the packaging. The first smokeless cigarette, Premier, was another good intention that missed. Soft-batch cookies, heralded as tasting like David's and Mrs. Fields, have almost disappeared from grocery shelves. Sony, RCA, Frito Lay, and Procter & Gamble were victims of technology mesmerization. They became enamored with the sex-appeal of the technology and oblivious to delivering a consumer benefit or need.[41]

These sorts of errors seem the most obvious, yet they can gather incredible momentum within a company. They are the kinds of product developments that catch management's imagination. The way to detect these errors is to keep checking to see if the products catch customers' imaginations as well.

Whereas some products are launched to the dramatic din of a rapid crash, many more are introduced with a whimper. New products do not generally fail immediately or entirely, but they may fail to excite customers, as is the case with many "no-brainer" product line extensions. Hodock observes that the most successful and excellent new products, such as the ones that the AMA recognizes through its Edison Awards, "are truly innovative products rather than warmed-over versions of 'me too.'" Last year's Edison winners included novelties such as Spiffits from DowBrands, the first premoistened towels for household cleaning; Souper Combos from Campbell, the first microwavable soup and sandwich combination; and Healthy Choice, the first microwavable frozen dinners with low levels of cholesterol, fat, and salt.[42] Campbell evidently took its own advice to heart and stopped chasing mindless line extensions. Of course, the line extension balances lower reward with lower risk—it usually costs far less to develop and introduce. But when it comes to new products, the old adage is certainly true—no guts, no glory!

What if you have a truly innovative idea, and you develop and introduce it with skill, only to find the new market rapidly filled with competitors? You may never recover the development costs. If you can't hold onto the market for a significant portion of the introductory phase, you are probably in big trouble. The failure to maintain a leadership position for long enough to benefit from the several advantages of being a "first-mover" firm is another common source of disappointing product launches. The advantages to being first include (or ought to include) the technological leadership that comes with being farther down the learning curve than competing firms, the ability to preempt competitors in the acquisition of scarce resources (which often include market niches), and the tendency for buyers to want to stick with first-movers to avoid switching costs.[43] An increasing number of companies seem to be pursuing what is known as the "fast follower" strategy, which involves rapid imitation of innovating competitors. Fast followers increase the threat that a competitor will steal the thunder—and some of the profits. Given this threat, how can you be sure a new product's competitive advantage will prove durable? What can be done to foil the efforts of those diabolical fast followers?

The advice offered by marketing experts is helpful, but not always consistent. For example, conventional wisdom has it that a skimming strategy is appropriate when rapid competition is not expected, and a penetration strategy when competition is expected. Skimming means a company keeps price and profits high, milking the least price-sensitive customers before pursuing the rest of the market. But if the company expects rapid competition, then it should use a penetration strategy, with lower pricing and aggressive promotion and distribution to capture as much of the potential market as possible at the outset, on the theory that this will give the firm a larger share in the long run. However, one recent academic journal contribution on this question suggests that managers should maximize short-run returns where fast imitation is likely. This strategy requires asking a premium price for a new product where imitation is projected in a relatively short time. Alternatively, a moderate price is warranted where followers are likely to be delayed.[44] In other words, this recommendation is the opposite of the thinking behind the penetration and skimming strategies. For our money, we'd prefer to bet on a penetration strategy when rapid competition is expected, but this boils down to management judgment rather than any firm principle of marketing.

This same journal article identifies the components of a new product that affect the durability of its competitive advantage, and the authors suggest some more logical prescriptive principles on this score. The idea is that management can do a better job both of anticipating the duration of a competitive advantage and of planning so as to maximize its duration by focusing on all the factors that make products easy or difficult to imitate. The factors, with specific ideas for how they can be used to make the product harder to imitate, are as follows:[45]

- *Product form*—Give the product a distinctive form and encourage customers to make inferences about product function from its form.
- *Product function*—Differentiate the product on one or more functional characteristics rather than introduce a generic or nonspecialized product. Consider developing more than one product to give consumers function that is closer to their specific needs.
- *Product intangibles*—Innovate in this area, adding value through warranties, financing, product availability, support to the customer, and so forth.
- *Pricing*—Use penetration pricing, and also price-based sales promotions, if appropriate, to encourage rapid trial and adoption.
- *Promotion*—Use advertising and other promotional efforts to stake out a desirable position within the market, building consumer awareness of this position and signaling possession of it to potential competitors.
- *Distribution*—Minimize transaction barriers (obstacles to customer purchase and use). Invest in building good distribution channels to make the product readily available and to support the user.
- *Firm characteristics*—A unique location or specialized skills and resources can provide the building blocks of durable competitive advantage. Basically, if your firm is less like its competitors, it is more likely to come up with hard-to-imitate innovations.

Perhaps you recognized the familiar four Ps in this schema: product, price, promotion, and place. Product is broken into three categories, but the rest of the schema is straight out of the textbook (with distribution referring to "place"). The article authors added characteristics of the firm to round out the picture.

The characteristics of the firm that affect ease of imitation include "any unique resource that isolates a new product from rivals."[46] This resource may offer protection because of customer perception—for example, a watch made by a Swiss firm gets a few points in customer perception merely because it is Swiss. The resource also may offer an economic advantage. Most simply, however, the reliance on different resources may minimize the likelihood of another competitor's having hit upon the same idea at almost the same time. This latter problem is, in our opinion, an especially troubling one.

The sad fact of the matter is that it is rare to have a completely original idea. Often an insight or invention is a product of circumstance. Both Alfred

Wallace and Charles Darwin thought up the theory of evolution in great detail, without knowing about the other's work, at virtually the same time. This kind of concomitant development happens too often in the history of invention for it to be treated as mere coincidence. You can assume that, if a customer need and a novel solution strike you as a natural, they may seem obvious to a competitor as well. No one should really have expected to dominate the laptop computer market, for example, because most PC makers knew that this is the direction their innovations had to go. They did not wait for a competitor to introduce a laptop before beginning their own product development. (Although one wonders why some did not take advantage of the obvious tide of events to swim against it and stake out a novel and unexpected new segment.)

Loel Bleeke of the consulting firm McKinsey and Company has identified a general problem he refers to as look-alike strategy, and it is applicable to product development as well.[47] He finds that companies within an industry often converge on the same or similar strategies without intending to. They do not ask each other what they should do, but all go off and do the same thing, and the end result often looks like they consulted together. They are surprised to find their competitors pursuing the same goals and markets they are, and their strategy is bound to run into trouble as they face unexpected, and unnecessary, competition via the look-alike mechanism. Alternatively, as in the case of laptop computers, the companies all fight it out on the same playing field by tacit agreement, even though only a few are likely to establish significant positions in the game. Look-alike strategy is especially problematic with new-product introductions, because the last thing a sane management team wants to do is to introduce a new product at about the same time competitors introduce similar new products. The first-mover advantage is lost to all parties.

Bleeke believes look-alike strategies develop because of five common errors in strategy formation:

1. Managers tend to focus on where to compete rather than on how to compete. *Where* is a two-dimensional issue, whereas *how* is three-dimensional. Thinking about how can lead to many creative and original ideas. How a company produces and delivers products or services is often a better source of novel new-product concepts than where it sells them. Yet a great deal of attention is given to the where's of marketing in new-product development and introduction: which markets to serve, which stores or channels to use in reaching markets, where to place products on the stores' shelves, and so forth.

2. Little emphasis is placed on uniqueness and adaptability. According to Bleeke, strategic plans ought to be evaluated on the basis of how unique and how adaptable they are, but management usually overlooks these two issues in strategy formulation. The same can be said for new-product development and introduction plans. If a company doesn't *specify* uniqueness in new products, it is unlikely to get uniqueness. Yet most product proposals are evaluated primarily based on financial expectations—what kind of revenues, market share, and

profits are forecast in a given period of time. However, because these forecasts are heavily dependent upon the uniqueness of the product, reality will fall short of the projections if similar products appear at the same time. Nevertheless, companies tend to underemphasize the more qualitative assessment of uniqueness in favor of the quantitative projections. The importance of adaptability is even more obvious. Will the new product prove adaptable enough to survive and profit from unexpected events? Will engineers be able to adapt the basic technical platform to create future generations of the product? Will marketing be able to reposition the product to pursue a segment of the market if a challenger stakes out another segment? These and many similar questions ought to be asked to determine adaptability.

3. Little attention is given to *when* to compete. One of the most common causes for new-product failure according to The Conference Board survey is bad timing. As product life cycles shorten (a commonly cited but poorly explained phenomenon), it is increasingly easy for a company to find itself out of step with the market. In technology-driven products, competing technologies can make products out-of-date rapidly. Products intended to take advantage of a change in public perception may precede the perceptual change and fall on ears that are not yet prepared for the message. Products chasing a demographic trend may similarly be out of step with microlevel change, even though they are on target as far as a long-term trend goes. For example, knowing that the population is aging does not guarantee that a company can succeed today by introducing a line of products or services targeted at the over-60 segment. There must be a self-defined segment consisting of people who see themselves as part of this over-60 cohort. Many people in our society, however, still have mixed attitudes about the elderly, and older people's self-images are often based on the values and images of people a decade younger. Public perception has not yet caught up with the demographic trend, so a product launch based on this trend could be out of step with customer attitudes. Even when the market timing for a new product is precisely right, the company must ask itself whether it is realistically able to be the first entrant and, if not, must modify its investment and development strategy to stake out a second- or third-entrant position.

4. Companies tend to focus on competing firms instead of competing individuals. When developing strategy in general, and new-product plans in particular, it is easy to limit the competitor analysis to a review of the facts on the major competing firms. But the market shares, growth rates, and financial ratios tell only one side of the story. In predicting competitor behavior, it is vital to incorporate an understanding of the personalities of the decision makers. Who is in charge of new-product development at each competitor? What did they study in school, and what kind of products have they developed previously? Are they supported by other managers, or are their hands tied? Are they aggressive or cautious (how many times have they brought out first-mover products)? The personal approach to competitor analysis can even be extended to the companies

as a whole by asking what their corporate cultures are like and how they are changing.

5. Companies use common performance measures. The fact that the major companies in most industries use the same measures reflects in part the increasing tendency for managers to move from company to company in their career pursuits, taking customs and practices with them. When it comes to strategy in general, and to new-product development in particular, a company is what it measures. For example, a company may decide to strengthen its brand franchise and market share in certain high-growth market segments through its product development and marketing effort. It also may continue to evaluate the key managers according to profitability of products from all segments in the short term. In such a case, the managers will continue to fight it out for short-term returns in the mainstream segments instead of innovating to pursue the growth segments that the company intended to target for long-term returns. Common performance measures lead to implementation that looks alike, even if the stated goals are divergent.

Academics who study organizations use the term *isomorphism*, which is the tendency toward consistency and constancy within the organization. It is the enemy of innovation and change, the inertia we spoke of early in this chapter. Bleeke's observations suggest that isomorphism can affect not only individual companies, but entire industries. The managers within an industry can be thought of as informal members of an intellectual community. They often come from similar backgrounds, and share ways of looking at and talking about business problems with the other managers in their industry. The culture of companies within any industry is often similar. Let's say you were plunked down inside a mystery company and had to guess whether its business was insurance or computers. You would probably guess immediately whether you were in an insurance or a computer company by the dress, manner, and speech of the people around you and the layout and decoration of the building. But you might have trouble guessing *which* computer company or insurance company, as individual companies differ little on these indicators of culture.

What happens, however, when a foreign company decides to enter the U.S. computer market? The company is not part of this informal industrial community, and it approaches management and marketing differently from U.S. competitors. Its approach to product development also differs. In short, it is not subject to the same isomorphic forces, at least at first. Thus, it is much more likely to generate novel product ideas. It is not subject to the dangers of look-alike strategy.

When U.S. managers talk about innovation, they always look over their shoulders to see if any Japanese companies are creeping up from behind. The subject of innovation, with its related issues of product quality, fast-cycle product development, entrepreneurship, and the like, is high on the management agenda largely because Japanese companies have outperformed U.S. companies in many industries by being better innovators.

The explanations for this phenomenon are many and varied, and some are quite farfetched and convoluted. But the Japanese success may reflect the simple fact that the Japanese companies entered the U.S. market with a fresh perspective, free of the blinders imposed by the U.S. industrial culture. While the big three in Detroit continued to develop autos that offered power and luxury, Japanese companies, with their new and distant view of the market, saw more clearly that fuel economy and reliability were becoming more important to consumers. The time it took for the U.S. automakers to see what should have been obvious to them from the outset is a testament to the power of the normative forces at work within their industry. They simply could not see what was obvious to the newcomers in their market; they did not understand their own customers.

If there is any overriding concern in the area of new-product development, this must be it: The basic scope and direction of the product development effort must be right, and they will not be unless management thought is liberated from the strictures of look-alike strategy and is able to focus on novel opportunities presented by the environment.

We began the chapter with the observation that products can be thought of as living and dying, according to a common architecture as described by the product life cycle. We have followed this life cycle from inception through development and introduction. In the next chapter, we follow it into its growth phase, maturity, and decline. It is also relevant, however, to remember that companies themselves have proven remarkably mortal. How many companies with which you do business have been around for 100 years? And how many are newly formed within the last decade or two? Most companies are young, and many—especially the majority that are privately owned—fail to survive beyond the span of a single generation of managers. One recent survey found that only a few U.S. companies can actually be traced back as far as the Civil War.[48] Why should companies prove so mortal?

One clue to this puzzle is provided by the product life cycle itself, and by the thought that companies seem to have trouble breaking out of traditional ways of thinking to maintain a healthy level of innovation. The isomorphic forces that crystalize organizations and entire industries into rigid, inflexible ways of thinking about their business and their markets put them at risk and open the door to newcomers, whether entrepreneurs from their own country or industrialists from abroad.

No company can live long if it ties itself to a single product. Even the longest lived products die eventually, at least according to theory. The railroads took the myopic view that their product was railroads, not transportation, and that their job was laying track, not moving people and goods the most efficient way.[49] Thus, the railroads went into a long slow decline as automobiles, trucks, and planes began to displace the railroad as the favored form of transportation. But what does the mortality of companies have to do with product development and introduction?

Everything—for it is in this core function of the business that new life is injected, or old life sucked out. The business that allows its product development to degenerate into mindless brand extensions soon has a portfolio of mature and declining products. The company, on the other hand, that is able to break away from the industry-think that limits the vision and imagination of its competitors, and manages to introduce a stream of exciting and unique new products, revitalizes itself by keeping its portfolio weighted toward development- and growth-stage products. Surely this is why some companies now set specific developmental goals for themselves. Rubbermaid insists that 30 percent of sales comes from products developed in the last five years, and 3M reports that 32 percent of its sales come from products that are fewer than five years old, for example.[50]

Thus, we can say that the vitality of the product development function is directly related to the vitality of the company as a whole. This makes sense, at least if we look at the basic purpose of a business. At its heart, the business exists to produce products and provide them to consumers through an exchange process that is convenient and profitable for both, or all, parties. Business is about products, and it is through products that a business provides value to its customers. As soon as management attention wanders from the customers, rigidity and clouded vision attack the product development efforts, and the company no longer innovates effectively for its customers. The product portfolio shifts toward older goods and services and uneventful extensions of them, and someone else takes the reins to provide the kind of leadership that McKenna was talking about when he said, "in marketing, what you lead, you own. Leadership is ownership."

In the beginning of this chapter, we hypothesized that management attention shifts slowly from customer needs to company needs as the product life cycle progresses. The antidote to the aging of the company via slowed innovation and look-alike strategy is thus a refocusing of management attention on the customer. As Charles Hooper of Helene Curtis states in the chapter's opening quote, "Good ideas don't begin around the conference table. They begin with the consumer." They also end with the consumer, as our examination of new-product introduction and failure illustrated. In the next chapter, we examine how to keep the company focused on the customer throughout the product's life cycle, as we follow the product from its introduction to the heady growth of its teenage years and on into maturity.

10 PRODUCT MANAGEMENT

Birth, Death, and Resurrection

MANAGING GROWTH IN THE PRODUCT LIFE CYCLE

In Chapter 9, we traced the product's progress from idea through market introduction. As a new product enters the market, its sales usually grow at a modest rate. Sometimes the product is so obviously a great idea that everyone rushes to buy it, but generally it takes a while for the word to get around. The majority of consumers in most markets do not want to be the first to try something; they wait for opinion leaders to evaluate it, or learn about it when their reference group adopts it. Also, companies rarely flood the market with their new product. They prefer a more cautious rollout, first with regional sales and advertising, allowing less risk on the introduction and greater learning as they proceed.

This caution by consumers and companies gives way to a gradual increase in momentum, presuming that the product is a success, until sales begin to grow at a rapid rate. Imagine that one person tries the product and likes it, then tells two more people about it. They try it, and each tells two more. Soon there is exponential growth. Unfortunately for managers, it is not always this simple to achieve exponential growth! But a successful product introduction generally moves to a rapid growth phase as it begins to penetrate the main portion of its target market. This growth does not accelerate indefinitely, however, because the market comprises a limited number of consumers. Eventually the bulk of the people who are likely to try the product have done so, and new customers become more scarce. If a healthy portion of the people who tried the new product continue to repurchase it, sales will not fall. But sales rarely continue to grow at the same rate. Thus, the growth phase is characterized by sales growth that accelerates at first, then begins to decline. When growth levels off—say to near the rate of growth of the GNP or of the targeted segment itself—the product is said to have moved out of growth and into maturity. At this point, most of the potential market has been exposed to the product, and all but the most conservative laggards have tried it. Because trial does not convert into ongoing usage in every case, however, companies commonly see sales growth flatten out well below 100-percent penetration of the potential market.

The growth phase of the product life cycle is characterized by increased competition. New brands are often launched by competitors who have noted the success of the first-mover's product and rushed to grab some of the market share. There are only two ways to capture market share: A company can take share away from a competitor by convincing customers to switch brands. This can be a tough, and costly, dog fight. Alternatively, a company can convince nonusers to try its product before they have adopted a competing brand. If consumers try and like the company's brand, the job of keeping them as customers is easier than the task of taking them away from a competitor. But if a company lets a first-mover spread a product through the entire market before the company enters with a competitive product, there is no second option—the company is forced to gain share by capturing it from the first-mover. The firm then must overcome any loyalty toward the competitive brand and convince consumers that another product is sufficiently different and better to be worth the trouble, risk, and cost associated with switching brands.

Although marketers and managers find it appealing to think of consumers as dedicated and loyal to their brand and its producer, in fact brand loyalty is not as strong as it might be. The combination of more products from which to choose and an increasing emphasis on price-oriented promotions has no doubt eroded brand loyalty in recent years. Nonetheless, sufficient brand loyalty exists in most categories to support the notion of a first-mover advantage. Exhibit 10.1 reports the results of a recent survey which asked product users if they were loyal to one brand.

Based on these statistics, one might wonder whether it is wise to focus the majority of a company's marketing expenditures on promoting a brand identity in categories such as TVs and running shoes, in which the majority of consumers do not profess to care about brand loyalty. Perhaps the firm's money would be better spent on product development to create sufficient differences between brands that consumers would have good reason to become loyal to a brand! But let's return to discussion of the growth stage, and the strategies available to a second entrant into a new market.

What if your product is as good as that of the first entrant into a new market, but not any better? If you enter quickly, before the first-mover has captured much of the market, you can attract almost as many first-time customers as the first-mover. But if you wait, you will have to convince consumers who already use the competing product to switch. The longer you wait to enter, the more dramatic the product advantage you need to gain a strong second or third place in the growing market. This is why competition grows so rapidly

EXHIBIT 10.1.   Product loyalty.

Product	Percentage of Users Loyal to One Brand
Cigarettes	71
Mayonnaise	65
Toothpaste	61
Coffee	58
Headache remedy	56
Film	56
Laundry detergent	48
Beer	48
Automobiles	47
Shampoo	44
Soft drinks	44
Underwear	36
Television	35
Batteries	29
Athletic shoes	27
Garbage bags	23

during the growth phase of the product life cycle. Competitors are eager to reach customers before the consumers have developed an affection for any other brand.

In the competitive environment associated with the growth stage, the life-cycle model prescribes a strategy aimed at establishing brand loyalty and building market share. Also important is the establishment of competition for distribution channels—whoever gets them first has an advantage. If you were to develop a new cola that most people liked better than Coke and Pepsi, you would still face a daunting task of defeating two major companies, whose strong dealer relationships give them a vise grip over shelf space at the retail level.

In response to the increasing competition of the growth stage, managers begin to stake out specific product positionings, the high ground in the consumer's mind from which the company will be able to defend its market share in the future. Companies begin to differentiate their products, in product attributes and consequently in customer perception. The initial single-product, mass-market focus gives way to an increasing number of more specialized products that compete better in the fights for specific segments of the growing market. Pricing is also used to focus offerings on multiple market segments; in fact, one often sees a range of product models, differentiated in large part on the basis of how much they cost and how elaborate they are. The main objective of promotion—the sales, discounts, and advertising used to sell the product—is to build brand loyalty. During introduction, promotion was directed at building primary demand—the desire for the product concept itself. But during the growth stage, promotion shifts toward building selective demand—the specific demand for the company's brand versus the general interest in the new category that is generated during the development of primary demand.

To clarify the impact of these forces, we use three product examples: compact discs, roller blades, and food processors. These products have two things in common: They are or recently were in growth stages, and they all spin. The latter similarity is quite unimportant, but an interesting coincidence nonetheless.

Compact Discs

Compact discs (CDs) were introduced to Europe and Japan in 1982, and to the U.S. market in 1983. At the time, many industry experts predicted that consumers would refuse to discard their records and tapes, and their turntables and tape players, for the uncertain benefit of digital recordings on compact discs. Some experts saw it differently, remembering that the history of the recorded music industry is one of new standards displacing old with superior sound. An oft-quoted commentary by the editor of a trade magazine comes from 1949, when $33^{1}/_{3}$-rpm (revolutions-per-minute) plastic records were first introduced to a market dominated by shellac 78-rpm records: "I ask readers if they want to feel that their collections of records are obsolete, if they really want to spend money on buying discs that will save them the trouble of getting up to change them, and if they really want to wait years for a repertory as good as what is available now to them?"[1] Much to the expert's surprise, consumers answered yes to these questions, both when long-playing records (LPs) were introduced in 1949 and when CDs were introduced in 1983.

Sales of CD players in the United States started at 35,000 in 1983, a decent showing for the introductory stage of the life cycle. In 1984, sales grew dramatically, to 208,000 units. Although this represents 494-percent growth, the percentage is not particularly important because the base was so small. The next year's growth rate of 188 percent, however, was striking because it represents growth on a fairly large base. This growth brought industry sales of CD players to 600,000 units by 1985, and put the product onto the classic accelerating growth curve characteristic of the first half of the growth stage of the product life cycle.[2] Interestingly, CD players were introduced by several companies at roughly the same time, including the original innovators, Sony and Philips. No single company could claim to have a significant time-lead advantage in this market, although, as the innovators, Sony and Philips turned out to have some advantages that allowed them to hold onto a strong position.

CD players on their own are of no more value than CDs are on their own. The consumer generally will buy neither a CD until he or she has a CD player, nor a CD player without being convinced that CDs are a desirable purchase. Thus, the growth of the CD market is dependent on the growth of the CD player market; their life cycles are linked. In 1983, total unit sales of CDs was 443,320. This is a pretty good showing for the first year in the U.S. market, and it represents about a dozen CDs per CD player. CDs cost consumers about $20 each at the time, so the average owner of a CD player invested about $240 in CDs during 1983. From these statistics, we can also compute that the total sales of CDs was almost $9 million—nothing to sneeze at for an introductory-stage product. Nevertheless, unit shipments of all forms of prerecorded music totaled about 600 million in 1983, which means that CDs accounted for less than one-thousandth of the total market for prerecorded music![3] The bulk of sales was accounted for by $33\frac{1}{3}$-rpm LPs, which accounted for 45 percent of unit sales; by 45-rpm singles, with 20 percent of sales; and by cassette tapes, with a little over 30 percent of sales. Eight-track tapes held only a few percentage points of market share, as cassette tapes had largely displaced them by 1982.

Since 1983, CD unit sales have grown much as the product life cycle might have predicted. Exhibit 10.2 shows CD sales plotted over time. Exactly when the product moved from introduction to growth is difficult to say—the definition of life cycle stage is based on judgment as much as anything—but it looks like the curve shifted upward in 1985, making this the first year of the growth phase. It is worth noting that the total market for prerecorded music did not grow at all during this time period; it has stayed fairly constant and even declined at times in recent decades, as is typical of a mature market.

A difficult strategic issue for the innovators in this case was how to capture a leading position in the CD market that their innovation had spawned. The innovators were Philips, which developed CD technology for video applications in the 1970s, and Sony, with which Philips entered into a joint venture for the purpose of developing and introducing CDs for prerecorded music. Although

EXHIBIT 10.2.   Compact disc unit sales, U.S.

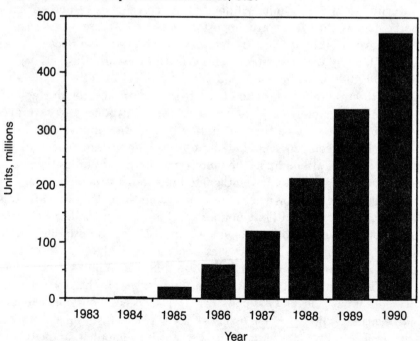

these companies focused on developing and marketing the CD players, not the CDs, they also had an active interest in CDs via Philips's record-producing subsidiary, Polygram, and via Sony's acquisition of CBS records. In other words, the joint developers of the CD technology stood to profit handsomely if their record-company subsidiaries could, between them, gain a preeminent position in the market for CDs. Although the companies could have prevented other companies from producing CDs, this would have ensured that the new technology would *not* become an industry standard.

The CD technology had to be adopted throughout the industry to provide consumers an extensive repertoire of music and to make the new product a viable competitor against the LP standard. In fact, Philips and Sony joined forces specifically to ensure that they would not create competing standards. It was essential to disseminate the new technology widely and encourage record producers to make the new CDs through generous licensing agreements. The necessity of creating an industry standard pushed the innovators to give their technology away, but the desire to profit from CD sales pushed them to maximize their shares of this new market. Further complicating this difficult situation was the fact that CD production capacity must be added in large, expensive increments. Building a new factory is no small investment. Yet Philips and Sony did not know how successful the new CD standard would be, and thus were not eager to invest in excess capacity. They could have preempted the market by building a huge factory, but they would have lost heavily on this investment had the market not grown as it did.[4] What happened? We will return to this case after discussing our other two products and reviewing some of the principles of product management.

Roller Blades

It's tough to be a 20-year-old entrepreneur in the United States. Ask Scott Olson, who probably had never heard of the product life cycle when he started Rollerblade Inc. in 1980 to manufacture roller skates with in-line wheels. His innovation was to take an old idea—the original design used by Rollerblades was from the eighteenth century—and reproduce it in modern materials. It worked much better with ski-boots and skate-board wheels and, after a slow start, the market entered its growth stage in 1987 and reached sales of about $100 million a year by 1990 (see Exhibit 10.3).[5]

Olson originally marketed the product to hockey players and skiers for off-season training. From 1980 to 1984, sales were modest and the company stayed small. Cash flow problems, that nemesis of entrepreneurial businesses, led Olson to sell 94 percent of his company to a private investor. By 1985, Olson and his investor were not seeing eye to eye on how to manage the business, and soon Olson resigned. It is little consolation to him that the company he founded still holds the largest share of the rollerblade market, since Olson now runs one of its eight competitors. Olson's new company, Innovative Sport Systems, holds only

EXHIBIT 10.3. Rollerblade growth stage.

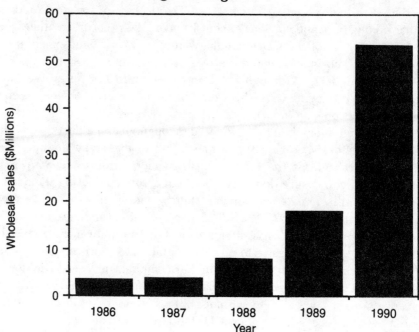

3 percent of the market to Rollerblade Inc.'s 66 percent, demonstrating at Olson's expense the dramatic advantage of being the first-mover in a new market.

From Rollerblade's perspective, Olson's new company is only a minor issue. More troubling is First Team Sports Inc., whose Ultra-Wheels brand was the second to enter, in 1987, and now holds 22 percent of the market. Third is Bauer with only 5 percent. This established maker of hockey skates was a late entrant, but its reputation for quality skates and its strong distribution to sporting goods stores probably worries Rollerblade's president, John Sundet, as much as First Team's large share does.

As the life cycle model suggests, the rapid growth of rollerblade sales since 1987 has attracted increasing competition, and Rollerblade Inc.'s grasp of the market has slipped as a result. In early 1990, its competitors gained considerably when Rollerblade's production lagged behind demand and store orders were not filled on time. This forced previously loyal retailers to seek other sources, and opened the door to the host of competitors that now crowds Rollerblade for shelf space. What does the life cycle model prescribe for Rollerblade Inc. at this stage? For starters, it needs to capture distribution channels before competitors do. Its recent move into department stores can be seen in this context. And it needs to begin advertising to build its brand name and establish a strong identity versus its competitors. The competitors are beginning to advertise too; a rush is on to sign up celebrity endorsers.

More than this, however, Rollerblade Inc. needs to maintain its leadership by continuing to lead the market in *product development* and *innovation*. When Olson's new company, Innovative Sport Systems, introduced Switchit, the most important thing about the event was that Rollerblade Inc. did not. Switchit skates are combination hockey and roller skates, with interchangeable wheels and blades. Rollerblade's innovation has been to make minor refinements to its initial product, for example, by adding a fifth wheel. But can it maintain the kind of leadership that Regis McKenna spoke of in Chapter 9, the leadership that establishes a company's ownership of the market? Without Olson's creativity, this may be Rollerblade's greatest strategic challenge. In the next case, we will find out what can happen to a company that fails to lead the market it created.

Food Processors

At the risk of taking the suspense out of this story, we will start by telling you that Cuisinarts Inc. introduced the food processor to American kitchens in 1973, struggled through two slow years of introductory-phase sales, rode the crest of growing sales through the rest of the 1970s and well into the 1980s, but lost share to competitors and ended in bankruptcy court in the fall of 1990.

Carl Sontheimer bought the U.S. distribution rights to Robo-Coupe's restaurant food processor, then adapted the product for the home market. An engineer and passionate cook, Sontheimer kept his company focused on quality and refused to expand the line by offering lower-cost, and in his view lower-quality, products. His short-line strategy held up better in the introductory phase than it did later, when competing lines from Farberware, Waring, General Electric, Hamilton Beach, and Moulinex entered the market.[6] Instead of expanding the line downward as many companies do during the growth phase, Cuisinart expanded it upward, introducing a more powerful model at $275 retail in 1979 when the competition sold for only $70 on average. Fortunately, Sontheimer's sense of the market was right, and the model fueled Cuisinart's growth. But when Sunbeam introduced a tiny, inexpensive version of the food processor in 1985, the market's mood had changed and the new product's sales went ballistic. However, Sontheimer still refused to compete at the low end.

Advisors and industry experts frequently urged Cuisinart to expand its line and to extend the brand name into related product categories. Sontheimer resisted. He was once quoted as saying, "We could put pebbles in a can, and if we put the Cuisinart name on it, it would sell. But after that, the name would be absolutely worthless."[7] This single-minded vision of the company's mission no doubt avoided cheapening the Cuisinart name in consumers' minds. But it did not position Cuisinart for the end of the growth phase and the onset of maturity, and when sales began to slow Cuisinart ran into big trouble.

What can we learn from these three cases? First, they all seem to support the general indications of the life cycle model. The often-sudden switch to fast growth, the changing competitive picture this brings, the need to alter marketing strategies for growth, the imperative of maintaining market position and leadership for the inevitable growth ceiling and transition to maturity; all these are indicated by the model, and all could have been anticipated by the innovators in each of these three cases. So far, management has not done too poorly. After all, Philips and Sony indirectly control a strong position in CDs, and Rollerblades still holds a majority share. But Rollerblades might have a stronger position if its grasp of distribution channels had not slipped, and its future no doubt depends on how many of the hot new products come out of its labs versus its competitors. That makes two out of three, since Cuisinart failed to hold onto the market it created. A willingness to listen to the market and to jump quickly on the new light-weight processors might well have saved Cuisinart.

The most obvious conclusion is that the growth stage is fraught with peril. It is not easy to take advantage of a high-growth market. Run-away demand puts a lot of strain on a company, making it extremely hard to know what to do next. There is no settled routine in a rapid-growth market, no simple way to look ahead and anticipate future sales, no guarantee that you will not have twice as many competitors next year; or that your sales will not suddenly stop growing. But on the other hand, growth-stage products are ultimately manageable, and the same obsession with customers and emphasis on marketing that succeeds in other markets can guide management in a growth market. We will review many of the strategies and tactics that make up the craft of product management in the next section of this chapter, then see how they help define the next steps for each of our case companies. The main focus of strategic choice concerns the nature of the product line—how and how far it is extended, how long it should be allowed to grow before a new generation is introduced—as it moves from introduction toward maturity and into decline. First, however, we will look at some of the product management strategies that are applied in growth and then in maturity.

PRODUCT MANAGEMENT STRATEGIES

It rarely makes sense to limit the company's offering to a single product. As we have seen already, the life cycle model indicates a tendency toward brand extensions and the creation of lengthening product lines during the growth stage. Most companies have one or more product lines as a result, and companies with many mature brands, like Campbell, may focus the majority of their development efforts on extending these lines (although this is not necessarily a wise focus, as we saw in the last chapter). Product lines must be managed with care to ensure that viable products are brought out and to ensure the firm's survival and growth. A number of strategies are available to aid in achieving this goal.

Full versus Limited Line

While the terms full and limited are a matter of degree, a full-line strategy refers to a strategy of providing product lines that are both wide in number and deep in assortment. (You can readily see that a full-line strategy is necessary to be a leader in the CD market.) A limited-line strategy entails offering a selected set of products. The full-line strategy has the advantage of greater flexibility to match the market's desires. As an executive of James River Corporation (a paper company) put it, "There's a big advantage in selling to clients from a full wagon."[8]

At the same time, a full-line strategy has some drawbacks. Marketers must be careful not to spread themselves so thin that each line receives less attention than it needs. And they must keep in mind that as product lines are added, the economies of scale associated with mass production (and mass marketing) can be reduced or destroyed. Sunbeam, the $1 million appliance arm of Allegheny International, is facing this problem as it enters international markets. The firm plans to reduce the number of parts in its products in response. For example, in 1985 the company realized it was marketing 27 different iron chassis around the world and resolved to cut these down to three. Sunbeam's competitor in kitchen appliances, the Conair Corporation, has a more limited line. But it plans to extend its line considerably now that it has acquired Cuisinart. Conair bought the bankrupt food processor company for $27 million and introduced Cuisinart microwave-oven accessories, coffee machines, juicers, and even coffee beans in 1990.

Many marketers believe that they must offer a full line of products in order to be successful. A broad mix gives them a competitive advantage, providing greater ability to meet customer needs, increased customer recognition, higher dealer demand, and greater promotional effectiveness. Yet when this strategy is relied upon in place of managerial judgment, it often results in the addition of inefficient and unneeded products.

American Biltrite's Boston-based Industrial Products Division provides an example. Over the years, this maker of hoses, belting, and shoe soling had tried to be too many things to too many customers. The company had a great many unprofitable products and customers as a result. In one product area, 48 percent of Biltrite's customers provided only 2 percent of its sales. After analyzing its product line strategy, Biltrite reduced the total number of items from 25,000 to 12,000 and eliminated 7,700 of 15,500 customers; revenues and profits benefited from these changes.

The Line-Filling Strategy

Closely allied to the two strategies just described is the line-filling approach. This involves developing products to fill gaps in the market that have not been noticed by competitors or have occurred as a result of changes in consumer preferences. Ideally, the added products will compliment existing ones, perhaps even enhance the sale of present products, and produce a satisfactory return on investment. When Sunbeam studied Cuisinart's market in 1984 and discovered that the majority of food processors were not used by their owners, they saw a gap that needed filling. Their Oskar, introduced in 1985, filled that gap by giving consumers a small, easy-to-use, easy-to-clean food processor that could be used much more casually and easily than the more complicated and bulky Cuisinart. As we saw, Cuisinart failed to copy this successful strategy. But the real question is why it had not done the market research first, seen the obvious market need, and preempted the competition by innovating to meet that need. You cannot continue with your current strategy if many of your customers have stopped using your products.

Line and Brand Extension Strategies

Armor All is a hundred-million-plus a year product, used by car owners to spruce up their dashboards, bucket seats, and tires. But in 1988, Armor All Products Corporation was a one-product subsidiary of McKesson Corporation. Its product was profitable—1987 profits exceeded $22 million—and its sales continued to grow. But the company had owned the well-known Armor All brand since its introduction in 1972 and never done anything with it. Compare this to Turtle Wax's line of 40 products, and you have a strong case for line extension. Armor All president Jeffrey Sherman decided to extend the brand, but not to the extent his competitors have. He introduced four new products: car wax, protectant, cleaner, and car wash, all of them targeted at the 18- to 49-year-old males who make up Armor All's traditional market, as well as a specially packaged paste wax targeted at women.[9]

Extension strategies are more typical of maturity than growth. Line extensions are new varieties of the same basic product. A different size or new dispenser for Armor All would be a line extension. Brand extensions take the brand name of one product category and extend it to another, as Sherman did when he introduced Armor All waxes, cleaners, and protectants. Brand extensions usually work best when the new categories are closely related to the old in the consumer's mind, as in the Armor All case. Sometimes they are taken much farther, however, as when Coca-Cola and MacDonald's licensed their names to clothing manufacturers. These ventures have not been as successful as the companies hoped, probably because the new categories are not mentally linked to the old ones. But sometimes brand names can be extended dramatically, and licensing of brand names continues to increase in popularity. For example, Caterpillar licenses its name to makers of work clothes on the theory that consumers can reasonably be expected to see the relation between them and the earth-moving equipment for which Caterpillar is famous.

The use of a brand or line extension has two distinct advantages. The cost of introduction is much lower because consumer education is not needed. Advertising and other promotional expenditures are more effective because they produce greater awareness and recognition of the brand. Moreover, the risk of introducing the product is reduced because the new product's image is already established. And since the development costs are reduced, the costs of a product failure are lower.

Brand extension is sometimes used by companies that find their competitive situation getting tougher—as typically happens near the end of the growth stage of the product life cycle. A simple way to conceive of this strategy is to imagine that heightened competition encourages consumers to experiment with products different from the one they have grown accustomed to. Since they have more choice, they exercise that choice more often. And in response, competitors add choice to their lines.

All other things being equal, if you offer the most choice within your line, you will capture experimenting consumers most often, and thus keep your competitors from capturing them. And no doubt this simple stratagem would lead to infinite line extensions were it not that all other things are never equal. The limit on this game is shelf space—or catalog space, or salesperson's time. The distribution channels simply cannot handle all this choice. We observed in the previous chapter that about 15,000 new products will be introduced to supermarkets in 1991. But on average, only 3,000 of them will be pushed to any single grocery store by wholesalers; they know the stores cannot handle all the available products, so focus their efforts where local or regional preferences make them most likely to pay off. Even so, there is no room for 3,000 new products a year in the average grocery store, and most of these will be weeded out quickly by store management or by disinterested shoppers.

Brand extension is also used in maturity and decline, as an antidote to dwindling markets. Thus Prince Manufacturing, the company that began the oversized tennis racket craze, sought growth in a level market by adding two more Prince lines—one smaller than its standard size and another superlarge racket that has been described as a "garbage can cover." But a caution is in order—brand extensions often fail to revive flat or falling sales. There generally has to be something new and exciting about the new product introductions for consumers to give them much attention. And unfortunately for Prince, an even larger tennis racket is not it.

Line-Stretching Strategies

Lines are not very stretchable. That is, they tend to resist being traded up or traded down, and it takes considerable marketing effort to stretch them in these directions. However, line stretching is often attempted, perhaps simply because markets are so often segmented on the basis of price and quality. If you want more customers in a market segmented in this manner, the most obvious alternative (although not necessarily the wisest) is to try to pursue both high- and low-quality segments.

When marketers who are known for selling low-priced products offer higher-priced (and presumably higher-quality) products, this is known as trading up. Kmart, long known as the king of mass merchandise discounters, conducted marketing research that found customer preferences shifting toward higher quality. So in 1984 the company began taking down its endless rows of pipe racks and refurbishing its decor. Greater emphasis was put on snappy displays and higher-profit national brands. Electronic centers were added, complete with computers, software, and video-game cartridges. The bed-and-bath areas were refashioned and "Kitchen Korners" were added (apparently management did not want to trade up so high as to necessitate proper spelling). But note that this makeover was launched over an 18-month period, and required a huge investment in store redesign and advertising aimed at repositioning the discounter.[10] And furthermore, Kmart did not try to dominate the rock bottom discount position any more, because this would have been too inconsistent with its new image.

Did it work? Well, not really. Certainly not in the 18 months management originally planned on and, in fact, the transformation is still in progress. Since 1984, Kmart has tried many strategies to bring its image upscale, including hiring actress Jaclyn Smith and decorator Martha Stewart to help design and promote apparel and housewares. It has spent millions on advertising to tell consumers about its new position and improved stores. But Louis Stern, a marketing professor at Northwestern who follows the industry, says that the stores do not live up to the advertised image: "Kmarts are depressing. I certainly don't see evidence that they are vastly different." Apparently management agrees, since $1.3 billion in store renovations is currently on the drawing board, along with a $1 billion computer to make Kmart's distribution system competitive with Wal-Mart.[11] Unfortunately its larger rival is a moving target. Wal-Mart recently unveiled the prototype for *its* new stores. According to a *The Wall Street Journal* report, "customers expecting the usual warehouse ambiance of discount stores will be shocked." Should they be so shocked as to become disoriented, the store's shopping carts feature video screens that constantly update the shopper concerning location and provide information about products and prices in each department.[12] As Kmart is learning, it is especially hard to trade up when competitors already dominate the desired position.

Trading down occurs when marketers make cheaper lines, and in general it is easy going compared to trading up. It's all down hill, so to speak. But while easy, it is dangerous. The problems come in when the higher priced line is jeopardized by the new, lower-quality line. Tiffany & Co., a marketer of upscale, high-status gift merchandise, was bought by Avon Products and lost its classy image as Avon traded the Tiffany brands down. Regular customers were no longer sure whether Tiffany's was closest to Kmart or Cartier.

In our discussion of segmentation, we reviewed a similar strategy that failed miserably for Jaguar. Its effort to introduce lower-priced Jaguar automobiles into the American market damaged its high-end market; the new line had to be withdrawn. It is important to note the relationship between segmentation strategies and line and brand extensions. Research may indicate a new segment worth pursuing, as it did in the Jaguar and Kmart cases. But whether the current product line can be stretched to cover the new segment, and what impact this will have on it in the original segment, is a separate issue and one that management often fails to appreciate fully.

Repositioning Strategies

We have already emphasized the importance of establishing a competitive position in the mind of the consumer. Marketers often attempt to change the consumer's perception of their brand or product. Thus *Playboy* magazine redefined itself as a more "tasteful sex" and "literary quality" publication during its turnaround in the early 1980s. Now Christie Hefner, the CEO, envisions an even more dramatic change. According to a recent profile of her, "Some consuming zeal drives her to attempt to refashion her father's sex-based company. She wants it to be a more diversified media concern offering several magazines, videos, television programs, and catalogues: in short, "quality fun for adults."[13] From raunchy sex to quality fun is a tall order, even for a repositioning strategy!

Repositioning generally involves the use of advertising and promotional campaigns to create a changed perception. In using this strategy, however, the marketers must guard against confusing the consumer about the product's position; confusion is likely to accompany Playboy's efforts to switch from a sex-based appeal to a wholesome entertainment position, since presumably the magazine itself will continue to feature provocative (or pornographic, depending on your perspective) centerfolds.

Planned Obsolescence

Marketers sometimes use the strategy of forcing a product in their line to become outdated, thereby increasing replacement sales. This strategy, planned obsolescence, takes four forms. Technological obsolescence results when technological improvements are made in the product. Compaq Computers introduces a dozen new products each year because it develops the underlying technology at a rapid rate—and because its competitors will beat it to the punch without this rapid rate of replacement. Postponed obsolescence occurs when technological improvements are available but are not introduced until the demand for existing products declines and inventories are depleted. Gillete follows this strategy in introducing new shaving products; the company held back on the introduction of Teflon-coated razor blades until consumers' interest in chromium blades had peaked. Physical obsolescence results when products are built to last only a limited time. Examples include car batteries, nylon stockings, and light bulbs. Style obsolescence occurs when the physical appearance of a product is changed to make existing versions seem out of date. This strategy is most obvious in the garment and automobile industries. Planned obsolescence—especially style obsolescence—has been strongly criticized because it appears to encourage the purchase of products that are not really needed. It gives the impression that marketers are dictating the buying behavior of consumers. Marketers counter this criticism with the argument that people desire change and that, in some cases, the costs of inventories that no longer sell would only raise the prices of new products. Furthermore, many times the costs associated with higher levels of quality are prohibitive. A car battery that would last as long as a car would probably cost two or three times as much. (Actually, that doesn't sound at all bad!) And, too, the quality should match the intended use—a product need not last forever if the consumer only intends to use it for a season or two.

That's the official response to the standard criticism of planned obsolescence, but one of the great advantages of a book like this is that we can cover the body of marketing knowledge without the reverence required of a standard textbook. And this particular topic deserves to be handled with the gloves off. Why? Because marketing has a surly, soiled reputation in some parts, and one of the reasons is the disrespect for the consumer suggested by practices like planned obsolescence. The management team that is dedicated to serving its customers would not make kids' toys that break after a few hours of use; it would never produce automobiles that suffered from innumerable warranty claims, recalls, and malfunctions as new American autos do; it would never build a washing machine using parts that were expected to fail in a few years. And the argument that customers do not care to pay more for better quality is overturned by the success of well-made toys like Lego, by the dramatic in-roads of almost defect-free Japanese autos into Detroit's traditional strongholds; by the success of Maytag's emphasis on long-term reliability in washers and driers.

On the one hand, consumers are frequently willing to pay a little more for products that they can have confidence in, and feel cheated and gypped when products break down with unseemly rapidity. Every time a child's toy breaks on the day it was bought, both the child and the parent know full well that the manufacturer has ripped them off, and their distrust of marketers and manufacturers in general is increased as a result. These experiences poison the exchange relationship throughout the economy, just as the single bad service encounter poisons the customer's relationship with a single company. In most cases, planned obsolescence makes the job of the manager harder by chipping away at the customer-company relationship; a relationship that is already built on remarkably little trust and information in comparison to personal relationships, as we saw in the introduction to this third section of the book.

On the other hand, while experts debate the extent to which consumers are or are not willing to pay more for better quality, a small group of companies has come to see that better quality can be provided at the same, or lower, cost. Quality guru Philip Crosby has been saying for years that "quality is free"—the title of his best-selling book. Companies like Whirlpool, Florida Power and Light, Xerox, and Corning have thrown themselves into careful person-by-person, process-by-process improvement of their work over the last five years, implementing Total Quality Programs that are loosely modeled on the successful Japanese approach to quality. As was discussed in the chapter on strategy, the early results of these and similar efforts show that when a real commitment is made and the corporate culture can be refocused on the pursuit of perfection, almost unheard of rates of improvement can be achieved. Defect rates can be lowered by orders of magnitude. Processes streamlined to reduce costs. Products redesigned to reduce component costs and improve performance and reliability. These programs are the antithesis of planned obsolescence. They show that if a company wishes to it can give the customer more for less, rather than less for more, which is really all that planned obsolescence boils down to.

Because of technological developments and other innovations, companies must anticipate and plan for product obsolescence. They must even strive to make their own and their competitors' products obsolete through innovation. But they should never plan obsolescence into the product design or packaging, for this is a serious abuse of the consumers' trust; it violates the underlying architecture of the exchange equation. If marketing really is getting harder to conduct— one of the themes that seems to recur as we survey the field—part of the blame must be assigned to the thousands of companies whose acceptance of the notion of planned obsolescence has weakened the foundations of the customer relationship. Innovation does not have to mean an endlessly increasing offering of new bells and whistles, as the rapid growth in new products implies; it can also mean a drive to make a small number of essential products better and better. The success of foreign competitors in the U.S. market can be attributed to the management philosophy that allows ideas like planned obsolescence to gain credence in U.S. companies in the first place, although it is far more often attributed to the allegedly more wily strategies and greater advantages of foreign competitors.

Product Deletion Strategies

As products decline or become obsolete, management must decide when to eliminate them from the line. Not all marketers have a well-defined approach to this situation, and they are often reluctant to phase out products. Since the company must bear the costs of continuing to market weak products, it is important to think through the reasons for retaining products when they have fallen below their point of maximum profitability. In general, products are retained if a segment of the market still prefers them. Often a minority of the market does not adopt new products until well after the majority, and are also laggards when it comes to abandoning them for the next upgrade. But if these customers are important to a company's mission, their needs must be considered when considering how to time product deletion. In other cases, the old product simply confuses customers and competes with the new for access to the distribution channel without really benefiting anyone. If the product was successful, management may be too attached to it to give it the boot. Specifically, the managers who were responsible for its success may find it hard to see their creation die. This decision is probably best given to more impartial members of the management team!

Marketers can choose among three strategies for pruning product lines. The *continuation strategy* involves following the past strategy until the product is dropped. The *milking strategy* cuts marketing expenses way back in an effort to reduce costs and secure profits in the product's concluding stages. Finally, a *concentrated strategy* entails aiming all marketing efforts at the strongest market segment and phasing out the other segments.

How do these strategies apply to our case companies, the three producers of rotating products? In CDs, there is an obvious advantage to offering consumers a broad selection of music. Sony and Philips benefited from rapid line extension, because this speeded consumer acceptance of the new standard. However, it was not at all clear in 1983 whether the CD standard would be adopted in the popular music category. Many industry opinion leaders predicted that CDs would be restricted largely to the classical music segment, where the higher quality and longer product life was expected to be more important to consumers. Forecasts for 1983 CD sales based on this assumption were in the $400,000 range, since classical and jazz LPs accounted for only 7.5 percent of total prerecorded music sales in 1982, and since it was assumed that initial penetration of this segment would be small.[14] In fact, the sales were about 20 times this forecast, largely because of unexpectedly high demand in the popular music segment. Of the 443,320 CDs sold in 1983, 410,166 were popular versus 33,154 classical and jazz CDs.[15] The accepted forecasts proved completely wrong.

As first-movers, Sony and Philips had a dramatic information advantage over potential competitors in the CD market. They manufactured many of these first discs for the U.S. market (initially in two off-shore plants), and as licensors of the technology, presumably knew what their licensees were manufacturing as well. As a result, they knew that the popular market had accepted CDs and they were able to revise their forecasts of demand quickly to reflect the unexpectedly high sales in this segment.[16] This permitted them to see that consumer pull would force the industry into extending CDs into the popular segment, and would make the market far larger as a result. The information allowed them to invest in the capacity needed to serve the popular segment before their competitors did. And this is a very important point. Their superior information made clear the broad nature of the CD product line at retail, and they were able to maintain their first-mover advantage by rapidly investing in U.S. production facilities. For example, while by 1988 there were a total of 32 plants producing CDs worldwide, Philips and Sony controlled four large plants that together were capable of producing 57 percent of all CDs bought in that year.[17]

The story is slightly different for Rollerblade. We concluded earlier in the chapter that Rollerblade needs to maintain its leadership by continuing to lead the market in product development and innovation. But it still holds a strong controlling position in the market, with 66 percent of wholesale sales in 1990. While small by comparison with Philips and Sony, Rollerblade is three times as big as First Team Sports, the second-place maker of rollerblades. How should it use its added size, and the marketing leverage and consumer brand awareness this gives it? One possibility would be to expand the brand by moving into hockey skates, skate boards, exercise clothing, and so forth. Does this make sense for the company? It may in the future, depending upon the synergy of each extension with the image and customer base of the core product. But as long as Rollerblade is in a rapid growth phase, it will probably do best by focusing its resources on meeting growing demand for rollerblades and trying to maintain its leadership of the category through innovation. We say probably, because it is never clear how soon the growth will end. What if rollerblades prove to be a fad item, their sales flatten, then fall into a rapid decline? Pet rocks went through the entire product life cycle in a year, so it is important to remember that anything is possible! The only way to reduce the risk that such a possibility poses to the company is to stay very close to the market and to constantly gather information that could provide early warning of such an event.

What about Cuisinart? For starters, it is interesting to note that the company pursued a very limited brand extension strategy during most of its history. Its founder, Carl Sontheimer, was often criticized for being too protective of the Cuisinart name to permit the company to cash in on its recognition in the kitchenwares market. After Cuisinart was acquired from Sontheimer in 1987, the new management must have hoped to make up for lost time. They pursued an aggressive trading-down strategy, pushing their food processors into discount outlets and angering the more upscale kitchen stores that were its traditional channel. Cuisinart's prices were high, even when discounted, so the new down-scale market did not make up for the resulting loss of sales in the upscale market. Cuisinart lost market share and, to make matters worse, the product category itself had quietly slipped out of its growth phase and entered maturity and then a sickly decline. In fact, category sales peaked in 1986 at 6 million units. By 1989, sales had declined to only 3 million units! With food processor sales down industry-wide, and its own share slipping due to the failure of its trading-down strategy, Cuisinart was so pinched for cash that it could no longer afford to extend its brand into new, faster-growing products. The window of opportunity had closed. (There is probably a lesson in this for the managers of Rollerblade Inc.)

A new Cuisinart is rising from the ashes of these strategic mistakes under the guidance of Lee Rizzuto, the chairman of Conair Corporation who acquired it out of bankruptcy in 1990. And he points to Cuisinart's "failing to add products to its existing lines of processor and cookware" as a key mistake, one he hopes to remedy.[18] The Cuisinart name is still well-known, even though the product has slipped into decline, and Rizzuto will probably be able to leverage brand recognition into a successful full-line strategy for the cookwares market.

MATURITY AND DECLINE

You no doubt noticed that our discussion of product management strategies led us into strategies most suitable for the end of the product life cycle. Perhaps it is fitting that our discussion has moved from the growth stage to maturity and decline without our quite realizing it. This is just what happens to companies like

Cuisinart, and perhaps Rollerblade soon as well. The managers in a growth-stage market easily come to take that growth for granted, and when it slows, their companies are strained, sometimes to breaking, by the shortfall in cash flow. One of the problems with the product life cycle model is that it does not offer any rules for forecasting when the current stage will end and the next one begin.

But once it becomes clear that growth is slowing, the model offers a clear description of what is in store for management. Sales become very sensitive to the ups and downs of the economy, and cost savings become the route to profits. (Cuisinart ignored the fact that new competitors were achieving significant cost savings by producing their machines in Taiwan.) The number of competitors stabilize and the competitive situation can best be described as an oligopoly or monopolistic competition, depending on the number of competitors that remain. As the less efficient and effective competitors disappear from the scene (the victims of increased price competition), the market becomes highly segmented and promotional programs must be designed for each segment. Thus, when the number of male joggers stabilized in 1982, running shoe companies began courting women runners and nonrunners with new, more targeted product offerings and advertising.

During the maturity stage, there are two main strategies: defensive and offensive. The goal of a defensive strategy is to keep the product's market share from being eroded by substitute products. The focus is on cutting production costs and eliminating weaknesses in the product. Some modifications may be made in the marketing mix, such as improved packaging or a change in the promotional theme. Pricing becomes important as consumers become less responsive to promotion.

Promotional efforts are aimed more at dealers than at consumers. Coca-Cola, for example, faced diminished demand for its soft drinks as the teenage market shrank. In response, it began shifting dollars from national media to point-of-sale displays and price promotions designed to increase the loyalty of the more than 500 independent bottlers that produce, warehouse, distribute, sell, merchandise, and market the company's products. (Never underestimate the importance of the distribution channel—especially in maturity!)

An offensive strategy focuses on finding new markets and untapped market segments, new product uses, and ways to stimulate increased use of the product by existing customers. This attempt to break out of a stagnant market is called product relaunch. Attention is given to improving the quality of the product, at least as far as its subjective features are concerned. "Ajax with Ammonia-D" and "Lemon-Scented Mr. Clean" are examples of this approach. But tangible features can be added to the product too. For instance, in the appliance industry manufacturers are pushing digital touch-pad controls in the hope that these will create sales growth.

As products approach maturity, management must either revitalize them through an offensive strategy or must look for new products to offset the anticipated decline and death of the existing product. Most companies try to add new, high-growth products regularly so that they have offerings in all stages of the life cycle. But remember that the life cycle applies to the category as a whole, not any particular brand; this means the new products must really be new, not just extensions of brands in a mature category! Although most companies invest in ongoing product development, many fail to allocate their effort appropriately between mature and growth products.

While the onset of maturity sometimes catches management unaware, you can't miss decline. Falling sales are always an attention-getter. However, sometimes companies are uncertain whether their sales decline represents lost share or whether the entire category is actually declining. Good ongoing tracking of competitor performance is a great help in diagnosing the onset of each stage of the product life cycle; without it, companies can miss a life cycle change for as much as a year or two, and their strategies can be hopelessly out of date as a result.

As product sales turn downward, profits usually decrease and competitors begin to leave the industry. During the decline stage, the typical strategy is to bring in whatever profits can still be made before the product is dropped. In this stage, marketers do little to change a product's style, design, or other features; improvement does not seem worth the investment any more. Prices tend to hold steady; they may even rise if costs go up and there is a loyal segment that will continue to buy the product. On the other hand, prices may go down if the firm wants to reduce inventories. Distribution outlets are phased out as they become unprofitable; promotional expenditures are curtailed; and market information is gathered only for the purpose of identifying the point at which the product should be phased out.

At the beginning of Chapter 9, we postulated that management attention is focused on the customer's needs at the beginning of the product life cycle, and slowly shifts toward a focus on the company's needs by the end. You can easily see how declining sales and profits would draw management's attention away from thoughts of customers and toward the bottom line. Elimination of promotional expenditures makes good sense from a financial point of view, but this eliminates management's primary channel for communicating with customers. Customers' primary channel for communicating with management, through marketing research, is also curtailed to save costs and because management assumes that it would not act on information about customer preferences at this point anyway.

Thus, the cycle is complete: an innovative idea, born of insight into the consumer's condition, develops into a growing product. Competition enters to challenge the first mover, shifting management attention from the initial concept of consumer need to one of competitive rivalry. Management begins to extend the product and pursue narrower and more defensible niches through segmentation and positioning. Finally the new market is saturated and, with any luck, management has held onto a dominant share of it. Now its higher volume allows it to drive costs below competitors, and it enters maturity with a strong brand franchise and the likelihood of milking considerable profit before sales head South for the decline phase. Management tightens belts (except for its own, of course) and tries to run an efficient operation in order to control the profit stream it has created. Control means rigidity, ushering in those twin enemies of innovation, routine, and procedure. The focus on customers is now a hollow ritual, filtered as it is through computerized sales reports and layers of bureaucracy. When the product enters decline, it is already dead in the sense that the life force provided by the initial consumer focus is gone.

Remember Theodore Levitt's observation (quoted in Chapter 1) that loss of growth reflects "a failure of management?" Management consultant Mack Hanan has found that many mature industrial products can be turned around and given new life with a new management approach. He argues that "maturity occurs when we lose margin control. When customers set our margins, it is they who are marketing to us. It is we who pay the price."[19] Loss of margin control occurs when competitors match your performance and price and you no longer have anything unique and exciting to offer customers. The antidote is simply to start giving customers something unique and exciting again, but the loss of customer focus over the course of the product life cycle makes this simple solution far from obvious in most cases. (Digital controls on the same old washing machine are *not* unique and exciting.) As Hanan puts it, "In most mature businesses, the most mature component is the manager." The changes in management structure and attitude over the course of the life cycle are what doom products to decline in most cases.

This may sound like a radical thesis at first glance, but there are many examples of product relaunches in which supposedly moribund categories have been given new life and returned to growth. One of the classics is the story of baking soda, which was revived by Arm & Hammer simply by promoting new uses for it. Whereas it's use in baking continues to decline, sales growth and increased profits come from consumer adoption of the product for use as a refrigerator deodorant, rug cleaner and deodorizer, tooth paste, and so on. But it took imagination on Arm & Hammer's part, that particular marketing imagination that is fueled by a creative focus on consumers and their needs, to find and promote these new product uses in the first place. Management had to be revived by a reacquaintance with the customer before the brand and product category could be revived!

Hallmark cards continues to grow in a mature industry because it also understands the secret of reviving the life cycle through refocusing on the customer. Most of the sales in the card industry are made up of special-occasion greeting cards, and this was Hallmark's emphasis as well, at least until two years ago. After (hopefully) exhausting what the cynical consumer might view as an ongoing effort to create more special occasions (did Congress invent Grandparent's Day and National Secretary's Week, or was it really Hallmark?), Hallmark discovered the brave new world of *non-occasion cards*. Now don't laugh—this is a bona fide market opportunity.

Starting with the observation that "children love to get mail. It builds their self-esteem and it's also supportive," as Christy Wilson of Hallmark puts it, the company developed a line of non-occasion cards for children in 1989.[20] The line took off, generating much of the growth in Hallmark's sales. Competitor Gibson entered with a similar line in mid-1990, and now the category makes up 15% of total card sales in the United States. This line was successful not only because children love to get mail, but also because demographic trends are straining parent-child communications. When both parents work, the children may not talk to their parents all day. So Hallmark sees a growing social need that it can help address through its card line. What next? Hallmark has just introduced a line of non-occasion cards for adults.

Many years ago, Henry Ford observed that "The man who will use his skill and constructive imagination to see how much he can give for a dollar, instead of how *little* he can give for a dollar, is bound to succeed." These two extremes can be said to represent the two ends of the product life cycle. Every successful innovation is based on the effort to see how much one can give customers for the dollar. This is what being customer-oriented really boils down to. And as the customer focus is displaced by concern for competitors, and finally in the decline stage, concern for the company itself, the emphasis shifts to seeing how little one can give for the dollar. If you look briefly at the prescriptions of the life cycle model again, you will notice that the prescribed strategies for the onset of decline are designed to maximize the profits to the company by giving the customer as little as possible. Many of the popular strategies in maturity share this fault, with planned obsolescence being the worst offender. Therefore one way to revive a mature or declining product is to stop and ask, perhaps for the first time since its inception, how the company can give its customers more for their dollar.

11 THE NATURE OF PRICING

Making Money and Capturing the Customer

The purpose of price is not to recover cost but to capture the value of the "product" in the mind of the customer.

—Daniel A. Nimer, president, The DNA Group[1]

Ads from Compaq declare in bold, two-page type, "Two bottom-line reasons for buying a Compaq PC." Not surprisingly, #1 is that the company "significantly reduced prices." Way down in the far corner if you look hard, comes reason #2: "It simply works better." It is clear what the main selling point for PCs is these days. Perhaps the company should change its slogan to "It simply costs less." We saw in Chapter 10 how price comes into play in the maturity stage of the PLC. This price-based competition is a sure sign of maturity.

When Kayser-Roth, the large hosiery maker, introduced its new Sheer Indulgence brand of panty hose in 1988–89, it ran into trouble because its premium pricing deterred consumer trial. According to the trade magazine *Marketing Week*, "Consumers wouldn't try the hose which sold for twice as much as the in-store competition."[2] The company had to relaunch Sheer Indulgence in 1990 with a coupon on packages that gave buyers one dollar off at the register—a high cost to pay for trial!

If you ask the purchasing manager for Kraft, how much his company pays for airline tickets, he will say "That's really none of anybody else's business." Why should this Philip Morris Company subsidiary be so touchy about airline prices? Because the prices it pays are probably much lower than the prices individual consumers pay. Secret corporate contracts give large companies discounts averaging 27 percent off standard fares.[3] Airlines have traditionally been able to cut these deals by raising the fares paid by individuals, and the Justice Department is not amused by this practice. It launched four investigations of possible price-fixing by airlines in the last two years. One mechanism for price-fixing is the electronic database all airlines now use for listing their fares. Carriers may send subtle signals to each other via this network. As Ian Ayers, a specialist in antitrust issues from Northwestern, puts it, "It's a serious problem . . . a way of facilitating collusion." With the electronic network "it's easier to reach agreements. It's easier to detect breaches of an agreement."[4] But, collusion or no, the drop in travel during the U.S.-Iraq war set off a new round of fare wars in the airline industry, with price-based advertising and coupon battles for individual buyers and deeper discounts for business travelers.[5]

Pricing also has its secrets in the auto industry, where the U.S. manufacturers are struggling to increase prices without attracting consumer attention. *The Wall Street Journal* report explains that they are "trying to soft-pedal the price increases by scattering them all over the window sticker, ending discounts on options and putting last year's middle-of-the-lineup name on this year's base model."[6] In fact, deceptive practices are surprisingly common in pricing.

When Starkist decided it was time to raise the price of its standard $6^1/_2$ ounces can of tunafish, it faced only one small problem: Consumers did not agree. So it decreased the size of the can to $6^1/_8$ ounces instead. Not enough that most consumers would notice; just enough to increase the effective price per ounce by 5.8 percent.[7] This deceptive practice, called *downsizing*, is a widespread but little-noticed alternative to direct price increases. And it has been used, at the consumer's expense, in categories ranging from diapers to paper towels.

When President Bush renewed China's "most-favored nation" trade status in May of 1991, human-rights advocates were shocked, but pricing experts and cynics (or are they synonymous?) probably were not. The bottom line is that China has the lowest prices. At a time when U.S. trade deficits have fallen dramatically, imports from China continue to grow by 25 to 30 percent a year (on a dollar basis) and the U.S.-China trade deficit rises almost as fast.[8] But nobody seems inclined to complain about a trend that would provoke calls for war if it characterized the U.S. relationship to Japan. Nobody wants to risk their access to the lowest-cost supplier and, as *Fortune* puts it, "a bowl of rice and $2 a day beats wage rates almost everywhere."[9]

How important is pricing? Most managers steer clear of pricing, and on first thought most will rate it far below the other marketing variables—product, place, and promotion—in terms of its on-going impact on the business. But as soon as you pry the cover off of pricing decisions and issues, as these stories do, the extent of its influence seems daunting. This impression is strengthened by most customer surveys, for even in markets considered the least price-sensitive—luxury goods; essential industrial components—consumers consistently rank price as one of the most important variables driving purchase decisions. *Marketing Week* announced with great fanfare that "suddenly, pricing is the hot button."

But while the recession certainly brought cost-consciousness to the fore, the truth is that pricing has always been the hot button.[10]

Prices go by many names—rent, tuition, fare, rate, interest, dues, premium, honorarium, even bribe. But all these names add up to one thing—what one must give up in order to obtain a product. In short, any transaction can be seen as an exchange of something of value, usually money, the price, for some amount of satisfaction, the product. The key to determining the product's price lies in understanding the value that consumers place on the product. And that value results from the consumers' perception of the total satisfaction provided by the product. When the price is higher than the perceived value, the exchange will not take place. When the two sides of the marketing management exchange equation are in alignment, exchanges take place. No one knows this better than IBM, even if it didn't have Compaq to remind it.

IBM found itself on the short end of the exchange equation in 1984 when it tried to give a shot in the arm to its faltering PC$_{jr}$. The PC$_{jr}$ was priced too high (at about $1,700) for a machine with its limited features when it was introduced in 1983. By the middle of 1984, IBM had corrected some technical deficiencies and began cutting the price. By Christmas, the PC$_{jr}$, with color display and $200 worth of software, was priced as low as $795—and seasonal sales took off.[11] Yet even adjustments in the marketing equation may not be enough; the PC$_{jr}$ was dropped from IBM's line in 1985.

As this book goes to press, Apple is engaged in a similar experiment and is hoping that a new lower-priced line of personal computers will combat the IBM challenge. IBM compatible PC's have driven prices so low that customer perception of value has changed in the market, forcing people to recalculate the equation. But most of Apple's products are aimed at the business and education markets, while the PC$_{jr}$ was aimed at the home computer market. The biggest difference is that personal computers have more—and more important—uses in the business than the home, so the marketers of business computers have more value to offer. As a recent *Consumer Reports* article explains:

> Less than a decade ago, the computer seemed headed into every home . . . heavyweights like IBM and Texas Instruments rushed "home computers" into department stores . . . Now 10 years later, the computer revolution in the home has still not begun . . . consumers quickly learned that inexpensive home computers didn't do much, while truly useful ones were costly.[12]

The article goes on to describe several new personal computers aimed at the home, including IBM's PS/1. This machine lists for as little as $999 (more if you choose options like color monitor and hard drive). And it does a lot more a lot faster than the old PC$_{jr}$. In 1985 dollars, it is no doubt a better value than the PC$_{jr}$ was. But will it crack the home market? Perhaps not—*Consumer Reports* explains that "Yet to appear is the one compelling application or group of applications that might make a computer as indispensable in the home as in the office." And without this perception of indispensability, it is hard to sell home computers at *any* price.

These examples from the personal computer industry illustrate the influence of cost, demand, and competition on price. The PC$_{jr}$, and perhaps the new PS/1, face lackluster demand making it difficult for IBM to sell them at a healthy margin above cost as a result. Apple's new lower pricing reflects the need to respond to aggressive pricing by competitors. In both cases, consumer response is driving prices down and squeezing the manufacturer's margins.

These examples illustrate an important point: Price is a large part of consumer satisfaction, and a product's value is what consumers perceive it to be. Thus buyers help set the values of products. Therefore, it is odd that price sometimes makes no difference to the buyer. This is particularly true in the case of products that are bought on impulse or in an emergency.

Because price is a hard number, usually firmly fixed, it is easy to forget that the value it represents is a soft, slippery concept, and thus seldom represented properly. Value is an action-oriented concept.

The changeable nature of value is expressed in these lines from the poet, Emily Dickinson (who all Amherst-based authors feel obliged to quote at least once in a book since she is our town's most famous deceased resident):

> Undue significance a starving man attaches to food . . . partaken, it relieves indeed, but proves that spices fly in the receipt. It was the distance was savory.[13]

If you think back to our discussion of Maslow's hierarchy of needs, or more prosaically, to the typical consumption pattern of desire-purchase-gratification, it is clear that "spices fly in the receipt." The perceived value of a product is never so high as just before we buy it, and unfortunately the price commonly reflects this. Once the purchase is made, the need temporarily satisfied, the price would have to be far lower to induce immediate repurchase. This means price usually represents perceived value *only* to those who happen to be in immediate need of the product. It is misleading to speak of this value as universally accepted; it is tightly linked to the context and condition of each consumer. And it is therefore also misleading to think that a slight drop in price will necessarily lead to a large increase in sales. In fact, the link between price and consumer behavior is a complex one, mediated as it is by perception of value. Perhaps this is what makes many managers wary of pricing; what seems at first to be a hard, quantitative science proves upon reflection to be largely behavioral, not mathematical. As a result, all pricing decisions are complex and difficult.

Because of their intangible nature, services can be even more difficult to price than goods. In the case of services, the tendency to use price as an indicator of quality is more pronounced. When the consumer is especially likely to expect differences in the quality of a service (for example, accountants, investment counselors, or convention speakers), and when the consumer runs greater risks if the service is of poor quality, price becomes even more critical.

In marketing services, price is frequently used to build confidence in the quality of the service offered. With these warnings, we will move on to the standard tools and techniques of pricing, even though they often seem too crude for such subtle decisions.

SETTING PRICES

Price-setting starts with an exploration of pricing objectives. There are a variety of possible objectives, and it is helpful to review the options before setting or adjusting prices.

Sales Objectives

Pricing objectives should be tied to the overall strategic objectives of the organization. And since a fundamental goal of most companies is to grow, it follows that sales growth would be a reasonable goal of pricing. Sales growth is often pursued through price reduction. Yet higher sales do not automatically produce higher profits. Too often marketers expect that an increase in unit sales will result in lower cost per unit. In fact, many companies find that the expense of increasing sales volume outweighs the savings in unit costs and that profits actually diminish.

Some companies attempt to avoid sales growth, aiming instead at maintaining sales. Such organizations realize that sales growth and expansion bring increased complexity, greater responsibility, and more problems. Companies that pursue a follower or "me too" strategy realize that aggressive pricing often spurs bigger, more powerful competitors to retaliate. For this reason, companies like Crown Cork & Seal (metal containers) and Union Camp Corporation (paper products) aim to make profits through cost reduction and market share maintenance.

Compagnie Generale des Établissements Michelin emphasized market share when it attempted to become the world leader in the tire industry. For 30 years, Michelin had stressed the quality of its radial tires and sold them at premium prices. But in the 1980s, it established the goal of increasing its share of the American auto tire market by 6 percent and its share of the truck tire market by 10 percent. To achieve these goals, it slashed its replacement tire prices.

The pricing objective of some companies is simple survival. Organizations that find it difficult to compete may drop their prices—sometimes drastically—in order to generate the cash they need to pay their bills and stay in business, hoping that conditions will change and allow them to regain a firm position in the marketplace. In the low-cost computer market, for example, a price war begun by Commodore International brought on survival pricing by Mattel, Texas Instruments, and Timex. By 1983, not only had Commodore won the war (Mattel, Texas Instruments, and Timex all left the industry), but it had grabbed 35 percent of the market. (When aggressive low pricing is used by an industry leader to drive others out, however, it is often treated as unfair competition or "predatory pricing" by the FTC.)

Profit Objectives

Cost pressures, such as those imposed on U.S. manufacturers by Chinese competitors, lead companies to seek to achieve their financial goals through pricing. One commonly cited profit objective is profit maximization, or obtaining the highest possible profit. Economic models are often used to describe how maximum profits can be attained in theory. In practice, however, this goal is unrealistic, since a firm can never know when it has achieved it. Data about costs and demand are difficult if not impossible to obtain or estimate accurately. In addition, profit maximization is often equated with "profit gouging," and neither consumers nor government officials take kindly to companies that seem to earn excessive profits. Moreover, if a firm's profits are excessive, competitors will be attracted to its markets.

Another profit-oriented objective, a more frequently used and attainable one, is target return on investment. A firm that sets this goal for itself seeks to regain a certain percentage of its investment as income. This return on investment (ROI) is the ratio of profits to invested capital. It may be described as the compensation that the firm expects to receive for the use of its capital. The target return on investment approach has traditionally been used by firms that are monopolies or leaders in their industries—such as General Motors, DuPont, International Harvester, and Union Carbide.

In recent years, the pricing objectives of many companies have emphasized cash flow as well as profits. This involves generating cash as fast as possible and maintaining a steady flow of cash into the company. This emphasis on cash flow is an outgrowth of the poor economic conditions of the 1970s and early 1980s, especially the high cost of borrowing money. To generate cash, many companies pruned their product lines and lowered their prices. It rose again to popularity during the 1990–91 recession.

Competitive Objectives

Many firms consciously price their products to meet or prevent competition. In a number of industries, there is a definite price leader; R.J. Reynolds in cigarettes and IBM in computers are examples. R.J. Reynolds sets cigarette prices and other companies follow its lead. Most competitors in the computer industry look to IBM in setting their prices, although recently IBM has been forced to follow the lead of lower priced competitors like Compaq in its PC line. (Leadership can be hard to maintain.) In other situations, a company may enter a market with extremely low prices in order to discourage other firms from entering the market. In still other cases, a marketer may set prices in such a way as to offset the effects of competitors' actions. In the "fare wars" in the airline industry, for example, carriers are often forced to cut their fares in response to the low fares set by their competitors. When fuel prices go up, as they did when Iran invaded Iraq, these fare wars can drive carriers to below-cost pricing, and even to bankruptcy. The pressure to end such pricing battles through illegal collusion is great.

A price war begins, like a real war, with each combatant believing it is possible to achieve their objectives at the expense of the competitors. But, like real wars, price wars tend to hurt all the parties in the long run. This certainly is the case in the ongoing mainframe computer price war. The average price for a used IBM 3090 mainframe fell from $3 1/4 million to $1 1/4 million in the first seven months of 1991.[14] New mainframes are selling at 40 to 50 percent off list. According to an executive V.P. of leasing company Comdisco, "There is no such thing as a price any more." The industry leader, IBM, is partly responsible for this raging strategic battle. It has dug in its heels, announcing that it refuses to lose any more market share to competitors like Amdahl, Hitachi, Data Systems, and Unisys. (Unisys' $1.3 billion loss in the 2nd quarter of 1991 may also fuel the war by forcing them to adopt survival pricing.) IBM also has introduced software and hardware upgrades in recent years that make it easier for customers to bring old machines up to the performance level of new machines. This has strengthened the linkage between used and new prices, meaning that the free-fall in used prices had a greater effect on new prices than manufacturers expected.[15] This hurts IBM and other manufacturers, but it is a real killer for the leasing companies. Their leases for used mainframes are based on the projected value of machines at the end of the leases. Their projections are going to be completely wrong.

With this introduction to the concepts and objectives of pricing, we are now ready to look at and use specific pricing strategies. These are presented in the following sections on cost-based, demand-based, and competitor-based pricing.

COST-BASED PRICING STRATEGIES

A product's price can be compared to a tripod; the initial price generally rests on three foundations: costs, demand, and competition.

We turn now to the first leg of the pricing tripod—costs. The costs associated with bringing a product to market are a crucial factor in setting prices. Costs represent the *floor*—the minimum that can be charged in an exchange; prices that are below costs yield no profit (or from the customer's perspective, costs that are above value will not be reimbursed). Some firms do set prices below costs for some products, but only for a short time. In the long run, the price must cover all the costs incurred in producing and marketing the product.

To say that "costs" are the basis of prices is simplistic; there are many kinds of costs, and they are related to price in different ways. We will look at the various kinds of costs and then examine some of the ways in which marketers use them to set the list price for a product. (See Exhibit 11.1.)

EXHIBIT 11.1.   Affect of costs on product price.

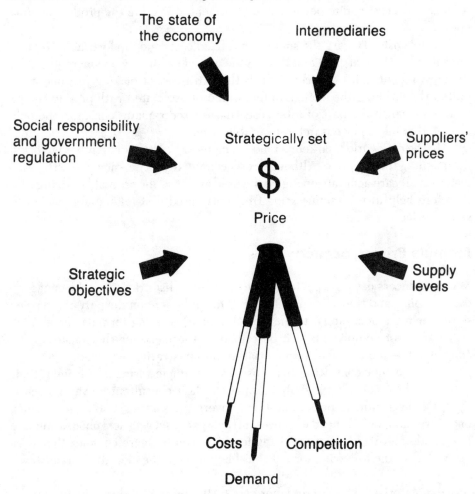

Total fixed costs (TFC) are costs that do not change, no matter what quantity of output is produced. Such costs normally include executives' salaries, plant and equipment depreciation, property taxes, employees' health insurance premiums, and the like. These costs exist whether the firm produces a million units of the product or chooses to produce no units at all. While fixed costs can change in the long run (for example, when a new plant is built), they remain constant in the short run. Yet fixed costs per unit decrease as the quantity produced increases.

Total variable costs (TVC) are costs that fluctuate, depending on the quantity of output produced. Variable costs typically include raw materials, fuel, workers' wages, packaging, sales commissions, freight, and other such charges. If no products are produced, no variable costs are incurred. In practice, variable costs can change as the level of output increases, since suppliers often give discounts for purchases of large quantities of raw materials, and because workers tend to become more efficient at making the product as time goes by.

Total costs (TC) are the sum of total fixed costs and total variable costs.

Finally, the marginal cost (MC) is the cost of producing one more unit than the most recent unit produced. This is the extra cost of making just one more unit of the product, the change in the total cost associated with producing one more unit. Since the part of total costs that is fixed remains constant, the only change that takes place is in total variable costs.

In the real world, marketers tend to emphasize costs over all other factors in determining the list price. Although costs cannot always be known exactly, estimates usually are accurate enough to be used as a basis for profitable pricing. It is therefore helpful to examine some frequently used cost-related approaches to setting prices.

Formula Pricing Strategy

Many producers use a simple formula to arrive at a list price. Such formulas are easy to apply, and they eliminate the need for judgment on the part of the price setter (or more accurately, the *use* of judgment). Pricing formulas emphasize either the cost components just described or the elements that make up the components—such as labor or materials or administrative overhead.

Management consulting firms use a very simple formula in pricing their services: They multiply the daily fees paid to their consultants (a variable cost) by 3. Of the resulting price, one-third covers the salaries of the consultants, one-third pays for overhead expenses (office space, secretaries, phones, and the like), and one-third is profit. Pricing formulas can be more complex than this. For instance, the following formula has been used in the electronics industry:

Price = Material cost + Direct labor cost + 100 percent of direct labor cost (to cover overhead) + 120 to 180 percent of direct labor cost (to cover all other costs and provide a profit

Formulas like these are used in the hope that the final price will be sufficient to cover all costs (even though they may not all be used in the computation) and still leave some profit. The main problem with this simple and quick approach, as with all cost-oriented approaches to pricing, is that it does not consider whether the customer will be willing to pay the price charged. In short, demand is ignored. Also, this approach neglects competitors' prices.

Cost-Plus Pricing Strategy

In cost-plus pricing, the list price is determined by adding a reasonable profit to the cost per unit, or average total cost. This approach ensures that all costs will be covered and that the desired profit will be achieved. However, it relies on cost forecasts. This can be dangerous, since costs often change rapidly. Moreover, this approach also fails to ensure that the quantity of output produced will actually be sold, since the marketer cannot know whether the price is in line with consumers' perceptions of the value of the product. And if fewer units are sold, the firm's profit picture may be bleak at best.

There are situations in which the cost-plus approach is appropriate, but in those cases the nature of demand is known. The level of consumption of some products is stable and not very sensitive to changes in price. Examples of such products are milk, bread, paper clips, and bobby pins.

Cost-Plus Pricing by Intermediaries

In setting their prices, wholesalers and retailers use a version of the cost-plus approach known as *markup pricing*. The price paid by final consumers is the end result of a series of markups that occur as the product moves through the distribution channel from the producer to the consumer. Let's see how this works.

A wholesaler pays a manufacturer $20 for a product. If the wholesaler adds $5 to the price and then sells the product to a retailer for $25, the markup is $5. This includes an amount to cover all wholesaling costs beyond the manufacturer's price for the product, plus something to ensure a profit. Since the markup is usually expressed as a percentage of the selling price, in this example the wholesaler's markup is 20 percent. (The markup is often computed as a percentage of cost.)

When a retailer purchases the product from the wholesaler, it will also add a markup to the price. The retailer's markup is frequently between 40 and 60 percent, depending on the type of product handled. Assuming a 50 percent markup on a product purchased for $25, the retailer would charge consumers $37.50 for the product.

Some intermediaries use the same markup for all products; others use a variable-markup policy, using different markups for different items. Grocery stores, for instance, use markups of 6 to 8 percent for soap and sugar, 15 to 18 percent for canned goods, and 25 to 35 percent for meats and produce. These are known as "customary" markups.

Target Return Pricing Strategy

In this popular approach, the marketer seeks to obtain a predetermined or "targeted" percentage return on the capital used to produce and distribute the product, or a specific total dollar return. This method is similar to the average-cost approach. An example will show how it works.

Assume that a company has fixed costs of $50 and must incur an additional $80 in variable costs to product eight items. (Eight is arbitrarily assumed to be the quantity of an order that management must set a price for.) Also assume that management wants a 10 percent return on its investment of $200 in developing the product; $20 is its targeted profit.

To compute the price, add the targeted profit to the fixed costs:

$$20 + 50 = 70$$

Compute the average:

$$150/8 = \$18.75$$

This price will cover all fixed and variable costs plus the targeted return, *if* all eight units are sold.

This approach, like other cost-related approaches, gets an "A" for simplicity. And if the company sells all the items it plans to sell, it will achieve its target return. However, this approach also ignores the demand side—as well as competitors' price strategies—and the targeted return is not guaranteed. What happens to return on investment if a firm sells five items rather than the eight items planned? The firm still has three items in inventory and is realizing a loss—and hence a negative ROI; the calculations are shown in Exhibit 11.2.

Until the early 1980s, the U.S. automobile industry used the target return approach. According to an industry expert, "It was a classic formula dating back to the 1920s. It made pricing a fairly easy task."[16] The car companies had pricing committees that decided how many cars they expected to sell, totaled up costs and threw in a healthy profit, and simply divided these costs by expected unit sales. Whenever costs rose or sales fell, prices were increased to make up the difference. But the high inflation rates of the late 1970s and fierce competition from Japanese automakers combined to change this pattern. According to a spokesperson for American Motors, "We found out what happens when you try to offset cost with higher prices: you stall the market."[17] In the early 1980s, marketers turned to rebates, savings certificates, contests,

EXHIBIT 11.2. ROI calculations.

Estimated Sales: 8 Items		Actual Sales: 5 Items	
Total revenue (estimated)		Total revenue (actual)	
(8 × $18.75) =	$150.00	(5 × $18.75) =	$ 93.75
Total fixed cost		Total fixed cost	
(excluding target return)	$ 50.00	(excluding target return)	$ 50.00
Total variable cost	$ 80.00	Total variable cost	$ 80.00
Total cost	$130.00	Total cost	$130.00
Profit (loss)	$ 20.00	Profit (loss)	($ 36.25)
Return on investment (ROI)		Return on investment (ROI)	
$=\dfrac{20}{200}=10\%$		$=\dfrac{(36.25)}{200.00}=-18.12\%$	

extended warranties, low-cost financing—even a money-back guarantee—to lure buyers. In the 1989 and 1990 seasons, the U.S. auto makers were engaged in a costly and unprofitable effort to stimulate demand and grab a share through these price-based incentives. By early 1991, it was clear that auto makers had lost control over their pricing, despite their efforts to disguise price increases. Regardless of sticker price, consumers are buying cars at lower actual prices by waiting to take advantage of promotional deals. So much for formulas!

Breakeven Pricing Strategy

Breakeven pricing focuses on the volume of sales at which total revenue equals total costs, that is, the volume at which no profit or loss is incurred. This approach requires a thorough knowledge of costs. The basic idea of breakeven analysis is that the price of a unit of the product must cover its own variable costs as well as the fixed costs of producing the product. As shown in Exhibit 11.1, the breakeven point is reached when enough units of the product have been sold to cover their own variable costs along with *total* fixed costs. At sales volumes below the breakeven point, total costs will not be covered and a loss will result. At sales volumes above that point, anything over the variable costs becomes profit.

The breakeven point can be determined by using the following equation:

$$\text{BE volume (units)} = \frac{\text{TFC}}{\text{Fixed-cost contribution}}$$

$$= \frac{\text{TFC}}{\text{Selling price} - \text{Variable cost per unit}}$$

The term *fixed-cost contribution* refers to the portion of the selling price that is left over after variable costs have been accounted for, as is indicated in the second equation.

When using this method, the marketer examines a number of different prices, as shown in Exhibit 11.3, and notes the volume of the product that must

EXHIBIT 11.3. Computation of the break-even point.

(1) Unit	–	(2) Unit Variable Cost	=	(3) Contribution to Fixed Cost	(4) Total Fixed Cost	(3) = (5) Breakeven Point
23		20		3	50	16.7
29		20		9	50	5.6
32		20		12	50	4.2
42		20		22	50	2.3

be sold at each price in order to break even. Breakeven analysis makes two simplifying assumptions.

First, it assumes that the variable cost per unit is constant—but we learned earlier that variable costs depend on the volume produced. Second, breakeven analysis assumes that any quantity can be sold at a given price. In reality, however, we know that for any given price there is a maximum quantity that will be sold and that this reflects the upper limit of demand. The marketer therefore must compare the breakeven volumes for various prices with estimates of the maximum volumes that can be sold at those prices. If the estimated maximum volume is below the breakeven quantity, that price is rejected. The price that is finally selected is the one that will yield the greatest amount of profit if the planned volume of sales is achieved.

Experience Curve Pricing Strategy

In general, the average total cost of a product declines steadily as more units are produced. This decrease is due to a combination of two separate cost-related phenomena—economies of scale and experience. Economies of scale result when fixed costs are spread over more units of the product. Economies of scale can also result from efficiencies that allow average variable costs to decline, such as greater employee skill due to experience. This can be further enhanced if fixed costs can be decreased over the long run.

Analyses of costs in many industries have proven that as the volume of production rises, cost per unit drops at a predictable rate. Specifically, each time the cumulative volume of production doubles, the per-unit cost declines by a fixed percentage. This is a result of learning—in other words, of experience. Producers that benefit from this effect are said to move down the experience curve. An 85 percent experience curve is shown in Exhibit 11.4. This curve, which is typical of many products and services, indicates that as cumulative volume of production doubles, costs per unit decrease by 15 percent.

Here we see that higher volumes of production are desirable, since they lead to cost reductions. This is one of the reasons that marketers fight to increase their market share. And when costs decline, the firm can pass on the savings in the form of lower prices, keep it as profits, or do some of both. Texas Instruments rode the experience curve when it brought the prices of digital watches from $2,000 to under $10 in five years. The price reduction followed a 60 percent decrease in production costs as the volume of units produced rose.

Experience curve pricing does not explain the success of Japanese auto firms in American markets. Detroit had (and still has) produced many more units than the Japanese auto makers, but Japanese producers nonetheless learned more rapidly, introducing a series of process and product innovations that allowed them to come into U.S. markets with low prices. Japanese companies quickly took the lead in markets where consumers were particularly price conscious. For example, at the beginning of the 1980s Japanese cars were

EXHIBIT 11.4.   An 85 percent experience curve.

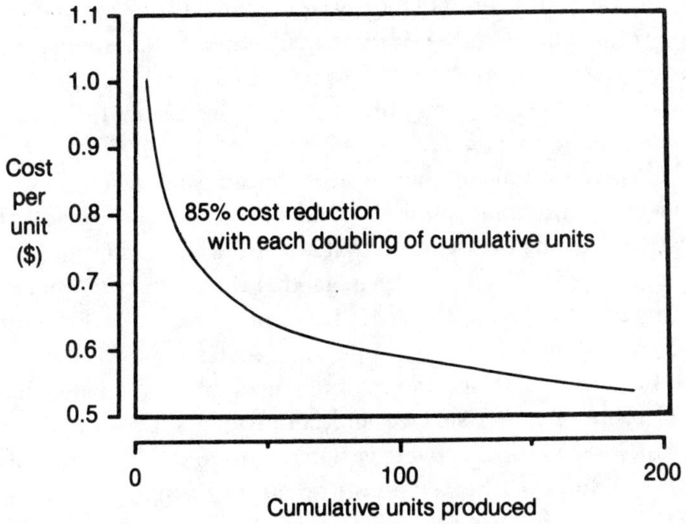

priced an average of $2,000 below U.S.-made autos and enjoyed a better qual-
ity image to boot. By 1984, Japanese auto producers had a $1,200 to $2,000
cost advantage over U.S. car makers! And a 1990 study shows that productivity
is still higher at major Japanese auto makers than in the United States. This
illustrates the point that the rate of learning in an organization may be what
really drives cost down, and the cumulative experience of the organization is
relevant only to the extent that it produces learning. A static, conservative
manufacturer may not learn as fast as an aggressive entrepreneur, for example.

Experience curve pricing has the drawbacks of other cost-oriented pricing
approaches. It focuses on the cost component without considering what consumers feel is an appropriate price and without taking account of competitors'
prices. It has been successful in cases in which the prices charged were in line
with demand and the low-price marketer was the market leader. Experience
curve pricing works best with products that are entering the rapid growth stage
of the product life cycle.

Marginal-Cost Pricing Strategy

In this approach, a firm sells an additional unit of a product for the extra cost of
producing that unit. In practice, the seller will not charge precisely the marginal
cost, but will charge somewhat more, though still less than the average total cost.

Pricing on the basis of marginal or near-marginal cost is not generally a
wise approach, since profits cannot be made unless all costs are recovered. But
there are times when such a strategy may be advantageous. For example, marketers that are just beginning to ride the experience curve can afford to price
below cost, knowing that as volume expands, the losses will turn into profits as

the effects of experience take hold. And if a firm is threatened with a plant shutdown but wants to keep its laborforce employed, this pricing method may produce the volume needed. In addition, marketers that are engaging in a price war may resort to this tactic to drive competitors away. Finally, when a store wants to attract customers it may price a few items below full cost; such low-priced items are called *loss leaders*.

The McCormick Inn in Chicago used an unusual variation on marginal-cost pricing to secure some publicity and induce people to stay there. In a program called "Rooms by Degree" that was in effect between November 16 and December 30, the room rate was pegged at the outdoor temperature. If the temperature was 20 degrees, the cost of the room was $20. If the temperature dipped to zero, the room was free. Hotels and motels have high fixed costs (the costs of the building, heating, and maintenance) and rather low variable costs (the costs of room cleaning service and laundry). As a result, the rental of a room even at a low rate often covers variable costs and adds something to cover fixed costs. In addition, the temperature rarely dropped below 40 degrees during the time that the program was in effect!

DEMAND-BASED PRICING STRATEGIES

While Production and marketing costs set a "floor" for the price, the level of demand establishes its upper limit, or "ceiling." As noted earlier, if the expected satisfaction that will come from the product is less than the price of the product, no exchange will take place. In short, demand reflects the upper limit on what consumers are willing to give up in order to obtain the product.

Demand is very difficult for price setters to estimate; consumers appear fickle, and their attitudes, values, needs, and wants change frequently—often very rapidly. Keeping on top of their moods and whims regarding what they will pay for products is extremely difficult. Marketing surveys can and do help to identify the level of demand, but there is often a big difference between what consumers say they will do and what they in fact do.

As further proof of the difficulty of estimating demand, we note that some high prices are not only accepted, but accepted enthusiastically. General Electric, for example, introduced its Touch 'n Curl mist hair curler for $27, and it outsold a similar hair curler priced at $15 by as much as 45 percent. Litton Industries' best-selling microwave oven-range combination was priced at $1,099 and far outsold similar models priced $400 lower. The difficulty in finding a price that is high enough to meet demand without being too high makes pricing decisions more of an art than a science.

In the typical demand situation facing most firms today, as the price of a product decreases, the quantity demanded goes up. Conversely, as the price goes up, the quantity demanded goes down. There is, in other words, an inverse relationship between price and quantity demanded.

In the real world, marketers need to know with some certainty that a given price will generate a given quantity sold, but this information is rarely available! In order to know that a slightly lower price would generate a specific quantity sold, that price would have to actually be charged, and the marketer would have to monitor purchases of the product. In practice, this kind of testing is not feasible. Furthermore, consumers are very changeable. By the time the experiment was complete, their reactions to various prices could have changed.

One company that has experimented with estimating demand is Noumenon Corporation, a California-based software manufacturer. When it introduced Intuit, a fully integrated program designed to run on an IBM or compatible computer, at a rather typical price of $395, the firm found little consumer interest in the program. Noumenon therefore decided to test-market various prices. It dropped the price to $50 and then raised it by $20 a week. Sales of Intuit rose steadily until the price reached $130. Beyond $130, sales were lower than at the prior price, and at $210 they stopped altogether. Analysis showed that sales were greatest at $90, so the company settled on a price of $89.95. After six months, it had sold 1500 programs.

Prestige Pricing Strategy

Not all products have the traditional downward-sloping demand curve. For some products, higher prices bring higher sales volumes—at least up to a point. Products do not have to be unusually expensive to show this kind of relationship between price and demand. It can be found in such product categories as baby foods and smoke detectors. Consumers tend to believe that a higher price indicates higher quality, especially where safety is a factor. Also, in some product categories, different brands differ greatly in prestige value. Price is also used as a clue to quality when no other information about the product is known.

Price Elasticity Strategy

Consumers are more sensitive to price changes in some product categories than in others. This is even more true at the level of individual brands.[18] This sensitivity to price is termed price elasticity of demand. It reflects changes in quantity purchased relative to changes in price. There are three types of price elasticity:

1. *Elastic demand*, in which a percentage change in price brings about a greater percentage in quantity sold (generally in the opposite direction).
2. *Inelastic demand*, in which a percentage change in price brings about a smaller percentage change in quantity sold (generally in the opposite direction).
3. *Unitary demand*, in which a percentage change in price brings about an equal percentage change in quantity sold (again, generally in the opposite direction).

In situations of elastic demand, consumers are quite sensitive to changes in price. For example, in the automobile industry the market was historically quite elastic. Lagging sales were often revived by rebates, savings certificates, and low-cost financing. As already discussed, however, these techniques have not been as effective recently. Demand for autos is becoming less elastic, probably because there is considerable overcapacity in the industry at present.

In situations of inelastic demand, the market is rather insensitive to changes in price. Thus demand for a product decreases by a relatively small amount as the price per unit increases. This occurs because consumers feel strongly enough about having additional units of the product to purchase it at a higher price. Examples are products for which consumers feel a strong need and for which there are few or no substitutes, such as salt, milk, and postage stamps. Thus sales of domestic postage stamps were hardly affected by the 16 percent increase in the price of stamps in 1991.

Situations of unitary elasticity usually occur when there are many sellers whose products can be readily substituted for one another. No one seller can influence the price to any great extent. The demand for many agricultural products reflects unitary elasticity, since a single farmer cannot control the prices at which farm products will be sold. The prices of these goods rise and fall in accordance with supply and demand.

Three influences have been found to affect the price elasticity of demand for a product. One is the extent to which other products can be substituted for it—the more alternatives there are, the more price elastic the product tends to be. Second, if the product is a necessity, it tends to be price-inelastic—price doesn't matter to the buyer. Third, when the price of the product is a significant portion of one's budget, demand for that product tends to be more price elastic. Cars and houses are price elastic whereas small, routine purchases like canned peaches and cereal are less so.

Products also exhibit "cross elasticity of demand." Changes in the prices of certain products affect sales of other products. For example, as the prices of videocassette recorders dropped to the $200 to $400 range, sales of blank videocassette tapes soared. Why? Many consumers could for the first time afford a second VCR, and therefore could copy movies for their own libraries.

Price Range Strategy

Consumers rarely seek products with a particular price in mind. Instead, they typically seek to satisfy a need or want within a range of prices. In fact, it appears that people refrain from buying a product when its price seems to be too low as well as when it seems to be too high. The lower limit on price is tied to the perceived relationship between price and quality. So while we usually talk about demand in terms of setting a ceiling on price, demand may provide a floor, or lower limit, as well. In sum, demand is not tied to a single price; it is related to a range of prices. The marketer's job is to set the price within that range.

THE THIRD LEG: COMPETITION

While costs set a floor for prices and are usually used to determine the list price, and demand sets the upper level, or ceiling, for that price, marketers must also consider the prices of competitors that offer buyers other ways of satisfying their needs. Most of the time, the marketer is concerned with direct competitors, but this is not always the case. Some competitors may offer innovative products that satisfy needs in new ways. For example, warm-up suits replaced sweatsuits for joggers and other sports enthusiasts; leather athletic shoes replaced canvas tennis shoes and sneakers; metal tennis rackets replaced wooden ones. In each case, the price of the traditional product could be used as a basis for evaluating the price of the new product.

Most often, though, buyers compare the prices of directly competing products—of Federal Express versus Express Mail, Nestlé's Souptime versus Lipton's Cup-a-Soup, or Blue Cross/Blue Shield health insurance versus a local health maintenance organization. In many such cases, competitors' prices become the key to price setting. This is especially true in price wars, such as the mainframe case described earlier.

Competitors can initiate price changes in either direction. Competitive price reductions are the most frequent maneuver. When this happens, the marketer can respond in a number of ways. It can maintain its price—but this strategy is best only if it has some competitive advantage, some perceived difference in the mind of the buyer that would justify a higher price. With commodities, this strategy would be a mistake. Along the same lines, a competitor can fight back with nonprice competition in the form of higher advertising budgets, improved packaging, or product modification. Most frequently, however, the competitive response to a price reduction is a similar price reduction. This happens constantly in the airline industry. A final approach is a very aggressive one—a price increase with some sort of product improvement. For example, when Heublein was attacked by Wolfschmidt with a $1 per bottle price reduction, it responded with a $1 increase on its Smirnoff brand coupled with additional advertising in an effort to protect its 23 percent market share.

Sometimes competitors take the lead and raise their prices. When the products of competing firms are homogeneous, the reaction to a price rise is to do nothing, since few buyers will pay more for something that they don't see as different from competing products. However, when buyers see differences between products, competitors have more choices open to them. If the price raiser is the market leader, the strategy of maintaining the lower price can create a competitive advantage.

In sum, competitive pressures are extremely influential in setting prices. Competitive pricing is the key marketing tool of discount department stores, cut-rate drugstores, and off-price apparel stores. Their appeal is in offering products at prices below those charged by direct competitors. But for most marketers, strategic pricing requires a solid understanding of the costs of producing and marketing the product and an indication of what consumers are willing to pay for it. The marketer must temper these two inputs with information about competitors' prices and how they are likely to react to price changes.

STRATEGIC PRICING

The tripod concept is helpful in organizing cost-based, demand-based, and competitor-based strategies. However, there are a number of pricing strategies that are more context-specific and best treated outside this scheme. For example, the pricing strategies used for new products are quite different from the typical strategies described previously. For the rest of this chapter, we will review pricing options in specific situations, and then we will close with a look at an emerging theory of pricing that is more closely allied to the marketing concept than are many of the traditional strategies. It is called *value pricing*. But first, let's quickly review situational pricing strategies.

New Product Introductions

There are two common strategies in this situation, although combinations of the two often are seen. In the skimming approach, the initial price is set at a high level with the goal of selling the product to the people who want it most—and are willing to pay a higher price for it. Later, when the high-demand market segment has been satisfied, the price is reduced to appeal to more price-sensitive customers. In this way, total revenue is maximized.

For a skimming strategy to be effective, a number of conditions must prevail. Demand should be rather insensitive to price. Otherwise the initial high price will not attract enough buyers to make the product profitable. Skimming is more effective when there are different price segments within a market. It works well, too, when consumers know little about the costs of producing and marketing the product—and are unlikely to realize that they are paying a premium for being among the first to acquire it. Finally, skimming works best when there is little likelihood that competitors will enter the market quickly with a similar product. Competition often leads to price cutting, which soon puts an end to the attractive profits that accompany a skimming strategy.

From the marketer's standpoint, skimming offers several advantages. As we have seen, the costs of developing a new product can be substantial, and a skimming strategy can help in recovering these costs. Moreover, if the firm initially produces the product on an experimental basis but plans to produce it on a larger scale later, a skimming policy can be used to limit demand for the product until mass production can be undertaken. And since a high price is often equated with high quality, a skimming policy can develop a prestige image for the product. Finally, marketers know that it is easier to lower the initial price than it is to risk consumer resistance to a price increase. So when the shape of the demand curve is not known, skimming makes sense.

For all its advantages, however, skimming has certain drawbacks. First, it attracts competitors. The initial high price yields high profits, thereby encouraging other firms to introduce similar products. And the higher the initial price, the more likely it is to attract competitors. An inappropriate price may hurt sales throughout a product's life and can even lead to an early death. Another drawback of skimming strategies is that they often make it necessary to revise the marketing mix to serve the new target markets that appear as prices drop. For example, advertising is likely to become more important than personal selling, and the distribution pattern is likely to shift from specialty stores to mass merchandise outlets.

In contrast to the skimming approach, a *penetration strategy* calls for low prices and high volume. Marketers who choose this approach believe that a low price will lead to such high sales volume that the total profits will be greater than could be achieved with a higher initial price. The idea is to reach the entire market with a low price, thus generating the greatest possible demand.

Penetration is often used when the market is not divided into price segments—when there is no "elite" market that is willing to pay a high price. Such a strategy is appropriate for new products that are not socially visible and do not symbolize high status. The penetration approach is generally useful when consumers are price sensitive and when a lower price will really result in a larger volume of sales. For example, Paramount released the home videocassette of *An Officer and a Gentleman* at a price of $39.95, substantially less than the then standard $59.95 to $79.95 price tag for a hit movie. The cassette took off and sold 80,000 copies at a time when 25,000 copies was considered the equivalent of a gold record. But note this success attracted copy-cats and helped drive the prices downward in this industry. It could not be done again at this price point. Penetration pricing is also used in situations in which competitors can enter the market rapidly, since lower prices may make the market less attractive to potential competitors. Finally, penetration pricing is useful when a firm can establish large-scale production plants and reap the benefits of economies of scale.

Like the skimming approach, however, penetration pricing has some disadvantages. Although the tendency to discourage competition is a major benefit of this approach, marketers should never feel that their market position is secure— even when they are offering an attractive low price. Thus, after Paramount came out with its $39.95 price, Warner released *Risky Business* at $39.98 and MCA offered *Jaws 3* at a similar price. In fact, a low price often results in losses during the introductory stage, while the product is gaining consumer acceptance. With a low-price strategy, the break-even point is not reached until a larger quantity is sold. A penetration approach, therefore, entails more risk than a skimming policy. On the other hand, penetration pricing can open up markets that have not been served before.

Skimming and penetration need not be viewed as either/or alternatives. Sometimes a skimming strategy is followed by a penetration strategy. For example, Texas Instruments was once a price leader in the digital-watch industry, setting both the upper and lower price levels. But once the low-price barrier of

$50 was broken by competitive pressures and price cutting, the company quickly adopted a penetration strategy. In the end, it became the first company to introduce a $10 watch.

Skimming and penetration are the major approaches to pricing new products, but they don't cover the full range of strategic options. Let's look at some of the other pricing strategies used by marketers.

Pricing When Intangibles Are Important

We have noted several times that for some consumers the intangible features of a product play a key role in the purchase decision. We have seen, too, that price can be an important element in conveying the product's image. In fact, some marketers make a point of presenting an image of quality through the price tag. Thus certain beers (Michelob and Lowenbrau), automobiles (Cadillac and BMW), cosmetics (Clinique), and liquors (Chivas Regal Scotch and Jack Daniels Sippin' Whiskey) are given a prestige image through pricing. (This is known as prestige pricing.)

Curtis Mathes, which markets a line of television sets, explicitly states in its advertisements that its sets are the most expensive on the market. In taking this approach, the company recognizes that there is a market segment that wants high quality and believes that price is a good indicator of quality. Polaroid has also used this approach. Its Polaroid 600 instant camera, called the Sun Camera, eliminates minor shadows from photographs. Polaroid priced it at $95, a far cry from the $25 price tag on its Polaroid Onestep.

Closely allied to the prestige pricing strategy is the notion of a price-quality relationship. It has been widely assumed that consumers equate high price with high quality and that a low price means low quality. Several studies have explored the validity of this relationship.[19] They have found that when price is the only piece of information used in evaluating a product, different price levels are in fact associated with different quality levels. However, when other information, such as brand name and product features, are taken into consideration, there is little evidence of a close link between price and quality in the mind of the consumer. It appears that consumers also use advertising, brand, store image, and other variables in evaluating the quality of a product. Marketers *should not* assume that a high price will produce a perception of high quality—or vice versa.

The perceived-value strategy is also appropriate in situations in which intangibles are important. We noted earlier that price should be equated with the consumer's perception of the product's value. This demand-oriented principle is the basis of the perceived-value pricing strategy, in which the price is equated with the amount of value the consumer expects to receive in the exchange. This approach seems sensible and may well be the best way to tap consumers' willingness to buy at the top end of the demand curve. And it avoids the tendency to price solely on the basis of costs.

In this approach, the marketer identifies all the benefits that the buyer will receive in the exchange. Those benefits are then priced individually in accordance with their perceived value. For example, Caterpillar sets high prices for heavy equipment such as bulldozers and tractors. When a customer asks why one should pay a premium price for the product, the Caterpillar dealer will list all the benefits that the customer will receive by buying, say a tractor from Caterpillar rather from J.I. Case or John Deere. The customer might be informed that a $2,500 premium is being paid for durability, $3,000 more for superior service, $1,500 extra for a better parts warranty, and $2,300 more for reliability. The price of the tractor is $22,000; the extra $9,300 is for the features that are not offered by competitors' products. Often the salesperson follows this speech with the offer of a discount and the shocked customer ends up feeling that the tractor is a bargain!

The value-in-use strategy is similar to the perceived-value strategy except that the benefits supplied by the product are not "unbundled." In this approach, the value that the product will provide when it is used becomes the focus of price setting. Industrial robots, for example, replace humans on an assembly line and reduce labor costs. Word processors do not replace secretaries, but they do make them more productive. A new form of light bulb that saves electricity can be priced to reflect that saving. This is a demand-oriented approach. If price should be equated with perceived value, surely the benefits and cost savings offered by the product ought to be included in the price. Because cost estimates are easier to obtain in industrial than in consumer situations, the value-in-use strategy is best suited to industrial pricing.

Pricing in Oligopolies

In some industries, especially oligopolies, one company sets prices for the entire industry. Such companies tend to be the dominant firms in their industries. Examples include DuPont, Kodak, Hershey, U.S. Steel, National Gypsum, and Gillette.

A price leader must take its role seriously and use care in setting its prices. The firm must be familiar with the cost and demand conditions in its industry. If it is too aggressive in its pricing, it may attract unwelcome attention from antitrust officials. IBM has drawn fire for what critics call "predatory pricing," aggressive low-price tactics that have humbled its competitors. But with the recent price wars in both PCs and mainframes, IBM's dominance of pricing has slipped. It can no longer use price-leader strategies.

Pricing When Buying Is Habitual

Customary pricing involves sticking to a traditional price level. The marketer tries to avoid changing the price from its accepted level. Instead, it adjusts the size and content of the product in order to hold the price. Candy bars are an example. The traditional 5-cent candy bar has given way to the 25-cent, the 30-cent, and now even the 50-cent bar—but not easily. Between 1949 and 1985, Hershey changed its price only 6 times, but the weight (quantity) of the bar changed over 30 times. As a result, in 1986 chocolate lovers paid 7 times as much for a Hershey bar as they did in 1949, but they got only 45 percent more candy.

Pricing to Reflect Buyer Behavioral Attitudes

In situations when consumers face many potentially confusing choices, it is helpful to adjust prices and their presentation to give them maximum appeal and clarity. This is often done at the retail level with lower-priced consumer products, or consumer nondurables as the economists like to call them. In some cases, the price should take into account certain demand-related consider-ations. Such considerations usually affect transactions at the retail level rather than those at the manufacturing or wholesaling level. Certain adjustments can make the final price more attractive to consumers and lead to higher sales. Price adjustments reflect how consumers view a product and its price.

Some prices seem to have greater appeal than others, either because they are traditional or because they match some inner logic of consumers. Thus prices like $14.31 for a necktie or $38.72 for a toaster may not feel "comfortable." For other products, however, such unrounded prices may be totally acceptable—63 cents for a packet of slivered almonds or $2.69 for Skippy peanut butter. While psychological pricing is often used to make a price more palatable, it can also be used to emphasize the relationship between price and quality. For instance, con-sumers may not be attracted to a skin lotion that is priced too low. An 8-ounce jar of lotion priced at 49 cents may not be as appealing as the same jar at $2.98. At 49 cents, the link with quality is missing. Let's look at some specific psychologi-cal pricing techniques.

The odd-pricing form of psychological pricing is achieved by making the end of the price an odd number or some number just below a round number (for example, 98 or 99). Odd pricing is based on the notion that a price of $9.99 appears lower to consumers than $10.00. This difference of only one cent gives the illusion that the price is in the range of $0.01 to $9.99 rather than in the range of $10.00 to $19.99. While it is customary for marketers to price in this manner, studies of consumers' sensitivity to such price distinctions do not con-clusively support this approach.[20] Given these findings, we can conclude that marketers use this pricing technique mostly because others use it.

Some marketers price products at even numbers, such as "3 for $1" for candy bars or $1,650 for a prestige watch. Some even go so far as to work backward so that the even-dollar price includes the sales tax. They believe that consumers feel more comfortable paying even amounts. This is known as the even-pricing approach.

Price lining is most often practiced by retailers, but some manufacturers and wholesalers also use this approach. It is based on the fact that most retailers have more than one product to price, and a number of substitute products or brands in each product category. For instance, a women's clothing store may offer a variety of silk scarves. But consumers will not respond to a series of similar prices such as $9.50, $9.60, $9.70, and so on. Instead, buyers prefer to choose among a few prices that sort products into "lines" based on some attribute such as quality, prestige, or style. The retailer therefore may price the scarves at $10, $17.50, and $25. These prices clearly indicate that there are scarves for the economy-minded woman at $10, medium-quality scarves at $17.50, and top-of-the-line scarves at $25.

The theory underlying price lining is that different market segments, or target markets, can be served best through different prices. But this approach raises some important issues for retailers. It is difficult to determine how many segments there are, or which ones it is profitable to serve. In addition, retailers must be careful to establish price lines that match the prices sought by various market segments. The price differences must be large enough so that consumers can distinguish among the various lines. At the same time, however, the lines must not be priced so far apart that some market segments are not served.

Many retailers recognize the appeal of a lower than normal "bargain" price. As a result, they use the price variable to draw customers into the store. The low-priced products are referred to as "traffic builders" or as loss leaders or price leaders. Such products are marked up by less than the usual percentage, and they are chosen for their promotional appeal. Most likely the retailer has large stocks of these items to sell. Price leaders are usually well known, highly desired, somewhat expensive branded goods.

Some marketers use what is known as *bait-and-switch pricing*, in which prices are set low to attract customers, but when they come to buy, an attempt is made to sell them more expensive models. Salespeople attempt to "trade-up" the customer to higher-priced, higher-margin items. Such pricing is often deceptive—and clearly is not socially responsible. The federal government, through the Federal Trade Commission, has made this practice illegal in interstate commerce.

Consumers often become confused when they try to compare products with different prices. Is a 7-ounce bag of potato chips priced at $1.39 a better buy than a 5-ounce bag at 99 cents? Marketers have responded with unit pricing, in which the price of the package is accompanied by the price of the product per ounce, pound, pint, or some other standard measurement of quantity. First used in the early 1970s, unit pricing has been employed extensively for grocery products.

The purpose of unit pricing is to help consumers make more economical purchases. Yet there are costs associated with its use—special labels, computer records, and labor costs for the retailer, as well as reduced brand loyalty as price competition increases. Research has found consumers shifting to store brands as a result of unit pricing. Yet those with the most to gain—the lower-income shoppers—tend to use it less than better-educated, higher-income shoppers.[21]

Sometimes manufacturers start with the list price that will generate a high enough sales volume for the retailer to make a profit. From that price, they subtract the markups added by each intermediary in the distribution system. In this way, they come up with a price that they, the producers, can charge. This backdoor approach assumes that the manufacturer can correctly assess the demand for the product and that it can compute its own costs so that it can be sure that the price it arrives at will be profitable. The quantity produced has a definite effect on the costs, so the relationship between quantity and the price charged to the customer needs to be known with reasonable accuracy.

Pricing and the Product Life Cycle

Pricing strategies must be adjusted throughout a product's life. Let's look at how pricing differs for new, mature, and declining products in different stages of the life cycle (Exhibit 11.5).

The Introductory Stage

Pricing a new product presents a real challenge. Little is known about the costs of making the product, how much consumers will be willing to pay, or how competitors will react. Yet this initial pricing decision is important, especially in view of the high rate of new-product failures.

The difficultly of pricing a new product depends to a large extent on the degree of newness. Innovative products are the most difficult to price, since they have no reference point in the consumer's mind. Products like cellular telephones, trash compactors, and jet skis are examples. The demand leg of the pricing tripod is particularly troublesome here. Costs can be estimated and

EXHIBIT 11.5.   Pricing over the product life cycle.

$	Introduction	Rapid growth	Slow growth	Maturity	Decline
Strategy	• Newer products are harder to price • Introductory price deal may make sense	• Reduce prices to discourage competition • Offer many price lines	• Lower price to broaden appeal • Price agressively to limit competition	• Avoid price cutting • Goal is price stability • Be flexible	• Cut prices to sell inventory, then eliminate product, —OR— • Cut costs and keep price stable

sometimes competitors' reactions gauged—but it is often impossible to guess the level of demand. With such unique products, the major choice is between skimming and penetration strategies.

New products that have identifiable substitutes or that replace existing products are classified as imitative products or adaptive replacements. In these cases, the marketer has more to go on. When Gillette's Eraser Mate was the first erasable-ink pen on the market, it still had to compete with regular ball-point and felt-tip pens. The key issue for marketers was how much consumers would pay for perceived differences in the product's function or appearance. When the consumer cannot perceive such differences, the price cannot vary much from the prices of alternative products or brands. For such products, the perceived-value and value-in-use strategies are appropriate.

Sometimes marketers offer an introductory price deal in which the new product is offered at a reduced price for a limited period. This is an attempt to induce trail of the product in the hope of building brand loyalty. This approach should not be confused with penetration pricing.

The Rapid Growth and Slow-Growth Stages

The tremendous demand that accompanies the rapid-growth stage encourages a policy of maintaining prices at a high level. Yet a sounder strategy is to reduce prices as the cost savings that come from experience are realized. Holding profit margins at a moderate level has the added benefit of discouraging competitors from entering the market. With consumers eager to buy the product, many price lines can be offered to meet every segment's needs—from low-end to premium models.

In the slow-growth stage, as sales start to decrease, the price strategy should aim to broaden the appeal of the product through price reductions. More aggressive pricing is used to boost sales and at the same time fight competition. This pricing strategy has been used extensively by the Japanese in American markets as they have slid down the experience curve with their electronic and automotive products.

The Maturity Stage

When products move from the growth stages into the maturity stage, price adjustments become a major strategic tool. Flexibility is the key to effective pricing at this stage. With mature products, most sales are replacement sales. Price increases are avoided, and when they do occur, they are usually due to increased costs rather than higher demand. If possible, a stable pricing strategy is the best approach at this stage.

While a price reduction may seem to be the logical way to stimulate sales of mature products, this tactic depends on the price sensitivity of consumers and on the competitive situation. With some products—such as hairpins or clothespins—a price reduction is not likely to increase sales and, in fact, would probably lead to lower profits, since the quantity sold is unlikely to change. Moreover, competitors are likely to react by also lowering their prices.

The Decline Stage

Once a product's sales begin to dip, marketers have two pricing options, depending on their long-run plans. If they want to prune the declining product from the line, the appropriate strategy would be to continue to lower the price, preferably in stages, until all inventory has been sold. An alternative is to maintain the price but cut costs. In the latter case, promotional expenditures are often curtailed.

As competitors leave the market, the product becomes less available. Often there is a certain market segment that still needs the product. Since this need can be quite strong, the firms that remain in the market during the later stages of the product's life cycle may actually be able to raise their prices.

EPILOGUE: VALUE PRICING AND THE MARKETING CONCEPT

A wonderful cartoon appeared in the papers a few years ago, showing a customer at the counter in a small shop. A sign in the window announced "best prices, highest quality." Inside, the storekeeper was talking to the customer, saying, "We got low cost or good quality. Which do you want?"

Not much of a choice for the customer. But often this is just what the consumer faces in the marketplace. We referenced a number of studies showing that consumers definitely do draw inferences about product quality from price, and this is an intuitively obvious point as well. In general, it makes sense that a higher-priced product will be better. One assumes that it is higher priced because it costs more to make, and that it costs more to make because the manufacturer used more expensive (and thus better quality) materials in its manufacture.

This is an appealing tautology, but based on circular reasoning nonetheless. Products are better because they have higher prices. They have higher prices because they cost more to make. They cost more to make because they are made out of better materials. The materials are better because they have higher prices. They have higher prices because they, in turn, are made out of better raw materials, which have higher prices, which . . .

It could well be that a car made out of heavier, larger pieces of metal is better. Detroit always assumed this was so, and paid no attention to the "little sardine cans" imported by foreign auto makers in the sixties. But the smaller, lighter cars, using less and in many cases less expensive materials, turned out to be superior in many ways. They were lighter and thus used less gas. They could be made by fewer people, in less time, on a smaller production line. Many of them were better engineered and more fun to drive. The front-wheel drive of many imported cars eliminated the long, heavy, and costly drive train of a rear-wheel-drive car, but gave better traction and handling. By the 1990s, consumers, and Detroit, have come to realize that less is often more when it comes to automobiles. It turns out that you *can* get better quality for a lower price.

But having said this, we must also point to the obvious counterargument: There is still a large price range in automobiles, with "better" cars generally costing more. Although innovation and marketing imagination have enabled individual manufacturers to introduce individual products that offer better quality for lower price, this happens within the context of a traditional cost-quality continuum. One way to look at this continuum is to draw a value curve, showing different combinations of cost and quality that are acceptable to consumers. As Exhibit 11.6 indicates, the value curve assumes that different combinations of price and quality are available, but that some tradeoff must be made. Further, products anywhere on this line represent different tradeoffs that have the same value to the consumer. At the upper end of this curve is high quality, at the lower end is low cost. Which do you want? Neither, really. What the consumer wants is low cost and high quality, which is not on this value curve.

When an innovator offers more for less, as foreign auto makers did, this does not follow the logic of the value curve. The new combination of cost and quality is off the curve. It is a better combination, a better value, from the customer's perspective. In theory, at least, everything on the curve is of equal value, but the innovation that moves beyond the curve is a better value to the consumer. Management has to take a creative, innovative approach to product development and marketing, but when it does, it can truly offer more for less.

EXHIBIT 11.6.　Price and quality value curve.

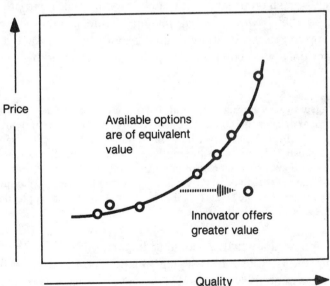

We quoted Henry Ford's advice in Chapter 1 discussing the essence of marketing, that "We have never considered any costs as fixed. Therefore, we first reduce the price to the point where we believe more sales will result. Then we go ahead and try to make the prices." This concept seems to best describe the Japanese auto makers, rather than today's Ford and its U.S. competitors. And it is diametrically opposed to the idea that you can have good quality or low prices, but not both. It ignores the accepted value curve, and strikes out confidently for a point far off the curve. When this point is reached, competitors must copy the innovation, and as they do, the entire value curve shifts.

Note that the "quality is free" claim of consultant Philip Crosby, also noted earlier in the book, is the other side of this coin. It is actually feasible to improve the quality of products by making them better, rather than by spending more money making them. As the few U.S. companies to experiment with total quality programs have discovered, you can do a lot better job with the existing equipment, material and people, just by changing the organizational structure and culture and focusing harder on quality. You do not have to hire more quality control inspectors, or throw more material and finished goods away; you can instead teach suppliers to provide better-made components and your factory can learn to produce fewer bad finished products. Thus the practical impact of a total quality program is to allow a company to offer consumers something that does not lie on the value curve.

If quality increases without a proportionate increase in price, there is a value premium that the company and the customer can share. The better-quality product can be sold at only a little higher price than its competitors. Or perhaps costs can be driven lower than the competition's at the same time quality is increased, so that the same pricing structure both offers a higher margin for the producer and a better value for the customer.

We aren't much on prognostication, but we are willing to predict that the 1990s will be the *decade of value pricing*. Value pricing is the term most commonly applied to the strategy of giving more for less. Take a recent consumer's experience with computer shopping, as recounted by *The Wall Street Journal*:

> Mr. Magyar was planning to buy an extra computer to handle mailing lists and word processing for the nonprofit business he runs. But he found out he could buy an Apple Macintosh Classic, with the same power and most of the same features as the Macintosh SE models he already had, for half the price of the old SE. So he bought two computers instead of one, spending a total of $2,590. "I wanted the biggest bang for the buck, and the Classics fit that bill nicely," he says. What's the new Macintosh Classic's secret? Simple, says Ann Arbor Apple dealer Richard Weir: "It's more for a hell of a lot less."[22]

Why is it more for a hell of a lot less? In part, this reflects the price wars in the computer industry. Apple is trying to gain share and move from being a niche player to a major player in the PC market at the same time that competing

IBM clones are slashing prices (and margins) in a fierce price war. So Apple has had to slash its prices too. And its margins are down as a result. But they are not down enough to explain the two-for-one pricing James Magyar took advantage of. A price war can give the consumer the same, or at best a little more, for a lot less. But it will never give a hell of a lot more for half the price. Nobody's margin has that much room for competitive pricing. The bulk of this extra value comes from Apple's ability to make a product that does more and costs less to make. It is simply passing on its experience and technical advances to the consumer in the form of extra value.

Value pricing is not just a pricing strategy, as the Apple case illustrates. Price is used to position the product off the value line—which in effect shifts the line and creates a new standard competitors must shoot for. But a great deal more must go into creating a product that has lower costs or increased quality. The product must lie on a different cost-quality curve than competing products for management to afford a pricing strategy that puts it on a different price-quality curve.

Toyota's 1991 Tercel illustrates this point. Again according to *The Wall Street Journal* reporter, "Toyota Motor Corp. engineers embarked on a mission to achieve what one Toyota planner calls an "epic-making cost-down" when it re-designed its least expensive model, the Tercel. The result, launched this fall, is a little car with a smooth, big-car external profile, and 7% more horsepower and a quieter ride than its predecessor. The base price starts at just $6,588, but Toyota officials say the car is a money maker."[23] The new Tercel combines better per-formance with a lower price because Toyota made this the focus of a major development effort, not simply because someone decided to cut the price.

Taco Bell is pursuing a positioning strategy akin to Tercel's. It slashed prices in order to push the price of most items on the menu below a dollar. But this move could not be made without major innovations. New items had to be developed and the layout and operation of its stores completely redesigned. Key to the strategy is a reduction in kitchen space, allowing the seating to take up two-thirds of a restaurant where it was confined to one-third of the floor space in the past.[24] The new value pricing at Taco Bell has allowed it to increase its profit margins at a time when other fast food companies are experiencing shrinking margins. Now McDonald's and other competitors will be forced to innovate to position themselves on the new value curve Taco Bell has created.

The only problem with the "more for less" claim is that it is not always credible. Consumers are so used to inflated advertising claims and deceptive pricing practices that they are generally skeptical about such claims, waiting to see whether there is substance behind them. And what happens if the claims are not rooted in fact? Presumably consumers will be disappointed if they have made a purchase on the basis of false expectations. They will experience post-purchase dissonance, as we discussed in the chapter on consumer behav-ior. They will be more wary and cynical in the future. Even if they are not deceived by the claims, they will have to wade through more confusion and contradictory information to make a wise purchase. The false claims add to the confusion and noise in the consumer's environment (already a problem, as we discussed in the chapter on promotion). This makes it harder for all marketers to communicate with the consumer, even those marketers who do have a better value to offer.

If you cannot offer a product that is exceptional—one that lies beyond the value curve—then perhaps it is in your interest to confuse the consumer. Think about the hocus-pocus and smoke screens employed by the average car salesman—they leave the customer uncertain about what the final price will be and what it includes, making it difficult to shop around for the best value. Compare this to Caterpillar's approach, as discussed earlier in this chapter. Although its prices are higher than competitors', its strategy is to offer quality in excess of the extra price paid, so the salespeople can use a more information-oriented sale and less of the traditional hocus pocus. No doubt the new Tercel can be sold in a straightforward manner, focusing on communicating the facts rather than conning the buyer. So if you use the value-pricing approach to offer something that really is a better value, then it is in your best interest to cut through noise and confusion and communicate the facts of the product without deception. The value pricing strategy goes beyond pricing, requiring a completely different approach to all the variables in the marketing mix.

A biological analogy is helpful in visualizing the difference between a value-based marketing strategy for a superior product and a persuasion-based strategy, such as might be used for a product that does not offer more value. Among butterflies (and a number of other animals) there are two common forms of mimicry. First, poisonous butterflies that live together tend to look alike, even though they may be of unrelated species. Each has bright warning colors so that predators can learn quickly to avoid it and its kind. And, as evolution has discovered, when all poisonous species use the same warning colors and patterns, the learning is even more effective. The predator is then faced with a very simple rule—don't eat any butterflies that are red with yellow spots (for instance), regardless of their shape, size, or species. They are all poisonous.

The other kind of mimicry involves fakery. Some species that are perfectly delicious have evolved the same warning colors as the poisonous species. Thus predators mistake them for the poisonous ones, and they benefit unjustly from the predators' learning.

But what happens if many good-to-eat butterflies look like poisonous ones? The learning process starts to break down. Say a naive young bird eats a red-with-yellow-spots butterfly, and it tastes great. It may do in any number of the poisonous ones as well before this first experience is overcome with new learning. And the smaller the proportion of poisonous butterflies to good-tasting fakes, the slower and less efficient the learning will be. At some ratio of mimics to models, the whole system breaks down and predators are just confused, but no longer wary of red-and-yellow butterflies. This is bad news for all the predators and butterflies.

This analogy may seem far afield, but the game is the same with the exception that marketers want their products to be consumed, while butterflies take the opposite view. Regardless, the communications objectives are similar, and the problem of consumer learning and choice parallels the problem of predator learning and choice. And when the proportion of true values is low compared to the mimics or fakes, the system will break down. Perhaps it already has.

Take the personal computer industry. While the value curve certainly does make periodic shifts due to technological advances, there is an increasing amount of noise to confuse the consumer and disguise genuine values. Competitors attempt to use both value pricing and deceptive strategies, depending upon whether they have something new to offer or not. And that is like being poisonous every now and then, but tasting delicious most of the time. A butterfly wouldn't last very long with that strategy! And in the computer industry, fat margins don't last very long either.

As this book goes to press, all the leading PC makers are running ads that claim they make the best computers. They even have survey results to back up their claims. The theory is that if a consumer survey ranks your brand higher than competitors, you can claim it is a better value for the price. The survey results are considered evidence of superior quality. But here are six recent surveys and their winners:[25]

Survey	*Winner*
Dataquest Annual Customer Satisfaction Survey	CompuAdd
IDC PC Reliability Study	Hewlett-Packard
J.D. Power Computer End-User Satisfaction Study	Dell Computer
InfoWorld Newspaper Product of the Year	Northgate Computer
PC World Service Excellence Award	CompuAdd
Datamation magazine Desktop Computing System Brand Preference Study	Hewlett-Packard

So which one is the best? There are so many surveys, of so many different samples (often magazines survey their readers), and the surveys contain so many categories, that everyone wins something . . . which makes research firms and magazines happy, since they sell more research and advertising space as a result. But it leads to lots of false value strategies and confusion for the consumer. According to PC maker CompuAdd's CEO, Edward Thomas, there are now so many surveys that "They're beginning to lose their meaning. It's like, 'Will the real survey please stand up?'"[26] But since CompuAdd copped the number one position in the Dataquest survey, Thomas still plans to run an ad campaign based on the survey results. Perhaps the company has nothing more definitive to say to its consumers!

But when it does have something new to trumpet, will customers take the claims at face value? Probably not. Which leads us to an important final point about the value-pricing strategy: It requires consistency to be optimally effective. But to be consistent in its use of the strategy, a firm must consistently innovate and offer superior value to its consumers. It must keep moving the value curve outward, and not resort to smoke and mirrors between moves. This strategy cannot be mixed with other strategies at will since it is predicated on a different relationship with the consumer. The strategy builds trust and adds value—thus it is the purest expression of the marketing concept. But it demands consistent commitment on the part of management, which may be the scarcest commodity of all.

12

PLACE AND TIME—THE DISTRIBUTION FUNCTION

Innovative Guidelines for Profitability

We want to be perceived as a tryly valued supplier—one which really cares about satisfying the needs of its customers. That spirit should be vested in all members of the marketing and logistic channels as well as in our own employees.

—*Howard Gochberg, Land O'Lakes*[1]

In 1987, the consulting firm Ernst & Whinney announced a revolution in distribution, and nobody paid any attention. The report of their study on the logistics of product distribution, conducted for The Council of Logistics Management, concluded that "logistics . . . can be a critical factor in ensuring the success of new products or other strategic initiatives. As testimony to this fact, the microcomputer industry boasts a graveyard filled with companies offering competitive products backed by fatally uncompetitive distribution/service operations."[2] Their report went on to identify 10 fundamental principles of logistics which, they argued, were as critical to the profitability of companies as the principles of excellence enumerated in Peters and Waterman's best-selling book, *In Search of Excellence*. By now, everyone in business knows about the Peters and Waterman book, while hardly anyone has even heard of the Ernst and Whinney report.

We have noted in previous chapters that distribution can be strikingly important, but also that it is often overlooked. (In fact, we have also argued that product development and pricing receive too little of management's attention—perhaps the truth is that all of the marketing activities suffer from lack of

319

upper-level understanding and attention!) Within the field of distribution, two distinct branches are recognized, but neither receives constant management attention. The development and management of the channels of distribution—the chain of intermediaries linking the producer with the ultimate consumer—is considered quite distinct from the logistics of moving the actual material in question. Distribution channels involve relationships between business partners: manufacturers, wholesalers, retailers, sales representatives, and the like. Physical distribution involves the actual movement of products, and thus focuses on how they are transported and warehoused.

From the customer's point of view, this distinction is meaningless. Either the product can be purchased conveniently and delivered quickly and reliably, or it cannot. But from the company's point of view, the activities associated with each branch of distribution are so different that they almost always receive separate treatment. Logistics is run more or less out of the loading docks, and thus has just about the lowest status of any activity. Logistics managers are paid less than other managers. Distribution channels are usually run out of the sales department, which traditionally ranks only slightly better than logistics in the corporate hierarchy. The sales and logistics people rarely talk to each other in the traditional U.S. company, locked as they are in the struggle for last place in the game of interdepartmental politics.

But back to the revolution in logistics. Has anything really changed, or is Ernst & Whinney just trying to drum up business for its National Distribution/Logistics Group? In truth, probably a good measure of both.

A recent *Harvard Business Review* article noted that,

> When communication was limited to telephones and letters, and transportation took weeks or months instead of hours or days, concentrating on a few products—and the vertical integration that let managers control every step of their production processess—made real sense. Now such traditional strategic formulas no longer hold.[3]

The change in strategic thinking described in Chapter 3 has been driven in large part by these two trends: the increased speed and quality of both communications and transportation. The authors of this article go on to say that managers can now "divide their companies' value chains, handle the key elements internally, outsource others advantageously anywhere in the world with minimal transaction costs, and yet coordinate all essential activities more effectively to meet customers' needs." The result is a new way of organizing the company, in which many of the activities that add value, even in the core manufacturing area, are now spread among suppliers, partners, and subsidiaries all around the world. "Under these circumstances, moving to a less integrated but more focused organization is not just feasible but imperative for competitive success."

This fundamental shift in strategy and organization means, according to these authors, that "managers need to break out of the mind-set that considers manufacturing . . . as separate from (and somehow superior to) the service activities that make such production possible and effective."[4] These service activities include distribution and logistics, as well as many of the other marketing crafts, including the collection and management of marketing information, product inception and development, the management of the customer relationship, and the management and revival of product life cycles. In fact, these activities are increasingly critical to the development and maintenance of a company's market position from the customer's perspective. Although we still think of Apple as a computer manufacturer, in fact, much of what Apple does of value to customers involves the management of software development, service and support activities, and all the other elements that go into taking a relatively useless, low-margin box full of electronics and turning it into a high-margin, highly useful piece of equipment.

Again according to the *Harvard Business Review* paper,

> True strategic focus means that a company can concentrate more power in its chosen markets than anyone else can. Once, this meant owning the largest resource base, manufacturing plants, research labs, or distribution channels to support product lines. Now physical facilities—including a seemingly superior product—seldom provide a sustainable competitive edge. They are too easily bypassed, reverse engineered, cloned, or slightly surpassed. Instead, a maintainable advantage usually derives from outstanding depth in selected human skills, logistics capabilities, knowledge bases, or other service strengths that competitors cannot reproduce and that lead to greater demonstrable value for the customer.[5]

Does this mean we should abandon all the good ideas presented in the product chapter, for example, in favor of yet another new "mindset"? How many times can the poor reader be expected to go through this process? Actually, the revolution in logistics and the revolution in product development are part of the same story, a story that was first revealed in the spill-over of marketing activities into nonmarketing functions at Omni in Part One, and that also explains the revolution in strategic thinking by which service management and total quality programs displaced the planner's traditional organization charts and industry matrices in Chapter 1. To find the key that relates these fundamental changes in the nature of management, it is necessary to look among the most prosaic and low-status activities of the organization, the logistics of acquiring raw materials and components on the one hand and of delivering finished goods and services on the other. Here, at the very bottom of the corporate hierarchy, in the warehouses, parts rooms, and loading docks, something fundamental is happening that will remake, or destroy, every business in the country.

It started in Japan, and it began with the relationship between a company and its suppliers. As Kaoru Ishikawa, the famous Japanese statistician explains,

> Twenty-five years ago . . . the average Japanese company purchased materials approximating 70 percent of its manufacturing cost from outside suppliers . . . If

the parts purchased were defective, no matter how hard the final assembler worked good products would not emerge. Knowing this, we began QC [Quality Control] education among subcontractors in the late 1950s. We also attempted to make these subcontractors specialists in their own fields. Today, Japan's automobiles and electronics are considered to be the best in the world. This is due in part to the excellence of their parts suppliers. In contrast, in Western countries companies try to produce all the parts they need in their own factories.[6]

He argues that generalist companies cannot compete with specialized suppliers. Ford's in-house steel mill, for example, "cannot compete against Japanese steel mills, which have many engineers and export everywhere in the world. In terms of quality and effectiveness, there is simply no competition."

Thus the development of total quality in Japan was not limited to the confines of single factories, but instead was focused in large part on the management of supplier relationships. It required far closer ties at all levels in order to allow for collaborative efforts to engineer quality into products and to produce products more consistently to specifications. And it required a dramatic elevation of the lowly field of logistics, for this greater reliance on specialized suppliers meant that the final assembler had to rely on each supplier delivering the right amounts of the right components at the right times.

This was both a practical and a philosophical change. On the practical level, since most components came from outside the factory, their transportation (the time and place utility provided to the factory by its suppliers) was of necessity a matter of grave concern. On the philosophical level, these suppliers were delivering into factories in which the principles of quality management were being implemented, just as they were at the suppliers' factories. Rather than allowing an inventory of rejected items to pile up at some inspection station at the far end of a production line, the factory tried to build quality into every unit on its way down the line. And, just as this wasteful inventory of rejects was eliminated, so too were the beginning inventories, those mounds of components that used to cram the factory's warehouses. Management began to see the manufacturing process as including the production and delivery of components by suppliers, and to manage the process all the way through, rather than just on the assembly line. With this new perspective, the costly stockpiling of components at the factory was replaced with just-in-time delivery of just the right components, all of them meeting performance standards. Suppliers became part of the manufacturing process, and sophisticated communication and transportation made it possible to integrate their activities with the company's seemlessly.

The Japanese electronics and auto factories harnessed the new information and transportation technologies to implement the concept of a new strategic focus that, as the authors of the *Harvard Business Review* article put it, provides maintainable advantage derived "from outstanding depth in selected human skills, logistics capabilities, knowledge bases, or other service strengths" instead of from the bricks and mortar investment in some monstrous, fully integrated and self-sufficient plant. Behind the Japanese successes in process management, and their resulting productivity and quality gains, was a simple but revolutionary new approach to logistics. And U.S. companies are now being exhorted to follow a similar strategy.

You have no doubt noticed that the story has so far focused on the logistics of supplier relationships, not customer relationships. From the suppliers' perspective, we are talking about customer relationships; but, even beyond this simple symmetry, the changes in logistics have had a dramatic impact on customer relationships. For as companies developed closer links to their suppliers, they also developed closer links with their customers. The same kind of opening-up happened on the down-stream side of the Japanese company, and is now happening at many U.S. companies. The entire purpose of the quality programs was to build in quality *for the customer.* Quality did not sell if designed to satisfy engineers, managers, or inspectors, or anyone but the person or organization that was expected to purchase the product once completed. To understand how customers defined product quality was no simple task, as you might imagine after our bout with marketing information in Part Two of this book. It required stronger ties and better information flow between customer and manufacturer, and through all the parties involved in distribution who stood in the way of this information flow. Japanese companies began to seek direct contact with customers in much the same spirit that had led to direct contact with suppliers.

And as they asked themselves and their customers penetrating questions about product quality, they came to see the product in a more expanded sense, realizing that it includes all sorts of supporting services, that the product is indeed an action-oriented concept dependent as much upon availability, for instance, as on its more tangible characteristics such as size, power, and so forth. To produce a high-quality product, they had to manage every aspect of it, including its physical distribution, and also including support services like repair and training, even though these might be performed by other parties in the distribution channel. The quest for quality-based competitiveness led management inevitably both up and down the chain of commerce in which it formed the central link, using the new information technologies and a new concept of management to turn the entire process into a single-purpose multicompany organization focused on the customer.

Logistics and distribution become one from this perspective, and their results are inseparable from the product attributes arising from design and production, for this is the customer's viewpoint seen through management's eyes. While it is convenient to read about these functions, and to manage them, as separate entities, it is now apparent that they must be envisioned as integral elements of the customer's satisfaction. The links must be so strong, both in how we think of them and in how we manage them, that they are no longer allowed to go their separate ways. Product development and production is part of the same story as logistics and distribution, and this story is a new one. There has indeed been at least the beginning of a revolution in distribution. That no one paid any attention to this argument when Ernst & Whinney made it in 1987 is indicative of the fact that it is ongoing, and indeed perhaps still in its infancy. But with the advantage of hindsight, managers will one day see this revolution for what it is.

It is easy to get carried away by the sweeping changes in management, and to neglect the fundamentals as a result. If distribution is helping to drive the customer revolution in management, you can be sure that it will in turn be driven by this revolution as well. The practical, day-to-day issues of distribution and logistics will be seen in a different light, and the company that can manage these areas effectively will be better at managing change in all areas. This means that there is more reason than ever to focus on the fundamentals. Without further ado, our review of the manager's essential knowledge base in distribution follows.

THE FUNDAMENTALS OF DISTRIBUTION

Distribution involves the movement of products in all stages of development—from resource procurement through manufacturing and on to final sales. Raw materials offer little satisfaction until they reach the hands of the producer and are turned into finished products. From this standpoint, distribution can be seen as adding value, or satisfaction, to raw materials by moving them to the manufacturer, to intermediaries, and finally to the ultimate consumer. Distribution accomplishes this by providing time and place utility, in other words, availability.

Reducing the distance between buyer and seller provides time and place utility. Consumers do not like to travel long distances or spend a lot of time shopping for products. In fact, they like it less than ever; surveys show consumer enthusiasm for shopping is waning. For example, research firm Yankelovich Clancy Shulman reports that 65 percent of Americans find clothes shopping frustrating, up from 60 percent just one year earlier. Almost half—47 percent—of shoppers dislike visits to the grocery store.[7] When a product is located close to its potential buyers, the satisfaction it offers is enhanced. Vending machines and mail-order retailing are excellent examples of how marketers bridge the time and place barriers to exchange.

Distribution also consists of making sure that products are in the *appropriate* place. Having the right product in the right place can help stimulate exchange. Ireland's Waterford Glass, one of the finest makers of handcrafted crystal, controls 25 percent of the U.S. market as a result of having created an elite image for its high-quality product. Ads in such magazines as *Gourmet* and *The New Yorker* and distribution limited to select department and specialty stores have made Waterford the best-selling fine crystal in America. By maintaining the appropriate places for its product, the company has maintained its upper-class aura; there's no appeal to owning a product that almost anyone can buy.

The broadened view of the product is closely tied to distribution. Services, for example, must be properly located—think about what automatic teller machines have done to make banking services more readily available. Such nonprofit organizations as Goodwill Industries and the Salvation Army understand that a convenient drop-off point stimulates donations—as does home pickup of unwanted appliances and used carpeting.

People also need to be "distributed." Aspiring actors, singers, and comedians know how important it is to be in the right place at the right time. Special kinds of products need to be distributed as well. For example, health and social services are distributed throughout communities to make them more accessible to the public. Doctors, HMOs, and even hospitals are putting up low-cost "urgent care centers" (referred to as "Doc-in-the-Box" or "7-Eleven Medicine" by critics and rivals) at easy-to-get-to locations such as shopping malls. In California, voter registration forms have been distributed through businesses, including fast-food chains like McDonald's.

Intermediaries

Intermediaries make the movement of products efficient and effective. They go by many names: middlemen, retailers, wholesalers, distributors, agents, channel members. Intermediaries provide various services as products move through the distribution system.

There are two types of middlemen who take title to products: retailers and wholesalers. Retailers are intermediaries who sell products primarily to ultimate consumers. They may also buy from other intermediaries as products move through the distribution channel. Wholesalers are intermediaries who distribute products primarily to commercial or professional users: to retailers; to manufacturers (who use the goods to make other products); to the government; and to large institutions that purchase in quantity, like colleges and hospitals. Wholesalers may also function as links in a distribution chain; that is, they buy and sell products among themselves.

Intermediaries exist because there are some real problems in the marketing of products, problems that are best solved by intermediaries. First, there's the matter of geographic distance—the physical separation of buyers and sellers. Second, as we have noted, products must be in the appropriate place in order to stimulate exchange. The process of matching product and market is complicated by distance, because consumers in different locations want different things. Thus a Vermont buyer is likely to want wool sweaters, while a buyer in Arizona would probably prefer polo shirts.

Discrepancies such as this fall into two categories: quantity discrepancies and assortment discrepancies. Manufacturers want to make large numbers of items to benefit from economies of scale. Yet each individual buyer in each region wants only one or a few items. This is the quantity discrepancy. At the same time, manufacturers must understand the assortment that the buyer wants. Buyers throughout the country have a host of unique wants and needs, and manufacturers must attempt to match them. Taken together, these two problems are the *assortment* problem, that is, the problem of assembling the quantity and assortment of products that will match the wants and needs of different markets.

The first two problems—distance and exchange stimulation—are solved by a process called *sorting,* which consists of two steps: concentration and dispersion. First products are brought together at one location (concentration). Then they are divided up and moved in smaller quantities to locations closer to the ultimate buyers (dispersion). As an example, consider the wheat grown by farmers in the Midwest. Many buyers in many locations can use this wheat. In Minnesota, Pillsbury uses it for flour and muffin mixes. Dreikorn's bakery in Massachusetts needs it for bread; and Mrs. Paul's in Pennsylvania uses it in pie crusts. How do farmers in Nebraska, Iowa, and Illinois get their crops to these and other companies throughout the nation? Each could load a truck with wheat and drive to all these places to sell it. But this distribution method would be inefficient. Instead, farmers throughout the Midwest pool their crops at a centrally located grain elevator, and then the wheat is shipped in large quantities to various points throughout the country.

By its very nature, sorting is economical. The tasks of concentration and dispersion reduce the number of transactions required to distribute products. Exhibit 12.1 shows the situation with four manufacturers and four consumers. When one intermediary is added, the number of transactions is halved. And since each transaction costs money, the cost of distribution is also reduced. The use of intermediaries allows each producer to transport a quantity of products that is sufficient to meet the needs of all four consumers; without an intermediary, each producer would have to transport a smaller quantity to each of the four consumers. And since the intermediary carries the products of all four producers, the entire assortment is available to each buyer.

Magazines provide an example. They are distributed through two channels—customer subscriptions and single-copy sales at drugstores, newsstands, convenience stores, supermarkets, and chain stores. As postal rates have risen, the single-copy channel has become more important. Ten national wholesalers move more than 33,000 different magazines to about 500 regional wholesalers. The regional wholesalers then distribute the magazines to retail outlets. Since magazines are perishable products, speed is very important. *TV Guide,* for instance, is stocked at more than 150,000 establishments within 36 hours of printing. Thus concentration and dispersion reduce the complexity of the task of getting magazines into the hands of the reading public.

Because intermediaries are located close to consumers, it is possible for them to assess the needs and wants of a particular market much more accurately than manufacturers can. Since intermediaries, especially retailers, actually talk and work with the buyers of products, they learn firsthand what those buyers

EXHIBIT 12.1. Product distribution.

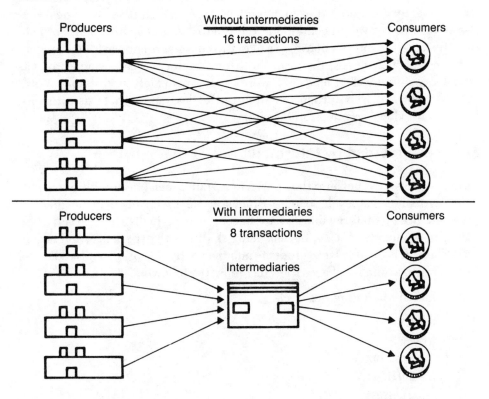

want. This knowledge is fed back to the producer so that the appropriate assortment of products can be manufactured. This communication between intermediary and producer helps solve the assortment problem.

In the magazine industry, $200 million worth of magazines are returned unsold each year and must be shredded. Without this cost, the industry could more than double its profits. In an effort to reduce this loss, wholesalers provide detailed information on returns and sellouts by area and by type of magazines. This information helps publishers regulate the number of magazines shipped and helps wholesalers and retailers select the proper combination of magazines for each area served.

Reducing Total Inventories

Within a distribution system, products must be stored so that they can be made available when the buyer wants them. Paradoxical as it may seem, when intermediaries are used to distribute products, the total inventory stored is lower than would be the case without intermediaries. From Exhibit 12.1, we see that with one intermediary there are five storage locations (four producers plus the intermediary); without that intermediary, there would be only four places in which inventory is stored (the four producers). Although it seems logical that five storage places would contain more inventory than four, this does not hold true. Because the intermediaries are closer to consumers and have a more accurate sense of their needs, they can, in theory, better forecast which products consumers will buy. This leads to fewer products being left in inventory. Without the intermediaries, producers would offer less appropriate assortments, leaving a backlog of products in inventory.

Services Provided by Intermediaries

Intermediaries exist because they perform certain special tasks within the marketing system—and they do so more efficiently and effectively than manufacturers could. Because intermediaries have become experts in distribution activities, they gain economies of scale, become more skillful with experience, and in general do a better job of getting products into the hands of consumers. In doing so, they perform a number of activities, including the following:

- Informal Marketing Research
- Buying
- Selling
- Bulk Breaking
- Price Setting
- Promotion
- Transportation
- Storage
- Financing (i.e., through credit policies)
- Risk Bearing (especially when they take title to products)
- Management Services.

The Channel of Distribution

The channel of distribution is the route taken by a product and its title as it moves from the resource procurer through the producer to the ultimate consumer. It is made up of all the intermediaries that perform the functions that put products into the hands of consumers.

As products move from producers to ultimate consumers, various exchange transactions take place. In the process, a number of tangible and intangible items are passed from one channel member to the next. First, there is the product or service itself. Raw materials are sold to manufacturers, which, in turn, produce finished products that are moved down the line to the ultimate user. The product is exchanged for some kind of payment, which usually takes the form of money. But that is not all that is exchanged. In most cases, the title to the product, or legal ownership, also changes hands. In addition, information is exchanged as products pass from one owner to the next. Communication backward through the channel lets manufacturers know consumers' needs, although long channels can filter and limit information. At the same time, information flows in the other direction in the form of promotion, enhancing the desirability of the product and stimulating exchange. Manufacturers promote not only to consumer markets but also to channel members. Throughout the distribution channel, then, there are a variety of exchanges—product, payment, title, and information—both forward and backward.

The most frequently used channels for distributing consumer products are shown in Exhibit 12.2. Channel A is the shortest, the simplest to manage, and often the quickest way to distribute consumer products. We know it in the form of door-to-door selling of products like life insurance, encyclopedias, magazines, some household items, and vacuum cleaners. Sales representatives from Amway and Avon come to our doors and present their goods, and industrial salespeople call on purchasing managers. Manufacturers' mail-order

EXHIBIT 12.2.   Product distribution channels.

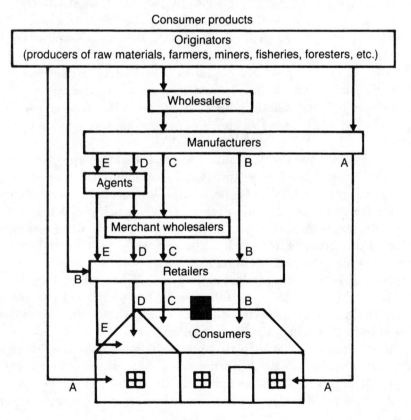

catalogs and farmers at roadside stands selling fresh fruits and vegetables are other examples. This channel employs no intermediaries; it is a "direct" or "short" channel, because products move directly into the hands of consumers from those of producers or originators.

Channel B is the type of channel that is most visible to us as consumers. We buy many kinds of products through this kind of channel—automobiles, paint, gasoline, and clothing, for instance. Many manufacturers have special outlets that sell directly to consumers; some own their own retail stores. Sherwin-Williams and Firestone, for example, use this approach.

Channel C is most often used by small manufacturers and retailers to distribute such products as drugs, lumber, hardware, and food items. Products that have a large market need such a channel, since manufacturers often do not have a large enough salesforce to reach the mass market effectively. Wholesalers provide a large web of contacts that otherwise would be beyond the reach of most manufacturers.

Channel D is the longest and most indirect of the frequently used distribution channels. The agents provide yet another layer of intermediaries with an even more extensive network of contracts. Candy is distributed to wholesalers through agents. This makes sense, since there are so many potential buyers of this impulse item.

Channel E shows that some producers bypass the wholesaler and employee agents to sell to retailers. Food-processing companies that do a great deal of business with large grocery chains don't need the services of wholesalers. Food brokers, are very common in the food industry. For example, Ocean Spray, which makes cranberry products and juices, uses 75 food brokers who sell to retail stores, another 20 who sell to food service buyers, and still another 25 who handle both types of outlets. Recently, it added H.J. Heinz' food service salespeople, who call on other wholesalers and provide access to the restaurant market.

Exhibit 12.3 shows the distribution channels that are typical of industrial products. Channel F is the most frequently used industrial channel. Because industrial markets usually require personal selling, a short, direct channel is most effective. Many metal manufacturers, conveyor belt producers, and makers of construction equipment use this channel. IBM has built its reputation in the mainframe computer market by selling directly to industrial customers through its expertly trained salesforce.

Industrial distributors are the counterparts of wholesalers. They take title to products and perform the same functions that wholesalers do for consumer products. In Channel G, industrial distributors act as the selling arm for many smaller manufacturers that serve industrial markets.

Channel H shows that industrial producers sometimes need the storage facilities provided by industrial distributors. In this channel, the agent facilitates the sale of products and the industrial distributor stores them until they are needed by users. The distributor thus can provide quick service to users.

EXHIBIT 12.3.   Industrial product distribution channels.

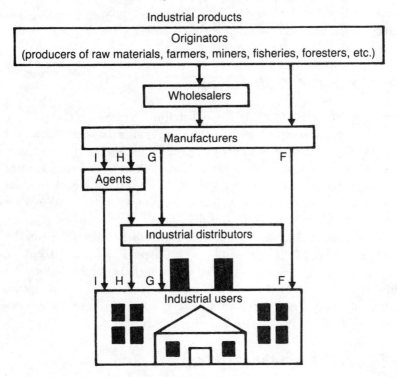

In Channel I, industrial distributors are bypassed because their services are not needed. This kind of channel is used to distribute many agricultural products.

A Broadened View of Distribution Channels

The concept of distribution channels is not limited to goods. Services, too, need channels of distribution. Some universities, for example, use telecourses to transmit lectures into the homes of students via dishes or public broadcasting systems. This is an alternative to the familiar on-campus distribution channel. Hospitals too are experimenting with alternative channels, such as providing services in clinics separate from the hospital itself.

Direct mail is another alternative distribution channel, a way to reach customers who do not want to go to the trouble of leaving their homes to shop. The development of alternative channels is one of the most important sources of opportunity for companies. Wholesale clubs are another example. The rapid growth of Costco, Sam's, Price, and other clubs in the last few years has created an alternative channel with the ability to reach most urban markets in the United States. Initially, these clubs picked up the leftovers of the established retail channels, but as they grew they were able to demand special pricing and packaging. Now manufacturers are beginning to design product offerings specifically for the wholesale clubs. For example, Heinz now produces packages condiments (ketchup, relish, and so on) in special variety packs for distribution in the channel, and also has added oversized ketchup bottles on pallets, ready for the clubs to display on their cement floors.[8]

Multiple Channels of Distribution

Marketers sometimes use more than one distribution channel; this is called dual distribution. Appliance manufacturers sell their goods through two very different channels. To reach the housing and mobile-home market (20 percent of industry sales), they submit competitive bids to meet builders' specifications. To reach the larger replacement market, they sell through retail outlets. Computer manufacturers need more than one channel as computers are sold to a growing market of home and business users as well as industrial customers.

Marketers may also choose to serve a single market through several different distribution channels. For example, STP Corporation sells oil and gasoline additives both in service stations and in supermarkets, while General Electric distributes many of its small electrical appliances through discount outlets as well as through catalog retailers. In this way, marketers reach consumers whose needs are similar but whose buying patterns are different.

Developing a Distribution Strategy

The distribution area of marketing involves both strategic and tactical decisions. The strategic decisions consist of choosing a distribution channel and the intermediaries that will make up the system for moving the product to the market. These decisions set the stage for the tactical decisions, for example, the choice of exactly which firms will serve as intermediaries and how the actual movement of the product will take place.

Remember the Porsche case? In August 1984, with the contract it had reached in 1969 with Volkswagen of America about to expire, Porsche planned to alter the distribution of its sports cars in the United States. The contract between Porsche and VW specified that VW dealers would be the outlets for Porsche products. Porsche's president, Peter Shutz, wanted to bring the company closer to the customer by "doing business like no one else." A research study had found that buyers of the pricey, quality cars were not impulse buyers but, rather, saw their purchase as an investment. Shutz did not think they needed the fast-talking sales pitch of a typical dealer's salesforce. However, because he underestimated the power of the dealers, his plan failed.

The new distribution plan called for eliminating dealers completely and using agents in their place. The agents would not buy the cars, and hence would avoid inventory holding costs; instead, they would buy the cars as needed to complete a sale. They would work on an 8 percent commission compared to the

16 to 18 percent markup generally charged by VW. A total of 40 company centers would be established to stock the Porsches—but they would also sell them in direct competition with the agents.

Shutz felt that the mass retailer was the wrong outlet for his low-volume, high-price ($21,400 to $44,000) autos. He had also heard that some dealers who did not have the cars desired by consumers were buying them from other dealers at a large premium that was passed on to the customer, making the cars even more expensive. He also knew that the Japanese would soon introduce a comparable high-performance sports car, and he wanted to set up a stronger distribution system for competitive reasons. Since the VW contract called for all VW dealers to handle Porsche cars, he had no control over the selection of dealers. Hence the new plan.

Shutz's plan was such a radical departure from the distribution system in America that it met with widespread resistance. In addition, VW dealers were asked to invest in partnerships to finance the Porsche centers. The dealers felt betrayed and insulted by the offer to invest in a distribution system that attacked their traditional franchise system, one that provided them with as much as $40 million in annual sales. Shutz had reasoned that the lower inventory carrying costs would be welcomed and that investment in the centers would foster greater commitment by the dealers. He was wrong.

Three weeks after presenting the plan to what he thought would be an excited and accepting dealer audience, Shutz had to scrap the new distribution system. The dealers were so angered that, with the help of the American International Automobile Association, they started a class action lawsuit. Dealers across the country sought damages of over $3 billion. Shutz issued a letter explaining that the company had decided against the new system. As part of his effort to rebuild the dealer network, Shutz had buttons made with the slogan, "Nobody's perfect."[9]

Strategic Criteria

Marketers are faced with a lot of distribution channel alternatives. How do they choose among them? In the case of products that are new to the firm but not to the marketplace, channels already exist. Given room on the channel member's shelf and sufficient demand, the product can take its place beside those of competitors. Sometimes marketers branch out from the traditional outlets for a particular product. This approach was successfully pursued by Hanes when it took its L'eggs line of pantyhose to supermarkets and drugstores instead of specialty and department stores. Other products are so innovative (for example, the original Apple Personal Computer or personal telephones once the AT&T monopoly was broken in the early 1980s) that no established channel exists for them. In such cases, channel decisions must be based on an assessment of the organization's goals and resources and an understanding of the market. All distribution strategies, however, are guided by three overall criteria: market coverage, channel control, and costs.

Market Coverage

We have seen how intermediaries decrease the number of transactions that are necessary to reach a particular market. While a producer could make four direct contacts with ultimate consumers, if the producer instead contacts four retailers, each of which makes four contacts with ultimate consumers, the total number of contacts in increased to 16. We can extend this line of thinking to still another layer of intermediary. The longer the channel of distribution, the greater the market coverage. Thus if the size of the potential market for a product is very large, a larger number of intermediaries is desirable.

Market coverage is an important consideration for many marketers. For example, almost all people in the United States over the age of 15 are potential buyers of Gillette Sensor razor blades. That's a lot of people, and it takes a long channel to ensure that this product is available when and where it is needed. Contrast this with the market for Mack trucks. The total market for heavy trucks is only about 300,000 customers, with 10 percent of them buying 90 percent of all the big rigs sold. In this case, less market coverage is needed. While most buyers of heavy trucks also purchase razor blades, very few razor blade buyers purchase heavy trucks!

Channel Control

The second major criterion in setting distribution strategy is channel control. When intermediaries gain title to a product, they can do almost anything they want with it. They own it. What most manufacturers want is the kind of aggressive selling and promotion by intermediaries that will move the product through the distribution system efficiently and effectively. They may also want to ensure that the product does not fall into the hands of intermediaries whose image does not match the manufacturer's goals. Both concerns were reflected in Porsche's effort to redesign its channel; although in the end it did not have sufficient power to make any changes.

Costs

Marketers cannot ignore the costs associated with different distribution channels. Many consumers believe that the shorter the channel, the lower the cost of distribution. We have seen, however, that the opposite is true. Intermediaries are specialists that perform the functions of distribution more efficiently and effectively than manufacturers could. Thus the costs of distribution to the producer are lower when a longer channel is used. A short, direct channel requires a substantial investment by the manufacturer, who must maintain a sizable salesforce and clerical staff for this purpose.

Other Factors

These three criteria—coverage, control, and cost—provide the overall guidelines for choosing a distribution channel. Marketers can analyze the situation more closely, however, using more specific factors like the ones presented in Exhibit 12.4. None of these factors alone should determine the strategy; rather, all relevant factors should be taken into consideration. Some variables will tell the decision maker which channel length is most appropriate. These are referred to as *determining factors*. Others will indicate whether enough profits will be achieved to offset the higher cost of using a short channel. These are called *qualifying factors*. Close scrutiny of Exhibit 12.4 will show that determining factors for a long channel tend to reflect the need for substantial market coverage while determining factors for a short channel reflect the need for control.

Intensity of Distribution

At this point, the basic strategic decisions have been made. The marketer has determined the channel length and what kinds of intermediaries to include or exclude. The next step is to determine the number of intermediaries in the channel. This is known as the intensity of distribution. There are three alternatives: intensive, selective, and exclusive distribution.

Intensive distribution has the goal of wide geographic coverage. This approach gives products the greatest exposure. At its extreme, intensive distribution means that every appropriate, suitable, available outlet where buyers might shop for the product carries it. Intensive distribution is necessary for convenience items and for some other goods, however. Retailers don't always find it so desirable since it means that they have to compete for customers.

Selective distribution involves the use of a limited set of outlets in a given territory. It is generally used for shopping products and some specialty products—those that are characterized by a high degree of brand awareness and brand loyalty. This is an increasingly frequent approach to distribution as manufacturers have realized that intensive distribution does not always lead to aggressive selling and promotion. With selective distribution, manufacturers gain because channel members are more loyal and cooperative. Retailers, for instance, know that they have some guaranteed sales; they face less competition from other retailers than in the case of intensive distribution. As a result, they are more willing to promote the manufacturer's product aggressively, provide service, and hold more stock in inventory. Peter Shutz's plan for Porsche would have made distribution more selective.

EXHIBIT 12.4.   Factors that affect the length of distribution channels.

Factors	Explanation	Channel Length
Market Factors		
1. Number of potential exchanges	1. When many individual exchanges are expected, a long channel is indicated. When relatively few exchanges are expected within a given period, as with industrial markets, the manufacturer may be able to serve them directly with a short channel.	1. Many→Long (Determining) Few→Short (Qualifying)
2. Expected size of an exchange	2. When the expected size of an individual exchange is likely to be small, intermediaries will probably be used. When the size of an order is large, it may be economical, in terms of contact cost, to use a short channel.	2. Small→Long (Determining) Large→Short (Qualifying)
3. Geographic concentration of the market	3. When consumers are concentrated within a specific geographic area, as with industrial markets, a short channel is feasible. But if consumers are dispersed across a large region, intermediaries are likely to be used to gain maximum contracts.	3. Concentrated→Short (Qualifying) Dispersed→Long (Determining)
Marketing Mix Factors		
1. Unit Price	1. The per-unit cost of distribution is generally higher with short channels. If the unit price and profit margin are large and can absorb the extra cost, a short channel is feasible. Otherwise a long channel is necessary.	1. High→Short (Qualifying) Low→Long (Determining)
2. Perishability (speed requirements)	2. Short channels are generally quicker than long channels. Products that are perishable generally use short channels.	2. Perishable→Short (Determining) Nonperishable→Long (Qualifying)
3. Width of product line	3. Sometimes other products in a product line throw off excess cash and profit that can be used to support a short channel for a low-cash-producing product in the short run.	3. Wide→Short (Qualifying) Not wide→Long (Determining)
4. Technical, specialized, or customized products	4. Technically complex or specialized products, especially industrial products, often require special service by the manufacturer, such as demonstration, training, customization, or maintenance. This calls for a short channel.	4. Specialized→Short (Determining) Not specialized→Long (Qualifying)

EXHIBIT 12.4. *(Continued)*

Factors	Explanation	Channel Length
5. Product type	5. Some products, such as impulse items or commodities, need intensive distribution so as to make them widely available to consumers. In such situations a long channel is in order. Other products, such as specialty or shopping goods, may require only selective or even exclusive distribution; hence, a short channel may be appropriate.	5. Commodity type→Long (Determining) Specialty type→Short (Qualifying)
6. Promotion	6. When a firm uses a promotional strategy, directed at the final consumer, to build demand, it is hoped that those consumers will then demand that retailers carry the product. This encourages other intermediaries to carry the product as well. In this way longer channels become available for distributing the product. When promotion is directed at intermediaries to gain their support for the product, shorter channels may be used because the producer can expect full cooperation from the few intermediaries it employs.	6. Promotion toward consumers →Long (Qualifying) Promotion toward intermediaries→Short (Qualifying)

Organizational Factors

Factors	Explanation	Channel Length
1. Number of other products or lines	1. When a firm has several products or product lines that can appropriately use the same channel system, together they may be able to support a short channel.	1. Many→Short (Qualifying) One→Long (Determining)
2. Financial resources	2. Distribution generally requires a sales force, transportation equipment, the ability to grant credit, and so on. Financially weak firms cannot establish these on their own and have to use intermediaries.	2. Strong→Short (Qualifying) Weak→Long (Determining)
3. Control desired	3. Firms that want to be able to control the distribution process, so that they may control the final selling price, the level of inventory, sales promotion activities, and activities of the sales force, will want to use a short channel. The shorter the channel, the easier it is for a manufacturer to control.	3. Control desired→Short (Determining) Not desired→Long (Qualifying)

EXHIBIT 12.4. *(Continued)*

Factors	Explanation	Channel Length
4. Management skill	4. Channel decisions are strategic decisions that require management know-how. Firms that lack the requisite skills may prefer to turn the job over to an intermediary.	4. Skilled→Short (Qualifying) Not skilled→Long (Determining)

Intermediary Factors

1. Economy in services required	1. For every product, distribution requires certain activities, such as advertising, bulk breaking, sorting, transporting, and storage. The efficiency and effectiveness of intermediaries should be compared with those of the producer itself.	1. Efficient intermediaries →Long (Qualifying) Inefficient intermediaries →Short (Determining)
2. Availability of intermediaries	2. The existence of a distribution structure is an uncontrollable variable. If no intermediaries exist that can accomplish the specific activities and services needed for a product's distribution, the producer will have to establish its own distribution system.	2. Available→Long (Qualifying) Not available→Short (Determining)

Regulatory Environment

1. Regulatory restrictions	1. When an industry is highly regulated, there are often restrictions on the activities in which producers may engage, for example, a prohibition on door-to-door selling. There may also be required activities. For instance, a bottle bill requiring deposits on cans and bottles will call for certain activities aimed at collecting the used containers. In such cases producers will need the assistance of intermediaries to comply with the regulations. In the absence of regulation, producers may be able to work with a short channel.	1. Heavy regulation→Long (Determining) Light regulation→Short (Qualifying)

Selective distribution allows producers to choose the best possible channel members, avoiding bad credit risks, unaggressive marketers, poor inventory planners, and others that will not do an adequate job for the producer. At the same time, this strategy puts more pressure on intermediaries to move the product. Manufacturers have higher expectations when only a few intermediaries are included in the channel. Often they place specific constraints on them in order to ensure aggressive selling of their product. For example, retailers may be expected to advertise locally and maintain well-stocked inventories.

In the case of exclusive distribution, the number of intermediaries is limited to one for each geographic territory. This is an extreme form of selective distribution, in which producers maintain the greatest possible control in a given market. Retailers are generally tied to the manufacturer by policies that guide their advertising, pricing, and sales promotion. Often, too, they are expected not to carry competing lines. This latter policy is risky. While not illegal per se, it can be interpreted as reducing competition and thereby violating the Clayton Antitrust Act of 1914.

From the intermediary's perspective, exclusive distribution guarantees all sales of the product in that territory. This strategy is generally employed with specialty goods, for which the manufacturer wants to ensure the proper image and buyers will seek out the outlet that carries the product.

An example of exclusive distribution is provided by Nexxus Products Co., the company that markets "polymeric tridimensional" hair conditioners and "botanically fortified" shampoos. Nexxus has chosen to distribute its products almost exclusively through hairstyling salons. To support its distributors, Nexxus keeps them stocked with free samples for salons, copious amounts of sales literature, and annual meetings in beautiful Santa Barbara, California, where the company has its headquarters. Each distributor has an exclusive territory, and over half of the 32 distributors carry only Nexxus products. As one distributor put it, "I feel like one of the family."[10]

Selecting Channel Members

Channel members must be chosen carefully. Not all available distributors can or will do an adequate job. Therefore, marketers must use some specific decision criteria in making their selections:

- Is the intermediary located close to the desired market?
- Is the intermediary able to provide the necessary services to the buyer?
- Does the intermediary have the talents and skills to advertise locally and arrange promotional displays?
- Are the product lines carried by the intermediary compatible with the marketer's product line?
- What competitive product lines are carried?
- Does the intermediary have sufficient financial resources?

- How many years has the intermediary been in business?
- Does the intermediary display a cooperative spirit?
- What is the image and reputation of the intermediary in the market served?
- Does the intermediary have the managerial talent needed to carry the marketer's product line?

The characteristics desired in channel members depend in part on whether the marketer uses a pull or push strategy as part of its overall marketing approach. In a pull approach, the manufacturer spends heavily to create consumer awareness and demand for the product. As a result, consumers request the product from retailers, which in turn request it from intermediaries. Here the flow is a backward one, with consumer demand putting pressure on the intermediaries to carry the product. This strategy has often been used in the packaged-goods industry, where heavy spending by the likes of General Foods, Procter & Gamble, and General Mills has pulled such products through the distribution system. The pull strategy is appropriate when the product is readily differentiated from others, has a mass market, and carries a low price.

In a push strategy, the emphasis shifts to aggressive personal selling by the manufacturer to encourage channel members to stock and promote its product. While promotion to consumers is not ignored, it receives less attention than promotion aimed at gaining the cooperation of distributors and retailers. This strategy is particularly useful for durable goods, for high-priced items, and for products with limited markets.

Channel Management

The distribution channel is a system of channel members—producers, intermediaries, and consumers—that are linked together through the exchange process in order to create time and place utilities. To meet this goal, the distribution system must be viewed as a totality. It is to the advantage of each channel member to cooperate with the other members of the channel, although in practice cooperation is often minimal.

In reality, most channel members operate somewhat independently. Each has its own goals—profits, sales volume, the development of a particular image, and so on—and the goals of one channel member may not be consistent with those of another. Furthermore, each channel member may deal with many others. Under these circumstances, it's difficult, sometimes impossible, for each individual channel member to satisfy all the suppliers and customers involved. In serving the diverse needs of retailers, for example, a food wholesaler may carry canned peas produced by Del Monte, Green Giant, and Stokely Van Camp. Each of these manufacturers would prefer the wholesaler to carry only its brand. Thus the wholesaler cannot completely satisfy both the retailers and the manufacturers. And most damaging, the wholesaler cannot be an objective conduit for consumer information.

In short, there is often conflict rather than cooperation among channel members. Marketers must anticipate and understand the sources of channel conflict and try to eliminate or minimize them.

Minimizing Channel Conflict

To minimize channel conflict, you must know how it arises. There are two types of channel conflict: vertical and horizontal. Vertical conflict arises between channel members at different levels of the distribution system—between producer and wholesaler, for instance, or between wholesaler and retailer. Each channel member is expected to perform certain functions and behave in certain ways. For example, a manufacturer expects a wholesaler to show its full line of products to a retailer. When this is not done, conflict arises. This is exactly the form of conflict that is depicted between Porsche and the VW dealers!

Horizontal conflict occurs between channel members at the same level—between two or more wholesalers or two or more retailers. Such conflict can occur between intermediaries of the same type (for example, two competing supermarkets) or between two different types of intermediaries (for example, a department store and a discount store). Generally, the second type of horizontal conflict is more common. So many retailers have turned to carrying a vast array of products, and in so doing have added product lines that formerly were carried by other types of retailers, that they must now engage in intense competition for customers. Drugstores, for instance, must compete with discount stores, supermarkets, small grocery stores, and even department stores. Similarly, specialty paint stores now have to compete with lumberyards, hardware stores, discount stores, and department stores.

Reducing Channel Conflict

Cooperation within a channel often comes from the ability of one channel member to influence the behavior of others, in other words, from the power of one member over the others.[11] Power results in control and thus fosters cooperation. The channel member that has such power is referred to as the channel captain. In most cases, the channel captain is the manufacturer; Procter & Gamble, Gillette, General Electric, and General Motors, for example, are clearly the dominant forces in the distribution of their products. Increasingly retailers or wholesalers are becoming the channel captain. Wal-Mart can pretty much dictate the design, price, and terms of sale of the products they buy from most of the manufacturers in their distribution channels. In Canada and some European countries, and increasingly in the United States, powerful retailers are requiring "slotting fees" of as much as $30,000 to cover the risk and costs of giving shelf space to new products. And if products do not sell as briskly as expected over say a three-month period, manufacturers are forced to pay failure fees of $2,000 to $5,000. Even more, these are fees demanded for in-store product sampling, promotional ads in circulars, and special displays.[12] A General Mills vice president offered this report: "Seven chains control about 75 percent of the business in Canada, and they are using their power to extract more money from us. So, we're very careful that we have a good new product that will last a long time."[13] The recent consolidation of retailers through acquisitions, failures, and the growth of giant discounters and wholesale clubs is increasing the power of retailers in the United States, too.

Channel leadership requires three conditions: The channel captain must want to exert influence; the other channel members must be willing to accept its control; and there must be significant differences in the power of the various channel members.[14] When a shift in power occurs, there is often disagreement over who should lead, and thus increased conflict.

A second approach to resolving channel conflict is to integrate the channel members into a single organization called a *vertical marketing system*. Such a system operates as a whole rather than as a set of individual parts. Also, certain economies of scale can be achieved in this way. For example, marketing research, accounting programs, and advertising personnel can be used by all the members of the channel. At the same time, however, inefficiencies are introduced as the channel is restructured—and the new channel can require a sizable financial investment. Legal restrictions may also interfere, since some vertical systems may be viewed as reducing competition. Nevertheless, more and more such systems are being established both in the United States and in other developed countries.

There are three types of vertical marketing systems: corporate, administered, and contractual. In a corporate vertical marketing system, control is gained through ownership of both production and distribution operations. The corporation can own some or all of the parts of the channel. Firestone, for instance, owns some of the retail outlets that distribute its tires; Coca-Cola owns some of the bottlers that distribute its soft drinks. Not all such systems are owned by the producer, though. Revco D.S., the nation's largest discount drugstore chain, has expanded into the production of drugs and related items.

In an administered vertical marketing system, cooperation results primarily from the economic power of one channel member; in other words, one member is informally designated as captain. This channel member usually has the most resources to invest in channel management and performs functions that win the loyalty of other channel members. General Foods Corporation, for instance, has developed computer software that will measure retailers' product turnover and should boost their profits. And now with scanner data, many supermarket chains are taking on the captain role; information is their power base.

Contractual vertical marketing systems offer a middle ground between the costly corporate system and the less controllable administered system. In this approach, channel members draw up a legal agreement that specifies the rights and responsibilities of each party. This is the fastest-growing type of vertical marketing system. The most common form of it is the franchise system.

For a fee, the franchise owner buys the right to sell the franchisor's product, but specific guidelines such as using only corporate-sponsored promotions and products and wearing corporate uniforms are set up to ensure a standardized image and level of quality.

The growth in franchising is striking. Over 3,000 companies now distribute through franchises in 60 different industries. A third of all retail sales are made by franchises (on a dollar basis) and at the current rate of growth the figure will be 50 percent in the year 2000.[15] What accounts for this remarkable transformation of distribution channels?

The conventional explanation falls short. Franchisors usually say people buy franchises because the failure rate is only 5 percent. But according to Rupert Bartlett of the American Bar Association's Forum on Franchising, "at best a third are doing very well, a third are in definite financial trouble and a third may be breaking even."[16] The high success rate of franchises is a myth, albeit certainly a useful myth for companies wishing to sell franchises. And the high risk of nonfranchise startups is also a myth. The conventional wisdom says that 9 out of 10 entrepreneurs fail, but the most extensive study to date reported a 77 percent survival rate three years after startup.[17] In fact, the risks of a startup are about the same, whether it is a franchise or not.

While entrepreneurs may select franchises on the basis of myth rather than reality, the real issue is why *customers* select franchises. More and more consumers are voting for franchises with their wallets, and the most likely explanation is that the franchises offer higher quality. The presence of a concerned owner (and often the owner's spouse and children) behind a retail counter can make a big difference in this era of miserably poor customer service. The franchise owner is management, but this management is on the front lines, interacting with customers daily. The franchise system's organization is inherently more customer-oriented than the centrally-managed chains with which franchises often compete. And while independent stores may also have on-site management, they lack the logistical advantages and economies of scale of a franchise system when it comes to activities like purchasing and advertising. The rise of franchising is a little told part of the story of the marketing revolution in America.

LEGAL ASPECTS OF DISTRIBUTION

Companies that attempt to control the distribution of their products are in danger of violating the Sherman Antitrust Act, the Clayton Antitrust Act, or the Federal Trade Commission Act. Four methods of control are frequently employed— usually by manufacturers. While none is illegal per se, each can be deemed illegal if it has the effect of reducing competition, creating a monopoly, or restraining trade.

In exclusive dealing situations, the manufacturer forbids dealers to carry competitors' products. While not all exclusive dealing is illegal, it tends to be unlawful when such an agreement is reached by a very large manufacturer and a very small dealer. In such cases, the power of the manufacturer is viewed as a restraint of trade. Exclusive dealing is also deemed unlawful when the manufacturer has a dominant share of a given market. When the exclusive contract actually improves competition—for example, when the manufacturer is small and/or just getting started—exclusive deals may be looked upon favorably by the courts.

Dealer selection involves selecting the dealers to which a manufacturer will sell, and not selling to any others. In 1919, the United States Supreme Court firmly established the right of producers to choose the organizations and individuals to whom they will sell—as long as the intent is not to create a monopoly. The courts have also said that dealers cannot be dropped for handling competitors' lines.

In the case of tying agreements, the producer forces the dealer to buy additional products in order to secure one highly desired product—or at least the dealer is restrained from buying that product from another source. Generally, such agreements are viewed as violating the antitrust laws. They are seen as legal when a new company is trying to enter a market, when the producer is trying to maintain a desired level of quality, or when an exclusive dealer is required to carry a manufacturer's full product line.

Manufacturers use exclusive territories to ensure that dealers sell only to customers within a specific territory. Where such arrangements reduce competition and restrain trade, they could be viewed as illegal. Generally, judicial bodies seek to foster competition among intermediaries handling the same brand.

So far we have looked at distribution channels from afar, as would a manager working on a distribution strategy. But it is also helpful to sweep down for a close look at retailing, since this aspect of the channel is of such scale and importance that it is the primary concern of many companies.

RETAILING

> One of the great inclinations of retailers is to find someone who's doing everything right and try to improve on it.[18]
>
> Allan L. Pennington, president
> Pennington Associates

Stew Leonard's is a specialty grocery store in Norwalk, Connecticut. But not your average specialty food store; with revenues of $115 million a year, or $3,470 per square foot of selling space, it probably sets the record. Its high sales do not reflect a broader selection; in fact, the store carries only 800 items versus two to three thousand at the typical grocery store. Instead, the store sells more of the items it does stock, simply because they are better. An anecdote told to a reporter by Stew Leonard, Jr., who recently took over the management of the store from his father, illustrates the philosophy that makes this store unique.

A couple of years ago, Stew Jr. and his brother, Tom, and some other managers from the store were getting ready to meet with a high-powered, high-priced consultant. Stew Sr. couldn't attend the meeting, so Stew Jr. asked him on the phone if there was anything particularly important he wanted discussed. "I bought some corn yesterday," Stew Sr. replied, "and had it for dinner last night, and it wasn't really sweet."

Stew Jr. gently remonstrated with his father: "Dad, this isn't that kind of meeting. We're talking about strategy, we're talking about merchandising. Isn't there anything really important that you want me to mention?"

"Yeah. The corn isn't really, really sweet."

From there, Stew Jr. recalls, their conversation turned immediately to how to get corn into the store the day it was picked. As it wound up, "we had to competely rearrange our trucking, and our farmer had to start picking earlier. But we got fresh-picked corn."[19]

The more limited selection means that the store buys a high volume of what it does sell, getting good prices on it and having enough power to demand quality from its suppliers. To sell better corn, the store had to convince the farmer to pick early in the morning, and had to alter the logistics so that the fresh-picked could be loaded and delivered by truck immediately. Even so, the store could not offer fresh-picked corn until 10:00 AM, but you can be sure it now sells a great deal more than the neighboring grocery stores that sell corn that has been in transit for days. So Stew Leonard's is able to sell better corn without buying it at a higher price. Its secret, according to Stew Sr., is that customers "come here to save money on good stuff." Better quality for a better price—a winning strategy, but only possible if you are willing to innovate and develop new processes. And if you have a better understanding of what customer's care about than competitors.

As we saw in our examination of product development, manufacturers offer more products to grocery stores every year. Those "mindless brand extensions" that Campbell management complained about, and even the hundreds of sincere efforts to innovate, have over the years produced an incredible variety of choice. But have they produced better quality, have they given consumers more value? The Stew Leonard's story suggests that they may not. As Joseph Palmer, owner of Palmer's Supermarkets in nearby Stamford, Connecticut, explains, "We don't need 16 flavors of health bars. The redundancy is out of control."[20] A quick trip to Norwalk would show him how the retailer can take control over product selection and build a quality-based strategy instead of the typical redundancy-based strategy of grocery stores.

Retailing includes all activities associated with selling goods and services to ultimate consumers. In the case of retailers, one might say, "The buck *starts* here," since the sale of a product at retail begins the movement of payments back through the distribution channel. Since it sells goods to the final member of the channel, the consumer, the retailer is in the best possible position to understand the specific wants and needs of the markets that drive the entire distribution and production system.

Although we usually think of retailers as merchant intermediaries who own stores, it's also accurate to consider teachers, lawyers, consultants, doctors, and dentists as retailers. Certainly not all retailing requires a store. We buy newspapers at a stand, have our shoes shined on a street corner, buy a hot dog or balloon from a street vendor. A Mary Kay cosmetics representative who comes to our door is a retailer, and so is a mail-order marketer. Anyone who markets to the ultimate consumer, by whatever name, is in the business of retailing. A hospital is a retailer to patients. Colleges are retailers of education, and such organizations as charities, funeral homes, and churches also fall into the retail category. Retailing thus has a very broad scope.

We tend to focus on the time and place utilities that come from the retailing function. But retailers also provide possession utility. By offering desired assortments and prices related to perceived value, the retailer encourages the customer to make a purchase and thereby obtain possession utility. Retailers of services—hairstylists, insurance agencies, landscapers—offer even more; they provide form utility as well as time, place, and possession utilities. Such retailers are virtually inseparable from their highly perishable products. Their services last only as long as they are performed and cannot be performed without the retailer.[21] Moreover, the intangible nature of services makes customer-retailer contact the basis for most of the form utility provided.[22] The cleanliness of the Chemlawn truck that fertilizes your lawn, the personality of the Hertz agent, the professional appearance of the booklet containing your H&R Block prepared tax forms—all of these features contribute to your perception of the product. Service retailers must pay strict attention to such details in order to create the form utility desired by their customers.

MODERN RETAILING STRATEGIES

In the past, retailers took a "supplier" approach to retailing; they saw themselves essentially as buyers of merchandise for consumers in their locality. But in the late 1970s, the "positioning era" came to retailing. The retail establishment began to be defined in terms of the market segment it served. Initially this segmentation was based on demographic variables, but now life-style segmentation appears to be taking hold as companies provide an image, a merchandise assortment, an entire feeling geared to a well-defined target market.[23] Wal-Mart, for example, has developed product lines, personnel, and policies that reflect the life styles of small-town, rural America. And we saw in an earlier chapter how Kmart tried to change its target market through trading up.

In sharp contrast to these merchandise strategies, other retailers have become specialty stores with a narrow set of product lines and deep assortments. The Gap, Toys'R'Us, B. Dalton, and Radio Shack are examples. In addition, there are numerous approaches that fall somewhere between the mass merchandise and specialty store strategies. In the rest of the chapter, we will take a brief look at some of the strategic options available to modern retailers.[24]

The Value Strategy

A retailer that adopts the value strategy attempts to offer greater overall quality at a lower price than its competitors. While price competition has long been a favorite strategy of retailers, it has become even more important since the inflationary 1970s, and the current recession has given discount-style retailers a boost as well. Today consumers are cautious and very value conscious, wanting to get their money's worth. Costco, Sam's, and Price are examples; these wholesale clubs are capitalizing on an opportunity to allow customers to buy leading brands at rock-bottom prices.

The Efficiency Strategy

Americans are time conscious, and many stores have taken advantage of this characteristic. The "place" in the 4P's ought to refer to place in *time* as well as space. Convenience stores emphasize proximity to the customer. Superstores stress one-stop shopping. Catalog and other mail-order retailers combine computer, telephone, and credit card technologies to minimize their customers' shopping effort. Catalog showrooms reduce the time the customer has to spend searching for a desired item. In the future, we are likely to see the expansion of videotex shopping (purchasing via computer) as well as catalogs on videodiscs, interactive cable television, and broadcast teletext, with orders being placed by telephone.

The Personal-Contact Strategy

In the United States today, consumers are increasingly concerned with individual well-being and quality of life. Such consumers crave highly customized and expert personal service. Nordstrom's pampers its customers with personal phone calls and notebooks full of information about their personal tastes. Other retailers are pursuing this strategy by offering a wider array of services. Abraham and Straus, for example, offers a special department called "The Office," where trained consultants help women executives make decisions about their wardrobes. Stew Leonard's is famous for its numerous well-trained and helpful staff.

The Sensory Strategy

Some retailers emphasize the shopping experience itself. Atmospherics play a large part in this strategy. Excitement is generated by special events and displays and by architectural and lighting effects. Harrod's, the London department store, uses live models in its floor displays. They stand motionless for about 30 seconds and then move just a little, creating a startling effect. Stew Leonard's uses animated model cows to add atmosphere to his diary goods' lines.

THE FUTURE OF RETAILING

We have looked at several recent developments and trends in retailing. But what is likely to happen in the future? One theory, known as the wheel of retailing, seems to be borne out by recent developments.[25] This theory states that each major innovation in retailing begins a cycle. At first the innovation is viewed skeptically, but over time it takes hold, usually because it makes possible lower prices. For example, at the turn of the century, department stores were an innovation based on low cost and high volume, replacing general stores and other small retailers. The first department stores were simple and sparse in their operations. But over time they escalated their services and thus their expenses—and in came the discounters. Now discounters are adding services, and what do we see? In comes the new wave of discounters, the factory outlet malls, the warehouse stores, and the off-price retailers. (See Exhibit 12.5.)

It is easy to imagine continued movement based on the value strategy, with larger and more efficient warehouse stores displacing other forms. But the success of Stew Leonard's stands in contrast, suggesting that the wheel may soon turn in a new direction. The appeal of quality to consumers can obviously be exploited in retailing, for those who are willing to listen hardest to their customers and think more creatively about their operations. After all, why shouldn't every grocery store sell *sweet* corn?

WHOLESALING AND PHYSICAL DISTRIBUTION

> In the past we have added value to our suppliers' product by buying in large quantities, storing, shipping, receiving and carrying receivables. Today—and more important, tomorrow—the value added is information processing.[26]
>
> W. A. Williamson
> Former Chairman of the Board
> National Wholesale Druggists Association

Wholesaling involves all of the activities provided by wholesaling intermediaries engaged in selling merchandise to retailers; to industrial, commercial, institutional, farm, and professional businesses; or to other types of wholesaling intermediaries. Broadly speaking, any transaction between one producer or intermediary and another is a wholesaling transaction. Thus, a retailer selling napkins to a restaurant or paper and pencils to another retailer is engaged in a

EXHIBIT 12.5. The wheel of retailing.

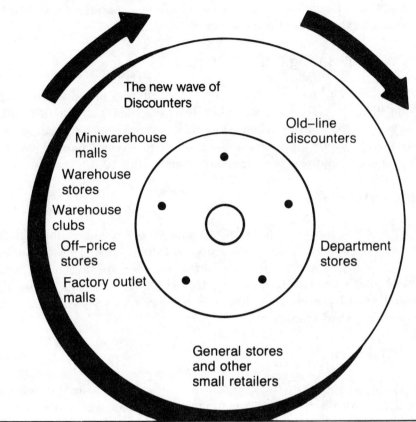

wholesaling transaction. In the same manner, a manufacturer's representative selling office equipment to a doctor or another kind of professional is also involved in a wholesaling transaction.

Wholesaling is an extremely important part of the distribution channel. Without wholesalers, another member of the channel would have to perform their functions. In some cases, this simply is not possible. For example, many small retailers would not be able to survive if they tried to perform all of the functions that a large chain performs. If food wholesalers did not exist, the grocery industry would be limited to major chain stores that can afford to perform wholesaling functions. Stew Leonard's would be out of business.

In a larger sense, wholesaling is very important to the U.S. economy. Wholesalers have been described as the nation's inventory managers. Wholesaling "helps the economy adjust, both in times of high growth and in times of recession, because of its ability to react rapidly to changing demand and supply."[27]

We have already seen that wholesalers provide a variety of services. In fact, they think of themselves as service providers rather than simply as suppliers of products. The activities of wholesalers include buying and selling, distribution, warehousing, and financing. Usually the wholesaler can perform these activities more efficiently than either the manufacturer or the retailer.

Types of Wholesaling Intermediaries

There are now a half million wholesaling intermediaries in the United States, which together generate over $2 billion in sales. Today, almost five million Americans are employed by wholesaling intermediaries.[28] Wholesaling intermediaries can be subdivided into three major categories: merchant wholesalers, agents, and manufacturers' sales branches. (See Exhibit 12.6.)

Merchant Wholesalers

Merchant wholesalers make up the largest segment of the wholesaling industry in terms of both number of establishments and sales volume. They account for 81 percent of all wholesaling intermediaries, and they are responsible for 58 percent of total wholesale trade in the United States. Merchant wholesalers have two distinct features: They take title to the goods they sell, and they are independently owned businesses.

Agent Middlemen

Agents and brokers make up the second major category of wholesaling intermediaries. The main difference between agent middlemen and other types of wholesaling intermediaries is that they do not take title to the merchandise they sell. An agent's or broker's primary function is to bring together buyers and sellers and facilitate exchanges. These intermediaries provide fewer services than other wholesalers and usually work on a commission basis.

Agents can be essential to small manufacturers for which they perform the selling function. This enables the manufacturer to keep expenses down.

EXHIBIT 12.6.   Services provided by wholesalers.

Service	For Customers	For Suppliers
Buying	✓	
Bulkbreaking	✓	
Warehousing	✓	✓
Transportation	✓	
Financing	✓	✓
Management services	✓	
Provide product/market information	✓	✓
Hold title to products	✓	
Sales and promotion		✓
Risk bearing		✓

Normally agents specialize in a particular type of customer or product line. They also tend to have a fairly large customer base within a specific geographic area.

Manufacturers' agents are the most frequently encountered type of agent. These are independent sales representatives who work for several manufacturers of related but noncompeting product lines. Manufacturers' agents receive a commission on every sale they make. One of the major benefits of using this type of intermediary is that it spreads the cost of a single sales call over many products. Complementary product lines can be added relatively easily, since a customer base has already been established.

To receive the saving in costs that results from the use of agents, the manufacturer must sacrifice some control over how its product is actually sold.

It is for this reason that Apple Computer recently made some drastic changes in its distribution system. It dismantled its network of manufacturer's representatives and in its place created a 400-person retail salesforce. It also set up a second salesforce to concentrate on specific market niches, such as business and educational markets. According to an industry analyst, "Apple wants to eliminate layers of marketing and get closer to dealers. . . . That's important because it will enable them to monitor their sales more closely, get dealer input on their marketing strategies, and better gauge what shipment rates and inventory positions should be."[29]

Manufacturers' sales branches and offices are the third major type of wholesaling intermediary. These are wholesaling establishments that are owned and operated by manufacturers but are separate from the manufacturers' factories. They account for 9 percent of wholesaling establishments and 31 percent of wholesale sales. The reason for the establishment of sales branches and offices is to improve selling, inventory control, and product promotion. Their relative success is due to the fact they are usually set up in the manufacturer's best markets.

Strategic Problems of Wholesalers

A recent survey of distributors identified five major problem areas; the first is unstable economic conditions. This is a pressing problem that has resulted from apprehension about interest rates, the memory of high inflation rates, plant closings, and government deficits. The next problem cited was the same one that retailers face; intense competition among distributors. Respondents to the survey mentioned numerous unethical practices, intense price competition, and too many distributors per trading area as indicators of this problem. The third major concern of wholesalers is the high cost of making a sales call—both in terms of salaries and in terms of the cost of maintaining cars and paying salespeople's expenses. This is forcing a change in distributors' selling practices.

Declining employee productivity is another problem faced by wholesalers. This cuts into profits because it raises operating expenses. Finally, manufacturer-distributor relationships are a frequently mentioned concern. Wholesalers often come into conflict with manufacturers over such matters as product return policies and discounts. In many cases, the real problem is poor communication.[30]

One strategic tool that is being used to solve some of these problems is computerization. Like retailers, wholesalers are turning to extensive use of computers and automation. More and more wholesalers are applying these technologies to inventory and cost control, warehouse and store design, and a variety of other uses. It has been said that in coming decades wholesalers will be in the information business as well as the distribution business. As one wholesaler has pointed out, "It is important to provide retail accounting services, inventory services, price file services, and computer back-up."[31]

In the not-so-distant past, wholesalers ordered all of their merchandise either by mail or by phone. Now over 40 percent are ordering foods via electronic devices, either directly through a wholesaler-to-manufacturer order entry system or through a computerized clearinghouse. For example, the National Wholesale Drug Association, in conjunction with Informatics Clearinghouse, has set up an order entry system called ORDERNET. In this system, orders from retailers or wholesalers are consolidated at a central location. At certain times during the day. each manufacturer's computer obtains all the relevant purchase orders from the ORDERNET file. This system has significantly cut down the time it takes to order merchandise.

Warehouse automation is another major strategic tool for wholesalers. Fleming Co., a wholesale food merchant, has invested heavily in this approach. Fleming spends as much as $30 million to build computerized warehouses in which orders from different affiliated supermarkets are sorted into categories (breakfast cereals, canned vegetables, etc.). When every item has been classified, a warehouse employee can make a single trip to a specific area for the needed goods. Fleming has also set up a system of laser scanners that will sort one load of, say, green beans and direct the cases to specific loading docks for shipment to different retailers.[32]

PHYSICAL DISTRIBUTION

We have examined in detail the components of the distribution channel, the intermediaries that bridge the gap between the producer and the ultimate consumer. And we have focused on the end of the channel, the retailer. Determining the length and composition of the distribution channel is a strategic decision; it establishes the overall plan for getting products into the hands of consumers. But the job of distribution is not yet complete; still missing are the activities that result in the actual movement of products through the distribution channel.

The physical-distribution system is responsible for actually moving products in such a way as to accomplish the goal of providing time and place utility. The objective of physical distribution is summed up in a statement by Robert Woodruff, former president of Coca-Cola: "Our policy is to put Coke within an arm's length of desire." An effective physical-distribution system can give a company a significant competitive advantage: a survey of 216 industrial purchasing agents showed that physical distribution ranked second only to quality as a factor in their buying decisions.[33]

The economic impact of physical distribution is awesome. It accounts for the largest component of marketing costs—about 20 cents out of every dollar you spend goes to pay for physical distribution. That amounts to over 15 percent of GNP. However, the cost of physical distribution varies dramatically from one industry to another. In the food industry, for example, it accounts for about one-third of each consumer dollar spent; in the textile and wood industries it amounts to only one-sixth of the price of goods.[34]

Physical distribution ensures that the right products are available when consumers want them—in the right place and at the right time. This overall objective can be summed up in one word: service. This applies to the distribution of services as well as goods.

Physical-distribution decisions need to be guided by a strategy. This strategy must reflect the firm's overall marketing strategy. At the same time, the physical-distribution strategy must mesh with all the other activities in the marketing mix. For example, low-priced impulse items with heavy advertising budgets need extensive coverage and therefore must have maximum exposure at the retail level. The physical-distribution strategy, therefore, must concentrate on making the product available wherever it is needed. A long distribution channel may need the support of many warehouses, fast and frequent transportation, and quick order processing. Consumer packaged-goods companies like Procter & Gamble, Frito-Lay, and General Foods all know the value of such a strategy.

Forecasting Demand

The key to effective and efficient movement of products throughout the physical-distribution system is correctly forecasting the demand for those products. Inaccurate forecasts can result in over- or understocking at intermediate points in the distribution system and may greatly reduce profits. Thus correctly forecasting the level of demand is critical to controlling the flow of products through the distribution system.

Order Processing

At each exchange point within a distribution system, the needs of the next channel are expressed by the placement of orders for products. Thus the retailer orders its inventory from the wholesaler, which, in turn orders replacement products from the distributor or manufacturer, and so on back through the entire channel. How well products flow between channel members depends on how well and how quickly orders are processed at each step along the way. This involves many clerical procedures that may take much time and present many opportunities for mistakes and delays.

Some firms have gained a decided advantage by investing in computerized ordering systems. Bergen Brunswig, a Los Angeles-based distributor of over-the-counter drugs and medical supplies, offers its retail customers a computer-based order entry program designed to speed ordering and delivery. And at Whirlpool Corporation, a major marketer of home appliances, a computerized system allows a distributor to dial into a computer from a dealer's showroom for information about current stock, production, and shipping dates. Orders are taken immediately, and goods can often be shipped straight to the retailer, bypassing the distributor's warehouse. Time and money are saved and damage due to handling is avoided.

Inventory Management

Products must be stored in a way that will make up for any inaccuracies in demand forecasts. Storage of products—that is, inventory management—is a way of safeguarding against inability to meet demand directly from the assembly line. It is an expensive activity, for it involves the costs of storage space, handling, and insurance, as well as costs associated with product obsolescence. These costs can be decreased by reducing the size of the inventory, but then the marketer runs the risk of losing sales when the product is unavailable. In the ideal situation, demand for the product can be forecast correctly and inventory can be built up at an appropriate time to meet that demand. In reality, however, marketers must balance the costs of holding inventory against the costs of lost sales.

As you will recall from the chapter's introduction, Toyota and other Japanese manufacturers have developed a new approach to inventory management. Called *just-in-time purchasing*, this concept involves buying in small quantities to reduce inventory carrying costs and obtain delivery just in time for use.[35] This system results in lower order quantities, frequent and reliable delivery times, shorter and extremely reliable lead times, and consistently high product quality.[36]

Just-in-time purchasing is now used by Toyota dealers, and has also been used to control inventory at the manufacturing level, but its use is not yet widespread in the United States.[37] To implement this system effectively, the firm must change its manufacturing process. This approach requires tight scheduling, insistence on high-quality materials, simplified materials-handling procedures, and lower inventory levels, all of which make interruptions of production more likely.

Storage

Storage management is concerned with the size, number, and location of facilities to house inventory. To store inventory, channel members can choose between private and public warehouses. Private warehouses are owned and controlled exclusively by their users, while public warehouses are owned by independent contractors that rent space as needed to various channel members. Since public warehouses do not require a large investment on the part of the marketer, inventories can be expanded or contracted as the need arises. This is particularly helpful when the firm markets products for which demand fluctuates widely. Public warehouses have lower unit costs, too, since their fixed costs are spread among a large number of users.[38]

There has been a shift away from storage and toward movement of goods. Distribution centers have replaced warehouses in many cases; these are streamlined storage facilities that are geared to taking orders and delivering products. Automated equipment and computerized inventory systems allow the firm to react rapidly to customer needs. Caterpillar Tractor has a distribution center housing 60 days' worth of inventory—more than 200,000 parts. Its computer network links dealers and other storage points around the world. At Levi Strauss' distribution center, the 48,000 items in inventory come from 10 manufacturing plants in the United States and are shipped to 17,000 American retailers as well as to 70 countries. Eastman Kodak maintains its distribution center at Chicago's O'Hare Airport, where products can be shipped anywhere in the world within a matter of hours.

Protective Packaging

Since products that are damaged at any point in the distribution system cause the smooth flow of goods to break down, distribution managers are very concerned about protective packaging. The packages and containers used to ship products should be compatible with the materials-handling system and should fit compactly into transportation equipment in order to reduce freight costs. In addition, shippers should be aware that some modes of transportation may have characteristics that make them unsuitable for transporting a particular product unless it is properly protected. For example, railroad cars are usually very hot, while airplane storage areas get extremely cold; many products that are shipped by either of these methods need to be protected against the temperature.

Transportation

Another major physical-distribution decision is determining the mode of transportation to use in shipping products through the distribution channel. Transportation companies are classified by law into four types: common carriers, contract carriers, private carriers, and exempt carriers.

Common carriers serve the general public by transporting products on a specified schedule and according to regulations and standards established by government regulatory agencies as well as by company rules. Most interstate transportation companies are common carriers. Contract carriers are independent firms that agree to transport a specified number of shipments to specific destinations for an estimated price. Many contract carriers specialize in certain types of goods: household movers and automobile trucking companies are examples. Private carriers are shippers that own the goods they ship. The company employs the drivers and either owns or leases the equipment used. Large grocery chains usually own their own fleets of trucks, for example. Exempt carriers, as their name indicates, are shippers that are exempt from state and federal regulation. They are involved mostly in moving unprocessed agricultural products, usually by truck.

Within these broad categories, there are five main transportation modes: railroad, truck, pipeline, waterway, and airplane. These alternative modes are generally compared on the basis of six characteristics: door-to-door delivery time (speed), number of geographic points served (availability), ability to be on time (dependability), ability to carry various products (capability), number of scheduled shipments per day (frequency), and cost per ton-mile (cost).

The main goal of physical distribution is to ensure that the right products are available when consumers want them—in the right place and at the right time. But this overall goal has several aspects that we should examine more closely.

Availability

The most basic objective of physical distribution is availability. Availability is in fact a key element of any product, although it is often assumed by management and customer alike. Suppliers at each point in the distribution system must anticipate demand and be able to furnish all items ordered by customers. This ability depends on the accuracy of forecasts. When any channel member is out of stock, customers are inconvenienced and must either search for another source or wait until the products have been restocked. In either case, they do not receive the level of service they expected and desired.

Accurate Order Filling

Few things are more maddening than to wait for an order and then receive the wrong items. This can be caused by mistakes made during order writing, order receiving, order filling. Often customers indicate their needs incorrectly, especially over the telephone. Errors also occur in the process of transcribing information from purchase orders to shipping orders, since different intermediaries may misunderstand each other's ordering systems or documents.

Delivering Undamaged Goods

Physical distribution must also pay attention to all activities that could cause damage to goods—materials-handling procedures, packaging, storage, and mode of transportation. Usually, faster transportation results in less damage, although it is more costly.

Speedy and Reliable Delivery

Many physical-distribution activities must be performed between the time when a need for products is recognized by a channel member and the time when those products are received. These activities—order writing and transmitting, order processing, order filling, and shipment—take time. Closely aligned with speed of service is the channel member's dependability. Customers often make plans that depend on the receipt of products as scheduled. But improved speed and dependability usually leads to higher costs. For example, computerized order processing is faster than manual processing, and air transport is faster than truck transport; but each method is more expensive than the alternative. Thus channel members must be keenly aware of their customers' needs in terms of time and dependability.

The Total-Cost Approach to Physical Distribution

By now it should be clear that there are two main objectives of physical distribution. The level of service is important because it ensures that channel members—and the ultimate consumer—will be satisfied. But as the service level is improved, the costs of distribution increase. Thus physical-distribution decisions involve a trade-off between minimizing total distribution costs and maintaining a satisfactory level of service.

It is difficult to define a satisfactory level of service; the firm needs to determine its customers' requirements and compare the service levels offered by competitors. Customers want fast, on-time delivery of undamaged goods. They also want to be sure that their emergency needs will be met, and sometimes they expect to have inventory held for them. With respect to the competition, the firm should expect to at least match the level of service offered by others—but going a step further can provide a competitive advantage. The higher costs of providing more service must be studied carefully. An analysis of customer needs may indicate that a low-service, low-price strategy is best, but offering superior service at a premium price may turn out to be a better strategy. And, increasingly, firms are accepting Philip Crosby's argument that "quality is free" and innovating to improve service without raising costs.

IN CONCLUSION

We left Porsche fumbling with its "Nobody's Perfect" pin back in 1984. What happened? The plan to replace dealers (a form of merchant middleman) with agents (who, unlike dealers, do not take title to the cars) backfired. Dealers refused to give up their franchises and balked at investing in the 20 distribution centers Porsche wanted to open. It turned out Porsche did not hold power over the dealers—they refused to acknowledge that it was the channel captain. No doubt the fact that Porsche dealers almost always carried other, higher-volume makes reduced Porsche's control over them.

With the failure of its plans to increase control over marketing in the distribution channel, Porsche focused more cautiously on the logistics side of the equation. The company left dealers in place, but broke away from its deal with Audi and set up Porsche Cars North America located in Reno, Nevada, to handle physical distribution. Dealers benefited by the company's better control over inventories and its use of closed trucks to insure that the cars were delivered in perfect condition.

But in 1986, U.S. unit sales of Porsches peaked at a little over 30,000 and began a precipitous fall: down to 25,000 in 1987, 15,000 in 1988,[39] and only about 6,000 in the current year. This slide has had a dramatic impact on the distribution channel. According to a Porsche dealer (who wishes to remain anonymous) "A Porsche franchise today is a loser. It probably costs each dealer to be a Porsche dealer today." The drop in sales reflects the impact of economic conditions, including the stock market crash of 1987 and the current recession. But it also reflects Porsche's retreat from its effort to trade down to lower-priced sports cars and concerns back at headquarters that too much of Porsche revenues (over 60 percent in 1986) were from the U.S. Porsche's new, narrower focus on the upper end of the market has helped it improve its own profits,[40] but has left dealers impoverished. Our anonymous dealer explains that "back in '86 we'd buy a car for $20,000 and sell it for $25,000, making 25 percent profit. Now we buy a car for $70,000 and maybe sell it for $71,000 just to move it." With lower volume and margins, "sales no longer cover the dealer's very high floor plan costs" on Porsches. According to the dealer, "About a third of their dealers have handed in their franchises and walked away," and remaining dealers are less inclined to invest in aggressive marketing efforts.

In this context, it is easy to see why Porsche is turning to direct mail to supplement dealer contact with prospective customers (as we described in Chapter 8). And the company is also staging "Porsche Experience" sessions to demonstrate the cars in locations like Chicago's huge Rosemont Horizon parking lot.[41] Despite the failure of its original plan, Porsche is slowly strengthening its control, both over physical distribution and over customer contacts. It will be interesting to see what this distribution channel looks like when the dust finally settles.

13 PROMOTION
The Many Faces of Marketing

Promotion is the face of the company; or its many faces, if it promotes multiple brands and lines, each having a unique identity. The task of promotion is to insure that targeted consumers know and like the company's products. Ads on TV and radio, print ads in magazines and newspapers, billboards, event sponsorship, contests and coupons, special packaging, telephone, direct mail, in-person sales pitches, and many other vehicles are used to animate this face and give it power in the eyes and mind of the consumer. And the cleverness with which the face is drawn is all-important since hundreds of other faces are crowding around every consumer, struggling to be seen and heard.

This image of promotion has a slightly nightmarish quality, and, in fact, promotion has a dark side, both for the company and the consumer. Some people believe that "Advertising has filled in all the cracks of people's lives to the extent that it is seen as an encroachment," as Steven Ewen, a professor of media studies at Hunter College, puts it.[1]

The expansion of ads into all the cracks in our environment certainly strengthens this impression. Ad space is for sale everywhere. Ads now appear over sinks and urinals in public bathrooms. The sponsorship messages on public TV and radio are quietly swelling until they sound for all the world like mini ads. Phones ring off the hook at dinner time with computerized sales pitches. Skiers seeking escape on the slopes are assaulted by small billboards on each post of the ski lift.

Ambushing the Consumer

And where ads aren't officially welcome, they find ways to sneak in. Game Show Placements, Ltd. advertises to marketers that giving their products away on game

359

shows is "the ultimate in low-cost mass exposure." "Product placements" in movies are a booming business, with companies paying from thousands to hundreds of thousands to appear in the likes of Back to the Future II and Rocky V. An MGM/UA Communications Company representative hyped "Rocky V" to marketers in 1990, saying there would be "opportunities to show 10 to 25 logos" in the film. Pepsi, Budweiser, and many others rose to the bait.[2] Perhaps worst of all is the assault on children with the new TV shows-that-are-commercials leading the charge. McDonald's produced an insipid "McTreasure Island." The new "Video Power" TV show is all about video games and features "infomercials" (lengthy documentaries or dramas with a subtle advertising message) that are "spliced into the show so seamlessly that kids might not know the difference."[3]

Some managers think advertising has gone too far. While Alex Szabo, president of movie theater ad distributor Screenvision Cinema Network crows that "We target viewers entering the theater, exiting the theater. We're taking it to the ultimate step," Richard Cook of Disney Studios says, "movie ads are an unwelcome intrusion," and Betsy Frank of ad agency Saatchi & Saatchi describes them as one of a number of new "ambush media." (These are media, like restroom and classroom ads, that are designed to play to a captive audience.)

Disney recently decided not to permit advertising shown with its movies.[4] The protests of managers are not always as convincing, however. While Ashland Oil Inc.'s 592 gasoline and merchandise stores will not be installing TV monitors on top of their pumps, they will be using print ads on signs above the pumps and ads in the music piped out of the stores. As John Pettus, president of Super America, puts it, "There's a limit to what you can do to exploit your favorite friend, the customer."[5]

While crassly put, this is the essence of the problem. From the marketer's perspective, the competition for attention intensifies yearly. Alberto Baccari, creative director of Armando Testa Advertising, felt compelled to use a violent image of a man's hand and arm (with advertised Breil watch) grasping and twisting a woman's upside-down head in order to attract attention to the watch in magazine ads. According to Baccari, "I don't believe in violence, but I needed to communicate on the edge. The client had a limited budget, and the ad worked. Sales went up."[6] The proliferation of brands and the incredible redundancy it creates is an obvious source of competition for the consumer's eye and ear, pushing marketers to communicate on, and sometimes over, the edge. The product life cycle may also be at fault—remember the natural proliferation of competition and segmentation of the market that occurs at maturity? There are an awful lot of mature product categories out there, and it seems like the efforts to innovate new ones have pushed introduction rates far higher than withdrawal rates. James Schroer of Booz, Allen & Hamilton recently published a study concluding that "Most consumer goods markets are static, so to gain a share you have to outspend the competition by a huge amount."[7]

CONSUMER ATTENTION: THE GROWING CHALLENGE

The challenge facing ad agency Saatchi & Saatchi in the introduction of the Salon Selectives line of hair care products from Helene Curtis is typical. As Amy Goldman of Saatchi & Saatchi puts it, "There are more than 250 advertised brands in the hair care category, all of them claiming to deliver beautiful hair."[8] This means an advertiser's "share of voice," or percentage of total promotional spending for the category, is often sickly. And if companies split up share of voice among many participants, they tend to split market share similarly. The alternative is categories like soft drinks in which one or a few large competitors spend so much on their 'voices' that no one else can possibly be heard. (Coke and Pepsi hold 70 percent of the U.S. soda market.)

Ironically, as the clamor for consumer attention swells, many companies are backing off from the conventional emphasis on heavy newspaper and TV advertising, shifting to more controversial (and less crowded) media like above-urinal and pre-movie placements. This movement is fueled by the rise in the number of alternative media (cable TV and the proliferation of radio station frequencies, for example), which pulls audience away from traditional media. Cost *per exposure* for advertisers in traditional media like network TV are rising as a result.

And there is also a shift away from advertising and toward trade and consumer promotions (such as coupons). Where advertising made up about 40 percent of the ad/promotion budget a decade ago, now it only accounts for 30 percent at the average U.S. company.[9] As we discuss later, this shift may represent a nonoptimal effort to maximize short-term sales at the expense of brand equity. But regardless, it is fueling a wave of panic in the ad industry that is made worse by the rising tide of necessary recessionary belt-tightening. As odd as it may sound, at the very time that consumers are complaining about increasingly intrusive advertising, advertisers are desperate for work! Newspapers, TV networks (but not cable), magazines, and even billboard companies report loss of advertisers, and the keynote speaker's address at the 1991 conference of the American Association of Advertising Agencies was entitled "Remembering a Year Best Forgotten."[10]

Advertising as Communication

Madison Avenue, no doubt, takes a dim view of Games Gang Ltd.'s promotional strategy. Their favored medium for new game introductions is word of mouth! Gender Bender, for instance, was introduced in the summer of 1990 by salespeople walking populous beaches to demonstrate the game. Rather than press for orders, the salespeople explained the game and handed out mini game packs. Says sales manager Kevin McNulty, "It would be nice if they all bought the game, but our goal is to get them at least talking about it."[11] Are these people crazy? Probably not—this is the company that launched Pictionary in 1986 with a word-of-mouth campaign that made it the best-selling game for three years running.[12] They seem to take the American Association of Advertising Agencies literally when it defines promotion as "interpreting to the public, or to desired segments of the public, information regarding a legally marketed product or service." Since Games Gang's strategy is to develop a small number of excellent and unique products, all they really need to do is to disseminate information about them and sales will take care of themselves (presuming effective distribution, of course).

Advertising as Persuasion

But what happens if your products are only a little better, or really not much different from hundreds of others—like a new shampoo, for example? You still wish to sell them, but you face an uphill battle before consumers want to buy them. In this (and most) cases, the purpose of promotion goes beyond the official definition as interpreter of information. Promotion has three main objectives: informing, persuading, and reminding. The first job of promotion is to inform the potential buyer about the availability and nature of a product. In the case of new products, the buyer obviously needs such information. But even when a product is not new, many potential buyers may not realize that it exists. And when an existing product is changed in any way, this too needs to be communicated to potential buyers.

Once buyers have been informed, they need to be persuaded that purchase of the product will lead to satisfaction. This is accomplished by transmitting a positive set of beliefs about the key attributes of the product. Promotion is a major force in "the battle for the consumer's mind." As we saw in Chapter 7, marketers strive to create a position for their product vis-à-vis competitive products and brands, and the key to accomplishing this is promotion. Then, knowing that potential buyers are not constantly thinking about its product, the marketer must continually remind them of its existence and availability. Thus in 1984, Pepsi-Cola paid a record $55 million fee to Michael Jackson and his brothers, spent another $1 million on production costs, and then paid $40 million for advertising time to launch its Jackson Brothers in Concert campaign touting the slogan, "Pepsi, the choice of a new generation." The campaign was so extensive that the average American would be exposed to the ads 12 times over a three-month period.

Influencing Demand

At a more specific level, the promotional strategy attempts to influence the shape of the demand curve. The goal is to push the demand curve to the right of its existing position (from D_1 to D_2 in Exhibit 13.1). This results in the sale of a greater quantity at a given price. Put another way, promotion helps reduce the impact of price on the buyer's decision. It stimulates nonprice competition. Through persuasion, it influences consumers to focus on attributes of the product rather than on its price. In more technical terms, promotion attempts to make the demand curve increasingly inelastic (price insensitive) at high prices and increasingly elastic (price sensitive) at low prices.

Promotion versus the Marketing Concept

Informing consumers is not particularly controversial, but when you take the further step of trying to persuade them, you risk irritating and even alienating them. As we discussed in Chapter 1, most promotional campaigns hit more people than they target—it's a symptom of the relative lack of focus of most media. As Steven Star of the Marketing Center at M.I.T.'s Sloan School put it, "If a marketing program satisfies a million people, distracts 500,000, and frustrates 300,000, what is the net effect?"[13] It may be alienated consumers. And worse, as Star points out, "assuming . . . that one wants to cater carefully to consumer wants and needs" is "not always a justified assumption—there are charlatans and sharp-shooters everywhere in all professions." Here the good talk about serving customers can give way to ugly talk like John Pettus' musings on how "to exploit your favorite friend, the customer."

The problem is that you *don't* exploit your favorite friend, and if the company wants to get truly customer-oriented, it must avoid crossing the sometimes

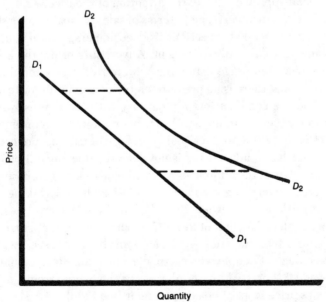

EXHIBIT 13.1.   Promotion shifts the demand curve.

faint line between friendly persuasion and unfriendly exploitation. If the promise of the marketing concept is to be fulfilled, it must carry through to promotion, shaping the face the company presents to its customers as much as the personality behind that face. Persuasion must only be undertaken with the best interests of the customer at heart, and it ought to be management's task to align these interests with the company's so that the customer does not have to feel cheated in order for the company to prosper! But this is a difficult challenge, requiring the active participation of senior management (and perhaps the entire company), not just the efforts of specialists at the ad agency. Promotion can be used to advance the marketing concept, or it can be allowed to conflict with it. At most companies, this key issue has yet to be addressed, let alone resolved. Promotion is still on the frontiers of the marketing concept, despite its being the most visible face of marketing from the customer's perspective.

With these thoughts as a backdrop, it is time to bring the full cast of promotional activities on stage.

Advertising

Advertising is any impersonal form of communication about ideas, goods, or services that is paid for by an identified sponsor. It is usually transmitted by mass media—newspapers, magazines, television, radio, direct mail, outdoor billboards, and transit cards. More than two-thirds of all advertising employs such media; the remainder uses things like matchbooks, circulars, calendars, catalogs, and special-event and trade show advertising. The message channel of advertising is not personal, and it is not as specifically targeted as other promotional methods. Consequently, advertising tends to use rather basic appeals—sex, prestige, hunger, social approval—to get the attention of the receiver.

The feedback from advertising in terms of sales is usually quite slow. While salespeople can get immediate reactions from customers, it is difficult to trace a given sale to any particular advertisement. Advertising offers the advantage of being able to convey a message many times. Moreover, it is offered in a relaxed atmosphere; generally there is no pressure on the consumer to make an immediate decision. And the combination of creativity with the impressiveness of the mass media can have quite an impact. It has been found that consumers make a strong connection between product quality and use of national advertising.[14]

On the other hand, advertising is not very flexible since it cannot be tailored to each member of the audience. And while mediocre advertising is easy to create, truly good advertising is a much more difficult undertaking. In fact, ad recall is always fairly low, between 25 and 30 percent, for print ads, and it has dropped from a high of 70 percent in 1987 down to 48 percent currently for TV ads, according to a tracking study by Video Storyboards Tests, Inc. Mind you, this is the percentage of people who can name an outstanding commercial—any commercial—and it is pretty low considering that anywhere from *1 to 17 percent* of most product's price is spent on advertising it (see Exhibit 13.2).

EHIBIT 13.2.   Advertising-to-sales ratios.

Industry	Ad Dollars as Percent of Sales[a]	Ad Dollars as Percent of Margin[b]
Air cond, heating, refrig equip	1.5	5.8
Air transport, scheduled	1.8	16.0
Apparel & other finished prods	2.9	8.0
Beverages	9.5	17.0
Bolt nut screw rivets washers	0.9	2.9
Btld & canned soft drinks, water	2.9	6.2
Can/frozen presrv, fruit, veg	6.9	17.1
Carpets & rugs	0.7	2.8
Catalog, mail-order houses	5.7	15.8
Computer & office equipment	1.2	2.7
Cutlery hand tools, gen hrdwr	10.9	21.6
Educational services	5.0	9.4
Electronic computers	5.1	10.3
Games, toys, child veh ex dolls	14.2	29.3
Groceries & related pds-whsl	1.5	10.7
Grocery stores	1.3	5.5
Guided missiles & space veh	5.3	170.1
Hospitals	5.0	29.7
Industrial inorganic chemicals	16.5	34.4
Investment advice	8.6	19.8
Iron & steel foundries	1.2	4.2
Lawn, garden tractors, equip	4.0	11.3
Lumber & other bldg matl-retl	1.8	6.9
Membership sport & rec clubs	11.0	13.5
Motion pic, videotape distrib	13.0	15.1
Perfume, cosmetic, toilet prep	10.4	16.1
Phono records, audio tape disc	8.3	23.2
Prepackaged software	4.8	9.2
Radio, tv consumer elec stores	5.3	23.8
Retail stores, all	5.8	12.7
Security brokers & dealers	3.1	7.3
Special clean, polish preps	14.5	24.8
Sugar & confectionary prods	10.6	28.9
Women's clothing stores	2.7	7.5

[a] Ad dollars as percent of sales = Ad expenditures/net sales.
[b] Ad dollars as percent of margin = Ad expenditures/(net sales − cost of goods sold). Based on 1989 industry data.

Source: Schonfeld & Associates, 1 Sherwood Drive, Lincolnshire, Ill. 60069, 1990.

Strategic Advertising Management

These statistics conceal complex and, in general, carefully managed advertising campaigns. It is interesting to look briefly at how campaigns are conceived, managed, and executed. This process, while not the direct responsibility of most managers, nonetheless ought to be a direct concern of all managers since it determines the character of the company's public face.

At the heart of advertising management is the concept of a campaign. Rarely is advertising undertaken on a one-time-only basis, or for that matter on a continuous basis either. A campaign is most easily understood as a series of messages with a single theme that are repeatedly conveyed to the target audience over an extended period. The repetition enhances consumer learning and reinforces the message—that is, if the message is appropriate and targeted at a receptive audience.

The development of a campaign starts with the establishment of objectives (which generally flow from the strategic objectives established in the planning processes described in Chapter 2). From one perspective, advertising has the same objectives as promotion in general—to inform, persuade, and remind. But there is more to it than this. Managers advertise in order to generate action in the marketplace, to stimulate the sale of goods and services. This often means immediate action by consumers is an important objective. This means applying the concepts of buyer behavior from Chapter 7 to the development of the campaign. Campaign objectives generally focus on stimulating action over an extended period, first making consumers aware of the brand or product and then building interest, desire, and ultimately intention to purchase. Post-purchase communication with consumers may also be included in the objectives—for instance, management may want to remind consumers about the product or brand.

These are strategic objectives. They cannot be implemented directly, because they do not specify specific actions. They need to be translated into more specific and action-oriented objectives such as the following:

- *Sales objectives.* Sales goals are frequently used despite the difficulty of correlating sales with advertising. Often goals include specific increases in sales dollars, unit volume, or market share.
- *Prepurchase objectives.* Goals are often based on the AIDA hierarchy:
    Awareness ⟶ Interest ⟶ Desire ⟶ Action.
    For instance, a new-product advertiser may set an exposure goal. Lowe's, the leader in the kitty litter industry, budgeted $10 million for an advertising campaign to introduce a new and improved kitty litter. Its goal for the campaign was to reach 95 percent of consumers more than 10 times. To achieve this goal it ran print ads in 18 magazines.
- *Image-building objectives.* Companies often undertake institutional advertising in an effort to improve their image, either with consumers or intermediaries. Omni's new corporate campaign in the Part One introduction is an

example of this kind of advertising. The "Black and Decker . . . ideas that work" campaign is another.

The core of effective advertising is translating the objectives into a specific message concept. The advertising message is based on an "advertising platform," which is a concise statement of the issues and benefits the advertiser wishes to convey. It may include a specific positioning strategy, as discussed in Chapter 8.

If all else fails, conventional wisdom has it that one can develop an advertising platform by answering three questions:

What features are unique to the marketer's product or brand?

What criteria do consumers employ to evaluate different products or brands?

How does the marketer's product or brand rate vis-à-vis those of competitors on these criteria (where is it strong or weak)?

The selling points that come out of the platform form an advertising theme, a message that is repeated in various forms throughout the advertising campaign. How this theme is expressed has a lot to do with the effectiveness of advertising. If stated clearly but unimaginatively, the theme may not cut through the clutter and make its way into the target's cerebellum. This is where the art in advertising comes in. Creativity, humor, surprise, excitement—something must be used to animate the theme, but care must be taken not to lose the underlying message in the pursuit of memorable advertising. It is a delicate balance, often missed. Here are some of the most common and successful message strategies.

- *Testimonials.* These use an authority to present the message strategy. Athletes and movie stars are often used for testimonial because their notoriety attracts viewer attention—but if their public image is inconsistent with the message strategy and product positioning, their testimonials will not be effective.

- *Humor.* Good humor can be particularly effective; poor humor can sometimes be devastating. There's nothing like a really humorous campaign to excite special-interest groups and generate negative publicity. The classic "Where's the beef?" campaign of Wendy's, for example, led many groups to complain that the elderly woman in it was a demeaning stereotype. Even well-received humor is not necessarily successful—some of the funniest campaigns ever, including the long series of humorous Alka-Seltzer campaigns in the 1980s, have had little measurable effect on sales or market share. But although it is hard to control, humor is nonetheless a popular message strategy because of its power to attract and hold attention.

- *Sensual/sexual message strategies.* Sex is often used in advertising messages. However, research shows that it generally is not very effective in getting the message across. Consumer attention may be captured, but it is difficult to focus on the message.

- *Comparative messages.* Pepsi strikes at Coca-Cola. Burger King attacks McDonald's. Until the mid-70s marketers viewed such comparisons as ill-mannered and risky. Naming competitors in an ad gives the competitor free exposure. However, the FTC took the novel position in 1973 that such ads could lead to better products, lower prices, and more information for consumers, and in 1981 the National Association of Broadcasters abolished their guidelines that restricted use of comparative advertising. Now comparisons are quite common, although they can still backfire. The 1990 TV campaign from Volvo that showed an oversized pickup driving over a line of cars, crushing all but the Volvo, was persuasive—until it came out that the Volvo had been secretly reinforced.[15]

- *Slice-of-life messages.* These use a popular song and a brief scene from life to position a product. The music is often key, for example, baby boomers may be targeted with an old Marvin Gaye song or something else from their teens, along with an appropriate fictional scene, in order to create a brand identity for the product.

- *Fantasy messages.* These stress the ideal self-image of the buyer. They relate a product or brand to some desirable person or situation, implying that the use of the product or brand will help the consumer achieve the desired state.

The choice of a medium to transmit the message obviously has a major influence on the way advertising ideas are carried out. We will look briefly at the issues involved in selecting a message channel, but first it is helpful to look at the common elements of advertising. Whatever medium is used, a typical ad includes copy, illustrations, and several other elements. Copy consists of all the written or spoken elements of the message. The headline tends to be the focal point of an advertisement—this may in fact be the only part of the ad the consumer sees or hears. Body copy (and sometimes subheadlines, extend the headline and elaborate on it. The body copy presents the major points of the message. Here the basic problem to be solved is set forth, the advantages of the focal point or brand are explained, a claim of superiority over competing brands is made, and a plea for action is made. Finally, the ad should contain a signature, the identifying name and other symbols of the sponsor of the ad. The signature needs to be distinctive and attention-getting; in TV and radio, it must be repeated to insure retention.

The illustrations in an ad consist of photographs, graphs, charts, drawings, cartoons, and any other visual devices that accompany the copy. They are used to gain attention, arouse interest and desire, and even stimulate action. The illustrations should be clearly related to the appeal and wording of the copy.

This sounds like obvious advice, but we guarantee that you can open any magazine and find that the majority of ads violate this rule.

The layout of an ad is its overall structure—the positions assigned to various elements of the copy and illustrations. The placement of headlines, copy, illustrations, and the marketer's signature are critical to the overall effect of the ad and also determine how, and how well, the ad will lead the viewer through the message. The same is true for a television or radio ad, except that the timing can be more tightly controlled by the advertiser. But in either case, the ad is not digested immediately. There is a sequence and timing to the ad that has a great deal of impact on its effectiveness.

The latest word from the advertising industry is that illustrations are displacing copy in ads. For example, Ron Jackson, the CEO of ad agency Jackson/ Ridey & Co., argues that "We don't read copy like we used to. We find out at the store. What we're seeing is a copyless generation."[16]

Hogwash. More likely, we don't *write* copy like we used to. But if you can write wonderful copy, it may sell better than any ad that is all header (or jingle) and illustration, because body copy can communicate a great deal more information. It can engage the consumer over a longer period of time, more meaningfully. According to ad guru David Ogilvy (who *can* write wonderful copy), "All my experience says that for a great many products, long copy sells more than short."[17]

To illustrate the above points about elements of an advertisement, and to show how they can be used to convey a powerful message, we have included Exhibit 13.3, a two-page magazine advertisement by OMON New York, Ltd. created for their client, Toyota, by art director Rodd Martin and copywriter Paul Bernasconi.

This ad illustrates the power of copy; the majority of the space is taken up by the copy and, to draw the eye strongly to the beginning of the body copy, the header is placed at the bottom instead of the top. The illustrations are small and treated almost like snapshots in a journal. They focus attention on the fish the children caught while out on Chesapeake Bay. This fish is used to symbolize the learning about nature and the environment that the Chesapeake Bay Foundation provides to inner-city kids. The body copy picks up the fish theme and expands on it powerfully.

But what does this foundation and the students and teacher it worked with have to do with Toyota? What is the campaign's message? What objective did Toyota have in mind, and is it accomplished?

This is an example of corporate advertising. It's objective is to build Toyota's image by highlighting socially-responsible investments made by the corporation. Toyota gave money to the foundation—this is implied without being discussed specifically in the ad. And it is interesting to speculate who the socially responsible image is targeted at. What group of consumers is Toyota courting in such a round-about manner? Probably baby-boomers, who are increasingly concerned about the environment, poverty, and other social problems.

©1990 Toyota Motor Corporate Services of North America, Inc.

THERE'S BEEN A LOT OF TALK about the environment lately. But out on Chesapeake Bay, sailing around on a vintage skipjack, a group of school kids are learning that when it comes to the environment, actions speak louder than words.

Myrtha Allen, Environmental Sciences teacher at P.S. 405, Baltimore, explains, "Most of my kids are city born and bred. They live in apartments, they get their milk in cartons, their eggs in those styrofoam containers. They were about as interested in the environment as they are in

"IT WAS THE FIRST FISH Jawan had seen that WASN'T SURROUNDED by french fries."

MYRTHA ALLEN, Teacher

370

EXHIBIT 13.3. *(Continued)*

homework." She smiles at a nearby eight-year-old. "And who can blame them? Some of them, like Jawan here, had never even seen a live fish before."

That's where the Chesapeake Bay Foundation stepped in. Since 1966, when it started in Annapolis, Maryland, with a rented fishing trawler and little else, the Foundation has taken more than 300,000 students out into the Bay to experience the environment first hand. And at the same time making them aware of how important their contribution is to the future of the planet.

Myrtha puts it simply. "To get these kids wanting to clean up the world, we've got to get their hands dirty."

And they do. They get very dirty.

"Oh yeah," chuckles Myrtha, "we do it all. Once we threw a net in just to see what we'd get. When we pulled it up, sure enough there were the milk cartons, the soda cans, the egg containers. And flapping around in the middle of it all was this big, cranky striped bass. You should've seen their faces.

"We took 20 little consumers out on a boat that day. We came back with 20 budding environmentalists."

At Toyota, we're proud that through the support we give to the Foundation more kids like Jawan will be able to experience our fragile environment first hand. And hopefully start playing an active part in preserving it.

Is the program working? "These kids are organizing neighborhood recycling drives,

they're writing letters to Senators. Take a look at these posters some of my students have been doing."

The classroom walls are alive with crayon and pencil. Bright orange crabs. Smiling oysters. Families of ducks.

And one poster that stops everyone. It's of a smiling little boy holding hands with a big striped bass. And boldly scrawled above both their heads is one word: "Brothers".

And it's signed by Jawan. Age eight.

TOYOTA
INVESTING IN THE INDIVIDUAL

This is an effective ad, but it uses the various elements of advertising very differently than most ads. Contrast it with Toyota's typical slice-of-life television advertising, which focuses on the good feelings associated with owning a Toyota. Why are the ads so different—how do the objectives and messages differ? (This is a good question for readers to apply the principles of marketing to.)

You can see why Omon selected magazine spreads for their corporate image campaign (which includes profiles of other nonprofits supported by Toyota as well). They need the full two pages to tell the story. These ads present their message—that Toyota is a responsible corporate citizen, involved and helpful in the United States—through interesting but lengthy stories. The copy takes a few minutes to read, and because it is about interesting nonprofits and their work, Omon can count on people wanting to read it. The slower pace of the magazine is perfect for story-telling. The message channel was well chosen for this campaign.

Each channel has unique characteristics that provide both advantages and disadvantages. Marketers must understand these characteristics in order to select the proper channel. Newspapers claim the largest share of advertising expenditures, but their ad revenues have not grown in recent years. They offer extensive market coverage on a local level; almost every household receives a newspaper every day. They permit flexible scheduling and the cost per contact is relatively low. But in general they do not permit the advertiser to target any narrowly defined segments. If you want to say something to cat-owners in the newspaper, you will have to say it to everyone else as well. Magazines give more specificity, and their better print quality makes possible a wider range of visual effects in advertising. Television advertising is split between the fast-growing cable channels and the slow-growth network advertising. TV offers the choice of national or local (or spot) exposure, and the video medium permits a wide range of techniques and effects. A good TV ad can have tremendous impact and high recall (although most do not). But TV is very expensive by comparison with other media.

Less common, but also important, are radio, outdoor, and direct mail. Radio offers extensive coverage of local markets, and can be highly selective. For example, rock stations appeal to young people while classical stations tend to attract mature listeners. Radio is also a relatively inexpensive and flexible medium. Our society's preoccupation with TV has probably blinded many managers to the power of radio advertising. Outdoor advertising options are growing, as we have already noted critically, but they do present a useful medium in some cases. Outdoor is great for awareness-building, since it can offer a large number of exposures at low cost. But it generally does not allow complex messages—who can read more than a few words while driving past a billboard? The more conventional outdoor ads, such as roadside billboards, are not at all selective. Newer types, such as those at ski resorts or in men's bathrooms, offer selectivity at the likely expense of irritating the customer. In general, there is considerable wasted exposure and the risk of negative connotations with this medium. Direct marketing is the most rapidly growing medium at present, and it is sufficiently important to justify its own section.

Direct Marketing

In recent years, marketers have made increasing use of a form of advertising called direct marketing: "An interactive system of marketing which uses one or more advertising media to effect a measurable response and/or transaction at any location."[18] The key words in this definition are measurable response. Direct marketing uses various kinds of message channels—coupons, catalogs, direct mail, consumer and business magazines, newspapers, telephone, television, and radio—to communicate an offer that will elicit an almost immediate response.

Direct marketing is distinguished from general advertising by the following characteristics (see Exhibit 13.4): (1) A definite offer is made; (2) all the information necessary to make a decision is provided; and (3) a response mechanism is given—a toll-free telephone number or a mail-in coupon, for example. In 1978, direct marketing accounted for $60 billion in annual sales; by 1985 the figure had shot up to over $200 billion. Jumping on the bandwagon, companies like General Foods, Nestlé, Thomas J. Lipton, Sunkist, Whitman's Chocolates, and R.J. Reynolds began marketing premium products via catalogs and toll-free 800

EXHIBIT 13.4. Comparison of direct marketing and general advertising.

Direct Marketing	vs.	General Advertising
• Selling to individuals. Customers are indentifiable by name, address, and purchase behavior.		• Mass selling. Buyers identified as broad groups sharing common demographic and psychographic characteristics.
• Products have added value or service. Distribution is important product benefit.		• Product benefits do not always include convenient distribution channels.
• The medium is the marketplace.		• Retail outlet is marketplace.
• Marketer controls product until delivery.		• Marketer may lose control as product enters distribution channel.
• Advertising used to motivate an immediate order or inquiry.		• Advertising used for cumulative effect over time to build image, awareness, loyalty, benefit recall. Purchase action deferred.
• Repetition used within ad.		• Repetition used over time.
• Consumers feel high perceived risk—product bought unseen. Recourse is distant.		• Consumers feel less risk—have direct contact with the product and direct recourse.

Source: Bob Stone, *Successful Direct Marketing Methods,* 3rd ed. (Chicago: Crain Books, 1985), p. 2.

numbers. Lipton, for instance, mailed out more than a million catalogs touting its Sir Thomas Lipton Collection of exotic teas, teakettles, and shortbreads.

Media Scheduling Strategies

Most advertising campaigns run for a stated period of time, often a year. Three broad approaches are available: the continuity, flighting, and massed (or concentration) strategies (see Exhibit 13.5). In the continuity strategy, advertisements are spread out over the entire planning period. When demand for the advertised product is evenly disbursed throughout the year, this strategy often works best.[19] Convenience items and other products with high repeat purchase rates warrant this approach. When demand for the product has distinct and identifiable peaks and valleys, the flighting strategy can be used. In this case, advertising follows a stop-and-go pattern. Typically, there is heavy advertising during some days, weeks, or months, and no advertising in between. A special form of flighting, called the pulse strategy, combines a continuous campaign with short bursts of heavier advertising. Supermarkets, for example, know that shopping is heaviest on Fridays and Saturdays, so they do most of their newspaper advertising on Thursdays and Fridays. Finally, in the concentrated strategy, the marketer bunches all of its advertising into specified periods and does no advertising in between. Makers of swimming pools, charcoal, and snow blowers use this approach. These contrasting strategies are illustrated in Exhibit 13.5.

Personal Selling

Personal selling is person-to-person communication in which the receiver provides immediate feedback to the source's message through words, gestures, expressions, and the like. Since personal selling is a conversation between two or more parties, the message can be tailored to the audience. This permits more precise customer targeting than advertising, but it limits the total number of contacts that can be made. Another disadvantage is that the cost of each contact is much higher than in the case of advertising. Even so, because of its adaptability and its "personal" nature, personal selling has a much greater persuasive impact than advertising.

Personal selling is especially appropriate when the unit of sale is large enough to support the cost of the contact; when the product is rather complex, so that detailed explanation or demonstration is needed; and when the product benefits have to be carefully matched to the customer's desires. Personal selling has the greatest potential to close the sale—the salesperson is there to complete the order or get the customer's promise to make the purchase.

What makes the difference between effective personal selling and wasted time? A great many salespeople make calls every day, but many of them have relatively low closure rates. Part of this is personal technique, and experience and training can make a difference. But much of it comes down to how well the

EXHIBIT 13.5.   Advertisement strategy approaches.

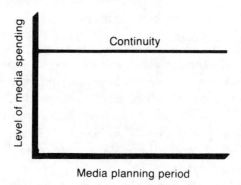

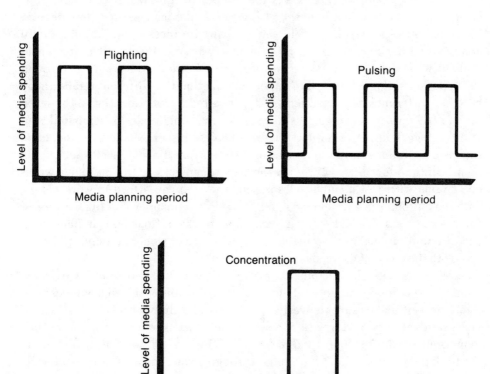

salesforce is managed. Every year the trade magazine *Sales & Marketing Management* uses a survey to identify the best salesforces in America. The categories against which salesforces are rated are:

1. Recruiting top salespeople
2. Retention of top salespeople
3. Quality of training

4. Opening new accounts
5. Product and technical knowledge
6. Reputation with customers[20]

These are the yardsticks against which many managers judge a sales program. But it is interesting to listen to managers from the 1990 winners talk about their sales strategies. While they do indeed excel on these attributes, they seem to emphasize building long-term, mutually-beneficial customer relationships over any of the specific items on the list. They actually use personal selling in the spirit of the marketing concept, to benefit customers over the long term, rather than just to write orders more rapidly.

Procter & Gamble (P&G) was the winner in the Health & Beauty Aids category. Here is Shelly Zimbler, P&G's general sales manager for this category. "It's a matter of survival. The old way of doing business—good products with good advertising copy—is history. We need to work creatively with customers to find out what they need to move our products. We've moved from a confrontational period of doing business to understanding that five different retailers may have five different ways of selling."[21] This required a reorganization of the sales-force. P&G now uses category selling, in which a single salesperson handles an entire category for certain retail buyers—P&G's direct customers. It used to be that every retailer would see dozens of different salespeople, each specializing in specific product lines. But with the new organization, the customer works one-on-one with just a single salesperson, one who can afford to work closely with the customer in a problem-solving, cooperative manner. For big customers, this salesperson is backed up by a team of people from finance, manufacturing, and distribution, making it possible for P&G to make significant changes in response to the customer's needs.

Working with the customer is also a theme at Nabisco Biscuit Company, winner in the Food Products category. This RJR Nabisco subsidiary focuses on the basics—it makes sure deliveries are timely and shelves stocked. But senior vice president of sales Harry Lees believes their success comes from their effort to make life easier for their retail customers. "First of all, we deliver product to the back door so they don't have to go through a warehouse. Then, we literally set up the biscuit department. We help our customers pick the best location—even the best aisle and shelves—for the products. Our salesperson can sit down with a customer and, using a laptop computer, share our information on what the retail outlet's position is in a market, who its customers are, what its average purchase is, and how to create the most effective merchandise mix for that environment." He adds that, unlike many competitors, Nabisco does not pay slotting fees, and is able to stick to this policy because of the high level of attention it gives to customers.[22]

Note the added value both these companies get from direct sales. They are not only taking advantage of the personal contact to make a lengthier, more personalized and more persuasive sales pitch. They are taking advantage of the relationship to build a long-term relationship in which their expertise and data is used to help the customer's business. They profit by selling soaps or cookies, but the customer profits by improving their business overall as well as by selling specific products. This kind of relationship goes far beyond anything possible with arms-length alternatives such as advertising and direct mail. (See Exhibit 13.4.)

SALES PROMOTION

The American Marketing Association defines sales promotion as "those marketing activities, other than personal selling, advertising, and publicity, that stimulate consumer purchasing and dealer effectiveness, such as displays, shows and expositions, demonstrations, and various nonrecurrent selling efforts not in the ordinary routine."[23] This very broad definition embraces many kinds of activities, including in-store displays, sampling, coupons, contests, trading stamps, trade shows, price-off deals, premiums, refund offers, sweepstakes, and rebates. Annual expenditures for such activities have been found to exceed total spending on advertising and to be increasing in importance.[24]

Sales promotion is typically used at the point of purchase to motivate consumers to complete an exchange. It is not a substitute for a promotional program; instead, it is used to supplement other promotional activities. Sales promotion, however, can go a long way toward creating awareness and favorable attitudes—generally the domain of advertising.

Sales promotion offers additional ways of reaching customers. It is generally used at infrequent intervals, since the response tends to diminish over time; this is called wearout. Advertising and personal selling, on the other hand, are used on a more continuous basis. Sales promotion is usually intended to increase sales over a short period, while personal selling and advertising have a long-term sales goal. Exhibit 13.6 depicts the "ratchet" effect of a short-term sales promotion carried out in conjunction with an advertising program.

EXHIBIT 13.6. Short-term sales promotion "ratchet" effect.

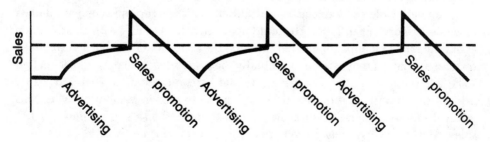

Public Relations

Public relations (PR) is a promotional activity that aims to communicate a favorable image of the product or its marketer and to promote goodwill. Every organization deals with many important groups, called publics, such as stockholders, the government, intermediaries, the community at large, employees, suppliers, customers, and the news media. Public-relations activities are directed toward these publics.

An activity that is usually considered to be part of public relations is publicity. This term refers to any message about the organization that is communicated through the mass media but is *not* paid for by the organization. Although public-relations personnel can send press releases, feature stories, and photographs to the media, marketers have much less control over publicity than they do over advertising, personal selling, and sales promotion. Perhaps for this reason, audiences tend to find such information more believable than information that comes from an identified sponsor.

Publicity can result in negative images as well as positive ones. Adverse publicity has affected companies that market breast implants, artificial sweeteners, tampons, products containing asbestos, and flammable sleepwear. Unfavorable publicity often leads to the banning of such products, or at least to consumer reluctance to use them. Thus Ford's Pinto, accused of having an unsafe gas tank, was taken off the market even though Ford was vindicated in the courts.

Advertising, personal selling, sales promotion, and public relations are the tools that marketers have available to them as they plan their promotional strategies and communication campaigns. In the next section, we will see how these tools are used in designing promotional strategies.

The conventional paths to successful promotion of a product or service no longer guarantee a safe arrival, and an increasing number of innovators are succeeding through creative bushwhacking. That is because promotion has become more difficult and challenging in recent years, driven as we have seen by many of the same factors that make management in general more difficult, factors that are behind the new wave of emphasis on the customer: increased competition, globalization, saturation of advertising and distribution channels, and proliferation of products. Consider these examples of nontraditional efforts to communicate with the customer:

Kenneth Cole needed to attract attention to his startup shoe company and its new line of footwear in 1982. He could not even afford to talk with an ad agency about the kind of campaign needed to match the visibility of established competitors. So he made a movie instead. Actually, he *pretended* to make a movie, called "The Beginning of a Shoe Company," so that he could obtain a permit to park a 40-foot trailer and giant display on a busy street corner in Manhattan. With this unusual jump-start, the business has grown to more than $100 million in 1991 sales. And it still uses novel promotions, such as a print ad in which a jet from (failed) Eastern Air Lines was pictured along with Cole's shoes under the headline, "some forms of transportation are more reliable than others."[25]

Another way to command attention is to fight dirty. Software company Borland International has gained against giant rivals Lotus and Ashton-Tate through aggressive direct mailings and a pricing policy characterized by *Business Week* as "uncivilized." Borland promoted its $495 Quatro Pro spreadsheet to Lotus 1-2-3 users for an unheard-of $99, and its $725 Paradox database program to database king Ashton-Tate's customers for only $150. Sales accelerated, and market share more than doubled in two years. Most recently, Borland has negotiated a stock-swap deal that will allow it to *acquire* Ashton-Tate for $439 million. Again, Borland seems to be stretching the rules in its pursuit of market share. Here is Borland's motivation according to the *New York Times*, "By combining (with Ashton-Tate), Borland will now have access to the millions of customers who already have (Ashton-Tate's) DBase installed and will some day need a fresh, more powerful version."[26]

But these successes reflect both a willingness to bend the rules and a solid grasp of the essentials. Bushwhackers will get lost without a compass, and strategy provides that compass for promotion efforts.

DESIGNING PROMOTIONAL STRATEGIES

Putting together a promotional strategy involves considering the various promotional activities as a whole. The main task of the strategic planner is to determine the blend of activities that will achieve the organization's promotional goals. Rarely will only one of those activities be used; usually a combination of activities is more effective. But even though several promotional tools may be used, one of those tools will receive the greatest emphasis.

There are many kinds of promotional strategies. Each can be defined in terms of how it allocates funds and effort among the various promotional activities. Any firm can have its own unique promotional program in which it uses promotional techniques differently than any other firm. The choice of particular techniques is determined mainly by the objectives of the promotional strategy itself and by the situation analysis, an evaluation of the internal and external factors that affect the strategy's chances of success. In the remainder of this section we will explore these key strategic considerations.

Promotional Objectives

The basic objective of promotion is to bring about an exchange. Yet that exchange may not be a sale in the usual sense. For example, we see marketers attempting to get consumers to accept an idea ("If you drink, don't drive"): And even when a sale is the ultimate goal, promotional efforts may not be aimed toward achieving immediate results. In general, then, we can say that the objective of promotion may be to communicate information as well as to stimulate sales.

The objectives of promotion follow the "hierarchy of effects" decision model knows as **AIDA**; Awareness leads to Interest, which in turn fosters **De**-sire, which ultimately leads to Action. Thus creating awareness must be the first goal of promotion. By providing information, the marketer arouses the interest of consumers; more persuasive communications arouse desire, and finally this leads to action in the form of an exchange. The various promotional tools are applied in different ways to achieve each of these goals.

Readers with previous training in marketing may recall the AIDA model as one of those dreadful multiple-choice favorites, and others may skim over it on the assumption that it is just another silly mnemonic. Wait! For all its simplicity, it is an essential concept, and a great many promotional efforts fail by trying to generate action before systematically building awareness, interest and desire. If you research nothing else before planning a promotion strategy, at least find out how many consumers in the target market are currently in each stage, and iden-tify the inter-stage transition at which the most potential customers are lost. There is no point in spending money on awareness—generating ads if awareness is high but poor distribution limits conversion of desire to action, for instance.

Some generalizations can be made about the relative effectiveness of each of the four promotional tools. Advertising, because of its mass market coverage, is thought to be highly effective in creating awareness, but it becomes less persuasive as time goes by. Personal selling with its lower contact rate is less effective in creating mass awareness but is most effective in creating desire and action. Sales promotion is most effective in getting consumers to complete an exchange; its impact is greatest at the point of purchase. Finally, public rela-tions and publicity are helpful in creating awareness, but they have little imme-diate effect on sales.

Potential buyers are more receptive to some promotional tools than to others. Their desire for information causes them to seek out particular promo-tional tools or media—a fact that can be very useful to marketers. Exhibit 13.7 charts various promotional tools according to their value as providers of infor-mation as well as the immediacy of their sales effect. Some promotional tools are not sought out, but when consumers and intermediaries become aware of them, they readily use them to gain information (for example, to find out if they have won a contest). In the figure, this is represented by a dotted line moving these techniques to the left.

What is the practical value of this insight? Simply put, if consumer information-seeking can be accommodated, the information, persuasion and reminder goals of promotion can all be accomplished far more easily. Best to try to communicate with the consumer when he or she wishes to communicate with you! So, for example, if you know that people read computer magazines when thinking about buying a new PC, you will focus your promotional efforts at them via public relations and display advertising in this medium, and you

EXHIBIT 13.7.   When to use promotional tools.

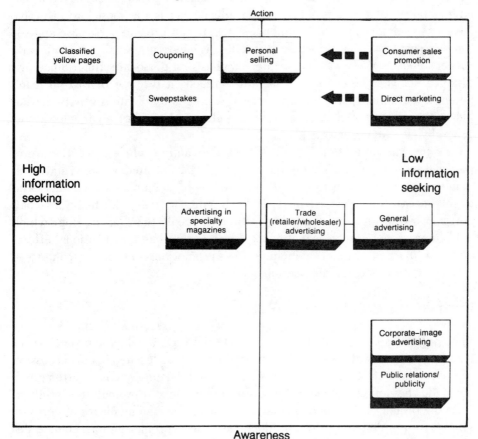

may also want to use reader service cards to establish direct contact with them in order to focus sales or telemarketing on these interested readers as well.

ANALYZING STRATEGIC ISSUES

Most companies have a mixture of promotional activities but usually one is emphasized. The main emphasis of the promotional strategy is determined by the external environment as well as by certain aspects of the marketing organization and its product. Let's take a look at some of the key issues that affect development of promotional strategy and determine which activity will be emphasized.

The Nature of the Market

Like other marketing decisions, promotional decisions should be based on a firm understanding of the market. Its size and nature can actually dictate the strategy.

For instance, a widely dispersed market like consumer packaged goods requires a large number of contacts. Mass media advertising is the most cost-effective means of accomplishing this. Good mass media exposure and persuasive appeals can be so effective that little personal selling is necessary. Small geographically concentrated markets warrant greater emphasis on personal selling. Since less distance needs to be covered in making contacts, it is less expensive to reach potential customers. This is why personal selling is used extensively to market industrial products. Industrial markets are clustered in relatively few locations, generally close to waterways.

When the promotion is aimed at retailers and/or wholesalers, the use of personal selling is also common. Large orders, concentrated markets, and small numbers of potential customers all require emphasis on personal contact. And as in the case of industrial buyers, the buying motives tend to be rational. Personal selling is better suited to rational appeals than advertising, which tends toward more emotional appeals. On the other hand, promotional efforts aimed at intermediaries often includes sales promotions—especially contests—and advertising in trade publications.

Push versus Pull Strategies

The "push-versus-pull" distinction refers to the ways in which a manufacturer tries to get intermediaries to carry its products. As we learned in our discussion of the product life cycle, in a push strategy each channel member attempts to persuade the next member in the system to handle and promote the product. Thus the product is "pushed" through the channel, often by means of personal selling. In a pull strategy, the producer uses mass promotion to stimulate demand in the consumer market, thereby causing intermediaries to want to carry the product so that they can satisfy customers who request it. This is the strategy that cosmetics companies like Maybelline have begun to emphasize—they are spending heavily on advertising to "pull" the product through the channel.

The Nature of the Product

The nature of the product also affects the methods used to promote it. Personal selling is emphasized when a product has a high unit value, since consumers often need to be prodded into making the exchange. When a demonstration is needed to show the product's main features, personal selling is far more effective than advertising. Personal selling is also important for goods and services that must be tailored to the needs of the customer, such as investment securities, insurance portfolios, industrial conveyor systems, or electrical or legal services.

Advertising is a more effective promotional tool for products that are purchased frequently, like convenience goods. Marketers of specialty and shopping products can use advertising to create awareness, but usually some personal selling is needed to point out the advantages of the product over competing ones.

Advertising is also appropriate for products that have hidden qualities (for example, the lack of phosphates in Tide detergent). Advertising helps, too, in communicating highly emotional appeals (for example, the U.S. Army's "Be all that you can be" and AT&T's "Reach out and touch someone") and in differentiating a product from competing products.

In addition to advertising, much sales promotion is directed toward consumers. Sales promotion is particularly effective for impulse items whose features can best be judged at the point of purchase. For example, many magazines need exposure at supermarket and drugstore checkout counters, where people can leaf through them while waiting to make their purchases.

Stage in the Product Life Cycle

In the introductory stage of the product life cycle, the promotional mix must provide information in order to create product (as opposed to brand) awareness. The marketer must stimulate primary demand, or demand for the product category itself. Consumers must understand the nature of a compact disc, roller blade, or food processor. They must know that the product exists and must learn about its attributes. Exposure is the key, and advertising is usually the best way to get it.

Also during the introductory stage, a product may need to be pushed through the distribution system. Getting intermediaries to accept the product may require a substantial investment in personal selling. Trade shows, fairs, and conventions are often a good way to sell the product to channel members, greatly reducing the number of contacts needed to make the product familiar and desired.

As the product enters the maturity stage of the cycle, the promotional mix calls for a shift from building primary demand to creating selective demand, or demand for a particular brand. As marketers face stiffer competition, the focus shifts toward persuasion. Promotion must stress the benefits and advantages of the product over those of competitors. In this stage, more and more consumers are responsive to product promotion; thus the promotional costs per contact are reduced. While mass advertising generally continues to get heavy use, personal selling is necessary in order to push the product through the distribution system.

In the maturity stage, organizations with strong brand recognition can use reminder advertising to keep the brand name in the consumer's consciousness. During the decline stage, new products overtake old ones, which are ultimately abandoned. Unless sales can be revived by repositioning the product or innovating to improve it, promotional expenditures will be reduced significantly or eliminated completely. Advertising, in particular, is ineffective when a product's primary demand takes an unfavorable turn. Any promotion that is undertaken is usually targeted toward consumers who still have a strong preference for the product.

Stage in the Adoption Process

New ideas and new products have been found to spread through society in a predictable set of five stages that parallel the **AIDA** model to some extent. The adoption curve in Exhibit 13.8 shows this process.[27]

Each stage of the adoption process requires a different promotional emphasis. In the first stage, a group of consumers known as innovators adopt the new idea. These risk-takers tend to be young, well educated, mobile, and sophisticated. They tend also to have a wide network of social contacts outside their immediate reference groups. They have less difficulty understanding and applying technical information than most people. They employ nonpersonal sources of information, especially technical and scientific journals, and

EXHIBIT 13.8.   Adoption curve.

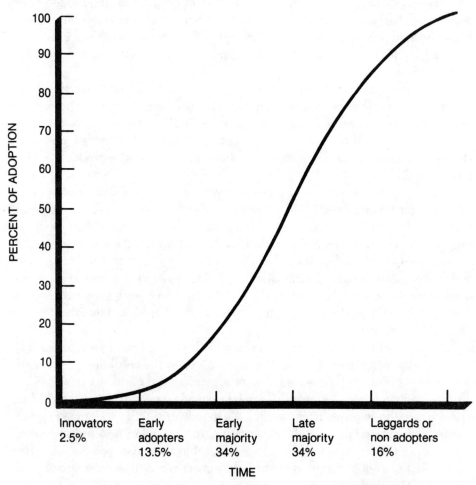

generally read advertisements for information, especially ads in specialty magazines and newspapers.

In the next stage, the product is bought by early adopters (also known as "opinion leaders"). Other people tend to be highly influenced by these individuals. Early adopters, like innovators, tend to be young and mobile. However, they have smaller networks of social contacts than innovators have. Salespeople are very useful in reaching this group, and the mass media are also important. Because of its size and influence, this is an important group from the standpoint of promotional strategy.

The early majority are less venturesome in adopting new products. This cautious group waits and watches others before accepting a new idea. Typically the product is in the rapid-growth stage of the product life cycle before these consumers will buy it. They need loads of information from as many sources as possible—salespeople and mass media advertising as well as early adopters among their friends and associates.

The late majority are skeptical of new ideas. They are older and more committed to familiar ways of doing things. This group usually needs strong social pressure to purchase something new. Its members have little contact with salespeople and are not greatly influenced by advertising. Getting to them generally means getting to early adopters or the early majority, who in turn influence these consumers.

The final group to adopt a product consists of the laggards or nonadopters, who are strongly oriented towards the past and very suspicious of new concepts. They are generally lower in social-class status and less educated than other consumers. They depend on other laggards for ideas and are very difficult to reach via promotional activities. In fact, it may well be that promotional efforts should avoid this group, since when its members are ready to buy, the marketer is likely to have newer products on the market.

Stage in the Buying Decision Process

We have seen how the individual goes through the process called AIDA. And in Chapter 5 we saw how the consumer first becomes aware of a problem and then searches for information, makes a decision, and finally evaluates that decision. If we collapse these processes into "prepurchase time" and actual "purchase time," we find that different promotional activities have varying degrees of effectiveness at different points in the process.

Corporate-image advertising, general consumer advertising, and publicity all are effective in creating prepurchase awareness but diminish in effectiveness as the sale becomes imminent. At that point, personal selling and sales promotion techniques such as point-of-sale displays have greater impact. But in the postpurchase stage the mass media become useful for reminder purposes and as an aid in positive evaluation. Many other forms of sales promotion remain effective throughout the process. Retailers' circulars, for instance, stimulate awareness, interest, and desire—and are often referred to after the sale.

In the case of trade promotion, what seems to be most effective are price deals and sales contests. Personal selling is continuously effective with trade buyers as is being listed in trade catalogs. In the case of direct marketing, techniques such as telemarketing and door-to-door selling are most effective in the purchase period. Catalogs, direct mail, and broadcast advertising create awareness and often lead to direct responses, as well as reminding consumers of the value of a purchase. Thus they are effective in both prepurchase and post-purchase periods.

DEVELOPING A PROMOTION MIX

After evaluating strategic issues such as the nature of the market and product, the applicability of push or pull strategies to the distribution channel, the stage of the product life cycle, the stage of the adoption process, and the stage of the buying decision process—deep breath now!—management should have suffi-cient insight to develop a promotion strategy.

At least the broad brush strokes should become apparent. For example, an early stage of the product life cycle for an innovative and exciting product, low awareness and interest, and a resulting desire to focus initially on the prepur-chase period will all point toward general consumer advertising and publicity. If the channel is very competitive and retail shelf space hard to obtain, a pull strategy will be favored, with consumer promotion emphasized over trade pro-motion. The selection of advertising medium will depend on which media best reach consumers when they are already seeking information and whether the sale is complex or simple, emotional or rational. And if these broad brush strokes are well executed, a decent result is highly likely. (The inverse is unfortunately also true.) The plan can (and must) be further refined by detailed consideration of the message to be communicated—this goes back to the product's positioning and how to make it clear and exciting—and also by the specifics of a promotional budget. Several common techniques are applied in budgeting.

Percentage of Sales

In the percentage-of-sales approach, the marketer first determines the percent-age of sales revenue that has been allocated to promotion in the past. The next year's promotional budget is determined by applying this percentage to the past year's sales, to some level of anticipated sales, or to some combination of the two. This approach is easy to use and provides a handy means of comparing the firm's expenditures with those of competitors. But it ignores the fact that promotion is intended to stimulate sales. When this approach is used, promotional expendi-tures are reduced when sales go down! At best, this approach should be used in making preliminary calculations; it should not determine the final budget. Yet because of its simplicity it is used by over 50 percent of major advertisers.[28]

Competitive Parity

Marketers—especially those with mature products—often match what competitors are spending on promotion. This approach adds a measure of competitiveness to the strict percent-of-sales approach. However, it assumes that competitors know what they are doing and that all the firms in the industry have the same goals. That, of course, often is not the case.

The Market Share Approach

Some promotional budgets are based on the assumption that market share is directly proportional to proportional expenditures. A firm with an 8 percent share would allocate an amount equivalent to 8 percent of the industry's total promotional expenditures to its promotional budget. Evidence shows, however, that this approach is ill-founded since it is rarely true that share of promotion is equal to share of market.[29] But, on the other hand, if your share of voice is far lower than your targeted market share, it is likely to limit your performance.

All Available Funds

In some cases, the marketer allocates all available funds to promotion. While this is an easy solution, it too has its drawbacks. "All available funds" essentially means all profits. But profits have little relationship to promotion, since they are a function of the firm's total costs, including manufacturing, executives' salaries, administrative overhead, and so on. Moreover, this approach may result in lost opportunities if promotional expenditures still fall below the amount needed to generate a sizable change in sales. That is, the investment of just a bit more in promotion (even if it means borrowing) could have a dramatic effect on sales.

The Task (Objective) Approach

In setting a promotional budget, marketers should first establish what they would like to accomplish; then they can decide what level of investment in promotion is needed to reach their goals. As noted earlier, sales goals are difficult to relate to promotional expenditures, but that approach makes the most sense. And some firms can arrive at a reasonable estimate of what they will require to reach certain objectives. Marketing research and past experience are good guides. Test markets provide an experimental setting in which various levels of promotional spending can be tested. Finally, long experience allows some marketers to make a reasonable estimate of the costs involved in reaching certain promotional goals. This approach, in fact, is the one that is used most frequently by large advertisers.[30]

IN SEARCH OF EXCELLENT PROMOTIONS

Talking about promotion strategy is one thing, but doing it is quite another. The problem is that the process alone cannot guarantee results—it takes a little inspiration as well. Many, probably most, promotion plans produce mediocre results even if the planners considered the situation thoroughly in advance. The truly excellent promotional campaign is terribly rare. Most ads are zapped or forgotten, most coupons ignored or lost, most telemarketing callers hung up on, most direct mail thrown out. Even personal sales calls often fail to close the sale. So when a promotional effort really works, it is as if a little magic has been thrown into the equation. Here are two examples with more than the average share of magic. Both were winners of 1990 Effie Gold Awards, the joint American Marketing Association/American Association of Advertising Agencies awards for effectiveness.

Salon Selectives

In the beginning of this chapter, we noted the difficulty of introducing a new line of hair care products when there are more than 250 advertised brands in the hair care industry, all claiming to deliver "beautiful hair." Since 1985 almost half of the 45 introductions in this market have failed. But Helene Curtis and its agency combined clever positioning with effective promotion to create a $200 million-a-year product line in three years.[31]

The new Salon Selectives line, as its name suggests, was positioned as a salon brand, using for its theme the line, "Like you just stepped out of a salon." Salon Selectives is "a unique level-type system of shampoos and conditioners at a popular mid-price," priced so as to fall between Helene Curtis' expensive Finesse and inexpensive Suave lines. The promotion mix favored awareness-building through TV and print ads, with awareness of the brand name exceeding 80 percent by 1990 (the line was introduced in 1987). The advertising used headers like, "Why some women look like they just stepped out of a salon." According to Amy Goldman of Saatchi & Saatchi, "the agency used . . . in-depth research (psychological probe and anthropological search) to leverage the power of the product premise, salon imagery . . . Consumers believe the products provide a 'magic potion' for hair care . . . The women used in the advertising dimensionalize the product end-benefits and define a unique brand character (e.g., confident, fashionable, professional women who are on the go.)"

The promotional campaign helped this product line become the most popular of the "salon" brands, and the advertising has proven memorable in tests measuring ad recall by consumers. *Salon Selectives* has proven that good product and promotion planning can make for a successful introduction, even in a mature, crowded category.

Samsung Semi-Conductors

This Korean firm hired ad agency Curtin Emerson Ransick in the spring of 1988 with the goal of establishing its semiconductors in the U.S. market. At the time, Samsung was an ugly duckling, ranking a sorry twentieth or worse in market share among suppliers of semiconductors (the chips out of which computers and the like are built). But its recent investment in high-capacity production facilities gave it swan potential—it was capable of supplying large volumes of high-quality products at very competitive prices.

Awareness of Samsung was low among electronic design engineers, purchasers and management at the companies that buy semiconductors in the United States. According to Neil Ransick of Curtin Emerson Ransick, "Research indicated that Samsung's standing was low," and it was considered weak on technology and thought of as a low-price, low-quality, impersonal and unfriendly company. "Overall, the company just wasn't anyone the prospect wanted to hear about."[32]

The promotion mix favored personal selling when Neil Ransick and his agency took Samsung on. Most sales were made by independent sales rep firms and distributors, and 10 percent of products were sold direct by Samsung's own salesforce. The agency could have focused on pushing products through these two personal sales-oriented channels, since personal selling is obviously important, at least with the more complex and expensive semiconductors. But the low recognition and negative image among customers suggested the necessity of a strong image-building pull strategy as well. As a compromise, the promotion plan used pull advertising and sales promotions to generate leads (not sales), and emphasized personal selling for closing sales, servicing customers, and building and maintaining the customer relationship. To complicate the task, the promotion budget was determined by a method that, although common, was not included in our earlier list of "official" techniques: management dictum. Samsung gave the agency a "modest advertising budget for the job to be done," according to Ransick.

The pull advertising had to succeed in a "highly cluttered media environment." There are lots of trade magazines read by the purchasers and purchase influencers, and they are bursting with competitive advertising. However, the agency noted that most competing ads were detailed, dull recitations of product features. But Samsung did not need to communicate details of its products, so much as it needed to communicate a new, "sophisticated, up-to-date" image and also convince customers it was a "supplier that you'd want to do business with," again according to Ransick.

To achieve this goal, and to stand out from the clutter, the agency chose a "benefit-oriented concept, addressed with an illustration by an eminent illustrator . . . something almost unknown in the industry." Translated (agency-speak is unintelligible to most managers), this means large, bold ads in trade magazines using humorous cartoons. Ransick explains that "the idea behind wit and fun as a key ingredient was, of course, to provide a friendly demeanor and build a sense that Samsung was a company you'd want to do business with."

Because of the budget constraints, the agency negotiated a special rate with "one of the giant trade publication organizations" that gave it access to magazines reaching electronics engineering management, engineers, and purchasing agents (these three members of the buying group read different magazines). They used a combination of two-page spreads and 12 page freestanding inserts (in order to provide more detailed coverage of the broad product line). In addition to the image-building cartoons and copy, ads included coupons designed to stimulate readers to contact Samsung. Ransick explains:

> Lead generation was a major objective. In the advertising inserts, we used a prominent coupon promising specific pieces of literature and sample products, with prompts [on each page] inviting the reader to turn to the coupon . . . page. An easy-to-find address and 800 phone number closed each spread ad.

Samsung's case illustrates the value of different promotional techniques at each stage of the purchase. Corporate image advertising, followed by coupons for free samples and literature, targets prospects in the prepurchase period. Personal selling takes over in the purchase period (using leads generated by the prepurchase promotions). Advertising continues to keep the company visible to provide reminders (and to reduce any post-purchase dissonance) after the sale. This is good promotion; the broad brush strokes are right. But it achieves excellence because it is executed with originality and care. The almost magical first-year results speak to this point.

- Awareness improved 13 percent.
- Attitude improved 11 percent.
- Purchase intent up 73 percent.
- 50,000 inquiries generated.
- Solid support for campaign in a survey of the salesforce.
- Samsung moved up to 11th place in its industry.

The program also had something very important going for it—a message that benefited both Samsung and the customer. As customers became aware of the breadth of products, quality, and low prices, and once they overcame their initial prejudice against the company, they were eager to use Samsung as a supplier. Perhaps this is the best promotion strategy in this age of adversity for marketers and managers—to communicate a message the customer will be pleased to receive!

AFTERWORD

Corporate Headquarters, Omni, 1998

"Call it my marketing imagination at work, Jim, but I think the 'less is more' movement is gonna be big. And that means more is going to seem like less to lots of consumers, too. So far we have been giving them more—portable and in-car food warmers and coffee makers along with their stationary ones, for instance. And chip makers, coffee roasters, and produce detoxers are crowding counters that already have mini-ovens, food processors, and coffee makers on them. And our joint venture with Xerox is churning out one office gadget after another. These things aren't recyclable, you know."

"What are you driving at, Ann? Are you trying to tell me we should give our customers *less*?" Jim Berman glanced at his wall calendar computer, which was beeping softly to attract his attention to the display panel: "October 12, 1998, 12:23" it read in soft LCD lettering, and under that, "You are late for your Rotary Club lunch, Jim."

"Damn the Rotary Club," Berman added irritably. "When is a manager supposed to find time to think?"

"Do you have to go Jim? We can finish later," interjected Ann Jones, Omni's vice president of customer interface.

"No, let's keep going. We need to come up with some novel customer usage scenarios for the board meeting this afternoon. It's supposed to be a strategy session, and the group does best when it has some future scenarios to chew on." Berman leaned back and talked quickly into the wall computer's microphone: "Cancel lunch. Warn me a half hour before the board meeting though." The screen darkened, then flashed: "Message uncodable. Please enunciate more clearly."

"Damn this thing. Who the hell makes it anyway?"

"We do, Jim." Jones scribbled a note and, stepping briefly out of the office, handed it to the chairman's secretary. "Bob will remind you about the meeting, Jim; he just got back from lunch. Now where were we?"

"Small is beautiful?"

"No, that was way back in the sixties and it didn't catch on. 'Less is more' they call it now. You've seen the new oven from Somitsu? It replaces three of their old products at once, with microwave, convection oven, broiler, and chiller all built in. And the controls are amazing. There is only one nob—an old-fashioned nob in place of the typical "active matrix" color liquid crystal display and keypad. No database of recipes, no color pictures of what the food is supposed to look like. You actually look through a window at the *food* as it cooks, instead of at an LCD image. You don't even have to read the directions to use it, Jim. You just plug it in."

"Is it doing well? Have we run it by our consumer panel?"

"It's the hottest product in the category right now, and we have nothing like it on the drawing board. By the way, I forgot to mention that it sells for 15 percent less than anything comparable. I think they reduced the number of components to push their costs down." Jones fished into her briefcase, pulling out her compupad and stylus. "I've got test results here, hold on." She scribbled on the surface for a moment, touched a series of database prompts, and switched the machine to audio. "Here is the speed summary of the panel reactions," Jones explained. "This is our regular monthly panel from San Francisco—the panelists are in the Consulting Customers Program we set up a few years ago. I'll play you highlights of their conversation."

"I can't fit another appliance in the trailer. But with this thing I might chuck some of the old ones and just use it."

"It reminds me of an old-fashioned oven from when I was a kid."

"How old did you say you were?" (Laughter.)

"Most of my appliances fell and broke in the big quake last month, but this one looks like it could survive Kuwait."[1]

"It's simple. I like that. I can't work half the things in my office or house anymore."

"It looks simple and solid, like it's built to last. And I can't believe the price is so low."

"I'm embarrassed by all the gadgets in my house. We even have computer-driven light switches. This is a nice, straightforward tool. It's a soft-impact product, you know—it seems environment friendly."

Berman broke in, his voice automatically tripping the off switch on the compupad's super-compact disc player. "I don't keep up with all the latest slang, Ann, but it sounds like the panel is anticomputer. Does this thing really not use a central processor?"

"Oh, it's all built in, sensors and everything, but it's hardwired with nothing but a manual override switch. You don't have to interact with it at all, or even see it. I think they didn't even realize it was an intelligent machine. Maybe that's one of the strategies for the less-is-more scenario: hide the intelligence and simplify the interface."

"Still waters run deep, huh? I can see a new personality for products. The strong, silent type."

"Are you saving these ideas on your desk recorder, Jim? You know you can have Bob edit them on screen and print them on the Xerox machine in the board room." Jones leaned over the new Xerox ExecuDesk and showed Berman how to select the command sequence. He hovered nervously over the project.

"I think I'm a candidate for your 'less is more' segment, Ann. I'm getting too old to keep up with the technology."

"That's another thing, Jim. You know the ElderOffice line we developed for in-home offices?"

"In the Xerox joint venture?"

"Right. The demographics are there—its our fastest growing segment. A whole line of products for elderpreneurs, old geezers like you who have second careers where they work out of their homes."[2] (Berman laughed at the comment, but without much conviction.) "But the point is, Jim, this segment is not only moving toward simplified interfaces, it's also embracing a breakdown of the traditional boundaries between professional and personal life. I think this breakdown trend may spread to other segments of the population—there's another scenario for your board to chew on."

"Yes, I remember when Xerox told us they had decided the office of the future was going to be in the home. I thought they were nuts. And I didn't believe the elderly would become the biggest source of new business formation and innovation in the country, either. I just went along with the idea because joining the Xerox Keiretsu seemed like the thing to do."

"Your secret's safe with me," Jones laughed. "Standardizing the customer interfaces on all the office and home appliances for that segment has been a big help, though. And Xerox teams came up with some of our hottest new products, like the personal publishing system that makes cards and does graphics for home use. And of course Omni benefits from Xerox's investments in its HBID." (HBID is the now-popular acronym for Home-Base Industrial Cluster, for all you time travelers.) "For instance we can get our LCDs cheaper from Corning than we used to from Hoya now that Xerox gives Corning the majority of its LCD business."

"Well, I keep waiting for the photocopy machine that can duplicate dinner when unexpected guests arrive. But tell me what you mean about this scenario."

"Well, you see we are finding that elderpreneurs no longer make a big distinction between work and personal lives. They often do cottage-industry types of jobs—programming, consulting, design, production brokering, and so forth. And they do their work whenever and wherever they want to—sometimes at the kitchen table. The entire home environment is becoming multifunctional. Kind of like a high-tech version of the traditional farmhouse, you know, where the farmer and his family kind of lived their work. In fact, in our panels we are hearing a lot more stories about elderbusinesses expanding to include the children and grandchildren. And with the housing crisis, many more extended families are living and working under the same roof."

"You think this is a major trend, Ann? Should we be making 'lifestyle' products rather than separate lines of home and office appliances?"

"Maybe. You've heard the popular expression, 'as the elders go, so goes the nation.'"[3]

"Okay, that can be scenario number two. What about this Zero Marketing thing? Do you think that's important?" Berman glanced furtively at his wall computer again and added, "How about a quick bite to eat? I'm starved and I've got this darn meeting in an hour." The machine's display remained blank, much to Berman's relief.

"Let's grab something from the sandwich machine in the cafeteria—or how about having Bob bring it so I don't have to listen to you cuss out the controls?"

Berman pushed the intercom button on his desk and ordered a tuna sandwich on whole wheat. "Do you want the no-cal option?" came Bob West's muffled voice. "No, lots of cals, please. And what do you want, Ann? Roast beef on rye, mustard and lettuce. What Bob? It only dispenses sprouts?"

With much back-and-forth, the meal was ordered and West dispatched to fetch it from the fresh food vending machines. But he was back in a minute with the report that his vending card was used up. Jones sent him off again with hers. "And remember to code it 'business expense' when you order," she called after him. "You know how hard it is to reallocate costs in those personal accounting systems," she muttered as he disappeared. "I think it's a conspiracy to keep us from falsifying our expense reports."

"Sony sells a hand-held re-coder now, you know," Berman interjected. "You can modify the entire magnetic record on any of your expense cards before you upload it to the central system. It's billed as an error-catching system, but its great for the criminal minded. I think Omni's travel expenses went up 15 percent the month it was introduced!"

Jones laughed at the thought. "Did that shake your faith in the total trust program?"

"Results, Ann, results. I don't care if people bend the rules a little, as long as we keep setting productivity records. They *make* the rules, after all. And I haven't seen such rapid improvement since we started the old total quality program back in 1990."

"Well, what were you saying about Zero Marketing, Jim?"

"You know, so many consumer products companies have eliminated their promotion spending that I wonder if there isn't an important lesson here for everyone."

"Did you see the new corporate campaign from IBM/A?" asked Jones.[4] "They are boasting about their 'Zero Marketing Pledge,' saying that they are committed to cutting message clutter and will communicate with customers only in interactive media where information is given in response to customer queries. They make it sound like a benefit, when in fact it's just a gimmick to control the escalating promotion costs. They still use rebates and other consumer promos, after all."

"I think it might be more than a gimmick. Message clutter is a big political issue now. Look at the new regulations on telemarketing and direct E-mail. You can't make a cold call to anyone's telephone or PC anymore, Ann. And direct mail was killed three years ago. Besides, some of these interactive electronic shopping networks are run by nonprofits now."

"Maybe you're right. After all Omni has to spend twice as much today as we did five years ago just to maintain share of voice. Advertising *is* out of control."

"What are we doing with the new interactive media, anyway? I don't think Omni is a leader in that area."

"Well Jim, that's my department of course, since it has to do with how we interact with consumers. And we do have full-text interactive stacks on line with all the major home-shopping services. Usage is up—I think 15 percent of our home products are purchased direct via the new interactive channels. But we get a lot of flack from our wholesalers and bigger retailers, so it's hard to push it. They see it as a competing channel. For example, we don't dare offer the kind of price promotions that some of the new direct-only competitors do, even though our margins are higher in the direct channel."

"Well, I'm going to put interactive media down as another area to look at this afternoon. But I agree that channel conflict is going to be a problem if we try to develop it. The strength of mass marketers is so great now it is hard for us to make a move without their approval. In fact, many of our distributors are so powerful that *they* are telling *us* what to sell and how to market it. And the Zero Marketing movement is adding to their power by reducing the power of brand names and emphasizing point-of-purchase information. I think it's a mistake for companies like IBM/A to stop advertising."

"You know, Jim, it's all well and good for IBM/A to say they don't advertise anymore, but in fact they are spending as much on their corporate TV and print campaign as they once did on product line campaigns. They have simply focused the message more narrowly and put more of their resources behind it. I think it's more a strategy to increase impact given the clutter problem than it is a real effort to wean themselves of advertising."

"You're probably right," Berman responded. "But there is definitely a message clutter problem, and there is growing public sentiment against broad-spectrum persuasion advertising. Companies that act as leaders on social problems seem to get a bottom-line return these days. Remember the boost McDonald's got when they went 'green' and switched to organic foods? We should consider a scenario where the industry moves away from advertising completely, just to see what kind of alternatives there are."

"I think relationship marketing is the alternative. With the rapid increases in longevity and the declining birthrate, we need to focus more on retaining customers than on finding new ones. Heck, today's teenage customer may be with us for 80 or 90 years, if we can build a strong customer bond. And that's a lot easier now because we capture so much information about them. We know a great deal about their personal lives from our interactive home appliance databases. The smart ovens, for instance, retain a full record of everything they cooked and all the recipes they accessed on the reference database. More of our ovens are going on-line with reciprocal access to data—they tap into our free centralized databases, and in return we can upload the usage data captured on their appliances. And we can tap into Xerox's business profile databases for financial and career information. My department is playing around with long-term latent need forecasting for the individual customer. We think we will be able to anticipate personal and career moves, travel plans, changes in taste—all sorts of things. If we can help them make these transitions, or at least offer them an adjusted set of product options when they do, we can keep them for life."

"What in the world do you do with records of what somebody ate? Speaking of eating . . ." Berman looked nervously at West's empty desk, then his own watch.

"Oh, you'd be surprised what long-term ethnographic data from a single household can reveal, especially if correlated with changes in travel patterns, career, health, family status, and the like. There's a whole new field of behavioral demographics that specializes in making sense out of the millions of bits of dull information that are now captured on individual consumers. You can build up a psychological profile over time that is a great deal more accurate than the old VALS-type profiles, although it's still not perfect of course. Did you know that American Express now collects 4,500 pieces of information about each cardholder?"

"How does this fit in with Zero Marketing?"

"The idea is that the better you understand the consumer's latent needs, the more narrowly you can focus your product offerings. You don't market everything to everyone; you simply select a narrow range of products that the individual consumer is very likely to be interested in now or in the future. You are able to cut down on misses, or unnecessary exposures, so this helps reduce message clutter. It can even work in mainstream media like print and cable, now that they are customizing their programming to behavioral segments of their viewers or readers. Two neighboring households subscribing to the same magazine can get different advertisements, for instance."

"Okay, let's get that down too. We can talk about a relationship marketing scenario. That gives us less-is-more, lifestyle product, Zero Marketing, interactive buying media, and relationship marketing for the board to chew on. Do you think that's too much on marketing, Ann?"

"You're the one who always says, 'marketing is everything,' Jim, although I think you stole that from Regis McKenna."

"He stole it from me. But you're right. By the way, where will you be this afternoon, Ann? Can I raise you on the tele-intercom if the board comes up with some technical questions on all this?"

"I'll be in my office. You can reach me there. But maybe you better bring Bob with you to work the controls."

"Jesus, where is he? He should be editing this thing instead of messing around!"

"The sandwiches, Jim. Remember?"

"Oh yes, and here they are."

West slid a tray onto the desk and went back out to his consol. "You're conversation's up on the screen," he reported. "I'll try to boil it down. You can watch on your desk as I do it if you want to make comments." Jones leaned over Berman's desk to switch on the desktop monitor as Berman unwrapped the sandwiches and prepared the meal.

"I'm starved, Ann, aren't you?" But a soft beeping interrupted his first bite, sandwich in mid-air. Both Berman and Jones turned toward the wall computer, its screen now flashing a message in red: "It's too late for lunch, Jim. You have to go to the board meeting now."

"And Bob," Berman shouted out the office door, "would you get me a meeting with the product manager for those damn wall computers ASAP?"

"I think it's one of the products we're managing by product team now, Jim," Jones added cautiously. "There is no product manager."

"No wonder," muttered Berman as he tore into a corner of his sandwich. "Hey," he added, I didn't want sprouts on this thing!"

Ann laughed. "Less *is* more, don't you agree?"

Chapter Notes

INTRODUCTION

1. Laszlo Papay, *Making Total Quality Happen*, Research Report #937, The Conference Board, 1990, p. 30.

2. As quoted in Philip Kotler, *Marketing Management*, 5th Edition, Englewood Cliffs, NJ: Prentice-Hall, 1984, p. 1.

CHAPTER 1

1. Edgar Woolard, "Creating a New Company Culture," *Fortune*, January 15, 1990, pp. 127–131.

2. L.L. Bean company catalogs and literature.

3. Howard Schlossberg, "Baldridge Winner Aims for 100% Satisfaction," *Marketing News*, February 4, 1991, pp. 1, 12.

4. Howard Schlossberg, "Author: Consumers Just Can't Wait to Be Satisfied," *Marketing News*, February 4, 1991, p. 13.

5. Peter M. Senge, "The Leader's New Work: Building Learning Organizations," *Sloan Management Review*, Fall 1990, pp. 7–23.

6. Ibid.

7. Howard Schlossberg, "Author: Consumers Just Can't Wait to Be Satisfied," *Marketing News*, February 4, 1991, p. 13.

8. Brian Dumaine, "The Bureaucracy Busters," *Fortune*, June 17, 1991, pp. 36–50.

9. Howard Schlossberg, "Baldridge Winner Aims for 100% Satisfaction," *Marketing News*, February 4, 1991, pp. 1, 12.

10. Brian Dumaine, "The Bureaucracy Busters," *Fortune*, June 17, 1991, pp. 36–50.

11. Cited in Theodore Levitt, "Marketing Myopia 1975: Retrospective Commentary," *Harvard Business Review*, September–October 1975.

12. Ibid.

13. Ibid.

14. Michael Miller, "Lawmakers are Hoping to Ring Out Era of Unrestricted Calls by Telemarketers," *The Wall Street Journal*, May 28, 1991, p. B1.

15. Ibid.

16. Steven Star, "Marketing and Its Discontents," *Harvard Business Review*, November–December 1989, pp. 148–154.

17. Dick Berry, *Marketing News*, December 24, 1990, p. 10.

18. Brian Dumaine, "The Bureaucracy Busters," *Fortune*, June 17, 1991, pp. 36–50.

19. Henry Ford, *My Life and Work*, New York: Doubleday Page & Co., 1923, pp. 146–147.

CHAPTER 2

1. Paul Schoemaker, "Strategy Complexity and Economic Rent," *Management Science*, 36(10), October 1990, pp. 1178–1192.

2. "The New Breed of Strategic Planner," *BusinessWeek*, September 17, 1984, p. 63.

3. Gary Reiner, "Getting There First: It Takes Planning to Put Plans into Action," *The New York Times*, March 12, 1989: Business Forum.

4. Ronald Hentcoff, "How to Plan for 1995," *Fortune*, December 31, 1990, pp. 70–77.

5. Michael Dertouzos, Richard Lester, and Robert Solow, *Made in America: Regaining the Competitive Edge*, New York: Harper Collins, 1989, p. 46.

6. Janice Castro, "Making It Better," *Time*, November 13, 1989, pp. 78–81.

7. "How to Plan for 1995," *Fortune*, December 31, 1990, p. 70.

8. "Levi Strauss Is Stretching Its Wardrobe," *Fortune*, November 19, 1979, p. 89.

9. "It's Back to Basics for Levi's," *BusinessWeek*, March 8, 1982, p. 77.

10. Andrew Feinberg, "The First Global Generation," *Adweek's Marketing Meek*, February 6, 1989, pp. 18–27.

11. Susan Faluti, "Levi Strauss's Net Surged 30% in 2nd Quarter," *The Wall Street Journal*, July 11, 1991, p. C13.

12. "How Do You Follow an Act Like Bud?" *BusinessWeek*, May 2, 1988, p. 119.

13. Robert Buzzell and Bradley Gale, *The PIMS Principles: Linking Strategy to Performance*, New York: The Free Press, 1987, p. 9.

14. Statistics for 2nd quarter 1990, from a September 24, 1990, report by Diana Temple of Salomon Brothers.

15. "Diversified Gillette still Depends on Blades," *The New York Times*, February 25, 1990.

16. Data for this example are from Mart-Charlier, "Brewers Shake Off a 3-Year Hangover," *The Wall Street Journal*, January 15, 1991, and originally collected by the trade magazines *Impact* and *Beer Marketer's Insights*.

17. For an explanation of other approaches, see Yoram Wind and Vijay Mahajan, "Designing Product and Business Portfolios," *Harvard Business Review*, 60(1), January–February 1981, pp. 156–165.

18. Based on telephone conversations with Bruce Bunch and William Rothschild. See Alexander Hiam, *The Vest-Pocket CEO: Decision-Making Tools for Executives*, Englewood Cliffs, NJ: Prentice-Hall, 1990, pp. 377–384.

19. "The New Breed of Strategic Planner," *BusinessWeek*, September 17, 1984, pp. 62–66.

20. Ibid.

21. Ibid.

22. Ibid.

23. This case based on Brian Dumaine, "How Managers Can Succeed Through Speed," *Fortune*, February 13, 1989, pp. 54–59.

24. Ibid., p. 56.

25. "The New Breed of Strategic Planner," *BusinessWeek*, September 17, 1984, pp. 62–66.

26. Frank Sonenberg, "Customer Satisfaction: The Strategic Edge for the 1990s," *Adweek's Marketing Week*, September 3, 1990.

27. Andrea Gabor, "The Front Lines of Quality," *U.S. News and World Report*, November 27, 1989, pp. 57–59.

28. Janice Castro, "Making It Better," *Time*, November 13, 1989, pp. 78–81.

29. Brian Dumaine, "The Bureaucracy Busters," *Fortune*, June 17, 1991, pp. 36–50.

30. Hideki Kaihatsu, "TQC in Japan," *Making Total Quality Happen*, New York: The Conference Board, 1990.

31. Robert Camp, "Competitive Benchmarking," *Making Total Quality Happen*, New York: The Conference Board, 1990.

32. Ibid.

33. Ibid.

34. Janice Castro, "Making It Better," *Time*, November 13, 1989, pp. 78–81.

35. Ibid.

36. Roy Stata, "Organizational Learning—the Key to Management Innovation," *Sloan Management Review*, Spring 1989, pp. 63–73.

37. Ibid, p. 64.

38. Nine senior managers worked with Peter Senge and Jay Forrester at MIT; the group is called the New Management Style Project.

39. Roy Stata, "Organizational Learning—the Key to Management Innovation," *Sloan Management Review*, Spring 1989, pp. 63–73.

40. Elliot Carlisle, *Mac: Managers Talk About Managing People*, New York: Penguin Books, 1982, p. 12.

41. Chris Argyris, "Teaching Smart People How to Learn," *Harvard Business Review*, May–June 1991, pp. 99–109.

42. Rosabeth Moss Kanter, "The New Managerial Work," *Harvard Business Review*, November–December 1989, pp. 85–92.

43. Brian Dumaine, "The Bureaucracy Busters," *Fortune*, June 17, 1991, pp. 36–50.

44. Patricia Sellers, "Pepsi Keeps on Going After No. 1," *Fortune*, March 11, 1991.

CHAPTER 3

1. Michael Waldholz, "Sudafed Recall Shows Difficulty of Halting Tampering," *The Wall Street Journal*, March 5, 1991, pp. B1, B4.

2. "Panicky Policy Holders Have Insurers Trembling," *BusinessWeek*, July 29, 1991, pp. 60–61.

3. "The Travel Business Still Has an Attitude Problem," *BusinessWeek*, March 18, 1991, p. 30.

4. John Berry, "While Patriots Soar in the Gulf, All Quiet on the Home Front," *Adweek's Marketing Week*, January 28, 1991, p. 4.

5. *Management Briefing, Business and Finance*, The Conference Board, January 1987. Also see Capsugel's Crisis Management Checklist and Vielhaber's Crisis Communication Strategies in Alexander Hiam, *The Vest-Pocket Marketer*, Englewood Cliffs, NJ: Prentice-Hall, 1991.

6. "Women in Japan: A Growing Force," *Advertising Age*, January 14, 1985, p. 40.

7. Condensed from Robert Bly, *Iron John: A Book about Men*, Reading, MA: Addison-Wesley, 1990, pp. 1–3.

8. Ibid, p. 235.

9. Two books that elaborate on this concept are Jay Conrad Levinson's *Guerilla Marketing Attack*, Boston: Houghton Mifflin, 1989, and Al Ries and Jack Trout's *Marketing Warfare*, New York: McGraw-Hill, 1986.

10. Noel Tichy and Ram Charan, "Citicorp Faces the World: An Interview with John Reed," *Harvard Business Review*, November–December 1990, pp. 135–144.

11. "Ready, Set, Merge," *Business Week*, July 29, 1991, pp. 24–27.

12. Michael Quint, "Challenged and Chastened, Citibank Pursues the Customer," *The New York Times*, July 14, 1991, p. F11.

13. Randall Smith, "Big Bank Mergers Come as Boon to a Wall Street Thirsty for Deals," *The Wall Street Journal*, August 16, 1991, p. C1. Ron Suskind, "BankAmerica Mulls Shawmut, Other Purchases," *The Wall Street Journal*, August 16, 1991, p. A3.

14. Fred Bleakley, "As Big Rivals Surge, Citicorp's John Reed Is at a Crossroads," *The Wall Street Journal*, August 16, 1991, pp. A1, A2.

15. "Ready, Set, Merge," *Business Week*, July 29, 1991, pp. 24–27.

16. "Don't Expect Citicorp to Play Copycat," *Business Week*, July 29, 1991, p. 26.

17. Ibid.

18. Michael Quint, "Challenged and Chastened, Citibank Pursues the Customer," *The New York Times*, July 14, 1991, p. F11.

19. Tichy and Charan, p. 137.

20. Ibid.

21. Ibid.

22. Ralph Winter, "R&D Outlays Slowing after Sharp Rise, *The Wall Street Journal*, December 27, 1990, p. A2.

23. Alan M. Kantrow, *The Constraints of Corporate Tradition: Doing the Correct Thing, Not Just What the Past Dictates*, New York: Harper & Row, 1987, p. 39.

24. Tomatoes are now bred to withstand 5 mph impacts which explains their lack of taste and toughness.

25. Lee Berton, "The CPA Jungle," *The Wall Street Journal*, July 24, 1991, pp. A1, A5.

26. Ibid.

27. "Now that the Recession Is Official, Three Experts Predict Recovery," *The New York Times*, January 13, 1991, p. F4.

28. "Business Outlook," *Business Week*, July 29, 1991.

29. Louis Uchitelle, "Optimism Is Disappearing for a Solid Recovery Soon," *The New York Times*, August 11, 1991, pp. A1, A20.

30. "Business Week Index," *Business Week*, July 29, 1991, p. 4.

31. Michael Doan, "Even Good Times Are Bad for Some," *U.S. News & World Report*, June 25, 1984, p. 64.

32. "Federal Consumer Actions in 1976," *Consumer News*, December 15, 1976, pp. 1–4.

33. Joanne Lipman, "Pediatric Academy Prescribes Ban on Food Ads Aimed at Children," *The Wall Street Journal*, July 24, 1991, p. B8.

34. See Ray O. Warner, "Marketing and the U.S. Supreme Court," *Journal of Marketing*, 41(1), January 1977, pp. 32–43.

35. Elaine Underwood, "Every Time It Snows, It's Pennies from Heaven," *Adweek's Marketing Week*, January 21, 1991.

36. "Break in Heat Wave Really Put a Chill on Some Business," *The Wall Street Journal*, July 24, 1991, p. B1.

37. Samuel Mathews and James Sugar, "Is Our World Warming?" *National Geographic*, October, 1990.

38. "A Warming World: What It Will Mean," *Fortune*, July 4, 1988, p. 107.

39. Janice Castro, "One Big Mac, Hold the Box!" *Time*, June 25, 1990, p. 44.

40. Quotes drawn from the following sources (with a few liberties taken in stage directions and the like): John Holusha, "Packaging and Public Image: McDonald's Fills a Big Order," *The New York Times*, November 2, 1990, pp. A1 and D5. John Holusha, "Talking Deals," *The New York Times*, August 9, 1990, p. D2. Daniel F. Cuff, "Lifelong 'Cheerleader' for McDonald's Way," *The New York Times*, November 5, 1990, "Business People" column.

CHAPTER 4

1. Hideo Sugiura, "How Honda Localizes Its Global Strategy," *Sloan Management Review*, Fall 1991, pp. 77–82.

2. Charles Ferguson, "Computers and the Coming of the U.S. Keiretsu," *Harvard Business Review*, July–August 1990, pp. 55–70.

3. *U.S. News and World Report*, December 3, 1990, p. 62.

4. Joshua Hammer, "From Russia with Hype," *Newsweek*, June 12, 1989, pp. 42–43.

5. William Doerner, "Too Far, Too Fast?" *Time*, October 10, 1988, pp. 50–51.

6. Susan V. Lawrence, "The Revolt of the Chinese Consumer," *U.S. News and World Report*, December 3, 1990, p. 62.

7. William Doerner, "Too Far, Too Fast?" *Time*, October 10, 1988, pp.50–51.

8. Bill Javetsky, "A New Economic Miracle?" *BusinessWeek*, November 27, 1989, p. 65.

9. Ibid, p. 63.

10. Ibid.

11. Kevin Cete, "East Germans Scout for Good Buys in West," *Advertising Age*, December 11, 1990, p. 40.

12. Dinah Lee, "Beijing Opens the Door to Bubble Gum and Band-Aids." *BusinessWeek*, August 8, 1988, p. 40.

13. Peter S. Green, "Czech Media Eye More Ad Space." *Advertising Age*, December 11, 1990, p. 40.

14. "How to Be a Global Manager," *Fortune,* March 14, 1988, pp. 53–54.

15. "Asking for Protection Is Asking for Trouble," *Harvard Business Review,* 65(4), July–August 1987, pp. 42–47.

16. Ibid.

17. "PepsiCo Accepts Tough Conditions for the Right to Sell Cola in India," *The Wall Street Journal,* September 20, 1988, p. 44.

18. "U.S. Products Still Hot in Philippines," *Advertising Age,* November 18, 1985, p. 70.

19. *Directory of Trade Statistics Yearbook,* International Monetary Fund, 1985, p. 6.

20. Many of the following examples are excerpted from David A. Ricks, *Big Business Blunders,* Homewood, IL: Dow Jones–Irwin, 1983.

21. Vern Terpstra and Kenneth David, *The Cultural Environment of International Business,* Cincinnati: South-Western, 1991.

22. Edward T. Hall, "The Silent Language in Overseas Business," *Harvard Business Review,* 38(3), May–June 1960, pp. 87–96.

23. Jeffrey A. Fadiman, "A Traveler's Guide to Gifts and Bribes," *Harvard Business Review,* 86(4), July–August 1986, pp. 122–136; "The New Export Entrepreneurs," *Fortune,* January 4, 1988.

24. Ernest Dichter, "The World Customer," *Harvard Business Review,* 4(4), July–August 1962, pp. 113–123.

25. Kathryn Rudie Harrigan, "Strategic Alliances: Their Role in Global Competition," *Columbia Journal of World Business,* 22(2), Summer 1987, pp. 67–69.

26. See J. J. Boddewyn, Robin Soehl, and Jacques Picard, "Standardization in International Marketing: Is Ted Levitt in Fact Right?" *Business Horizons,* 29(6), November–December 1986, pp. 69–75; W. Chan Kim and R. A. Mauborgne, "Cross-Cultural Strategies," *Journal of Business Strategy,* 7(1), Spring 1987, pp. 28–35; "The Issue Globalists Don't Talk About," *International Management,* 42(9), September 1987, pp. 37–42; James F. Bolt, "Global Competitors: Some Criteria for Success," *Business Horizons,* 30(1), January–February 1988, pp. 34–41.13.

27. Theodore Levitt, "The Globalization of Markets," *Harvard Business Review,* 61(3), May–June 1983, pp. 92–102.

28. "Europe's New Mass-Market Appeal," *Adweek,* June 1, 1987, p. G.A.7.

29. Hidea Sugiura, "How Honda Localizes Its Global Strategy," *Sloan Management Review,* Fall 1990, pp. 77–82.

30. Ibid., p. 78.

31. Ibid., p. 82.

32. Christopher Bartlett and Sumantra Ghoshal, "Organizing for Worldwide Effectiveness: The Transnational Solution," *California Management Review,* Fall 1988, pp. 54–74.

33. Ibid., p. 73.

34. Ibid., p. 66.

35. Warren Keegan, "Multinationals Product Planning: Strategic Alternatives," *Journal of Marketing, 33*(1), January 1969, p. 59.

36. Michael L. Dertouzos, Richard K. Lester, and Robert M. Solow, *Made in America: Regaining the Competitive Edge,* New York: Harper Perennial (Harper Collins), 1989.

37. Charles Ferguson, "Computers and the Coming of the U.S. Keiretsu," *Harvard Business Review,* July–August 1990, pp. 55–70.

38. Roy Manns, "A Nation of Shopkeepers and Shoppers," *Sloan Management Review,* Spring 1991, p. 3.

39. Charles Ferguson, "Computers and the Coming of the U.S. Keiretsu," *Harvard Business Review,* July–August 1990, p. 55.

40. Michael Porter, "Why Nations Triumph," *Fortune,* March 12, 1990, pp. 94–108. Also see Michael Porter, *The Competitive Advantage of Nations,* New York: *The Free Press,* 1990.

41. "Have We Lost Our Faith in Competition?" (an interview with Michael Porter), *Across The Board,* September 1990, pp. 37–46.

42. Ibid., p. 39.

CHAPTER 5

1. Joshua Levine, "Desperately Seeking 'Jeepness'," *Forbes,* May 15, 1989, pp. 134–138.

2. John Paul Newport, Jr., "American Express: Service That Sells," *Fortune,* November 20, 1989, pp. 80–94.

3. John Paul Newport, Jr., "American Express: Service That Sells," *Fortune,* November 20, 1989, pp. 80–94.

4. "How Procter & Gamble Fumbled Citrus Hill," *Adweek's Marketing Week,* March 7, 1988, pp. 1, 6.

5. John Paul Newport, Jr., "American Express: Service That Sells," *Fortune,* November 20, 1989, pp. 80–94.

6. Maryanne E. Rasmussen, "Measuring Bottom-Line Impact of Customer Satisfaction," *Making Total Quality Happen,* New York: The Conference Board, 1990, pp. 55–59.

7. Ibid.

8. "Marketing Trends: The 'Bloodbath' in Market Research," *Business-Week,* February 11, 1991, pp. 72, 74.

9. Ibid.

10. Sources: "How to Snoop on your Competitors," *Fortune,* May 14, 1984, pp. 29–33; "George Smiley Joins the Firm," *Newsweek,* May 2, 1988,

pp. 46–47; "Strategies for Playing the Global Game," *The New York Times,* June 26, 1988, p. F3.

11. Vern Terpstra, *International Marketing,* 4th ed., Chicago: The Dryden Press, 1987, pp. 178–185.

12. Charles S. Mayer, "The Lessons of Multinational Marketing Research," *Business Horizons, 21*(6), December, 1978, pp. 7–13.

13. David Kilburn, "Putting Out Feelers: Japanese 'Antenna Shops' Aid Research." *Advertising Age,* January 2, 1989, pp. 3, 25.

14. Donald F. Cox and Robert E. Good, "How to Build a Marketing Information System," *Harvard Business Review, 45*(3), May–June 1967, p. 145.

15. John D. C. Little, "Decision Support Systems for Marketing Managers," *Journal of Marketing, 43*(3), Summer 1979, p. 9.

CHAPTER 6

1. Peter F. Drucker, *Innovation and Entrepreneurship: Practice and Principles,* New York: Harper & Row, 1985, p. 90.

2. "Playing the Demographics Game," *The New York Times,* December 4, 1983, p. F12.

3. As quoted in *Newsweek* special edition, "The 21st Century Family," Winter–Spring 1990, p. 11.

4. Andrew Feinberg, "Bust or Boom?" *Adweek's Marketing Week,* December 5, 1988, 20–30.

5. C. Northcote Parkinson, *Parkinson's Law,* New York: Random House, 1957, pp. vii–viii. By the way, Parkinson's law is, "Work expands so as to fill the time available for its completion."

6. "Teen-Age Shoppers; Desperately Seeking Spinach," *The New York Times,* November 29, 1987, p. F10.

7. Charles D. Schewe, "Gray America Goes to Market," *Business: The Magazine of Managerial Thought and Action, 35*(2), April–June 1985, pp. 3–9; Hale N. Tongren, "Determinant Behavior Characteristics of Older Consumers," *Journal of Consumer Affairs, 22*(1), Summer 1988, pp. 136–157.

8. Ganesan Visvabharathy and David Rink, "The Elderly: Neglected Business Opportunities," *Journal of Consumer Marketing, 1*(4), 1984, p. 39.

9. "Soon, Most People May Have 'Lived in Sin'," *The Wall Street Journal,* June 13, 1988, p. 37.

10. Charles D. Schewe, "Marketing to Blacks: Research Implications for Managers," *Atlanta Economic Review, 36*(5), September–October 1976, pp. 34–40.

11. Henry Assael, *Consumer Behavior and Marketing Action,* Boston: Kent, 1981, p. 274; David Loudon and Albert J. Della Bitta, *Consumer Behavior: Concepts and Applications,* 2nd ed., New York: McGraw-Hill, 1984, pp. 210–216.

12. "Fast Times on *Avenida Madison*," *BusinessWeek*, June 6, 1988, p. 64.

13. "A Correction: How the Population Has Shifted." *The New York Times*, January 4, 1989, p. D20.

14. "Proceeding with Caution," *Time*, July 16, 1990, p. 60.

15. World Bank statistics, as reported in *The New York Times*, December 1, 1989, p. A23.

16. Peter F. Drucker, *Innovation and Entrepreneurship*, New York: Harper & Row, 1985, p. 91.

17. David M. Georgoff and Robert G. Murdick, "Manager's Guide to Forecasting," *Harvard Business Review*, 86(1), January–February 1986, see table.

18. John Naisbitt, *Megatrends*, New York: Warner Books, 1982; John Naisbitt and Patricia Aburdene, *Re-Inventing the Corporation*, New York: Warner Books, 1985.

19. "Back Issues," *Census '90*, The Wall Street Journal Research Reports, March 9, 1990, pp. R7, R27.

20. "For Better or Worse?" *Newsweek Special Issue: The 21st Century Family*, Winter–Spring 1990, p. 18.

CHAPTER 7

1. Abraham Maslow, *Motivation and Personality*, 3rd Ed., New York: Harper & Row, 1970, p. 7.

2. As quoted in Robert Johnson, "In The Chips," *The Wall Street Journal*, March 22, 1991, pp. B1-2.

3. Ibid. Many of the details in this chapter concerning Frito Lay and chip marketing come from the above article.

4. Ibid.

5. "Children's Hour: As Kids Gain Power of Purse," *The Wall Street Journal*, January 19, 1988, p. 1.

6. Ibid.

7. Alfred L. Kroeber and Talcott Parsons, "The Concepts of Culture and of Social System," in Gardner Lindzey and Elliot Aronson, *Handbook of Social Psychology*, Vol. 2, New York: Random House, 1985, p. 994.

8. Michael J. McCarthy, "Marketers Zero in on Their Customers," *The Wall Street Journal*, March 18, 1991, pp. B1, B8.

9. Ibid.

10. Ibid.

11. Janice Castro, "The Simple Life," *Time*, April 8, 1991, pp. 58–65.

12. Ibid.

13. Benjamin DeMott, *The Imperial Middle: Why Americans Can't Think Straight about Class*, Morrow, 1990.

14. Andrew Hacker, "Class Dismissed," *The New York Review of Books,* March 7, 1991.

15. *Money Income and Poverty Status in the United States 1989,* Bureau of the Census, 1990.

16. Jonathan Kozol, "The New Untouchables," *Newsweek Special Issue: The 21st Century Family,* Winter–Spring 1990.

17. William O. Bearden and Michael J. Etzel, "Reference Group Influence on Product and Brand Purchase Decisions," *Journal of Consumer Research,* 9(2), September 1982, pp. 183–194.

18. Dave DiMartino, "Frito-Lay Takes Off with MCA's Jets Promo," *Billboard,* July 23, 1988, p. 38.

19. "The High-Priced Call of the Wild," *Newsweek,* February 1, 1988, p. 57.

20. Isabella Cunningham and Robert Green, "Purchasing Roles in the U.S. Family, 1955 and 1973," *Journal of Marketing, 30*(4), October 1974, pp. 61–64.

21. Charles M. Schaninger and W. C. Buss, "Intergenerational Transfer of Task Allocation within the Family," paper presented at the American Marketing Association Winter Educators' Conference, Fort Lauderdale, Florida, 1984.

22. "If I Have the Doctor . . . ," *Forbes,* March 30, 1981, p. 64.

23. Abraham H. Maslow, *Motivation and Personality,* New York: Harper & Row, 1954.

24. According to Michael Rothschild of the University of Wisconsin, in Michael J. McCarthy, "Mind Probe," *The Wall Street Journal,* March 22, 1991, p. B3.

25. John B. Hinge, "Critics Call Cuts in Package Size Deceptive Move," *The Wall Street Journal,* February 5, 1991, pp. B1, B8.

26. James Ryan, "Tom Waits Wins 'Sound-Alike' Suit, *Billboard,* May 19, 1990, pp. 6, 82.

27. John Deighton, Daniel Romer, and Josh McQueen, "Using Drama to Persuade," *Journal of Consumer Research, 16,* December 1989, pp. 335–343.

28. Kathleen Deveny, "Copycat Cold Medicines Proliferate, Creating Confusion among Consumers," *The Wall Street Journal,* February 1, 1991, pp. B1, B8.

29. For more on low involvement, see Harold H. Kassarjian, "Low Involvement: A Second Look," in Kent B. Monroe, ed., *Advances in Consumer Research, 8,* Ann Arbor, Michigan: Association for Consumer Research, 1981, pp. 31–34; Michael J. Houston and Michael L. Rothchild, "Conceptual and Methodological Perspectives on Involvement," in Subash C. Jain, ed., *Research Frontiers in Marketing: Dialogues and Directions,* Chicago: American Marketing Association, 1978, pp. 184–187.

30. Jennifer Lawrence, "Crunch Time," *Advertising Age,* January 16, 1989, p. 4.

31. Sue Shellenbarger, "McDonald's Low-Fat Burger to Go National," *The Wall Street Journal*, March 13, 1991, p. B1.

32. "For the Poor Athletes Who Blame Their Tools, New Ones Are Coming," *The Wall Street Journal*, May 14, 1985, p. 31.

33. "Problem Recognition: The Crucial First Stage of the Consumer Decision Process, *The Journal of Consumer Marketing*, 5(1), Winter 1988, pp. 53–63.

34. "Doctored Strategy: Food Marketers Push Products through Physicians," *Advertising Age*, March 28, 1988, p. 12.

35. Joseph W. Newman, "Consumer External Search: Amount and Determinant," in Arch Woodside, Jagdish Sheth, and Peter Bennett, eds., *Consumer and Industrial Buying Behavior*, New York: North-Holland, 1977, p. 86.

36. William B. Locander and Peter W. Hermann, "The Effect of Self-Confidence and Anxiety on Information Seeking in Consumer Risk Reduction." *Journal of Marketing Research*, 16(2), May 1979, pp. 233–246.

37. Jennifer Lawrence, "Frito Heavies Up on 'Light' Items, *Advertising Age*, August 1988, p. 42; also "Frito Lay Tests Low-Oil Doritos," *Advertising Age*, January 18, 1988, p. 91.

38. Michael J. McCarthy, "Marketers Zero In on Their Customers," *The Wall Street Journal*, March 18, 1991, pp. B1, B8.

CHAPTER 8

1. Stann Rapp and Tom Collins, *Maxi Marketing*, New York: McGraw-Hill, 1987.

2. Cleveland Horten, "Porsche 300,000: The New Elite," *Advertising Age*, February 5, 1990, p. 6.

3. For its beginning, see Wendell R. Smith, "Product Differentiation and Market Segmentation as Alternative Marketing Strategies," *Journal of Marketing*, 20(3), July 1956, pp. 3–8.

4. "Global Marketing: How Marketing Executives Really Feel," *Ad Forum*, April 1985, pp. 30–31.

5. Franklin B. Evans, "Psychological and Objective Factors in the Prediction of Brand Choice, Ford versus Chevrolet," *Journal of Business*, October 1959, pp. 340–369; Ralph Westfall, "Psychological Factors in Predicting Product Choice," *Journal of Marketing*, 26(2), April 1962, pp. 34–40; Shirley Young, "The Dynamics of Measuring Unchange," in Russell I. Haley, ed., *Attitude Research in Transition*, Chicago: American Marketing Association, 1972, pp. 61–82.

6. Fred D. Reynolds and William R. Darden, "An Operational Construction of Life Style," in M. Venkatesen, ed., *Proceedings of the 3rd Annual Conference for Consumer Research*, 1972, pp. 482–484.

7. Arnold Mitchell, *The Nine American Lifestyles: Who We Are and Where We Are Going*, New York: Macmillan, 1983.

8. Jennifer Stewart, "Maybe It Will Work Here," *Viewpoint*, 1984, pp. 27–30.

9. "Coach Hopes to Bag Sales Overseas," *Advertising Age*, August 29, 1988, p. 32.

10. Based on research reported in "People's Choice," *Advertising Age*, January 16, 1984, p. 10, and "The Touch Is Light on Women's Market," *Advertising Age*, January 16, 1984, pp. 14–16.

11. Kevin J. Clancy and Mary Lou Roberts, "Toward an Optimal Market Target: A Strategy for Market Segmentation," *Journal of Consumer Marketing*, *1*(1), Summer 1983, p. 66.

12. "Looking Downscale—Without Looking Down." *BusinessWeek*, October 8, 1990, pp. 62–67. Low-income households are defined as those with $15,000 or less in annual incomes in 1984 dollars.

13. Ibid.

14. Kathleen Deveny, "Segments of One," *The Wall Street Journal*, March 22, 1991, p. B3; Stan Rapp and Tom Collins, *The Great Marketing Turnaround*, Englewood Cliffs, NJ: Prentice Hall, 1991.

15. Ibid.

16. Ibid.

17. Al Ries and Jack Trout, *Positioning: The Battle for Your Mind*, New York: Warner Books, 1982.

18. Yoram J. Wind, *Product Policy: Concepts, Methods, and Strategy*, Reading, Massachusetts: Addison-Wesley, 1982, pp. 79–81; David A. Aaker and J. Gary Shansby, "Positioning Your Product," *Business Horizons*, *24*(3), May–June 1981, pp. 56–62.

19. Teresa Domzal and Lynette Unger, "Emerging Positioning Strategies in Global Marketing," *The Journal of Consumer Marketing*, *4*(4), Fall 1987, pp. 23–40.

20. "Pepsi Challenges Japanese Taboo as It Ribs Coke," *The Wall Street Journal*, March 6, 1991, pp. B1, B3.

21. "Marketing Firm Slices U.S. into 240,000 Parts to Spur Clients' Sales," *The Wall Street Journal*, November 3, 1986, p. 1.

22. References: Arnold Mitchell, *The Nine American Lifestyles: Who We Are and Where We Are Going*, New York: Macmillan, 1983. Martha Farnsworth Riche, Psychographics for the 1990s, *American Demographics*, July 1989.

23. Regis McKenna, "Marketing in an Age of Diversity," *Harvard Business Review*, September–October 1988. (And Alexander Hiam, "Adversity and Market Diversity," *Harvard Business Review*, March–April 1989, for the influence of marketing and other factors.)

24. Aimee Stern, "Tired of Playing Mind Games," *Adweek's Marketing Week*, July 13, 1987, pp. 1, 6.

CHAPTER 9

1. Howard Schlossberg, "Experts Share Formulas for Innovative Success," *Marketing News,* April 15, 1991, pp. 11, 26.

2. Michael Ray and Rochelle Myers, *Creativity in Business,* New York: Doubleday, 1986, p. 93.

3. "Nurturing Those Ideas," *BusinessWeek,* Innovation in America, 1989, pp. 105–118.

4. "I Can't Work This Thing!" *BusinessWeek,* April 29, 1991, pp. 58–66.

5. Ibid.

6. Yuichi Okumura, general manager of the product-planning unit at JVC's Video Products Division; ibid.

7. Regis McKenna, "Marketing Is Everything," *Harvard Business Review,* January–February 1991, pp. 65–79.

8. Howard Schlossberg, "Experts Share Formulas for Innovative Success," *Marketing News,* April 15, 1991, pp. 11, 26.

9. William Taylor, "The Business of Innovation: An Interview with Paul Cook," *Harvard Business Review,* March–April 1990, pp. 97–106.

10. "Marketing Briefs," *Marketing News,* April 15, 1991, p. 26 (quoting *Gorman's New Product News*).

11. "Another 15,000 New Products Expected for U.S. Supermarkets," *Marketing News,* June 10, 1991, p. 8. "Fewer New Products in '91," *Marketing News,* January 20, 1992, p. 1.

12. Alexander Hiam, "Campbell's New Product Rules," in *The Vest-Pocket Marketer,* Englewood Cliffs, NJ: Prentice-Hall, 1991.

13. *New Product Management for the 1980s,* New York: Booz, Allen & Hamilton, 1982, p. 9.

14. "How Chesebrough-Ponds Put Nail Polish in a Pen," *BusinessWeek,* October 8, 1984, p. 196.

15. *New Product Management for the 1980s: Phase I,* New York: Booz, Allen & Hamilton, 1981.

16. Regis McKenna, "Marketing Is Everything," *Harvard Business Review,* January–February 1991, pp. 65–79.

17. Actually, we argued in Chapter 4 that a strong home base, plus a "think globally, act locally" strategy, was key to global success. They are, but in large part because they improve the quality of innovation.

18. Howard Schlossberg, "Experts Share Formulas for Innovative Success," *Marketing News,* April 15, 1991, pp. 11, 26.

19. "The Brakes Go On in R & D," *BusinessWeek,* July 1, 1991, pp. 24–46.

20. See Tom W. White, "Use of Internal, External Sources to Garner and Screen New Product Ideas," *Marketing News,* September 16, 1983, sec. 2, p. 2.

21. Eric von Hippel, "Has a Customer Already Developed Your Next Product?" *Sloan Management Review, 18*(4), Winter 1977, p. 63.

22. *New Products: Best Practices—Today and Tomorrow*, New York: Booz, Allen & Hamilton, 1982.

23. See "Osborn's Brainstorming" and "Crawford Slip Writing" for detailed instructions on two brainstorming methods, in Alexander Hiam, *The Vest-Pocket CEO: Decision-Making Tools for Executives*, Englewood Cliffs, NJ: Prentice-Hall, 1990.

24. *Management of New Products*, 4th ed., New York: Booz, Allen & Hamilton, 1968, and *New Products: Best Practices*.

25. David Kilburn, "Putting Out Feelers: Japanese 'Antenna Shops' Aid Research," *Advertising Age*, January 2, 1989, p 3.

26. David B. Montgomery and Glen L. Urban, "Screening New-Product Possibilities," in Robert Rothberg, ed., *Corporate Strategy and Product Innovation*, 2nd ed., New York: Free Press, 1981.

27. Alexander Hiam, "Center for Concept Development's Evaluation Form," *The Vest-Pocket Marketer*, Englewood Cliffs, NJ: Prentice-Hall, 1991, pp. 104–106.

28. "Bik 'n' Bop," *Marketing News*, April 15, 1991, p. 26.

29. "Trouble at Campbell's Soup," *BusinessWeek*, September 25, 1989, pp. 68–70.

30. Ibid.

31. Ibid.

32. *New Product Management for the 1980s: Phase I*, New York: Booz, Allen & Hamilton, 1981.

33. "Bucket Brigade vs. Fast Cycle Development," *BusinessWeek, Innovation in America*, 1989, p. 107.

34. "Product Development: Where Planning and Marketing Meet" (Interview). *The Journal of Business Strategy*, September–October. 1990, 13–16.

35. Tom Peters, *Thriving on Chaos: Handbook for a Management Revolution*, New York: Harper & Row, 1987, Chapters 1–2.

36. As quoted in William Taylor, "The Business of Innovation: An Interview with Paul Cook," *Harvard Business Review*, March–April 1990, pp. 97–106.

37. "RCA's Rivals See Life in Videodiscs," *BusinessWeek*, April 23, 1984, p.88.

38. C. Merle Crawford, *New-Product Management*, Homewood, Illinois: Richard D. Irwin, 1983, pp. 25–28.

39. As reported by *Marketing News*, February 8, 1990, p. 1.

40. C. Merle Crawford, "New-Product Failure Rates—Facts and Fallacies," *Research Management*, September 1979, pp. 9–13.

41. Calvin L. Hodock, "Strategies Behind the Winners and Losers," *The Journal of Business Strategy*, September–October 1990, pp. 4–7.

42. Ibid.

43. Marvin B. Lieberman and David B. Montgomery, "First-Mover Advantages," *Strategic Management Journal,* 9, 1988 pp. 41–58.

44. Michael W. Lawless and Robert J. Fisher, "Sources of Durable Competitive Advantage in New Products," *Journal of Product Innovation Management,* 7(1), March 1990 pp. 35–44.

45. Ibid.

46. Ibid.

47. "Making Strategy Look Different," *Management Briefing: Marketing,* February–March 1988, The Conference Board.

48. "America's Oldest Companies," *Nation's Business,* July 1976, pp. 36–37.

49. Theodore Levitt, "Marketing Myopia 1975: Retrospective Commentary," *Harvard Business Review,* September–October 1975. Levitt points out in this important article (probably the most important article ever written on marketing) that "The railroads are in trouble today not because the need [for transportation] was filled by others (cars, trucks, airplanes, even telephones), but because it was *not* filled by railroads themselves." Here lies the key issue in determining whether product decline and death is inevitable. This issue is addressed in detail in the next chapter.

50. "Masters of Innovation," *BusinessWeek,* April 10, 1989, pp. 58–67.

CHAPTER 10

1. Compton MacKenzie, Editor of *The Gramophone,* as quoted in E. Levin, "CDs: To Buy or Not To Buy," *People Weekly,* March 11, 1985, p. 11.

2. "Compact Discs Now the Hottest Sound in Town," *U.S. News and World Report,* June 17, 1985, p. 62.

3. These calculations are based on data collected by Anita M. McGahan in "Market Segmentation and Capacity Commitment in the American Compact Disc Industry," Working Paper, Harvard Business School, October 1990.

4. This issue is addressed in Anita McGahan's working paper, noted above, and our discussion relies heavily upon this source for information and ideas.

5. "A Craze May Outsprint Its Creator," *New York Times,* August 7, 1990, pp. D1, D6.

6. This case is based largely on N. R. Kleinfield, "How Cuisinart Lost Its Edge," *The New York Times Magazine,* April 15, 1990, pp. 46, 66–67.

7. Ibid.

8. "Fort Howard: New Marketing Muscle from Maryland Cup," *BusinessWeek,* July 18, 1983, p. 132.

9. Julie Schlax, "A Good Reason to Mess With Success," *Forbes,* September 19, 1988.

10. "K Mart: The No. 2 Retailer Starts to Make an Upscale Move—At Last." *Business Week*, June 4, 1984, p. 51.

11. David Woodruff, "Will K Mart Ever Be a Silk Purse?" *Business Week*, January 22, 1990, p. 46.

12. Kevin Hellikee, "Wal-Mart's Store of the Future Blends Discount Prices, Department-Store Feel," *The Wall Street Journal*, April 17, 1991, p. B1.

13. Roger Cohen, "Ms. Playboy," *The New York Times Magazine*, June 9, 1991, pp. 32, 55–56, 84.

14. Anita McGahan, pp. 11–12.

15. Ibid.

16. Ibid.

17. Ibid. Extrapolated from the data in McGahan's working paper.

18. "Conair Head Planning Strategy for Cuisinarts," *The New York Times*, January 2, 1989.

19. Mack Hanan, *Re-Competitive Strategies: How to Regain Growth Profits for Mature Businesses*, American Management Association (AMACOM), 1986.

20. Isadore Barmash, "Sending the Very Best, For No Particular Reason." *The New York Times*, June 9, 1991, p. F12.

CHAPTER 11

1. "Pricing for Profit: The 1% Solution," HIDA Management Seminar, Boston, September 1983.

2. Dan Koeppel, "A Panty Hose That Couldn't Make the Stretch," *Adweek's Marketing Week*, June 19, 1989, p. 28.

3. "Business and the Airlines Play Let's Make a Deal," *Business Week*, March 4, 1991, p. 54.

4. Asra Q. Namani, "Fare Game," *The Wall Street Journal*, June 28, 1990, pp. A1, A8.

5. Brett Pulley and Asra Q. Namani, "American, Delta Shoulder Arms as Fare Wars Spread," *The Wall Street Journal*, March 13, 1991, pp. B1, B6.

6. Joseph P. White, "Car Makers Seek to Mask Price Increases," *The Wall Street Journal*, August 16, 1989, p. B1.

7. John B. Hinge, "Critics Call Cuts in Package Size Deceptive Move," *The Wall Street Journal*, February 5, 1991, pp. B1, B8.

8. Ford S. Worthy, "Making It in China," *Fortune*, June 17, 1991, pp. 103–104.

9. Ibid.

10. John Berry, "Suddenly, Pricing Is the Hot Button," *Adweek's Marketing Week*, November 5, 1990, p. 5.

11. "IBM's PC$_{jr}$ Computer Is Fulfilling Its Promise After a Faltering Start," *The Wall Street Journal*, December 13, 1984, p. 33.

12. *Consumer Reports,* "The Return of the Home Computer," January 1991, pp. 23–29.

13. From Poem CXXXI, *Collected Poems of Emily Dickinson,* Avenel Books, 1982.

14. Paul Carroll, "Truce Is Elusive in Mainframe Price War," *The Wall Street Journal,* July 24, 1991, p. B1.

15. Ibid.

16. "Auto Makers Rethink Pricing Policies to Woo Still-Reluctant Buyers," *The Wall Street Journal,* October 23, 1981, p. 1.

17. "Detroit's Merry-Go-Round," *Business Week,* September 12, 1983, p. 75.

18. Scott A. Neslin and Robert W. Shoemaker, "Using a Natural Experiment to Estimate Price Elasticity: The 1974 Sugar Shortage and the Ready-to-Eat Cereal Market," *Journal of Marketing,* 47(4), Winter 1983, pp. 44–57.

19. J. Douglas McConnell, "Effect of Pricing on Perception of Product Quality," *Journal of Applied Psychology,* 52(4), September 1968, pp. 331–334; Ben M. Enis and James Stafford, "The Price-Quality Relationship: An Extension," *Journal of Marketing Research,* 6(4), November 1969, pp. 256–258; Jacob Jacoby, Jerry Olson, and Rafael Haddock, "Price, Brand Name, and Product Composition Characteristics as Determinants of Perceived Quality," *Journal of Applied Psychology,* 55(6), December 1971, pp. 470–479; David M. Gardner, "Is There a Generalized Price-Quality Relationship in an Experimental Setting?" *Journal of Advertising Research,* 21(4), August 1981, pp. 49–52.

20. Zarrell V. Lambert, "Perceived Price as Related to Odd and Even Price Endings," *Journal of Retailing,* 51(3), Fall 1975, pp. 13–22.

21. Kent B. Monroe and Peter J. LaPlaca, "What are the Benefits of Unit Pricing?" *Journal of Marketing,* 36(3), July 1972, pp. 16–22; Michael J. Houston, "The Effect of Unit Pricing on Choices of Brand and Size in Economic Shopping," *Journal of Marketing,* 36(3), July 1972, pp. 51–54; David A. Aacker and Gary T. Ford, "Unit Pricing Ten Years Later: A Replication," *Journal of Marketing,* 47(4), Winter 1983, pp. 118–122.

22. Joseph White, "'Value Pricing' Is Hot as Shrewd Consumers Seek Low-Cost Quality," *The Wall Street Journal,* March 12, 1991, p. A1.

23. Ibid.

24. Ibid.

25. From Jim Bartimo, "In Polls Ranking PCs, Everybody Wins," *The Wall Street Journal,* July 31, 1991, p. B1.

26. Ibid.

CHAPTER 12

1. "True Partners Operate on a Handshake and Shared Values," *Marketing News,* June 24, 1991, p. 29.

2. Ernst & Whinney, *Corporate Profitability & Logistics: Innovative Guidelines for Executives*, Council of Logistics Management, 1987, p. vii.

3. James Brian Quinn, Thomas L. Doorley, and Penny C. Paquette, "Beyond Products: Services-Based Strategy," *Harvard Business Review*, March–April 1990, pp. 58–68.

4. Ibid.

5. Ibid.

6. Kaoru Ishikawa, *What Is Total Quality Control? The Japanese Way.* Translated by David J. Lu, Englewood Cliffs, NJ: Prentice-Hall, 1985, p. 32.

7. Patricia Sellers, "Winning Over the New Consumer," *Fortune*, July 29, 1991.

8. Patricia Sellers, "Winning Over the New Consumer," *Fortune*, July 29, 1991, pp. 113–124.

9. "Porsche's Civil War with its Dealers," *Fortune*, April 16, 1984, pp. 63–68.

10. "The King of Shampoo," *Fortune*, September 2, 1985, p. 48.

11. Robert F. Lusch, "Sources of Power: Their Impact on Intrachannel Conflict," *Journal of Marketing Research*, *13*(4), November 1976, pp. 382–390.

12. "Want Shelf Space at the Supermarket? Ante Up." *BusinessWeek*, August 7, 1989, pp. 60–61.

13.. "Retailers Exert More Influence in Selling of Packaged Goods," *The Wall Street Journal*, April 25, 1985, p. 33.

14. Adel I. El-Ansary, "Perspectives on Channel System Performance," in Robert F. Lusch and Paul H. Zinszer, eds., *Contemporary Issues in Marketing Channels*, Norman, OK: University of Oklahoma Press, 1979 p. 50.

15. Lisa J. Moore, "The Flight to Franchising," *U.S. News & World Report*, June 10, 1991, pp. 68–71.

16. Ibid.

17. National Federation of Independent Business, *Profiles of Success: An American Express Study of New Business*, 1989 (Available from Ketchum Public Relations).

18. "Boom Times in a Bargain-Hunter's Paradise," *BusinessWeek*, March 11, 1985, p. 120.

19. Michael Barrier, "A New Sense of Service," *Nation's Business*, June 1991, pp. 16–24.

20. "Another 15,000 New Products Expected for U.S. Supermarkets," *Marketing News*, June 10, 1991, p. 8.

21. Richard M. Bessom and Donald W. Jackson, "Service Retailing: A Strategic Marketing Approach," *Journal of Retailing*, *51*(2), Summer 1975, pp. 75–76.

22. Theodore Levitt, "Marketing Intangible Products and Product Intangibles," *Harvard Business Review*, *59*(3), May–June 1981, pp. 94–102.

23. Roger D. Blackwell and W. Wayne Talarzyk, "Life-Style Retailing: Competitive Strategies for the 1980s," *Journal of Retailing*, 59(4), Winter 1983, pp. 7–27.

24. Leonard L. Berry, "Retail Positioning Strategies for the 1980s," *Business Horizons*, 25(6), November–December 1982, pp. 45–50.

25. Malcolm P. McNair, "Significant Trends and Developments in the Postwar Period," in A.B. Smith, Ed., *Competitive Distribution in a Free, High-Level Economy and Its Implications for the University*, Pittsburgh, PA: University of Pittsburgh Press, 1958, pp. 1–25. For a refinement of this theory, see Stanley C. Hollander, "The Wheel of Retailing," *Journal of Marketing*, 26(3), July 1960, pp. 47–42.

26. "Computers Are the Key to Wholesalers' Strength," *American Druggist*, December 1983, p. 16.

27. U.S. Department of Commerce, *1985 U.S. Industrial Outlook*, Washington, D.C., 1985, p. 53–1.

28. Ibid.

29. "Apple-Polishing the Dealer," *Sales and Marketing Management*, September 10, 1984, p. 47.

30. "Key problems Facing Industrial Distributors" in James A. Narus, N. Mohan Reddy, and George L. Pinchak, *Industrial Marketing Management, 13*, September 1984, pp. 139–147.

31. "What Makes Retailers Switch," *Supermarket Business*, March 1985, p. 24.

32. "Fleming's Fast Rise in Wholesale Foods," *Fortune*, January 21, 1985, p. 54.

33. William D. Perreault, Jr., and Frederick A. Russ, "Physical Distribution Service in Industrial Purchase Decisions," *Journal of Marketing, 40*(2), April 1976, pp. 3–10.

34. Ronald H. Ballou, *Basic Logistics*, Englewood Cliffs, NJ: Prentice-Hall, 1978, pp. 17–18.

35. Richard J. Schoenberger and Abdolhossein Ansari, "'Just-in-Time' Purchasing Can Improve Quality," *Journal of Purchasing and Materials Management*, Spring 1984, pp. 2–7.

36. Chan K. Hahn, Peter A. Pinto, and Daniel J. Bragg, "'Just-in-Time' Production and Purchasing," *Journal of Purchasing and Materials Management*, Fall 1983, pp. 2–10.

37. Richard C. Walleigh, "What's Your Excuse for Not Using JIT?" *Harvard Business Review, 86*(2), March–April 1986, pp. 38–54.

38. Louis W. Stern and Adel I. El-Ansary, *Marketing Channels*, 2nd ed., Englewood Cliffs, NJ: Prentice-Hall, 1982, p. 167.

39. Gail Schares, "Jaguar and Porsche Try to Pull Out of the Slow Lane," *Business Week*, December 12, 1988, pp. 84–85.

40. "Profits double at Porsche," *New York Times*, January 25, 1990, p. D7.

41. "No One Tires of the Toys at Porsche's Playground," *Chicago Tribune*, July 29, 1990, sec. 17, p. 5.

CHAPTER 13

1. Mark Landler, "Consumers are Getting Mad, Mad, Mad, Mad at Mad. Ave.," *BusinessWeek*, April 30, 1990, pp. 70–72.

2. Laura Loro and Marcy Magiera, "Philly Products Angle for Ringside in 'Rocky V'," *Advertising Age*, February 5, 1990, p. 20.

3. Joseph Pereira, "Kids' Advertisers Play Hide-and-Seek, Concealing Commercials in Every Cranny," *The Wall Street Journal*, April 4, 1990, pp. B1, B6.

4. Joshua Hammer, "Advertising in the Dark," *Newsweek*, April 19, 1990, p. 44.

5. "Had it up to Here with Ads? Better Not Fill'er Up," *The Wall Street Journal*, February 2, 1990, p. B1.

6. Thaddeus Rutkowski, "Unnecessary Roughness," *Adweek*, January 11, 1988, p. B.R.22.

7. James C. Schroer, "Ad Spending: Growing Market Share," *Harvard Business Review*, January–February 1990, pp. 44–48.

8. American Marketing Association & American Association of Advertising Agencies, *1990 Winners: The Effie Gold Awards*, 1991.

9. Robert Buzzell, John Quelch, and Walter Salmon, "The Costly Bargain of Trade Promotion," *Harvard Business Review*, March–April 1990, pp. 141–149.

10. Joanne Lipman, "Executives Tackle Biggest Marketing Task," *The Wall Street Journal*, May 16, 1991, p. B6.

11. John Duggleby, "Games Gang Ltd. Finds That Talk Is Cheaper," *Adweek's Marketing Week*, July 17, 1989, pp. 46–47.

12. Ibid.

13. Steven H. Star, "Marketing and Its Discontents," *Harvard Business Review*, November–December 1989, pp. 148–154.

14. Arch C. Woodside and James J. Taylor, "Consumer Purchase Intentions, Perceptions of Product Quality and National Advertising," *Journal of Advertising*, Winter 1978, pp. 48–51.

15. Howard Schlossberg, "The Simple Truth: Ads Will Have to Be Truthful," *Marketing News*, December 24, 1990, p. 6.

16. Ibid.

17. David Ogilvy, *Ogilvy on Advertising*, New York: Vintage Books, Random House, 1983, p. 84.

18. Bob Stone, *Successful Direct Marketing Methods*, 3rd ed., Chicago: Crain Books, 1985, p. 1.

19. Julian Simon, "What Do Zielske's Real Data Really Show About Pulsing?" *Journal of Marketing Research, 16*(3), August 1979, pp. 415–420.

20. William Keenan Jr., "America's Best Sales Forces: Six at the Summit," *Sales & Marketing Management,* June 1990, pp. 62–82.

21. Ibid., p. 72.

22. Ibid, p. 75–76.

23. American Marketing Association, Committee on Definitions, *Marketing Definitions: A Glossary of Marketing Terms,* Chicago, 1960, p. 20.

24. Roger A. Strang, "Sales Promotion—Fast Growth, Faulty Management," *Harvard Business Review, 54*(4), July–August 1976, pp. 115–124.

25. Kenneth Cole: Doing the Old Soft-Shoe to Success," *BusinessWeek,* July 1, 1991, p. 65.

26. Lawrence Fisher, "Borland to Acquire its Rival," *The New York Times,* July 11, 1991, pp. D1 and D5.

27. "New? Improved?" *BusinessWeek,* October 21, 1985, p. 109.

28. Charles H. Patti and Vincent Blasko, "Budgeting Practices of Big Advertisers," *Journal of Advertising Research, 21*(6), December 1981, pp. 23–29.

29. "Advertising and Sales Relationships: A Current Appraisal," *Nielsen Researcher, 1* (1980), pp. 2–9.

30. Patti and Blasko, op. cit.

31. This and the following case history is based on *1990 Winners: The Effie Gold Awards,* AMA/New York and AAAA, 1991.

32. Ibid.

AFTERWORD

1. For those readers not up to date on current events in 1998, the comment refers to the surprise terrorist attack on the U.S. oil fields in Kuwait that destroyed large parts of the colony with small-scale nuclear weapons. One of Omni's smaller production facilities was badly damaged and is now too radioactive to be repaired.

2. The term *elderpreneurs,* now in common usage, was introduced in the 1994 best seller on entrepreneurship among the elderly by well-known authors Hiam and Schewe.

3. Now that elders make up such a large and fast-growing segment of the population, they have taken on a leadership role in politics and popular culture.

4. Readers may not recall that IBM and Apple merged their PC and VPC businesses in 1995, or that VPC stands for very personal computer—their name for the now-popular hand-held super-portables.

Glossary

ADMINISTERED VERTICAL MARKETING SYSTEM: A vertical marketing system in which one member is informally designated as captain.

ADVERTISING: Any impersonal form of communication about ideas, goods, or services that is paid for by an identified sponsor.

ADVERTISING CAMPAIGN: A set of messages with a single theme that is repeatedly conveyed to the target audience over an extended period.

ADVERTISING PLATFORM: The issues and product benefits that a marketer wishes to convey in an advertising message.

ADVERTISING TARGET MARKET: The specific audience toward which an advertising message is aimed.

ADVERTISING THEME: The parts of an advertising message that are repeated throughout the campaign.

AFFECTIVE COMPONENT (OF AN ATTITUDE): The emotional feeling of favorableness or unfavorableness that results from a person's evaluation of an object.

AGENT: A wholesaling intermediary that does not take title to merchandise but serves primarily to bring buyers and sellers together and facilitate exchanges.

ANNUAL PLAN: A plan in which the organization's managers set goals for a single year.

AREA SAMPLE: A probability sample in which respondents are chosen at random from a complete list of the population in a specific geographic area.

ATTITUDES: Feelings that express whether a person likes or dislikes objects in his or her environment.

AUCTION COMPANY: A wholesaling intermediary that sells merchandise on an agency basis by means of auctions.

AUGMENTED PRODUCT: An expected product that has been enhanced by a set of benefits that consumers do not expect or that exceed their expectations.

BACKTRANSLATION: A process in which a questionnaire is translated into a second language and then translated back into the original language.

BAIT-AND-SWITCH PRICING: A pricing strategy in which a product is given a low price in order to lure customers into a store, where an attempt is made to persuade them to buy a more expensive model or product.

BAROMETRIC TECHNIQUES: Forecasting techniques that use analyses of past trends to predict the future.

BARTER: The exchange of one good for another without using money as a means of valuation.

BASING-POINT PRICING: A geographic pricing policy in which the seller designates one or more geographic locations from which the rate that a buyer will be charged is calculated.

BRAINSTORMING: A method of generating new-product ideas that consists of holding group discussions in which a specific problem or goal is set and no suggested solution is criticized.

BRAND: A name, term, symbol, design, or combination of these elements that is intended to identify the goods or services of one seller or group of sellers and differentiate them from those of competitors.

BRAND COMPETITOR: An organization that competes with others to satisfy consumers' demand for a specific product.

BRAND EXTENSION: A new product category that is given the brand name of an existing category.

BRAND MARK: The portion of a brand that consists of a symbol, design, or distinctive coloring or lettering.

BRAND NAME: The portion of a brand that consists of words, letters, or numbers that can be vocalized.

BREAKDOWN METHOD: An approach to salesforce design in which the size of the salesforce is determined by dividing the forecasted annual sales volume by the expected sales volume per salesperson.

BREAK-EVEN PRICING: An approach to pricing in which the price of a unit of the product is set high enough to cover the variable costs of producing that unit as well as the fixed costs of producing the product.

BROKER: A wholesaling intermediary whose primary function is to supply market information and establish contacts in order to facilitate sales for clients.

BUSINESS DEFINITION: The way an organization answers the questions, "What business are we in?" and "What business *should* we be in?"

BUYER: In the exchange process, the purchaser of a product.

BUYING CENTER: All the individuals and groups participating in the buying process that have interdependent goals and share common risks.

CASH-AND-CARRY WHOLESALER: A limited-service wholesaler that sells on a cash-only basis and does not provide delivery.

CASH COW: An SBU that has a higher market share than its competitors and is in a low-growth market.

CASH DISCOUNT: A discount that is offered to buyers who pay their bills within a stated period.

CASH FLOW: The flow of cash into a company; maintaining a steady cash flow is sometimes used as a pricing objective.

CATALOG SHOWROOM: A discount store at which customers review catalogs and then place orders and wait for delivery.

CAUSAL STUDIES: Research in which the cause-and-effect relationships between various phenomena are explored.

CHAIN STORE: A retail organization that consists of two or more units under a single ownership.

CHANNEL CAPTAIN: A channel member that is able to influence the behavior of the other members of the channel.

CHANNEL MANAGEMENT: The activities involved in anticipating and understanding the sources of channel conflict and trying to eliminate or minimize them.

CHANNEL OF DISTRIBUTION: The route taken by a product and its title as it moves from the resource procurer through the producer to the ultimate consumer.

COGNITIVE COMPONENT (OF AN ATTITUDE): A person's evaluation of the characteristics of an object.

COGNITIVE DISSONANCE: The state of anxiety or uneasiness that follows a purchase decision and creates a need for reassurance that the decision was the best one.

COMBINATION STORE: A type of superstore that places emphasis on nonfood items and on services.

COMMISSION MERCHANT: An agent that performs selling functions for manufacturers, normally on a one-time basis.

COMMON CARRIER: A transportation company that transports products on a specified schedule and according to regulations and standards established by government regulatory agencies.

COMMON COSTS: Costs that must be allocated among two or more functional areas.

COMMUNICATION: The process of exchanging meaning.

COMPARATIVE ADVANTAGE: A theory that states that if a country has a relative cost advantage in a particular product, specializes in the production of that product, and trades it for products in which other countries have a relative cost advantage, more products will be available at lower prices than would be the case without specialization and trade.

COMPETITIVE ADVANTAGE: Differential access to resources (such as distribution channels, expertise, or technology) that can give a firm cost and quality advantages compared to its competitors.

CONATIVE COMPONENT (OF AN ATTITUDE): The intention or tendency to act that results from a person's evaluation of an object.

CONCENTRATED STRATEGY: A media scheduling strategy in which the marketer limits its advertising to specified periods.

CONCENTRATION STRATEGY: A marketing strategy that aims at a single market segment.

CONCLUSIVE STAGE: The stage of the research process in which the researchers develop a plan for collecting data, implement the plan, and provide the resulting information to decision makers.

CONSOLIDATED METROPOLITAN STATISTICAL AREA (CMSA): A population unit that contains a major metropolitan area and has a total population of more than 1 million.

CONSUMER: In the exchange process, the person who uses a product.

CONSUMER MARKET: A market in which goods and services are actually used up.

CONSUMER PANEL: A variation of the mail survey in which respondents are given some form of remuneration for participating in an ongoing study by filling out a series of questionnaires or keeping detailed records of their behavior.

CONTAINERIZATION: The use of large, standardized, easy-to-handle containers in which smaller packages can be loaded for shipping.

CONTEST: A sales promotion technique in which consumers are offered prizes for performing a task such as making up a slogan.

CONTINUITY STRATEGY: A media scheduling strategy in which advertisements are spread out over the entire period of the campaign.

CONTINUOUS IMPROVEMENT: Frequent incremental improvements driven primarily by customer requirements and competitor actions. Requires active organizational learning.

CONTRACT CARRIER: A transportation company that agrees to transport a specified number of shipments to specific destinations for an estimated price.

CONTRACTUAL VERTICAL MARKETING SYSTEM: A vertical marketing system in which channel members draw up a legal agreement that specifies the rights and responsibilities of each party.

CONTRIBUTION MARGIN TECHNIQUE: An approach to cost analysis that ignores nontraceable common costs.

CONTROL: The process of monitoring action programs, analyzing performance results, and, if necessary, taking corrective action.

CONVENIENCE PRODUCTS: Inexpensive, frequently purchased goods and services that consumers want to buy with the least possible effort.

CONVENIENCE SAMPLE: A nonprobability sample in which respondents are selected to suit the convenience of the researchers.

CONVENIENCE STORE: A store that is located near the residences or workplaces of its target customers and carries a wide assortment of products.

COOPERATIVE ORGANIZATION: A retail organization that consists of a set of independent retailers that combine their resources to maintain their own wholesaling operation.

CORE COMPETENCY: A constellation of closely related areas of expertise that, combined, give a firm a long-term advantage over competing firms.

CORPORATE CULTURE: A set of values that create a distinct pattern that is reflected in all of an organization's activities.

CORPORATE MISSION: A statement of an organization's overall goals, usually broadly defined and difficult to measure objectively.

CORPORATE VERTICAL MARKETING SYSTEM: A vertical marketing system in which one member gains control through ownership of both production and distribution systems.

COST-PER-THOUSAND: The dollar cost of an advertisement per 1000 readers or viewers.

COST-PLUS PRICING: An approach to pricing in which the list price is determined by adding a reasonable profit to the cost per unit.

COUPON: A certificate that entitles a consumer to a price reduction or a cash refund.

CROSS ELASTICITY OF DEMAND: A situation in which a change in the price of a product affects sales of another product.

CUE: An environmental stimulus that is perceived as a signal for action.

CULTURE: A set of values, ideas, attitudes, and other meaningful symbols created by human beings to shape human behavior and the artifacts of that behavior as they are transmitted from one generation to the next.

CUMULATIVE QUANTITY DISCOUNT: A quantity discount that is applied to a buyer's total purchases over a set period.

CUSTOMARY PRICING: A pricing strategy in which the marketer maintains a traditional price level.

CUSTOM RESEARCH FIRM: A research firm that assists a marketer in designing a study, collecting information, and preparing a report.

DATA BANK: The component of an MIS that stores raw data that come in from both the external environment and internal records.

DEALER BRAND: A brand that is created and owned by an intermediary.

DECIDER: In the exchange process, the person who chooses an alternative that will satisfy a want or need.

DECODING: The process whereby a receiver extracts meaning from a transmitted message.

DELEGATION: Assigning specific responsibilities to specific people.

DELPHI TECHNIQUE: A forecasting technique in which a panel of experts is asked to assign rankings and probabilities to various factors that may influence future events.

DEMAND: The composite desire for particular products as measured by how consumers choose to allocate their resources among different products in a given market.

DEMARKETING: A marketing tool whose objective is to persuade consumers to use less of a product while maintaining the same level of satisfaction.

DEMOGRAPHICS: Statistics about a population, such as sex, age, marital status, birthrate, mortality rate, education, income, and occupation.

DEPARTMENT STORE: A store that offers a wide variety of product lines and is divided into departments to facilitate marketing and merchandise management.

DERIVED DEMAND: Demand that is dependent on the demand for another product.

DESCRIPTIVE LABEL: A label that explains the important characteristics or benefits of a product.

DESCRIPTIVE STUDIES: Research that focuses on demographic information about markets and their composition.

DETERMINING (BEHAVIORAL) VARIABLES: A set of variables that determine whether or not a consumer is a member of a particular market segment.

DIFFERENCE THRESHOLD: The smallest change in the intensity of a stimulus that can be noticed.

DIFFERENTIATED MARKETING: A marketing strategy that aims at several market segments, varying the marketing mix for each segment.

DIRECT COSTS: Costs that can be assigned to a specific functional area.

DIRECT MARKETING: An approach to marketing that uses one or more advertising media to effect a measurable response.

DISCOUNT: A deduction from the list price in the form of cash or something else of value.

DISCOUNT STORE: A self-service general-merchandise store that combines low price with high volume.

DISCRETIONARY INCOME: The amount of disposable income that is left over after spending on essentials such as food, shelter, and clothing.

DISPLAY UNIT: The component of an MIS that permits the user to communicate with the system.

DISPOSABLE INCOME: The amount of income available for spending after taxes have been deducted.

DISTINCTIVE COMPETENCIES: Activities that a firm can perform better than other firms.

DISTRIBUTION: The process of making sure that a product is available when and where it is desired.

DISTRIBUTION CENTER: A storage facility that takes orders and delivers products.

DOG: An SBU that has a low relative market share and is in a low-growth market.

DRIVE: A strong motivating tendency that arouses an organism toward a particular type of behavior; see also *motive*.

DROP SHIPPER: A limited-service wholesaler that sells goods but does not stock, handle, or deliver them.

DUMPING: A situation in which a product is sold at a lower price in a foreign market than in a domestic one, or at a price below the cost of production.

EARLY ADOPTERS: Consumers who buy a product early in its life cycle and influence other people to buy it.

EARLY MAJORITY: Consumers who wait and watch others before adopting a new product.

ECONOMIC ORDER QUANTITY: The optimum quantity of a product to order at a given time.

ECONOMIC SYSTEM: The way in which society organizes its resources to produce goods and services that will satisfy its members' wants and needs.

ECONOMIES OF SCALE: The savings that result when fixed costs are spread over more units of a product.

EFFECTIVE DEMAND: The combination of desire to buy and ability to buy.

80/20 RULE: A term used to refer to the fact that a large percentage of a company's sales and profits may come from a relatively small percentage of its customers or products.

ELASTIC DEMAND: A situation in which a percentage change in price brings about a greater percentage change in quantity sold.

EMERGENCY PRODUCTS: Goods or services that are needed to solve an immediate crisis.

ENCODING: The process whereby a source translates a message into words and signs that can be transmitted, received, and understood by the receiver.

ENGEL'S LAWS: A set of statements concerning the proportional changes in expenditures that accompany increases in family income.

ENVIRONMENT: A set of forces external to the organization that the marketer may be able to influence but cannot control.

ENVIRONMENTAL SCANNING: A set of procedures for monitoring the organization's external environment.

EVALUATOR: In the exchange process, an individual who provides feedback on a chosen product's ability to satisfy.

EVEN PRICING: A form of psychological pricing in which the price is an even number.

EVOKED SET: The set of alternatives that come immediately to mind when a consumer seeks a solution to a problem.

EXCHANGE: An exchange occurs when two or more individuals, groups, or organizations give to each other something of value in order to receive something else of value. Each party to the exchange must want to exchange; must believe that what is received is more valuable than what is given up; and must be able to communicate with the other parties.

EXCLUSIVE DEALING: A method of control over distribution in which the manufacturer forbids dealers to carry competitors' products.

EXCLUSIVE DISTRIBUTION: An approach to distribution in which the number of intermediaries is limited to one for each geographic territory.

EXEMPT CARRIER: A company that is exempt from state and federal transportation regulations.

EXPECTED PRODUCT: A generic product plus a set of features that meet additional expectations of consumers.

EXPERIENCE CURVE: A graphic representation of the effect of experience on the per-unit cost of producing a product.

EXPERIMENT: A research method in which the effect of a particular variable is measured by making changes in the conditions experienced by a test group with respect to the variable and comparing the results with those of a control group that did not experience the change.

EXPLORATORY STAGE: The stage of the research process in which the problem is defined, objectives are set, and possible solutions are explored.

EXPRESS WARRANTY: A statement that specifies the exact conditions under which a manufacturer is responsible for a product's performance.

EXPROPRIATION: A situation in which a host country denies a foreign corporation the right to engage in business there and seizes its assets.

EXTENDED FAMILY: A nuclear family plus aunts, uncles, grandparents, and in-laws.

EXTENSIVE DISTRIBUTION: An approach to distribution that seeks the widest possible geographic coverage.

FACTORY OUTLET MALL: A shopping center that focuses on quality, name brand items offered at lower than usual prices.

FAMILY OF ORIENTATION: The family into which a person is born.

FAMILY OF PROCREATION: The family that a person establishes through marriage.

FEEDBACK: Information that tells an organization's managers about the performance of each marketing program.

FIXED-COST CONTRIBUTION: The portion of a selling price that is left over after variable costs have been accounted for.

FLEXIBLE-PRICE POLICY: A pricing policy in which the marketer offers the same products and quantities to different customers at different prices, depending on their bargaining power and other factors.

FLIGHTING STRATEGY: A media scheduling strategy in which there is heavy advertising during some parts of the campaign and no advertising in between.

F.O.B. PRICING: A geographic pricing policy in which buyers pay transportation costs from the point at which they take title to the product.

FOCUS GROUP: A form of personal interview in which a group of 8 to 12 people are brought together to offer their views on an issue, idea, or product.

FORM COMPETITOR: An organization that competes with others to satisfy consumers' wants or needs within a specific class of products or services.

FORM UTILITY: The satisfaction that buyers receive from the physical characteristics of a product (e.g., its shape, function, or style).

FRANCHISE: A legal contractual relationship between a supplier and one or more independent retailers. The franchisee gains an established brand name and operating assistance, while the franchisor gains financial remuneration as well as some control over how the business is run.

FREIGHT ABSORPTION: A geographic pricing policy in which the seller charges the same freight rate as the competitor located nearest to the buyer.

FREIGHT FORWARDER: A transportation company that pools many small shipments to take advantage of lower rates, passing some of the savings on to the shippers.

FREQUENCY: The average number of times that the average prospect will be exposed to a specific advertisement in a specified period.

FULL-COST APPROACH: An approach to cost analysis that takes both direct and common costs into consideration.

FULL-SERVICE WHOLESALER: A merchant wholesaler that performs a full range of services for its customers.

FUNCTIONAL ACCOUNT: An accounting category that reflects the purpose for which money is spent.

FUNCTIONAL SATISFACTION: The satisfaction received from the tangible or functional features of a product.

GENERAL-MERCHANDISE RETAILER: A retailer that carries a wide range of products.

GENERAL-MERCHANDISE WHOLESALER: A full-service wholesaler that carries a wide variety of product lines.

GENERIC COMPETITOR: An organization that competes with others to satisfy consumers' wants or needs within a general category of products or services.

GENERIC NAME: A brand name that has become associated with a product category rather than with a particular brand.

GENERIC PRODUCT: A set of tangible or intangible attributes that are assembled into an identifiable form.

GLOBALIZATION: The tendency for markets to expand across national boundaries, leading to increasing competition among firms from different nations and a growing dependence on diverse, multinational and multicultural customer bases.

GOVERNMENTAL MARKET: A set of federal, state, county, or local agencies that buy goods and services for use in meeting social needs.

GRADE LABEL: A label that identifies the quality of a product by a letter, number, or word.

GROSS RATING POINTS: The reach of an advertisement multiplied by its frequency.

HORIZONTAL CONFLICT: Conflict that occurs between channel members at the same level of the distribution channel.

HORIZONTAL COOPERATIVE ADVERTISING: Advertising in which marketers at the same level in the distribution system advertise jointly.

HORIZONTAL MARKET: A market that is made up of a broad spectrum of industries.

HORIZONTAL PRICE FIXING: A form of price fixing in which marketers at the same level of the distribution system get together and decide the price at which all of them will sell the product.

HYPERMARCHE: A combination department store and supermarket.

HYPOTHESIS: A statement about possible relationships between objects or events.

IDEAL SELF-IMAGE: Our mental picture of ourselves as we would like to be.

IMPLEMENTATION: The actual execution of a strategic plan.

IMPLIED WARRANTY: A legal promise that a product will serve the purpose for which it is intended, whether stated by the manufacturer or not.

IMPRESSIONS: The total number of exposures to a specific advertisement in a specified period.

IMPULSE ITEMS: Convenience products that are purchased not because of planning but because of a strongly felt need.

INDEPENDENT RETAILER: A retailer that owns a single outlet that is not affiliated with any other retail outlet.

INDUSTRIAL DISTRIBUTOR: An independently owned operation that buys, stocks, and sells industrial products.

INDUSTRIAL MARKET: A producer market that consists of firms that engage in the manufacture of goods.

INDUSTRIAL MARKETING: The process of anticipating, discovering, and designing product and service specifications that will satisfy the requirements of industrial customers.

INDUSTRIAL MARKETING RESEARCH: The systematic gathering, recording, and analyzing of data for use in solving problems related to the marketing of industrial goods and services.

INELASTIC DEMAND: A situation in which a percentage change in price brings about a smaller percentage change in quantity sold.

INFLUENCER: In the exchange process, an individual who provides information about how a want or need may be satisfied.

INFORMATIVE LABEL: A label that advises consumers about the care, use, or preparation of a product.

INITIATOR: In the exchange process, the person who first recognizes an unsatisfied want or need.

INNOVATORS: Consumers who are ready and willing to adopt a new idea.

INSTITUTIONAL ADVERTISING: Advertising that develops and maintains a favorable image for a particular industry or company.

INSTITUTIONAL MARKET: A set of not-for-profit organizations that buy goods and services for use in achieving a particular goal or mission.

INTENSIVE DISTRIBUTION: An approach to distribution that seeks the largest possible number of outlets in a given territory.

INTERACTIVE MIS: A computer-based marketing information system that allows managers to communicate directly with the system.

INTERMEDIARY: An independent or corporate-owned business that helps move products from the producer to the ultimate consumer.

INTERMEDIATE MARKET: A set of wholesalers and retailers that buy goods from others and resell them.

INTRAPRENEURSHIP: An approach to new-product development in which a small team of employees is set apart from the rest of the organization and freed from ordinary bureaucratic requirements long enough to develop a particular product.

JOINT DEMAND: Demand for two products that are complementary.

JUDGMENT SAMPLING: Nonprobability sampling in which respondents are selected on the basis of criteria that the researchers believe will result in a group that is representative of the population being surveyed.

JURY OF EXECUTIVE OPINION: A forecasting technique in which executives from various departments of the company are asked to estimate market potential and sales and then try to reach a consensus.

JUST-IN-TIME PURCHASING: An approach to inventory management in which products are bought in small quantities to reduce inventory carrying costs and obtain delivery just in time for use.

LABEL: A tag or part of a package that supplies information about a product or its seller.

LAGGARDS: Consumers who are strongly oriented toward the past and very suspicious of new concepts; they are the last to adopt a new product.

LATE MAJORITY: Consumers who are committed to familiar ways of doing things and skeptical of new ideas.

LEAD: The name of any individual or organization that may be a potential customer.

LEARNING: The process by which people's experiences produce changes in their behavior.

LEVELING: A cognitive process in which the information retained becomes shorter and more concise.

LIMITED-LINE RETAILER: A retailer that offers only one or a few lines of related merchandise.

LIMITED-SERVICE WHOLESALER: A merchant wholesaler that performs a limited number of services for its customers.

LINE EXTENSION: A new variety of a basic product.

LIST PRICE: The initial price of a product; also termed the *base price.*

LONG-RANGE PLAN: A plan in which the organization's managers set goals for a period of more than one year.

LOSS LEADER: A product that is given a lower than normal price in order to attract customers to a store.

MACROMARKETING: Bringing about exchanges between individuals and/or groups so as to provide satisfaction of a society's wants and needs.

MACROSEGMENTATION: A process in which an industrial market is divided into segments based on types of buying organizations.

MAIL INTERVIEW: A survey technique in which questionnaires are mailed to potential respondents.

MAIL-ORDER WHOLESALER: A limited-service wholesaler that sells to industrial, institutional, and retail customers by means of catalogs.

MAJOR INNOVATION: An item that has never been sold by any other organization.

MANUFACTURER'S AGENT: An independent sales representative who works for several manufacturers of related but noncompeting product lines.

MANUFACTURER'S BRAND: A brand that is owned and marketed by the manufacturer that produces it.

MANUFACTURER'S SALES BRANCH: A wholesaling establishment that is owned and operated by a manufacturer separately from its factories.

MANUFACTURER'S SALES OFFICE: A wholesaling establishment that is similar to a manufacturer's sales branch except that it does not carry inventory.

MARGINAL COST: The cost of producing one more unit than the most recent unit produced.

MARKET: A group of people with unsatisfied wants and needs who are willing to exchange and have the ability to buy.

MARKET AGGREGATION: A marketing strategy that uses a single marketing program to offer the same product to all consumers.

MARKET ATOMIZATION: A marketing strategy that treats each individual consumer as a unique market segment.

MARKET BREAKDOWN TECHNIQUE: A forecasting technique in which the sales forecast for a large unit is broken down into forecasts for smaller units.

MARKET BUILDUP TECHNIQUE: A forecasting technique in which information on a few specific market segments is aggregated to arrive at a total sales forecast.

MARKET-DRIVEN ECONOMY: An economic system in which supply, demand, and price determine what products will be produced and who will receive those products.

MARKETING AUDIT: A comprehensive, systematic, independent, and periodic examination of an organization's marketing environment, objectives, strategies, and activities.

MARKETING CONCEPT: The management philosophy that recognizes that the consumer should be the focal point of all activity within an organization.

MARKETING CONTROL CHART: A chart that combines trend analysis with the performance standards set by the organization.

MARKETING DECISION SUPPORT SYSTEM: A coordinated collection of data, models, analytic tools, and computing power by which an organization gathers information from the environment and turns it into a basis for action.

MARKETING INFORMATION SYSTEM (MIS): A set of procedures and methods for regular, planned collection, analysis, and presentation of marketing information.

MARKETING INTELLIGENCE SYSTEM: Within a marketing information system, the set of activities whose purpose is to monitor the external environment for emerging trends or events.

MARKETING MIX: The combination of activities involving product, price, place, and promotion that a firm undertakes in order to provide satisfaction to consumers in a given market.

MARKETING RESEARCH: A systematic, objective approach to the development and provision of information for decision making regarding a specific marketing problem.

MARKET SEGMENT: A group of buyers within a market who have relatively similar wants and needs.

MARKET SEGMENTATION: A marketing strategy in which a large, heterogeneous market is broken down into small, more homogeneous segments and a separate marketing program is developed for each segment.

MARKET SHARE: The total number of units of a product (or their dollar value) expressed as a percentage of the total number of units sold by all competitors in a given market.

MARKET SHARE ANALYSIS: A forecasting technique in which it is assumed that the firm's market share will remain constant and sales forecasts for the firm are based on forecasts for the industry.

MATRIX ORGANIZATION: An organizational structure in which projects are assigned to task forces made up of people drawn from various functional departments.

MEAN: The sum of all the numbers in a set of scores divided by the number of scores.

MEDIAN: In a list of numbers, the number above which half of the numbers in the list fall and below which the other half fall.

MERCHANT MIDDLEMAN: An intermediary that takes title to the products it distributes.

MERCHANT WHOLESALER: A wholesaling intermediary that is an independently owned business and takes title to the goods it sells.

MESSAGE: An idea that is to be conveyed from a source to a receiver.

MESSAGE CHANNEL: A vehicle for delivering a message.

MICROMARKETING: Strategically managing human and organizational exchange relationships so as to provide socially responsible want and need satisfaction throughout the world while achieving the marketer's objectives.

MICROSEGMENTATION: A process in which industrial market segments are subdivided on the basis of characteristics of the buying center and individual participants.

MILL SUPPLY HOUSE: A general-merchandise wholesaler that operates in an industrial setting.

MINIWAREHOUSE MALL: A type of shopping center in which a large warehouse offers space to a variety of sellers, including both retailers and wholesalers.

MINOR INNOVATION: A product that was not previously sold by the company but has been marketed by some other company.

MODE: In a set of data, the number that occurs most frequently.

MODEL BANK: The component of an MIS that contains mathematical marketing models that show relationships among various marketing activities, environmental forces, and desired outcomes.

MODIFICATION: Any adjustment of an existing product's style, color, or model; any product improvement; or a brand change.

MODIFIED REBUY: A purchasing situation in which the organization has bought the good or service before, but some aspect of the situation has changed.

MONOPOLISTIC COMPETITION: A competitive situation in which there are many buyers and sellers, imperfect market information, some barriers to entry, and differentiated products.

MONOPOLY: A competitive situation in which there is only one seller of a product and entry to the market is restricted.

MOTIVE: A need or want that is activated by a particular stimulus and initiates behavior toward some goal.

MULTINATIONAL CORPORATION (MNC): A corporation that operates in more than one country and makes all of its decisions within a global framework.

NATIONALIZATION: A situation in which a national government becomes involved in the ownership or management of a business organization.

NATURAL ACCOUNT: An accounting category that reflects how money is actually spent.

NEED: Something that is lacking that is necessary for a person's physical or psychological well-being.

NEW-TASK PURCHASE: A purchasing situation in which the organization is making the purchase for the first time.

NOISE: Any distraction that interferes with the effectiveness of a communication.

NONCUMULATIVE QUANTITY DISCOUNT: A quantity discount that is offered on each sale made to a particular buyer.

NONPROBABILITY SAMPLING: A sampling technique in which respondents are selected partly on the basis of researchers' judgment.

NONTRACEABLE COSTS: Common costs that are assigned to functional areas on an arbitrary basis.

NORMS: Rules that tell the members of a particular cultural group what behavior is correct in certain situations.

NUCLEAR FAMILY: A husband and wife and their children.

NUTRITIONAL LABELING: A form of labeling in which consumers are informed of the amounts of protein, fat, carbohydrates, and calories in a processed food product.

OBSERVATIONAL APPROACH: A research method in which researchers observe people's behavior and record what they see but avoid direct interaction.

ODD PRICING: A form of psychological pricing in which the price is an odd number or a number just below a round number.

OFF-PRICE STORE: A discount store that buys manufacturers' overruns and end-of-season goods at below-wholesale prices and resells them at prices significantly lower than the regular department store price.

OLIGOPOLY: A competitive situation in which a few firms account for a large percentage of the industry's sales and in which there are substantial barriers to entry.

ONE-PRICE POLICY: A pricing policy in which the marketer assigns a price to the product and sells it at that price to all customers who purchase the same quantity of the product under the same conditions.

OPEN DATING: A form of labeling in which consumers are informed of the expected shelf life of a product.

OPPORTUNITY: An unsatisfied want or need that arises from a change in the organization's environment.

ORGANIZATION: All the activities involved in getting ready to carry out a strategic plan.

ORGANIZATIONAL LEARNING: The process whereby individuals within an organization learn as a group and apply that learning to their work. Traditionally thought to vary with amount of experience (as measured for example by number of units produced), but increasingly seen as an independent variable that can be managed as a source of competitive advantage.

ORGANIZATIONAL STRUCTURE: A set of relationships among individuals with different responsibilities.

ORIGINAL-EQUIPMENT MANUFACTURER (OEM): An organization that purchases industrial goods to incorporate into other products.

OTHERS SELF-IMAGE: Our mental picture of ourselves as we believe others see us.

PACKAGING: All activities that are related to designing and producing the container or wrapper for a product.

PENETRATION: A pricing strategy in which the initial price is set at a low level in order to generate the greatest possible demand for the product.

PERCEPTION: The process by which a person attaches meaning to the various stimuli he or she senses.

PERFECT COMPETITION: A competitive situation in which there are many buyers and sellers, perfect market information, few or no barriers to entry, and homogeneous products.

PERSONAL INTERVIEW: A survey technique in which respondents are questioned in a face-to-face setting.

PERSONAL SELLING: Person-to-person communication in which the receiver provides immediate feedback to the source's message.

PHANTOM FREIGHT: A term used to refer to the difference between the true freight cost and the cost charged to the buyer in situations in which the buyer is charged an amount greater than the actual cost.

PHYSICAL DISTRIBUTION: All the activities that provide for the efficient flow of raw materials, in-process inventory, and finished goods from the point of procurement to the ultimate consumer.

PHYSICAL OBSOLESCENCE: Obsolescence that results when products are built to last only a limited time.

PIGGYBACK SERVICE: A transportation service in which loaded trucks are taken directly onto railroad flatcars.

PLACE UTILITY: The satisfaction that buyers receive from having a product available at the appropriate place.

PLAN: A written document that specifies resource requirements, costs, expected benefits, and activities necessary to achieve a goal.

PLANNED OBSOLESCENCE: A product management strategy in which a marketer forces a product in its line to become outdated, thereby increasing replacement sales.

PLANNING: The process of predicting future events and using those predictions to set courses of action that will achieve the organization's goals.

POINT-OF-PURCHASE PROMOTION: A sales promotion technique that consists of locating an attention-getting device at the place of actual purchase.

POSITIONING: A process in which a marketer communicates with consumers to establish a distinct place for its product or brand in their minds.

POSSESSION UTILITY: The satisfaction that buyers receive from having the right to use or own a product.

POSTPONED OBSOLESCENCE: Obsolescence that occurs when technological improvements are available but are not introduced until the demand for existing products declines.

PREMIUM: A product that is offered free or at less than the regular price in order to induce the consumer to buy another product.

PRICE: That which the buyer gives up in exchange for something that provides satisfaction.

PRICE LINING: A pricing strategy in which prices are used to sort products into "lines" based on an attribute such as quality, prestige, or style.

PRICE-OFF: A price reduction that is used to induce trial or increase usage of a product.

PRIMARY DATA: Data that are collected specifically for use in a particular research project.

PRIMARY DEMAND: Market demand for a product class rather than a particular brand.

PRIMARY DEMAND ADVERTISING: Advertising in which the marketer attempts to create awareness of and provide information about a type of product.

PRIMARY GROUP: A group that is small and intimate enough so that all of its members can communicate with one another face to face.

PRIVATE CARRIER: A company that owns the goods it transports.

PRIVATE WAREHOUSE: A warehouse that is owned and controlled by its users.

PROBABILITY SAMPLING: A sampling technique in which all members of the population being surveyed have a known chance of being included in the sample.

PRODUCER COOPERATIVE: A member-owned wholesale operation that assembles farm products to sell in local markets.

PRODUCER MARKET: A set of buyers that purchase goods and services and use them to make other products.

PRODUCT: A combination of functional and psychological features that provides form utility; the entire set of benefits that are offered in an exchange, including goods, services, ideas, people, places, and organizations.

PRODUCT DIFFERENTIATION: A marketing strategy that uses promotion and other marketing activities to get consumers to perceive a product as different from and better than those of competitors.

PRODUCT LIFE CYCLE: A sequence of stages in the marketing of a product that begins with commercialization and ends with removal from the market.

PRODUCT LINE: Within a company's product mix, a broad group of products that are similar in terms of use or characteristics.

PRODUCT MIX: The various products that a company offers to consumers.

PRODUCT PORTFOLIO: A company's product mix viewed from a strategic perspective; a set of products or brands that are at different stages in the product life cycle.

PRODUCT RELAUNCH: A product management strategy that focuses on finding new markets and untapped market segments, new product uses, and ways to stimulate increased use of a product by existing customers.

PROFESSIONAL ADVERTISING: Advertising that focuses on the benefits offered by professional services.

PROGRAM EVALUATION AND REVIEW TECHNIQUE (PERT): An implementation technique that uses detailed flowcharts showing which tasks can be carried out only after certain other tasks have been completed and which tasks can be done simultaneously.

PROMOTION: Any technique that persuasively communicates favorable information about a seller's product to potential buyers; includes advertising, personal selling, sales promotion, and public relations.

PROMOTIONAL DISCOUNT: A discount that is offered to intermediaries as compensation for carrying out promotional activities.

PROSPECTING: The process of locating and classifying potential buyers of a product.

PROTECTIONISM: The erection of barriers to trade in an attempt to protect domestic industries from foreign competition.

PSYCHOLOGICAL PRICING: A pricing strategy in which the product is given a price that is psychologically appealing to consumers.

PSYCHOLOGICAL SATISFACTION: The satisfaction received from the intangible benefits of a product, such as a feeling of self-worth.

PUBLICITY: Any message about an organization that is communicated through the mass media but is not paid for by the organization.

PUBLIC RELATIONS: A promotional activity that aims to communicate a favorable image of a product or its marketer and to promote goodwill.

PUBLIC WAREHOUSE: A warehouse that is owned by an independent contractor, which rents space to users.

PULL STRATEGY: A promotional strategy in which each channel member attempts to persuade the next member in the system to handle and promote the product.

PULSING STRATEGY: A media scheduling strategy in which a continuous campaign is combined with short bursts of heavier advertising.

PUSH STRATEGY: A promotional strategy in which the producer uses mass promotion to stimulate demand in the consumer market, thereby causing intermediaries to want to carry the product.

QUALIFYING (DESCRIPTIVE) VARIABLES: A set of variables that allow or qualify an individual to be a member of a particular market segment.

QUALITY CONTROL: The traditional approach to quality in which problems are detected after manufacturing and an effort is made to remove sub-standard products before shipping to customers.

QUANTITY DISCOUNT: A discount offered to buyers that purchase larger than normal quantities of the product.

QUESTION MARK: An SBU that has a low relative market share and is in a high-growth market.

QUOTA: A specific limit on the number of items of a particular kind that may be imported.

QUOTA SAMPLING: A form of judgment sampling in which the population is divided into subgroups on the basis of one or more characteristics and a specified proportion of respondents are chosen from each subgroup.

RACK JOBBER: A limited-service wholesaler that supplies nonfood products to supermarkets, grocery stores, and drug retailers.

REACH: The percentage of total prospects that are exposed to a specific advertisement in a specified period.

REAL INCOME: Income that has been adjusted for the effects of inflation.

REAL SELF-IMAGE: Our mental picture of ourselves as we think we really are.

RECEIVER: The audience that is the target of a message.

RECRUITING: The activity of locating skilled salespeople and inducing them to apply for employment.

REFERENCE GROUP: Any set of people that influences an individual's attitudes or behavior.

REINFORCEMENT: The extent to which satisfaction is derived from a response to an aroused need.

RELATIVE MARKET SHARE: An organization or SBU's market share divided by that of its largest competitor.

REPATRIATION: The transfer of profits to a parent firm from an affiliate in a foreign country.

RESEARCH DESIGN: An overall plan for conducting a research project, including the choice of the method that will be used to achieve the goals of the research.

RESPONSE: Whatever occurs as a reaction to an aroused need.

RETAILER: An intermediary that sells products primarily to ultimate consumers.

RETAILING: All activities undertaken by intermediaries whose primary function is to sell goods and services to ultimate consumers.

RETENTION: The extent to which one remembers what one has learned.

REVERSE ELASTICITY: A situation in which anticipation of a steady increase (decrease) in price causes buyers to make more (fewer) purchases of a product.

ROLE EXPECTATIONS: The rights, privileges, duties, and responsibilities that are associated with a particular role.

ROLE THEORY: An approach to the study of group influence that recognizes that people conduct their lives by playing many roles, each of which is accompanied by a certain range of acceptable behaviors.

ROLLOUT: An approach to new-product introduction in which the product is launched in a series of geographic areas over an extended period.

SALES MANAGER: The person who designs and manages the activities of an organization's salesforce.

SALES POTENTIAL FORECAST: A forecast of total potential sales for the firm for a specific time period.

SALES PROMOTION: The array of techniques that marketers use to stimulate immediate purchase.

SALES VARIANCE ANALYSIS: A method of data analysis in which data on actual sales are compared with quantitative sales objectives.

SAMPLE: A group of respondents who are representative of the population being surveyed.

SAMPLING: Giving free samples of a product to consumers or offering a trial size at a very low cost.

SCENARIO ANALYSIS: A forecasting technique in which researchers develop a subjective picture of several possible futures by identifying cause-and-effect relationships and following them to their logical conclusions.

SCIENTIFIC METHOD: A research process that involves the development of a hypothesis that can be confirmed, modified, or rejected on the basis of information gathered by objective means.

SCRAMBLED MERCHANDISING: The practice of carrying any product line, however dissimilar from other lines carried, as long as it yields a profit.

SEASONAL DISCOUNT: A discount that is offered to customers who purchase a product during a season when demand for that product is low.

SECONDARY GROUP: A large group whose members have a shared goal but do not engage in face-to-face communication.

SECONDARY SOURCE: Data that have been collected for a purpose other than the research project in question.

SELECTIVE DEMAND: Demand for a particular brand.

SELECTIVE DEMAND ADVERTISING: Advertising in which the marketer attempts to create awareness of and provide information about a specific brand.

SELECTIVE DISTRIBUTION: An approach to distribution that involves the use of a limited set of outlets in a given territory.

SELF-LIQUIDATING PREMIUM: A premium for which the buyer pays all or part of the cost.

SELLING: The process of assisting and/or persuading a prospective customer to buy a good or service or to act favorably on an idea.

SELLING AGENT: An agent that handles the entire marketing function for a manufacturer.

SENSORY THRESHOLDS: The upper and lower limits on the ability of human sensory processes to perceive increases or decreases in the intensity of a stimulus.

SERVICE: A deed, act, or performance.

SHARPENING: A cognitive process in which the information retained becomes more vivid and important than the event itself.

SHIPPERS' COOPERATIVE: A group of shippers that pool shipments of similar items in order to benefit from lower freight rates.

SHOPPING CENTER: A group of retail stores at a single location that is planned, developed, and controlled by one organization.

SHOPPING MALL INTERCEPT: A form of personal interview in which respondents are approached or intercepted as they pass a particular spot in a shopping mall.

SHOPPING PRODUCTS: Goods and services about which consumers will seek information before making a purchase.

SHOPPING STORE: A retail outlet that is favored by consumers who are shopping for a certain type of product.

SIMPLE RANDOM SAMPLING: Probability sampling in which respondents are chosen at random from a complete list of the members of the population.

SIMPLE TREND ANALYSIS: A forecasting technique in which managers review historical data and use the rates of change to project future trends.

SINGLE-LINE WHOLESALER: A full-service wholesaler that carries only one or two product lines but offers considerable depth in each.

SKIMMING: A pricing strategy in which the initial price is set at a high level with the goal of selling the product to people who want it and are willing to pay a high price for it.

SLICE-OF-LIFE ADVERTISING: Advertising that portrays consumers in realistic situations that are consistent with consumers' perceptions of their own life styles.

SOCIAL CLASS: A relatively permanent and homogeneous category of people within a society. The members of a class have similar values, life styles, interests, and behavior.

SOCIALIZATION: The process by which we learn the values and norms of our culture.

SORTING: A process in which products are brought together at one location and then divided up and moved in smaller quantities to locations closer to the ultimate buyers.

SOURCE: The originator of a message.

SPECIALTY LINE SUPPLIER: A research firm that specializes in one aspect of the marketing research process.

SPECIALTY-LINE RETAILER: A limited-line retailer that carries only one or two product lines, but offers substantial depth and expertise in those lines.

SPECIALTY-LINE WHOLESALER: A full-service wholesaler that carries a limited number of products for customers with specialized needs.

SPECIALTY PRODUCTS: Goods and services for which there are no acceptable substitutes in the consumer's mind.

SPECIALTY STORE: A retail outlet for which customers develop a strong preference based on the assortment of products offered, the service, or the store's reputation.

SPOKESPERSON: The person who delivers the message in a testimonial.

STANDARD METROPOLITAN STATISTICAL AREA (SMSA): The Census Bureau's standard urban population unit. An area is classified as an SMSA if it contains a city with a population of at least 50,000 or an urbanized area of 50,000 with a total metropolitan population of at least 100,000.

STAPLE ITEMS: Convenience products that consumers plan to buy.

STAR: An SBU that has a high growth rate and a high relative market share.

STATISTICAL BANK: The component of an MIS that offers statistical techniques to be used in analyzing data.

STATISTICAL PROCESS CONTROL: The use of statistical analysis (usually by line employees) to measure and manage specific work processes. Commonly used in total quality programs.

STRAIGHT REBUY: A purchasing situation in which the organization has bought the good or service before and is likely to reorder from the same vendor.

STRATEGIC BUSINESS UNIT (SBU): One or more products, brands, divisions, or market segments that have something in common, such as the same distribution system. Each SBU has its own mission, its own set of competitors, and its own strategic plan.

STRATEGIC INFORMATION SCANNING SYSTEM: A formal structure of people, equipment, and procedures to obtain and manage information to support strategic decision making.

STRATEGIC MARKET PLANNING: The managerial process of developing and implementing a match between market opportunities and the resources of the firm.

STRATEGIC PLAN: A long-term plan covering a period of 3, 5, or sometimes 10 years.

STRATEGIC PLANNING: The process of developing a long-range plan that is designed to match the organization's strengths and weaknesses with the threats and opportunities in its environment.

STRATIFIED RANDOM SAMPLING: Probability sampling in which the total population is divided into subgroups, or *strata,* and a random sample is chosen from each subgroup.

STRUCTURED QUESTION: A question that limits respondents to a specific set of replies.

STYLE OBSOLESCENCE: Obsolescence that occurs when the physical appearance of a product is changed to make existing versions seem out of date.

SUBCULTURE: A smaller cultural group within a society that reflects geographic, religious, or ethnic differences.

SUPERMARKET: A large self-service store that carries a full line of food products and, often, a number of nonfood products.

SUPERSTORE: A combination of a general-merchandise discount operation and a supermarket.

SURVEY APPROACH: A research method in which researchers use personal interviews, telephone interviews, or mailed questionnaires to question a group of people directly.

SWEEPSTAKES: A sales promotion technique in which prizes are tied to chance and consumers are encouraged to buy a product as part of the entry procedure.

SYNDICATED SERVICE: A research firm that periodically compiles specific types of data for sale to marketers.

TACTICAL PLAN: A short-term plan that specifies the activities necessary to carry out a strategic plan.

TARGET MARKETING: A process in which the marketer evaluates a number of market segments, decides which one or ones to serve, and develops and implements a unique marketing mix for the targeted segment(s).

TARGET RETURN ON INVESTMENT: An amount of income equivalent to a certain percentage of the firm's investment; this amount is set as a goal to be achieved through pricing.

TARGET RETURN PRICING: An approach to pricing in which the marketer seeks to obtain a predetermined percentage return on the capital used to produce and distribute the product.

TARIFF: A tax on imported goods.

TECHNOLOGICAL OBSOLESCENCE: Obsolescence that results when technological improvements are made in a product.

TELEMARKETING: The sale of goods and services by telephone.

TELEPHONE INTERVIEW: A survey technique in which respondents are questioned by telephone.

TESTIMONIAL: An advertising message that is presented by someone who is viewed as an expert on the subject.

TEST-MARKETING: The controlled introduction of a new product to carefully selected markets for the purpose of testing market acceptance and predicting future sales of the product in that region.

THREAT: An unfavorable trend or situation that could prevent the organization from satisfying a want or need.

TIME UTILITY: The satisfaction that buyers receive from having a product available at the appropriate time.

TOTAL FIXED COSTS: Costs that ordinarily do not change over time, no matter what quantity of output is produced.

TOTAL QUALITY PROGRAM: The most common rubric for Japanese-inspired efforts to build quality into a product or service as it is produced or performed. Quality may be defined as closeness of fit to specifications, customer needs, or (in the most sophisticated programs), fit to latent customer needs. Total quality programs require the active involvement of the line workers themselves, which generally is best achieved via a radical change in corporate culture led by the chief executive.

TOTAL VARIABLE COSTS: Costs that fluctuate, depending on the quantity of output produced.

TRACEABLE COSTS: Common costs that can be assigned to two or more specific functional areas.

TRADE DEFICIT: The amount by which a nation's total imports exceed its total exports.

TRADE DISCOUNT: A discount that is offered to intermediaries as compensation for carrying out various marketing activities.

TRADEMARK: A brand that is given legal protection because it has been appropriated exclusively by one marketer.

TRADING DOWN: A product management strategy in which a marketer that is known for selling high-priced products offers lower-priced products.

TRADING STAMPS: A sales promotion technique in which customers receive stamps in quantities depending on how much they purchase, and can redeem the stamps for merchandise.

TRADING UP: A product management strategy in which a marketer that is known for selling low-priced products offers higher-priced products.

TRANSACTION: An exchange between two or more parties.

TRANSFER PRICING: Raising the price of a product shipped to a foreign affiliate in order to increase the amount of profit transferred from the affiliate to the parent firm.

TRIAL: The consumer's initial purchase and use of a product or brand.

TRUCK WHOLESALER: A limited-service wholesaler that specializes in selling and delivery services.

TRUE PROSPECT: A lead that can benefit from the use of the product, can afford to buy it, and has the authority to do so.

TYING AGREEMENT: A method of control over distribution in which the producer forces the dealer to buy additional products in order to secure one highly desired product.

UNIFORM DELIVERED PRICING: A geographic pricing policy in which the seller offers the same delivered price to all buyers, regardless of their location and the actual freight expense.

UNITARY DEMAND: A situation in which a percentage change in price brings about an equal percentage change in quantity sold.

UNIT PRICING: A form of pricing in which the price of the package is accompanied by the price of the product in terms of some standard measure of quantity.

UNSOUGHT PRODUCTS: Goods and services for which consumers have no felt need.

UNSTRUCTURED QUESTION: A question that allows respondents to answer as they wish and does not limit the length of responses.

VALUE-ADDED TAX: A tax that is levied every time a product is sold to another member of the distribution channel.

VALUES: The deeply held beliefs and attitudes of the members of a particular society.

VARIETY STORE: A retailer that offers a wide assortment of low-priced items.

VERTICAL CONFLICT: Conflict that occurs between channel members at different levels of the distribution system.

VERTICAL COOPERATIVE ADVERTISING: Advertising in which marketers at different levels in the distribution system advertise jointly.

VERTICAL MARKET: A market that consists of a single industry.

VERTICAL MARKETING SYSTEM: A distribution channel whose members are integrated into a single organization.

VERTICAL PRICE FIXING: A form of price fixing in which marketers at different levels of the distribution system get together to set retail prices.

VOLUNTARY CHAIN: A retail organization that consists of a set of independent retailers that agree to buy most of their merchandise through a single wholesaler.

WANT: Something that is lacking that is desirable or useful. It is formed by a person's experiences, culture, and personality.

WAREHOUSE CLUB: A no-frills, cash-and-carry discount store that operates in a poor location; to shop there, the customer must become a member and pay dues.

WAREHOUSE SHOWROOM: A discount store that follows a strategy based on low overhead and high turnover; customers pay cash and must transport the merchandise themselves.

WAREHOUSE STORE: A no-frills supermarket that stocks a wide variety of food and nonfood items and sells them at lower prices than the typical supermarket price.

WARRANTY: A manufacturer's promise that a product will serve the purpose for which it is intended.

WEAROUT: The tendency of consumer response to a sales promotion to diminish over time.

WHOLESALER: An intermediary that distributes products primarily to commercial or professional users.

WHOLESALING: All of the activities provided by wholesaling intermediaries involved in selling merchandise to retailers; to industrial, institutional, farm, and professional businesses; or to other types of wholesaling intermediaries.

WHOLESALING INTERMEDIARY: Any firm that engages primarily in wholesaling activities.

WORKLOAD APPROACH: An approach to salesforce design in which the size of the salesforce is determined by dividing the total workload in hours by the number of selling hours available from each salesperson.

ZERO-BASED BUDGETING: An approach to budgeting in which each part of the organization must justify each item in its budget before it will be granted the funds it needs.

ZONE PRICING: A geographic pricing policy in which the seller divides a geographic area into zones and charges each buyer in a given zone the base price plus the standard freight rate for that zone.

Resources

H. Igor Ansoff. *The New Corporate Strategy*, New York: John Wiley, 1988.

Leonard L. Berry and A. Parasuraman. *Marketing Services: Competing Through Quality*, New York: The Free Press, 1991.

Robert D. Buzzell and Bradley T. Gale. *The PIMS Principles: Linking Strategy to Performance*, New York: The Free Press, 1987.

Jan Carlson. *Moments of Truth: New Strategies for Today's Customer-Driven Economy*, New York: Harper & Row, 1987.

C. Merle Crawford. *New Product Management*, Homewood, IL: Richard D. Irwin, 1983.

Philip B. Crosby. *Quality is Free: The Art of Making Quality Certain*, New York: McGraw-Hill, 1979.

William H. Davidow and Bro Uttal. *Total Customer Service: The Ultimate Weapon*, New York: Harper & Row, 1989.

Michael Dertouzos, Richard Lester, and Robert Solow. *Made in America: Regaining the Productive Edge*, New York: Harper Collins, 1990.

Peter F. Drucker. *Innovation and Entrepreneurship: Practice and Principles*, New York: Harper & Row, 1985.

Peter F. Drucker. *Management: Tasks, Responsibilities, Practices*, New York: Harper & Row, 1973.

Leonard M. Fuld. *Competitor Intelligence: How to Get It—How to Use It*, New York: Ronald Press, 1984.

Gary Hamel and C. K. Prahalad. "Corporate Imagination and Expeditionary Marketing," *Harvard Business Review*, vol. 69 no. 4 (July–August 1991) pp. 81–92.

Harvard Business Review paperback No. 90089. *Unconditional Quality* (a collection of HBR articles), Boston: Harvard Business School, 1991.

Alexander Hiam. *The Vest-Pocket Marketer: Classic Marketing Tools for Executives*, Englewood Cliffs, NJ: Prentice-Hall, 1991.

Alexander Hiam. *Closing the Gap: How America's Leading Companies Are Responding to the Quality Challenge*, Englewood Cliffs, NJ: Prentice-Hall, 1992.

Kaoru Ishikawa. *What Is Total Quality Control? The Japanese Way,* Englewood Cliffs, NJ, Prentice-Hall, 1985.

Thomas C. Kinnear and James R. Taylor. *Marketing Research: An Applied Approach,* New York: McGraw-Hill, 1987.

Theodore Levitt. "Marketing Intangible Products and Product Intangibles," *Harvard Business Review,* vol. 59, no. 3 (May–June 1981), pp. 94–102.

Thomas T. Nagle. *The Strategy and Tactics of Pricing,* Englewood Cliffs, NJ: Prentice-Hall, 1987.

Tom Peters and Nancy Austin. *A Passion for Excellence: The Leadership Difference,* New York: Random House, 1985.

Thomas J. Peters and Robert H. Waterman, Jr.. *In Search of Excellence: Lessons from America's Best-Run Companies,* New York: Harper & Row, 1982.

Michael E. Porter. *Competitive Advantage: Creating and Sustaining Superior Performance,* New York: The Free Press, 1985.

Michael E. Porter. *Competitive Strategy: Techniques for Analyzing Industries and Competitors,* New York: The Free Press, 1980.

C. K. Prahalad and Gary Hamel. "The Core Competence of the Corporation," *Harvard Business Review,* (May–June 1990) pp. 79–91.

Stan Rapp and Thomas L. Collins. *Maximarketing,* New York: McGraw-Hill, 1987.

Al Ries and Jack Trout. *Marketing Warfare,* New York: McGraw-Hill, 1986.

Al Ries and Jack Trout. *Positioning: The Battle for Your Mind,* New York: Warner Books, 1982.

Everett M. Rogers. *Diffusion of Innovations,* New York: The Free Press, 1983.

F. G. "Buck" Rogers. *The IBM Way: Insights into the World's Most Successful Marketing Organization,* New York: Harper & Row, 1985.

Ernan Roman. *Integrated Direct Marketing,* New York: McGraw-Hill, 1989.

William E. Rothschild. *How to Gain (and Maintain) the Competitive Advantage,* New York: McGraw-Hill, 1984.

W. Earl Sasser, Jr., Christopher W. L. Hart, and James L. Heskett. *The Service Management Course: Cases and Readings,* New York: The Free Press, 1991.

Leon G. Shiffman and Leslie Lazar Kanuk. *Consumer Behavior,* Englewood Cliffs, NJ: Prentice-Hall, 1987.

Louis W. Stern and Adel I. El-Ansary. *Marketing Channels,* Englewood Cliffs, NJ: Prentice-Hall, 1988.

Valerie A. Zeitland, A Parasuraman, and Leonard L. Berry. *Delivering Quality Service: Balancing Customer Perceptions and Expectations,* New York: The Free Press, 1990.

INDEX